Encyclopedia of
Money

Encyclopedia of
Money

Larry Allen

ABC-CLIO

Santa Barbara, California
Denver, Colorado
Oxford, England

Library of Congress Cataloging-in-Publication Data

Allen, Larry.
     Encyclopedia of money / Larry Allen.
       p. cm.
     Includes bibliographical references and index.
     ISBN 1-57607-037-9 (alk. paper)
     1. Money Encyclopedias.   I. Title.
   HG216.A43   1999
   332.4'03—dc21   99-38048
                                   CIP

03 02 01 00   10 9 8 7 6 5 4 3 2

ABC-CLIO, Inc.
130 Cremona Drive, P.O. Box 1911
Santa Barbara, California 93116–1911

This book is printed on acid-free paper ∞.

Manufactured in the United States of America

Contents

Preface

This book is written for the general reader, who may use it as a reference source to the important monetary experiences that have either shaped the evolution of money and banking systems or that for other reasons are regarded as interesting monetary experiments. The reader who does not know where to start may want to read the book from beginning to end. In the spirit of the adage that all sides of an issue cannot be seen from just one angle, this book approaches the subject of money as seen from every angle represented by important monetary systems and experiments in history.

Innovations in monetary systems invariably entail a redistribution of income, and therefore the subject of money is not one we expect to see handled without prejudice. This book, however, strives to treat the subject without trying to prove or disprove current theories in monetary economics. Some value judgments can hardly be avoided in descriptions of episodes of hyperinflation, which remind us of the monetary insanity that lurks beneath the surface of fiat money systems. Also, complex scenarios of monetary debacles often seem clearer when seen through the trained eyes of the leading economists in history and theories can lend organization to an otherwise chaotic series of events. In this book theories are advanced only to bring to light the order that exists where there appears to be no order, and to enliven the discussion with thought-provoking ideas. The main organizing principle in this book consists in the common characteristics shared by various types of money and monetary systems, rather than unifying theoretical threads that can be traced from the first page to the last.

This book presents the subject of money in the form of more than 300 topics ranging from whale tooth money, fur money, and tobacco money to the mechanisms of the modern international monetary system. Individual topics are intended to stand on their own merits, each striving to penetrate as a roving spotlight all the nooks and crannies of monetary systems, lingering over the idiosyncrasies, and looking for archaic relics in modern systems and modern traits in ancient systems.

The professionally trained economists will miss in this book much of the technical jargon and sophisticated mathematical and statistical analysis associated with the science of monetary economics. Perhaps the absence of theory and jargon will be repaid in the revelation of the almost endless variety of monetary systems and experiments that deserve our attention, and can teach us something about the nature of money.

The composition of this book was enriched substantially by conversations with Dr. Ron Fritze, professor of history at Lamar University, whose far-flung knowledge of history and ancient societies gave me many clues concerning the whereabouts of unique monetary experiences. In discussing the treatment of various subjects, I always benefited from the clarification that any issue received at his hands. The hearty cooperation of the librarians at the Mary and John Gray Library on the Lamar University campus impressed me during the process of assembling materials for this book. They seemed never at a loss for tools that helped me find particular references and books. A word of appreciation is due to Todd Hallman and others at ABC-CLIO who patiently guided me through this project. The considerate thoughtfulness of the people at ABC-CLIO could always be counted on to inspire a sense of fresh confidence. Finally, my daughter earned my appreciation for always allowing me to baby-sit my granddaughter while she unsnarled my computer.

Introduction

Money serves four basic functions in an economic system. It acts as: (1) a medium of exchange; (2) a unit of measure; (3) a store of value; and (4) a standard of deferred payment.

As a medium of exchange, money must be universally accepted in exchange. It must be something always accepted in trade. In prisoner-of-war camps cigarettes have served as a medium of exchange, and in the northern reaches of the earth furs have circulated as a medium of exchange. Livestock and precious metals have a long history of service as mediums of exchange.

Money must also act as a unit of measure, comparable to yards, gallons, tons, cubic feet, or any other measure. Pounds sterling, American dollars, Japanese yen, German marks, and French francs all serve as units of measurement. A consumer can buy 10 gallons' worth of gasoline or $10 worth of gasoline. The Hudson Bay trading posts in Canada measured sales and profits in terms of beaver pelts, and Virginia colonists priced goods in terms of pounds of tobacco.

Anything meeting all of the demands placed on money must be satisfactory as a store of value. That is, it must preserve its value over a length of time. Perishable commodities rarely serve as money because wealth stored in perishable commodities is doomed to extinction. Precious metals such as gold and silver, known for resistance to corrosion and natural deterioration, are the most prized as monetary commodities and have few rivals as commodities that preserve value over time. Livestock reproduce, allowing them to preserve value over time, and even earn a form of interest. Inflation is the chief enemy of paper money because it renders the paper money useless as a store of value.

Money should also furnish society with a standard of deferred payment, enabling debtors and creditors to negotiate long-term contracts. Creditors want assurance that debtors cannot legally discharge debts with money possessing less purchasing power than the money originally borrowed. An unanticipated depreciation of the currency shortchanges creditors and gives debtors a windfall gain, arbitrarily redistributing income from creditors to debtors.

On the other hand, if money becomes unusually abundant, debtors easily find the means to repay debts, and creditors find the money repaid to them is worth less. Debtors are at risk if currency unexpectedly appreciates, increasing what debtors have to repay creditors in real terms. Unexpected currency appreciation redistributes income in favor of creditors over debtors. Because those who need to borrow money are usually worse off than those who have money to lend, an income redistribution favoring creditors is likely to cause hard feelings among those who already feel they get less than their share of income. Monetary issues are the focal point of a not-so-secret war between debtors and creditors.

Money falls within two broad categories, commodity money and fiat money. Commodity money makes use of some commodity, such as tobacco, rice, gold, or silver, that has an intrinsic value, or market value independent of any government decree sanctioning the commodity as legal tender for payment of private and public debts. Commodity monetary standards may make use of tokens or paper circulating money, but the circulating money can always be redeemed in a monetary commodity at an official rate. Under the gold standard the United States government committed itself to selling gold for $35 per ounce. Fiat money has no intrinsic value; that is, it has no market value independent of a government decree establishing it as legal tender for private and public debts. Modern monetary systems are called inconvertible paper standards, because the fiat money issued by these systems cannot be converted into a commodity at an official rate. Fiat money has value because governments give themselves a monopoly on the privilege to issue fiat money, enabling them to limit its supply, and governments use their power to adjudicate disputes to make the money legal tender for all debts. By limiting the supply and creating a need, the government confers value on paper money that has little or no intrinsic value.

Two commodities, gold and silver, have been lifted up as the aristocrats of commodity money. Until the nineteenth century silver usually prevailed as the predominant form of commodity money, punctuated by intervals of bimetallism, which made use of both gold and silver and established a fixed ratio that set the value of each metal in terms of the other. Aside from the Byzantine period, when gold reigned supreme, the hegemony of silver lasted from the time of Alexander the Great until the nineteenth century.

Historically, precious metals have had a funny way of showing up and disappearing as civilizations waxed and waned. The silver mines of Laurium helped finance the golden age of Greece, and the decline of the Roman Empire coincided with the exhaustion of the silver mines in Spain and Greece. The stagnation of Western Europe during the Middle Ages may be explained by the virtual disappearance of precious metals during that era. The economic expansion of Europe that led to the eventual world dominance of European civilization in the nineteenth century followed the European discovery of vast precious metal deposits in the New World.

The much-vaunted gold standard, the demise of which is still mourned by a few true believers, actually represents a relatively late development in monetary history. The gold standard is a recent upstart compared to silver and bimetallic standards. Only in

the 50 years preceding World War I (1914–1918) did gold become the sole standard of purchasing power, completely eclipsing the role of silver in the world's monetary system.

The fascination with gold may be a relic of the awe that surrounded money in some primitive societies. The word *taboo* originated from the sacred character and atmosphere of mystery that surrounded primitive money in islands of the South Pacific. On the Fiji Islands sperm whale teeth, called *tambua,* a variant of *taboo,* acted as money and conferred social status on their owners. The power of a whale tooth guaranteed compliance with any request that accompanied it as a gift. On Rossel Island some of the most valuable units of shell money could only be handled in a crouched position, and many of these units were thought to have been handed down from the beginning of time. In parts of the Philippines women were not allowed to enter sacred storehouses where rice money was kept.

John M. Keynes, a famous English economist in the first half of the twentieth century, observed in his *Treatise on Money,* Volume II (1930), that gold had "enveloped itself in a garment of respectability as densely respectable as was ever met with, even in the realms of sex or religion." Concerning the power that a relatively small amount of gold played in the world's monetary affairs, Keynes wrote in the same work that "[a] modern liner could convey across the Atlantic in a single voyage all the gold which has been dredged or mined in seven thousand years." The world's supply of gold has increased since Keynes wrote these words, but the supply remains small in comparison to the important role it has always played in monetary affairs. Even during Keynes's time monetary gold lay out of sight in the underground vaults of central banks, and gold transactions took the form of changing the designated owners of gold by paper notations (earmarking), rather than physically moving gold to different locations.

The strength of gold as a monetary commodity lay in the hold it commanded upon the human imagination, but its weakness lay in its restricted supply, which failed to keep pace with the growth of trade. The gold standard forced the world's economies to struggle constantly against what today would be called a tight money policy. Although fresh supplies of gold occasionally burst forth, furnishing a brief respite from tight money, the long-term trend was one of deflation owing to the limited money supplies.

The world's trading partners severed the connection between domestic money supplies and domestic gold reserves in the 1930s, hoping that more lax monetary policies would reinflate the depression-ridden economies of that era. Under the Bretton Woods system of the post–World War II era, domestic currencies remained convertible into gold at the request of foreign central banks, but not at the request of private individuals. During the Bretton Woods era, gold reserves failed to keep pace with the need for monetary growth, and by agreement of the members of the Bretton Woods system, a form of "paper gold" was created called standard drawing rights. Standard drawing rights are really only entries in accounting logs, but they act as reserves of gold or foreign currencies.

Since 1971 the world's major trading partners have been on inconvertible paper standards. The United States dollar and other major currencies became strictly fiat money, inconvertible into gold even at the request of foreign central banks.

The burst of inflation of the 1970s may be due partially to a void in monetary discipline left by the departure from the last vestiges of the gold standard. The world's monetary authorities learned, however, to restrict the rate of monetary growth to noninflationary levels, and by the mid-1990s inflation had subsided to insignificant levels virtually worldwide.

A

Act for Remedying the Ill State of the Coin (England)

In 1696 Parliament enacted the Act for Remedying the Ill State of the Coin, after one of the famous currency debates in history that pitted those who favored return to a historical currency standard against those who favored ratifying past depreciation.

Toward the end of the seventeenth century the old hammered silver coinage accounted for the bulk of England's circulating coinage. The coinage was worn and clipped, some dating back to Elizabeth I, effectively reducing the silver weight relative to the face value of each coin. Freshly struck milled coins disappeared as fast as they left the mint as Gresham's law played itself out—bad money chasing out good. The milled coins, immune from clipping, enjoyed greater silver value and were far more beautiful.

Once the government committed itself to recoinage, two schools of thought rose up about the principles that should guide it. John Locke, the famous philosopher who influenced the American Revolutionaries, stood firmly in favor of maintaining the historical weight standard of English coins. Locke's proposal required that the lost silver content of worn and clipped coins be restored in recoinage, substantially increasing the government's costs. William Lowndes, secretary to the Treasury, proposed recoinage at a lower silver content for a given face value, bringing the silver content of freshly minted coins into line with the silver content of worn, clipped coins. Wear and clipping had on aver-

age cost the coinage 20 to 25 percent of silver content. Supporting Lowndes's proposal were numerous historical precedents for stabilizing depreciated coins at current levels. Locke described the proposal to reduce the silver content relative to face value as "a clipping done by public authority, a public crime." Lock was also concerned that reducing the silver content enabled the government to repay debt with cheaper money.

Sir Isaac Newton, another towering figure who was a player in this drama, served as warden of the mint during recoinage. Newton appears to have favored devaluation, and apparently foresaw that refusing to devalue would increase the amount of silver each gold coin would buy, increasing the value of gold at home, causing gold to flow in and silver to flow out.

Parliament sided with Locke, and the Act for Remedying the Ill State of the Coin, with minor exceptions, mirrored Locke's views. The cost of the recoinage surpassed all expectations, totaling 2.7 million pounds, more than half of the government's revenue. In the spirit of the Enlightenment, the government enacted a tax on windows to help pay for the recoinage. In addition to the Tower mint, several branch mints were pressed into service, and the recoinage was completed in three years.

The mechanics of the plan for calling in the old coinage caused no small amount of discontent. For a certain period of time, the government accepted at face value worn and clipped coins for the payment of taxes and government obligations. Landowners with

John Locke stood firmly in favor of maintaining the weight standard of English coins. (Library of Congress)

property taxes to pay, and merchants with customs' duties to pay, benefited from the plan, buying up worn and clipped coins at a discount and paying their taxes with them. Wage earners and the poor had less need of the money to pay taxes, and often found the soon-to-be discontinued money accepted only at a discount by shopkeepers.

The act struck a blow for upholding the sanctity of a monetary standard, even at great expense, to protect the interest of creditors, especially when government was a major debtor. Newton correctly anticipated, however, that the act would put England on the road to the gold standard. Gold flowed into England, where it could purchase silver cheaply. The silver was then sold abroad at a profit.

See also: Clipping, Fleetwood, William, Great Debasement, Pound Sterling

References: Chown, John F. 1994. *A History of Money.* Feavearyear, Sir Albert. 1963 *The Pound Sterling.* Horton, Dana S. 1983. *The Silver Pound and England's Monetary Policy Since the Restoration, Together with the History of the Guinea.*

Aeginetan Silver Standard

Aegina was the first Greek city-state to make use of techniques for coining precious metals developed on the Asian side of the Aegean Sea. In the ninth and eighth centuries B.C. Aegina was the leading trade center in Greece proper, and carried on a lively trade with the cities in Asia Minor that first developed methods of coinage.

Whereas the cities of Asia Minor coined a metal called *electrum,* a mixture of silver and gold, Aegina coined silver exclusively. Silver was readily at hand from the Greek islands and the mines of Laurium in the south of Attica. As the premier commercial power on the west side of the Aegean Sea, Aegina monopolized the shipment of silver and was the logical place for minting silver for the export trade. The value of silver coinage rested on the importance of trade with Egypt, where silver was valued above gold.

Aegina probably began striking silver coins around 750 B.C., and its coins bore an image of a turtle or tortoise, the symbol of Aegina. The opposite side had only a punch mark. Greek tradition bestows the credit for this first Greek coinage on Pheidon, tyrant of Argos, whose rule cannot be precisely dated.

Aeginetan silver coins superseded an iron spits currency that circulated in ancient Greece. Aristotle, writing in the fourth century B.C., gives the following account of the development of money:

> As the reciprocity in importing articles that were wanted and exporting those that were surplus spread more widely, they were obliged to employ coin. For it is not easy to value the necessaries of life one against another: so, for purposes of exchange it was agreed to give and receive some commodity that was readily adaptable for practical use, such as iron and silver and so forth: this was first regulated simply by bulk and weight, but finally had a stamp impressed on it, to save measuring it: for the stamp was meant as an indication of quantity. (Aristotle, 1952)

Aegina gave to Greece two denominations of coinage that were to outlast the Aeginetan standard—the *obol,* derived from the Greek word for "spits," referring to iron spits, and *drachma,* equal to six obols, or a "handful" of six spits. The standard coin of Aegina, called a *stater,* equaled two drachmas in value.

Aegina seems to be the first state to coin money and stand ready to maintain its value in terms of an

Both sides of the Aeginetan stater. Note the tortoise, symbol of Aegina. (Smithsonian Institution, National Numismatic Collection)

objective measure, such as six spits. The cities of Asia Minor contented themselves with letting their currency fluctuate in value with the market for precious metals.

In the seventh century B.C. the Greek city of Corinth introduced its own coinage, improved in many respects and rivaling Aeginetan coinage as the favorite medium of Greek commerce. The Aeginetan coinage was losing ground to Corinthian coinage in the sixth century B.C. when Athens began its own coinage, which soon dominated Mediterranean trade.

See also: Attic Silver Standard, Corinthian Silver Standard, Temple Coinage in Ancient Greece

References: Aristotle. 1952. *Politics.*
Burns, A. R. 1927. *Money and Monetary Policy in Early Times.*
Carridice, Ian. 1995. *Greek Coins.*
Freeman, Kathleen. 1976. *The Work and Life of Solon.*
Milne, J. G. 1931. *Greek Coinage.*

Alchemy

Alchemy was a pseudoscience that flourished during the Middle Ages. Its chief aims were the transmutation of base metals into gold and silver, and the discovery of an elixir of eternal youth. The alchemists searched in vain for the philosopher's stone, a substance that, if properly treated, would allegedly transmute lead, iron, copper, or tin into gold or silver—but particularly gold.

Perhaps it is only coincidental that Sir Isaac New-

ton, the master of the London mint from 1699 to 1726 and one of the towering intellects in the history of humanity, spent years conducting experiments in alchemy, leaving behind manuscripts on alchemy of 100,000 words. Between 1661 and 1692 experiments in alchemy accounted for most of Newton's laboratory work. He experimented with alchemy while he was writing his masterpiece, the *Principia.*

The origins of alchemy stretch back into the murky recesses of history. One legend suggests that Jason's golden fleece was actually a papyrus manuscript describing the gold-producing secrets of alchemy. Probably a combination of Greek speculation, Eastern mysticism, and Egyptian technology conspired to make Alexandria, Egypt, one of the first centers of alchemical studies in the West. The Roman emperor Diocletian ordered all Egyptian texts on alchemy destroyed after crushing an Egyptian rebellion at the end of the third century. Apparently his action was taken only to punish the Egyptians. Evidence of alchemical studies in China show up as early as the second century B.C., and India also boasts of an ancient tradition of alchemy.

The Arabs inherited both the Eastern and Western traditions of alchemy, and went far toward developing the science of chemistry while practicing alchemy. The greatest of the Islamic alchemists was the Great Geber, regarded in medieval Europe as the father of alchemy. To the Arab alchemists we owe the terms *alcohol, alkali, borax,* and *elixir.*

Alchemists were often suspected of heretical practices. (Library of Congress)

The study of alchemy passed from the Arabs into Europe through Spain. In 1181 the University of Montpellier was founded in southern France. It became the birthplace of European alchemy, producing in the thirteenth century several of the most famous alchemists, including Albertus Magnus and Roger Bacon, the most renowned of the medieval scientists. Another famous graduate, St. Thomas Aquinas, also wrote on alchemy. Like their Arab predecessors, the European alchemists believed that all metals were constituted of varying proportions of two metals, mercury and sulfur. Much of their research centered on the quest for an elusive elementary solvent with which metals could be broken down into these two basic elements and then reconstituted in different proportions, resulting in different metals.

It was with good reason that alchemists were perceived as charlatans promising more than they could deliver, yet at the same time they were suspected of being in league with dark forces and, akin to sorcerers, using black magic and charms.

The European monarchies also suspected alchemists of fraudulent and heretical practices, but were always in a bind for money. Although fearing alchemists as potential counterfeiters, they could not resist the lure of the alchemists' promise to convert lead and other base metals into gold. James II of Scotland is reported to have dabbled in alchemy himself. King Charles II of England inherited a bare treasury and sought a solution to his fiscal problems in the magic of alchemy. He built his own laboratory for alchemical investigations connected to his bed-chamber by a secret staircase. France also turned to alchemists to help finance wars with England, and both countries issued gold-colored currency as soldiers' pay. In the twentieth century Adolf Hitler is reported to have sought the services of scientists engaged in alchemical studies, hoping to bolster Germany's gold reserves.

The famous English philosopher Sir Francis Bacon, in his book *Advancement of Learning* (1605), may have caught the significance of alchemy when he wrote, "Alchemy may be likened to the man who told his sons that he had buried gold in the vineyard; where they by digging found no gold but by turning up the mold about the roots of the vines procured a plentiful vintage."

See also: Gold
References: Bacon, Sir Francis. 1952. *Advancement of Learning.*
Cummings, Richard. 1966. *The Alchemists.*
Marx, Jennifer. 1978. *The Magic of Gold.*

Alexander the Great (356–323 B.C.)

If the Greek city-states perfected the coinage that Lydia invented, Alexander the Great spread Greek coinage throughout an empire that stretched from Egypt to India, and north to Samarkand. The Egyptians had not coined money before Alexander, and the Romans did not begin coining money until after his death.

Macedonia, the country of Alexander, began its rise to world leadership with vast holdings of mineral deposits, including iron, copper, silver, and—unlike the Greek city-states—gold. The king of Macedonia owned these resources as personal property under his sole authority. Macedonian coinage made its appearance around 479 B.C. Over a century later King Philip II minted a golden *stater* bearing an image of the head of Zeus on one side and a depiction of his kingly victory in an Olympic chariot race in 356 B.C. on the other side. These coins found their way to the Celtic tribes of central and northwestern Europe, and are among the oldest coins discovered in England. Some observers saw Philip himself in the image of Zeus, and these coins helped raise the prestige of Macedonia in the Greek world. Before his death, Philip had accumulated a large stock of gold *philippeioi* and silver tetradrachms to finance an invasion of Persia.

Both sides of a silver tetradrachm. Hercules is depicted on the obverse. Zeus, holding an eagle, is pictured on the reverse.
(Smithsonian Institution, National Numismatic Collection)

Alexander ascended the throne in 336 B.C. already commanding this huge stock of gold and silver coin, which he could use to pay mercenaries. The chief Macedonian mints were at Pella and Amphipolis, and these mints began to rival Athens as the largest source of coinage in the Mediterranean world. Alexander put both the gold and silver coins on the Attic standard, and he used his large reservoirs of gold to maintain a ten-to-one ratio between silver drachmae and gold drachmae. Alexander's own golden stater bore the head of Athena wearing a Corinthian helmet on one side, and on the other side a winged Victory with a wreath and a stylus. His silver tetradrachm bore the head of a young Hercules with a lion-skin headdress, and the other side a Zeus, complete with throne, scepter, and eagle. Alexander never struck coins bearing an image of himself, but after his death coins with his image appeared in parts of his empire.

Perhaps Alexander's greatest contribution to the spread of coinage was his practice of paying his soldiers in cash. Cavalrymen averaged two drachmae a day, infantrymen one drachma, and a common mercenary two-thirds of a drachma. Midway through his Asia Minor campaign, Alexander was spending 20 talents (half a ton of silver) per day paying and rationing his army. The Persian campaign brought virtually unlimited supplies of gold and silver bullion under Alexander's control. He coined bullion that he found hoarded in temples and royal treasuries.

Amphipolis was the most prolific of the mints in Alexander's empire, minting some 13 million silver tetradrachms alone over an 18-year period. Alexander turned the mint of Babylon into the most productive in Asia, second only to Amphipolis in his empire, and he established lessor mints at Tarsus, Sicyon in the Peloponnese, Lampsacus, Sardis, Miletus, and Sidea in western Asia Minor, at Ardaus and Sidon in Phoenicia, at Citium in Cyprus, at Alexandria in Egypt, and at Ecbatana, now in Iran. Alexander's army accepted the Attic standard, which acted to spread that standard throughout the empire.

In the course of Alexander's coinage, the image of the head of Hercules on his coins began to resemble an idealized engraving of Alexander himself, marking a departure from the emphasis on religious themes of the more democratic Greeks. Under the influence of the example set by Alexander, the Romans would be the first to put the head of a living person on a coin. Alexander also paved the way to making coinage a jealously guarded sovereign prerogative, and he infused coinage into the economies of the ancient world on a greater scale than had ever been seen before. One of his legacies was a vast increase in the use of coins as a form of money.

See also: Attic Silver Standard, Celtic Coinage
References: Hammond, G. L. 1980. *Alexander the Great: King, Commander, and Statesmen.*
Milne, J. G. 1931. *Greek Coinage.*

Stewart, A. 1993. *Faces of Power, Alexander's Image and Hellenistic Politics*.

Troxell, Hyla A. 1997. *Studies in the Macedonian Coinage of Alexander the Great*.

Almonds

J. B. Tavernier traveled through India during the seventeenth century, and he observed in an account of his travels:

> For small Money they make no use of these Shells [in the Province of Gujerat] but of little Almonds which are brought from about Ormuz and grow in the Dessarts of the Kingdom of Larr. If you break one of the shells it is impossible to eat the Almond for there is no *coloquintida* [colocynth] so bitter; so that there is no fear lest the children should eat their small Money. Some years the Trees do not bear and then the price of this sort of Money is very much raised in the Country and the Bankers know how to make their benefit. They call these Almonds *Baden*. They give for a *pecha* sometimes 35 sometimes 40. (Tavernier, 1985)

Nineteenth-century authors reported the use of bitter almonds, unfit for consumption, circulating in the Sudan as money.

The fact that the almonds were bitter, and not desired as food, leaves one wondering what was the appeal that made these almonds attractive as money. For use as money societies have often raised up commodities that had food value, either nutritionally or as a stimulate or depressant, or had religious significance, or conferred social status. There is no mention that almonds possessed any of these characteristics. However, almonds are reasonably durable, which may have made them useful as a store of value. The use of almond money was restricted to small change, perhaps because almonds never commanded the economic and social significance of most commodities that rise to the status of money.

See also: Commodity Monetary Standard
References: Einzig, Paul. 1966. *Primitive Money*. Quiggin, A. Hingston. 1949. *A Survey of Primitive Money*. Tavernier, J. B. 1985. *Collections of Travels through Turkey into Persia and the East-Indies*.

American Penny

The penny in the United States is a one-cent coin. Presently the United States Mint strikes about 13 billion pennies annually, accounting for two-thirds of all coins struck by the mint. If all the pennies struck by the U.S. Mint since its inception were lined up edge to edge, the pennies would circle the earth 137 times.

Historically, the penny was a copper coin. Copper coinage came slowly to the English-speaking countries, perhaps because of its long association with currency debasement. Early in the seventeenth century Spain had debased its silver coin with copper alloy, eventually striking coins that were virtually all copper with face values commensurate with high silver content. The prevailing opinion in England was that only gold and silver met the standard of a monetary metal. A shortage of small change among tavern keepers and tradesmen, however, prompted the introduction of private tokens. To meet the need for small change the English government in 1613 first struck copper coins. England struck the first copper pennies for home use in 1797.

In 1722 the English government authorized William Wood to mint pennies and halfpence for Ireland and the colonies. These pennies were a mixture of copper, tin, and zinc, and had a touch of silver. In 1681 New Jersey sanctioned as legal tender copper coins called Patrick's Pence, after the Irishman who brought the coins to the colonies.

Under the Articles of Confederation several states established mints that turned out copper coins. The Coinage Act of 1792 established the cent and the half cent and set the weight of the cent at 264 grains of copper. The act made no provision for the actual coinage of copper and the legal tender provisions of the act failed to mention copper coins. Congress soon amended the act to provide for the purchase of copper and necessary arrangements for the coinage of copper cents and half cents. Congress also began to think of the copper coinage as a fiduciary issue, and authorized the president to substantially reduce the copper weight of the cent and half cent.

Congress also banned the circulation of foreign copper coins, a restriction that did not apply to foreign gold and silver coins. The Spanish silver dollar circulated clearly as legal tender currency while the legal tender status of the copper cents and half cents remained in doubt. After President Washington

Both sides of the first American penny. Congress had to amend the Coinage Act of 1792 to provide for the coinage of pennies. (Smithsonian Institution, National Numismatic Collection)

reduced the copper content of the cent to 168 grains, the coinage of cents and half cents accelerated as a profit-making venture.

In 1857 Congress substantially increased the seigniorage on the copper coins. It abolished the half cent, and reduced the weight of the one-cent coin to 72 grains with 88 percent copper and 12 percent nickel. In 1864 Congress again changed the composition of the cent, raising the copper content to 95 percent, and making up the remaining 5 percent with zinc. Congress also made the one-cent coin legal tender.

In 1909, to mark the one-hundredth year since his birth, Abraham Lincoln became the first historical figure to adorn a United States coin. Fifty years later an image of the Lincoln Memorial appeared on the reverse side, and today both sides of the penny commemorate Abraham Lincoln.

Rising copper prices in the 1970s caused a shortage of pennies, then worth more as copper than as money. Pennies were melted down for copper, and to keep pennies in circulation the government reduced the penny's copper content to 2.5 percent, the remaining 97.5 percent composed of zinc.

At the end of the 1990s the penny's future is somewhat uncertain. Inflated price levels may have made the penny coin obsolete, but proposals to discontinue the penny have not met with widespread approval. The U.S. Mint contends that coinage of the penny is profitable to the government, and other large major industrialized countries, including Great Britain, Canada, Japan, Germany, France, and Italy, have kept the penny, or penny equivalents, in production.

See also: Coinage Act of 1792, Copper
References: Carothers, Neil. 1930. *Fractional Money*; Gadsby, J. William. 1996. *Future of the Penny: Options for Congressional Consideration.*

American Revolution Hyperinflation

On 22 June 1775 the First Continental Congress, struggling to finance the Revolutionary War effort without power to tax or borrow, authorized the issuance of $2 million in bills of credit. These bills of credit, soon to be known as *continentals*, were issued with the understanding that individual states would redeem them according to an apportionment based upon population. The Congress had considered, but rejected, another option that would have assessed to each state a sum of money to be raised by the issuance of state notes on the authority of each state government.

Congress issued an additional $4 million in bills of credit before the year was out. These were scheduled for redemption between the years 1779 and 1986, and, contrary to a suggestion from Benjamin Franklin, paid no interest. The plan for each bill of credit to bear the signature of two members of Congress fell by the wayside, and Congress hired 28 individuals to sign the bills. Congress continued to run the presses, authorizing the issuance of $241,552,780

An assortment of paper money issued by several colonial governments during the American Revolution. (Library of Congress)

in bills of credit before voting to limit circulation to $200 million in bills of credit toward the end of 1779. After 1779 Congress ceased the issuance of bills of credit (continentals).

Congress issued the continentals because the states did not want to levy taxes to finance a war that was partially sparked by anger over English taxation of the colonies. Desiring to tread lightly on taxes, the individual state governments issued $210 million of their own notes between 1775 and 1780, further fanning the flames of inflation.

Although the states shied away from levying taxes to redeem continentals, they complied with the request from Congress to declare continentals legal tender. To reinforce the state action, Congress passed resolutions to shame people into accepting continentals in payment for goods. After hearing of one instance of an individual refusing to accept continentals, Congress resolved (23 November 1775): "That if any person shall hereafter be so lost to all

virtue and regard for his country as to refuse, such person shall be deemed an enemy of his country." Until the end of 1776 price inflation remained relatively tame, but then inflation began to gather momentum, becoming runaway in 1779 when the ratio of continentals to specie in face value increased from 8:1 to 38:1.

In December 1776 the New England states held a price convention in Providence, Rhode Island, that called for less paper money and more taxation, and that developed a recommended set of prices for farm labor, wheat, corn, rum, and wool. The New England states enacted these price recommendations into law and Congress urged other states to do the same. Congress also gave its blessing for states to assume the authority to confiscate hoarded goods. Citizens held mass meetings denouncing price increases, and irate women raided shops that reportedly were hoarding goods. Merchants had to defend themselves in court. Philadelphia protesters hanged in effigy a specie dollar to protest dealers refusing to accept paper money.

In 1778 a second price convention set forth a list of recommended prices, and Congress seemed ready to legislate, calling for a price convention in 1780. Congress also asked the states to formulate price recommendations on the assumption that prices were 20 times higher than they were in 1774. Congress gave up on the idea of fixing prices, however, and in March 1780 Congress asked the states to remove punitive legislation against those refusing to accept continentals.

After 1779 the depreciation of continentals continued, raising to 100 to 1 the face value ratio of continentals to specie by January 1781. The ratio of 100 to 1 became the official ratio at which Congress converted continentals into interest-bearing, long-term bonds under the funding act of 1790.

The experience of the continentals became a lesson in the evolution of paper money—a lesson that had to be relearned many times. The issuance of inconvertible paper money became the accepted practice worldwide as governments learned to maintain its value by restricting its supply.

See also: Confederate Hyperinflation, French Revolution Hyperinflation, German Hyperinflation, Inconvertible Paper Standard, Russian Revolution Hyperinflation

References: Bezanson, Anne. 1951. *Prices and inflation during the American Revolution, Pennsylvania, 1770–1790.*

Hepburn, A. Barton. 1967. *A History of Currency in the United States.*

Myers, Margaret G. 1970. *A Financial History of the United States.*

Paarlberg, Don. 1993. *An Analysis and History of Inflation.*

Stabile, Donald R. 1998. *The Origins of American Public Finance: Debates over Money, Debt, and Taxes in the Constitutional Era, 1776–1836.*

Ancient Chinese Paper Money

In the second book of *The Travels of Marco Polo,* Chapter XVIII is entitled: "Of the Kind of Paper Money issued by the Grand Khan, and made to pass current throughout his Dominions." In this chapter Marco Polo, who lived in China from 1275 to 1292, described the paper money system as follows:

In this city of Kanbulu is the mint of the grand khan, who may truly be said to possess the secret of the alchemist, as he has the art of producing money by the following process. He causes the bark to be stripped from those mulberry-tree the leaves of which are used for feeding silk-worms, and takes from it that thin inner rind, which lies between the coarser bark and the wood of the tree. This being steeped, and afterwards pounded in a mortar, until reduced to a pulp, is made into paper, resembling (in substance) that which is manufactured from cotton, but quite black. When ready for use, he has it cut into pieces of money of different sizes, nearly square, but somewhat longer than they are wide. The coinage of this paper money is authenticated with as much form and ceremony as if it were actually of pure gold or silver; for to each note a number of officers, specially appointed, not only subscribe their names, but affix their signets also; and when this has been regularly done by the whole of them, the principal officer, deputed by his majesty, having dipped into vermilion the royal seal committed to his custody, stamps with it the piece of paper, so that the form of the seal tinged with the vermilion remains impressed upon it, by which it receives full authenticity as current money, and the act of counterfeiting it is punished as a capital offense. Nor dares any person, at the peril of his life, refuse to accept it in payment. When any persons happen to be possessed of paper money which from long use has become damaged, they carry it to the mint, where, upon the payment of only three percent, they may receive fresh notes in exchange. Should any be desirous of procuring gold or silver for the purposes of manufacture, such as of drinking-cups, girdles, or other articles wrought of these metals, they in like manner apply at the mint, and for their paper obtain the bullion they require. (Polo, 1987)

Marco Polo's account of the paper money system in China may have been a bit optimistic. China had been issuing paper money since A.D. 910 and had already suffered at least one round of hyperinflation before Marco Polo's visit. Around 1020 inflation and currency depreciation became such a problem that the authorities resorted to perfuming the paper money to make it more attractive. China seemed to have experienced phases of reformed currencies, punctuated with bouts of inflation. By 1448 the Ming note was worth only 3 percent of its face value,

The earliest known paper money. (Smithsonian Institution, National Numismatic Collection)

and no further references to paper money are found after 1455.

Paper money lost its charm in China owing to inflation, leading to its extinction as a form of state-sponsored money in China until the twentieth century. When the Western world saw a renaissance of paper money toward the end of the seventeenth century, inflation again reared itself as a rock of danger for any paper-money system. Despite the inflation dangers of paper money, however, the societies experiencing the fastest economic development since the beginning of the seventeenth century have been those that learned to use paper money.

See also: Chinese Leather Money
References: Hewitt, V., ed. 1995. *The Banker's Art*.
Polo, Marco. 1987. *Travels of Marco Polo*, ed. W. Marsden.

Arab Dinar

The gold *dinar* of the Arabs rivaled the Byzantine *solidus* as the preferred international currency from the eighth century until the thirteenth century.

By the middle of the seventh century the Arabs had wrested Syria and Egypt from the Byzantine

Empire, and had conquered Iran and Iraq. Within another 50 years the Muslim empire stretched from Spain and Northern Africa to India. The victorious Arabs fell heir to the Byzantine gold coinage in the west, the principle coin of which was the solidus, and to the Iranian silver coinage, the principle coin of which was the drachm, named after the Greek drachma.

The first generation of Arabs contented themselves with the existing monetary standards and coinage, but in A.D. 696 the caliph Abd al-Malik established a uniquely Islamic coinage. Its principle coin was called the gold dinar because the Arabs had called the Byzantine solidus a dinar. The term *dinar* seems to have stemmed from the word *denarius*, referring to a silver coin in ancient Rome. The gold dinar was equal to 4.25 grams of gold, compared to 4.55 grams of gold content in the Byzantine solidus.

Typical of the age, a religious dispute seems to have sparked the decision to establish an Islamic monetary system. Apparently, the caliph Abd al-Malik received word that the Byzantines were importing papyrus decorated in Egypt with a Greek inscription reading "Father, Son, and Holy Ghost." Abd

Islam disapproved of the use of any image of a ruler, deities, or animals on coinage. (Smithsonian Institution, National Numismatic Collection)

al-Malik then sent written instructions that the words "Allah is witness that there is no God but Allah" replace the words "Father, Son, and Holy Ghost." When the Byzantine emperor learned of these developments he sent word to Abd al-Malik, pointedly observing that the Byzantines dominated world coinage. He threatened that soon Byzantine coins would bear messages insulting to the prophet Mohammed unless the Christian inscription was restored to the Egyptian papyrus. This threat provoked the Arabs to erect their own mint, and begin striking their own coinage.

The new Arab dinar bore an inscription on one side affirming the unity and uniqueness of God, and an inscription on the reverse side denying the Christian doctrine of the Trinity. Islam frowned on the use of images of rulers, deities, or animals within a religious context, which in Islam encompassed the coinage.

Plans for an Arab coinage were left in the hands of Al-Hajjaj bin Yusuf, governor of Iran and Iraq. He apparently established the first Arab mint in Wasit in A.D. 702–703. The government tattooed moneyers and moneychangers employed at the mint, and closely supervised them to guard against any sort of fraud. Mint employees caught in fraudulent acts had their hands cut off as punishment. On advice of Al-Hajjaj bin Yusuf, Abd al-Malik ordered that old coins be melted down and minted into Islamic coins, that the new coins be used throughout Islam, and that

anyone refusing to accept the new coinage receive the death penalty.

Between A.D. 813 and 833 the caliph Al-Ma'mun reformed the Arab coinage, providing for greater uniformity in the coinage from different parts of the Muslim empire. The coin types of his reforms lasted until the eleventh century among the secular rulers within the Abbasid caliphate, and until the mid-thirteenth century in Iran and Iraq. By the end of the thirteenth century the gold coinage of Venice and Florence began to displace the Byzantine and Muslim coinage systems.

See also: Byzantine Debasement, Mughal Coinage, Ottoman Empire Currency

References: Cipolla, Carlo M. 1956. *Money, Prices, and Civilization in the Mediterranean World.*

Williams, Jonathan, ed. 1997. *Money: A History.*

Argentine Hyperinflation

Between 1988 and 1991 Argentina saw the climax of more than a half century of inflation, sending runaway annual inflation rates into four-digit territory.

Unlike Chile, Argentina was no stranger to paper money in the early nineteenth century. In 1822 the Bank of Buenos Aires issued bank notes that traded at a premium, but war with Brazil in 1826 led to the suspension of convertibility of these notes into gold. The notes depreciated significantly before resumption of convertibility in 1867. Convertibility was suspended again in 1876, and Argentina's peso depreciated by more than 50 percent.

In 1899 Argentina adopted the gold standard and began an era of price stability that, aside from the interruption of World War I, lasted until Argentina and the world abandoned the gold standard early in the depression of the 1930s. Argentina's wholesale price index (based upon 1943 prices equaling 100) stood at 31.6 in 1907, rose to 38.3 in 1914, and climbed steadily—reaching 68.0 in 1920. Then Argentina saw prices decline steadily until reaching a trough of 42.1 in 1933.

From 1934 until 1990 prices rose and inflation fluctuated with a long-term upward trend. Inflation averaged over 50 percent between in 1940 and 1950, and then subsided to an average slightly over 23 percent between 1961 and 1965. Inflation began to creep upwards and really took off in the early 1970s, averaging nearly 109 percent between 1973 and 1976. Inflation finished the decade of the 1970s in the 170 percent range, and approached 400 percent in the mid 1980s. By 1989 the annual inflation rate exceeded 3,000 percent. Inflation exceeded 2,000 percent in 1990 and declined to 84 percent 1991. By the mid-1990s Argentina had tamed inflation to well within the single-digit range and had become a model of monetary stability.

The root cause of the inflation originated in isolationist foreign trade policies, political instability alternating between military dictatorships and civilian governments, interventionist domestic economic policies emphasizing subsidies, and the failure of the tax system to fund public expenditures. The unfortunate episode of the Falklands war in 1982 may have helped put Argentina on the road to bankruptcy and collapse. Between 1980 and 1990 real wages fell 20 to 30 percent. Between 1973 and 1990, per capita income fell 26 percent. Tax revenue as a percentage of the gross national product (GNP, a measure of total national output and income, comparable to the gross domestic product in use today) fell in the 1980s and the public debt surpassed 100 percent of GNP. Printing money became a substitute for taxation.

Dissatisfaction with economic chaos helped bring a democratic revival in Argentina, and early in the 1990s a democratic government brought inflation under control, a feat that had eluded military governments. Worldwide inflation in the 1970s had led some observers to doubt the ability of democratic governments to face up to the disease of inflation.

In March 1991 the Argentine legislature enacted the Law of Convertibility, creating a new Argentine peso convertible into one U.S. dollar. The new monetary base was backed by 100 percent of reserves in gold, dollars, or other foreign currencies. United States dollars were also accepted as a currency for domestic transactions. The value of the peso was pegged at 1 dollar, and the central bank maintained convertibility between pesos and dollars. This currency reform not only broke the back of inflation, but made Argentina's monetary system a model for other developing countries. Monetary reform coincided with a capitalist revolution in Argentina, emphasizing privatization, less government intervention, and openness to foreign trade.

See also: Bolivian Hyperinflation, Brazilian Hyperinflation, Chilean Inflation, French Revolution Hyperinflation, German Hyperinflation, Inflation and Deflation

References: De la Balze, Felipe A. M. 1995. *Remaking the Argentine Economy.*

Meiselman, David. 1970. *Varieties of Monetary Experience.*

Assignats
See French Revolution Hyperinflation

Athenian Owls
See Attic Silver Standard

Attic Silver Standard
Athens capitalized upon the invention of coinage more than any other Greek city. The city owed no small part of its success to the Laurium mines, which Aeschylus called a "fountain of running silver." Athens' coins became the most popular in the Greek world, and the city forced the client states in the Athenian empire to replace their own currency with Athenian currency, creating the Attic silver standard.

Before the sixth century B.C. Greece and Macedonia could lay claim to only two small mines that held deposits of pure silver. Silver was relatively rare, and valued among the ancient Egyptians more highly than gold. Athens had at its doorstep mines at Laurium that held vast deposits of argentiferous lead ores, awaiting only the technology to separate the silver from the lead. The mines got their name from

The Athenian tetradrachm, bearing the image of the goddess Athena on one side and the image of an owl on the other. (Smithsonian Institution, National Numismatic Collection)

the *laurai*, or horizontal alleys, that entered into the hillsides before deeper mining methods were employed. The Greeks learned to free the silver from the lead by heating molten metal on cupels of porous material and exposing it to the air, thereby separating a metal that was 98 percent silver. In 546 B.C. the tyrant Peisistratus, the first Athenian ruler to see the value of the silver mines, coined the first *owls*, the Athenian coins that would become the most famous coins of the Greek world, remaining in circulation for nearly 600 years. Around 490 B.C. a prospector discovered the first really profitably veins of silver, touching off a silver rush and supplying the financial resources that would propel Athens to commercial supremacy. The Laurium mines remained an important source of silver to the ancient world before playing out around 25 B.C.

The basic monetary unit throughout the Greek world was the *drachma*, from a word meaning "handful of grain." The precise weight seemed to range between less than 3 grams in Corinth, and more than 6 grams in Aegina. The famous Athenian owls were usually struck in one-, two-, and four-drachma pieces, and on rare occasions in eight-, 10-, and 12-drachma pieces. Perhaps the most famous coin in antiquity was the four-drachma, or *tetradrachm*, bearing the image of an owl on one side and the head of the goddess Athena on the other. The owl was the sacred bird of Athena. Before the Athenian owl there were a few scattered instances of coins

bearing human heads, but the owl started the fashion of putting the head of a deity or famous person on one side of a coin, a practice that has survived into modern times.

The smallest Athenian coins were made of copper and were called *chalkous*. Eight chalkoi made an *obol*, a reference to its resemblance to nails or spits, *obeliskoi*. Six obols made a drachma, and two drachmae made a silver stater. One hundred drachmas, or 50 staters, equaled a mina. And 60 minae, or 6,000 drachmae, equaled a talent. Two obols were a day's pay for a laborer.

In 456 B.C. Athens forced Aegina to give up minting its own turtle coinage in favor of the Athenian owls. In 449 B.C. Athens issued an edict requiring that all foreign coins be brought to the Athenian mint, and that all allies adopt the Attic standard of weights, measures, and money. These were probably measures to promote commerce, and certainly acted to further Athenian commercial ambitions.

The Athenian government's stubborn avoidance of debasement through all its vicissitudes deserves some credit for the esteem that the owls commanded among Mediterranean trading centers. The one exception was an episode during the Peloponnesian War, when Sparta stopped the flow of silver from the Laurium mines in 407 B.C., causing Athens a severe coin shortage. The Athenian government first melted down golden statues and other treasures that adorned the Acropolis, and minted 84,000

The Augustalis bore an image of Fredrick II on one side and an eagle on the other. (Smithsonian Institution, National Numismatic Collection)

golden drachmae. When the coin shortage worsened between 406 and 405 B.C. Athens issued bronze coins with silver coating, giving history one of the first examples of Gresham's law in operation. During the wartime bronze debasement, the famous Greek comedy playwright Aristophanes, wrote: "In our Republic bad citizens are preferred to good, just as bad money circulates while good money disappears." (Angell, 1929). Athenian citizens hoarded gold and silver coins and spent the bronze coins. Athens demonetized the bronze coins in 393 B.C. and Athenian coinage again established itself as the preferred currency in the commercial world.

The Attic silver standard gave the Western world a shining example of a monetary policy committed to sound money for an extended period of time. In contrast, the lack of rectitude in Roman monetary policy left the world a legacy of monetary disorder and rapid inflation.

See also: Aeginetan Silver Standard, Corinthian Silver Standard, Solon

References: Angell, Norman. 1929. *The Story of Money.*
Burns, A. R. 1927. *Money and Monetary Policy in Early Times.*
Davies, Glyn. 1994. *A History of Money.*
Figueira, Thomas J. 1998. *The Power of Money: Coinage and Politics in the Athenian Empire.*
Freeman, Kathleen. 1976. *The Work and Life of Solon.*
Milne, J. G. 1931. *Greek Coinage.*

Augustalis

The *augustalis* was the first gold coin of commercial importance struck in western Christendom after the disappearance in the eighth century of the old Roman Imperial coinage.

The Emperor Frederick II (1194–1250), the most gifted, innovative, and scholarly ruler of the age, first struck the augustalis in 1231, preceding by about 20 years the European return to large-scale gold coinage. Frederick II's gold coinage is often judged an extension of Islamic and Byzantine gold coinage, rather than Western European coinage, depriving Frederick II of credit for minting the first European gold coinage after the disappearance of European gold coinage in the Middle Ages. Nevertheless the augustalis was an important step in the reintroduction of gold coinage to Western Europe.

Frederick II was emperor of what was later called the Holy Roman Empire, which Voltaire described as "neither holy, nor Roman, nor an empire." The Empire encompassed what is now Austria, the Czech Republic, eastern France, Germany, large parts of Italy, the Netherlands, Belgium, Luxembourg, Sicily, and Switzerland.

After the Carolingian reform in the eighth century, the silver denier was the highest denomination of coin minted in Europe. The shilling and pound were imaginary denominations that passed as multiples of the denier. As trade grew, and the purchasing power of silver fell, Europe needed coinage of greater value.

Probably an annual tribute extracted from Tunisia by treaty supplied the sizable quantities of gold coinage and gold dust that enabled the imperial mints of southern Italy to coin the augustalis. The new gold coin bore an image of the emperor on one side and an eagle on the other side. The coin contained $4^1/_2$ grams of gold alloyed with an admixture of silver at a rate of $2^1/_2$ carats of silver per $20^1/_2$ carats of gold and a bit of copper. The total weight of the coin was 5.28 grams. The alloyed composition of the augustalis was not uncommon at the time, and the scrupulously maintained weight of the augustalis made it more attractive than the pure gold Islamic dinar. In France, England, and the Holy Land, the augustalis displaced the tar, a coin that Lombard princes in southern Italy and Sicily struck as a quarter of a dinar.

The augustalis maintained its popularity for 50 years, but was supplanted by the pure gold coinage that Genoa and Florence first minted in 1252. From Genoa and Florence gold coinage quickly spread to the rest of Italy and Europe. France and England had issued gold coins before the end of the century, and Germany began gold coinage in 1328.

See also: Florentine Florin, Venetian Ducat
References: Chown, John F. 1994. *A History of Money.* Lopez, Robert S. 1986. *The Shape of Medieval Monetary History.*

Augustan Monetary System

Augustus, Roman emperor from 30 B.C. to A.D. 14—the first emperor after the fall of the Roman Republic, established a monetary system that provided a degree of monetary order to the Romans for two centuries. The system gradually gave ground to currency debasement and inflation, which grew to unbearable proportions during the third century A.D., when the emperors Aurelian, Diocletian, and Constantine instituted major reforms of the Roman currency.

The early Roman Republic adopted a bronze monetary standard, but wars brought in larger supplies of silver, making it the dominant monetary metal in last 150 years of the Republic. Bronze became only token money and under Julius Caesar Rome regularly minted gold coins.

Under the Augustus system, the gold *aureus* was equal to one-forty-second of a pound of gold, down a bit from the standard of the Republic that put an aureus at one-fortieth of a pound of gold. The system continued the later Republican standard for the silver *denarius,* fixing its weight at one-eighty-fourth of a pound of silver. By government decree, 1 aureus equaled 25 denarii, making the Augustan system a bimetallic monetary standard. The ratio by weight between gold and silver was 1:12.5. Like all bimetallic standards the system had difficulty maintaining a fixed ratio between two metals, the values of which were free to fluctuate in open markets.

Augustus also minted a gold *quinarius* worth one-half of an aureus, and a silver quinarius, equaling one-half of a denarius. He minted two bronze coins, the *sestertius* and the *dupondius,* the latter worth half as much as the former. A sestertius was equal to about one-half of a silver quinarius. Further down the scale of coins was the copper *aes,* equaling one-quarter of a sestertius, and a copper *quadrans,* equal to one-half of an aes. The bronze and copper coinage belong in the category of token coinage, and was mostly sold to the moneychangers who found buyers in need of small change. The gold and silver coins were almost pure in precious metal content and were used to pay for government expenditures, including the wages of the soldiers.

Augustus followed the example of Julius Caesar in having an effigy of himself struck on one side of the coins. After his death coins appeared with an image of Augustus and referred to him as a deity. The idea that coins were struck and issued by deities may have encouraged later Romans to think that coins had value independent of their precious metal content. Toward the end of the first century the emperor Domitan put the words "Dominus et Deus" on coins bearing his image.

The emperor Nero reduced the weight of the aureus to one-forty-fifth of a pound of gold, and the denarius to one-ninety-eighth pound of silver. The relative values of the two coins stayed fixed at 1 aureus to 25 denarii. Also the silver was alloyed 10 percent with another metal. As government expenditures outpaced tax revenues, Roman emperors turned to the practice of secretly debasing silver coins. Under the philosophic emperor Marcus Aurelius, the silver content of silver coins fell to 75 percent, and by the second decade of the third century the silver content had fallen to 50 percent. Then the debasement and inflation became a much more frenzied affair until the silver content of coins fell to 4 percent by A.D. 270. With the monetary reforms of Aurelian, Diocletian, and Constantine the Romans would learn to live with inflation and perhaps slow it down slightly before it took off again in the fourth century A.D. The problem of currency debasement and inflation became one of the subplots of the decline and fall of the Roman Empire.

See also: Bronze Standard of Ancient Rome, Constantine I, Roman Empire Inflation

References: Burns, A. R. 1927. *Money and Monetary Policy in Early Times.*
Duncan-Jones, Richard. 1998. *Money and Government in the Roman Empire.*
Jones, A. H. M. 1974. *The Roman Economy.*
Mattingly, Harold. 1968. *Roman Coins.*

Austrian Hyperinflation

After the close of World War I, Austria, one of the states that emerged from the division of the Austro-Hungarian Empire, experienced an episode of soaring hyperinflation, registering an annual inflation rate of 10,000 percent between January 1921 and August 1922. A legacy of food shortages and high unemployment after World War I helped send Austria on a monetary path of economic insanity. The creation of new states, coupled with the scarcities of war, disrupted traditional flows of trade, and Austria, a loser in the struggle, owed war reparations.

The government of Austria met the crisis by incurring large expenditures on food relief and unemployment relief. From 1919 until 1922 the Austrian government collected less than 50 percent of public expenditures in taxes, and financed the remainder selling treasury bills to the Austrian section of the Austro-Hungarian Bank, which paid for the treasury bills with fresh bank notes, denominated in Austrian crowns. From March 1919 until August 1922 the Austro-Hungarian Bank multiplied Austrian bank note circulation by a factor of 288, increasing the supply of bank notes in circulation from the equivalent of $4.7 million to over $1.3 billion. Aside from public borrowing, the bank continued to make private sector loans at favorable interest rates.

As inflation mounted, Austrians began a "flight from the crown." They spent the bank notes sooner after receiving them and Austrian crowns held as a form of wealth were spent. Austrians put wealth in foreign exchange or real assets, minimizing holdings of Austrian currency. Contemporary economists might describe the flight from the crown as an increase in the velocity of money, meaning money is spent more frequently on goods and services. The government instituted exchange controls in a rather ineffective effort to stop Austrians from converting Austrian crowns to foreign exchange. The value of Austrian crowns in the New York foreign exchange market dropped sharply. In January 1919 one U.S. dollar bought 17.09 Austrian crowns, and in August 1922 one U.S. dollar bought 77,300 Austrian crowns.

The flight from the crown caused prices to rise faster than the money supply growth rate. Between January 1921 and August 1922 retail prices rose by a factor of 110, while bank note circulation rose by a factor of only 39.

The depreciation of the crown in foreign exchange markets stopped abruptly in August 1922, and the upward spiral in retail prices ended the following month. The League of Nations arranged for the Austrian government to receive a loan of 650 million crowns. In return the Austrian government had to end deficit spending and establish a central bank independent of the government. The mere spread of knowledge of the agreement was sufficient to stabilize retail prices and the crown in foreign exchange markets.

The central bank of Austria continued to rapidly infuse bank notes into the Austrian economy but inflation subsided, appearing to defy the laws of economics. These bank notes, however, were backed with gold, foreign assets, or commercial paper, rather than government securities. The change in the composition of the assets of the central bank accounted for the end of the monetary disorder.

At the end of 1924, long after the inflation subsided, Austria issued a new unit of currency, the shilling, worth 10,000 crowns.

See also: German Hyperinflation, Hungarian Post–World War I Hyperinflation, Polish Hyperinflation

References: Sargent, Thomas J. 1993. *Rational Expectations, and Inflation.* 2d ed.
Wicker, E. 1986. Terminating Hyperinflation in the Dismembered Hapsburg Monarchy. *American Economic Review* 76(3):350–364.

Automatic Transfer Service (ATS)
See Monetary Aggregates

Ayr Bank

The Ayr Bank was a Scottish bank of the latter eighteenth century that caused one of the most famous banking debacles in European history. In part the bank owes its notoriety to Adam Smith, who, in the *Wealth of Nations*, devoted a good bit of space to describing its story.

The Ayr Bank, more accurately called the firm of Douglas, Heron, and Company, came into being in November 1769. It was founded along the lines of the land bank schemes suggested by John Law, but unlike Law's schemes, it was a purely private initiative without official backing. As a copartnership, as opposed to an incorporated business, its owners were fully liable for all the debts of the business. Its founders were landowners of the first order, one of whom, the Duke of Buccleuch, had accompanied Adam Smith on a tour of Europe and had the benefit of the famous economist's advice. Land owned by the founders was the ultimate security for the bank's notes.

The Ayr Bank burst upon the scene when the Scottish economy was in a contraction and many observers felt that a shortage of circulating money acted as a drag on the Scottish economy. According to Smith, writing in the *Wealth of Nations*:

> This bank was more liberal than any other had ever been, both in granting cash discounts, and in discounting bills of exchange. With regard to the latter, it seems to have made scarce any distinction between real and circulating bills, but to have discounted all equally. It was the avowed principle of this bank to advance, upon any real security, the whole capital which was to be employed in those improvements of which returns are the most slow and distant, such as the improvements to land. (Smith, 1952)

The liberal lending policy of the bank led to a rapid expansion of bank notes, greater than what the bank's resources could support. The Ayr Bank expansion of credit found its way into speculation in real estate and the London stock market. Bank notes were redeemed with bills of exchange drawn on London banks in amounts that exceeded the bank's London resources. In 1772 a London-Scottish banking house with close connections with the Ayr Bank failed, and the Ayr Bank's house of cards collapsed. Scotland's public banks refused to grant credits to the failing bank. The bank was liquidated, and the income from the land was pledged to the redemption of outstanding bank notes. The founders of the bank lost everything, some of whom were apparently unaware that their liability was unlimited.

The failure of the Ayr Bank was probably due more to mismanagement than to faults in the land bank principle. The bank may have actually spurred the economic development of Scotland, but its failure weakened public confidence in land banking schemes, leaving gold and silver as the most acceptable security for bank notes. The bank's history shows how easily an expansion of bank notes leads to a speculative bubble that ends in collapse. History has continued to repeat itself, with Tokyo being the last scene of a speculative bubble fed by overly generous credit policy.

See also: Bank of Scotland, Free Banking, Land Bank System, Scottish Banking Act of 1765

References: Checkland, S. G. 1975. *Scottish Banking History: 1695–1973.*

Kroszner, Randy. 1995. *Free Banking: The Scottish Experience as a Model for Emerging Economies.*

Smith, Adam. 1952. *An Inquiry into the Nature and Causes of the Wealth of Nations.*

B

Babylonian Grain and Silver Standard

By 2000 B.C. Babylonia had evolved into a highly developed commercialized society, complete with a sophisticated monetary and credit system. Barley and silver functioned side by side in a dual monetary system that made use of both as mediums of exchange and standards of value. Historically, barley preceded silver as the chief form of currency, but both were legally sanctioned currencies in the heyday of Babylon's commercial preeminence. A legal ratio established the value of silver in terms of barley and vice versa. Creditors accepted payments in either silver or barley, depending upon a debtor's preference. Silver grew in importance relative to barley, and later in the ascendancy of Babylon gold became a competing metal currency.

The standard monetary unit was a *shekel,* equal to 180 grains of barley, or a fixed weight of silver. "To weigh" was the term for payment in silver, and "to measure" was the term for payment in grain. Silver was melted into small ingots that circulated as money and was usually tested for fineness at each transaction. Some of the ingots bore the image or superscription of the god whose temple guaranteed the fineness of the silver. An extant Babylonian contract refers to payment of "fifty shekels of white silver in single shekel pieces," suggesting that silver came in pieces equal to a shekel, and multiples of a shekel. Sixty shekels made a mina, and 60 minas made a talent.

The Code of Hammurabi (ca. 2123–2108 B.C.)
specified grain money for certain payments and metal for others. This code required grain to pay for hired oxen or field laborers, and silver to pay for surgeons, veterinary surgeons, artisans, brick makers, and tailors. Merchants who insisted upon payment in the wrong currency could face severe penalties. Article 108 of the code read: "If a wine-seller does not receive grain as the price of traffic, but have wish to receive money (or silver) they shall call that wineseller to account and they shall throw her into the water" (Einzig, 1966).

Temples lent goods from their stores for repayment in kind. These loans charged no interest as long as they were repaid on time. Some merchants carried on a banking business of sorts, making loans in silver and grain, and holding deposits of customers that earned interest. These customers could pay obligations by writing drafts on these deposits. The statutory rate of interest was 20 percent, but silver loans often earned 25 percent and grain loans more than 33 percent. Bills of exchange have survived written on clay tablets, showing the names of the drawer and drawee, the amount of money changing hands, including interest, and the place and date of payment.

After the Hittites sacked Babylon in 1758 B.C., silver remained mostly as a fictitious unit of account while grain, slaves, domestic animals, and garments served as a tangible means of payment. Primitive currencies often surface in advanced economies when established money either loses its value or, as in Babylon, becomes too scarce. The Hebrew scriptures always measure gold and silver in shekels, making shekels a recognizable unit of money in the Western world.

See also: Mosaic Silver Standard, Phoenician Weight Standard
References: Burns, A. R. 1927. *Money and Monetary Policy in Early Times.*
Einzig, Paul. 1966. *Primitive Money.*
Postgate, John Nicholas. 1994. *Early Mesopotamia: Society and Economy at the Dawn of History.* Rev. ed.

Balance of Payments

The balance of payments for a country summarizes all the international transactions that involve either an outflow or an inflow of money. It is composed of three major elements: (1) the current account, (2) the capital account, and (3) the official reserves transactions account. The official reserves transactions account reflects the official transactions between central banks that must occur when the combined balance of the current and capital accounts is in either the deficit or surplus column.

Transactions that lead to an outflow of money are registered as a debit in the balance of payments, and are entered with a negative sign. Transactions that lead to an inflow of money are registered as a credit, entered with a plus sign. Imports of foreign goods cause an outflow of money, entered with a negative sign in the balance of payments. Exports of domestic goods to foreign buyers lead to an inflow of money, registering as a credit with a plus sign. The balance of trade is total exports minus total imports.

A balance of trade deficit causes a net outflow of money, and a surplus causes a net inflow of money. Income earned from foreign investments and money transferred between citizens of different countries can also influence the balance of payments. When these types of flows are figured into the balance of trade, the outcome is the balance on current account.

Capital flows between countries show up in the balance of payments on the capital account. When domestic investors purchase financial or nonfinancial assets in foreign countries, capital flows out, and money also flows out, registering with a negative sign on the balance of payments. When U.S. citizens purchase stock on the Tokyo stock exchange, dollars flow out, just as when U.S. citizens purchase a Toyota. When foreign investors purchase financial or nonfinancial investments in the domestic economy, capital flows in, and money flows in, registering as a positive sign in the balance of payments. The sale of U.S. government bonds to Japanese investors causes dollars to flow into the United States. If a domestic seller exports goods abroad on credit, the sale of goods is entered as a plus sign in the balance of payments, and the grant of credit is a capital outflow and is entered with a negative sign.

Capital flows often offset imbalances in the balance of trade, as can be observed in the bilateral relationship between the United States and Japan. United States exports to Japan fall well short of U.S imports from Japan, contributing to a deficit on the balance of trade, and an outflow of dollars. In turn Japan invests significantly in the United States, building factories, and purchasing real estate and U.S. government bonds. Japan earns dollars by selling goods in the United States, and invests those dollars back in the United States, causing dollars to flow out on the current account, and flow in on the capital account.

If the outflow of money exceeds the inflow of money, the central banks must settle accounts by compensating adjustments in holdings of gold, foreign exchange, or other reserve assets. An excess of money outflow over money inflow will draw down the reserves of the domestic central bank, while an excess of money inflow over money outflow will build up reserves of the domestic central bank. An excess in the outflow of money leaves foreigners with a claim on domestic resources, and excess in the inflow of money has the opposite effect.

Persistent deficits or surpluses on the combined current and capital accounts cause changes in the value of domestic currency in foreign exchange markets. A deficit causes supplies of domestic currency to build up in foreign exchange markets, and the domestic currency will lose value. As the currency loses value, imports become more expensive, and exports become cheaper in foreign markets. Together these forces will remove the deficit. A surplus causes domestic currency to gain value in foreign exchange markets, making imports cheaper, and exports more expensive in foreign markets. These forces act to remove the surplus.

See also: Foreign Exchange Markets, Gold-Specie-Flow Mechanism, Mercantilism
References: Appleyard, Dennis R., and Alfred J. Field, Jr. 1992. *International Economics.*
Daniels, John D., and David Vanhoose. 1999. *International Monetary and Financial Monetary Economics.*

Banco del Piazza del Rialto, Il
See Bank of Venice

Bank

The term *bank* apparently owes its origin to the "bank" or bench used by the moneychangers during the Middle Ages. Historically, some banks were called banks of deposit, and mainly held deposits of foreign and domestic currencies and arranged payment in foreign trade transactions. The Bank of Amsterdam was a bank of deposit.

Other banks created deposits that acted as a circulating medium of money in a society. One of the earliest banks in this category, the Bank of Venice, was formed when a group of the government's creditors combined and began using government debt as a means of payment in trade. The famous merchant bankers, such as the Rothschilds, acted largely as brokers marketing government and corporate securities to wealthy patrons.

Central banks are bankers' banks, and these banks trace their history from the Bank of England. These banks buy government debt, have a monopoly on the issuance of paper money, and often act as a lender of last resort to commercial banks. The term *bank* nowadays refers to these commercial banks.

Commercial banks in modern capitalist societies act as financial intermediaries, raising funds from depositors and lending the same funds to borrowers. The depositors' claims against the bank, their deposits, are liquid, meaning banks are expected to redeem deposits on demand, instantly. Banks' claims against their borrowers are much less liquid, giving borrowers a much longer span of time to repay money owed banks. Because a bank cannot immediately reclaim money lent to borrowers, it may face bankruptcy if all its depositors show up on a given day to withdraw all their money. Protecting banks and bank customers from bank failures of this sort is the aim of much government banking regulation.

The principle of fractional reserve banking lies at the heart of the modern commercial banking system. During a given period of time a bank will receive fresh deposits while existing deposits are withdrawn. Normally the fresh deposits and the withdrawn deposits cancel each other out. Despite daily deposits and withdrawals, a bank maintains an average level of deposits that represents funds the bank can largely keep loaned out. For safety banks hold back a certain fraction of deposits, called reserves (thus fractional reserve banking), to cover themselves over periods of time when withdrawn deposits exceed fresh deposits. Because these reserves earn no interest, banks are tempted to cut the margin of reserves a bit thin. If adequate, these reserves enable a bank to weather a crisis of confidence when masses of people suddenly withdraw deposits out of fear.

When a bank fails the bank's customers, the depositors, suffer as much or more than the bank's owners. This makes the banking industry an excellent candidate for government regulation. Bank lending policy can also aggravate the business cycle. During an economic downswing banks can become overly cautious, restricting the availability of loans and sending the economy into a steeper downward spiral. On the upswing, however, banks lose their caution, generously granting loans and propelling the economy into an inflationary boom. Government regulation strives to protect bank depositors from bank failures and to encourage banks to become a stabilizing force in the economy.

See also: Bank of Amsterdam, Bank of England, Bank of Venice, Central Bank, Depository Institution Deregulation and Monetary Control Act of 1980, Goldsmith Bankers, Glass-Steagall Banking Act of 1933, Medici Bank, Swiss Banks, Wildcat Banks, World Bank

References: Baye, Michael R., and Dennis W. Jansen. 1995. *Money, Banking, and Financial Markets: An Economics Approach.*
Richards, R. D. 1929. *The Early History of Banking in England.*

Bank Charter Act of 1833 (England)

With passage of the Bank Charter Act of 1833, Parliament renewed the Bank of England's charter until 1855. The act also included provisions that strengthened the bank as the prime note-issuing institution in England, an important step toward giving a single institution a monopoly on the privilege of issuing bank notes.

In 1832 Parliament formed a committee of inquiry to look at various issues from all sides, including the Bank of England's monopoly on joint-stock banking within 65 miles of London. The law forbade incorporated banks with more than six shareholders from engaging in London's banking business. Other joint-stock banks wanted to enter the London market, and existing law seemed to suggest that other banks were free to set up business in London as long as they did not issue bank notes. The Bank of England hotly contested this viewpoint and Parliament made timely use of the expiration of the Bank of England's charter to review the matter.

One outcome of the inquiry was a recommendation that did not make it into the law, but nevertheless represented an important principle. Horsely Palmer, governor of the bank, formulated the principle that all demand deposits and bank notes, that is "all liabilities to pay on demand," should be backed by gold reserves equaling one-third of such liabilities. The remaining two-thirds could be invested in securities. The gold reserves were necessary to ensure the convertibility of bank notes and other bank liabilities. Parliament failed to act on Palmer's recommendation, but the quantification of a reserve policy remained an important issue in banking.

One provision of the act stated "That any Body Politic although consisting of more than six persons may carry on the Trade of Business of Banking in London, or within sixty five miles thereof provided they did not issue notes." The forbidden notes were notes payable on demand or within less than six months. Other banks could open for business in London but the Bank of England held a monopoly on the privilege of issuing bank notes.

The act also made Bank of England notes more than 5 pounds legal tender in England and Wales but not in Scotland and Ireland. These notes were legal tender everywhere except at the Bank of England. This provision enabled country banks to hold Bank of England notes as reserves in lieu of gold, reducing the drain on gold reserves in times of contraction, and centralizing gold reserves in the vault of the Bank of England.

Another important provision lifted the 5 percent usury ceiling on bills of exchange payable within three months. This provision was the beginning of the famed "bank rate" that became a powerful policy instrument for the Bank of England. If gold began to flow out, threatening England's gold reserves, the bank raised the bank rate, attracting funds from abroad and ending the outflow.

With the Bank of England's growing power came responsibility for public disclosure of activities. The act required the Bank of England to began sending weekly statistics on notes issues and bullion reserves to the Treasury and monthly summaries were to be published in the *London Gazette*.

The Act of 1833 was important in the history of money because it made Bank of England notes legal tender during peacetime, it effectively made the Bank of England the custodian of England's gold reserves, and it gave the Bank of England the bank rate with which to control the inflow and outflow of gold. It laid in place principles fundamental to the operation of England's nineteenth-century gold standard, a standard that ruled the monetary world by the end of the century.

See also: Bank Charter Act of 1844, Bank of England, Central Bank

References: Chown, John. 1994. *A History of Money*. Roberts, Richard, ed. 1995. *The Bank of England: Money, Power, and Influence, 1694–1994*.

Bank Charter Act of 1844 (England)

The English Bank Charter Act of 1844 represents an important step in the evolution of the Bank of England as a central bank with a monopoly on the issuance of bank notes (paper money), one of the defining characteristics of a central bank. Today all modern economies have central banks with a monopoly on the issuance of bank notes, the Federal Reserve System in the United States being a good example. In the early 1800s a multitude of commercial banks issued their own bank notes in England, France, the United States, and other countries.

Sir Robert Peel, who was prime minister when Parliament passed the Bank Charter Act of 1844, shared with the famous economist David Ricardo the view that the issuance of currency should be a government monopoly with the profits accruing to the government. Peel considered establishing a new system of currency, with a board independent of government but responsible to Parliament, charged with the issue of paper, convertible into gold, and valid as legal tender. In reality Peel chose a more moderate course that made use of existing institutions:

Important provisions in the Bank Charter Act are paraphrased as follows:

1. The note issuing department of the Bank of England became separate and distinct from other departments. The bank removed it to a different building.

2. The Bank of England was required to hold gold bullion equal in value to the volume of its bank notes issued in excess of 14 million pounds. The government debt secured most of the first 14 million pounds.

3. The Bank of England was required to stand ready to redeem its bank notes into gold at the rate of 3 pounds 17 shillings and 9 pence per ounce of gold.

4. The creation of new banks with the privilege to issue bank notes was prohibited.

5. Banks currently issuing bank notes continued to issue notes as long as their total notes in circulation never exceeded their average for the 12 weeks preceding 27 April 1844.

6. If a bank became insolvent it lost the right to issue bank notes.

7. If a bank stopped issuing notes for any reason, it could never again put notes into circulation.

8. If two or more banks combined and ended up with more than six partners, the new bank could not issue bank notes.

9. The Bank of England was allowed to issue new bank notes backed by securities up to two-thirds of the value of discontinued country bank notes.

The act had the desired effect. The issuance of bank notes gradually became the exclusive privilege of the Bank of England, which by World War I had made its monopoly complete. By monopolizing the issuance of paper money, the Bank of England was able to limit the money supply, helping to maintain its value, which is equivalent to avoiding inflation. The act helped bring stable prices, but its restrictions on the issuance of bank notes hampered the Banking of England's ability to act as a lender of last resort.

The government was forced to suspend the convertibility of Bank of England notes into gold during major financial crises. The financial crises of 1847, 1857, and 1866 all saw suspensions of convertibility.

The Bank of France has enjoyed a monopoly on the issuance of bank notes since 1848, and the Federal Reserve System, established in 1914, has always had a monopoly on the issuance of bank notes. With the demise of the gold standard in the 1930s, the practice of maintaining the convertibility of bank notes into gold disappeared, giving central banks more freedom to inject liquidity into a financial system during a crisis.

See also: Bank Charter Act of 1833, Bank of England, Central Bank

References: Davies, Glyn. 1994. *A History of Money.*
Powell, Ellis. 1915. *The Evolution of the Money Market: 1385–1915.*
Roberts, Richard, ed. 1995. *The Bank of England: Money, Power, and Influence, 1694–1994.*

Bank Clearinghouses (United States)

In the United States, bank clearinghouses partially fulfilled the functions of a central bank before the establishment of the Federal Reserve System. Bank clearinghouses facilitated interbank settlement of accounts, a necessary part of check clearing processes. Also, during financial crises, when currency and coin was scarce, bank clearinghouses issued certificates representing claims on bank assets. These certificates replaced cash in the interbank settlement of accounts and infused additional liquidity into the banking system, allowing banks to survive the outflow of currency and coin typical of financial crises. On rare occasions these certificates circulated as currency.

New York City banks established the first clearinghouse in 1853. Two years later the concept spread to Boston and soon all the nation's largest cities had bank clearinghouses. The New York clearinghouse remained the most important because of New York's (Wall Street's) strategic role as the financial nerve center of the United States.

Under a bank clearinghouse system, an individual bank, Bank A, presents all its claims against other banks (deposited checks written on other banks) to the clearinghouse each day. The clearinghouse credits Bank A's clearinghouse account accordingly. All other banks that have received deposits of checks written on Bank A will take these checks to the clearinghouse also, and Bank A will find its clearinghouse account debited to pay for these checks. Whatever discrepancy exists between debits and credits is settled with cash. The clearinghouse system substantially reduces the amount of cash that changes hands in the check clearing process.

Banks operate on the principle that, despite daily withdrawals and new deposits, the average level of deposits at a bank remains steady during normal business conditions, and therefore banks can keep the vast proportion (80 to 95 percent) of customer deposits loaned out. Banks keep reserves, such as vault cash, for those periods of time when withdrawals exceed new deposits. Sound banks, however, often fell prey to their own success by loaning out too much of depositors' money and coming up short of reserves to redeem deposits during a financial crisis. Bank clearinghouses help banks resist the temptation to overextend loans by forcing banks to speedily honor checks written on their accounts. Also, the New York clearinghouse required weekly reports from associated banks showing customer deposits, assets, and reserves.

The New York clearinghouse issued certificates against bank assets to substitute for cash in interbank settlements during financial crises when accelerated withdrawals of deposits often left banks without cash reserves. The clearinghouse issued certificates against a bank's assets when a bank put up 100 percent collateral either in bonds, or short-term commercial loans rated at 75 percent of face value. In a financial crisis a bank experiencing a drain on reserves could use certificates to settle up with the clearinghouse. The use of clearinghouse certificates was not legally sanctioned until 1908, but certificates helped ease the strain in every financial crisis from 1873 until 1914. The clearinghouse was essentially serving as a lender of last resort, one of the important functions of a central bank.

Although clearinghouses were strictly private organizations, acting on private rather than public initiatives, they met some of the regulatory needs of the banking system before the United States turned to central banking in 1914 with the establishment of the Federal Reserve System.

See also: Central Banks, Federal Reserve System, National Bank Act of 1864

References: Gorton, Gary. 1984. *Clearinghouses and the Origin of Central Banking in the U.S.*
Hepburn, A. Barton. 1924. *A History of Currency in the United States.*
Myers, Margaret G. 1970. *A Financial History of the United States.*

Bank of Amsterdam

The Bank of Amsterdam, established in 1609, rose to become a major hub of world monetary affairs in the seventeenth and eighteenth centuries. As a so-called bank of deposit, the Bank of Amsterdam hardly resembled anything we now call a bank. It rarely even made loans, with the exception of loans to Dutch municipalities and to the Dutch East India Company. The bank held deposits of major currencies and facilitated payment in foreign trade transactions.

The model for the Bank of Amsterdam were banks in the small Italian city-states of Venice and Genoa, where the circulating money consisted of a medley of currencies issued by home governments and neighboring states. Currency that flowed in to these areas from trading partners was often clipped and worn, creating uncertainty about the value of foreign bills of exchange paid in these currencies. To remove this uncertainty these small city-states required that foreign bills of exchange above a certain amount be paid in transfers between accounts in a bank rather than in domestic currency. Special banks enjoying full government backing were established to handle these transactions.

Before 1609 the prevalence of worn and clipped coins had depreciated the value of Amsterdam's currency by 9 percent below the value of currency fresh from the mint. With Amsterdam's merchants running short of good money to pay bills of exchange, the government created the Bank of Amsterdam as a means of providing a currency of uniform value. The bank was a bank of deposit, accepting deposits of currencies at face value, foreign or domestic, worn, clipped, or freshly minted. Depositors paid a small recoinage and management fee deducted from each deposit. The balance on a depositor's account constituted a form of money called money of account or bank money and it never suffered any kind of debasement. Its value remained the same as if it were fresh from the mint. Along with the establishment of the bank came the legal requirement that foreign bills of exchange drawn on Amsterdam, equal to or greater than 600 guilders, be drawn for payment in bank money.

The Bank of Amsterdam also took deposits of bullion, giving each customer a receipt valued in bank money for a deposit of bullion, and crediting the customer's account of bank money in an amount equal to the value of the bullion deposit. The receipt entitled the customer to buy back the bullion with bank money at the price stated on the receipt. The customer paid a modest fee to the bank for storage of the bullion, and if the customer defaulted on the storage fee, the bank took possession of the bullion and sold it as part of the bank's profit. The bank money was much more convenient to handle than bullion and just as good in the eyes of European bankers. Vast deposits of coin and bullion made the Bank of Amsterdam an important holder of the reserves of the European monetary system, putting the bank in a position to play a regulatory role.

Because the Bank of Amsterdam was not a lending institution it stored all the currency and bullion deposited with it in readiness to redeem its outstanding bank money. Bank money was superior to currency and merchants were willing to pay a premium for it, enabling the bank to earn income by selling its bank money at a premium.

In the 1780s wartime difficulties forced the bank to underwrite loans to merchants in difficulty, and the bank saw its reserves drop substantially relative to the deposits of bank money owed to the public. The public turned cautious, and when the French invaded in 1795, caution turned to panic. Unable to redeem all the deposits of coins and bullion, the bank closed down. In 1802 a forced loan allowed the bank to reopen its doors, but it was not successful, and in 1820 the Bank of Amsterdam was liquidated.

See also: Bank of Deposit, Bank of Venice, Bills of Exchange, House of St. George

References: Braudel, Fernand. 1984. *Civilization and Capitalism.* Vol. III.

Davies, Glyn. 1994. *A History of Money.*

Israel, Jonathan I. 1989. *Dutch Primacy in World Trade: 1585–1740.*

Smith, Adam. 1952. *An Inquiry into the Nature and Causes of the Wealth of Nations.*

Van Houte, J. A. 1977. *An Economic History of the Low Countries: 800–1800.*

Bank of Deposit

From the fifteenth through the eighteenth centuries banks of deposit flourished in European cities with heavy traffic in international trade. Banks of deposit accepted deposits of domestic and foreign currency and held them as 100 percent reserves, as opposed to using the deposits to finance loans. This policy of retaining possession of the deposits maximized the safety of depositors' money. Records of each merchant's deposits were kept in account books, and funds were shifted from one depositor's account to another's account without coinage leaving the bank. These deposits constituted so-called bank money, which is a form of money that changes ownership by bookkeeping entries without any coinage or receipts changing hands. This bank money became the principle circulating medium in commercial transactions.

When Italian banks of deposit first emerged in the fourteenth century they required the payer and the payee to appear in person to transfer money in the bank's account books from one account to another. Later it became possible for the payer and payee to meet elsewhere if a notary was present. In 1494 Fra Luca Pacioli, a Renaissance mathematician and friend of Leonardo da Vinci, published a book famous for including the first written treatment of double-entry bookkeeping. In the tract on double-entry bookkeeping, he gave the following description of banks of deposits:

> It is common practice to deal directly with a transfer bank, where you can deposit your money for greater security or for the purpose of making your daily payments to Piero, Giovanni, and Maratino through the bank, because the registration of the transferred claim is as authoritative as a notarial instrument since it is backed by the government. Now suppose you are a banker performing a transfer: If your creditor, without withdrawing cash, orders payment to another party, in your journal you debit that depositor and credit the assignee. Thus you make a transfer from one creditor to another, while you yourself remain debtor. Here you function as an intermediary, a witness and agent of the parties and you justly receive a commission." (Lane & Mueller, 1997)

Adam Smith, in a famous digression in the *Wealth of Nations* (1776), described the class of banks called banks of deposit. He identified the banks of Venice, Genoa, Amsterdam, Hamburg, and Nuremberg as institutions founded as banks of deposit. According to Smith, the currency of small states was made up almost exclusively of the coinage of neighboring states, leaving a small state virtually no control over the quality of its circulating medium. These foreign currencies, becoming worn and clipped, traded at a discount in foreign exchange markets, acting as a hindrance to merchants in the small states. Because small states could not reform domestic currencies, which was mostly foreign, they established public deposit banks as a substitute. Banks of deposit accepted deposits of all currency, new and worn, and exacted a discount of perhaps 5 percent for currency depreciation from wear and tear. The government of the state guaranteed the value of the bank deposits. These deposits, which changed ownership only by means of bookkeeping entries in the bank, represented a uniform quality and, for that reason, often traded at a premium over metallic coinage. According to Smith, the premium on the bank money of the Bank of Hamburg was 14 percent over the clipped, worn, and otherwise diminished currency that poured in from surrounding states.

Aside from the state's commitment to maintain its integrity, bank money had several advantages over metallic currencies of varying consistencies. According to Smith in his *Wealth of Nations* (1776):

> Bank money, over and above its intrinsic superiority to currency, and the additional value which this demand necessarily gives it, has likewise some other advantages. It is secure from fire, robbery, and other accidents; the city of Amsterdam is bound for it; it can be paid away by a simple transfer, without the trouble of counting, or the risk of transporting it from one place to another. (Smith, 1952)

Perhaps the growth of paper money during the Napoleonic era put an end to banks of deposit. Unlike coins, paper money could not be debased by "clipping" bits off of it. Thus, the problem of coins with varying degrees of wear and tear was no longer an issue after the advent of paper money. The Bank of Hamburg inherited the precious metal trade from the Bank of Amsterdam and remained active in that trade until 1814, when the Bank of Hamburg was converted into the Netherlands Bank, a different type of institution.

See also: Bank of Amsterdam, Bank of Venice, House of St. George

References: Kindleberger, Charles P. 1984. *A Financial History of Western Europe.*

Lane, Frederic C., and Reinhold C. Mueller. 1997. *Money and Banking in Medieval and Renaissance Venice.*

Bank of England

The Bank of England is the central bank of the United Kingdom. It acts as the government's bank, regulates the money stock growth rate and the availability of credit, and serves as a banker's bank for commercial banks, making loans and holding deposits. Like all central banks, it holds the exclusive privilege to issue bank notes (paper money). Sometimes referred to as the Old Lady of Threadneedle Street, the Bank of England sits at the center of the London financial center.

The English Parliament granted the Bank of England a corporate charter in 1694 when England was waging a costly war with France. The government needed money, and the Bank of England began as a plan to help raise funds for the government. Parliament imposed a tax on shipping tonnage, and earmarked the proceeds to go to such persons as should voluntarily advance money to the government.

The government planned to borrow 1.2 million pounds at a moderate 8 percent interest. To attract funds on the scale needed at that interest rate, Parliament granted the subscribers to the loan the privilege of pooling their funds and incorporating themselves under the name of the Governor and Company of the Bank of England. The debate in Parliament over this act raised quite a howl, including predictions that the Bank would encourage fraud, gambling, and the corruption of national morals.

Initially, Parliament granted the Bank of England a charter for 10 years. This charter authorized the bank to trade in gold, silver, and bills of exchange, and to issue bank notes equal in amount to its capital. It prohibited the bank from selling merchandise, excepting what had been held as security for unpaid loans. The charter put the management of the Bank of England in the hands of a governor, deputy governor, and 24 directors, elected yearly by the stockholders.

Parliament continued to renew the bank's charter, usually in return for loans to the government, often at lower interest rates. Parliament renewed the bank's charter in 1709 and added a provision that no other joint-stock company with more than six partners could issue bank notes, a provision that eventually gave the Bank of England a dominant position in the issuance of bank notes. In 1751 the bank took over the administration of the national debt, and by 1780 the bank had a virtual monopoly on the

The Bank of England, known as the "Old Lady of Threadneedle Street," ca. 1909. (Library of Congress)

issuance of bank notes in London. The Bank of England began to wear the aspect of a central bank as smaller banks began the practice of keeping funds on deposit with it.

Originally conceived to raise money to fight a war, the bank underwent a particularly innovative period of development during the wars with revolutionary France and Napoleon. Over the protests of the bank's directors, the bank was forced to accommodate the financing needs of the government for unlimited amounts. The bank began issuing notes in much smaller denominations, and in 1797 the bank, with approval from Parliament, suspended the convertibility of its bank notes into specie. Government borrowing had weakened the bank's reserve position and bank note holders were making a run on the bank. Even though they were now inconvertible, the value of Bank of England bank notes stood up well because the government accepted them at par value in all payments and in 1812 made them legal tender. Country banks began to hold Bank of England notes as reserves for their own bank notes.

After resuming convertibility of its bank notes into specie in 1821 the Bank of England saw its bank notes grow in acceptability relative to gold. The country banks found the notes just as useful as gold for managing a cash drain, and began to look to the Bank of England as a place to borrow funds in a liquidity crisis. In 1833 the British government again declared Bank of England notes legal tender for sums above 5 pounds so long as the notes remained convertible. As Bank of England notes replaced gold as the circulating medium, the bank became the major holder of gold reserves.

At first the Bank of England resisted the pressure to become a lender of last resort in financial crises, still seeing itself as a bank competing with other banks, rather than a source of succor to competing banks in a financial crisis. The bank discovered, however, that adjusting its bank rate of interest to compete with other banks destabilized markets. After the crash of 1847 the bank began accepting its role as a lender of last resort and using adjustments in its bank rate of interest to stabilize money markets.

The years preceding World War I saw the bank become the custodian of the gold standard, and develop methods of using the bank rate of interest and open market operations to regulate interest rates, and the inflow and outflow of gold. During World War I the government outlawed the export of gold, and after the war the bank became a strong voice favoring restoration of the gold standard, notwithstanding the high interest rates required to prevent an outflow of gold reserves. The high interest rates needed to maintain the gold standard were out of step with the needs of the time, and in 1931 Parliament passed the Gold Standard (Amendment) Act, suspending the gold standard. The bank was never quite the same after the loss of the gold standard, and the government gave the bank very little guidance as to what policies to follow after the suspension.

During the years between the two world wars the Bank of England's policies came under closer scrutiny and drew more criticism. In particular the Macmillan Committee in Parliament inquired into the full range of activities of the bank and criticized the bank for not being more committed to the methods of monetary management used by central banks —perhaps because of the bank's loyalty to the outmoded gold standard.

The success of the government-directed war economy led a new Labour government in Parliament to embark upon a program of nationalization of major industries after World War II. Controversy over the policies of the Bank of England before the war made it an obvious target. It was nationalized in 1946 and brought under the authority of the Exchequer, or British treasury. With elected officials exerting much more influence over monetary policy, the Bank of England lost some of its reputation for financial probity. During the inflation-ridden 1970s Britain suffered much higher inflation rates than Japan, the United States, and West Germany. During the 1980s tight monetary policies brought down inflation, and by the late 1990s there was talk of again privatizing the Bank of England.

The Bank of England is represented on the General Council of the European Central Bank, but so far England has opted not to participate in the introduction of the *euro,* the all-European currency. The euro will eventually replace the German mark, the French franc, and the currencies of other participating European countries.

See also: Bank Charter Act of 1833, Bank Charter Act of 1844, Bank of France, Banking Acts of 1826, Central Bank, Federal Reserve System, Pound Sterling
References: Bank for International Settlements. 1963. *Eight European Central Banks.*
Clapham, Sir J. 1970. *The Bank of England.*

Roberts, Richard, ed. 1995. *The Bank of England: Money, Power, and Influence, 1694–1994.*
Sayers, R. S. 1976. *The Bank of England: 1881–1944.*

Bank of France

The Bank of France is the central bank in France. It compares to the Bank of England or the Federal Reserve System in the United States, and is responsible for regulating the money stock, interest rates, and credit conditions in France.

When Napoleon assumed the reins of power in 1799 he knew the French government had lost all credibility as a borrower, a factor that had helped spark the French Revolution. His government needed to raise money, but selling government bonds was not a practicable means to do so as there was no market for discredited government debt at the time. In 1800 Napoleon created the Bank of France to help with this problem. It was initially capitalized at 30 million *livres.* Three years later livres were replaced by the new currency, *francs,* making the capitalization 30 million francs. Openly calling the new institution a bank was itself a bold move. After the disaster of John Law's bank in 1720 the very term *bank* had fallen into disrepute in France and disappeared from the names of French financial institutions.

The financial capital for the Bank of France came partly from the capital of the Caisse des Comptes Courants, a Paris discount bank issuing bank notes (paper money) that dissolved and merged into the new institution. Other capital for the bank was raised from public subscriptions, and an additional sum came from the government. The Bank of France was organized as a corporation, the stockholders of which elected a governing committee.

In 1803 the government granted the Bank of France the exclusive privilege to issue bank notes in Paris. The other main note-issuing bank in Paris, the Caisse d'Escompte du Commerce, had been merged unwillingly with the Bank of France in 1802. Other note-issuing banks in Paris were required to withdraw their bank notes before a certain date. Any new note-issuing banks in the provinces had to have the approval of the government.

From the beginning Napoleon wanted the Bank of France to purchase government bonds at the lowest possible interest rates and pay for the bonds with bank notes. In 1804 the bank caved in to government pressure and issued too many bank notes amid rumors that Napoleon had shipped the metallic reserves to Germany for military purposes. A crisis forced the bank to partially suspend convertibility of its bank notes into specie, and the notes depreciated 10 to 15 percent, while the bank—rather than the government—took the blame for the crisis.

In 1806 the governance of the bank underwent a major overhaul. A government-appointed governor and two deputy governors replaced the committee elected by the stockholders. Another partial suspension of convertibility came in 1814.

Napoleon emphasized low interest rates as a means of softening the blow of his continental blockade. He pressured the bank to keep its discount rate (central bank interest rate to borrowers) in the 4 to 5 percent range, a practice the bank continued until the mid-nineteenth century. He also encouraged the bank to act as a lender of last resort.

The Bank of France took advantage of its authorization to set up branch banks in the provinces. However, these branch banks were unsuccessful at first, even in places where they had regional monopolies on the issuance of bank notes. A few private banks opening in the provinces were also unprofitable at first, mainly because of strict government regulation. However, by 1840 private banks began to be a threat in the provinces. After 1840 the government refused to grant charters for new private banks with authority to issue bank notes. Between 1841 and 1848 the Bank of France opened 15 branch banks in the provinces.

In the political crises of 1848 the French government counted on the Bank of France for financial support. The public, remembering the worthless *assignats* of the Revolution, began to convert bank notes into specie and hoard it. The government responding by declaring Bank of France bank notes legal tender throughout the nation, and putting a limit on the number of bank notes the Bank of France could issue. The Bank of France now achieved a clear advantage over the private provincial banks, whose bank notes were only legal tender in their respective regions. The private provincial banks then merged with the Bank of France, and the Bank of France acquired a nationwide monopoly on the issuance of bank notes.

The Bank of France kept its discount rate fairly constant until the 1850s, when it began the practice of adjusting its discount rate to regulate the flow of specie. An increase in the discount rate could halt a specie outflow. In 1857 the bank became exempt from the usury law setting a 6 percent ceiling on interest rates.

By 1900 the Bank of France had some kind of office in 411 French towns, and had as many as 120 full branches, substantially more than the eight branches that the Bank of England had in Britain. The Bank of France played a much greater role in the French money and banking system than the comparable Bank of England played in the British system. The tight control that the Bank of France held over the development of banking in France may have inhibited French economic growth in the nineteenth century. During World War I and World War II the French government relied heavily on the Bank of France to buy government bonds with the issuance of bank notes as a measure of war finance. Bank notes increased 400 percent between 1940 and 1945, but controls suppressed inflation until 1944. The government nationalized the Bank of France in 1945. Inflation grew to acute levels in the 1950s.

On 4 August 1993 the Bank of France won its independence from political authorities in a piece of landmark legislation. With its newly won independence came a renewed commitment to price stability as its top priority regardless of domestic political pressures.

In 1998 the Bank of France joined the European System of Central Banks, which on 1 January 1999 assumed responsibility for implementing a single monetary policy for all member states of the European Monetary Union.

See also: Bank of England, Central Bank, Deutsche Bundesbank, Federal Reserve System, First Bank of the United States, Monetary Law of 1803, Second Bank of the United States

References: Davies, Glyn. 1994. *A History of Money.*
Kindleberger, Charles P. 1984. *A Financial History of Western Europe.*
Wilson, J. S. G. 1957. *French Banking Structure and Credit Policy.*

Bank of Japan

Japan was the first non-Western country to intentionally transform its economy into a developed capitalist system. In 1882 the Japanese government established the Bank of Japan on the European model of central banks. This was three decades before the

United States created the Federal Reserve System and occurred at a time when feudalism was still a fresh memory in Japan.

After the Meiji Restoration in 1868 the government launched Japan on an intensive program of Westernized economic development. The new government found gold, silver, and copper coins circulating alongside paper money issued by feudal lords and merchants. Like previous revolutionary governments, including the Continental Congress of the United States, the Meiji Restoration government turned to the issuance of inconvertible paper money to finance government spending. Inconvertible paper money is paper money not convertible into any type of precious metal. In 1877 the government issued another round of inconvertible paper money to suppress a rebellion. This touched off an inflationary surge from 1877 to 1881.

The Japanese government learned from European and American models. In 1872 Japan had adopted a system of national banks patterned after the national banking system in the United States. Like their counterparts in the United States, these banks held government bonds as collateral for bank notes. The government's inconvertible paper currency was redeemable in government bonds, but the system broke down after the government allowed national banks to issue inconvertible bank notes in the late 1870s.

In 1881 the Japanese minister of finance visited Europe to study central banking systems. The National Bank of Belgium had been created in 1850 and appeared to the Japanese as the most advanced institution of its type. The United States had no central bank, and the Bank of England had evolved over nearly two centuries without a written constitution.

The Bank of Japan Act of 1882 provided for the establishment of the Bank of Japan. The bank was organized as a private joint-stock company. The government furnished half of the capital. Government officials not only appointed the governor of the bank and other bank officers, but also supervised the policies and administration of the bank. The bank held a monopoly on the issuance of bank notes, and served as a lender of last resort to other banks.

The Bank of Japan was set up to serve as the fiscal agent of the government, to stabilize seasonal and regional fluctuations in the flow of funds, to finance international trade, and to hold specie reserves. The Japanese Treasury exerted strong influence on the operations of the bank. In 1897 Japan went on the gold standard, making the bank notes of the Bank of Japan fully convertible into gold.

In 1868 precious metal specie accounted for 75 percent of the money supply. By 1881 that percentage had decreased to 20 percent. Bank deposits accounted for 7 percent of the money supply when the Bank of Japan was formed. By 1914 this percentage had grown to 44 percent. Japan's economy became highly monetized, complete with bank notes and bank deposits.

In June 1997 the Japanese Diet enacted new legislation, the Bank of Japan Law, which provided that the autonomy of the Bank of Japan be respected. In 1998 the Bank of Japan began a major reorganization aiming at streamlining operations and reducing unnecessary holdings, such as surplus real estate.

The process that led to the formation of the Bank of Japan reveals something of the method that lies behind the Japanese economic miracle. Today Japanese commercial banks are among the largest in the world.

See also: Bank of England, Central Bank, Bank of France, Federal Reserve System, Yen

References: Davies, Glyn. 1994. *A History of Money,* 1994. Cameron, Rondo. 1967. *Banking in the Early Stages of Industrialization.*

Bank of Scotland

The Bank of Scotland claims the honor of being the first incorporated bank owned exclusively by private shareholders and devoted exclusively to the business of meeting the banking needs of the private sector. The Scottish Parliament chartered the Bank of Scotland in 1695, and it remains the only surviving institution created by that body. The life of the Scottish Parliament came to a close in 1707 when England and Scotland merged.

In 1695 the larger continental states, France, Prussia, and Austria, depended solely upon private bankers, such as the famous Fugger family of bankers who held sway in the fifteenth and sixteenth centuries. These countries remained strangers to public banks. Italy, Holland, England, and Sweden had founded public banks, but they all had strong connections to governments. The Bank of Amsterdam was founded in 1609, the Bank of Sweden in 1656, and the Bank of England in 1694. The Bank of England was closest in character to the Bank of Scotland but Parliament chartered it mainly to raise money for the government. Some of the Italian public banks were little more than societies of government creditors. The Bank of Scotland was expressly forbidden in its charter to make loans to the monarchy.

The Bank of Scotland began as a pure corporation, entailing limited liability for its shareholders and the same standing as an individual in the eyes of the law. The Scottish Parliament gave the Bank of Scotland a monopoly for its first 21 years, and made its dividends free from taxation for that period. Anyone could purchase stock in the bank, including foreigners. Edinburgh was headquarters for the bank, but branch offices were opened in Glasgow, Aberdeen, Dundee, and Montrose.

Over the protest of the Bank of Scotland, the English Parliament in 1727 chartered a second public bank in Scotland, the Royal Bank of Scotland. Intense rivalry existed between these two banks from the outset. By 1745 Scotland had a highly developed banking system, and notes of these banks were an important means of payment. In 1746 a third public bank, the British Linen Company, received a charter.

By 1730 the Bank of Scotland on three separate occasions had seen the necessity to suspend payment on its bank notes. In that year its directors approved the insertion of the so-called optional clause on its bank notes. The optional clause committed the bank to either redeeming its bank notes on demand, or suspending redemption for six months, and paying a specified interest rate during the interval of suspension. The English Parliament banned the optional clause in the Scottish Banking Act of 1765.

The Act of 1765 also opened up Scotland to "free banking," rendering it easier to organize banks that issue notes. Under Scotland's system of free banking, the Bank of Scotland took the lead in policing the issuance of bank notes by the smaller, provincial banks. In 1776 Adam Smith heaped high praise on the Scottish banking system, writing that "the business of the country is almost entirely carried on by means of the paper of those different banking companies. Silver very seldom appears and gold still seldomer."

In the nineteenth century Parliament began to concentrate the note-issuing authority in the hands of the Bank of England. In 1833 the Bank of England's notes became legal tender in England, a sta-

tus not enjoyed by other bank notes. In 1844 Parliament restricted the further issuance of bank notes by any other bank than the Bank of England. As the Bank of England assumed the role of Britain's central bank, the Bank of Scotland lost its position of leadership in Scottish banking. Mergers between Scottish banks in the nineteenth and twentieth centuries periodically rearranged the rankings of Scottish banks in terms of size, but the Bank of Scotland has remained one of the largest banks in Scotland. A 1989 survey by the *Economist* found the Bank of Scotland to be the bank most admired by its peer bankers.

See also: Bank of England, Royal Bank of Scotland, Scottish Banking Act of 1765
References: Checkland, S. G. 1975. *Scottish Banking, A History, 1695–1973.*
Colwell, Stephen. 1859. *The Ways and Means of Payment.*
Davies, Glyn. 1994. *A History of Money.*

Bank of Spain
See Spanish Inconvertible Paper Standard

Bank of Venice
The history of the Bank of Venice reveals something of the forces that led to the evolution of central banks.

In 1171 the government of the Republic of Venice extracted forced loans of specie from wealthy citizens. The government kept a record book that showed the amounts it owed individual citizens but otherwise issued no bonds, promissory notes (IOUs), certificates of indebtedness, or other proof of indebtedness. The government's creditors received 4 percent interest per year, but the government did not pay down the principal on the loans. The citizens of Venice began exchanging ownership of these government obligations to transact business, turning these government obligations into a circulating medium of exchange like any other form of money. Money transactions settled by entries in books were much more convenient than coined money transactions, particularly when large amounts were involved. The citizens of Venice soon voluntarily deposited specie with the "bank" in return for book entry deposits that could be transferred to other depositors in any amount.

In 1587 the Venetian government established the Bank of Venice as the Banco del Piazza del Rialto. As early as 1374 a committee of scholars had proposed the formal organization of a public bank, but no action was taken for over two centuries. By the late 1500s other Italian cities had already established public banks, costing Venice claims of priority in the history of banking. The credit for the first beginnings of modern banking practices, however, belongs to Venice.

The Venetian practice of banking on the security of government loans survived into the modern period. Today in the United States the Federal Reserve System issues Federal Reserve Notes and deposits at Federal Reserve Banks, holding government bonds as securities against these notes and deposit liabilities.

See also: Bank of Amsterdam, Bank of Deposit, House of St. George, Medici Bank, Venetian Ducat

References: Kindleberger, Charles P. 1984. *A Financial History of Western Europe.*
Knox, John Jay. 1903. *A History of Banking in the United States.*
Lane, Frederic C., and Reinhold C. Mueller. 1997. *Money and Banking in Medieval and Renaissance Venice.* Vols. I–II.

Bank Rate
See Bank Charter Act of 1833, Gold Standard

Bank Restriction Act of 1797 (England)

The Bank Restriction Act of 1797 began England's first experience with inconvertible paper currency—that is, paper currency that was not convertible into precious metal at an official rate. From 1797 until 1821, roughly coinciding with the Napoleonic Wars, the Bank of England suspended payments, meaning that bank notes were no longer redeemable in specie or cash. During this era England managed a system of inconvertible paper currency that met the needs of trade without triggering a destructive episode of hyperinflation.

Prior to the suspension of payments, banks in England, Ireland, and Scotland issued bank notes that circulated as paper money, and these banks stood ready to redeem bank notes into gold and silver specie, assuring the acceptability of bank notes in trade. Beginning in 1793 banks had difficulty maintaining sufficient specie reserves to satisfy all requests for redemption of bank notes. Heavy government borrowing, coupled with subsidies to foreign allies and military expenditures, caused a major outflow of gold, draining the gold reserves of

the Bank of England. The memory was still fresh of the financial debacle that followed John Law's attempt to multiply without limit the paper money in France in 1720. Rumors of a French invasion of Ireland sparked a run on banks, further drawing down gold reserves at the Bank of England. The Privy Council at an emergency meeting on 26 February 1797 decided that the Bank of England should suspend payments, and on 3 May 1797 Parliament confirmed the action with enactment of the Bank Restriction Act. The suspension of payments, advanced as a temporary measure, was continually renewed, lasting six years after the end of the Napoleonic War in 1815. It dominated discussions of monetary issues in Parliament for 24 years.

Measures of inflation during the suspension of payments period were not available because the science of index numbers was still in its infancy. The values of gold and foreign currencies, priced in British pounds, were the main indicators that gauged the value of the paper pound. The Irish pound dropped significantly on foreign exchange markets in 1801, sparking serious discussion. In 1809 the other monetary shoe fell when the British pound dropped significantly on the Hamburg foreign exchange market. The House of Commons appointed a committee, the Select Committee on the High Price of Gold Bullion, to investigate the monetary situation and report to Parliament. The report of this committee, the Bullion Report, fastened the blame on excessive issue of bank notes and recommended the return to convertibility within two years. Thomas Malthus and David Ricardo, famous economists of the time, supported the Bullion Report, while most businessmen and bankers, particularly officials of the Bank of England, defended the suspension policy, arguing that banking policy had no effect on foreign exchange rates. In hindsight the Bullion Report represented sound monetary economics, surprisingly advanced for its time, but the exigencies of war forced England to remain on an inconvertible paper standard. Someone summed up the issues saying that the bankers turned out to be bad economists, and the economists bad politicians.

Two factors seemed to have spared England the ravages of a paper money system out of control. First, England had a developed capital market for long-term financing of government debt. Second, Parliament enacted an income tax that became effective in

1799. The government's use of taxation and long-term borrowing lifted much of the pressure on the monetary system to pay for the war by printing bank notes.

When the war ended in 1815, contrary to expectations, the Bank of England still faced a drain on its gold reserves, and Parliament postponed the resumption of cash payments. In 1819 Parliament passed the Resumption of Cash Payments Act calling for the resumption of payments by 1823. The Bank of England's reserve position improved faster than expected and full convertibility into gold was restored in May 1821. The Resumption of Cash Payments Act also put England squarely on the gold standard, which England had been moving toward during the eighteenth century.

See also: Bank of England, Inconvertible Paper Standard, Liverpool Act of 1816, Pound Sterling
References: Chown, John F. 1994. *A History of Money.*
Clapham, Sir J. 1970. *The Bank of England.*
Fetter, F. W., and T. E. Gregory. 1973. *Monetary and Financial Policy in Nineteenth-Century Britain.*

Banking Acts of 1826 (England)

The Banking Acts of 1826 banned the issuance of bank notes of less than 5 pounds and ended the Bank of England's 100-year monopoly on joint-stock banking.

The Act of 22 March 1826 put an end to notes of less than 5 pounds and required the redemption of the smaller notes by 5 April 1829. Apparently the number of people hanged for the capital offense of forging notes, even small ones, was one thing that moved Parliament to act. Scotland, where 1 pound notes were highly popular, was exempted from the act. Before the act passed Parliament, the eminent author Sir Walter Scott had written letters to the *Edinburgh Weekly Journal* that ridiculed the abolition of small notes in Scotland. Another prominent Scot, Adam Smith, in the *Wealth of Nations,* had argued against the issuance of small notes in 1776, observing:

Where the issuing of bank notes for such very small sums is allowed and commonly practiced, many mean people are both enabled and encouraged to become bankers. A person whose promissory note for five pounds, or even for twenty shillings, would be rejected by everybody, will get it to be received without scruple when it is issued for so small a sum as sixpence. But the frequent bankruptcies to which such beggarly bankers must be liable may occasion a very considerable inconveniency, and sometimes a very great calamity to many poor people who had received their notes in payment. (Smith, 1952)

Arguments in favor of small notes cited the conservation of precious metal reserves when precious metal was no longer needed as a circulating medium. Scotland continued to circulate 1 pound notes throughout the nineteenth century, while Britain relied upon the gold sovereign coin to circulate as the 1 pound piece. Subsidiary silver coinage gradually replaced the role played by the small notes.

The Act of 26 May 1826 ended the Bank of England's monopoly on joint-stock banking. In addition to giving the Bank of England a monopoly on joint-stock banking, an act of 1707 had prohibited banking partnerships with more than six members from engaging in the banking business. Small-scale partnerships dominated English banking in the countryside, while the Bank of England enjoyed a preeminent position within a radius of 65 miles around London. Joint-stock banks were organized as modern corporations, affording the owners (stockholders) the protection of limited liability. Unlike corporations, partnership banks, in the event of bankruptcy, exposed all the personal assets of partners to the demands of creditors. Scotland had pioneered the proliferation of joint-stock banking, but England had tended to reserve to the Bank of England the exclusive privilege of joint-stock banking.

The Act of 1826 preserved the Bank of England's monopoly on joint-stock banking within a 65-mile radius of the center of London, but outside the London area it authorized the establishment of note-issuing banking corporations with an unlimited number of partners. To compensate for its loss of privilege, the Bank of England was authorized to set up branches anywhere in England or Wales. The Bank of England promptly opened branches in major cities, and for a while England flirted with the Scottish system of banking that emphasized competition between note-issuing incorporated banks. The Banking Act of 1833, however, made the Bank of England's notes legal tender, and the Bank Charter Act of 1844 marked a sharp shift toward a policy of concentrating note-issuing authority with the Bank of England.

See also: Bank of England, Free Banking, Scottish Banking
    Act of 1765
References: Checkland, S. G. 1975. *Scottish Banking, A
    History: 1695–1973.*
Davies, Glyn. 1994. *A History of Money.*
Richards, R. D. 1929. *The Early History of Banking in
    England.*

Banking School

Between 1819 and 1844 England was the battle-ground of one of the most important monetary controversies in history: the debate between the banking school and the currency school. The resumption of specie payments following the Napoleonic Wars had not spared England the trauma of periodic financial crises. Financial crises in 1825, 1833, and 1839 became thought-provoking grist for the monetary debating mill.

The currency school found the answer to England's financial turbulence in tighter linkages between domestic money supplies (defined as gold specie and paper money) and domestic gold supplies that varied with the import and export of gold.

The banking school saw domestic money supplies as a much more passive player in the drama of economic boom and crisis, and argued that the currency school's definition of money supplies was narrow and unrealistic. To the banking school a more workable definition of domestic money supplies would, in addition to specie and paper money, include bank deposits and bills of exchange. Banks supplied these forms of money to meet the needs of trade. Part of the thinking of the banking school hinged upon the "law of reflux," stating that every bank note or deposit issued on a loan was canceled when the loan was repaid. The "law of reflux" was akin to the "real bills doctrine" of a similar vintage.

The banking school felt it was unrealistic to attribute a close linkage between prices (inflation) and money supplies as narrowly conceived by the currency school, given the obvious importance of other types of money. The banking school further doubted if circulating domestic money supplies, even if totally metallic, would fluctuate in step with international gold flows as the currency school predicted. Rather than altering circulating money supplies, international gold flows might only lead to hoarding and dishoarding gold, especially within the banking community.

At the time of the debate between the banking school and the currency school, hundreds of banks issued their own bank notes. The banking school essentially defended the status quo, arguing that regulating the issuance of bank notes should be left to the wisdom of commercial bankers, subject to the requirement of convertibility. The bankers left to their own discretion would provide an elastic currency able to expand and contract to meet the needs of trade.

The Bank Charter Act of 1844 largely followed the recommendations of the currency school, especially in laying groundwork for monopolization of bank note issues by the Bank of England. Nevertheless, consistent with the thinking of the banking school, the act gave the Bank of England some discretion to expand and contract bank notes independently of gold flows.

See also: Currency School, Inconvertible Paper Money, Real
    Bills Doctrine
References: Chown, John F. 1994. *A History of Money.*
Spiegel, Henry Williams. 1971. *The Growth of Economic
    Thought.*

Barbados Act of 1706

In 1706 the colonial assembly of Barbados, a British colony, enacted legislation that led to one of the more unusual monetary experiments in history, creating a fiat domestic currency that was virtually legal tender. The legislation sparked a strong protest from merchants, slave traders, and other English traders, the creditors in the economy of Barbados. The British Board of Trade acted to force the redemption of the paper money, but the episode reveals the secret war between debtors and creditors that often surfaces when monetary institutions are evolving.

Sir Bevill Granville, the lieutenant-governor at the time, favored a party of debt-ridden planters in the colonial assembly. With Granville's patronage, the planter party, controlling leadership positions in the assembly, successfully sponsored the legislation, which passed in the lower house by a vote of 10 to 9. The planters clothed their proposal in arguments citing the shortage of coin as a contributing factor to the declining state of trade. To assure the successful execution of the plan, the assembly adopted the Triennial Act, which extended its own life for three years.

This proposal to create a locally issued paper money allowed each planter to receive "bills of credit" equaling in value to one quarter of the planter's estate. The institution issuing these bills was a bank, and the bank manager was called the holder. Among other duties the holder had sole responsibility for appraising the estates of the planters, one of the many objections of the creditors. The legislation called for the acceptance of the bills at face value in all domestic transactions, and required creditors to forfeit half of a debt for refusing to accept the bills in payment. Planters had to redeem the bills in one year, or renew them. Renewed bills remained in circulation. When the planters who first drew the bills failed to redeem them or were unable to pay the interest and renew them, they faced something like a foreclosure sale on that part of their property pledged as security for the bills.

The major flaw of the bills in the eyes of the creditors was that they paid no interest to their holders. The planters paid 5 percent interest on the bills, which went to the bank to cover the administrative cost of issuing, redeeming, and renewing the bills. The merchants and traders who received the bills in payment earned no interest while they held them, a factor that assured the rapid depreciation of the bills in value.

The Royal African Company, a slave-trading company, was among the major critics of the law, and vigorously objected, with other merchants and traders, to the British Board of Trade. The British government recalled Granville, and sent as a replacement Mitford Crowe, an individual in good standing with the merchants. The British government ordered Barbados to redeem the bills held by creditors involuntarily. Meanwhile leadership in the assembly lost confidence in the new bills, and, failing to persuade the assembly to take action, dissolved it, calling for new elections. The new election became a battleground for a clash between creditors and debtors, and the creditors came out on top. The new assembly passed the Relief Act of 1707, which forced planters to redeem their paper bills in one year or face foreclosure auctions.

The experience of colonial Barbados illustrates the difficulty of developing a fiat money standard acceptable to creditors, who bear the burden when money loses its value. Perhaps there is a lesson in the fact that the same New World that flooded the Old World with an influx of precious metals, was also inventive in coming up with new variants of paper money.

See also: Land Bank System, Sugar Standard of the West Indies
References: Brock, Leslie V. 1975. *The Currency of the American Colonies, 1700–1764.*
Nettels, Curtis P. 1934. *The Money Supply of the American Colonies before 1720.*

Barter

Barter is a rude form of exchange, based upon directly swapping goods for goods without the intermediary of money.

Exchange becomes more important as individuals specialize in the production of goods and services. Money considerably facilitates exchange because everyone accepts it in trade. In a money economy, individuals devoting all their energies and skills to the production of one commodity, such as cattle, can trade cows for money, and take money to town and buy groceries, televisions, automobiles, etc. In an economic system based upon barter, a cattle rancher must find someone who wants to trade cows for everything else he or she may want to acquire. Wanting to buy a television, the cattle rancher would have to find someone with more televisions than he or she needs for personal use, and who is in need of a cow. The cattle rancher, having more cows than needed for personal use, will trade a cow for a television. Economists call this conglomeration of circumstances a double coincidence of wants.

Barter exchange is necessarily time consuming and inefficient. It is hard to imagine someone working in a propeller shop making propellers for airplanes, and receiving pay in a bundle of propellers, and then trading propellers for everything they needed to maintain themselves. Money simplifies exchange and results in a constant ratio in the exchange rate between propellers, say, and televisions.

Historically, barter exchange precedes the use of money, but it has experienced resurgence at times. During the Middle Ages, metallic coinage became scarce in Europe, and barter exchange began to play a larger role. Serfs paid manor lords in certain hours of labor, and a noble would make payment in military service. In the American colonies, barter flourished because of a shortage of metallic currency. During the 1970s in the United States, barter again grew in popularity as a means of avoiding income taxes. Individuals with goods to sell, or services to be rendered, formed bartering organizations, with lists of goods that could be bartered.

In the 1990s an antiquated system of barter appeared in Russia just at the time that Western observers expected the emergence of a market economy. Some estimates suggest that as high as 70 percent of the transactions in Russia involve barter. City taxes may be paid in the form of clothes for policemen. Farmers bring food to factories in exchange for sheet metal, paint, and other useful items, and the factories pay workers in the food supplied by the farmers. Workers may be paid in kind: Workers at a timber factory received a bundle of plywood on payday. About 50 percent of industrial sales take the form of barter. A cannery trades its finished product, 12-ounce cans of meat, for livestock to slaughter, aluminum to make the cans, canning machinery, electricity, and cardboard boxes suitable for shipping canned meat.

In a country such as Russia barter emerges only after a complete breakdown of the currency. Companies must arrange deals involving several other companies in order to pay their own suppliers. They must find out what goods their suppliers will accept in payment, then set out to trade what they have to some other company that will accept these goods in order to get what their suppliers need. All kinds of imbalances develop. A police department might receive a large shipment of woolen socks but no new shoes.

Despite the obvious advantages of money exchange over barter exchange, metallic coinage, the most acceptable medium of exchange, was not freely embraced by ancient societies. Complaints against money were perhaps best expressed by the Chinese scholar Gong Yu (ca. 45 B.C.), who favored the abolition of coinage. He wrote:

Since the appearance of the uruzhu coins over seventy years ago, many people have been guilty of illicit coining. The rich hoard housefuls of coins, and yet are never satisfied. The people are restless. The merchants seek profit. Though you give land to the poor, they must still sell cheaply to the merchant. They become poorer and poorer, then become bandits. The reason? It is the deepening of the secondary occupations and the coveting of money. That is why evil cannot be banned. It arises entirely from money. (Williams, 1997)

Ancient Chinese scholars were not alone in voicing skepticism about money. The New Testament has the often repeated refrain that the "love of money is the root of all evil." The ancient Spartans legislated that only huge round metal discs could serve as money, hoping to discourage the accumulation and carrying of large sums of money. Metallic coinage was often blamed for the vices associated with the large seaport cities.

Despite reservations about money use, economies based upon money exchange rather than barter exchange support a much higher level of specialization among individuals, businesses, and regions, and this specialization fosters productivity. Greater specialization requires greater exchange, and money facilitates exchange. Economies using money are more efficient and productive, eclipsing economies based upon barter exchange.

See also: Commodity Monetary Standard, Montesquieu, Spartan Iron Currency

References: Baye, Michael R., and Dennis W. Jansen. 1995. *Money, Banking, and Financial Markets.*
Higgins, Andrew. 1998. Twilight Economy: Lacking Money to Pay, Russian Firms Survive on a Deft System of Barter. *Wall Street Journal,* 27 August, at A1:1.
Paddock, Richard C. 1998. Russians Bank of Bartering. *Los Angeles Times,* 28 December, at A1:1.
Williams, Jonathan. 1997. *Money: A History.*

Beer Standard of Marxist Angola

During the late 1980s imported beer became a medium of exchange on the black market in Angola. By that time the economy of Marxist Angola was beginning to break under the strain of a 13-year war against rebels supported by the United States and South Africa. The inflationary wartime finance left the official currency of Angola, the *kwanza,* trading on the black market for 2,000 kwanzas per dollar, compared to the official rate of 30 kwanzas per dollar. As goods disappeared from the shelves of the state-operated stores, a black market rose up right in the middle of the garbage dump of Luanda, the capital of Angola. At the black market consumers purchased all kinds of goods with imported beer. The depreciating kwanzas were pegged to the price of beer.

Initially, the government tried to squelch the black market, which continued to grow as the state-owned industry ground to a halt. The state economists began to visit the black market to get ideas for

Angola's economy, which caught the same distemper as the other socialist economies of that era. The government learned to tolerate the black market as it sought to decentralize its own bureaucratic economy, which was suffering shortages of raw material and manpower arising from the war effort. Government officials turned to studying the black market as a crash course in capitalism. Soon the policeman at the black market were there only for crowd control. The black market had a name, the *Roque Santeiro,* the title of a popular Brazilian soap opera played in Angola, a former Portuguese colony.

Consumers acquired imported beer in one of two ways. If they had dollars, they went to one of the government-owned hard currency stores and bought a case of imported beer—Heineken, Beck's, or Stella Artois—for $12. Only the middle classes, however, were likely to have dollars, which they acquired from foreign travel. Workers often got on the beer standard through their employers, who often paid them partially in coupons that they could spend in company-owned stores. These stores were owned by the multinational corporations that had employees in Angola. Workers could go to one of these stores, buy a case of imported beer, take it to the black market, sell it for 30,000 kwanzas, and then fill their grocery list shopping at the black market, or even buy a plane ticket to Lisbon. The plane ticket cost about two cases of imported beer. The black marketeer would break up the case of beer and sell it for about 2,000 kwanzas per can, turning a nice profit of 12,000 kwanzas.

The debasement of Angola's currency amidst civil war sounded a very familiar note in history. Hyperinflation attended the War of Independence of the American colonies, one example of many that could be cited. The adoption of imported beer as a medium of exchange appeared, however, to have no precedent, and seemed a bit comical. It may have been a reaction to the tendency of socialist economies to emphasize austerity in the production of consumer goods, even in peacetime. The free market that rose up from the ash heap of Angola's Marxist economy adopted as a monetary standard a symbol of Western variety and luxury in consumer goods—imported beer.

See also: Commodity Monetary Standard, Liquor Money
References: *Wall Street Journal.* 1988. In Marxist Angola, Capitalism Thrives, Using Beer Standard. 19 September, at 1.

Belgian Franc
See Belgian Monetary Reform: 1944–1945

Belgian Monetary Reform: 1944–1945

The Belgian monetary reform, although not radical, was among the most thorough in post–World War II Europe. Numerous European countries, freshly liberated from Germany, found themselves awash in currency that had been spent lavishly to pay soldiers and finance military expenditures. Monetary reform aimed at soaking up a flood of currency was common in the liberated countries, including France and Italy, in an effort to avoid the hyperinflation debacles that followed World War I.

The Belgian government-in-exile returned to Brussels in September 1944 with plans in hand to reform the Belgium currency. In the course of the war the Belgian money supply had climbed 250 percent without commensurate increases in price levels, creating a situation ripe for a round of runaway inflation. Bank notes were up 350 percent and bank account money was up 125 percent. Either the money stock needed to decrease rapidly, or prices would soar.

Few European countries thought in terms of returning to prewar exchange rate parities, and Belgium was no exception. Before the war, the Belgian franc had traded at 145 francs to the pound sterling and 30 francs to the U.S. dollar. The postwar Belgian authorities aimed to maintain an exchange rate of 176.6 francs to the pound sterling, and 43.70 francs to the U.S. dollar.

The Belgian government had new currency printed in England. In October 1944 all Belgian notes over 100 francs were frozen. In five days a census of circulating cash was completed, and the process of distributing the new currency began. Each family could exchange 2,000 of the old francs for the new francs on a one-to-one basis. More exchange took place, up to certain limits, to replace old francs in notes, bank accounts, and post office accounts. Up to 60 percent of these funds were blocked, unavailable for conversion into new francs. These blocked funds could be used for certain purposes, such as special taxes, including war profiteering taxes, which ran as high as 100 percent for German collaborators. Non-collaborators paid war-profiteering taxes up to 80 percent.

The immediate result of these actions was the reduction of note circulation from 300 billion Belgian francs to 57.4 billion. By December 1944 the Belgian money stock had grown to 75 billion, and it grew rapidly in the following year as British and American troops used Belgium as a base.

Belgium's gold holdings had been moved to France for safekeeping, which, however, did not prevent the Germans from capturing them. The Belgian government sued the French government in American courts, charging French negligence in securing Belgium's gold. The American courts ruled in favor of Belgium, and awarded Belgium compensation out of French gold reserves held in the United States. Later all gold that the Germans confiscated from Allied governments was recovered, allowing France to recoup its payment to Belgium.

With heavy British and American expenditures in Belgium, coupled with the recovery of its gold reserves, Belgium emerged from the war with an abundance of monetary reserves, sufficient to support a stable currency.

See also: Deutsche Mark, French Franc, Swiss Franc
References: Dupriez, Leon H. 1946. *Monetary Reconstruction in Belgium.*
Kindleberger, Charles P. 1984. *A Financial History of Western Europe.*

Billon
See Byzantine Debasement

Bills of Exchange

Bills of exchange developed during the Middle Ages as a means of transferring funds and making payments over long distances without physically moving bulky quantities of precious metals. In the hands of thirteenth-century Italian merchants, bankers, and foreign exchange dealers, the bill of exchange evolved into a powerful financial tool, accommodating short-term credit transactions as well as facilitating foreign exchange transactions.

The invention of the bill of exchange greatly facilitated foreign trade. The mechanics of this can be seen in the following example: Assume that a merchant in Flanders sold goods to a Venetian merchant and accepted in payment a bill of exchange drawn on the Venetian merchant promising to pay an agent of the Flemish merchant in Venice at a certain date

in the future, and in a certain currency. The bill of exchange allowed the Venetian merchant to accept delivery on the goods from Flanders, sell them, and take the proceeds to redeem the bill of exchange in Venice, probably in Venetian currency.

Bills of exchange were also instruments for foreign exchange transactions. Merchants in Italy and major trading centers in Europe bought bills of exchange payable at future dates, in other places, and different currencies. In the example above, the Flemish merchant could sell the bill of exchange to an exchange dealer for currency of his own choosing. In turn, the exchange dealer could sell the bill of exchange to a Flemish merchant engaged in buying goods in Venice. When the bill came due for payment in Venice, the Flemish merchant would use it to buy goods in Venice where the bill of exchange was paid. While this process seems complicated, it substantially reduced the transportation of precious metals. In our example, a Venetian merchant bought goods from Flanders, and a Flemish merchant bought goods from Venice without any foreign currency leaving Venice or Flanders.

Bills of exchange gave cover to bankers evading usury laws by hiding interest charges in exchange rate adjustments that governed foreign exchange transactions. A Florentine bank could advance a sum to an Italian merchant and receive a bill of exchange payable at a future date to an agent of the Florentine bank in a foreign market. When the bill of exchange matured, the Florentine agent in the foreign market would draw another bill of exchange on the Italian merchant, payable at a date in the future at the Florentine bank that drew the first bill of exchange on the Italian merchant. The Italian merchant would be borrowing the use of money for the time it took for these transactions to be completed, and the interest would be embedded in the fees for handling the bills of exchange. Bills of exchange drawn only to grant credit were called dry bills of exchange.

Credit transactions involving bills of exchange are difficult to untangle, even challenging the talents of Adam Smith, who cited the difficulty of the subject of bills of exchange as credit instruments in the *Wealth of Nations:*

> The practice of drawing and redrawing is so well known to all men of business that it may perhaps be thought unnecessary to give an account of it.

But as this book may come into the hands of many people who are not men of business, and as the effects of this practice are not perhaps generally understood even by men of business themselves, I shall endeavor to explain it as distinctly as I can. (Smith, 1952)

Smith goes on to describe a process by which bills of exchange are drawn and then redrawn with interest charges added, turning the bill of exchange into a form of long-term credit.

Bills of exchange circulated as money substitutes, partially playing the role of paper money, and economizing on the need to move specie between countries. When London became the financial center of world during the eighteenth century, bills of exchange became less important as credit instruments. Uninfluenced by church doctrines toward usury, the London financial markets developed financial instruments that clearly stated what interest rate was paid.

See also: Medici Bank

References: Davies, Glyn. 1994. *The History of Money*.
Homer, Sidney. 1977. *A History of Interest Rates*.
Kindleberger, Charles P. 1984. *A Financial History of Western Europe*.
Roover, Raymond de. 1966. *The Rise and Decline of the Medici Bank: 1397–1494*.
Smith, Adam. 1952. *An Inquiry into the Nature and Causes of the Wealth of Nations*.

Bimetallism

Under a bimetallic standard, a unit of money, such as a dollar, is defined in terms of two metals, usually gold and silver. The United States started out on a bimetallic standard that defined a dollar as equal to either 371.25 grains of silver or 24.75 grains of gold, fixing the relative value of silver to gold at 15 to 1. Bimetallic monetary standards date to the ancient world, and after the twelfth century they are well documented in European history. The use of two metals instead of one appeared as a reasonable means of supplementing money supplies.

A bimetallic monetary standard owes its complexity to the relationship between the price of metals fixed at a mint and the freely fluctuating market price of metals. A bimetallic system functions smoothly in the rare instance in which the market price and the mint price remain equal.

The true nature of a bimetallic standard is best examined when mint prices and market prices vary. If the mint ratio of silver to gold is 15 to 1 and the free market ratio is 16 to 1, citizens have an incentive to take silver to the mint for coinage, convert the silver coins into gold coins, and exchange the gold coins for a larger amount of silver on the free market. According to the theory of bimetallism, the actions of the mint in buying silver will lift the value of silver in the free market, reducing from 16 units to 15 units the amount of silver equal to a unit of gold in the free market. In thirteenth-century Genoa and Florence, a bimetallic system appeared to work according to the theory that market prices will gravitate toward mint prices.

Subsequent experience suggested that bimetallic systems do not work as the bimetallic theory suggested. Between 1792 and 1834 in the United States the mint ratio of silver to gold was 15 to 1 while the free market ratio was 15.5 to 1. This discrepancy between mint prices and market prices led to the disappearance of gold from circulation, because no one had an incentive to bring gold to the mint for coinage. Valued in silver, gold was worth more on the open market than at the mint. When Congress tried to remedy the situation by boosting the mint ratio to 16 to 1, above the free market ratio of 15.5 to 1, gold replaced silver as circulating money. Gold rather than silver was brought to the mint for coinage, and the United States began moving toward a gold standard. Under a bimetallic system, experience taught that the metal overvalued at the mint, compared to the free market, tended to drive the other metal out of circulation as predicted by Gresham's law.

The last half of the nineteenth century saw a vigorous rivalry develop between bimetallism and the gold standard. The United States and France were the strongest supporters of bimetallism, and England championed the cause of the gold standard. The difficulties of keeping mint prices and market prices in line were a severe drawback to bimetallic standards, and the major trading partners of the world turned to the gold standard toward the end of the century.

See also: Coinage Act of 1792, Crime of '73, Free Silver Movement, Gresham's Law, Latin Monetary Union, Monetary Law of 1803, Symmetalism

References: Chown, John F. 1994. *A History of Money*.
Klein, John J. 1976. *Money and the Economy*. 6th ed.
Kindleberger, Charles P. 1984. *A Financial History of Western Europe*.

Bisected Paper Money

Cutting notes into two or more pieces has seemed the answer to monetary and financial difficulties in more than one situation.

Immediately following World War II, the government of Finland, strapped for resources, bisected notes in denominations of 500, 1,000, and 5,000 markkaa. The left halves of the notes continued to circulate at half of the original face value, without any type of government overstamp, and the right halves became a forced loan to the government.

Greece implemented a similar expedient on two occasions. In 1915 the 100-drachma note was cut into a 75 drachmai and 25 drachmai note, mainly to meet a shortage of small change. In 1925 the Greek government bisected notes as a means of raising a forced loan. Similar to the Finnish episode, the Greek government bisected circulating notes, letting one half of each note circulate at half of its original face value and holding the other half as a loan certificate. These bisected notes also circulated without a government overstamp or overprint signifying their new value.

In 1944 Colombia faced a shortage of small change because people were hoarding coins to sell to tourists at inflated prices and to convert into buttons. The Banco de la Republica de Columbia withdrew one-peso notes dated 1942 and 1943, bisected the notes, overprinted each half note as now equal to a half peso, and recirculated the half pesos.

Toward the close of World War I officials of the Ottoman Empire cut one-livre bank notes into quarters, each equaling one-quarter of a livre. New denominations and signatures were overprinted on each note. The one-quarter-livre notes were apparently needed to meet the need for small change.

With the onset of World War I, Australia faced difficulty shipping currency to the 740 or so Fanning Islands. Virtually everyone on the islands was in the employ of Fanning Island Plantation Limited, a company engaged in exporting coconuts. The local manager of the plantation, with the aid of the United States military, arranged to have one-pound "plantation notes" printed in Hawaii and delivered to the islands. At the end of the war, Australian currency again circulated on the island, and most of the plantation notes were withdrawn, but some were bisected and used as movie tickets. The left half bore a one-shilling mark and the right half bore a two-shilling mark, reflecting the cost of attending movies on the islands.

The Bank of England has bisected notes as a security measure. After 1948 the new state of Israel sent bisected bank notes to the Bank of England for redemption. The notes were bisected and sent in two separate shipments, as protection against robbery.

The common theme in the history of bisected paper money is the exigencies of war. Bisected notes either replace disappearing small coinage or enable the government to arrange a forced loan on the government's terms. The bisection of notes as protection against robbery does not affect money in circulation. It therefore is not a tool of monetary policy, but only a detail of handling banking operations.

See also: Greek Monetary Maelstrom: 1914–1928
References: Beresiner, Yasha. 1977. *A Collector's Guide to Paper Money.*
Freris, A. F. 1986. *The Greek Economy in the Twentieth Century.*

Black Death

During an 18-month period starting in 1348 the bubonic plague, or Black Death, claimed the lives of at least one-third of the people living in Europe, perhaps the worst physical calamity in historic times. People avoided congregating at markets, fairs, or wherever goods were bought and sold. With no one to purchase them, goods at first piled up and prices fell, but after the plague had run its course, production fell off sharply. The labor force had fallen by one-third, while the amount of land, capital, and metallic coinage remained unchanged.

With the same amount of circulating money chasing fewer goods, prices rose. The shortage of labor tightened labor markets and wages appear to have doubled in a few years. Land lay uncultivated and rents fell as other prices climbed. As prices rose, albeit slower than wages, coinage began to leave in search of foreign markets where goods were cheaper, and governments debased coinage to make it less attractive in foreign markets and to stop the outflow of precious metals.

In 1351 Edward III, king of England, called Parliament together for the first time after the plague, "because the peace was not well kept, because servants and labourers would not work as they should, and because treasure was carried out of the kingdom and the realm impoverished and made destitute of money" (Feavearyear, 1963). Edward debased the English currency, and Parliament enacted laws to hold down prices and particularly wages. Workers felt hard pressed and when the bankrupt government raised taxes in 1380, revolt broke out.

France, already desolate from war with England, also turned to coinage debasement. Even priests struck for pay raises. In 1358 France saw revolt break out in towns and rural areas.

The monetary dimensions of the Black Death show that not all monetary disturbances began as shocks to the money supply. Rather than the money supply increasing sharply, output fell precipitously after the Black Death. Either a sudden money supply increase or a sudden output drop reduces the ratio of output to money, usually causing prices to increase. The pattern of internal inflation followed by currency devaluation in foreign exchange markets has been a familiar pattern in the post–World War II era. Although the mechanics of the metallic coinage systems was a bit different, the results were the same, as monetary history immediately following the Black Death illustrates. Once prices start to rise, governments often react by putting a lid on prices, a strategy that nearly always fails. The redistribution of income puts different income classes on edge, often ending in social revolt, and, on occasion, political revolution.

The monetary disorder following the Black Death prompted a French theologian and one of the greatest thinkers of the age, Nicholas Oresme (c.1320–1382) to write the first treatise on monetary economics, entitled *A Treatise on the Origin, Nature, Law, and Alternations of Money*. In this treatise Oresme explained Gresham's law two centuries before Gresham lived.

See also: Cross Coinage, Great Debasement

References: Cipolla, Carlo M. 1980. *Before the Industrial Revolution: European Society and Economy, 1000–1700.* 2d ed.

Feavearyear, Sir Albert. 1963. *The Pound Sterling.*

Miskimin, Harry A. 1963. *Money, Prices, and Foreign Exchange in Fourteenth-Century France.*

Bland-Allison Silver Repurchase Act of 1878

The Bland-Allison Silver Repurchase Act of 1878 reaffirmed the status of the silver dollar as legal tender, and provided for the limited coinage of silver dollars. The Coinage Act of 1873 made no provision for the coinage of silver dollars, and dropped the silver standard from the definition of the dollar. It left preexisting silver dollars as legal tender—though none were in circulation at the time—but an amendment to coinage laws in 1874 made silver coins legal tender only for debts up to five dollars. The act failed to establish so-called free silver; that is, it did not commit the government to mint all the silver brought to the mint. Silver coinage was limited and gold coinage was unlimited. Congressman Richard P. Bland of Missouri introduced the bill in the House of Representatives, and Senator William B. Allison of Iowa guided the bill through the Senate. The act provided:

> That there shall be coined, at the several mints of the United States, silver dollars of the weight of four hundred and twelve and a half grains troy of standard silver, as provided in the Act of January 18, 1837, on which shall be the devices and superscriptions provided by said act; which coins together with all silver dollars heretofore coined by the United States, of like weight and fineness, shall be legal tender at their nominal value, for all debts and dues public and private, except when otherwise provided by contract.

The bill that passed the House of Representatives provided for the free coinage of silver. It read that "any owner of silver bullion may deposit the same with any United States mint or assay office, to be coined into such dollars for his benefit upon the same terms and conditions as gold bullion is deposited for coinage under existing laws." The Senate amended the bill, substituting the free silver provision with a limit on the coinage of silver to not less than $2 million or more than $4 million per month. An amendment making the silver dollars convertible into gold failed, as did an amendment that forbade the use of silver dollars in payment for interest on the public debt. Measures to increase the silver content of silver dollars also failed.

Also, the act directed the president of the United States to invite European nations to "join the United States in a conference to adopt a common ratio between gold and silver, for the purpose of establishing internationally the use of bimetallic money, and securing fixity of relative value between those metals."

This provision led to the International Monetary Conference of 1878 in which the United States urged the adoption of a gold-silver bimetallic standard, but the European nations were not interested.

President Rutherford B. Hayes vetoed the Bland-Allison Act, citing the deterioration in the value of silver, and the injustice to creditors receiving payment in silver. The Senate voted 46 to 19 to override Hayes's veto, and the House voted 196 to 73 to override the veto, making the Bland-Allison Act the law of the land.

President Hayes had vowed to veto a free silver bill, and he attached little significance in the Bland-Allison bill to the provision that limited the coinage of silver. The silver advocates were not happy, and the push for free silver took on the aura of a populist movement as the century progressed. The government apparently kept its silver purchases to the minimum allowed of $2 million per month. The coinage of silver continued until 1890, when the Sherman Silver Act required the government to almost double its silver purchases, but substituted the issuance of treasury notes for the coinage of silver. After the enactment of the Sherman Silver Act, concern over the future of America's gold standard sparked a financial panic and Congress repealed it in 1893. The government discontinued the purchase of silver under the Bland-Allison and Sherman Acts.

See also: Bimetallism, Crime of '73, Free Silver Movement, Sherman Silver Act of 1890, Silver

References: Friedman, Milton. 1992. *Money Mischief.*
Laughlin, J. Laurence. 1896. *A History of Bimetallism in the United States.*
Meyers, Margaret G. 1970. *A Financial History of the United States*
Nugent, Walter T. K. 1968. *Money and American Society: 1865–1880.*

Blood Money

In primitive societies, a murderer often could compensate his or her victim's relatives with blood money, which the relatives were expected to accept in lieu of exacting violent revenge. Although the demand for some commodities tends to ebb and flow with fashion, commodities accepted as blood money tended to be goods that a tribe or people held in permanent high esteem, and these commodities often began to fill other roles of money, including as a medium of exchange.

In pre–World War II Samoa, a group of islands in the South Pacific, mats fulfilled the purpose of blood money. These prized mats could also compensate an injured husband, and bridegrooms received mats from the relatives of the bride. On the Fiji Islands, a single whale's tooth, comparable in value to a big canoe, was the expected blood money for a murdered man. On the Santa Cruz Islands and Reef Islands, blood money came in the form of red feathers of the parrot *Trichoglossus massena*. In 1871 the murderer of a bishop paid a fine of four coils of feather money.

On the island of New Britain, northeast of New Guinea, sacred shells were strung, stored in coils, and used to fulfill many of the roles of money. The next of kin of a murdered individual received between 20 and 50 strings. Intertribal wars and feuds between individuals could be ended with the payment of these strings of sacred shells, called *tambu* or *diwara*. When an intertribal conflict came to an end, the number of people that each side lost was counted, and a balance of compensation paid to the side that lost the most members. In the Congo, cowrie shells were accepted as blood money.

In areas of Kenya, livestock met the need for blood money, and medieval Ireland also furnished instances of cows paid as blood money. In medieval Wales the murder of a king could be atoned with the payment of 1,000 cows. The murder of a Welsh tribesman (probably including women and children) cost the murderer 126 cows—120 for the murder, and 6 for the implied insult. The cows had be normal cows, bearing no more than five calves, and producing milk. It is probable that only a well-to-do man could afford this blood money. At that time a cow in Scotland was equal to 6 shillings or 72 pence, and pence was the largest denomination coin in circulation. The pence equivalent of 126 head of cattle would have been far more than an average Welsh tribesman could have marshaled, assuming that the value of cattle in Scotland and Wales was in a similar range. Otherwise coins of larger denominations would have been minted. Those who could not pay the blood money were subject to the eye-for-an-eye and tooth-for-a-tooth brand of justice. In medieval Sweden the fine for killing a slave was either three marks of woolen goods, or six marks of *pfennige*, or 4 good oxen. A slave could purchase his or her freedom for identical amounts.

Blood money was an important institution in primitive societies where no powerful state authority could avenge every wrong committed against tribal members. Acceptance of blood money was expected of tribe members as the only means of avoiding internecine warfare. Moreover, blood money was often the only thing that stood between a murderer and a sentence of execution. Blood money commodities tended to be hoarded because nobody knew when they would need them, and trying to purchase them after the commission of a murder was not always easy. Because it was payment for a human life, blood money tended to be paid in commodities most highly prized by a society. To settle blood disputes between tribes, common units of blood money evolved that facilitated other types of intertribal exchange. Blood money commodities, always in demand and evolving a store of value, represent the emergence of money at its most embryonic point.

See also: Feather Money of Santa Cruz, Whales Tooth Money in Fiji

References: Davies, Glyn. 1994. *A History of Money*. Einzig, Paul. 1966. *Primitive Money*.

Bolivian Hyperinflation

During the 1980s Bolivia experienced an episode of hyperinflation that reached annual rates of 24,000 percent during the peak years of 1984 and 1985. Cups of coffee sold for 12 million pesos. A 1 million peso note that was equivalent to $5,000 in 1982 was worth only 55 cents by 1985. During the period of raging hyperinflation, the Bolivian peso depreciated 40,000 percent, sometimes losing 1 to 2 percent per hour.

Paper pesos were counted in bundles of identical bills, and sometimes pesos were measured by the height of stacks of bills. In some cases, paper pesos were weighed. A university professor received pay in a stack of bills about 19 inches in length. A secretary received a stack of bills from 9 to 10 inches in length.

Despite the shortcuts in counting money, an airline desk clerk would spend 30 minutes counting the 85 million pesos charged for an airline ticket. Small-denomination bills became nearly worthless and were often seen blowing in the wind, piling up in muddy clumps alongside sewage ditches and in bushes on vacant lots.

The Bolivian government had to rely on foreign countries to print its paper pesos on the scale needed to satisfy the hunger of a hyperinflationary economy. Paper pesos measured in thousands of tons were flown in from Germany, Brazil, and Argentina, arriving at the La Paz airport on pallets.

Checking account and credit card transactions lost favor because the clearance process took up valuable time as the inflation clock ticked away. Banks had no money to finance mortgages for households and businesses, which paid for construction on a pay-as-you-build basis.

The United States dollar became the de facto, unofficial standard of value in Bolivia during the hyperinflation. Bolivia's bustling cocaine trade with the United States supplied the Bolivian economy with dollars that fed a black market in currency. Currency traders walked the streets, offering to buy and sell dollars and pesos. Consumers came to town with dollars, traded the dollars for pesos before entering a store, then made their purchases with the pesos. The shopkeeper owner hardly received the pesos before going out on the street and converting the pesos back into dollars. Legally, transactions had to be conducted in pesos, but no one kept pesos longer than necessary. According to an article in the *Wall Street Journal* describing the Bolivian hyperinflation,

> Civil servants won't hand out a form without a bribe. Lawyers, accountants, hairdressers, even prostitutes have almost given up working to become money-changers in the streets. "We don't produce anything. We are all currency speculators," a heavy equipment dealer in La Paz says. "People don't know what's good and bad anymore. We have become an immoral society." (*Wall Street Journal*, 1985)

The blame for the Bolivian inflation has to be put at the feet of government finance. Tax revenues covered only 15 percent of the Bolivian government's expenditures, and the government's budget deficit equaled 25 percent of the country's annual output. As late as 1990 the annual inflation rate was still 7,000 percent, well below the levels of the mid-1980s, but still high. In the 1990s the inflation rate began to subside substantially as the government reduced deficit spending.

See also: Argentine Hyperinflation, Brazilian Hyperinflation, Chilean Inflation, German Hyperinflation, Inflation and Deflation

References: *Wall Street Journal.* 1985. Precarious Peso—
  Amid Wild Inflation, Bolivians Concentrate on Swapping
  Currency. 13 August, at 1.
Weatherford, Jack. 1997. *The History of Money.*

Brazilian Hyperinflation

Between 1989 and 1994 Brazil saw inflation soar
into hyperinflation dimensions, registering annual
inflation rates from 1,600 to 2,500 percent.

Brazil can boast of a long history with inconvertible paper money. Notes of the Bank of Brazil appeared no later than 1808, and copper displaced gold
and silver as the only metallic currency in circulation. In 1833 the government took over the issuance
of paper notes, and in 1835 these notes were made
legal tender. The currency system was reformed several times, but periods of monetary disorder became
part of economic life in Brazil, although they never
reached hyperinflation proportions until 1989.

Brazil shared an inflationary trend with the rest
of the world during the post–World War II era, but
with greater intensity. Between 1948 and 1965 the
inflation rate in Brazil averaged 2 percent per
month, lifting prices by a factor of 79 over the same
time period. Annual inflation rates finished the
decade of the 1960s in the 20 percent range. During
the decade of the 1970s, when worldwide inflation
gathered momentum, Brazil saw annual inflation
rates reach 77 percent by 1979.

The dynamics of inflation seem to require that
inflation persistently rise above the expected range.
Brazilian inflation rose above 110 percent in 1980,
and in 1988 entered four-digit territory. The year
1989 saw annual inflation exceed 1,700 percent. Inflation subsided to the three-digit range before soaring to 2,500 percent annually in 1993. The government began anti-inflation policies in earnest, cutting
the inflation rate by half in one year. Annual inflation
then dropped rapidly, reaching the 4 to 5 percent
range in 1997.

Unlike other famous examples of hyperinflation,
the blame for Brazilian hyperinflation cannot be
pinned on wartime expenditures or war reparations. Brazil did bear a heavy debt burden, and
much of the debt was owed to foreigners. Brazil's
central bank was a buyer of last resort of short-term
government bonds, which was the immediate cause
of the inflation.

Before inflation reached hyperinflation levels,
Brazil had adopted a system of indexation, making
inflation more bearable to average citizens. Under
indexation, government bonds, wages, and other
long-term contracts were automatically revised upward to adjust for inflation. The system of indexation contributed additional inertia to inflation, and
initially may have slowed the rate of acceleration of
inflation.

Taming inflation required deep and substantial
economic reforms. Brazil underwent a capitalist revolution, emphasizing discipline in government
spending, privatization, trade liberalization, and
stringent monetary control. Brazil also phased in a
new currency, and when the old currency was extin-
guished, prices stabilized. The new currency was
tied to the United States dollar, and backed by foreign exchange reserves, including dollars.

See also: Argentine Hyperinflation, Bolivian Hyperinflation,
  Chilean Inflation, Indexation, Inflation and Deflation

References: Pereira, Luiz Carlos Bresser. 1996. *Economic
  Crisis and State Reform in Brazil.*
Wachter, Susan M. 1976. *Latin American Inflation.*

Bretton Woods System

From 1946 until 1971 the Bretton Woods System
governed foreign exchange rate policies in the world
economy. The foreign exchange rate is the rate at
which one country's currency can be converted into
another country's currency. The system took its
name from Bretton Woods, New Hampshire, the
1944 site of the international conference of monetary officials who created it.

For an individual country foreign exchange rates
determine the cost of imported products to domestic consumers and the price of domestic exports to
foreign buyers. For example, the foreign exchange
rate between British pounds and United States dollars determines the cost of a British pound if purchased by a United States dollar, and conversely, the
cost of a United States dollar if purchased by a
British pound. Therefore this exchange rate will determine the cost in dollars of British goods sold in
the United States, and the cost in pounds of United
States goods sold in Britain. Thus, foreign exchange
rates determine the competitiveness of a country's
goods and services in the world market. Economies
rise and fall with changes in foreign exchange rates.

Before World War I, the world economy was on a
gold standard, which fixed the value of each country's

currency in terms of a fixed weight of gold, thereby setting exchange rates between currencies in the process. After World War I governments returned to the gold standard, but the result was unsatisfactory. The same governments abandoned the gold standard during the Great Depression, leaving foreign exchange rates free to float with varying degrees of government involvement.

The Bretton Woods System proposed to combine the stability of fixed exchange rates with the flexibility of floating exchange rates in a system of so-called adjustable peg exchange rates. Under an adjustable peg system, each country declared a par value of its currency in terms of gold and committed itself to buying and selling foreign currency and gold reserves to maintain this par value in foreign exchange markets. An individual country could not change the pegged value of its currency more than 10 percent without permission of the International Monetary Fund, a permanent international institution created by the Bretton Woods System.

In 1971 the Bretton Woods System came to an end because the United States needed to devalue its currency. The United States experienced a large outflow of dollars relative to inflow because of foreign expenditures from the Vietnam War and other obligations in foreign countries. By that time, however, most countries kept their currencies pegged to the value of the dollar rather than the value of gold, a practice that crept into the Bretton Woods System because gold monetary reserves were in short supply. In an effort to save the Bretton Woods System, the United States devalued its dollar relative to gold, but the outflow of dollars remained excessive. In 1973 the world economy went on a system of flexible exchange rates.

The Bretton Woods System kept alive a vestige of the gold standard when gold monetary reserves were inadequate to support the growth in world trade and money stock. It also provided stable exchange rates that reduced the risk and uncertainty associated with foreign trade, a factor that might have helped world trade recover from the disruption of world war. Perhaps its greatest accomplishment was the cooperation it fostered among trading partners in an important area of common interest.

See also: Balance of Payments, Gold Bullion Standard, Foreign Exchange Markets, International Monetary Fund, World Bank

References: Acheson, A. L. K. 1972. *Bretton Woods Revisited*. De Vries, Margaret Garritsen. 1987. *Balance of Payments Adjustment, 1945-1986: The IMF Experience*. Snider, Delbert. 1975. *Introduction to International Economics*.

Bride Money
See Feather Money of Santa Cruz, Ivory, Pig Standard of New Hebrides, Whale Tooth Money in Fiji

British Gold Sovereign
During the nineteenth century, the British gold sovereign coin was the pride of the British Empire, the last coin to achieve significant international stature before the era of paper money superseded metallic coinage. Sir Charles Oman, an author on English coinage, praises the sovereign as "the best piece ever produced from the English mint." J. H. Clapman, author of a well-known economic history of England in the late nineteenth century, wrote that the sovereign had become "the chief coin of the world."

Lord Liverpool's Coinage Act of 1816 had established gold as the sole standard measure of value for English coinage, and had provided for the coinage of a 20 shilling gold piece containing 123.3 grains of gold. Under the Carolingian system, which survived in Britain until 1971, one pound sterling equaled 20 shillings, which equaled 240 pence. The new coin was called the *sovereign*. Over a span of approximately 100 years the sovereign lived up to Lord Liverpool's dictum that gold coins should be made as perfect and kept as perfect as possible.

The sovereigns were popular in foreign countries and many left England permanently. Sometimes fluctuations in exchange rates made it profitable to melt down sovereigns, and resell the gold bullion to the English mint, where it was recoined. One Treasury official, referring to the burden of keeping the world supplied with coins, observed that "although it is certainly no part of our duty to provide coins for foreign Governments, the facilities afforded to our commerce by the diffusion of a sound circulating medium throughout the world may justify a voluntary burden for that purpose" (Challis, 1992). Sovereigns were also struck in Sydney, Australia, and Bombay, India.

Britain continued to mint sovereigns until 1914, when gold coinage ceased to circulate domestically.

The British gold sovereign was the last coin to achieve the stature of an international coin. (Smithsonian Institution, National Numismatic Collection)

During the interwar period Britain returned to a gold bullion standard, but gold coins were not minted. During the post–World War II era sovereigns were minted intermittently and sold as a hedge against inflation, but not as circulating currency.

The famous historian Arnold Toynbee, in Volume 7 of his *Study of History,* cited evidence that famous coins, such as the Athenian owls, continued to circulate in out-of-the-way parts of the world long after the disappearance of the government that issued them. According to Toynbee, "it may be anticipated that the English gold 'sovereign,' of which Englishmen saw the last in A.D. 1914, might still be circulating in Albania for generations, and in Arabia for centuries after that portentous date" (Toynbee, 1954).

The British pound sterling was the preeminent international currency during the nineteenth and early twentieth centuries, comparable to the United States dollar in the post–World War II era. The pound sterling, however, was the last international currency, the prestige of which was dependent on a precious metal coin of unquestioned weight and purity.

See also: Gold Standard, Pound Sterling

References: Challis, C. E., ed. 1992. *A New History of the Royal Mint.*
Feavearyear, Sir Albert. 1963. *The Pound Sterling.* 2d ed.

Bronze Standard of Ancient Rome

Early Romans replaced a cattle standard with a raw copper or bronze metallic standard. Various authors report the standard as copper or bronze, depending upon the translation of the Latin, which apparently used the same word to refer to both copper and bronze. This metal was used to make farm implements, rendering it valuable as money when the Romans changed from a pastoral to an agricultural society. The Romans remained on a bronze standard until the end of the Republic in 30 B.C.

The earliest bronze money, called *aes rude,* consisted of rude chunks of raw copper or bronze. These chunks began circulating as money while the Romans were on a cattle standard and were in use during the sixth century B.C. Specimens of this currency range in size from over 12 pounds to less than one ounce, and sometimes have an oblong or square shape. They must have been valued on the basis of weight.

During the fifth century B.C. a bit more refined form of bronze (or copper) money appeared, called *aes signatum.* This money took the form of regularly shaped bronze (or copper) bars with a specific weight. In the beginning one aes equaled a pound of bronze (or copper). These bars were stamped with an impressive variety of figures, including oxen and sheep, perhaps to create a psychological link between the new metallic money and livestock money. Swords, tripods, anchors, the Roman eagle, and fishbone-like markings are among the list of figures found on these bronze (copper) bars. During the fourth century B.C. the Romans began casting heavy round coins, known as *aes grave*. These coins, definitely circulating under the auspices of the government, came in sizes of various fractions or multiples of a pound of bronze (or copper), and often bore the image of a sheep, cow, or hog.

With the enactment of the Tarpeian law of 454 B.C., the government began the official transition to a metallic currency, providing that fines assessed in terms of cattle or sheep might be paid in the form of marked copper or bronze.

The weight of the aes steadily fell. According to Pliny, during the first Punic War in the third century B.C., "the Republic not having means to meet its needs, reduced the *aes* to two ounces of copper; by this contrivance a saving of five-sixths was effected, and the public debt liquidated" (Frank, 1959). During the second Punic War the weight of the aes was reduced to one ounce, and in 87 B.C. it was reduced to half an ounce to help pay for the Social War, a civil war that led to the end of the Republic.

The Roman language of money left an impressive legacy on our modern languages. The bronze coins were called *pecunia,* a reference to the images of livestock stamped on them. *Pecos* was the Latin word for cow, and in English money considerations are nowadays called *pecuniary*. The Latin word for pound, *libra,* was the predecessor of the English pound, the French *livre,* and the Italian *lira*. The word *expenned* meant "weighed out," referring to the weighing of the *asses* in payment for goods. The English words "money" and "mint" evolved from the word *moneta,* the Latin term for the coins struck at the Senatorial Mint located in the Roman temple for the goddess Juno Moneta. Also, the English words "estimate" and "esteem" came from the Latin *aestumare,* meaning "to value in copper."

During the third century B.C. the Romans began coinage of silver. These coins were struck, rather than cast, as the bronze coins had been. (Struck coins are stamped with hammers and cast coins are melted in molds.) By the middle of the second century B.C. bronze coins had lost much of their importance, and Augustus put the Romans on a bimetallic gold and silver standard in the last century B.C.

See also: Copper, Lex Aternia-Tarpeia of 454 B.C., Lex Flaminia of 217 B.C.

References: Burns, A. R. 1927. *Money and Monetary Policy in Early Times.*

Frank, Tenny. 1959. *Rome and Italy of the Republic.* Vol. 1.

Harl, Kenneth. 1996. *Coinage in the Roman Economy, 300 B.C. to A.D. 700.*

Byzantine Debasement

In the eleventh century A.D. the Byzantine Empire began debasing its gold coinage. For seven centuries Byzantium had maintained the purity of a gold coinage inherited from the reforms of the Roman emperor Constantine I.

Until the eleventh century, Byzantine gold coins show a gold content ranging between 22 and 24 carats fine, probably the highest standard of purity obtainable with the technical processes of the time. The Byzantine emperor Michael IV (r. 1034–1041) had practiced the money-changing profession before his elevation to emperor, and under his rule the Byzantine mints turned out coins varying between 12 and 24 carats. The purity of the gold coins continued to decline. Under Nicephorus III Botaneiates (r. 1078–1081), gold coinage averaged about 8 carats. By 1090 gold coins consisted of an alloy containing a bit of gold, more silver, and much more copper.

In 1092 Alexius I (r. 1081–1118) introduced a reformed coinage based upon four metals. A standard gold coin was struck with a fineness of 20.5 carats, a silver/gold alloy coin was struck with a fineness of 5 and 6 carats, a billon coin was struck containing 6 to 7 percent silver with the remainder of copper, and two copper coins were struck. This system provided the Byzantine Empire with a stable coinage throughout the twelfth century.

In 1204 Constantinople fell to Latin crusaders in the Fourth Crusade, and the gold coinage of Byzantium began a downward slide toward debasement. In 1253 William of Rubruck recorded an incident that occurred when the Tartars of Crimea were handed Byzantine gold coinage: "When our servants offered them *ipperpera* they rubbed them with their fingers and held them to their noses to sense by smell whether they were copper *(utrum essent cuprum)*" (Hendy, 1985). Apparently the Tartars were trying to detect a sour smell associated with copper, and the Byzantines debased their gold coinage with copper. It was said that India produced a copper that was bright, clean, corrosion resistant, and virtually indistinguishable from gold. Supposedly, Darius had drinking cups of gold and of copper, and these cups could not be distinguished except for smell.

In 1261 the Byzantine Empire was restored under a new dynasty, but the new government continued to strike debased gold coinage. In the fourteenth century debased gold coins ranged between 11 and 15 carats and a reformed silver coinage began to displace gold coins. The final blow to Byzantine gold coinage came when Constantinople fell to the Turks in 1453. Leonard of Chios, archbishop of Mitylene, gave the following account of monetary affairs during the siege:

> But the troubled emperor did not know what he was to do; he consulted his chief men; They advised that the citizens should not be disturbed through the exigencies of the occasion, but that recourse should be had to ecclesiastical property. He therefore ordered the holy vessels of God to be taken from the sacred churches, just as we have read the Romans to have done on account of the needs of the moment, to be melted down and struck into coin *(in pecuniam insigniri),* and to be given to the soldiers, the ditch-diggers, and the builders, who were concerned with their own interest, not those of the public, and who refused to work unless paid. (Hendy, 1985)

Byzantium's monetary disorder mirrored the deterioration of Byzantine society. Travelers and diplomats at the time noted the palaces, churches, and monasteries that were in ruins, and the destroyed houses and neglected fields.

The Byzantine shift from a gold coinage to a silver coinage marked a geographical shift in metallic coinage. Between the seventh century and the twelfth century, the Eastern world depended primarily on a gold-based coinage and the Western world depended on a silver-based coinage. During the thirteenth and fourteenth centuries a reversal occurred, and the Eastern world shifted to a silver-based coinage and the Western world to a gold-based coinage.

See also: Constantine I, Gold

References: Durant, Will. 1957. *The Reformation.*

Hendy, Michael F. 1985. *Studies in the Byzantine Monetary Economy.*

Williams, Jonathan, ed. 1997. *Money: A History.*

C

Caisse d'Escompte

The Caisse d'Escompte performed some of the functions of a central bank in pre-Revolutionary France. After the hyperinflationary fiasco of John Law's Banque Royale in the 1720s, the term *bank* acquired a negative connotation in France, and it was not used until the foundation of the Bank of France in 1800. Despite its name, the Caisse d'Escompte was a bank.

The failure of John Law's Banque Royale thoroughly soured the French people on banks that issued bank notes, thus retarding the continued development of French banking for several decades. In 1767 a so-called Caisse d'Escompte was established to purchase commercial paper and government securities, paying 4 percent interest (5 percent during war) and charging a 2 percent commission. The Caisse d'Escompte also enjoyed a monopoly on the issuance of coinage.

The first Caisse d'Escompte failed, but Finance Minister Turgot established by government decree another Caisse d'Escompte in 1776. This institution was empowered to discount bills of exchange and commercial paper at 4 percent, buy and sell gold and silver, and act as the government's bank. It could accept deposits from the public, but could not borrow funds at interest, or accept any debt that was not payable on demand. It could issue bank notes, because they paid no interest and were payable on demand, but could not issue less liquid assets, such as interest-bearing bonds. At first the bank notes were not legal tender. Perhaps as a lesson learned from the Banque Royale, the Caisse d'Escompte could not engage in any commercial or maritime enterprise, including insurance.

By 1783 the French government was already inching toward the abyss of bankruptcy that would provide the spark for the French Revolution. The Caisse became overly generous issuing bank notes to purchase government debt, and public confidence suffered. The government, however, was able to float a lottery loan and repay its debt to the Caisse. Also the capital of the Caisse was increased from 12 million to 15 million livres, the term of discounted commercial paper was restricted to 90 days, and the minimum coin reserve against bank notes was raised to 25 percent. The interest rate on commercial paper maturing past 30 days was increased to 4.5 percent. With these reforms, the Caisse won a reprieve from public distrust.

By 1783 the fiscal crisis of the *Ancien Regime* had deepened, and the Caisse and its stockholders became captives of the French government. In February of that year the Caisse was granted a privilege to issue bank notes for 50 years in return for a loan of 70 million livres to the French government. Now the state absorbed virtually all the financial capital of the Caisse. In August public confidence crumbled, panic erupted, and the Caisse had to redeem 33 million livres in bank notes before the panic subsided. The governing council of the Caisse refused a government offer to make the bank notes legal tender, but did request that the government repay the 70 million livre loan. The government was in no shape to meet such a request, as that money would never be seen again. Public confidence continued to wane, mainly because of the close association between the Caisse and government. Panic broke out again in August 1788, draining the Caisse's coin reserves from 50 million to 25 million livres, and convertibility was suspended. Although repayment of the 70 million livre loan was out of the question, the government came to the aid of the Caisse by making its bank notes legal tender. It also authorized the redemption of bank notes in discounted commercial paper.

The Caisse advanced more funds to the government before revolution broke out in July 1789. The revolutionary government continued to receive advances as the National Assembly debated proposals to transform the Caisse into a national bank. The National Assembly issued its own paper money, the infamous *assignats,* and the Caisse received payment in these inconvertible, legal tender notes. The Caisse wobbled on, still making advances to the government, until August 1793 when the revolutionary government took over its assets.

The first two French experiments with public banking, the Banque Royale and the Caisse d'Escompte, ended in hyperinflation, a reminder of the importance of discipline in note-issuing banks. England had a much more successful experience with the Bank of England. Despite two unhappy experiences with public banks, France under Napoleon established the Bank of France, and the organization of the Bank of France strongly influenced the design of the Federal Reserve System in the United States.

See also: Bank of France, French Revolution Hyperinflation, Law, John
References: Kindleberger, Charles P. 1984. *A Financial History of Western Europe.*
Wilson, J. S. G. 1957. *French Banking Structure and Credit Policy.*

Calderilla
See Vellon

Cappadocia
The ancient Near Eastern country of Cappadocia (located in modern-day Turkey) may deserve credit for issuing the first metal ingots stamped by a state authority sanctioning the metal for monetary use. Between 2250 and 2150 B.C. stamped ingots circulated among Cappadocian traders.

Cuneiform tablets record commercial transactions with references to payments made in money of a particular seal, for example, "of my seal," or "of your seal." Some evidence suggests that state-stamped ingots circulated at values exceeding the market value of their metal content. Apparently, different magistrates put their own seals on metal ingots, and some debt contracts called for differential interest rates, depending upon the seal of the money received in repayment.

The Cappadocian monetary units were *shekels* and *minae,* the latter a significant multiple of shekels. Silver and copper accounted for virtually all the metallic currency, although lead frequently showed up as an article of trade. No evidence suggests that the stamped ingots commanded a legal-tender status in the eyes of the law. Neither is it clear that a magisterial stamp vouched for a uniformity of weight or standard of purity.

Stamped ingots of Cappadocia predate the *electrum dumps* issued by the kingdom of Lydia (seated on what is now the western coast of Turkey) 500 years later, a challenge to Lydia's boast of being the inventor of coinage. The difference between the Cappadocian stamped ingots and Lydia's punched dumps is a matter of degree only. In each case an official stamp or punch identified the metal as money. Cappadocia's monetary history represented a very primitive stage in the development of state-guaranteed money.

See also: Lydian Coinage
References: Einzig, Paul. 1966. *Primitive Money.*

Carolingian Reform
Around A.D. 755 the Carolingian Reform established the European monetary system, which can be expressed as:

1 pound = 20 shillings = 240 pennies

Originally the pound was a weight of silver rather than a coin, and from a pound of pure silver 240 pennies were struck. The Carolingian Reform restored the silver content of a penny that was already in circulation and was the direct descendant of the Roman *denarius.* The shilling was a reference to the *solidi,* the money of account that prevailed in Europe before the Carolingian Reform. The solidi money of account originated from the Byzantine gold coin that was the foundation of the international monetary system for more than 500 years. The shilling acted to bridge the new monetary system to the old, an important role because debts contracted prior to the Reform were defined in solidi.

For three centuries following the reform, the only coin minted in Europe was the silver penny. Shillings and pounds were ghost monies—convenient shorthand for keeping accounts, but not actual coins. Rather than writing down 2,400 pennies, it was easier to write or say 10 pounds, and rather than write or say 12 pennies it was easier to write or say 1 shilling. The silver penny was the linchpin of the Carolingian system, but major transactions required unwieldy numbers of pennies, counting into the tens or even hundreds of thousands, and the pound and shilling were handy measures of pennies.

The Carolingian Reform was the work of Pepin the Short (r. 751–768), the first king of the Carolingian dynasty and father of Charlemagne. In addition to establishing the Carolingian monetary system, the Reform also reduced the number of mints, strengthened royal authority over the mints, and provided for uniform design of coins. All coins bore the ruler's name, initial, or title, signifying royal sanction of the quality of the coins.

Charlemagne spread the Carolingian system throughout Western Europe. The Italian *lira* and the French *livre* were derived from the Latin word for *pound*. Until the French Revolution, the unit of account in France was the livre, which equaled 20 *sols* or *sous*, which in turn equaled 12 *deniers*. During the Revolution the franc replaced the livre, and Napoleon's conquest spread the franc to Switzerland and Belgium. The Italian unit of account has remained the lira, and in Britain the pound-shilling-penny relationship survived until 1971.

Even in England the pennies were eventually debased, leaving 240 pennies representing substantially less than a pound of silver and the concept of a pound as a money unit of account became divorced from a pound-weight of silver.

After the breakup of the Carolingian Empire pennies debased much faster, particularly in Mediterranean Europe, and in 1172 Genoa began minting a silver coin equal to four pennies. Rome, Florence, and Venice followed with coins of denominations greater than a penny, and late in the twelfth century Venice minted a silver coin equal to 24 pennies. By the mid-thirteenth century Florence and Genoa were minting gold coins, effectively ending the reign of the silver penny (denier, denarius) as the only circulating coin in Europe.

See also: English Penny, Ghost Money, Pound Sterling, Silver
References: Chown, John F. 1994. *A History of Money.* Cipolla, Carlo M. 1956. *Money, Prices, and Civilization in the Mediterranean World.*

Case of Mixt Monies

At the turn of the seventeenth century the *Case of Mixt Monies* (1601), one of the most famous legal-tender cases in English history, upheld the principle in English-speaking countries that sovereign governments command the prerogative to confer legal-tender status on a monetary unit.

On 23 April 1601 Elizabeth Brett purchased 200 pounds of wares from a London merchant. Brett paid 100 pounds up front and committed herself to pay in September another 100 pounds sterling in current and lawful money of England. The September payment was also to be paid in Dublin, Ireland. An important complication occurred on 24 May when Queen Elizabeth sent to Ireland certain "mixt monies" from the Tower Mint, with official stamps and inscriptions, and proclaimed that the mixed money would be the lawful and current money of Ireland, at rate of a shilling for a shilling, and a sixpence for a sixpence, and that none should refuse it. The queen also proclaimed that after 10 July other money in Ireland would be valued only as bullion, and not as current money. The mixed money was of a baser alloy than England's coinage and was not current and lawful in England. On the day of payment, Brett tendered payment in 100 pounds of the mixed money, which, according to proclamation of the English crown, was current and lawful money in Ireland.

The London merchant protested, not wanting to accept the baser currency when the original contract specified sterling, and brought the dispute to court. The issue at hand was whether a time contract among parties required payment in the money that was current and lawful at the time the parties entered into the contract, or the money that was current at the time in the future when the contract specified that payment be made. The court found in favor of Brett, firmly sanctioning the right of the sovereign power to endow a monetary unit with legal-tender status.

The Constitution of the United States did not expressly confer upon Congress the power to endow a monetary unit with legal tender status, and forbade the states from declaring any money as legal tender other than gold and silver coins. In 1883 the Supreme Court upheld the right of the Congress to make a paper money issue legal tender, citing, among other things, that historically such a right belonged with the prerogatives of sovereignty.

See also: *Juillard v. Greenman*, Legal Tender
References: Breckinridge, S. P. 1903. *Legal Tender.*
Dunne, Gerald T. 1960. *Monetary Decisions of the Supreme Court.*

Cattle

A Gothic translation of the Bible (A.D. 340–388) made use of the Gothic term for cattle, *faihu,* to stand for "money." The English word *fee* is a descendant of the German word for cattle, *Vieh.* In the language of the Anglo-Saxons, *Vieh* evolved into the word *feoh,* which referred to cattle, property, treasury, price, reward, levy, tribute, and money. *Feoh* became *fee* in modern English, a reminder of the importance of cattle as money in early England. Likewise, the English word *pecuniary* stems from the Latin word for cattle, *pecos.* The modern monetary unity of India, the *rupee,* evolved from the Sanskrit word for cattle, *rupa.*

At some point in history, cattle have filled a niche in the money supply in virtually every geographical area of the globe, from the most northern Asiatic people of Russia, to the southernmost people of Africa. The Europeans brought cattle to the New World, where they again played the role of money in remote areas.

Homer's *Iliad* and *Odyssey* make numerous references to the use of oxen as a standard of value. A big tripod, the first prize in a competition, was worth 12 oxen, and a woman with many skills was worth 4 oxen. An unfired caldron was valued at one ox. When two opposing heroes held a friendly exchange of arms in the midst of battle, one set of arms was valued at 100 oxen, and the other at only 9 oxen. A son of Priam, king of Troy, was captured and sold into slavery for 100 oxen, and Priam ransomed him for 300 oxen. In the *Odyssey* one of the suitors who invaded Odysseus's house during his absence sought to appease him, offering to give him bronze and gold equal in value to 20 oxen, suggesting that oxen were a standard of value but not a medium of exchange.

One of the most advanced cattle monetary standards could be found in medieval Iceland. Icelandic law fixed the standard unit of value as a cow of 3 to 10 winters in age. The cow had to fall within a medium size, be unblemished and horned, have given birth to less than three calves, and be giving milk. A cow meeting these standards was called a *kugildi,* the standard monetary unit of Medieval Iceland. According to the law, values ranged from two-thirds of a kugildi for a sterile cow to $1\frac{1}{4}$ kugildi for a five-year-old ox, $1\frac{1}{2}$ kugildi for a six-year-old ox, and so forth. The law also fixed the value of horses, rams, ewes, goats, and pigs in terms of kugildi.

Cattle monetary standards have survived into the modern era, particularly in Africa. In some of these areas cattle have become an ecological problem. They are overstocked because they are a prestigious form of wealth that is valued beyond the bounds of economic practicality. The excess numbers of cows have overgrazed the land, eroding the soil. Traditionally, tribal raids killed off excess supplies of cattle, helping to hold the cattle population in check. Now a growing cattle population is an unwanted side effect of the demise of tribal warfare. Government authorities search for ways to introduce modern money as a means of reducing the cattle population and sparing the ecology. One proposal in a report of the Kenya Agricultural Commission suggested that the government issue coins bearing images of cows or goats, and provide special tokens shaped in the image of livestock and convertible into money.

Cattle were close to the ideal monetary medium in the earlier stages of economic development of many societies. They were a source of food and clothing, a store and symbol of wealth, and were objects of religious veneration. Well-formed and unblemished cattle were in demand as religious sacrifices. They were moveable, they reproduced, earning a crude form of interest, and they could fulfill all the basic roles of money, acting as a medium of exchange, a store of value, or a standard of value.

See also: Commodity Monetary Standard, Commodity Money, Goat Standard of East Africa
References: Davies, Glyn. 1994. *A History of Money.*
Einzig, Paul. 1966. *Primitive Money.*

Cellini, Benvenuto (1500–1571)

Benvenuto Cellini, Renaissance artist, author of a famous autobiography, and perhaps the most famous goldsmith in history, added coinage to the lists of arts he practiced. He won praise from popes and political figures for the beauty of his coins and his writing on the techniques of coinage. His work and reputation aided the spread of advanced techniques of coinage to the rest of Europe.

Cellini, notorious for a boastful and self-confident disposition, tells a story in his autobiography of how newly elected Pope Paul III sought him out to strike coins for the mint at Rome. After receiving word of a murder charge lodged against Cellini, the pope, not to be discouraged, ordered that Cellini be given safe conduct to Rome. When a friend of the murdered man objected, saying, "In the first days of your papacy it were not well to grant pardons of this kind." The pope answered: "You know less about such matters than I do. Know then that men like Benvenuto, unique in their profession, stand above the law, and how far more he, then, who received the provocation that I have heard of " (Cellini, 1931).

During the Renaissance a passion for beauty made itself felt in the practice of coinage as it had never been felt before. Before this episode with Pope Paul III, Cellini had served a stint as stamp master of the mint during the papacy of Clement VII. He tells a delightful story of how he landed the position at the mint:

So I went off, and very quickly made two dies of steel; then I stamped a coin in gold, and one Sunday after dinner took the coin and the dies to the Pope, who, when he saw the piece, was astonished and greatly gratified, not only because my work pleased him excessively, but also because of the rapidity with which I had performed it. For the further satisfaction and amazement of his Holiness, I had brought with me all the old coins which in former times had been made by those able men who served Popes Giulio and Leo; and when I noticed that mine pleased him far better, I drew forth from my bosom a patent, in which I prayed for the post of stamp-master of the Mint. The Pope took my patent and handed it to the Datary, telling him to lose no time in dispatching the business. The Datary began to put it in his pocket, saying: "Most blessed Father, Your Holi-

ness ought not to go so fast; these are matters that deserve some reflection." To this the Pope replied: "I have heard what you have to say; give me here the patent." He took it, and signed it at once with his own hand; then, giving it back, added: "Now, you have no answer left; see that you dispatch it at once, for this is my pleasure; and Benvenuto's shoes are worth more than the eyes of all other blockheads." (Cellini, 1931)

Cellini wrote treatises on goldsmithing and sculpture, translated into English as *The Treatises of Benevenuto Cellini on Goldsmithing and Sculpture.* Chapter XIV of the work, entitled "How to Make Steel Dies for Stamping Coins," describes some of the coins that Cellini struck. One coin had the head of the pope on one side and on the other side it had "St. Peter, just the moment after he has plunged into the sea at the call of Christ, and Christ stretches out his hand to him in the most pleasing wise" (Cellini, 1967).

Cellini traveled to Paris, where he struck medals for Francis I, king of France, and transmitted his techniques for stamping medals and coins to France, from which it passed to the other capitals of Europe.

See also: Da Vinci, Leonardo, Papal Coinage

References: Cellini, Benvenuto. 1931. *The Life of Benvenuto Cellini.* Trans. John Addington Symonds.
Cellini, Benvenuto. 1967. *The Treatises of Benvenuto Cellini on Goldsmithing and Sculpture.* Trans. C. R. Ashbee.
Ryan, John Carlin. 1989. *A Handbook of Papal Coins.*

Celtic Coinage

The coinage of the Celtic tribes in northern Europe and England has often been little more than a footnote in the history of the vast coinage of Greece and Rome, perhaps with reason because some of the Celtic coins were imitations of Macedonian and Roman coins. Nevertheless, hundreds of thousands of Celtic coins have been discovered, sometimes in hoards of up to 40,000 pieces. And these coins tell more about the life and thought of the Celts than any other artifacts from a society that left little in terms of written records. Certain Celtic rulers are known to history only because of their representation on coins.

The earliest dated coins found in England are the golden *staters* struck by Philip II of Macedon, and imitations of this stater are among the earliest Celtic coins found in northwestern Europe. Philip's golden

Coins tell more about the life and thoughts of the Celts than any other artifacts. (Smithsonian Institution, National Numismatic Collection)

stater found its way to the Celts either through Celtic mercenaries in the pay of Alexander the Great, through the migration of peoples, or through a trickling trade between England and the eastern Mediterranean. Between the first century B.C. and the first century A.D. the Celts struck imitations of the Macedonian golden stater. In addition, the Celts minted coins from silver, bronze, and a mixture of tin and copper called *potin*. The potin coins were cast rather than hammered or struck and passed as everyday token money. As Celtic coinage evolved beyond the imitation stage, it abandoned the Greek images, displacing them with images of things that reflected the pastoral life of the Celts—horses, boars, or stalks of wheat, among other things.

As Rome pushed the frontiers of its empire northward and across the channel to England, indigenous Celtic coinage disappeared in favor of Roman coinage. After the disintegration of the Western Roman Empire in the fifth century A.D. all coinage disappeared in the former Celtic countries for nearly 200 years. During the sixth and seventh centuries the Merovingian Gauls began minting gold and silver coins, and the winds of trade carried these coins to Anglo-Saxon England. During the seventh century these gold coins were progressively debased with silver.

Evidence of Anglo-Saxon gold coinage appears in the seventh century. The prime denomination of these coins was the *thrysma*, a reference to one-third of a gold solidus. These coins also succumbed to debasement, leaving silver as the principle monetary metal. Silver coins were often debased with copper or brass, until the eighth century, when full-weighted silver coins again appeared, and the English silver penny began its long history, lasting 1,000 years.

See also: Alexander the Great, English Penny
References: Allen, D. F. 1980. *Coins of the Ancient Celts.*
Davies, Glyn. 1994. *A History of Money.*
Van Arsdell, Robert D. 1989. *Celtic Coinage of Britain.*

Central Bank

Central banks are banks that serve as banker's banks, holding deposits of commercial banks and making loans to commercial banks. Typically, a central bank also acts as the government's banker, and holds a monopoly on the issuance of paper money. Commercial banks can turn to a central bank as a lender of last resort in financial crises. The Federal Reserve System in the United States, the Bank of England, the Bank of France, and the Bundesbank of Germany rank among the worlds leading central banks.

Monetary systems regulated by a central bank became the preferred form of monetary regulation in the latter part of the nineteenth century. The alternative to central bank regulation is what is called free banking, pioneered by Scotland in the late eighteenth century. In the high tide of nineteenth-century laissez-faire capitalism central banks were not fully evolved and free banking became a trend in England and the United States. The United States abandoned the Second Bank of the United States and turned to a form of free banking. Free banking was a system composed of a multitude of competing commercial banks, each of which issued its own bank notes. Under the free banking system no one bank commanded a monopoly on the issuance of bank notes, which is the position that a central bank enjoys.

Free banking denotes a banking system in which note-issuing banks are established according to the same principles that govern the establishment of any other new business enterprise. The ability to start a new bank requires sufficient financial capital and public confidence to make the new bank notes acceptable to the public and to help the new bank reach a profit-making scale of operation. A new bank need not clear any legal hurdles, such as charters or grants that require a special act of government. Each bank issues its own bank notes that it converts on demand into an acceptable medium of exchange—often, but not necessarily—gold. None of the banks issue notes bearing the legal status of legal tender, or in any way favored by the government. A bank's refusal to redeem its bank notes into an acceptable medium of exchange is equivalent to a declaration of bankruptcy.

A system of independent commercial banks can cause instability in the economy. In an economic upswing, banks have an incentive to make as many loans as possible, and the loans stand an excellent chance of being repaid. This expansion of loans can turn an economic upswing into an overheated boom and inflationary spiral. In an economic downswing, on the contrary, banks find extending loans more risky, and curtail lending activities accordingly. This restriction on credit and money can push the downswing over the precipice into a depression. Individual banks, driven by the profit motive in a free banking system, add to the severity of cyclical fluctuations.

Central banks seek the public interest rather than strive to maximize profits. In the downswing central banks supply more credit to the system rather than less. In the upswing central banks restrict the supply of credit. The monopoly on the issuance of bank notes and commercial bank reserve deposits gives the central bank control over the money supply, interest rates, and credit conditions. These can be adjusted to counter the cyclical swings in order to smooth out these economic fluctuations.

In the twentieth century the preference for central banking over free banking is dogma. Nearly all the discussion weighing the relative merits of these two systems took place in a 50-year interval in the nineteenth century.

See also: Bank of England, Bank of France, Bank of Japan, Deutsche Bundesbank, Federal Reserve System, Free Banking

References: Broz, J. Lawrence. 1997. *The International Origins of the Federal Reserve System.*
Mittra, Sid. 1978. *Central Bank Versus Treasury: An International Study.*
Smith, Vera C. 1990. *The Rationale of Central Banking and the Free Banking Alternative.*
Solomon, Steven. 1995. *The Confidence Game: How Unelected Central Bankers are Governing the Changed Global Economy.*
Timberlake, Richard Henry. 1978. *The Origins of Central Banking in the United States.*

Certificate of Deposit

Certificates of deposit (CDs) are interest-bearing receipts for funds deposited with banks or other depository institutions. Depositors purchase CDs in fixed denominations ($1,000, $10,000, etc.) and for a fixed time to maturity, which typically ranges between six months and five years for CDs of less than $100,000. At maturity, the owner of a CD receives the original purchase price of the CD plus interest. A purchaser of a one-year, $1,000 CD bearing 5 percent interest would receive at the end of a year $1,000, plus $50 interest. Certificates of deposit in denominations less than $100,000 are not negotiable and cannot be sold in a secondary market. Also, the issuing institution imposes a substantial penalty for early withdrawal. Since the deregulation of interest rates, CDs pay interest rates slightly higher than the treasury bill interest rates.

Negotiable certificates of deposit come in denominations of $100,000 and up. The most common denomination is $1 million, and time to maturity is usually six months or less. These CDs are sold mainly to corporations, state and local governments, foreign central banks and governments, wealthy individuals, and financial institutions. They can be sold in a secondary market before maturity if the owner needs cash, but most negotiable CDs are held to maturity. In 1961, First National City Bank of New York, now Citibank, first offered the large denomination CDs to its largest customers. Large CDs grew rapidly in popularity, and by 1973 the Federal Reserve Bank had lifted all interest rate ceilings on these large denomination, negotiable CDs.

Negotiable CDs quickly became a financial instrument for the Eurodollar market. Eurodollar CDs are CDs denominated in dollars but issued by foreign banks, or foreign branches of U.S.-owned banks. Eurodollar CDs first appeared in 1966 and owed their success to the high interest rates paid by institutions beyond the reach of U.S. banking regulations and interest ceilings. In 1968 U.S. and British banks began issuing sterling pound CDs.

The small denomination CDs (less than $100,000) came into being in the late 1970s and were intended to give small savers the advantages of market interest rates. The Federal Reserve Bank includes CDs of less than $100,000 in the calculation of M2, a monetary aggregate often regarded as the best measure of the money supply. The larger CDs are included in the calculation of M3, the most broadly defined monetary aggregate.

Negotiable CDs enable banks to attract deposits that they can count on having for a fixed period without losing to withdrawal, and the owners of negotiable CDs may always sell them for cash, albeit at a sacrifice of part of the interest yield. In contrast to demand deposits, which allow depositors to withdraw funds on demand, CDs assure the bank that deposits will be left with the bank for a while, taking some pressure off the bank. For thrift institutions, CDs are a powerful tool for raising funds, but at the price of higher interest rates for small savers.

See also: Monetary Aggregates, Money Market Mutual Funds Account, Negotiable Order of Withdrawal Accounts

References: Klein, John J. 1986. *Money and the Economy.* 6th ed.
Rose, Peter S. 1986. *Money and Capital Markets.* 2d ed.

Check

A check (or *cheque* in Britain) is a written order for a bank to pay money. The term *check* seems to have evolved from orders for payment called *Exchequer orders* that were drawn on the Exchequer, the name for the British treasury. The British Exchequer got its name from the checkered cloth that covered the tables in the rooms where cash payments were counted, or *checked*. The cloth was either black lined with white, or green with redlined squares. Government officials, pensioners, or whoever had a claim on government revenue received written orders that authorized an Exchequer official, or teller, to pay cash in the amount owed.

Checks were not called *checks* when they first came into use in the last half of the seventh century, but were called *drawn notes*. These notes, an innovation of the British goldsmith bankers, allowed an individual to order his or her goldsmith banker to make a payment of gold to a third party. In 1686 a young nobleman wrote the following drawn note on his father's banker:

> Pray do mee the favor to pay his bird-man four guineas for a paire of parakeets that I had of him. Pray don't let anybody either my Ld or Lady know that you did it and I will be sure my selfe to pay you honestly againe. —Arthur Somerset. (Nevin & Davis, 1970)

Early English checks always began with "pray" or "pray pay."

Checks grew in popularity in the nineteenth century. In England the Bank Charter Act of 1844 pushed banks toward deposit banking with checks and away from the issuance of bank notes. During the Civil War the United States federal government put a tax on bank notes issued by state banks, forcing the state banks to take up deposit banking with checks. In 1865 France simplified its law on the use of checks, and deposit banking with checks became widespread.

Checks are now the most common means of payment in the developed countries. They circumvent the need to carry large sums of cash and can be written for any amount. Checks are usually less acceptable than cash, but cashier's checks and certified checks are on par with cash as an acceptable means of payment. A cashier's check is issued by a bank against itself, and bears the signature of a bank officer. A certified check is a check guaranteed by the bank on which the check is written. Checks are negotiable, meaning they can be transferred to another person by endorsement.

See also: Bank, Goldsmith Bankers, Promissory Notes Act of 1704

References: Davies, Glyn. 1994. *A History of Money.*
Nevin, Edward, and E. W. Davis. 1970. *The London Clearing Banks.*
Richards, R. D. 1929. *The Early History of Banking in England.*

Chilean Inflation

Few countries have suffered sustained inflation rates lasting for more than 100 years, often in the double-digit and occasionally triple-digit ranges, but that has been a fact of economic life in Chile.

For a country that has persistently succumbed to the temptations of paper money excesses, Chile was slow to accept the idea that paper could circulate as money. Paper money was rarely observed in circulation before 1860, and Chileans were known for an abhorrence of paper money that only began to soften after 1850. From the colonial period until 1879 Chile remained on a bimetallic standard.

In 1879 Chile began its long inflationary career when Chilean banks stopped redeeming bank notes in specie, turning Chilean bank notes into inconvertible paper money. A fall in export prices precipitated the crisis and the War of the Pacific (1879–1882) pitted Chile against Peru and Bolivia for control of the nitrate mines in the Atacama Desert.

During the nineteenth century countries on a bimetallic or gold standard often suspended convertibility during war, but Chile never permanently returned to convertibility, although abortive efforts were made in 1887, 1895 through 1898, and 1925 through 1931. Although success in the War of the Pacific gave Chile control over the nitrate mines, Chile's exports continued to fall. Between 1878 and 1915, Chile's share of the world's copper production declined from 44 percent to less than 5 percent. The decline in export earnings, coupled with heavy foreign debt and internal inflation, crippled Chile's effort to reassert monetary order.

Between 1879 and 1904 inflation registered an average annual rate of 2 percent, a modest inflation rate but significant in light of the worldwide trend of deflation during that period. Annual inflation averaged 7 percent between 1904 and 1931. By 1914 prices were growing 10 percent a year. From 1931 until 1955, despite the depression decade, price increases averaged 20 percent. In 1931 inflation stood at 8.5 percent, rose to 15.1 percent by 1940, and crested at 47.8 percent in 1952.

From the 1950s through the 1960s annual inflation rates fluctuated in the 20 to 40 percent range. In 1971 inflation, repressed by wage and price controls, fell to 20 percent, but in 1972 inflation soared to 178 percent. As inflation accelerated in 1973 General Pinochet led a military coup that overthrew the democratically elected socialist president, Salvador Allende, and established a military dictatorship noted for brutality and violations of human rights.

As inflation accelerated in the 1970s, rising to 374 percent in 1974, the right-wing military dictatorship used its power to enforce a strict monetarist anti-inflation policy, relying upon restricted monetary growth rather than price controls to tame inflation. Monetarists argue that inflation is solely a function of excessive monetary growth rate, and the optimal economic policy is a constant, predictable 3 to 5 percent annual growth rate in the money supply. The Chicago school of economics, a leader in monetarist economic theory, had become influential in Chilean universities, and the Chilean war against inflation became a test case of the monetarists' anti-inflation policy.

Despite the strict monetarists' diet of slow money growth, inflation subsided slowly in Chile. By 1981 the inflation rate stood at a hefty 35.1 percent, but it fell below the 10 percent level the following year. A major economic slowdown in 1982 led the government to ease up on its unforgiving monetary policy and inflation began to creep up. Toward the end of the decade inflation was in the 30 percent range. Chile began the 1990s faced with an inflation problem of moderate proportions by its own historical standards.

See also: Argentine Hyperinflation, Brazilian Hyperinflation, Bolivian Hyperinflation, German Hyperinflation, Inflation and Deflation
References: Behrman, Jere R. 1976. *Foreign Trade Regimes and Economic Development: Chile.*
Valdes, Juan Gabriel. 1995. *Pinochet's Economists.*

Chinese Hyperinflation

From 1937 until 1949 China experienced a bout of inflation no less spectacular and no less fraught with social and political consequences than the hyperinflation of post–World War I Germany. The inflation began in Free China, the part of China not invaded by the Japanese, and continued until the communist government solidified control of the mainland in 1949 through 1950.

Chinese inflation falls into three eras. Between 1937 and 1939, the early war years, prices did not fully give way to inflationary pressures. Between 1940 and 1945, the war years, the Chinese people began to loose confidence in currency, and inflation accelerated. The end of World War II saw a brief lull in inflation before inflation rose to stratospheric heights, ending in the collapse of the currency system just before the nationalist government fled to Taiwan.

Japan's invasion of China left Free China robbed of 90 percent of its industrial capacity, and the Chinese government bereft of the tax revenue of the wealthiest provinces of China. Japan's blockade of ports serving Free China also reduced supplies of imported goods. The Chinese government sought to finance a military resistance and an industrialization of Free China without recourse to significant taxes, instead relying upon voluntary sacrifices and foreign aid. The government ran up massive deficits and expanded bank credit for industrial expansion. However, good harvests kept the prices of consumer goods down and wholesale prices increased 200 percent between December 1937 and December 1939, a modest increase in light of the inflationary pressures.

During the war years, 1940 through 1945, Japan tightened its noose around China, blocking virtually all imports into China, and crop failures further reduced the supplies of goods. China's archaic tax system, in which revenue rose with the number of transactions rather than prices, failed to produce added revenue commensurate with the rate of inflation. Government expenditures rose with inflation but tax revenue tended to stand still, causing the budget deficit to increase fourfold from 1939 to 1941. Prices rose nearly 600 percent between December 1939 and December 1941. Between December 1941 and December 1945 the government budget deficit increased over 100-fold, and prices increased 10,000 percent. The public lost confidence in the currency, and the velocity of circulation increased, further fueling the inflation. The government made a half-hearted effort at price controls, but China had neither the administrative apparatus nor the statistical information to carry out a plan for fixing prices.

The end of the war brought a stabilizing influence to prices, which actually fell from August to December 1945. In 1946 peace negotiations with the communists broke off, and the nationalist Chinese government continued heavy military expenditures and deficit spending. In 1946 government expenditures increased threefold, and revenue covered only 37 percent of the expenditure. Between June 1946 and August 1948 prices rose 146,772 percent in Shanghai. In August 1948 the government discounted the old currency, issued a new currency at a rate of 1 unit of the new currency to 3 million of the old. The government also imposed price controls. Inflationary pressures burst through the price ceilings, and prices continued to rise at a feverish pitch. From August 1948 until April 1949 prices rose 112,390 percent. The communists occupied Shanghai in May 1949, the nationalist government was in confusion, and the compilation of price information was suspended. As the communists consolidated control of Mainland China, the nationalists' currency became completely unacceptable.

The Chinese inflation experience adds further corroboration for Lenin's comment that the surest way to overthrow the capitalist system was to debase the currency. The rapid inflation was probably a major factor causing the climate of cynical corruption in the nationalist government, and helped contribute to its demise.

See also: American Revolution Hyperinflation, French Revolution Hyperinflation, German Hyperinflation, Inflation and Deflation, Russian Revolution Hyperinflation

References: Chou, Shun-Hsin. 1963. *The Chinese Inflation, 1939–1949.*

Friedman, Milton. 1992. *Monetary Mischief: Episodes in Monetary History.*

Kai-Ngau, Chang. 1958. *The Inflationary Spiral: The Experience in China, 1939–1950.*

Paarlberg, Don. 1993. *An Analysis and History of Inflation.*

Chinese Knife Money

Bronze knife money circulated in China from the seventh to the second century B.C. The blade and the handle constituted one piece of metal of even thickness that was shaped into a ring at the end of the handle.

The history of knife money is a bit murky, but knife money might have gotten its start as a measure to placate discontented troops. Prince Hwan, running short of funds, allowed his restless troops to use their knives to barter with the people. The knives

Knife money may have originated when soldiers used knives as barter items with civilians. (Smithsonian Institution, National Numismatic Collection)

were a popular item with the population and became a generally accepted medium of exchange. According to another story, Prince Hwan launched knife money when his government began accepting knives as payment for small fines in place of the legal ring currency. Perhaps history can be sifted from legend between these stories, which are not mutually exclusive.

Credit for the introduction of knife money may belong to sea traders from the Indian Ocean who established a colony in Shantung around 670 B.C. These

traders brought large bronze knives inscribed with a distinctive mark or emblem. The knives were of a regular weight and were used as money. The practice of inscribing an emblem may have been borrowed from the recently developed coinage of western Asia. A Chinese word, *tao,* originally meaning "knife," came to denote a unit of currency instead.

The bronze knife money of China experienced its own form of debasement, gradually shrinking in size. At first the blades were shortened but the weight of the knife was maintained. The knives gradually shrank, however, until only the ring of the handle was left as symbol of the knife that it represented.

Practical agricultural implements such as hoes have surfaced as money in several societies and weapons such as arrows and guns have commanded the characteristics of money in some societies. Knives perhaps fit into either one of these categories and rank among those eminently useful items that have made their way into lists of monetary commodities.

See also: Chinese Leather Money, Commodity Monetary Standard

References: Burns, A. R. 1927. *Money and Monetary Policy in Early Times.*

Einzig, Paul. 1966. *Primitive Money.*

Williams, John. 1997. *Money: A History.*

Chinese Leather Money

Arnold Toynbee in his famous work, *A Study of History,* which spans 11 volumes, relates an interesting episode in China's monetary history in which leather money temporarily supplemented coinage.

Under the emperor Hsiao Wen (r. 180–157 B.C.), China struggled with a shortage of coinage, probably because coinage of precious metals was still of relatively recent origin. The imperial government held an exclusive monopoly on the privilege to coin money but was not purposely keeping tight reins on the afflux of coinage into the economy. To ease the dearth of coinage, the imperial government gave up its monopoly and began to grant local governors and princes licenses to mint copper coins. Soon a flood of coinage inundated the economic landscape, and the monetary pendulum swung to inflation. In 119 B.C. the emperor Wuti put into action a plan to help restore the soundness of the currency and supply the government money. Toynbee quotes a fascinating passage from C. P. Fitzgerald's *China, A Short Cultural History* that explains this entertaining episode in monetary history. According to Fitzgerald:

> In the imperial park at Ch'ang Ngan the Emperor had a white stag, a very rare beast, which had no fellow in the empire. On the advice of a minister the Emperor had this animal killed, and made a kind of treasury note out of its skin, which, he believed could not be copied. These pieces of skin were a foot square, and were made with a fringed border and decorated with a pattern. Each piece was assigned the arbitrary value of 400,000 copper coins. The princes, when they came to pay their respects to the Throne, were compelled to buy one of these pieces of skin for cash, and present their gifts to the Emperor upon it. This precaution ensured the circulation of the "White Stag Notes." The skin of the white stag was, however, a limited quantity, and the time soon came when this device ceased to supply the Treasury with much needed money. (Toynbee, 1954)

Inflation continued to ravage the Chinese economy and in 113 B.C. the government demonetized all coinage, and returned to an imperial monopoly on coinage. The issuance of a new imperial currency minted exclusively by imperial officials cured the inflation.

Nine hundred years after this short-lived experiment with leather money, China introduced the world's first paper money. Although vague evidence suggests that China may have preceded Lydia in the invention of coinage, there is no doubt that China pioneered the development of paper money. Historians of money cite China's leather money episode as the beginning of the type of monetary thinking that led to paper money.

Skins would continue to play a monetary role in other parts of the world. Russian laws of the eleventh and twelfth centuries make numerous references to the use of skins, often squirrel skins, as money. Settlers in colonial America used deerskins as money. Each skin was known as a *buck,* a word that still signifies a dollar in the United States.

See also: Ancient Chinese Paper Money, Leather Money
References: Carter, T. F. 1931. *The Invention of Printing in China and its Spread Westward.*
Fitzgerald, C. P. 1935. *China, A Short Cultural History.*
Toynbee, Arnold. 1954. *A Study of History.* Vol. VII.

Chinese Silver Standard

By the early twentieth century China and Mexico were the only large countries remaining on a silver standard, and China was by far the largest. As the world's major trading partners abandoned the gold standard in the early 1930s China found itself in the clutches of worldwide monetary turmoil and abandoned the silver standard.

After the discovery of vast silver deposits in the New World, silver flowed to the Far East, sometimes directly from Latin America and Mexico, and became the metallic currency of choice in that area. After the opening of China to European trade in the mid-nineteenth century, and the subsequent influx of foreign investment, China ran balance of trade surpluses. Excesses of exports over imports brought in a steady stream of silver, which became the basis of China's currency.

Silver bullion circulated in different weights and shapes. Silver dollars, some minted in China and others in foreign countries, such as the United States, Mexico, or England, circulated along with subsidiary silver coins and copper coins. In 1895 England, itself on the gold standard, began issuing silver dollars, called trade dollars, specifically for trade with the Far East. English trade dollars bore inscriptions in English, Chinese, and Malay-Arabic. Briefly during the late nineteenth century the United States issued a special trade dollar designed specifically to compete with the Mexican dollar in Far Eastern trade. The Chinese called these various silver dollars *yuan,* meaning "round things," and yuan became the standard monetary unit in China and modern Taiwan.

At the end of the nineteenth century Chinese banks reintroduced bank notes into China and banks held silver as reserves. The public demanded that banks maintain the convertibility of bank notes into silver, and banks that suspended convertibility saw their bank notes depreciate rapidly. In 1916 Yuan Shih-kai, president of the Republic of China, tried to enforce a regime of inconvertible paper money, instructing banks to cease redemption of bank notes and directing the public to accept notes at par relative to silver coinage. Yuan Shih-kai wanted to seize the silver reserves in government banks and divert those resources to help himself emperor. The public put up a strong resistance and the effort failed. Provincial governments met

Silver bullion like this was circulated in different weights and shapes. (Smithsonian Institution, National Numismatic Collection)

with similar resistance to issues of inconvertible bank notes. When the Bank of Three Eastern Provinces could not redeem its notes in silver, the Manchurian government decreed the death penalty for anyone who circulated these notes at less than par. Nevertheless, irredeemable bank notes circulated at heavy discounts.

By 1922 the government banks had retrieved their irredeemable bank notes, and the public's confidence in bank notes strengthened. Banks began publishing reports of their reserve positions and by the eve of the worldwide depression of the 1930s, sound bank notes had virtually displaced inconvertible bank notes issued by provincial banks.

At the beginning of the depression, prices—including the price of silver—fell precipitously in the gold standard countries, making China's exports much more attractive in foreign trade, but making imported goods more expensive in China. China experienced a mild boom while most of the world slid into depression. As the world's major trading partners abandoned the gold standard and began reinflating their economies, China began to feel some of the effects of the depression. The Japanese invasion of Manchuria in 1931 reinforced the depressionary forces making themselves felt in China. When the United State abandoned the gold standard in 1933 and began reinflating its economy, the price silver began to rise significantly, and China's silver standard began to change from an advantage to a disadvantage. The rising price of silver meant that Chinese-produced goods were more expensive to the rest of the world, and foreign goods imported into China were cheaper.

The crowning blow to China's silver standard came with the enactment by the United States Congress of the Silver Purchase Act of 1934. This law authorized the United State government to purchase large amounts of silver, sufficient to significantly raise the market value of silver. As the market value of silver rose, Chinese silver was melted down and exported, decreasing the Chinese money supply. Also, the high price of silver made Chinese goods expensive in foreign markets, sharply cutting into Chinese exports. To avoid the deeper ramifications of a deflationary spiral, China officially abandoned the silver standard in 1935. With the abandonment of the silver standard and the Japanese invasion in 1937, China began a descent into a hyperinflation debacle.

See also: Balance of Payments, Chinese Hyperinflation, Silver, Silver Purchase Act of 1934

References: Chang, Kia-Ngau. 1958. *The Inflationary Spiral, the Experience in China: 1939–1950.*

Friedman, Milton. 1992. *Money Mischief: Episodes in Monetary History.*

Clipping

Clipping was a form of grassroots coinage debasement that flourished in the Middle Ages and the early modern period. Clipping occurred when private citizens removed (or clipped) small bits of precious metal from the circumference of coins and then passed the clipped coins on at face value. It required a certain amount of judgment to know how much metal could be removed without rendering a coin unacceptable in payment for goods and debts. Moneychangers, merchants, and other private individuals engaged in clipping accumulated valuable stores of gold and silver bullion. The law dealt harshly with clippers and counterfeiters, both of whom often met their fate at the gallows. The adoption of milled-edge coinage in the seventh and eighth centuries was intended to make clipping more easily detected, and therefore more difficult.

A variation of grassroots debasement, equal in effect to clipping, was known as sweating. Sweating was performed by putting gold or silver coins in a leather bag and shaking the bag violently, removing gold and silver from the coins in a process that more closely resembled the natural wear and tear that coins sustained from jingling in pockets and purses over several years of circulation. It was an accelerated process of natural wear and tear and captured small but valuable amounts of gold and silver.

The activities of clippers and sweaters, coupled with natural wear and tear, would eventually lead to the complete breakdown of a coinage system. If a freshly minted coin contained 20 grains of silver, but the typical coin circulating at face value averaged only 18 grains, then the 20-grain coins in circulation would be culled out and melted down for bullion or shipped to foreign countries, where they would be sold at a premium. Under these conditions, governments would stop striking new coins until all the clipped coins were called in under a program of recoinage, perhaps minting new coins at a lower weight than the original coins.

The growth of paper money, bank deposits, milled-edge coins, and token coinage rendered the methods of the clipper obsolete, and clipping ceased to be an issue faced by monetary authorities.

See also: Act for Remedying the Ill State of the Coin, Fleetwood, William, Milled-Edge Coinage
References: Challis, C. E. 1978. *The Tudor Coinage*. Chown, John F. 1994. *A History of Money*.

Cloth

From the Far East to Europe and Africa, cloth has surfaced as a medium of exchange and a unit of measurement. During the second millennium, silk cloth passed as money in China, circulating in pieces of a uniform size. The Chinese word *pu* began as a word referring to "cloth," but came to denote "money," reflecting the importance of silk cloth as money. Silk money survived the advent of metallic coinage in China. In 460 B.C. the government formed three separate boards for management of currency, one for gems, one for gold, and one for coins and silk.

Northern Europe furnishes numerous instances of cloth money during the medieval era. The Baltic Slavs used linen as a means of payment in commercial transactions, and small strips of thin textiles circulated as coin. In the language of the Northern Slavs the word *platni* meant "linen," and the word for "to pay" was *platiti*. Up to the fourteenth century Sweden made use of a hand-woven woolen cloth currency called *wadmal*. Creditors had to accept wadmal in the payment of money debts, and coined money and wadmal were linked in a fixed exchange ratio. Medieval Iceland also called its hand-woven woolen cloth money wadmal. Iceland's wadmal met

the need for a general standard of value, circulated as money, and even in modern times parts of Iceland valued land in units of wadmal. Certain districts of medieval Norway accepted cloth as legal-tender currency, and a district of medieval Germany had a cloth standard that set a certain length of cloth to *Reilmark,* or *Gewandmark,* predecessors of the modern-day German mark. In pre-Christian Prussia pieces of cloth adorned with bronze rings passed as money.

Cloth also enjoyed wide acceptance as money, lasting in some cases into the early twentieth century in several areas of Africa. In Zambia calico found favor as currency and was used in wages and marriage dowries. On the west coast of Africa a unit of money called a *long* served as a unit of account. Originally, a long referred to a length of cloth, but later evolved into an abstract unit of account used only for setting and quoting the prices. White shirts of the sort commonly worn for everyday dress circulated as money in parts of equatorial Africa. In the Congo barter transactions were conducted on the basis of prices set in pieces of cloth. A piece was 12 yards of standard quality cloth. In districts of the Sudan the unit of account for pricing moderately priced goods was bundles of 20 cotton threads.

Certain tribes in the Philippines used European cloth as a monetary standard. A monetary unit of cloth was a piece of cloth as long as the spread of a man's arms. The natives priced jars, glassware, gongs, and perishable items in terms of cloth, and fines were paid in cloth. An adulterer paid a fine of 215 meters of cloth. In Borneo standard rolls of cloth were a sort of legal tender of money.

In the nineteenth century cloth passed as money on Button Island of the Indonesian archipelago. The cloth money was called *kampuna,* meaning the "head cloth of a king," and it was woven on official looms, which validated its use as currency. Ordinary cloth bore no special value as currency and was traded only for its utility.

See also: Commodity Monetary Standard, Icelandic Saga Money
References: Einsig, Paul. 1966. *Primitive Money*. Quiggin, A. Hingston. 1949. *A Survey of Primitive Money*. Williams, Jonathan, ed. 1997. *Money: A History*.

Cocoa Bean Currency

At the time of the Spanish conquest, cocoa bean currency in the commercially active economy of the Aztec empire ranked above gold dust as the principal form of money. The Aztecs kept cocoa beans in bags holding 24,000 beans. Columbus met with a Yucatan ship hauling goods to trade for cocoa. One early observer of the Aztec society, Peter Martyr, noted regarding Aztec money: "Oh, blessed money which yieldeth sweete and profitable drinke for mankinde, and preserveth the possessors thereof free from the hellish pestilence of avarice because it cannot be long kept hid underground" (Einzig, 1966). The Aztecs also used copper hatchets as money and Cortez, in a letter to the king of Spain in 1524, referred to a copper hatchet as worth 8,000 cocoa beans. During the eighteenth century reports from Mexico indicated that the cultivation of cocoa beans was restricted to maintain the value of cocoa beans as money. Cocoa bean currency was not even spared the episodes of debasement that haunted the early history of precious metal currencies. Debasement of cocoa bean currency was accomplished simply by removing the stone of the cocoa bean and replacing it with dirt.

Girolamo Benzoni, writing in 1572, said that the Spanish inhabitants of Guatemala held their wealth in the form of cocoa. Henry Hawks, a merchant who spent five years in Central America, writing in the same year, claimed that in Guatemala cocoa "goeth currently for money in any market or faire, and may buy any flesh, fish, bread or cheese, or other things" (Einzig, 1966). When Thomas Cavendish landed at Aguatulco in 1587 he found 400 bags of cocoa beans stored in the Customs House, "every bag whereof is worth ten crownes." Master Francis Petty, who accompanied Cavendish, wrote "These cacaos goe among them for meate and money. For a hundred and fifty of them are in the value of one rial of plate" (Einzig, 1966). To preserve the local supply of money, Guatemala enacted an ordinance banning the export of cocoa unless payment was in coin. Cocoa bean currency stretched into Latin America. In 1712 a royal decree in Brazil listed cocoa, cloves, sugar, and tobacco as commodities that legally circulated as money and troops were paid in these commodities. In nineteenth-century Nicaragua 100 cocoa beans bought a serviceable slave.

The use of cocoa beans as money continued into

Cocoa bean currency. A copper hatchet could cost 8,000 beans. (Smithsonian Institution, National Numismatic Collection)

the nineteenth century, and remote Indian tribes in Mexico and Central America continued to make small change with cocoa beans into the twentieth century. Within these tribes the smallest silver coin equaled 40 cocoa beans.

The history of cocoa beans as money stands as a reminder that money evolves in a social context. Money is something that everyone will accept in exchange. Any product that holds up as universally acceptable to everyone necessarily has social significance, whether it be cocoa beans among the Aztecs, or cigarettes in a prisoner-of-war camp. Cocoa beans were perishable and bulky to transport in large quantities—serious drawbacks as a form of money. Aztecs, however, placed an important ceremonial value on a bitter cocoa bean drink, the precursor to hot chocolate. Montezuma, the Aztec ruler of Mexico, always drank one of these drinks before visiting his harem.

See also: Commodity Monetary Standard
References: Berdan, Frances F. 1982. *The Aztecs of Central Mexico: An Imperial Society.*
Einzig, Paul. 1966. *Primitive Money.*
Weatherford, Jack. 1997. *The History of Money.*

Coconut Standard of Nicobars

On the Nicobar Islands, located on an ancient trade route between India and the East Indies, coconuts fulfilled the various roles of money, serving as medium of exchange, store of value, standard of value, and standard of deferred payment. As a store of value coconuts took a backseat to less perishable silver-plated spoons and forks, but in every other respect coconuts served as the principle form of money on the Nicobars. Extensive evidence of coconut money existed in the nineteenth century and the first half of the twentieth century.

Although coconuts cannot be stored for indefinite periods, Indian traders held sizable stores of coconuts to transact business with the islanders and to export. The islanders also kept stores of coconuts in anticipation of future transactions. The Indian traders kept coconuts stored in courtyards protected by fences made from palm leaves; the British government found it necessary to adjudicate disputes between Indian traders and islanders whose pigs had crashed through the palm leaf fences and eaten the coconuts of the Indian traders.

Coconuts involved in a single transaction could mount into the thousands. Every year the Island of Car Nicobar bought 25 ships from the Chowra Island for 100,000 coconuts. Coconuts were counted in pairs up to a score, and then counted in scores of scores.

An exchange rate existed between coconuts and the silver *rupee* of India, and interestingly enough the silver rupee constantly depreciated relative to coconuts. Up to 1885 a silver rupee was the monetary equivalent of 500 coconuts. In 1901 official information put the value of one silver rupee at 100 coconuts. Following World War I the islands decided to impose an export duty, and fixed an official exchange rate of one silver rupee per 200 coconuts. In the post–World War I era, the silver rupee continued to fall relative to coconuts, equivalent to less than 100 coconuts by the beginning of World War II.

Coconuts served as a standard of value even when exchange took place in other articles. An official document cites an instance in 1896 when the people of Car Nicobar purchased a canoe from Chowra valued at 35,000 coconuts, but made payment in other articles, including cloth, spoons, baskets, Indian currency, silver wire, silver rings, knives, forks, pigs, fowls, beads, fishhooks, rupees, and axes. Each article had a coconut equivalent contributing to the total cost of the canoe.

Islanders contracted for debts payable in coconuts. A British government agent found that islanders were in debt to Indian traders for millions of coconuts, leading to the creation of a commission that studied the debts of natives to Indian traders with a view to scaling back indebtedness. After the

rupee was made legal tender, acceptable in the payment of all debts, islanders continued to contract debts in coconuts.

See also: Commodity Monetary Standard
References: Einzig, Paul. 1966. *Primitive Money.* Quiggin, A. Hingston. 1949. *A Survey of Primitive Money.*

Code of Hammurabi
See Babylonian Grain and Silver Standard

Coinage Act of 1792 (United States)
The United States Constitution, in Article I, Section 8, conferred upon Congress the power "To coin Money, regulate the Value thereof, and of foreign Coin." The first legislation Congress passed under this authority granted by the Constitution was the Coinage Act of 1792. The act was based on a report that Alexander Hamilton made to Congress a year earlier.

The act provided for the establishment of a mint, including naming the officers, specifying their duties, and setting their compensation. The act called for what was known as free coinage, indicating that anyone could bring gold or silver bullion to the mint for coinage at no cost to the owner. The gold and silver coins struck at this mint were legal tender for all debts, public and private.

The act also provided "that the money of account of the United States should be expressed in dollars or units, dismes or tenths, cents or hundredths, and milles or thousandths, a disme being a tenth part of a dollar, a cent the hundredth part of a dollar, and a mille the thousandth part of a dollar." The dollar was intended to be same in value as the Spanish milled dollar that was then in circulation in the former colonies. The act called for the minting of eagles, equivalent to $10; half-eagles, equivalent to $5; and quarter-eagles, equivalent to $2.50. The eagles were gold coins. Coins minted in smaller denominations were made of silver and included dollars, half-dollars, quarter-dollars, dismes (ancestor of the current dime), and half-dismes. The act also called for minting cents and half cents from copper. The act held out the threat of the death penalty to discourage any employee of the mint from secretly debasing the coins (reducing the precious metal content) for personal gain or embezzling precious metals or freshly minted coins.

President Washington placed responsibility for

the operation of the mint under the secretary of state, much to the disappointment of Alexander Hamilton, who was then secretary of the treasury. Hamilton later made his disappointment known, and Washington moved control of the mint to the Treasury Department. David Rittenhouse, an eminent scientist and philosopher from Philadelphia, became the first director of the mint.

Imperfections in the system soon made themselves apparent. The act had established an official exchange ratio between gold and silver at 15 pounds of silver to 1 pound of gold. It turned out that gold was worth more than 15 pounds of silver in world markets, causing gold to leave the United States. The overvalued silver coins should have stayed in the United States, but the freshly minted American dollars were more attractive than the Spanish dollars that actually contained more silver. Therefore the American dollars tended to disappear. The Coinage Act of 1793 made some foreign coins legal tender in the United States, and the Spanish dollar circulated as legal-tender money in the United States until 1857.

Although much of the culture and the social institutions of the early United States came from England and France, the dollar is one institution borrowed from the Spanish, a descendent of the Spanish milled dollar that circulated in the American colonies. *Milled* referred to the corrugated edge, now universal among coins, that made evident any clipping or other efforts to remove precious metal from the edges. Alexander Hamilton, a strong admirer of English political institutions, recommended the dollar to Congress as the money of account in the United States, citing the fact that the Spanish dollar had been in actual use in all the states and that the decimal system was superior to the duodecimal of England.

See also: Coinage Act of 1834, Dollar
References: Chown, John F. 1994. *A History of Money.*
Hepburn, A. Barton. 1924. *A History of Currency in the United States.*
Watson, David K. 1899. *History of American Coinage.*

Coinage Act of 1834 (United States)

The Coinage Act of 1834 put the United States on the monetary path that led to the adoption of the gold standard. By increasing the official value of gold, the act caused gold to flow to the mint for coinage be-

cause its mint price exceeded its free market price. Holders of silver found it advantageous to convert silver into gold at free market prices, and take gold to the mint, rather than to take silver directly to the mint. Thus the flow of silver to the mint vanished.

The Coinage Act of 1792 had overvalued silver relative to gold. According to official values fixed by the Act of 1792, 15 ounces of silver equaled 1 ounce of gold. In the free market, 1 ounce of gold purchased nearly 16 ounces of silver, meaning gold was worth more on the free market than at the mint. Holders of gold could obtain a larger value of coinage in face value by first purchasing silver on the free market and taking silver to the mint for coinage, rather than taking gold directly to the mint. Therefore only silver arrived at the mint for coinage, and gold coins disappeared from circulation as gold coinage came to a standstill. The overvaluation of silver in the act of 1792 was unintentional and—in the eyes of many observers—cost the states their prosperity.

Senator Thomas Hart Benton, one of the staunchest supporters of gold in United States history, apparently wanted to attract Latin American gold to the United States. In the book Benton wrote of his 30 years in the United States Senate, *Thirty Years' View,* he put the issue in crystal-clear terms:

> Gold goes where it finds its value, and that value is what the laws of the great nations give it. In Mexico and South America, the countries which produce gold, and from which the United States must derive their chief supply, the value of gold is 16 to 1 over silver; in the island of Cuba it is 17 to 1; in Spain and Portugal, it is 16 to 1; in the West Indies it is the same. It is not to be supposed that gold will come from these countries to the United States, if the importer is to lose one dollar in every sixteen that he brings; or that our gold will remain with us, when an exporter can gain a dollar upon every fifteen that he carries out. Such results would be contrary to the laws of trade, and therefore we must place the same value upon gold that other nations do, if we wish to gain any part of theirs, or regain any part of our own. (Hepburn, 1924)

Congress enacted the Coinage Act of 1834 on 28 June with only 36 representatives and 7 senators voting against the legislation. Another piece of legislation, passed on the same day, gave Spanish dollars minted in the newly independent states of the former Spanish colonies the same legal-tender status enjoyed by the Spanish dollars minted in Spain.

The Coinage Act of 1834 decreased the grains of pure gold in the *eagle,* a $10 gold piece, from 247.4 grains to 232 grains, a decrease of 6.26 percent. The gold content of the two other gold coins minted by the Treasury, the half eagle and quarter eagle, were decreased proportionately. The act left the silver content of silver coinage untouched. The increase in mint value of gold raised the official ratio of silver to gold from 15 to 1 to 16 to 1, essentially making an ounce of gold more valuable in terms of a fixed weight of silver.

By 1834 the United States was on a de facto silver standard, and term contracts were written under the expectation that payment would be made in silver dollars, a factor that might account for the interest in keeping silver a part of the monetary standard. Proponents of the Coinage Act of 1834 saw clearly, however, that the provisions of the act pushed the United States toward a de facto gold standard. The passage of the Coinage Act of 1834 marked the first time that the United States Congress debated monetary questions, and it revealed that the majority opinion in the United States favored a gold standard over a silver standard, a view that was in step with future world trends. The California gold discoveries of the 1840s further depressed the market value of gold relative to the mint price, further adding to gold showing up at the Treasury for coinage, and the sight of a silver dollar became a rarity.

See also: Coinage Act of 1792, Free Silver Movement, Gold Standard

References: Hepburn, A. Barton. 1924. *A History of Currency of the United States.*
Nettels, Curtis. 1962. *The Emergence of a National Economy.*
Schwarz, Ted. 1980. *A History of United States Coinage.*

Coinage Act of 1853 (United States)

The Coinage Act of 1853 nudged the United States closer to single monetary standard based upon gold. It provided for the coinage of subsidiary silver coins to support small transactions without endangering the precedence of gold as the preeminent monetary metal.

The conditions that spurred Congress to approve the Coinage Act of 1853 grew directly out of the Coinage Act of 1834. That act had decreased the gold metal content of gold coins relative to face value, drawing gold to the mint for coinage at the expense of silver. At United States mint prices, 16 ounces of silver matched in value an ounce of gold, more ounces of silver than was needed to purchase an ounce of gold on the free market. The flow of silver to the mint fell to a trickle, and speculators melted down silver coins and sold them for bullion.

The proponents of the Act of 1834 had foreseen that the act would lift gold to preeminence as the primary monetary standard, and that overvalued gold coins would drive undervalued silver coins out of circulation. They did not anticipate that the disappearance of the small denomination silver coinage would impose a hardship on retail businesses. Under the pre–Civil War coinage system, the mint struck the gold *eagle,* gold half eagle, and gold quarter eagle in face values of $10, $5, and $2.50, respectively. In silver coinage the mint struck the silver dollar, the half dollar, the quarter, the dime, and half dime. Ten dimes had the same silver content as a silver dollar. As speculators sold silver coinage for bullion, merchants and consumers stood without the coinage to settle minor transactions.

The Coinage Act of 1853 reduced the silver content of the half dollar, the quarter, and the dime and half dime, but left the silver content of the silver dollar untouched. The silver content of a silver dollar remained at 371.5 grains of pure silver, but a dollar's worth of half dollars, quarters, dimes, and half dimes dropped to only 345.6 grains of pure silver, about a 7 percent reduction. The Treasury continued to stand ready to accept unlimited amounts of silver for coinage into silver dollars, but the act authorized the Treasury's purchase of only limited amounts of silver to mint subsidiary coinage, that is, half dollars, quarters, dimes, and half dimes. The act gave the Treasury the authority to decide the amount of silver to purchase for subsidiary coinage, an amount that would necessarily be less than holders of silver would want to bring to the Treasury at overvalued prices. The purpose of the act was to maintain gold as the primary monetary metal while furnishing the public with a subsidiary silver coinage. Theoretically, the United States remained on a bimetallic standard because silver dollars enjoyed a legal-tender status, but in practice no silver dollars were coined.

The act provided that subsidiary coinage was legal tender for amounts up to $5.00, raising issues that would surface later when the government made paper money legal tender. A flavor of how antagonistic feelings ran on this issue is echoed in the remarks of the bill's major opponent, Andrew Johnson, later vice president, and then president upon the death of Lincoln.

I look upon this bill as the merest quackery—the veriest charlatanism—so far as the currency of the country is concerned. The idea of Congress fixing the value of currency is an absurdity, notwithstanding the *language* of the Constitution—not the meaning of it. If we can by law make $107 out of $100, we can by the same process make it worth $150. Why, Sir, of all the problems that have come up for solution, from the time of the alchemists down to the present time, none can compare with that solved by this modern Congress. They alone have discovered that they can make money—that they can make $107 out of $100. If they can increase it to that extent, they can go on and increase it to infinity, and thus, by the operation of the mint, the government can supply its own revenues. (Watson, 1970)

The Coinage Act of 1853 achieved its purpose. Small coinage increased in circulation, and after 1857 foreign coins were no longer legal tender in the United States. After the outbreak of the Civil War, all metallic coinage went into hiding, and the United States turned to an inconvertible paper standard. In the last quarter of the nineteenth century, the battle between gold and silver was fought anew before the United States settled firmly on a gold standard, without even the pretence of a bimetallic standard based upon gold and silver.

See also: Bimetallism, Coinage Act of 1792, Coinage Act of 1834, Free Silver Movement, Gold Standard

References: Chown, John. 1994. *A History of Money*.
Hepburn, A. Barton. 1924. *A History of Currency of the United States*.
Laughlin, J. Laurence. 1896. *A History of Bimetallism in the United States*.
Schwarz, Ted. 1980. *A History of United States Coinage*.
Watson, David K. 1970. *History of American Coinage*.

Coinage Act of 1965 (United States)

The Coinage Act of 1965 removed all silver content from dimes and quarters, and cut the silver content of half dollars from 90 to 40 percent.

Two separate trends conspired to substantially reduce the use of silver coinage. First, a coin shortage was making itself felt despite a triple increase in mint output of coins from mid-1959 to mid-1964. The rapid growth in vending machines, pay telephones, parking meters, and sales taxes fueled a corresponding increase in the demand for small change, including dimes, quarters, and half dollars. Also, collectors may have been absorbing coins at a faster clip. By mid-1964 merchants were facing difficulty making change and some banks were rationing dimes and nickels.

Second, world demand for silver exceeded world production, and the United States Treasury had been filling the gap by selling off silver reserves. By mid-1965 the Treasury faced a serious depletion of its silver reserves, and the market price of silver was rising, raising the specter that the price of silver might exceed the trigger price of $1.3824, at which point the silver content of small change would exceed the face value. Once the price of silver rose above $1.3824, silver coins would be worth more melted down and sold as bullion, leading to a disappearance of silver coins from circulation.

The Treasury proposed the complete removal of all silver from coinage, preferring to completely circumvent the threat that the price of silver would rise high enough to make melting down silver coins profitable. The role of silver in the monetary affairs of the United States, however, has been a politicized issue for over a century and Congress compromised by maintaining a 40 percent silver content in half dollars. The act provided for the coinage of dimes and quarters composed of a cupronickel plating over a copper core. Cupronickel is a copper and nickel alloy.

See also: Free Silver Movement, Silver, Silver Purchase Act of 1934

References: Jastram, Roy W. 1981. *Silver, the Restless Metal*.
Rickenbacker, William F. 1966. *Wooden Nickels, Or the Decline and Fall of Silver Coins*.
Schwarz, Ted. 1980. *A History of United States Coinage*.

Commodity Monetary Standard

Under a commodity monetary standard, a medium of exchange and unit of account is either a commodity or a claim to a commodity and the commodity is a good that would have value even if it were not used for money. Put differently, the commodity has an intrinsic value, in contrast to the paper money of an inconvertible paper standard that has value only by government fiat and is called fiat money for that reason.

In the purest form of commodity money, the commodity itself may change hands. History furnishes numerous examples of livestock, necessary staples, stones, shells, metals, etc., that have acted as a medium of exchange, a unit of account, a standard of deferred payment, and a store of value. The most famous and enduring commodity standard in history is the gold standard, but silver can boast of a history as a monetary standard that almost rivals the history of gold.

In more sophisticated commodity standards, paper claims to the commodity change hands in exchange, while the commodity itself is stored in warehouses or vaults. The gold standard of the nineteenth and early twentieth centuries perhaps offers the best example of a commodity standard in which paper claims to the commodity replace the commodity itself as the circulating medium. Less-developed countries of the world operated silver standards on the same principle, until inconvertible paper standards replaced all precious metal commodity standards in the twentieth century.

Although gold, and to a lesser extent silver, have been the most widely embraced commodities to act as the basis of the more sophisticated commodity standards, they do not stand alone. The colonists of Virginia stored tobacco in warehouses, and issued tobacco notes representing titles of ownership to the tobacco. The colonists quoted prices in tobacco, and tobacco notes exchanged hands instead tobacco itself. The colonists could freely convert tobacco notes into tobacco as needed. In the eighteenth and nineteenth centuries, Japan operated a similar system based upon rice. Rice notes circulated as money and even the value of gold and silver coins was expressed in terms of rice. In 1760 the Japanese government specifically forbade landowners from issuing rice notes in excess of the amount of rice they had stored, a common abuse in all commodity systems using paper claims to a commodity. Although in practice gold and silver have dominated commodity standards, in theory a whole range of commodities could serve the same purpose.

Under a commodity standard, the value of money is the price, determined by supply and demand, of a commodity that is costly to produce. A government agency sets the price at which it stands ready to buy and sell the commodity, and production of the commodity will expand to a level necessary to stabilize prices. If the official price of gold is $35 per ounce, as it was for a number of years under the United States gold standard, gold production expands to the point at which an ounce of gold costs just under $35 to produce. If gold is not profitable to produce at $35 per ounce, gold production contracts, reducing the world money supply and causing prices to fall. The average level of prices continues to fall, reducing the cost of producing gold, until gold becomes profitable to produce at $35 per ounce, at which point the world money supply (and prices) stabilize. If gold is highly profitable to produce at $35 per ounce, the gold production expands, adding to the world's money stock, and prices rise, increasing the costs of producing gold relative to its selling price. Theoretically, gold production expands and contracts to keep price stable, creating a self-correcting mechanism for maintaining price stability. Although governments have more experience with the gold standard than other commodity standards, in theory the same principles work regardless of the commodity.

More complicated commodity standards can be devised using more than one commodity. The bimetallic standard that figured prominently in nineteenth-century monetary history was a commodity standard based on gold and silver. The inflation surge of the 1970s renewed interest in commodity standards among monetary economists. One idea that surfaced was a variable commodity standard based on a composite commodity. A composite commodity is a weighted combination of several commodities. Thus a variable commodity standard makes a currency convertible into a weighted basket of several commodities.

See also: Bimetallism, Commodity Money, Credole and Tratte, Gold Standard, Rice Currency, Symmetallism, Variable Commodity Standard, Virginia Tobacco Act of 1713

References: Bordo, Michael D. 1981. The Classical Gold
    Standard: Some Lessons for Today. *Monthly Review*
    (published by the Federal Reserve Bank of St.
    Louis)(May): 2–17.
Fisher, Irving. *The Purchasing Power of Money,* 1911.
Yeager, Leland B. 1983. Stable Money and Free-Market
    Currencies. *Cato Journal* 3 (Spring): 305–326.

Commodity Money (American Colonies)

Stable commodities produced in the American colonies often filled the gap in the colonial money supply left by the outflow of most hard specie for European goods. Colonial assemblies sanctioned commodity money as legal tender and set the price of commodities for the retirement of public debts.

Typical of colonial assembly legislation sanctioning the use of commodity money was an act of the South Carolina assembly adopted in 1687. This act read:

> that all debts, accounts, contracts, bargains and judgments, and executions thereupon which are not made expressly for silver or money or some other particular commodity att a certain price shall and may bee paid and discharged by Corne att two shillings the bushel, Indian Peas at two shillings six pence the bushel, English Peas at three shillings sixpence the bushel, Pork at twenty Shillings per cwt., Beefe at twopence the pound, Tobacco at two pence the pound, Tar at eight shillings per barrell. (Brock, 1975)

Around the same time New York allowed pork, beef, and winter wheat to serve as money, and east New Jersey included wheat, Indian corn, butter, pork, beef, and tobacco as commodity money. New Hampshire's list of commodities serving as money for the years 1701 through 1709 had eight kinds of boards or staves and four kinds of fish, as well as pork, beef, peas, wheat, and Indian corn. The Caribbean colonies often made use of sugar as a medium of exchange, and tobacco dominated the commodity money supply in Maryland and Virginia. Curtis P. Nettels quotes a statement from the Virginia House of Burgesses regarding the salaries of the clergy, which states that "[f]or every marriage by license the laws give them twenty shillings or two hundred pounds of tobacco and if at a private house they marry any person they have for it one hundred pounds of tobacco at least" (Nettels, 1934). The difference between a marriage by license and a marriage at a private house is unclear, but tobacco was an important means of paying clergy.

Colonial assemblies set legal prices for all public payments, such as taxes, but prevailing market prices often set the rate for all private payments. Colonial assemblies invariably set the legal prices for public payments above the market prices, often chafing public officials who received income in commodity money at legal prices. The higher the legal price of a commodity relative to its market price, the smaller would be the quantity of the commodity received by the public official.

One of the problems with the use of commodity money is that commodities often vary substantially in quality. Creditors and government officials in jurisdictions that allowed commodity money often found themselves pressured to accept low-quality commodities in payment. To address this problem, the colony of New Haven (later absorbed into Connecticut Colony) in 1654 required that on:

> every plantation there shall be a viewer of corn, that in case of difference may judge, whether it be well dressed and merchantable or no, which man is to be chosen by each plantation, and shall be under oath to judge faithfully when called to it, and is to be paid for his time spent and pains therein by him whose corn is faulty, or who unnecessarily occasions the trouble. (Nettels, 1934)

Connecticut adopted a similar measure for both grains and pork. In Virginia and Maryland a debtor presenting tobacco to a creditor who refused to accept it could ask for two impartial judges. If these judges declared the tobacco good and merchantable, and the creditor still refused to accept it, the debt was counted as paid.

Another problem associated with commodity money is the expense and difficulty of transporting it. In the Massachusetts Bay Colony the General Court said that in the case of cattle driven to Boston for payment of taxes:

> if they be weary, or hungry, or fall sick or lame, it shall be lawful to rest and refresh them for a competent time in any open place, that is not corn,

meadow or inclosed for some particular use. (Nettels, 1934)

The widespread use of commodity money reveals the severity of the shortage of coins and other forms of money in the American colonies. It shows that forms of money will develop from the ground up when governments fail to infuse economies with sufficient money to finance trade.

See also: Commodity Monetary Standard, Virginia Tobacco Act of 1713

References: Brock, Leslie. 1975. *The Currency of the American Colonies, 1700–1764.*

Galbraith, John Kenneth. 1975. *Money, Whence It Came, Where It Went.*

Nettels, Curtis P. 1934. *The Money Supply of the American Colonies before 1720.*

Confederate Hyperinflation

From October 1861 to March 1864 price increases averaged 10 percent per month in the states of the Confederacy, putting the Confederate price index when Lee surrendered at 92 times its prewar base. In the history of the United States only the hyperinflation of the American Revolution compares in intensity with the hyperinflation of the Confederacy.

Like the revolutionaries that spearheaded the American Revolution, the leaders of the Confederacy faced a populace that was in no mood to pay additional taxes. Southerners felt that the present generation bore the burden of a war that would primarily benefit future generations, and as much of the expense as possible should be passed to future generations. Union blockades of Confederate ports precluded any effort to implement a revenue tariff on imports, the main source of federal government tax revenue. The Confederate government enacted a property tax but lacked the machinery to collect it in the face of uncooperative state governments. By October 1864 tax revenue accounted for less than 5 percent of all revenue that found its way to the Confederate treasury.

The Confederacy met with slightly more success in trying to finance public expenditures with bonds. In May 1861 the Confederate Congress approved a $50 million bond issue. The bond issue faltered on a depressed cotton market that resulted from the use of cotton as a bargaining chip with European governments whose recognition the Confederacy needed, leaving angry planters unable or unwilling to subscribe to bonds on the scale needed. By October 1864 bond sales had raised less than 30 percent of all revenue that had entered the Confederate treasury.

The remaining source of revenue was Confederate money. On 9 March 1861 the Confederate Congress authorized printing notes in an amount not exceeding $1 million, but the Treasury Department over four years printed $15 million of notes. Treasury employees at the note-signing bureau rose from 72 in July 1862 to 262 in July 1863. As printers, paper,

Assorted Confederate currency. Printing presses financed more than 68 percent of government spending between July 1861 and October 1863. (Library of Congress)

A Confederate $100 bill. (Smithsonian Institution, National Numismatic Collection)

and engravings became scarce, the Confederate government granted credit for counterfeit bills, which were stamped valid and reissued. From 1 July 1861 to 1 October 1863 the paper money column of the Confederate Treasury ledger accounted for 68.6 percent of all government revenue.

Surprisingly, private banks in the Confederacy were restrained in the issuance of bank notes. The uncertainties of war encouraged private banks to hold large quantities of vault cash, which actually tempered the inflationary thrust of the excess paper money.

Much of the Confederate currency bore the option to buy interest-bearing Confederate bonds up to a certain date, after which that option expired. As inflation gathered force early in 1864 the Confederate Congress enacted a currency reform that brought a lull in the inflation rate. The reform provided that all currency in bills greater than $5 could be converted into 4 percent bonds, dollar for dollar. Currency not converted into bonds by 1 April 1864 had to be exchanged for new currency at a rate of three for two. Inflation subsided until December 1864 when the Confederate government again had to turn to the printing presses.

From the first quarter of 1861 until 1 January 1864 prices in the Confederacy rose 28-fold while the money supply rose only 11-fold. Prices rose even faster than the money supply because of wartime disruptions in the supply of goods, and the phenomenon of velocity. Velocity is the average number of times per year that a dollar is spent, and in a hyperinflationary environment, recipients of money rush to spend it before it loses its value. An increase in the velocity of money has the same effect on the economy as an increase in the money supply.

The experience of the Confederacy shows what happens when the supply of money exceeds what is demanded by the normal transactions of business and the desire for liquidity. When the supply of money exceeds the demand, the value of money falls, meaning it buys less because of price increases.

See also: American Revolution Hyperinflation, Inflation and Deflation, Velocity of Money

References: Lerner, Eugene M. 1956. Inflation in the Confederacy, 1861–1865. In *Studies in the Quantity Theory of Money*, ed. Milton Friedman.
Myers, Margaret G. 1970. *A Financial History of the United States*.
Slabaugh, Arlie. 1998. *Confederate States Paper Money*, 9th ed.

Constantine I

Cosmas Indicopleustes, a sixth-century A.D. merchant, observed that the eastern Roman Empire owed its prosperity to two causes, Christianity and coinage. The history of these two valued attributes of the eastern empire leads back to one person, Constantine I, who made Christianity the official religion of the Roman Empire and introduced the golden *solidus* coin, which the Byzantine Empire continued to mint without debasement until the eleventh century.

Constantine rose to power in a portion of the western empire in A.D. 306, and after nearly two decades of piecemeal war with rivals, made himself sole emperor of the Roman Empire in A.D. 323. The Roman Empire

The golden solidus became one of the most famous coins in history, maintaining its purity and weight for several centuries. (Smithsonian Institution, National Numismatic Collection)

had been in the clutches of rampant inflation for half a century. The emperor Diocletian had issued full-weighted gold and silver coins, but the inflation showed no signs of easing up. In A.D. 301 Diocletian issued his famous Edict of Prices, which made raising prices above legal limits a capital offense. The Roman government had continued to debase its silver and copper coinage, but it had never significantly reduced the weight or purity of its gold coins. With inflation still out of control, Constantine put the reform of the currency close to the top of his priorities.

Constantine minted the solidus at a weight equal to one seventy-second of a pound of gold. Each pound equaled 12 ounces, and each ounce equaled 24 *scruples*. A solidus weighed 4 scruples. The greatest challenge Constantine faced was finding adequate supplies of gold and silver bullion. He required that a certain share of taxes be paid in silver and gold and he enacted new taxes payable in silver and gold. Also rents on imperial lands were collected in gold. He inherited a practice from previous emperors of placing a levy on cities in gold bullion. His most famous action to secure large supplies of gold and silver, enabling him to launch new gold and silver coinage on a large scale, was the seizure of the gold and silver stored in pagan temples. In the words of an anonymous observer writing a generation later:

In the time of Constantine there was lavish expenditure: he assigned gold to mean transactions, instead of bronze, which formerly used to be held of high value. The origin of this avarice is believed to have come from the following cause. When gold and silver and a great quantity of precious stones, which had been stored in ancient times in the temples came into public use, it inflamed the desire of all for giving and possessing. And whereas the expenditure even of bronze . . . already seemed heavy and excessive, nevertheless owing to a kind of blindness there was a more lavish zeal for expenditure in gold, which is considered more valuable. (Jones, 1964)

During the time of Constantine, the solidus was mainly used to pay large government expenditures, but it steadily grew in popularity as a means of settling private transactions. During the fifth century A.D., both the eastern and western governments discontinued all but the smallest copper coins, and silver coinage also dropped to a trickle. Gold coinage became the principle medium of exchange for public and private transactions. The gold solidus became the international coin par excellence, accepted from one end of the world to the other, and constituting further proof of Rome's sovereignty and divine favor.

The gold solidus was the most prestigious coin of the Middle Ages, and became one of the most famous coins in history. In the hands of the Byzantine government it maintained its weight and purity for 700 years, a record for any coinage.

See also: Byzantine Debasement, Dissolution of
    Monasteries, Roman Empire Inflation
References: Duncan-Jones, Richard. 1998. *Money and
    Government in the Roman Empire.*
Frank, Tenney. 1959. *An Economic Survey of Ancient Rome.*
    Vol. IV.
Jones, A. H. M. 1964. *The Later Roman Empire: 284–602.*
    Vols. I, II.

Consumer Price Index
See Value of Money

Copper

After gold and silver, copper has the longest and most varied history as a monetary metal. Resistant to corrosion and malleable, copper was used by ancient peoples to make utensils, hammers, knives, and vessels of great beauty. As early as 5000 B.C. ancient Egyptians buried copper weapons and tools in graves for use in the afterlife. The Chinese epic *Shu Ching* makes references to the use of copper around 2500 B.C.

In the Mediterranean world, Cyprus was a major producer and the sole supplier of copper to the Romans, whose first metallic monetary system was based on a copper or bronze standard. The Romans called it *aes cyprium*, later shortened to *cyprium*. The English word "copper" stemmed from the word *cuprum*, a corrupted form of *cyprium*. The chemical symbol for copper, Cu, comes from the first two letters of the Latin name.

The Ancient Egyptians operated on a copper monetary standard. The standard unit of weight was a *uten* or *deben* of copper, and it was subsided into the *kit* or *kedet*. Some writers contend that the copper units were mainly used to value goods for barter, but others claim that copper rings, equal to multiples or fractions of the copper unit of weight circulated as a medium of exchange.

Copper or bronze remained the monetary standard of Rome until the end of the Roman Republic in 30 B.C. The Latin word for copper also denotes bronze, leaving some confusion about Rome's monetary system. Bronze is copper alloyed with tin, and is a tougher metal than either copper or tin separately.

Copper had many practical uses for shaping weapons and tools, but ancient cultures never seemed to have invested copper with the religious significance that enveloped silver and particularly gold in a cloak of reverence. The Old Testament makes only one reference to copper (Ezra 8:27), but makes countless references to gold and silver, beginning in Genesis. Nevertheless, a certain Father Allouez, traveling through the area of Superior Bay (also called Allouez Bay) on Lake Superior in the 1660s observed:

There are often found beneath the waters of Lake Superior pieces of copper, well formed and of the weight of 20 pounds. I have seen them in the hands of Indians; and, as the latter are superstitious, they keep them as so many divinities, or as presents from the gods beneath. (Del Mar, 1968)

Before the Spanish Conquest, copper was more valuable than gold in North America, Mexico, and Peru. In modern European history copper has clearly been a second-class monetary metal. In the sixteenth century Spain debased its silver currency with copper alloy. The currency was called *vellon* and by 1599 it was virtually pure copper. Copper money was sometimes called black money because when mixed with a bit of silver it blackened quickly. In the seventeenth century Sweden, which had vast copper deposits, adopted a copper monetary standard that lasted over a hundred years. During the Napoleonic era the French government tried to make copper legal tender in the settlement of debts in amounts up to one-fourth of the amount owed, but the effort fizzled. In August 1800 the government instructed the Bank of France to pay no more than one-twelfth of the government's debt service in copper.

In the nineteenth century the demand for small change created a new demand for copper as a monetary metal. In 1797 England began issuing penny and twopenny coins made of copper. The first coinage legislation of the newly constituted United States authorized the coinage of cents and half cents made of copper. Copper coinage in the United States continued into the 1970s, when the high price of copper made pennies more valuable melted down and sold by weight.

The three metals that have served as money in the Western world are gold, silver, and copper. Although copper was not as valuable as gold or silver as a unit of weight, it filled a niche in the monetary system. A person planning to purchase a house would find it very difficult to transport the amount

The head of Athene was stamped on one side of the Corinthian stater, with the image of Pegasus on the reverse. (Smithsonian Institution, National Numismatic Collection)

of copper needed to make the payment. For large commercial transactions, gold was ideal, because of its high value per unit of weight. For the purchase of a soft drink, however, the amount of gold needed would be a very small quantity, too small to be easily measured and handled. Silver was preferable for intermediate transactions, but for small retail transactions, copper was most suitable.

See also: American Penny, Bronze Standard of Ancient Rome, Egyptian Copper Standard, Sweden's Copper Standard

References: Del Mar, Alexander. 1968. *The History of Money in America.*
Kindleberger, Charles P. 1984. *A Financial History of Western Europe.*
Williams, Jonathan. 1997. *Money: A History.*

Corinthian Silver Standard

Corinth was the first Greek city-state to successfully launch a rival coinage that competed with the Aeginetan standard. The beginning of coinage in Corinth gives some credence to the theory that geography is a determinant of history. The harbor of Corinth stood astride the isthmus connecting Peloponnesus with Attica, looking east toward Aegina, the birthplace of Greek coinage, and west, toward Italy and supplies of silver that it could control. Aegina controlled eastward trade into the Aegean Sea, but to the west the Corinthian gulf opened into the Ionian and Adriatic Seas, giving Corinth a free

field to establish colonies on the route to the Adriatic and across the sea to Sicily. Corinth learned about coinage from its eastward trade, and from control of the western sea routes won access to the silver mines of the Illyrian Mountains, breaking the Aeginetan monopoly on Greek supplies of silver.

Corinthian coinage may have been born of a political revolution that displaced an aristocracy and empowered the merchant classes. The first coinage in Corinth roughly coincided with the ascendancy to power in 655 B.C. of Cypselus, who established himself as a despot favoring the merchant classes. Corinthian coinage probably began as a measure to promote the commercial interests of Corinth.

Because it had to transport silver from long distances, Corinth could not coin silver on terms comparable to Aegina. Whereas the Aeginetan silver *drachma* weighed 96 grains, the Corinthian silver drachma weighed 43 grains, giving the coins of Aegina a sizable edge in Greece and the Aegean trading area. In Sicily and southern Italy, however, the advantage lay with the Corinthian coins that could be shipped directly from the Corinthian Gulf, whereas shipments from Aegina had to round the Peloponnesus, a longer, more dangerous, and therefore more expensive route.

In style and craftsmanship, Corinthian coins utterly outshone the Aeginetan coins. First, they bore the image of Pegasus, the winged horse of Greek mythology, a more charismatic and spirited concept than the clumsy tortoise image on Aeginetan coins. Also, the Corinthians stamped both sides of their coins and designed different coins for various denominations—another departure from the practice of Aegina, which stamped coins of all denominations only on one side and with the same image. In Aeginetan coinage, different coin sizes represented different denominations, a source of confusion to people in distant lands unfamiliar with Aeginetan weights and standards. One side of Corinthian coins always bore the image of Pegasus, but the reverse side bore different images for different denominations. The head of Athena was stamped on the reverse side of the *stater,* and the head of Aphrodite on the reverse side of the drachma.

The colonies of Corinth adopted the Corinthian coinage system, and sometimes restamped the Corinthian coins with images of their own choosing. Coins have been found upon which the second stamping left vestiges of the original Corinthian stamping. The Corinthian coinage was edging out the Aeginetan coinage when Athens began its own coinage during the sixth century B.C. Athenian coinage would supersede the Aeginetan coinage and substantially overshadow the Corinthian coinage.

See also: Aeginetan Silver Standard, Attic Silver Standard, Temple Coinage of Ancient Greece

References: Burns, A. R. 1927. *Money and Monetary Policy in Early Times.*
Carridice, Ian. 1995. *Greek Coins.*
Freeman, Kathleen. 1976. *The Work and Life of Solon.*
Milne, J. G. 1931. *Greek Coinage.*

Corn Banks of Egypt

Ptolemaic Egypt (323–30 B.C.) developed a highly sophisticated system of warehouse banking based on corn, a traditional form of money in Egypt. The Egyptians applied the knowledge of Greek banking to scattered government granaries that dotted the landscape in every locality of any consequence, and turned them into a national network of corn banks with headquarters in Alexandria. Even after Greek coinage spread to Egypt with the conquest of Alexander the Great, corn remained an important standard of value in the feudal economy of Egypt. The government and rich merchants jealously hoarded coins and precious metals to finance foreign transactions. Lower- and middle-class Egyptians transacted business in the domestic economy with deposits in corn banks, habituating the entire population to using banks.

Originally, farmers stored their annual crop of corn in government granaries for safety and convenience. The government collected taxes in corn, which was also deposited in granaries. The Egyptians lumped corn of the same quality together in the granaries and learned to exchange the ownership of corn without the corn leaving the granary—the first step in the development of corn banking. The owners of the corn could pass written orders of withdrawal of corn to pay debts and taxes, or to purchase goods and services. By the time of the Ptolemies, Egyptians had become accustomed to paying debts through the bank, a practice that had the additional advantage of creating an official record of transactions that could be helpful in the event of litigation.

The Ptolemaic Egyptians developed the banking expertise to centralize the accounting and management of a nationwide network of corn bank granaries from one headquarters in Alexandria. The centralized accounting and management afforded depositors the ability to transfer funds to other regions, creating one of the first money transfer systems. A thousand years before the development of double-entry bookkeeping, the Egyptians developed a system of debit and credit entries and deposit transfers that made use of the grammar of their language. Credit entries fell under the genitive or possessive case, and the dative case stood for debit entries. Records show that often deposits were transferred from one account to another without corn leaving the granary. Referring to the bookkeeping principles, M. Rostovtzeff, in his *Social and Economic History of the Hellenistic World,* says "I have mentioned this detail in bank procedure, familiar in modern times, because many eminent scholars have thought it improbable that such transfers were made in ancient times."

The grain bank network of Ptolemaic Egypt is the only banking institution of the ancient world that bears comparison with the greatest banks of the nineteenth and twentieth centuries. Sufficient records concerning the volume of accounts, number of branches, and employees are extant to form a picture of the vast influence it wielded over the Egyptian economy. In addition, the Ptolemies of Egypt probably deserve the distinction of being first to advance banking as a government enterprise.

The royal grain bank of Egypt demonstrates that precious metals are not a necessary component of a sophisticated monetary system. Any commodity that has a dependable market value can fill the role of a monetary standard. The annual flood of the Nile river helped stabilize corn production in Egypt and shield it from the whims of the weather, making the supply of corn sufficiently stable to form a monetary base.

See also: Commodity Monetary Standard, Egyptian Copper Standard

References: Davies, Glyn. 1994. *A History of Money*.
Rostovtzeff, M. 1941. *The Social and Economic History of the Hellenistic World*. Vols. I–III.

Corso Forzoso (Italy)

The famous *Corso Forzoso,* meaning "forced circulation," refers to the suspension of convertibility of Italy's paper *lira* from 1866 to 1881, which put Italy on a paper standard inconvertible into a precious metal. Before the Corso Forzoso Italy was on a gold and silver bimetallic standard, and holders of Italian bank notes could redeem notes in gold and silver specie.

The origin of the Corso Forzoso can be traced to costly wars waged to unify Italy, disorderly public finances arising from consolidation of budgets and taxation systems of separate Italian governments, and heavy public works expenditures in the name of industrialization. Between 1 January 1862 and 1 January 1867 the public debt grew from 3,131 million lire to 6,929 million lire. The debt was financed by short-term treasury bonds, a third of which were held by foreign investors sensitive to crises of confidence, and expecting bond redemption in gold and silver. The end of the American Civil War, bringing cancellation of war contracts, demobilization, and renewed competition from cheap American cotton, sent the economic tremors that pushed Italy over the monetary precipice. The price of Italian bonds on the Paris Bourse tumbled from 80 percent to 36.44 percent of par value and Italian bondholders and Italian correspondents of foreign bondholders asked for redemption in gold, causing a shortage of gold, and a crisis of confidence in the banking system. A run on the banks forced the government's hand and on 1 May 1866 the government, with prior approval from the legislature, decreed the inconvertibility of bank notes—the Corso Forzoso.

Notwithstanding the Corso Forzoso, the National Bank of Italy avoided the runaway issuance of bank notes that brought to ruin many past experiments with paper money. The index of wholesale prices rose modestly from 0.897 in 1866 to 1.051 in 1873. The gold price index rose from 1.046 to 1.137 over the same time period.

Defenders of the policy of Corzo Forzoso argue that the consequent depreciation of the lira in foreign exchange markets made Italian exports cheaper in foreign markets, and foreign goods expensive in Italian markets, together acting as a powerful boost to Italian industry. Also the Corzo Forzoso accustomed the Italian people to the acceptance of bank notes. In 1865 only one-tenth of the circulating money had consisted of bank notes. Critics of the policy point to the fear that Corzo Forzoso struck in the minds of potential foreign investors at a time when Italy badly needed foreign capital.

After achieving a balance budget early in the 1870s the Italian government began taking steps to restore convertibility of the lira. As the government paid off its debts to the National Bank of Italy in gold, the bank was able to restore convertibility, and on 7 April 1881 the Corzo Forzoso came to an end.

The Corso Forzoso ranks among the more successful early efforts to circulate fiat money, or money not supported by precious metals or other commodities. During the Napoleonic Wars England maintained control over its monetary affairs despite the adoption of an inconvertible paper standard. Before the Corso Forzoso, however, the more normal consequence of inconvertible paper money had been a whirlwind of inflation. France lamented two disastrous experiences with inconvertible paper, John Law's paper money, and the French Revolution's *assignats,* both of which caused runaway or hyperinflation.

See also: Bank Restriction Act of 1797, Inconvertible Paper Standard

References: Chown, John F. 1994. *A History of Money*.
Clough, Shepard B. 1964. *The Economic History of Modern Italy*.

Counterfeit Money

Counterfeit money is mostly forged or faked paper money, sometimes referred to as funny money. Counterfeit paper money is almost as old as paper money, and the practice of counterfeiting money survives into our own day as governments strive to remain one technological step ahead of the counterfeiters.

Counterfeiting became a flourishing activity early in the nineteenth century because of the proliferation of banks issuing their own bank notes. England was one country that did not spare the rod in handing out justice to counterfeiters. Between 1805 and 1818 the Bank of England successfully brought 501 counterfeiters to the bar of justice, and 207 met their fate at the gallows. Not only was it illegal to counterfeit money but having a forged note in one's possession was illegal and ignorance was no defense. A public outcry rose up against savage sentences meted out to people who accidentally came into possession of forged notes. In 1819 the Society of the Arts, concerned about the hanging of innocent people, published its *Report on the Mode of Preventing the Forgery of Bank Notes*. The report found fault with the Bank of England for issuing bank notes too easily counterfeited, and proposed a distinct set of copper plates and employment of highly skilled artists to design notes and engrave plates.

The sight of two women hanged for passing forged notes led George Cruikshank, cartoonist and political satirist, to produce an antihanging note: His "Bank Restriction Note" bore an image of Britannia with a skull instead of a head against a background of despairing figures and highlighting 11 individuals hanging from scaffolds. The note also bore the signature of Jack Ketch, a notorious public hangman. Cruikshank's note sparked riots in London, and the government appointed a royal commission to find ways of producing notes that could not be imitated. England turned to the American firm of Murray, Draper, Fairman & Company, which had revolutionized bank-note printing using a siderographic transfer process and highly complicated background patterns. The siderographic process facilitates the exact duplication of engraved steel plates by using alternating hardened and softened steel cylinders to pass on imprints. An employee, Jacob Perkins, inventor of these processes, offered his services to the Bank of England, won a contract, and the firm of Perkins Bacon became the premier producer of postage stamps and paper money worldwide during the nineteenth century.

Counterfeiting is sometimes a state-sponsored activity, with the object of producing confusion and social unrest in enemy countries. The Bank of England counterfeited vast numbers of *assignats,* the famous French paper money of the French Revolution that touched off a wave of hyperinflation. One of the largest counterfeiting schemes in history was Operation Bernhard, the code name for Nazi Germany's vast program for counterfeiting Bank of England notes. Apparently the Soviet Union also resorted to counterfeiting as a weapon in the arsenal of revolution.

Thanks to an international conference held in Geneva in 1929 counterfeiting laws are relatively uniform among various countries. Counterfeiting either domestic currency or foreign currency is illegal, and counterfeiters are subject to extradition. Printing counterfeit money is invariably a felony offense drawing a prison sentence, but incidental offenses, such as owning counterfeiting equipment or possessing counterfeit money, usually draw lesser sentences.

The development of high-quality color copying machines and sophisticated offset printing operations has complicated the problem of combating counterfeiters. The United States now impresses a thin polyester thread into its federal reserve notes. The thread runs vertically to the left of the Federal Reserve seal, and can be seen when the note is held up to a light. The notes also have the words "United States of America" microprinted in letters that can only be read with magnification. Despite these innovations, counterfeiting remains a major problem in the United States.

See also: Operation Bernhard
References: Angus, Ian. 1975. *Paper Money.*
Beresiner, Yasha. 1977. *Paper Money.*
Dacy, Joe. 1993. How to Spot Bogus Bills. *Nations Business* 81, no. 7 (July): 30.

Cowrie

The cowrie enjoyed a longer history as a circulating medium than any other type of money, stretching back to the dawn of history in China, and rivaling modern currencies in twentieth-century Africa. The *I-Ching,* among the oldest Chinese books, makes references to the use of cowrie money. For thousands of years, Africa, the Middle East, and the Far East swept up money from the shallower areas of the Indian Ocean and Pacific Ocean, home to a mollusk whose ovoid shell was called a cowrie. Perhaps part of the attraction of cowrie money was its variety; it occurs in different colors and ranges in size from as small as the end-joint of the little finger to as large as a fist. The cowrie probably first secured its hold on the human imagination as a commodity with religious and ornamental significance.

The use of cowries as money in China dates back to at least the fourth century B.C. when the first Chinese invaders found cowrie shells in use as money among the pre-Chinese population. In the Chinese language words denoting buying, selling, riches, prices, cheapness, and dearness, make use of the ideographic sign for the word "shell." In 1375 B.C. P'an Keng of the Shang dynasty expressed his displeasure at his greedy ministers hoarding cowries and gems. In 221 B.C. the government of China banned the use of cowries as money. In A.D. 10 Wang Mang, seeking a return to ancient traditions, revived the use of cowries, establishing an elaborate system of five different sizes of cowries to serve as monetary units with specific value. The commercial classes raised a howl over the return to an antiquated monetary system, and Wang Mang desisted.

Visiting Bengal India in the sixth century, Pyrard de Laval reported the use of cowries as ordinary money, although gold and silver were available. Kings and lords stored up shells in treasury houses especially built for the purpose. Without counting, merchants faithfully accepted in payment baskets of 12,000 cowries.

At least as early as the sixth century cowrie money had found its way to Timbuktu, where it was used for smaller transactions. During the nineteenth century the French colonial authorities in the Sudan managed the supply of cowries to smooth out local fluctuations, sending cowries to communities short of cowrie money. In Timbuktu the authorities fixed the exchange rate of cowries at 1,000 cowries per French franc.

By the sixteenth century cowrie money had become an important component of the money supply in Nigeria. Even after World War I cowries were hoarded as a store of wealth, piling up in treasure houses like heaps of newly threshed corn.

Arab traders introduced cowrie money to Uganda at the end of the eighteenth century, where it became the dominant medium of exchange and store of value during the nineteenth century. A woman cost 2 cowries at the beginning of the century, rising to 1,000 cowries by 1860, probably reflecting a massive influx of cowries rather than an increase in the value of women. By 1911 2,500 cowries were sufficient to fetch a cow, 500 cowries a

goat, and 25 cowries a fowl. An ivory tusk weighing 62 pounds brought 1,000 cowrie shells.

Cowries were durable, easy to clean, and impossible to counterfeit, making them a useful form of money over a vast geographical area. Unlike another primitive money, cattle, which were highly practical in the struggle for survival, cowries were valued by cultures for aesthetic, and in some cases religious, reasons. Cowrie shell money gives meaning to the phrase "shell out" as a popular expression for making payment.

See also: Commodity Monetary Standard
References: Einzig, Paul. 1966. *Primitive Money*. Davies, Glyn. 1994. *A History of Money*. Williams, Jonathan, ed. 1997. *Money: A History*.

Credit Union Share Drafts (CUSD)
See Monetary Aggregates

Credole and Tratte

Credole were warehouse warrants for grain that circulated as money in sixteenth-century Sicily. At that time Sicily was a major exporter of grain and home to a major Mediterranean grain market. The ports of Sicily were the sites of vast grain elevators called *caricatori*. Landowners brought their grain to the caricatori and either sold it immediately or received warehouse warrants, or credole, if they wished to sell it later. Moneylenders accepted credole as security from landowners who needed advanced payment for grain.

The credola system came unraveled toward the end of the sixteenth century. Grain speculators purchased credole from landowners at heavy discounts, and some landowners felt swindled when the market for grain improved. Many preferred to let their grain rot rather than fall into the hands of speculators. Forgeries of credole entered into circulation, sometimes with the complicity of the *magazinieri* (the owners of the caricatori) and government officials. Nonexistent grain was sold and some magazinieri wound up in bankruptcy. The government tried to stem the tide of scandal by threatening to send offenders to the galleys, demanding declarations of sincerity, and forbidding futures trading. The government also banned contracts that involved wagers on the future price of grain.

During the same period Naples also issued a

paper money instrument related to export trade. The viceroy of Naples sold *tratte,* which were licenses to export cereals and vegetables. The tratte were sold in advance and in much greater numbers than were needed, precipitating a depreciation in value. Venetian merchants claimed to have saved up to 32 percent in customs duties by making payment in depreciated tratte.

The Sicilian and Neapolitan experiences with credole and tratte show how natural it is for paper money to come into existence and that, while paper money comes in many forms, it always entails the same risk—overissuance.

See also: Commodity Monetary Standard
References: Braudel, Fernand. 1972. *The Mediterranean.*
   Vol. 1.
———. 1981. *Civilization and Capitalism.* Vol. 1.

Crime of '73 (United States)

The Coinage Act of 1873, a piece of legislation that caused hardly a political ripple in Congress, subsequently acquired the odious title of the "Crime of '73." The act rather informally dropped the bimetallic standard in the United States in favor of the gold standard, an action that incurred the wrath of debtors and western farmers as deflationary trends gathered force in the late 1800s. Since the days of Alexander Hamilton the United States had been on a bimetallic standard combining gold and silver in a fixed ratio. The Crime of '73 made it into the folklore in the United States, including references in the famous book, *The Wizard of Oz.*

A movement of economic and social protest lifted William Jennings Bryan to the leadership of the Democratic Party, and inspired his famous "Cross of Gold" speech, which compared the gold standard to the crucifixion of mankind on a cross of gold. Debt-ridden farmers and unemployed workmen quite rightly pointed the finger of suspicion to the unforgiving discipline of the gold standard, and saw something sinister in quietly removing silver from the monetary standard without the airing of a public debate. With vast holdings of silver in western states, coinage of silver could have infused additional monetary reserves in the economy, raising prices and easing pressure on debtors.

The offensive portion of the act downgraded the silver dollar to subsidiary coinage of the same proportional weight and fineness as the half dollar, quarter, and dime. These silver dollars were legal tender in amounts up to $5 but in 1877 the Treasury discontinued minting the silver dollars, due to a lack of interest.

Before the act silver owners could sell silver to the mint for $1.292 per ounce, but the market value of silver was $1.298 per ounce, creating an opportunity to melt down minted silver and sell it for a profit, causing silver dollars to disappear from circulation. The high market value of silver in 1873 probably accounts for the lack of public controversy at the time Congress passed the Coinage Act of 1873. The discovery of additional silver reserves in the western states, coupled with deflationary trends, pushed the market price of silver below the mint price. As deflationary trends made themselves felt, culminating in the depression of the 1890s, the silver interests missed the Treasury market for silver and depressed regions saw silver coinage as the answer to economic woes.

Abandonment of the bimetallic standard and cessation of silver as a monetary standard of value were in step with international currents at the time. Europe was rapidly turning to a gold standard that was associated with England's commercial success. The failure of William Jennings Bryan to win a presidential bid assured that the United States would remain on a gold standard, which became official with the Gold Standard Act of 1900. The discovery of new sources of gold relieved the monetary tightness of the late 1800s, effectively defusing the silver protest, and letting the Crime of '73 fade into political oblivion.

See also: Bimetallism, Bland-Allison Silver Repurchase Act of 1878, "Cross of Gold" Speech, Free Silver Movement, Gold Standard Act of 1900, Sherman Silver Act of 1890, *The Wizard of Oz*
References: Friedman, Milton. 1992. *Money Mischief.*
Myers, Margaret G. 1970. *A Financial History of the United States.*
Nugent, Walter T. K. 1968. *Money and American Society: 1865–1880.*

Croesean Reform

Croesus, king of Lydia from 570 to 546 B.C., reformed the Lydian currency by suspending the coinage of electrum and introducing the rudiments of a bimetallic system based upon gold and silver.

Lydia is credited with inventing coinage between 640 and 630 B.C. These first coins were struck from electrum, a naturally occurring mixture of gold and silver, sometimes called white gold. Lydia owned vast deposits of electrum and the export of electrum, often in the form of coinage, was a major industry.

By mid-sixth century other cities along the coast of Asia Minor were striking gold coins that competed with Lydia's electrum coinage. King Alyattes, Croesus's father, had sent Croesus on military expeditions in areas where these gold coins were popular, and he returned convinced of the importance of gold coinage. By then Lydian metallurgy had progressed sufficiently to enable the separation of the gold and silver in electrum. King Alyattes continued the coinage of electrum but did begin the coinage of gold.

Croesus, succeeding his father as king, undertook a major reform of the Lydian currency. He abandoned the coinage of electrum, which ceased to circulate as coinage in Asia Minor, and he established a currency system of gold and silver that would later supply the model for the currency of the Persian Empire.

The gold unit was called a *stater,* and the Greeks called the gold stater the Croesean stater. It bore the images of a bull and a lion, thought to have been introduced by Croesus. The Greek historian Herodotus wrote that Croesus sent two gold staters to each of the citizens of the Greek city of Delphi because of a prophesy that he—mistakenly, as he learned later—took as favorable for his prospects in a war against the Persians. Herodotus also recounts in detail many gifts of gold and silver objects that Croesus gave to the oracle of Delphi, many of which were still extant when Herodotus wrote in the fifth century. According to Herodotus, Solon, the famous lawgiver who reformed the monetary system of Athens, visited Croesus, who displayed to him his vast treasures, and hinted that Solon must regard him as the happiest man alive because of his wealth. Solon demurred, citing the many hazards that any living person faced, and after Croesus was overcome by Persia, he expressed admiration for Solon's wisdom.

The gold stater was made of 130 grains of pure gold, and smaller coins equaled one-third, one-sixth, and one-twelfth of the full-size coin. A silver stater was made of 220 grains of pure silver. The silver stater equaled one-tenth the value of the gold stater. Smaller silver coins equal to one-half, one-third, and one-twelfth of the value of the silver stater were also struck. The smallest silver coin equaled one-twentieth of the gold stater, providing a range of coins to handle transactions of varying sizes. All the coins were full bodied, making no use of cheaper alloys. Relationships between coins of the same metal were based upon the duodecimal system, while relationships between coins of different metals were based upon the decimal system. The duodecimal system uses 12 as the base number, as opposed to the decimal system, which uses 10.

Croesus is credited with introducing the world's first bimetallic monetary system. He did not invent either gold coinage or silver coinage, but perhaps because Lydia's electrum deposits held both gold and silver, he furnished the world with the first coinage system based upon both metals. A bimetallic monetary system was the prime rival to the gold standard in Europe during the late nineteenth century.

See also: Bimetallism, Lydian Coinage

References: Burns, A. R. 1927. *Money and Monetary Policy in Early Times.*
Williams, Jonathan, ed. 1997. *Money: A History.*

Cross Coinage: 1180–1554 (England)

Cross coinage, so named because it depicted a cross on one side, prevailed in England for a period of three and one-half centuries. During that period it appeared in three different versions. The so-called short cross coinage was minted from 1180 to 1247. The void long cross coinage made a brief appearance from 1247 to 1279, and the long cross coinage lasted from 1279 to 1544.

By the twelfth century production of English coinage had slowed to a trickle, and England and much of Europe virtually reverted to a barter and subsistence economy. In 1180 Henry II, king of England, ordered a major recoinage and recruited a Frenchman, Philip Emery, from the famous mint city of Tours, to direct the effort. The obverse side of the new coins bore an image of the full-faced king; bearded, wearing a crown, and holding a scepter. The king's name was inscribed on the coins as "Henricus" even during the subsequent reigns of Richard and John. The king's portrait was not true to life. By 1205 the coins had become sufficiently worn and clipped to necessitate another recoinage. King John ordered a recoinage using the same design. The government supplied at its own expense the extra silver needed to bring the coins up to standard weight, a feat that proved expensive and was not repeated by future governments.

In 1247 King Henry III ordered another recoinage, this time at the expense of those who held the worn and clipped coins. The obverse side retained the image of the king's face, but the reverse side bore an image of a cross that extended through the legend. The legend identified the mint and the moneyer (the individual who physically struck the coins). This English practice of identifying the maker of the coins probably helped to maintain the quality of English coinage. This coinage is called the voided long cross coinage because of its double cross design. It lasted only until 1279.

Edward I returned from the Crusades to find English coinage had suffered badly from wear and clipping. In 1279 he ordered a recoinage, and reduced the weight of each coin as a way of sparing the government or the people the expense of bringing the coinage up to standard weights. Edward I was the first English monarch to mint coin denominations higher than the penny. The obverse side bore a profile, as opposed to a facial, view of the king—shorn of his beard, but wearing a five-point crown. The reverse side bore an image of a broad simple cross, and the legend identified the mint but not the moneyer. This design, called the long cross design, lasted until Henry VIII's debasement of the coinage during the years 1542 to 1551.

Edward I's long cross design became synonymous with sound currency and was widely copied, particularly in the Low Countries.

See also: Clipping, English Penny, Moneyer, Pound Sterling
References: Challis, C. E. 1992. *A New History of the Royal Mint*.
Chown, John. 1994. *A History of Money*.

"Cross of Gold" Speech

In one of the epochal orations in United States history, William Jennings Bryan won himself the 1896 Democratic nomination for president in a spellbinding performance castigating the gold standard. The speech came to be known as the "Cross of Gold" speech because of a reference to crucifying humanity on a "cross of gold." Bryan made unsuccessful bids for the presidency in 1896, 1900, and 1908, mounting a serious challenge to well-financed Eastern money interests with his populist message, which struck a cord with debtors, farmers, and workers.

Bryan's answer to the depression of the 1890s was the free coinage of silver, replacing the gold standard with a bimetallic standard. To the charge that the gold standard was necessary for the prosperity of the business interests, Bryan answered in rhetoric that was music to the ears of hard-pressed farmers and manual laborers. Here are a few select morsels from his 1896 "Cross of Gold" speech:

[T]he farmer who goes forth in the morning and toils all day, who begins in the spring and toils all summer, and who by the application of brain and muscle to the natural resources of the country created wealth, is as much a business man as the man who goes upon the Board of Trade and bets upon the price of grain; the miners who go down a thousand feet into the earth, or climb two thousand feet upon the cliffs, and bring forth from their hiding places the precious metals to be poured into the channels of trade are as much business men as the few financial magnates who, in a back room, corner the money of the world. (Birley, 1943)

After setting the mood, Bryan took up the "paramount issue":

[I]f [tariff] protection has slain its thousands, the gold standard has slain its tens of thousands. No private character, however pure, no personal popularity, however great, can protect from the avenging wrath of an indignant people a man who will declare that he is in favor of fastening the gold standard upon this country, search the pages of history in vain to find a single instance where the common people of any land have ever declared themselves in favor of the gold standard. There are those who believe that if you will only legislate to make the well-to-do prosperous, their prosperity will leak through to those below. (Birley, 1943)

Bryan closed his speech in a rising crescendo of oratory that would lift him from an unknown member of Congress to the leadership of the Democratic Party at the age of 36:

If they dare to come out in the open field and defend the gold standard as a good thing, we will

A fifteenth-century moneyer weighing out coins, from a painting by Marinus van Reymerswaele. (Art Resource)

fight them to the uttermost. Having behind us the producing masses of this nation and the world, supported by the commercial interests, the laboring interests, and the toilers everywhere, we will answer their demand for a gold standard by saying to them: *You shall not press down upon the brow of labor this crown of thorns, you shall not crucify mankind upon a cross of gold.* (Birley, 1943, emphasis added)

The Eastern establishment saw Bryan as a reckless demagogue, spreading a message—abandonment of the gold standard—that held no charm to respectable financiers during the heyday of the gold standard from 1875 to 1914. Nevertheless, Bryan's message was in step with the forces of history, and most of the world abandoned the gold standard in the 1930s. Although Bryan was ahead of his time on many economic issues, his stances on other social is-

sues have received a less clear verdict from history. He ended his public career prosecuting a schoolteacher charged with teaching the theory of evolution against state law in the famous *Scopes* trial in 1925.

See also: Crime of '73, Gold Standard, *Wizard of Oz*
References: Birley, Robert, ed. 1943. *Speeches and Documents in American History.* Vol. III.
Friedman, Milton. 1992. *Money Mischief.*
Myers, Margaret G. 1970. *A Financial History of the United States.*

Culture of Money

The effects of money and coinage on Western culture began to make themselves felt in the sixteenth and seventeenth centuries. Up to that time money and coinage rarely played a pivotal role in works of art or literature. It was quite beneath the pride of the tragic heroes of antiquity to struggle over money or

At the Procuress, *a seventeenth-century painting by Dutch artist Jan Vermeer van Delft. (Art Resource)*

coins, nor would a medieval epic poet find considerations of money a suitable backdrop for moral conflict. Greek tragedies and medieval epics explored themes of war, love, hate, revenge, power, and honor but money was rarely, if ever, the grist for the mill.

In Shakespeare the pursuit of money and wealth appears as an issue worth addressing in dramatic conflict.

The Merchant of Venice perhaps goes further than any other Shakespearean play in making money its

central focus. Changes in attitudes toward money can also be detected in the works of artists. Sculpture and paintings of antiquity emphasized religious and mythological themes, a trait that continued through the Italian Renaissance. In paintings of less exalted themes, people were shown with some possessions—for example, dogs or horses—but not with a view toward idealizing the luxuries that money could purchase.

Interest in money and coins as artistic themes

reached a peak with the Dutch and northern European painters during the seventeenth century. Rather than painting the Last Supper, these painters were more likely to picture Judas returning the 30 pieces of silver. Typical themes for these artists were bankers counting their money and scenes of domestic tranquillity adorned with boxes of coins on tables. They painted group pictures of the masters of mints and their assistants. Samuel van Hoogstraeten painted the masters and wardens of the Holland mint at Dordrecht twice, once in 1654 and again in 1674. Unknown artists painted *The Master of the Mint of Nijmegen* and *Maastricht and His Assistants*. Rembrandt also painted a group picture of mint master and assistants. Dirck van Baburen and Jan Vermeer painted scenes of men procuring women with the flash of coins. Scenes of alchemists at work also showed up in Dutch paintings of the period.

The weighing of gold in balancing scales was also a common theme in Dutch painting. Vermeer's painting, *Woman Weighing Gold,* shows a young woman carefully balancing scales with gold coins on the table and a painting of the Last Judgment hanging in the background, a reminder of the transience of earthly beauty and wealth.

The role of Amsterdam as a banking center at a time when most money was in coinage may have contributed to artistic interest in themes of money. The seventeenth century saw coins from all over the world flow into the Bank of Amsterdam. As capitalism took hold in the large nation-states, and the middle and working classes made a bid for power, larger questions loomed on the horizon during the eighteenth century and artistic focus shifted away from money. It is hard to imagine either the American or the French revolutionaries being interested in pictures with scales weighing gold, or tables with gold coins. For a trading society such as the Dutch, however, money genuinely was the lifeblood of the economy.

Wealth may be more idealized today than ever, perhaps because highly commercialized societies such as the United States and Britain survived the major wars of the twentieth century and won their antagonists over to their way of thinking in economic matters. In a world based on economic competition, money has become a way of keeping score, replacing the medals, badges of honor, stripes, and other symbols of achievement associated with military and feudalistic regimes.

Although wealth continues to be highly idealized, mediums of exchange such as coins or bank notes hardly hold the aesthetic interest today as they did to the Dutch. People have been cheated by inflationary paper money too often, and with the gaping income inequality of modern capitalism, flashing money around might be seen as an invitation for poorer individuals to ask for help, or for one's workers to strike for higher pay or form a union. Perhaps it is revealing that the Dutch workers, who were among the highest paid in Europe, never made a bid for political power, as did workers in other centers of capitalist development. As with the proverbial saying about children, today's motto for money is that money should be heard (i.e., "money talks"), but it should not be seen. Nevertheless, symbols of wealth are as important as ever, but today these symbols represent wealth in a less liquid form—such as expensive tennis shoes, automobiles, luxurious houses, and other trophies of conspicuous consumption.

References: Haak, Bob. 1984. *The Golden Age, Dutch Painters of the Seventeenth Century.*
Schama, Simon. 1987. *The Embarrassment of Riches: An Interpretation of Dutch Culture in the Golden Age.*
Weatherford, Jack. 1997. *The History of Money.*

Cupro-Nickel
See Coinage Act of 1965, Liverpool Act of 1816

Currency Act of 1751 (England)
The Currency Act of 1751 sought to restrict the issuance of fiat paper money and to ban its use as legal tender for the settlement of private debts in the New England colonies.

The beginning of the eighteenth century saw several New England colonies, led by Massachusetts, issue fiat paper currency. They turned to paper currency partly because of the financial pressures of wars involving the French and the Indians, and partly as a measure to relieve domestic shortages of acceptable mediums of exchange for financing business activity. Colonial governments issued paper currency on the condition that they would accept the currency as payment for taxes at a future time, perhaps within a year or possibly as long as seven years later. When governments issued more paper currency than they reclaimed in taxes, the paper currency lost value relative to British currency, and colonial prices inflated.

British merchants who had claims of debt against the colonists suffered because the depreciated currency they had to accept in repayment had less value than the credit they had extended.

The Act of 1751 opened by citing the failure of previous acts of Parliament to stem the tide of depreciating paper currency in New England, and by observing that because of the legal-tender status of this paper currency "all debts of late years have been paid and satisfied with a much less value than was contracted for, which hath been a great discouragement and prejudice to trade and commerce."

The act provided that:

1. Effective 29 September 1751 governors, councils, or assemblies in Connecticut, Massachusetts Bay, New Hampshire, or Rhode Island, were forbidden to enact legislation authorizing the issuance of additional bills of credit (paper currency), and could not extend the period of outstanding bills of credit. Any actions along these lines were "declared to be null and void, and of no force or effect whatsoever."
2. Colonial governments were required to retire all outstanding bills of credit at the scheduled date.
3. Colonial governments could issue bills of credit to finance current government expenditures if sufficient taxes were levied to retire the bills within two years.
4. In the event of unusual public emergencies, such as war or invasion, bills of credit could be issued in excess of what the government would reclaim in taxes within two years. These extra bills had to pay interest and be reclaimed by a tax fund within five years.
5. None of the bills issued after 29 September 1751 were to be legal tender in private transactions, and none of the bills then in circulation should be legal tender.

The act allowed governments to continue to issue bills of credit as an instrument of government finance, but prohibited the attachment of the legal-tender sanction for settling private debts. The Currency Act of 1751 was followed by the Currency Act of 1764, which applied the same principles to the remaining colonies. The latter act sought to deny the legal-tender status of paper currency even in the payment of public debts. This was a confusing point, however, and the colonial governments continued to issue paper currency that could be used in payment of taxes. The Currency Act of 1773 clarified the issue by specifically allowing colonial governments to issue paper currency that was legal tender for the payment of public debts. The 1773 act allowed the use of paper currency as legal tender for the payment of taxes but, in deference to British creditors, not for private debts.

The Currency Act of 1751, and its sister act, the Currency Act of 1764, contributed to a shortage of circulating money in the American colonies, adding to the discontent that led up to the American Revolution. The American colonies were not blessed with the abundance of gold and silver mines found in the Spanish colonies. The hard specie that was won by exporting goods to Europe had to be used to import the numerous European goods needed in the American colonies. Entrepreneurs in the American colonies enjoyed practically unlimited supplies of natural resources, but harnessing these resources required a rapidly growing domestic money supply, with opportunities for borrowing money as the need arose. Because the availability of money fell far short of the business opportunities afforded by such a land, the colonists tried to find ways to invent their own money supply. The failure of the British to appreciate the need for an elastic money supply in a land of boundless resources contributed to the tension that resulted in revolution.

See also: Currency Act of 1764, Land Bank System, Massachusetts Bay Colony Paper Issue

References: Brock, Leslie V. 1975. *The Currency of the American Colonies: 1700–1764.*
Ernst, Joseph Albert. 1973. *Money and Politics in America, 1755–1775.*

Currency Act of 1764 (England)

The Currency Act of 1764 removed the authority of colonial governments in the middle and southern American colonies to issue legal-tender paper money for either private or public debts. The act passed Parliament following the French and Indian War (1754–1763) when colonial governments, particularly Virginia, freely turned to the issuance of paper money to defray military expenditures.

Parliament first acted to restrict the issuance of

colonial paper money in the Currency Act of 1751. That act circumscribed the ability of New England colonies to issue paper money, and banned the circulation of paper money as legal tender for private debts. The Act of 1751 enabled governments to declare paper money legal tender for public debts—that is, taxes—but not for private debts. England's Board of Trade moved to extend the provisions of the Act of 1751 to colonies south of New England, but the French and Indian War intervened, and the Board of Trade tended to wink or look away as colonial governments issued paper money to finance war expenditures. British merchants, however, saw the issuance of legal-tender paper money as a conspiracy of American debtors to defraud British creditors by repaying debts in depreciated paper money. They lobbied the Board of Trade and Parliament to stop the colonies' issuance of legal-tender paper money. To be sure, the paper money invariably depreciated relative to British pounds, reducing its value to British merchants.

Unlike the Currency Act of 1751, the Currency Act of 1764 did not restrict the authority of colonial governments to issue paper money, but did ban the designation of any paper money as legal tender for the payment of either private or public debts, thus making the issuance of paper money impractical. The prohibition on the issuance of paper money as legal tender for public debts put colonial governments in a financial crunch. These governments issued paper money and then levied taxes payable in the paper money, automatically providing for the retirement of the paper money issues, and preventing paper money from depreciating in value. Government treasuries rather than monetary authorities, contrary to current practice, issued this paper money. In addition, the issuance of this paper money helped relieve a shortage of coinage that hampered economic activity in colonial economies. Therefore, the Currency Act of 1764 was the equivalent of England enforcing a tight money policy in the colonies in the aftermath of the French and Indian War.

The legal-tender provisions of the act seemed perplexing and ambiguous to the colonists, who found it difficult to understand how a government could issue paper money and not accept it as taxes. Also, several colonies operated loan offices that issued paper notes against the security of real estate. The Act of 1764 seemed to suggest that loan offices could not accept in repayment the notes they had issued. The colonial governments appear to have worked around the act and continued to accept their own paper money in payment for taxes, but the colonists lobbied with Parliament to have the legal-tender restriction on public debts lifted. The colonies needed the paper money to supplement domestic money supplies, which were limited and thus acted as a brake on domestic economic growth. The restrictions on the issuance of paper money added to the tension between the colonies and the English government. With the Currency Act of 1773, Parliament amended the Currency Act of 1764, and lifted the ban on paper money as legal tender for public debts.

See also: Currency Act of 1751, Virginia's Colonial Paper Currency
References: Brock, Leslie V. 1975. *The Currency of the American Colonies: 1700–1764.*
Ernst, Joseph Albert. 1973. *Money and Politics in America, 1755–1775.*

Currency Act of 1773 (England)
See Currency Act of 1751, Currency Act of 1764

Currency School
The currency school emerged as an important body of monetary thinking following England's resumption of specie payments after the Napoleonic Wars in 1821. England had suspended specie payments from 1797 to 1821 because of the financial stress of wars with France. The fundamental principle of the currency school lay in the concept of a money supply composed of coin and paper money acting just as if all money was entirely metallic.

Before the development of paper money, domestic supplies of metallic currency fluctuated with the ebb and flow of foreign trade. Buying goods from foreigners caused metallic currency to flow out, and selling goods to foreigners caused metallic currency to flow in. A net outflow of metallic currency depressed domestic prices, rendering domestic goods more competitive at home and abroad, and a net inflow of metallic currency lifted domestic prices, rendering domestic goods less competitive at home and abroad. Economic competition between countries ensured monetary stability.

The resumption of specie payments—that is, the

return to convertibility of the pound in 1821—had not ended fits of monetary and financial disorder and adherents of the currency school saw variations in the money supply as the culprit. England had suffered major crises in 1836 and 1839, a mere three-year interval that many regarded as a wake-up call. According to the thinking of the currency school domestic money supplies were fluctuating, not with the ebb and flow of international trade, but with variations in bank notes issued by banks. Everyone agreed that banks could expand or contract the supply of bank notes within a wide range without endangering their ability to convert bank notes into specie.

The currency school argued that fluctuations in money supplies were the major cause of economic swings, an idea that is commonplace now, and that banks were causing these fluctuations. The solution to the problem lay in establishment of a state authority exercising a monopoly privilege on the issuance of bank notes, a practice that is universal in modern monetary institutions. Unlike current monetary arrangements, however, the currency school contended that the issuance of bank notes should be kept strictly proportional to domestic metallic currency and bullion. A loss of gold to other countries should cause domestic bank notes to decrease an equivalent amount, putting downward pressure on domestic prices. A gain in gold from other countries worked in reverse. At that time in England hundreds of banks issued bank notes without coordination, and the principle of convertibility had not assured that gold flows would drive domestic money supplies.

Opposed to the arguments of the currency school was the banking school. The banking school argued that bank notes expanding and contracting with the needs of trade were not a source of instability and that an elasticity of currency was needed to pave the way for economic expansion. The banking school preferred leaving the management of bank notes to bankers whose discretion was tempered by the requirement of convertibility.

The Bank Charter Act of 1844 was a great victory of the currency school over the banking school. The act included provisions that would ultimately give the Bank of England a monopoly on the issuance of bank notes. The act also separated the Bank of England's note-issuing authority from its other banking business. In a departure from the principles laid down by the banking school, the act left the Bank of England with some discretion to regulate the issuance of bank notes independent of changes in gold reserves.

The currency school shares with the modern-day monetarist school the idea that the money supply should be managed by fixed rules rather than left to the discretion of bankers and policy makers. Modern-day monetarists would agree with the currency school that management of the money supply is the foundation of macroeconomic policy. Imbedded in the thinking of both the currency school and the monetarist school was skepticism about the wisdom of government policy makers, and a preference for policies founded on fixed principles rather than subjective judgments made in the midst of economic disturbances.

See also: Bank Charter Act of 1844, Bank of England, Banking School, Central Bank, Monetarism

References: Chown, John F. 1994. *A History of Money*. Spiegel, Henry William. 1971. *The Growth of Economic Thought*.

D

Da Vinci, Leonardo

The modern methods of coinage that surfaced in fifteenth-century Italy probably owe their origin to Leonardo da Vinci, who spent time at the papal mint during a stay in Rome. In *The Notebooks of Leonardo Da Vinci* can be found the following references to the coinage of money:

> All coins which do not have the rim complete, are not to be accepted as good; and to secure the perfection of their rim it is requisite that, in the first place, all the coins should be a perfect circle; and to do this a coin must before all be made perfect in weight, and size, and thickness. Therefore have several plates of metal made of the same size and thickness, all drawn through the same gauge so as to come out in strips. And out of these strips you will stamp coins, quite round, as sieves are made for sorting chestnuts; and these coins can be stamped in the way indicated above; &c. The hollow of the die must be uniformly wider than the lower, but imperceptibly. This cuts the coins perfectly round and the exact thickness, and weight; and saves the man who cuts and weighs, and the man who makes the coins round. Hence it passes only through the hands of the gauger and of the stamper, and the coins are very superior. (Richter, 1883)

Leonardo's technique brought a measure of precision to the coinage of money that had eluded even the best goldsmiths and silversmiths before the time of the Renaissance. The old method produced irregularly shaped coins that easily fell prey to clippers who could remove a bit of the precious metal without leaving any tell-tale signs. It began by casting precious metal in sand to form ingots roughly equal to the desired thickness of the coins. The ingots were reheated and hammered closer to the desired thickness. Then they were cut into squares, trimmed and weighed, and reheated. The squares were then hammered into a circular shape. Rolls of these blank coins were hammered into some degree of uniformity, making it possible to stack the coins. A hammer and a die struck the desired design on these blank coins to complete the finished product. The lack of uniformity in the coins made it easier for forgers to pass off inferior coins, and the whole process was a slow method for striking coins.

Leonardo's contribution to coinage was the work of Leonardo the mechanical engineer, rather than Leonardo the artist. During the Italian Renaissance, however, the minting of coins engaged the talents of the best artists of the age. Some of the coins, minted by famous artists and distinguished for their beauty, became collectors' items and sold for high prices. The famous Renaissance artist, Benvenuto Cellini, perhaps the most celebrated goldsmith in history, wrote a chapter in a treatise on goldsmithing and sculpture entitled "How to Make Steel Dies for Stamping Coins." With respect to one coin he struck for Pope Clement VII, Cellini wrote: "This coin brought me much honor, for I put great labor into it." The methods perfected by the Renaissance artists

Persian soldiers received one gold daric per month. This primitive coin was comparable in weight to the British gold sovereign. (Smithsonian Institution, National Numismatic Collection)

spread to France, and from France to Germany and Spain.

See also: Cellini, Benvenuto, Papal Coinage
References: Richter, Jean Paul, ed. 1970. *The Notebooks of Leonardo Da Vinci.*
Usher, Abbott Payson. 1929. *A History of Mechanical Inventions.* Rev. ed.

Daric

The *daric* was a monetary unit and royal gold coin of ancient Persia, first struck during the reign of Darius I, king of Persia from 521 to 485 B.C. According to the Greek historian, Herodotus, Darius regarded his coinage as no laughing matter, as revealed in the following anecdote taken from Herodotus's *History:*

> Now Aryandes had been made governor of Egypt by Cambyses. He it was who in after times was punished with death by Darius for seeking to rival him. Aware, by report and also by his own eyesight, that Darius wished to leave a memorial of himself, such as no king had ever left before, Aryandes resolved to follow his example and did so, till he got his reward. Darius had refined gold to the last perfection of purity in order to have coins struck of it: Aryandes, in his Egyptian government, did the very same with silver, so that to this day there is no such pure silver anywhere as the Aryandic. Darius, when this came to his ears, brought another charge of rebellion, against Aryandes, and put him to death. (Bk. IV) (Herodotus, 1952)

Soldiers received 1 daric per month as pay. Xenophon's Anabasis makes a reference to Cyrus agreeing to pay his soldiers $1^1/_2$ daric per month. The daric is mentioned in the Bible, in Ezra 2.69: "according to their ability they gave to the treasury of the work sixty-one thousand darics of gold."

Evidence of smaller coins is scanty but it seems that the Persians accepted the duodecimal system common in ancient Asiatic monetary systems. Under the duodecimal system, fractional coins came in amounts of one-third, one-sixth, and one-twelfth of the gold unit, the daric in the case of Persia. The largest silver unit was usually one-tenth of the gold unit, but in the case of Persia the *shekel* was apparently equal to one-twentieth of the gold unit. The silver unit usually followed similar subdivisions as the gold unit. The only known subdivisions of the daric represent one-twelfth and one-fourth pieces, and the only known subdivisions of the shekel represent one-third and one-sixth pieces. The Persians seemed to have preferred simplicity in monetary affairs, and may have shunned a proliferation of fractional coins.

The daric consisted of 130 grains of gold, comparable to the 123 grains of gold for the *sovereign,* the famous British gold coin of the classic gold standard era from 1875 to 1914.

For 200 years darics were the only gold coins of the Greek world, circulating alongside the silver coinage of the Greek city-states. To the Persian kings the supremacy of their gold coins reflected their own

The obverse of the De a Ocho Reales bore an image of two columns, symbolizing the pillars of Hercules. (Smithsonian Institution, National Numismatic Collection)

personal supremacy. The Persian system was bimetallic, based on official silver to gold ratio of $13^1/_3$ to 1. This unvarying ratio was preserved until the invasions of Alexander the Great, accounting for some of the stability of the system. Toward the end of the empire, silver rose in value relative to gold and was exported, effectively leaving Persia on a gold standard. The daric never suffered the debasement that many currencies suffer in the declining phases of societies.

See also: Gold, Lydian Coinage

References: Burns, A. R. 1927. *Money and Monetary Policy in Early Times.*
Carradice, I, ed. 1987. *Coinage in the Administration of the Athenian and Persian Empires.*
Einzig, Paul. 1970. *The History of Foreign Coinage.* 2d ed.
Williams, Jonathan, ed. 1997. *Money: A History.*
Herodotus. 1952. *History.*

De a Ocho Reales (Pieces-of-Eight)

Toward the end of the sixteenth century, Spanish coins, particularly the *de a ocho reales,* had become the international currency and held that position until eclipsed by the pound sterling in the nineteenth century. The pieces of eight was the immediate forerunner of the United States dollar.

The pieces of eight, called the Spanish dollar in the United States, was equal to eight *reales,* a Spanish monetary unit. *Reales* was a word for "royal" in Spanish. Today the monetary unit of account in Saudi Ara-

bia is called the *riyal,* and in Oman and Yemen the monetary unit is the *rial,* both derivatives of the *real.* Spanish coins dominated Far Eastern trade, Mediterranean trade, and trade with the New World.

The Spanish real, a silver coin, came into existence in 1497 with the monetary reform of Ferdinand and Isabella, the Spanish monarchs who financed Columbus's voyage to the New World. Originally, the real consisted of one-sixty-seventh of a mark of silver and was coined in multiples, quadruples, and octuples (the piece of eight reals), and in fractions of a real. The real was sometimes called a *bit.* The pieces of eight were eight bits. A fourth of a real equaled two bits, a half a real equaled four bits, and three-fourths of a real equaled six bits. The division of the dollar into bits lives on in the cheer-leading yell that can be heard at any high school football game, "Two bits, four bits, six bits, a dollar, all for the [name of team] stand up and holler." Ferdinand's and Isabella's monetary reform set out to provide Spain with a unified coinage system. Charles V popularized the pieces of eight, equal to the Bohemian or Saxon *thaler,* which gave its name to the United States dollar.

Mints in Mexico City and Peru turned out vast quantities of Spanish reals. Mexico City boasted of the largest mint in the world, and minted a pieces-of-eight coin called the pillar dollar, because of its symbol on the obverse side denoting the Pillars of Hercules, the strait that opens the Mediterranean into the Atlantic Ocean. The dollar sign "$" may have originated from this symbol of the Pillars of Hercules with the "S" portion a reference to a banner hanging from one pillar.

Mexico, after winning independence from Spain in 1821, minted its own *peso* with a bit more silver than the old Spanish pieces of eight. The new Mexican *peso* was called the Mexican dollar in Far Eastern trade, where it was the most popular coin throughout the nineteenth century, competing with the U.S. silver trade dollar and a British silver trade dollar. Spanish pieces of eight and Mexican pesos were legal tender in the United State in much of the pre–Civil War era. Mexico remained on a silver standard while most of the world adopted the gold standard, and Mexican silver pesos remained important in Far Eastern trade. During the Great Depression of the 1930s Mexico abandoned the silver standard, just as the United States abandoned the gold standard.

With the loss of Mexican silver, and the European shift toward the gold standard after 1875, Spanish coinage receded into the background as international currency.

See also: Dollar, Silver

References: Braudel, Fernand. 1972. *The Mediterranean and the Mediterranean World in the Age of Phillip II.* Vol. I.
Hamilton, Earl J. 1947. *War and Prices in Spain, 1651–1800.*
———. 1965. *American Treasure and the Price Revolution in Spain, 1501–1650.*
Weatherford, Jack. 1997. *The History of Money.*
Vives, Jaime Vicens. 1969. *An Economic History of Spain.*

Debit Card

Debit cards, similar in shape and size to credit cards, substantially advanced the replacement of coins, paper money, and checks with electronic money. These plastic cards with a magnetic strip on one side enable individuals to convert bank deposits into instant cash or pay for purchases by electronically shifting money from a buyer's bank account to a seller's bank account. The development of the debit card may rank with coinage, printed paper money, and checks as one of the great innovations in money, creating a new monetary era that supplants the era of paper money.

The debit card burst upon the world in 1971 when a banker in Burbank, California, connected the idea of money with the idea of a vending machine. A vending machine dispensing cash would free customers from the rigor of fixed banking hours, enabling customers to withdraw cash 24 hours a day, seven days a week. Thus the automated teller machine came into being.

The next important step in debit card development occurred in 1974 when the First Federal Savings and Loan of Lincoln, Nebraska, installed debit card reading machines at the cash registers of the Hinky Dinky supermarket. Rather than withdrawing cash, these machines enabled customers to transfer funds from their own bank accounts to the supermarket's bank accounts, abolishing the need to carry cash or a checkbook to the supermarket. Debit card transactions take less time than check transactions and eliminate the need for protection against bad checks.

Debit cards have not been an unmixed blessing. There have been numerous instances in which authorized individuals have used debit cards to empty out someone's bank account. The use of debit cards at automatic teller machines usually requires a personal identification number, which makes unauthorized use more difficult. Some of the debit cards that double as credit cards may be used at some retail outlets without personal identification numbers, and these cards have the greatest potential for fraudulent misuse.

Debit card transactions require an intricate telecommunications network that is only cost effective in grocery stores, department stores, and other large retail outlets that handle large volumes of sales. Small transactions that take place at small retail stores and even vending machines still depend heavily on coins and paper money. A new debit card, sometimes called the smart card, removes the need for an expensive telecommunication network, making it feasible for use with vending machines and small retailers. The smart card has an embedded computer chip that allows the card to be programmed for a fixed amount of money. The smart card can be used to make purchases up to a fixed or approved amount without a telecommunication network that connects a card-reading machine with a bank computer. The smart card can be used at isolated retail sites, or at vending machines, without the necessity for correct change.

The latest development in the smart card is an electronic payment system called Mondex. Under the Mondex system, a machine transfers money from a customer's card to a merchant's card, without going through the intermediary of a bank. The merchant can then pass on the electronic money from his or her card to the card of another person. The Mondex system, still in the testing stage in the last years of the twentieth century, allows blips of electronic money to change hands without going through the intermediary of a bank, holding the greatest promise of revolutionizing the currency system and ending the use of coins and paper money.

References: Bray, Nicholas. 1995. Future Shop: No Cash Accepted. *Wall Street Journal*, 13 July.

Weatherford, Jack. 1997. *The History of Money*.

Decimal System

The decimal system, a number system based upon the number 10, became a distinguishing characteristic of currency systems during the nineteenth and twentieth centuries. The currency system of the United States offers a typical example of a decimal currency system, with one dime equal to one-tenth of a dollar, and one cent equal to one-tenth of a dime, or one-one-hundredth of a dollar.

From the ninth century until the end of the eighteenth century the Carolingian currency system held sway in Europe. Under the eighth-century Carolingian reform, instituted by Charlemagne's father, King Pepin, 12 *pence* equalled 1 *shilling*, and 20 shillings made 1 *pound*.

The Carolingian reform established a new silver coinage in which 240 *denarii* (pennies) equaled a *livre*, or pound weight of silver. The Norman Conquest brought the Carolingian system to England, where it survived until 1971.

The Russians deserve credit for giving the modern world the decimal system of currency. By 1535 the Russians were trading in a Novgorod *ruble*, and a smaller unit, the *denga*, equal to one-one-hundredth of a ruble. Under Peter the Great the denga became the *kopek*, but otherwise Russia's decimal currency system has remained intact up to the present day.

The Russian decimal system met with a cold reception in the courts of Europe, which had elaborated upon the Carolingian system into currency systems susceptible to manipulation because of a multiplicity of coins that could be selectively debased. Also, the royal courts of Europe were not impressed with innovations from countries such as Russia, which were mired in economic backwardness.

The American revolutionaries, eager to depart from the practice of European monarchies, found no charm in coins called *crowns* and *sovereigns,* bearing portraits of British monarchs. The Spanish milled dollar was a popular coin in the American colonies, but the Spanish dollar was subdivided into eight *reales.* In 1782 Robert Morris, U.S. superintendent of finance, sent a report to the Congress of Confederation recommending that the states coin their own money as a substitute for the medley of foreign coins then circulating, and that the state coinage systems uniformly follow a decimal system. The reasons for preferring the decimal system were:

> that it was desirable that money should be increased in the decimal Ratio, by that means all calculations of Interest, exchange, insurance and the like are rendered much more simple and accurate, and of course, more within the power of the mass of people. Whenever such things require much labor, time and reflection, the greater number, who do not know, are made the dupes of the lessor number who do. (Watson, 1970)

Thomas Jefferson forwarded the idea that the hundredth part of the dollar be called a *cent,* after the Latin word for "one hundred," and that the tenth of the dollar be called a *dime,* which means "tenth" in Latin. Alexander Hamilton incorporated these ideas into his *Report on the Establishment of a Mint,* and the Coinage Act of 1792 called for the adoption of a decimal currency system in the United States. Because the Russian currency system made use of coins outside the decimal system, the United States can boast of the first completely decimal currency system.

The arguments favoring the decimal system impressed the revolutionary imagination of France, and on 7 October 1793 the French revolutionary government replaced the coinage system of the Bourbon dynasty with a decimal currency system. In 1795 the French revolutionary government changed the name of the livre to the *franc,* which equaled the sum of 100 *centimes.* The conquest of Napoleon helped launch the decimal system in Europe, where it spread rapidly during the nineteenth century. England held out until 1971, becoming one of the last countries to adopt a decimal currency system. A pound now equals 100 pence, instead of 240 pence.

See also: American Penny, Carolingian Reform, Coinage Act
of 1792, Dollar, Monetary Law of 1803
References: Crown, John F. 1994. *A History of Money*.
Watson, David K. 1970. *History of American Coinage*
Weatherford, Jack. 1997. *The History of Money*.

Denarius
See Augustan Monetary System, Carolingian
Reform, Florentine Florin, French Franc, Lex
Flaminia of 217 B.C., Roman Empire Inflation

Depository Institution Deregulation and Monetary Control Act of 1980 (United States)

In 1980 Congress passed the Depository Institutions
Deregulation Monetary Control Act (DIDMCA), the
most important piece of banking legislation in the
United States since the Glass-Steagall Banking Act of
1933. The DIDMCA signaled a marked shift in government banking policy in the direction of a deregulated banking system. This was a sharp contrast to
the banking legislation of the 1930s, which had
added to the regulation of the banking industry.

One of the more important provisions of the
DIDMCA authorized all depository institutions to
offer negotiated order of withdrawal (NOW) accounts. These accounts are interest-bearing savings
accounts with check-writing privileges that depositors basically treat as checking accounts. The banking legislation of the 1930s had forbidden banks
from paying interest on checking accounts. In the
1970s thrift institutions, faced with an outflow of
funds and hoping to make their savings accounts
more attractive, received permission from banking
regulators to let thrift depositors write checks on savings accounts. Before the DIDMCA only savings and
loans (S&Ls), credit unions, and other thrift institutions offered NOW accounts. In practical terms, the
DIDMCA enabled all depository institutions, including commercial banks, to pay interest on checking
accounts. The DIDMCA also removed interest-bearing deposits from the restrictions of state usury laws.

A related provision of the DIDMCA made automatic transfer accounts legal, further lifting restrictions on interest-bearing checking accounts. These
accounts let commercial banks automatically transfer unused checking account funds into interest-
bearing savings accounts. Because checking ac-

counts could not pay interest before the DIDMCA,
the ability to switch funds from checking to savings
as needed gave checking accounts some of the advantages of interest-bearing accounts.

By the mid-1970s technology had made switching
an inexpensive procedure, but the courts had ruled
that automatic transfer accounts violated the law
against the payment of interest on checking accounts. Therefore legislation was necessary to remove the prohibition on automatic transfer accounts.

The DIDMCA called for the formation of a Depository Institutions Deregulation Committee
charged with overseeing the removal of interest-rate
ceilings on all deposits, except business deposits at
commercial banks. This committee was composed
of the heads of the Treasury Department, the Federal
Reserve Board, the Federal Depository Insurance
Corporation, the Federal Home Loan Bank Board,
and the National Credit Union Administrator. The
Comptroller of the Currency served as a nonvoting
member.

The DIDMCA freed from state usury ceilings res-
idential mortgages and agricultural and business
loans in excess of $25,000 and extended partial ex-
emption to other loans made by state-chartered
banks, savings and loan institutions, and credit
unions. States had the option to reinstate state usury
ceilings on these loans, but action had to be taken by
1 April 1983.

The DIDMCA gave federally chartered S&Ls permission to make consumer loans, and invest in commercial paper and corporate debt securities. Up to
20 percent of a savings and loan's assets could be
committed to these uses. The DIDMCA also added
credit cards, trusts, and fiduciary services to the
range of services offered by S&Ls. In a nutshell, the
S&Ls now compete with commercial banks in a
wider range of services.

The DIDMCA authorized mutual savings banks
with federal charters to enter the market for business loans. These institutions could invest up to 5
percent of their assets in these loans, and the business borrowers could not receive checking privileges
associated with these loans

The DIDMCA put all federally insured depository
institutions under the reserve requirements imposed by the Federal Reserve System. Before the
DIDMCA the Federal Reserve System set reserve requirements of federally chartered commercial

banks. (Reserve requirements set the percentage of checking and savings deposits that must be retained in the form of vault cash or a deposit at a Federal Reserve Bank.) Reserve requirements protect depositors (or the FDIC) by making bank assets more liquid and less risky, but they also leave bank assets less profitable because reserves pay no interest. State laws had invariably set lower reserve requirements, as a percentage, for state-chartered banks. The DIDMCA increased the power of reserve requirements as a tool of monetary regulation, and leveled the playing field between federally chartered institutions and state-chartered institutions.

The consumer is the clear beneficiary of competition in most industries, but when a bank fails the bank's customers suffer as much as the bank's owners. Depression-era legislation reduced competition between banks to stem the tide of bank failures. The DIDMCA took an important step toward restoring competition to the banking industry.

See also: Federal Reserve System, Glass-Steagall Act of 1933
References: Baye, Michael R., and Dennis W. Jansen. 1995. *Money, Banking, and Financial Markets: An Economics Approach.*
White, Lawrence J. 1986. The Partial Deregulation of Banks and other Depository Institutions. In *Regulatory Reform: What Actually Happened?* Ed. Leonard W. Weiss and Michael W. Klass.

Deutsche Bundesbank

The Deutsche Bundesbank is the central bank of Germany, comparable to the Federal Reserve System in the United States. The youngest addition to the ranks of European central banks, the Deutsche Bundesbank gained a position of preeminence among European central banks during the post–World War II era.

The Reichsbank, the central bank of Nazi Germany, came to an end in 1948. In West Germany the allied occupation authorities established a new currency, the *Deutsche Mark,* and organized a regional system of autonomous central banks, called *Landeszentralbanken.* At the apex of this system stood the Bank Deutscher Länder. This bank had the exclusive privilege to issue bank notes and acted as a lender of last resort. It was a two-tier structure, the lower layer composed of legally independent entities, and the structure may not have been organizationally efficient.

The Bundesbank Act of 1957 reorganized West Germany's central banking system, merging the independent Landeszentralbanken and the Bank Deutscher Länder. The act incorporated these entities as the Deutsche Bundesbank, a corporation wholly owned by the West German government. The head office remained at Frankfurt am Main, and each of the 11 Länder central banks operated its own system of branch banks. In 1990 the state banking system of East Germany was integrated with the Bundesbank, and the latter assumed the responsibility for monetary policy in the unified Germany. The system is spread out into more branches than the Federal Reserve System in the United States; one of the Länder central banks may oversee as many as 50 branch banks.

The distinguishing characteristic of the Bundesbank is its independence from government officials. The German people, having suffered through two episodes of hyperinflation in the twentieth century, were committed to establishing a central bank that would protect the integrity of its currency. The law creating the Bundesbank conspicuously ignored any economic goals other than price stability. In the words of the statute:

> The Bundesbank, making use of the powers in the field of monetary policy conferred upon it under this Law, shall regulate the money circulation and the supply of credit to the economy with the aim of safeguarding the currency and shall ensure the due execution by banks of payments within the country as well as to and from foreign countries. (Bank of International Settlements, 1963)

The supreme policy-making body of the Bundesbank is the Central Bank Council, composed of a president, vice president, up to eight additional members of a directorate, and the presidents of the 11 Länder central banks. The president of the Federal Republic of Germany appoints the members of the directorate, each serving eight-year terms. The president of the directorate is appointed for an eight-year term, and is highly secure in that appointment. The president of the Federal Republic appoints the presidents of the Länder central banks upon the recommendation of the directorate of the Central Bank Council.

Because of its independence from government officials, the Bundesbank could concentrate solely on controlling inflation during the post–World War II era when other central banks, less independent of government authorities, pursued policies aimed at reducing unemployment. During the 1970s when most Western countries were racked by inflation, West Germany kept inflation to modest levels, and the Bundesbank rose to become the most influential central bank in Europe. In 1993 the European Monetary Institute, the precursor to a European central bank, was set up in Frankfurt, symbolizing the European Union's commitment to sound monetary policies.

See also: Bank of England, Bank of France, Central Bank, Federal Reserve System

References: Bank of International Settlements. 1963. *Eight European Central Banks.*
Kennedy, Ellen. 1991. *The Bundesbank: Germany's Central Bank in the International Monetary System.*
Padoa-Schioppa, Tommaso. 1994. *The Road to Monetary Union in Europe.*

Deutsche Mark

The *Deutsche Mark,* or German mark, is the currency unit of Germany, comparable to the dollar for the United States. After the collapse of the Bretton Woods System in 1973, the U.S. dollar, no longer convertible into gold and subject to depreciation from inflation, lost some of its position as an international currency. As the U.S. dollar lost ground as an international currency, the German mark began to play the same role in the European economy as the U.S. dollar played in the world economy.

Compared to the British pound sterling, which can boast of a 1,300-year history, the history of the German mark is a bit short in light of the prestige that it now commands in international trade. In the immediate aftermath of World War II, the *Reichsmark,* the currency of Nazi Germany, no longer functioned as a medium of exchange. Trade took place on a black market, outside the system of German price controls, and commodities such as cigarettes and coal acted as mediums of exchange. Barter also flourished; city dwellers walked to the countryside with whatever goods they had and traded them for food.

The victorious Allies originally planned to introduce monetary reform in 1946, but an agreement between France, the Soviet Union, Britain, and the United States to treat Germany as single economic unit broke down, delaying monetary reform from May 1946 to June 1948. Part of the difficulty was that France, Britain, and the United States did not want to entrust the Soviet Union with plates to print currency, fearing that the Soviets would print up extra currency to impose an inflation tax on Germany. As the rift between the Western occupation powers and the Soviet Union widened, the decision was made to print the currency in England. The plan to replace the Reichsmark with a new currency, the Deutsche Mark, was a closely guarded military secret, given the code name Operation Bird Dog.

On 20 June 1948 the Western powers issued to every inhabitant in the three Western zones 40 Deutsche Marks in exchange for 40 Reichsmarks. Two months later another 20 Deutsche Marks were exchanged for 20 Reichsmarks. Aside from the per capita distribution, Deutsche Marks replaced the Reichsmarks on a 1:10 basis, one Deutsche Mark equaling 10 Reichsmarks. All debts were written down at this ratio, including government debt, mortgages, bank loans, and insurance policies. Bank deposits and balance sheets of businesses were adjusted on the same basis, deflating the asset side and the liability side to one-tenth of their original amounts. The authorities decreed that all new debts had to be contracted in Deutsche Marks. A central bank, patterned somewhat after the Federal Reserve System, was created from the branches of the Reichsbank. It was called the Bank of Deutscher Länder (Bank of German States), and in 1957 it was transformed into the Deutsche Bundesbank.

All price controls were lifted on 24 June 1948. With the new currency, goods suddenly showed up at stores where shelves had been empty for years. Apparently many goods had been hiding in the underground economy.

The Soviet authorities were forced to follow the example of currency reform in order to keep the Reichsmarks no longer usable in the Western zones from flooding the Soviet zone. The Soviets issued the *Deutsche Mark East* and for a while the western Deutsche Mark circulated side by side with the Deutsche Mark East at equal value. By the end of July 1948 the Deutsche Mark East traded at about half the value of the Deutsche Mark, a factor that contributed to the political separation of East and West Germany.

A noted economist, Charles Kindleberger (1984), wrote, "I regard the German monetary reform of 1948 as one of the great feats of social engineering of all time." The Deutsche Mark evolved into the most prestigious currency in Europe. During the inflation-ridden 1970s West Germany kept inflation to modest levels, and in the 1980s West Germany led Europe in the disinflation process. As Europe moved toward economic integration the Deutsche Mark played a major role in the monetary affairs of Europe. In the 1990s economic turmoil from combining the two Germanys cost the Deutsche Mark a bit of its reputation for stability. Also, France began to rival Germany in reputation for price stability.

On 1 January 1999 the European System of Central Banks launched a new European currency, the *euro,* that will eventually replace the national currencies of participating countries. The *euro* will replace the Deutsche Mark, the French franc, and several other European currencies.

See also: German Hyperinflation, Gold Mark of Imperial Germany, Rentenmark

References: Kindleberger, Charles P. 1984. *A Financial History of Western Europe.*

Padoa-Schioppa, Tommaso. 1994. *The Road to Monetary Union in Europe.*

Stolpher, Gustav. 1967. *The German Economy: 1870–Present.*

Dissolution of Monasteries (England)

Between 1534 and 1540 King Henry VIII, showing the same hasty, thoughtless stubbornness that marked his quest for a son, dissolved most of the English monasteries and confiscated their property.

Early in the sixteenth century England's enemy was Charles V, emperor of the Holy Roman Empire, which Voltaire later described as "neither holy, nor Roman, nor an empire." The Catholic world looked to Charles V to champion the cause of Catholicism against the impious king of England, and precious metals from the New World poured in to Charles, enlarging his vision of possibilities.

The dissolution of the monasteries occurred against the backdrop of the Reformation, the sixteenth-century religious movement that began as an effort to reform the Catholic Church, and ended with the establishment of the Protestant churches. Thus the forces of the Reformation in England made monasteries a clear and open target. In addition, expenses for public works impelled Henry VIII along a course that ended in the confiscation of vast holdings of ecclesiastical properties. Aside from extravagant court expenditures, Henry VIII financed a major enlargement of the English navy, and a significant improvement of England's harbors and ports. Paying for these public expenditures with more taxes was not workable. Taxes were already high and any increase would have prompted tax evasion, perhaps increasing collection costs as much as revenue. Henry VIII resorted to currency debasement, the worst such episode in English history, and to the confiscation of ecclesiastical properties. Monasteries had large landholdings that generated income and were also storehouses of gold and silver candlesticks, crosses, plate, and other precious metal objects.

Legislative action began in 1534 with the Act for the Suppression of the Lesser Monasteries. This law covered all monasteries with annual incomes of less than 200 pounds, accounting for about two-thirds of all the monasteries in England. In 1538 Henry expanded the policy of dissolution to friaries, and in 1539 he expanded it to the larger monasteries.

The monasteries were stripped and sometimes destroyed. About 75,000 pounds sterling in gold and silver was sent to London from dissolved monasteries. Bells were melted down and recast as cannon, and lead from roofs and gutters was exported. By 1540 nearly all ecclesiastical orders had ceased to exist, although a few survived until Henry's successor, Edward VI, dissolved them in 1547, thus completing Henry's policy.

The abbots of targeted monasteries resorted to various stratagems to hide precious metals when the king's agents came to dispose of monastery property. Some abbots placed gold and silver objects with private individuals in hopes of getting them back later. Some objects were hidden in secret vaults and walls, and some were sold for money, converting ecclesiastical property into private property. Nevertheless, the king's agents were tenacious, and uncovered much property that had been concealed or secretly sold.

Where possible, gold and silver were coined directly, but in some cases embedded jewels, wood, or other materials had to be extracted and separated. Gold and silver either went straight to the mint or ended up at the goldsmiths.

The sanctity of religious temples, churches, and monasteries had always enabled these facilities to accumulate larger quantities of gold and silver than private individuals could safely shelter. During the Reformation the Catholic institutions lost some of their inviolability in countries destined to be predominately Protestant, and governments pressed for funds tended to expropriate the precious metals for their own use.

See also: Constantine I, Great Debasement, Knights of the Templars, Silver Plate
References: Challis, C. E. 1978. *The Tudor Coinage.* Davies, Glen. 1994. *A History of Money.*

Dollar

The *dollar* is the official name for the United States currency, the closest approximation to a world currency, and is also the name for numerous other national currencies.

The term *dollar* is apparently a variation of the term *thaler,* a common term for coins in Germany and Eastern Europe that may have been derived from a valley named Joachimsthal where coins were minted in the sixteenth century. The coins were called *Joachimsthalergroschen,* soon shortened to *thaler,* and later to *taler*. In the sixteenth century the Scots adopted the term *dollar* to distinguish their currency from that of the English. The Scots were not always compliant subjects of the English Crown, and from the outset the term *dollar* bore an anti-English and antiauthoritarian connotation. Scottish emigrants brought the term *dollar* to the British colonies.

Although England forbade its colonies to mint coins, Spain put no such prohibition on its colonies, which were rich in precious metals. Mexico boasted of one of he world's largest mints. Spanish coins were the most readily accepted worldwide, including in the British colonies, but the colonists called the coins dollars rather than their Spanish names of *reales* and *pesos*. The Spanish pieces of eight coins had a face value of eight reals, and in the United States the phrase "two bits' is still used to refer to a quarter, one-fourth of a dollar.

The most common Spanish coin circulating in the British colonies was sometimes called the pillar dollar because the obverse side bore an image of the Eastern and Western Hemispheres with a large column on each side. The columns represented the Pillars of Hercules, and the words *plus ultra,* meaning "more beyond," embellished a banner hanging from one of the columns. The coin was apparently a means of publicizing the discovery of America. The dollar sign probably evolved from the pillar dollar, with the two vertical parallel lines representing the columns, and the "S" shape representing the banner.

The dollar had established itself as the primary money unit of account in the 13 colonies, and the Congress of the new republic declared on 6 July 1785 that the "money unit of the United States of America be one dollar" (Weatherford, 1997). In 1794 the United States began minting silver dollars containing $371\frac{1}{4}$ grains of silver, an amount based on the average weight of Spanish dollars circulating in the United States. Spanish and Mexican dollars remained legal tender during the early days of the Republic.

Popular usage made dollars, whether United States, Spanish, or Mexican, the accepted currency in the New World. Canada created an official currency, the Canadian dollar, pegged at a one to one exchange rate with the United States dollar. Among the British colonies in the Caribbean, dollars became the official currency in Anguilla, Saint Kitts and Nevis, Antigua and Barbuda, Montserrat, Dominica, Saint Lucia, Saint Vincent, Guyana, the Bahamas, Belize, Barbados, the Cayman Islands, the British Virgin Islands, Trinidad and Tobago, the Turks and Caicos Islands, and Jamaica. Most Latin American countries adopted as their official currency the peso, which shares with the dollar a common ancestor, the Spanish *real*.

Spain also popularized the use of dollars in the Pacific basin. In the latter nineteenth century Mexican dollars dominated Pacific basin trade but both the United States and Britain issued so-called trade dollars for foreign trade with the area. The Chinese called silver dollars *yuan,* meaning "round things," and yuan became the standard currency in China and Taiwan. The Japanese shortened *yuan* to *yen* and established a yen currency. Initially 1 yen approximately equaled 1 dollar.

The term *dollar* became the name of the official currencies in Australia, New Zealand, Fiji, the Cook Islands, Kiribati, Brunei, Singapore, Hong Kong, the Solomon Islands, Pitcairn, Tokelau, Tuvalu, the Marshall Islands, and Western Samoa. By 1994, the term *dollar* denoted the official currencies in 37 countries and autonomous territories. Europe, the birthplace of the original dollar, is one of the few places in the world where *dollar* is not a designation for an official currency. In 1991 the newly independent country of Slovenia, part of the former Yugoslavia, adopted *tolar,* a variation of *dollar,* to denote its official currency. Zimbabwe, among the latest African countries to join the ranks of independent nations, named its official currency the *dollar.*

See also: Coinage Act of 1792, De a Ocho Reales, Taler
References: Nussbaum, Arthur. 1957. *A History of the Dollar.*
Weatherford, Jack. 1997. *The History of Money.*

Dollar Crisis of 1971

In August 1971 the United States government suspended the convertibility of dollars into gold for foreign official holders of dollars, marking the final break with the gold standard in the world economy. Uneasiness about the dollar reached crisis levels in 1971 as the rest of the world became increasingly aware that the United States did not own enough gold to redeem all the foreign-owned dollars. The drain on its gold reserves also concerned the United States government. Before the suspension, foreign official holders of dollars (foreign central banks and foreign governments) had been able to convert dollars into gold at the rate of $35 per ounce. (Domestic holders of dollars had been unable to convert dollars into gold since the 1930s.) Gold has remained an important component of international monetary reserves, but currencies are no longer convertible in gold at a fixed, official rate.

The Bretton Woods System, created in 1944, established a world gold standard for international purposes, requiring each country to define a par value of its currency in terms of a fixed weight of gold. A shortage of world gold reserves, however, led countries to define domestic currencies in terms of United States dollars, and the United States stood ready to redeem dollars into gold at the official rate for foreign official holders. The redemption of dollars into gold drained the United States gold stock from $25 billion in 1949 to $12 billion in the early 1970s.

Largely because of worldwide military and political obligations, the United States ran what are called balance of payments deficits after World War II, infusing additional dollars into a world economy hungry for monetary reserves. A balance of payments deficit occurs when the outflow of dollars from U.S. imports and investment abroad exceeds the inflow of dollars from U.S. exports and foreign investment in the United States. The consequence in 1971 was an increase in the number of foreign-owned dollars that the United States was committed to redeeming in gold. After the mid-1960s, the U.S. balance of payments deficits grew at a faster tempo because of military involvement in Vietnam and heavy investment abroad. The rest of the world saw that the United States gold stock was insufficient to redeem all foreign-held dollars in gold. In August 1971 President Nixon announced that the United States would no longer convert dollars into gold for foreign official holders. Between August 1971 and May 1973 world governments endeavored, without success, to save the Bretton Woods System with a dollar devalued in terms of gold.

After 1973 the value of the dollar was no longer defined in terms of a fixed weight of gold, and other currencies were no longer defined in terms of dollars. The exchange rates between currencies floated freely and were based upon supply and demand. Today governments manage the floating exchange rates, but currencies are not tied to each other in fixed exchange rates.

Historically, the suspension of convertibility of paper money into precious metal has occurred during wartime—the Civil War and the War of 1812 being prime examples in the United States. The suspension of the convertibility of the dollar in 1971 occurred when the United States was engaged in an expensive cold war with the Soviet Union, coupled with a lengthy effort in Vietnam. Some observers attribute the inflation of the 1970s to the collapse of the gold standard, and the loss of the discipline that the gold standard had imposed on monetary growth. As control over monetary growth brought inflation down in the 1980s, however, a connection between the gold standard and price stability seemed less necessary.

See also: Balance of Payments, Bretton Woods System, Dollar, Gold Standard
References: De Vries, Margaret Garritsen. 1987. *Balance of Payments Adjustment, 1945 to 1986: The IMF Experience.*
Snider, Delbert A. 1975. *Introduction to International Economics.*

Drachma
See Aeginetan Silver Standard, Attic Silver Standard

Drum Money

The people of Alor, a small island close to Indonesia, used brass kettledrums and brass gongs as the principle forms of money. The drums, called *mokos,* played the dominant role in this monetary system, while gongs played a lesser role, and small change was made with arrows. Gongs without defects were treasured for their ceremonial value, but damaged gongs changed hands as money. Pigs also filled a niche in the monetary system of Alor, and one pig was worth a certain type of *moko* valued at 5 *rupiah,* a money of account that originated with the *rupee* in India. Pigs were highly valued because of their ceremonial importance in festivities.

Mokos came in a range of monetary denominations, each with its own name, and varying in value from 1 rupiah to 3,000 rupiahs. Most of these drums entered Alor from East Java, but some of the drums were reported to have been discovered buried in the ground. Although some drums were regarded as fake imitations of the real article, they nevertheless were readily accepted in exchange. Right before World War I the Dutch government sought to displace drum currency with modern money, banning the importation of drums, and purchasing hundreds of mokos for scrap.

Drums functioned as a medium of exchange, store of value, and standard of deferred payment, but seemed not be used as a unit of account for pricing other goods, aside from the fixed ratio between mokos and pigs. Most trade took the form of barter.

The accounts of debtors and creditors were composed almost exclusively of drums and gongs. Owners of drums and gongs were eager to lend them, partly to prevent their own creditors from seizing them. Ceremonial festivals were occasions for settling accounts, usually with passionate haggling and quarreling. Whenever a creditor found a debtor and demanded repayment, his own creditors crowded around the transaction, and demanded repayment of their own loans when drums and gongs passed from the first debtor to the first creditor. Subsidiary creditors of second or third degree might get involved. The islanders were enmeshed in a web of creditor-debtor relationships that focused the attention of the men while the women did much of the work. A women who got involved in financial affairs was called a man-woman and a man who gathered wood and gardened was called a woman-man.

Poetry of the Alor was known to take up the unromantic theme of quarrels between debtors and creditors on a scale that might suggest a lack of refinement to the people of the highly commercialized societies of the industrialized world. Debtors and creditors were put on a level with star-crossed lovers and tragic heroes of Western literature.

See also: Commodity Money Standard, Pig Standard of New Hebrides

References: Du Bois, Cora Alice. 1986. *The People of Alor: A Social-Psychological Study of an East Indian Island.* Einzig, Paul. 1966. *Primitive Money.*

Duodecimal System
See Croesean Reform, Daric

E

Edict of Prices of A.D. 301 (Roman Empire)

The Edict of Prices of A.D. 301 was the most famous government decree enacted in the ancient world to override the economic laws that govern the value of money. At first glance inflation seems to be an upward drift in the prices of all goods on the market. Penetrating the subject more deeply brings one to the realization that the steadily upward trend in prices means that money buys less, that is, money is declining in value. The Edict of Prices of A.D. 301 was an effort to stop inflation with wage and price controls.

The last half of the third century A.D. saw the economy of the Roman Empire swept up in a spiraling updraft of inflationary momentum, triggered by debasement of the coinage. Coins that had 40 percent silver content in A.D. 250 dropped to 4 percent or less silver content by A.D. 270. The government also infused the money supply with a hefty helping of grossly inferior copper coinage.

Diocletian assumed the royal purple in A.D. 284 and ruled until A.D. 307. He first sought to meet the challenge of inflation by reforming the currency—issuing new coins full valued in precious metal. The inflationary surge continued to ravage the economy, robbing the soldiers of purchasing power, and pushing the poor further into poverty while the rich found ways to shield themselves from inflation. Something of the frustration the government felt over the stubborn persistence of the inflation shows through in the wording of the legislation:

If, indeed, any self-restraint might check the excesses with which limitless and furious avarice rages—avarice which with no thought for mankind hastens to its own gain. Since, however, it is the sole desire of unrestrained madness to have no thought for the common need and since it is considered among the unscrupulous almost the creed of avarice, selling and rising with fiery passions, since, as a guide, fear is always found the most influential preceptor in the performance of duty—it is our pleasure that anyone who shall have resisted the form of this statute shall for his daring be subject to a capital penalty. Nor is he exempt from the same penalty who believes that subsequent to this regulation he must withdraw them [commodities] from the general market, since the penalty should be even more severe for him who introduces poverty than for him who harasses it against the law. (Frank, 1940, Vol. 5)

The edict set maximum prices for a detailed list of goods, and wages for a range of skills from architects to stonemasons. Those who sold goods above the maximum were subject to the death penalty. The same punishment awaited buyers who conspired with sellers to pay prices above the maximum, and sellers who hoarded goods to avoid selling them at legal prices.

The edict failed miserably. Sellers hoarded goods, and production fell off. Diocletian eased the restrictions of the edict, which Constantine revoked completely. The language of the edict sounds familiar tones that often are heard when government policy fails to tame inflation, and governments turn to wage and price controls out of frustration.

See also: Constantine I, Roman Empire Inflation
References: Duncan-Jones, Richard. 1998. *Money and Government in the Roman Empire.*
Frank, Tenney. 1940. *An Economic Survey of Ancient Rome.* Vols. I–VI.
Jones, A. H. M. 1974. *The Roman Economy.*

Egyptian Copper Standard

A weight of copper was the unit of account in ancient Egypt before the invasion of Persia and Alexander. Various writers refer to this unit of account as either the *uten,* or *utnu,* or *deben,* or *tabnu.* Smaller denominations were called the *kit, chat,* or *kedet.*

Apparently, copper was hard to come by in ancient Egypt. In the fourteenth century B.C., the king of Cypress wrote to the king of Egypt, informing him that "a present to my brother I have sent as copper (or bronze) is not common in thy midst."

In ancient languages copper and bronze often share the same word, rendering precise translation difficult. According to the Papyrus Anastasi, around 1200 B.C. a garrison of soldiers in the town of Pa-Ramses in lower Egypt received 100 uten of copper to celebrate the visit of King Minephtah.

Only scanty evidence points to the actual use of copper as a medium of exchange. The one surviving tax record omits any mention of copper on a list that includes gold and silver, hides, apes, chest of linen, staves of cedar wood, and many other commodities. There is some evidence that coiled copper wire served as money in an early period of Egyptian development. An ideograph of a bent wire is the hieroglyphic representation for money. Also the term *deben* meant "circular," or "encircling." Wall paintings depict people weighing metal rings and trading metal rings for goods, but do not identify the rings as copper.

Archeological evidence clearly shows that prices were frequently expressed in copper. An ox brought 119 uten (or deben), and temple workmen earned 5 deben per month and a grain ration. Three deben bought a knife, and 2 deben bought a tanned hide. Although the Egyptians quoted prices in copper, gold may have been popular as a medium of exchange.

See also: Bronze Standard of Ancient Rome, Copper
References: Einzig, Paul. 1966. *Primitive Money.*
Williams, Jonathan, ed. 1997. *Money: A History.*

Electrum
See Aeginetan Silver Standard, Lydian Currency, Symmetallism

English Penny

The English silver penny circulated for at least 1,100 years, first appearing in the eighth century, and remaining in circulation until 1820, setting a record of longevity for a circulating coin that has probably never been matched.

At the opening of the eighth century, small silver coins circulated, known to modern scholars as *sceattas,* and mentioned in the laws of Ine, a local English ruler, as *pennies.*

The clearest point of departure for a history of the penny begins about A.D. 760 with King Offa, ruler of Mercia, an Anglo-Saxon kingdom in central England. King Offa enjoys the added distinction of being the only English king ever to strike coins bearing the name and bust of his consort. He minted over a million pennies—by some estimates several millions—and he surpassed all of his predecessors in the quality of his coinage, as well as its quantity. Beginning with King Offa's coinage, the penny remained the only English coin in circulation for 500 years. Initially 240 silver pennies weighed one pound, beginning the history of the English sterling pound.

The weight of the penny probably varied. In 1266 the English government defined a silver penny to be the weight of "thirty-two wheat corns in the midst of the ear." In 1280 the English government fixed the weight of the penny equal to 24 grains, setting the precedent that makes a pennyweight today equal to 24 troy grains. The 32 grains of wheat were comparable to 24 grains. During the thirteenth century a penny was worth a day's wages or could buy a sheep. The value of the penny was sufficiently high that the government turned to minting halfpenny coins in the fourteenth century, and three-halfpenny coins in the sixteenth century. The weight of the penny steadily fell until silver pennies struck in 1816 weighed 7.27 troy grains.

In 1257 Henry III minted gold pennies that were worth 20 silver pennies. Per unit of weight gold was 10 times as valuable as silver, and Henry III's gold pennies weighed twice as much as the silver pennies. The issue of gold coins failed, being too valuable to meet the needs of the English economy.

The English silver penny first appeared in the eighth century. (Smithsonian Institution, National Numismatic Collection)

The word *penny* may have originated from the word *pending,* which was the name of a coin issued by Penda, a king who ruled Mercia in the second quarter of the seventh century. Nevertheless, linguistic forms of *penny* are widely spread with equivalents in Dutch and Friesian. The Danish word for money is still *Penge,* resembling *penig,* the Old English word for "penny." Variants of the word *penny* may have evolved from an old Danish word for the pans that were used to coin money.

The smallest denomination of coins minted in the United States are called pennies. They are token coins but were formerly minted from copper. The purchasing power of the United States penny is a bit modest to justify the phrase, "a pretty penny," referring to a large sum of money. Sixpenny nails now denote nails of a certain length, but originally denoted nails that sold for six pennies per 100.

See also: American Penny, Copper

References: Davies, Glyn. 1994. *A History of Money.* Feavearyear, Sir Albert. 1963. *The Pound Sterling.*

Equation of Exchange

The equation of exchange identifies the exact mathematical relationship that exists between the money supply, the price level, and the volume of economic activity. The economist Irving Fisher (1867–1947) first formulated the equation of exchange, and his version took the following form:

$$MV + M'V' = PT.$$

Here M stands for the stock of currency in a given year, V stands for the velocity or number of times a dollar bill changes hands during a year, M' measures the quantity of checkable deposits, and V' the velocity of checkable deposits. P stands for the price involved in a typical transaction, and T represents the number of transactions.

Contemporary economists make use of a simplified equation of exchange that takes the following form:

$$MV = PY$$

Here M stands for a measure of the money stock that includes, at a minimum, currency in circulation plus checkable deposits. Time deposits and other highly liquid assets may also be included. V stands for the income velocity of money, defined as being equal to the money value of income and output divided by the money stock. P stands for the price level and Y stands for real output. In practice PY stands for Gross Domestic Product (GDP) unadjusted for inflation, called nominal GDP, and Y stands for GDP adjusted for inflation, called real GDP. P is a factor standing for the price level and is calculated by dividing nominal GDP by real GDP. Velocity is calculated by dividing nominal GDP by the money stock.

Nominal GDP divided by M equals V, which can be converted to the form $MV =$ nominal GDP. Furthermore, nominal GDP divided by real GDP *(Y)* equals the price index *(P),* which is mathematically equivalent to saying that nominal GDP = PY. Therefore $MV = PY$ is what is called an identity in mathematics, true by definition.

The equation of exchange is often converted to a percentage change form, expressed as:

$$\% \text{ change in } M + \% \text{ change in } V =$$
$$\% \text{ change in } P + \% \text{ change in } Y$$

A school of economists called quantity theorists assumes that velocity is relatively stable, suggesting that the percentage change in V is always zero. They also assume that the percentage change in Y is at the long-term growth rate of real GDP, approximately 3 percent. With these assumptions the inflation rate (percentage change in P) will always be 3 percent less than the growth rate of the money stock (percentage change in M). If the money stock grows at 10 percent a year, the inflation rate will be 7 percent a year. Therefore, inflation is an exact mathematical function of the money stock growth rate, and the equation of exchange furnishes us with a theory of inflation.

Empirical evidence bears out the close correspondence between money stock growth and inflation, but there is still room for some economists to argue that increases in the inflation rate force authorities to increase monetary growth, instead of the other way around. These issues still stand to benefit from further study.

See also: Monetarism, Velocity of Money
References: Mankiw, N. Gregory. 1996. *Macroeconomics.* 3d ed.
Klein, John J. 1986. *Money and the Economy.* 6th ed.

Euro Currency

On 3 May 1998 leaders of the European Union (EU) concluded an agreement to establish a European Monetary Union (EMU) and, on 1 January 1999 to launch a common EMU currency, called the *euro.* Euro notes and coins will enter into circulation and replace national currencies by 1 July 2002.

Initially, 11 countries have agreed to adopt the euro, Germany, France, Italy, Spain, Portugal, Belgium, Luxembourg, the Netherlands, Austria, Finland, and Ireland. Greece will probably join the euro zone by 2001, and for now Britain, Sweden, and Denmark plan to retain their own national currencies. Some economists have named the new monetary zone Euroland.

The historic agreement to form the EMU pro-

vides that responsibility for management of monetary policy in Europe falls to a newly established European Central Bank (ECB). Central banks regulate money supplies, interest rates, and credit conditions, and currently each member of the EMU has its own central bank to manage its domestic monetary policy. A major challenge facing the ECB will be the search for a monetary policy that can meet the needs of such diverse economies as Germany and Portugal. A single European monetary policy will mean a single interest rate all across Europe, regardless of economic conditions in each country.

The president of the ECB will normally serve an eight-year term but the first president, Dutchman Wim Duisenberg, has promised to step down after four years in favor of Frenchman Jean-Claude Trichet. Frenchman Christain Noyer will serve as vice-president of the ECB, and a four-member board, with representatives from Germany, Italy, Spain, and Finland, will oversee the management of the bank. Reaching an agreement on the leadership of the ECB was the last major hurdle to finalizing the agreement.

A common European currency will make transparent differences in wages, labor costs, and prices among European countries, forcing high-cost countries to enact reforms to improve efficiency and lower costs. Uncompetitive countries will no longer have the option of devaluing their currencies, rendering their exports cheaper to foreigners and their imports more expensive compared to domestic goods. The new currency system, by increasing competition between European national economies and coming on line amid an inflation-free recovery, has been spared the fears of currency weakness that might be expected to undercut a new currency without a track record. Also, to bolster the euro EMU countries have five times more gold and currency reserves than the United States.

By increasing cross-border competition and trade, the EMU should economically strengthen Europe in the global economy. European leaders envision that the euro, supported by an economic bloc with more inhabitants than the United States, is well positioned to challenge the dominance of the dollar in the global market place.

Nevertheless, the introduction of the euro has not been met with universal applause. Europe currently suffers from high unemployment rates—in some countries the highest since the 1930s—and much of the blame is pinned on the economic integration of Europe. The euro is seen as a further step down the road of economic integration, forcing companies to undertake more streamlining to remain competitive by laying off more workers. So far Britain, Denmark, and Sweden have remained aloof, fearing the euro will aggravate economic ills and involve some loss of sovereignty.

See also: Latin Monetary Union, Monetary Unions of Ancient Greece, Wendish Monetary Union
References: Karouf, Jim. 1998. Start the Presses: Euro Set to Debut. *Futures* 27, no 9 (1 September):30
Wall Street Journal. 1998. Economic Climate Looks Good for Launch of New Currency. 4 May, at A17–18.

Eurodollars

Eurodollars come into existence when the ownership of dollar deposits in United States banks passes into the hands of foreign banks. The dollar deposits, more commonly called demand deposits or checking accounts, remain in United States banks, but the owners of the deposits are foreign banks, or foreign branches of United States banks. Individuals in foreign countries have dollar deposits in United States banks, but these deposits do not count as Eurodollars. Dollar deposits owned by foreign banks count as Eurodollars because these banks conduct a business of attracting dollar deposits and making dollar loans. Eurodollar deposits in foreign banks are interest-paying time deposits, usually of large amounts, and borrowers of dollars can turn to these foreign banks for dollar loans.

In the late 1950s European banks first began holding deposits denominated in dollars, and borrowing and lending in dollars. The probable cause of the growth of the Eurodollar market lay with interest rate ceilings in the United States. Regulation Q, promulgated by the Federal Reserve Board, put a legal ceiling of less than 6 percent on interest rates that time deposits could pay in United States banks. The payment of interest rates that exceeded the legal interest rate ceiling in the United States constituted one of the major attractions of Eurodollar deposits. When interest rates soared in the 1970s, foreign banks, not subject to United States banking regulations, were able to pay much higher interests on time deposits, and make dollar loans on favorable terms. In the 1980s the deregulation of United States banking took away some of the competitive advantage of

Eurodollars, but the Eurodollar market had already established itself. From 1976 until 1992, Eurodollars grew from $14 billion to $56 billion.

The growth of multinational corporations, major customers in the Eurodollar market, may have contributed to the expansion of Eurodollars. Growth was further facilitated because the Eurodollar market made dealing in dollars a daytime affair in European time zones. Large United States banks also have borrowed funds in the Eurodollar market, and during the cold war, the Soviet government kept dollar deposits in European banks to prevent the United States government from freezing Soviet assets in a political dispute.

London is the headquarters for the Eurodollar market, but Eurodollar transactions take place worldwide. Banks in the Bahamas, Cayman Islands, Canada, Hong Kong, and Singapore hold dollar deposits and lend dollars.

Eurodollars are a subspecies of Eurocurrencies, all of which have extraterritorial markets such as the Eurodollar market. Other important Eurocurrencies are Japanese yen, German marks, British pounds, French francs, and Swiss francs. Luxembourg is headquarters for Euromark deposits, and Paris and Brussels for Eurosterling deposits.

See also: Euro Currency, European Currency Unit
References: Daniels, John D., and Lee H. Radebaugh. 1998. *International Business*. 8th ed.
Terrell, Henry S., and Rodney H. Mills. 1983. International Banking Facilities and the Eurodollar Market. *Staff Study No. 124* (published by the Board of Governors of the Federal Reserve System)(August).

European Currency Unit

The European Currency Unit (ECU) began in 1979 as what is called a basket currency, a composite currency based upon a weighted average combination of European currencies. It had a predecessor in the European Unit of Account (EUA), which dated back to the 1950s and was used for official transactions between countries. The ECU was similar in concept, but it experienced a totally unforeseen growth in private sector use, suggesting that there might be a strong demand for an international currency. The initials, ECU, were consciously devised as a reference to the ancient French coin, *ecu,* which was equal to three French *livres*.

The ECU acts as a unit of account for keeping

books and defining the terms of contracts, but does not circulate in the form of a paper currency. The European Monetary Fund kept its funds designated in ECUs. The ECU was an intermediate step toward a common European currency that European Union countries launched in mid-1998.

At its first introduction, an ECU consisted of specified amounts of the following currencies:

West German mark 0.828
French franc 1.15
Belgian franc 3.66
Luxembourg franc 0.14
Italian lira 109.00
Danish krone 0.217
Dutch guilder 0.286
Irish pound 0.00759
British pound sterling 0.9885

Later the ECU basket incorporated the currencies of Spain, Portugal, and Greece. As various currencies were devalued or revalued, the weights were reconfigured accordingly.

ECUs could be expressed in terms of single ECU units or in terms of equivalent amounts of separate national currencies. Member countries of the European Monetary System cooperated to maintain desired exchange rates between individual national currencies and the ECU.

The ECU began as a basket currency, but it soon took on characteristics of an independent currency. A market for ECU-denominated assets developed independently of the market for assets denominated in component currencies, and ECU deposits earned interest, which was often different from a weighted average of interest rates paid on deposits of component currencies. By 1985 ECU transactions in Paris ranked third, after the U.S. dollar and the German mark, and by 1987 ECU futures on the Chicago Mercantile Exchange approached 3 million transactions. Financial assets denominated in ECUs included certificates of deposit, commercial paper, bank loans, and fixed rate and variable rate bonds. Central banks created ECUs for settling payments between individual countries, and private banks bundled individual currencies to create ECU financial instruments as needed.

The ECU represented an important step in the development of a European currency. Presumably with the introduction of the *euro* in 1998, a Euro-

pean basket currency such as the ECU will no longer serve a purpose.

See also: Euro Currency, Snake
References: Kenen, Peter B. 1955. *Economic and Monetary Union in Europe.*
Padoa-Schioppa, Tommaso. 1994. *The Road to Monetary Union in Europe.*

European Monetary Union (EMU)
See Euro Currency

Exchequer Bills
See Exchequer Orders to Pay (England)

Exchequer Orders to Pay (England)
Exchequer orders of payment, which appeared during the seventeenth century, were the first paper money issued by the English government. The orders were what might be called state notes, in contrast to bank notes, which completely displaced state notes as circulating money in England, and later the United States. State notes are issued by government treasuries to finance government spending. Bank notes are liabilities of banks and are secured by the assets and investments of the issuing bank. Virtually all paper money today is bank notes issued by central banks.

In 1667 Parliament authorized Charles II to issue paper orders, or assignments of revenue, to whoever advanced cash or supplied goods to the government. A record book kept a list of the Exchequer orders according to their order of issuance. As tax revenue poured in, the Exchequer redeemed in cash the orders in the same sequence as they were issued. The first order issued was the first redeemed and so on. At first, the government assigned revenue from a particular tax to redeem an issue of orders, but later the government issued orders for redemption out of general revenue.

The Exchequer orders supplemented and eventually replaced tallies, which were the notched wooden sticks split into matching parts. Tallies served the same purpose as the orders but were not as amendable to written endorsements, and therefore were not as suitable as currency. The orders, like the tallies, were negotiable; that is, they were transferable to another party with a written endorsement. This rendered them serviceable as a medium of exchange.

The government issued Exchequer orders to department heads who either paid for supplies with orders or discounted orders to goldsmiths in return for cash. As a loan to the government, orders bore interest, sometimes as high as 8 to 10 percent, a handsome interest rate to goldsmiths who paid depositors as much as 6 percent interest to attract funds for discounting orders. The goldsmiths made a ready market for the orders, rendering them liquid and even more acceptable as money. The orders supplemented the scarce coinage in the English economy and offered an interest-bearing investment in small denominations (20 pounds or so) for the small investor.

In late 1671 the market for Exchequer orders became saturated, even at the high interest rates, and the goldsmiths stopped discounting orders for the government. On 2 January 1672 Charles II issued a proclamation, the infamous Stop of the Exchequer, suspending the redemption of the orders. The goldsmiths were left with vast holdings of unredeemable orders, and many went bankrupt. Interest payments were suspended until 1677. The money owed by the government later became part of the British public debt, but the credit of the British Crown was seriously impaired, and the issuance of Exchequer orders came to an end.

In 1696 the English government began issuing Exchequer bills. These bills paid interest, were acceptable in payment of most taxes, transferable by written endorsement, and convertible into cash on demand at the Bank of England. The popularity of these bills as a form of currency, allowed the government to drop the interest rate to as low as 1 percent per annum. Private banks complained that the bills competed with their own bank notes.

Later, in the eighteenth century, the government's financing requirements outgrew the small denomination Exchequer bills, around 20 pounds, that were payable on demand. The government opted for bills paying higher interest rates and payable after a fixed time period. These bills were not suitable as a medium of exchange, and bank notes became the only paper money circulating in England.

The experience with the Exchequer orders struck a hard blow against the credibility of state paper money in England. If the Exchequer orders had turned out to be a successful experiment in paper money, England might have developed a monetary system based on state paper money, rather than bank notes.

See also: Bank of England, Stop of the Exchequer, Tallies

References: Davies, Glyn. 1994. *A History of Money.*
Feavearyear, Sir Albert. 1963. *The Pound Sterling: A History of English Money.*
Nevin, Edward, and E. W. Davis. 1970. *The London Clearing Banks.*
Richards, R. D. 1929. *The Early History of Banking in England.*

F

Faust

A theme of the dangers, temptations, and blessings of paper money made its way into Part Two of *Faust,* one of the most famous epic poems in history. *Faust* came from the pen of Johann Wolfgang von Goethe (1749–1832), a many-sided scientist, statesman, and literary figure whose works can be found on any list of the greatest books in the history of mankind. Line 317 of *Faust* reads "Man errs as long as he doth strive," a thought particularly pertinent to a history of paper money that is filled with errors made by societies striving to do too much with too few resources.

Part Two of Faust was finished in 1832. A historical figure, Dr. Johann Faustus, furnished the main subject of Goethe's poem. The real Faust, living in the sixteenth century, practiced medicine, studied astrology, and conducted experiments in alchemy. The goal of alchemy was to find a method for transforming base metals into gold. Faustus was thought to be a magician and according to legend had dealings with the devil. The story of Faustus passed down to Goethe was probably much more mythical and legendary than historical.

Goethe's Faust is a restless striving soul disappointed with the brevity of beauty and the never-ending search for elusive truth. He offers to sell his soul to the devil on condition that the devil show him a pleasure that brings lasting satisfaction, one that he would not tire of, but would want to "Tarry a while, you are so fair." Second only to Faust in Goethe's play is the devil, Mephistopheles.

In Part One Faust seduces a young maiden, gets her pregnant, kills her brother, and abandons her. None of the pleasures in Part One are able to calm Faust's striving and enable him to feel fulfilled.

In Act 1 of Part Two, Faust and Mephistopheles visit the emperor of the Holy Roman Empire. They catch the emperor amidst a budget crisis with the pay of soldiers and servants in arrears, and moneylenders demanding payment on debts. Mephistopheles holds out the promise of the alchemist's dream, the secret to making gold that is as simple as printing paper money. The paper money is secured because "In veins of mountains, walls far underground, gold coined and uncoined can be found." The emperor, on learning the bills have been paid and seeing joy on so many faces, has to be reminded that the night before he authorized the issuance of paper money. The treasurer tells him that the night before:

The chancellor came and spoke in words that
  ran:
"A lofty festal joy do for thyself attain:
Thy people's weal—A few strokes of the pen!"
These you did make, ten thousand fold last night
Conjurers multiplied what you did write;
And that straightway the good might come to
  all,
We stamped at once the series, large and small;
Tens, twenties, thirties, hundreds, all are there.
You cannot think how glad the people were.
Behold you city, one half dead, decaying,
Now full of life and joy, and swarming and
  playing!

The notes bore the emperor's signature, and on each note could be read:

To all whom it concerns, let it be known:
Who hath this note, a thousand crowns doth own.
As certain pledge thereof shall stand
Vast buried treasure in the emperor's land,
Provision has been made that ample treasure,
Raised straightway, shall redeem the notes at pleasure. (Goethe, 1952)

Faust puts the money to good use, digging canals, draining marshes, building factories and new farms. At first the money spreads happiness, but sins are committed in the name of progress. New government functionaries appear on the scene with names such as Quick-loot and Getquick, and soon the emperor faces a rebellion.

At the end Faust's pleasure at his good works seems to have met his requirement for a pleasure that never grows stale. As the devil takes his soul, angels redeem Faust, saying redemption is possible for those who never cease striving.

Goethe correctly anticipated the era of paper money. Before the nineteenth century virtually every experiment with inconvertible paper money had ended with disaster. Inconvertible paper money is money that cannot be converted into precious metals at a fixed rate. A century after Goethe wrote Part Two of *Faust,* most of the countries of the world adopted inconvertible paper standards.

See also: *Oedipus Tyrannus*
References: Binswanger, Hans Christopher. 1994. *Money and Magic: Critique of the Modern Economy in the Light of Goethe's Faust.*
Goethe, Johann Wolfgang von. 1952. *Faust, Parts One and Two.* Trans. George Madison Priest.
Jackson, Kevin, ed. 1995. *The Oxford Book of Money.*

Feather Money of Santa Cruz

The use of feather money survived on the Santa Cruz Islands, a group of islands in the southwestern Pacific Ocean, into the post–World War II era. The red feathers of this money came either from the parrot *Trichoglossus massena,* or from a red-scarlet honey-eater named *Mzomela cardinalis.* The feathers were integrated into striplike coils of fiber extending 15 feet in length and 2 to 3 feet in width. The outer side of these coils was blanketed with overlapping rows of red feathers.

The feather money owed its high monetary value to the labor-intensive effort required to produce it. Capturing the birds was no small task, and each bird furnished only a few of the feathers suitable for the purpose of making a coil. Each coil was made by hand, further adding to the labor invested in each unit of money. The attachment of wooden emblems and charms partially accounted for the value of each feather coil. The production of a coil of feather money took 500 to 600 man-hours.

The feather money was too valuable to be useful for an everyday medium of exchange, but it was much in demand as a store of value. It was stored away with great care in a secure place that was dry and warm in order to preserve the color and elasticity of the coils. Wealthy individuals stored their feather money in huts built specifically for that purpose. The coils lost value as their feathers wore off.

The islanders paid fines, ransoms, and blood money in feather money. When a Bishop Patterson was murdered in 1871 on nearby Reef Islands, his murderer paid a fine of four coils of feather money, which was about the same amount that was needed to purchase an oceangoing canoe. A bride brought 10 coils or more, depending upon her beauty and habits of industry.

The trouble that went into the production of feather money helped keep the supply down, making the feather money scarce and valuable. Feathers probably became acceptable for money because of their beauty, which made them highly esteemed, and because significant prestige became attached to the their ownership. Gold and silver may have started as money for similar reasons. As Australian money began to invade the Santa Cruz Islands as a medium of exchange, the price of feather money in Australian money steadily rose, showing the hold of the feather money on the minds of the islanders. The attraction of feather money appears to have been purely aesthetic, independent of religious significance or physiological need.

See also: Commodity Monetary Standard
References: Einzig, Paul. 1966. *Primitive Money.*
Krieger, Herbert William. 1943. *Island Peoples of the Western Pacific: Micronesia and Melanesia.*

Federal Deposit Insurance Corporation (FDIC)

See Glass-Steagall Banking Act of 1933

Federal Reserve System

The Federal Reserve System is the central banking system for the United States, established by the Federal Reserve Act of 1913. Most countries have only one central bank, such as the Bank of England, or Germany's Bundesbank. The Federal Reserve System makes up a system of 12 regional central banks. Central banks are bankers' banks, holding deposits of commercial banks, making loans to commercial banks, and serving as lenders of last resort to commercial banks in an economic downturn. The Federal Reserve System also acts as a bank for the United States government, and has a monopoly on the issue of bank notes, called Federal Reserve Notes. The term *reserve* in the title refers to the role central banks play in determining the liquidity of commercial banks. The Federal Reserve System regulates the money supply, interest rates, and credit conditions in the United States.

The United States was slow to adopt the concept of central banks as systems of monetary control. The early years of the Republic saw the creation of the First Bank of the United States in 1791, but Congress failed to renew its charter in 1811. Congress chartered the Second Bank of the United States in 1816, but President Jackson vetoed the renewal of its charter in 1832. These two banks, similar in structure, were early experiments in central banking, but were unpopular. The United States government's control over the management and policies of these banks was limited to the voting rights of a minority stockholder. Fear of East Coast domination of the banking industry helped undermine support for the Second Bank of the United States.

The decentralized and unregulated banking system of the latter 1880s constantly buffeted the country with money panics and financial crises, leading public officials to see the necessity for overcoming the political objections to a central bank. Political objections came from several angles, including government officials who felt that the banking industry could not be trusted to regulate itself, and leaders in banking who felt that elected politicians lacked the necessary knowledge to regulate banking and were

Headquarters of the Federal Reserve System in Washington, D.C. (Courtesy Board of Governors of the Federal Reserve System)

often irresponsible in financial matters. In addition to the distrust between leading bankers and elected politicians, there was distrust between regions of the country. Many regions presumed that a central bank would be located in New York City, subjecting the country to Wall Street domination. These contending forces helped shape the Federal Reserve Act of 1913 that created the Federal Reserve System.

To diffuse the fear of Wall Street domination of banking the Federal Reserve Act created a system of 12 regional central banks. The Federal Reserve Bank of New York is the most important for policy purposes, but there are Federal Reserve Banks in Boston, Philadelphia, Atlanta, Cleveland, St. Louis, Kansas City (Mo.), Richmond, Dallas, San Francisco, Chicago, and Minneapolis.

Like the First and Second Bank of the United States, the Federal Reserve Banks are privately owned. Private ownership helped appease the banking community's arguments that knowledgeable bankers can best regulate the banking industry. Commercial banks in each district that are members of the Federal Reserve System own the stock in the regional Federal Reserve Bank. The Federal Reserve Act requires all banks with national charters to be members of the Federal Reserve System.

The final authority for monetary policy lies with the Board of Governors of the Federal Reserve System. The president of the United States makes appointments to this seven-member board, subject to the approval of the Senate. The seven board members serve 14-year terms that are staggered so that one member's term expires every other year. This constant rotation on the board dilutes the power of any one president to bias the board politically. One of the board members acts as chairman of the Board of Governors, and the president—with the approval of the Senate—appoints that person. The chairman serves a four-year term that is renewable. Congress organized the Board of Governors to be independent of either the banking industry or the elected politicians.

Despite the trend toward deregulation in banking, Congress has not limited the authority of the Federal Reserve System, except in certain areas such as fixing interest rates on savings accounts. The Depository Institution Deregulation and Monetary Control Act of 1980 gave the Federal Reserve System the authority to set reserve requirements for state-chartered banks in addition to its existing authority to set reserve requirements for national chartered banks. (The reserve requirement is the percent of money deposited in checking and savings accounts that a bank has to retain in the form of vault cash and deposits at Federal Reserve Banks.)

Because the Federal Reserve System's governing board is composed of unelected officials who are somewhat immune to political pressure, the Federal Reserve System often bears the brunt of the responsibility for combating inflation in the United States. Anti-inflation policies are often accompanied by high unemployment, rendering these policies unpopular with elected officials, who like to earn credit for reducing unemployment rather than increasing it. Therefore the elected officials often defer to the unelected officials that compose the Board of Governors the responsibility for slowing down the economy and taming inflation.

See also: Bank of England, Bank of France, Central Bank, Deutsche Bundesbank, First Bank of the United States, Second Bank of the United States

References: Board of Governors of the Federal Reserve System. 1984. *The Federal Reserve System: Purposes and Functions.*

Broz, J. Lawrence. 1997. *The International Origins of the Federal Reserve System.*

Greider, William. 1987. *Secrets of the Temple: How the Federal Reserve System Runs the Country.*

Timberlake, Richard Henry. 1978. *The Origins of Central Banking in the United States.*

Fiat Money
See Inconvertible Paper Standard

First Bank of the United States

The First Bank of the United States (1791–1811) met the needs of a central bank in the early years of the Republic. It helped regulate the issuance of bank notes by state banks and acted as the bank of the United States government. The First Bank received its charter from the national government in 1791 when President George Washington signed the bill authorizing its incorporation.

The First Bank of the United States was a brainchild of Alexander Hamilton, who saw such a bank as a means of raising short-term capital for the government and handling bills of exchange needed for making payments to foreign holders of the national debt. Hamilton patterned the First Bank after the Bank of England, and got many of his ideas from the role the Bank of England played in the English economy and government finances. He also promoted the bank as a means of increasing the circulation of bank notes, which was needed at that time because of a shortage of specie.

Hamilton's *Report on a National Bank* went to Congress in December 1790. The proposal drew fire from critics concerned that the bank was a monopoly sanctioned by Congress. As the debate on this issue waned, constitutional questions arose that were to haunt the bank for the duration of its existence. The Constitutional Convention of 1787 had chosen not to give Congress the power to grant charters of incorporation and the Constitution itself was silent on the subject.

The bill for the bank's charter passed by a two-to-one vote in the House and by a majority vote in the Senate, but Washington balked at signing it, partly at the urging of such luminaries as Thomas Jefferson. Washington signed the bill chartering the bank after Hamilton wrote a very able paper in its defense. The First Bank made Philadelphia its headquarters and, over Hamilton's opposition, set up branches, one as far away as New Orleans.

The charter authorized a capital stock of $10 million. The U.S. government purchased one-fifth of the stock, paid for by a loan from the First Bank, and the remaining four-fifths was opened for public subscription. The bank was fully capitalized within an hour after shares became available to the public. Public subscribers could pay one-fourth in specie and four-fifths in government obligations and foreigners eventually held much of the stock. The charter prohibited the bank from trading in anything besides bills of exchange, gold and silver bullion, and goods held as security for defaulted loans. The total debt of the First Bank could not exceed its capital and money held on deposit. The bank needed congressional approval before it could make loans in excess of $100,000 to the U.S. government, any state government, or to purchase any of the public debt.

Commercial loans accounted for most of the bank's lending, and the bank served some of the functions of a central bank. At that time bank loans were paid out in bank notes, convertible into specie on demand. The bank held other commercial banks accountable by presenting to them their bank notes for redemption in specie. The First Bank's role in controlling the issuance of bank notes won the support of the large commercial banks. The bank particularly helped control the overissuance of bank notes by country banks, often the source of inflationary pressures.

When the charter for the First Bank came up for renewal in 1811, it failed by one vote in the House. Constitutional issues and foreign ownership cost the First Bank much of its support in Congress. The vote in the Senate was a tie, and the vice president broke it by voting against the First Bank.

Congress soon missed the First Bank and in 1816 Congress chartered the Second Bank of the United States, but that bank lost its charter in 1832. The Federal Reserve System, established in 1913, was the first central bank in the United States to establish itself in the confidence of the voters.

See also: Bank of England, Central Bank, Free Banking, Federal Reserve System, Second Bank of the United States

References: Myers, Margaret G. 1970. *A Financial History of the United States.*

Timberlake, Richard H. 1978. *The Origins of Central Banking in the United States.*

Fishhooks

Fishhooks have served as money in the Maldives Islands, the islands of Micronesia, mountainous regions of the West African country of Cameroon, and portions of Nigeria.

The Maldives Islands, located southwest of the southern tip of India, were famous as a hunting ground for cowries, seashells that circulated widely as money in Asia and Africa. Cowries were the islands' main export, and were used as local currency. In the 1800s, however, the main currency was a corrupted silver fishhook called the *larin*. The king of the Maldives issued larins, and put an official stamp on them, making them a state currency. For small change larins were divided into pieces, but a divided larin was worth only one-twelfth of a whole larin. The use of larins as currency seems to have gotten its start in the city of Larr in southern Persia.

In the Gilbert Islands in the west central Pacific Ocean, fishhooks circulated as money and were reported to be highly valuable. Pearl shells were cut into the shape of fishhooks, and were called fishhook money. Seashells strung on cords, sperm whale teeth, and discs of coconut also acted as currency on these islands.

In the mountains of Cameroon, called the Cameroons by the British in the nineteenth century, fishhooks served as a medium of exchange, along with cowries, soap, and gunpowder. Cameroon is on the west coast of equatorial Africa. Cowries were the chief medium of exchange in the Cameroons, while wives, goats, and bead necklaces acted as a store of value. Fishhook currency could also be found in parts of Nigeria.

Fishhook money fits into the category of nail money in Scotland, or needle money in India. Fishhooks are small and durable, easily stored and transported, serve a necessary need, and are restricted in supply because they can be produced only with labor. The logistics of storing and exchanging fishhooks is simple, and the restricted supply relative to demand preserves the value of fishhooks. Though of a small size, fishhooks are highly productive tools. The combination of smallness and utility contributes to their value as money.

See also: Commodity Monetary Standard

References: Einzig, Paul. 1966. *Primitive Money.*

Meek, Charles Kingsley. 1950. *Law and Authority in a Nigerian Tribe: A Study in Indirect Rule.*

Fleetwood, William

William Fleetwood, Royal Chaplain in England during the late seventeenth century, preached a sermon, the Sermon against Clipping, in the Guildhall chapel on 16 December 1694. Clipping was a means of debasing coins by removing precious metal from around their edges. Perfectly round coins with a ribbed edge, called a milled edge, were introduced to prevent clippers from robbing domestic currency of its precious metal content. Before the development of the milled edge, governments constantly struggled with the problem of clipped coins, often enacting legislation governing the use of clipped coins.

Fleetwood took the text for his sermon from Genesis 23:16, a passage in which Abraham paid for land to bury his dead:

> Abraham agreed with Ephron; and Abraham weighed out for Ephron the silver which he had named in the hearing of the Hittites, four hundred shekels of silver, according to the weights current among merchants.

Before plunging into the hellfire and damnation portion of his sermon, Fleetwood gave a reasoned treatment of monetary theory, citing the importance that money be portable, durable, and beautiful. According to Fleetwood, in the days of Abraham, silver:

> was valued both by Buyer and Seller according to its weight but because it was too troublesome, and took up too much time, to carry Scales Men found it convenient to have a stamp or Mark set upon every piece, to signify its weight and value. Yet something was still needed to secure the truth of Payments: Men might be fraudulent and false. (Chown, 1994)

Fleetwood proceeded to denounce the sin and evil of clipping, arguing that the failure of the clipper to identify or see a specific victim of his sin did not absolve him of moral responsibility. He exclaimed that the convicted "can be sorry for their great misfortune, but they know not how to repent the sense of these offenses affects them little or nothing" (Chown, 1994).

He told of the punishment in past times for the crime of clipping, such as severing the right hand. In past times some "who were found to Adulterate the King's Coin, were so punished as if the Laws intended to prevent Adultery itself" (Chown, 1994). He noted that in his own time society had become merciful, letting clippers off with a modern execution, "a short and easy death."

In the following year Parliament again legislated against clipping and counterfeiting, prompting one observer to say, "But did this prohibition, tho by Act of Parliament, cure the evil? Alas no. The forbidden Fruit, was of too luscious a relish to be so easily relinquished. It was not in the power of any paper spell to stop the spreading Gangrene" (Chown, 1994).

Despite the pessimism expressed in the above passage, the government was already laying plans to replace all coinage in circulation with milled-edge coins. The milled-edge coins effectively discouraged the clipper by making the effects of clipping very noticeable.

See also: Act for Remedying the Ill State of the Coin
References: Chown, John F. 1994. *A History of Money*. Feavearyear, Sir Albert. 1963. *The Pound Sterling: A History of English Money*.

Florentine Florin

The Florentine *florin* was the first European gold coin to achieve the status of an international currency after the disappearance of European gold coinage in the eighth century. Florence first issued the florin in 1252. It weighed 3.53 grams or 72 grains of fine gold and took its name from the fleur-de-lis, the iris flower whose image adorned one side of the florin. The florin preceded the era of milled coins with corrugated edges that protected coins against the clippers. To circumvent the clippers, florins circulated in leather bags sealed by the mint. The seal was intended to vouch for the integrity of the coins inside. Thus anyone who wished to clip coins had also to be able to counterfeit the seal.

The florin did not burst upon the world without European rivals. Genoa also commenced gold coinage in 1252, but Genoa's coins never commanded the international stature of the florin. Frederick II of Sicily may have struck gold coins a few years earlier than Florence, but his coinage was a descendant of Moslem and Byzantine coinage, despite its popularity in Europe.

Originally Florence struck the florin as a gold pound, equal to 20 *soldi* or *shillings,* or 240 *deniers,* or *pennies.* The Florentine version of the Carolingian

The Florentine florin rose to become the equivalent of the modern dollar in international trade. (Smithsonian Institution, National Numismatic Collection)

system soon broke down amidst fluctuating exchange rates between gold and silver, and an imaginary money of account developed based upon a pound *affiorino,* in which 20 florins equaled 29 affiorinos. A separate silver standard evolved that set the value of the silver pound equal to 20 silver soldi, or 240 silver deniers. Market forces overrode government efforts to establish official exchange ratios between gold and silver such as existed with the European bimetallic system in the nineteenth century.

From the outset Florence groomed the florin to play the part of an international currency. Florentine law provided that only international merchants of the Calimala Guild, the moneychangers, the cloth and silk manufacturers, the grocers, and furriers, could keep books and conduct business in florins. Silver currency was used in retail trade, payment of wages, and small transactions. Wholesale prices were often quoted in florins, while retail prices were quoted in silver currency.

San Antonino (1389–1459), archbishop of Florence, complained of the government debasing the silver currency used by the lower classes, while maintaining the purity of the gold currency used by the wealthier classes. The employer-controlled government of Florence could effectively reduce real wages by debasing silver coins used to pay wages while maintaining the purity of gold florins in which wholesale goods were priced. Separate gold and silver standards, with separate prices, exposed one segment of the population to the ravages of inflation

through debasement, while another segment remained untouched by inflation. From 1252 until the beginning of the fifteenth century, the florin rose in value 700 percent relative to silver coinage, largely reflecting debasement of silver.

In the second half of the thirteenth century and the first part of the fourteenth century the Florentine florin rose to become the equivalent of the modern-day dollar in international trade. As often happens in currencies, the florin was unable to dodge the pitfalls of success. Foreign governments minted florin imitations from lighter metal, and at the beginning of the fifteenth century Florence minted florins of a lighter weight. The florin may have owed part of its success to the strength and expansion of the Florentine economy. During the fifteenth century the Venetian *ducat* displaced the Florentine florin as the international currency par excellence.

See also: Carolingian Reform, Gold, Sealed Coin Purses, Venetian Ducat

References: Chown, John. 1994. *A History of Money.*
Goldthwaite, Richard A. 1980. *The Building of Renaissance Florence: An Economic and Social History.*

Food Stamps

Food stamps are coupons redeemable in food at grocery stores. The government allots food stamps to low-income families to assure that minimal nutritional needs are met. Because they are redeemable in food, food stamps have circulated as money in ghetto areas. Although the food stamp program is a federal program, supervised by the United States Department of Agriculture, the process of identifying qualified families and issuing food stamps is left to the individual state governments.

The first food stamp program grew out of the contradictions of the Great Depression of the 1930s in which agricultural surpluses mocked the problems of rising unemployment, hunger, destitution, and falling farm incomes. The government's initial response of destroying agricultural commodities seemed unreasonable in light of growing poverty and hunger. The first food stamp program began in 1939 and continued until 1943 when the wartime boom had solved the unemployment problem, and agricultural surpluses were no longer accumulating.

The food stamp program was revived in the 1960s, partly because President Kennedy, when campaigning in West Virginia, had observed schoolchildren taking home leftovers from school lunches. Various pilot programs were put into operation until Congress enacted the Food Stamp Program Act of 1964. Later in the 1960s and early 1970s Congress increased the benefits and eased the eligibility requirements. At first food stamp recipients had to pay for the stamps, but in the 1970s the stamps became free.

To qualify for food stamps families must fall below certain income levels, after allowances are made for housing costs, childcare, etc. The lower a family's income, the more food stamps the family can receive.

In the 1970s and early 1980s food stamps became a sort of second-class currency in low-income neighborhoods. Although food stamps could legally be used only to purchase food, some merchants fudged and sold alcohol and other grocery store items for food stamps. On the streets food stamps are traded for cash, but at steep discounts. Individuals traded food stamps for cash and used the cash to purchase items that could not be purchased with food stamps.

Partly because of the fraudulent use of food stamps, the federal government during the Reagan years cut back on food stamp expenditures. The program remained in place, however, and the 1990s saw many states implement electronic benefit transfer programs that substituted a debit card for coupons. The use of the cards requires identification, rendering the transfer of food stamp benefits to parties other than the cardholder almost impossible. By 2002 all states are expected to have electronic benefit transfers.

Given that food items such as livestock, rice, corn, and many others have historically emerged as mediums of exchange, it should not be surprising that coupons redeemable in food should began to wear the aspect of money and circulate accordingly. Presumably, food stamp money will disappear in time because it involves an illegal use of food stamps, and the government will work to improve its regulation of the program.

See also: Commodity Money

References: Berry, Jeffrey, M. 1984. *Feeding Hungry People*. Weatherford, Jack. 1997. *The History of Money*. Weinstein, Steve. 1998. True Benefits. *Progressive Grocer* 77, no. 5 (May): 80–86.

Forced Savings

Forced savings refers to the use of money creation and inflation to divert resources into the production and acquisition of capital goods. A government that prints up money, as opposed to levying taxes or selling bonds, to pay for the construction of a hydroelectric generation facility is pursuing a policy of forced savings. Less-developed countries, particularly in Latin America, turned to forced savings policies in the post–World War II era as a means of financing economic development. At least some of the inflation in Latin America has its roots in economic development strategies based on forced savings.

The mechanics of forced savings operates through the medium of inflation. The government prints up money to purchase capital goods, attracting resources into the production of capital goods at the expense of consumer goods. Consumer goods production falls relative to demand, and consumer goods prices increase, reducing the amount of consumer goods that households can afford. This forced reduction in consumer goods acquisition translates as forced savings. Consumers still spend the same amount of money, it just does not stretch as far as it did before inflation. Thus the consumers do not come out with any more savings, but society does, because society is extracting resources for the production of capital goods. The forced reduction in consumer goods production is the key to forced savings.

Savings always involve a reduction in current acquisition of consumer goods. Ordinarily, households elect to divert a share of income away from consumption expenditures, and set that share of income aside as savings. Financial institutions and stock and bond markets channel these savings into businesses that need financing to purchase capital goods. Savings are always at the expense of consumption expenditures, but normally savings are a voluntary choice of households. Societies must save, that is, depress current consumption, in order to make resources available for the production of capital goods.

Economists and policy makers have advanced several arguments in favor of forced savings as an attractive vehicle for financing economic development. First, vast portions of the populations of less-developed countries live at the margin of subsistence, too poor to voluntarily engage in much saving. Second, many less-developed countries do not have the financial institutions necessary to mobilize the small savings of individual households. Third, wars have shown that governments can print up money to finance major public undertakings without destroying economic systems. The same effort that goes into financing a war can theoretically be tapped to finance industrialization.

Notwithstanding arguments favoring forced savings, the anti-inflation bias in current economic thinking emphasizes the downside of any policy that can only be activated with inflation. There has been no evidence of a correlation between inflation and growth, and many countries, such as Britain and the United States, experienced rapid economic development in the nineteenth century without inflation. Also inflation disrupts society and the burden of inflation is not evenly shared. Unionized workers can often strike and gain wage increases that compensate for inflation and some businesses may receive government aid that compensates for inflation. Other groups in society, those on fixed incomes or living on past savings, are likely to bear the bulk of the inflation burden. Inflation encourages households to invest voluntary savings in hedges against inflation such as land, buildings, jewelry, gold, silver, or stocks of grocery and household necessities. Investment in hedges against inflation diverts voluntary savings away from the purchase of capital goods such as factories, machinery, etc. After inflation has become expected, creditors extort high interest rates as inflation protection, further discouraging risk-bearing entrepreneurs from accessing sources of borrowed funds.

In countries that insist upon printing up money to finance government expenditures, forced savings strategies may make more sense than the acquisition of military goods, or the construction of lavish government buildings and monuments. Nevertheless, forced savings, because of its inflationary effects, entails major complications for the efficient operation of the economy, and seems to hold little charm for contemporary policy makers.

See also: Inflation and Deflation

References: Friedman, Milton. 1972. *Money and Economic Development.*
Hogendorn, Jan S. 1987. *Economic Development.*

Foreign Exchange Markets

Foreign exchange markets are markets in which national currencies are bought and sold with other national currencies. In a foreign exchange market U.S. dollars may purchase British pounds, German marks, French francs, Japanese yen, etc.

Prices of foreign currency are expressed as exchange rates, the rate at which one currency can be converted into another currency. On 12 March 1997 it took $1.59 to purchase a British pound in foreign exchange markets, or, alternatively 0.6256 British pounds could purchase one U.S. dollar. Exchange rates are reported daily in large metropolitan newspapers and financial papers such as the *Wall Street Journal.*

Foreign exchange markets are as old as coinage itself. In the ancient world religious temples were a popular site of foreign exchange markets because the sacredness of the grounds acted to safeguard treasuries of coin. The modern term *bank* evolved from the moneychangers' "bench" of the Middle Ages. Today modern communication and computers have made possible a worldwide integrated foreign exchange market where trades are conducted electronically 24 hours a day during the business week. The big players in the foreign exchange markets are the large commercial banks with foreign branches.

Under the current international monetary system, foreign exchange markets are highly competitive and exchange rates can change daily. (Between 1946 and 1971 the world was on a fixed exchange rate system, and exchange rates were pegged at certain levels by governments.) A supply of U.S. dollars is created in foreign exchange markets when Americans buy goods, or make investments, in foreign countries where dollars are not accepted. A demand for U.S. dollars is created in foreign exchange markets when the rest of the world wants to buy American goods, or make American investments, which require payment in dollars. Exchange rates fluctuate to balance supply and demand, clearing the market for U.S. dollars as foreign exchange. Markets for other currencies emerge in a similar fashion.

Exchange rates can exert strong influences on domestic economies. If the market value of the dollar appreciates relative to the Japanese yen—meaning it takes fewer dollars to purchase a yen—Japanese goods become cheaper to American consumers, increasing the importation of Japanese goods and reducing demand for domestic goods in competition with Japanese goods. If the market value of the dollar depreciates relative to the Japanese yen—meaning it takes more dollars to purchase a yen—Japanese goods become more expensive to American consumers, diminishing the importation of Japanese goods and making domestic goods more competitive. In summary, a depreciation of the dollar increases the demand for American-made goods, and an appreciation of the dollar decreases the demand for American-made goods.

Foreign exchange rates are quoted in spot rates and forward rates. The spot rate is the rate at which foreign currency can be purchased for delivery within two business days. A forward rate is the rate at which a foreign currency can be purchased for delivery after a length of time, such as 90 days. A forward market enables an American importer to strike a deal to import French goods and purchase French francs to pay for the goods when they arrive at some date in the future, protecting the importer from fluctuations in exchange that could make the goods much more expensive than expected.

Unless the world adopts a common currency, foreign exchange markets will remain a vital part of the international trade framework, the connecting link that allows trade between countries with different currencies. On 1 January 1999 Europe launched the *euro*, a European currency that will eventually replace German marks, French francs, Swiss francs, and other European currencies, and will abolish the need for foreign exchange markets to establish rates for the convertibility of one European currency into another. If the world follows the path of economic integration followed in Europe, then a world currency could become a reality some day. On the upside a world currency would remove the risk and uncertainty of exchange rate fluctuations that can disturb the flow of international trade, and promote trade between the regions of the world. On the downside a world currency would preclude the use of localized monetary policies to help specific areas. Currently, the Japanese economy is stagnant and the Bank of Japan is free to expand the Japanese money supply to stimulate the economy. If the world was on a worldwide currency system, and Japan was the only country suffering stagnation, world monetary authorities could not expand the money supply worldwide just to help Japan—and besides, increasing the money supply worldwide might not help Japan anyway.

See also: Balance of Payments, Gold-Specie-Flow Mechanism, Temple Moneychangers
References: Baye, Michael R., and Dennis W. Jansen. 1995. *Money, Banking, and Financial Markets*.
Daniels, John D., and Lee H. Radebaugh. 1998. *International Business*. 8th ed.
Daniels, John D., and David Vanhoose. 1999. *International Monetary and Financial Monetary Economics*.

Forestall System

The Forestall system of Louisiana banking regulation, established in the middle of a depression in 1842, was one of the most successful and influential systems of state banking regulations, establishing principles that became standard in banking regulation.

The Panic of 1837 had thrown the United States economy into a deep depression that lasted until 1843. The depression was sparked by President Andrew Jackson's Specie Circular, requiring that only gold and silver specie (coinage) be used to pay for land purchased from the government. The Specie Circular put the brakes on a land boom. Banks across the United States, including Louisiana, suspended payments, meaning they could no longer redeem their bank notes with specie. At that time each bank issued its own bank notes, in contrast to the current practice of issuing checking accounts. Louisiana boasted of nine commercial banks when the Forestall system was put in place. All nine banks had suspended payments.

Among the detailed regulations of the Forestall system was the requirement that customers' deposits could be loaned out only for 90 days. The capital contributed by bank owners was exempt from this limitation. These short-term loans could not be renewed, and the law required that banks publish the names of borrowers requesting renewals.

The Forestall system also forced banks to maintain specie reserves equal to 30 percent of their bank-note and deposit liabilities. The remaining 70 percent had to be backed by short-term commercial loans.

Amidst the Panic of 1857 an epidemic of payment suspensions spread through the United States. Thanks to the Forestall system, however, Louisiana banks were among the few banks that continued to make specie payments. Other state legislatures, noting the panic-proof resilience of the Louisiana banks, began to insist upon cash reserves. The reserve policy of Louisiana banks enabled them to continue to make remittances to their New York correspondents long after the Civil War had started.

The success of the Forestall system created a predilection for cash reserves in American banking regulation that remains an important element of national banking regulation today. Commercial banks in the United States are required to hold reserves either in the form of vault cash or deposits at a Federal Reserve Bank. Deposits at another financial institution, government bonds, or other forms of seemingly safe assets are not acceptable as legal reserves. The Federal Reserves System usually requires commercial banks to hold reserves that range between 10 to 20 percent of demand deposits.

See also: Federal Reserve System, Free Banking, New York
  Safety Fund System, Suffolk System
References: Cameron, Rondo, ed. 1972. *Banking and*
  Economic Development: Some Lessons of History.
Davis, Lance E., Jonathon Hughes, and Duncan M.
  McDougall. 1969. *American Economic History.*

Fort Knox

Fort Knox, a United States Army post, is the location of the largest United States gold bullion depository. Located about 31 miles southwest of Louisville, Kentucky, Fort Knox began as a post for army maneuvers in 1918 and was called Camp Knox. Its name was changed to Fort Knox in 1933. The post covers about 110,000 acres and is home to 57,000 residents. In addition to guarding the gold bullion depository, Fort Knox is famous for training armored divisions in the United States Army. Construction of the Fort

Knox Bullion Depository was finished in 1936. Because of the security surrounding the depository, which lies in the middle of the military base, Fort Knox has become a universal symbol of an impregnable store of wealth. No tourists are allowed on the military base.

Early in the Great Depression of the 1930s the United States nationalized privately owned gold, and devalued the dollar from $20.67 per ounce of gold to $35 per ounce of gold. The rise in the price of gold triggered an inflow of gold into the United States, and by 1939 the United States had swept into its vaults over half of the world's gold stock. The United States Treasury built the new gold depository at Fort Knox to help store its newly acquired gold treasure.

The Fort Knox Bullion Depository is a granite building constructed from 16,000 cubic feet of granite, 4,200 cubic yards of concrete, and 750 tons of steel for reinforcement. The legend United States Depository, engraved in gold, adorns a marble-lined entry, along with the gold seal of the Treasury Department.

Today the depository holds approximately 4,600 tons of pure gold with a market value of approximately $58 billion. The gold is stored in bars of 1,000 ounces each. Because gold does not deteriorate, gold in the vaults of Fort Knox could be hundreds of years old, probably including gold seized from the Aztecs and the Incas. Some of the gold that flowed into the United States from France in the 1930s was still in the wrappings that held the gold when the Jefferson administration had sent the gold to France to pay for the Louisiana Purchase. The United States government maintains smaller gold caches at West Point and in Denver.

The world's largest hoard of gold is not stored at Fort Knox. The Federal Reserve Bank of New York maintains an air-conditioned vault about 80 feet below street level in the bedrock of Manhattan Island, New York. This Federal Reserve vault holds about 11,000 tons of gold at a market value of about $176 billion, accounting for about a third of the gold reserves in Western economies. The gold mostly belongs to foreign governments and foreign central banks that store the gold in New York as a matter of convenience. Some of this gold was shipped over on the eve of World War II for security, but much of it European governments purchased from the United States during the 1950s and 1960s, but kept in the United States to spare shipping costs. In 1971 the

Benjamin Franklin's involvement in the printing trade likely contributed to his interest in paper money. (Library of Congress)

United States stopped redeeming dollars presented by foreign governments into gold.

See also: Gold, Gold Exchange Standard, Gold Reserve Act of 1934, Gold Standard
References: Green, Timothy. 1981. *The New World of Gold.* Marx, Jennifer. 1978. *The Magic of Gold.* Weatherford, Jack. 1997. *The History of Money.*

Fractional Reserve System of Banking
See Bank, Monetary Multiplier

Franklin, Benjamin (1706–1790)

In addition to filling the roles of diplomat, newspaper publisher, inventor, scientist, and signer of the Declaration of Independence, Benjamin Franklin, perhaps the most American of the American revolutionaries, was a tireless advocate of paper money in the American colonies. As early as 1729 he wrote a pamphlet, *A Modest Enquiry into the Nature and Necessity of a Paper Currency,* and continued to advance proposals for paper money as an answer to economic ills that afflicted the colonies. Perhaps the same practical turn of mind that led Franklin to invent the lightning rod, bifocal glasses, and the Franklin stove also led him to take up the currency problems of the colonies, and seek answers in paper money schemes. By the time of Franklin's death, and owing partly to his efforts, North America had experimented with more paper money issues than any other part of the world up to that time. Even today the United States 100-dollar bill bears an engraved portrait of Benjamin Franklin, symbolizing his long association with paper money in the United States.

The young Franklin apprenticed himself to the trade of printer, and in later years was publisher of the *Pennsylvania Gazette.* Franklin's pamphlet on paper currency helped secure approval of a proposal continuing the issuance of paper money in Pennsylvania, paving the way for Franklin to receive the task of printing the paper money, which he described as "a very profitable job, and a great help to me." Franklin's involvement in the printing business may have favorably disposed him toward paper money.

The Colony of Pennsylvania had created a land bank that issued paper money as loans against real estate and precious metal plate. In 1765 British government officials asked for proposals to raise revenue from the American colonies in the least objectionable way. Parliament enacted the infamous Stamp Act to help service wartime debt and pay part of the expense of defending the colonies. Franklin argued forcibly with the British government for his "paper money scheme," which would generate income from loans and at the same time supply the American colonies with a continental currency. Franklin wanted the English government to establish a loan office that would make loans secured by real estate. The interest-paying loans would be taken out as paper money issued under the authority of the British government, infusing the American colonies with much-needed money and raising revenue for the British government. According to Franklin, an annual interest rate would act as a general tax, but not "an unpleasing one." This paper money would have been legal tender for public debts, including repayment of loans to the land bank. If England had adopted Franklin's plan rather than the Stamp Act, perhaps history would have taken a different turn.

Franklin was noted for conservative philosophy in financial matters, and famous for sayings such as "A penny saved is a penny earned," and "Early to bed and early to rise makes a man healthy, wealthy, and wise," and "God helps them that help themselves." That Franklin's philosophy of thrift, honesty, and commerce could embrace the concept of paper money should have been taken as unerring signal that paper money was the wave of the future. Nevertheless, history has held up many examples showing that the abuses of paper money are harmful of the virtues that Franklin preached.

See also: Land Bank System
References: Ernst, Joseph Albert. 1973. *Money and Politics in America, 1755–1775.* Weatherford, Jack. 1997. *The History of Money.*

Free Banking

Free banking was a trend toward a highly decentralized monetary system that originated in Scotland and in the early nineteenth century, appeared on a modest scale in England, and developed on a wider scale in the United States, beginning in 1838 and ending with the National Banking Act in 1864.

Before the era of free banking, bank charters were granted for political favors, regarded as matters of political patronage. Rising inflation from 1834 to

A two-dollar certificate of deposit issued by the Clinton Bank, New York. (Smithsonian Institution, National Numismatic Collection)

A two-dollar note, issued by the City Trust and Banking Company of New York in 1839, promised to pay the bearer on demand nine months after date of issue.

1837, followed by a money panic and a rash of bank failures, elevated public concern about privilege and political corruption in the banking system. New York acted first with the Free Banking Act of 1838. This act allowed any person or group of persons to obtain a bank charter who could meet capitalization criteria requiring that bank notes be 100 percent backed with mortgages and state bonds, plus an extra 12.5 percent in gold and silver specie. The reserves of gold and silver specie enabled bank customers to count on redemption of bank notes in gold and silver, and when banks failed the state sold the mortgages and state bonds to compensate bank customers.

About 18 states adopted free banking laws similar to the New York act. They usually allowed anyone, without political connections, to deposit suitable financial securities with a state banking authority, receive a bank charter, and make loans and discount bills by issuing their own bank notes.

Free banking was not the only solution to the crisis of confidence in banks. In 1845 the fledgling state of Texas completely outlawed banks in its first constitution, and by 1857 four other states had enacted similar legislation.

The success of the free banking system depended on a delicate balance of state regulation and freedom of enterprise. A certain amount of chaos ensued. Bank notes circulated from defunct banks, and "wildcat" banks established in remote areas issued bank notes that would never be redeemed in specie. Some scholars argue that by the eve of the Civil War state regulation had began to shape the free banking system into a workable and orderly system.

Free banking aroused fears of inflation because there was no one entity regulating money supplies, and the perplexing assortment of bank notes, trading at different discounts, hampered trade between regions. The development of the national banking system during the Civil War ended the free banking era in the United States.

During the 1970s the slow progress of the monetary authorities toward taming inflation brought a renewed interest and attention to the free banking system. Under a properly regulated free banking system, bank notes remain convertible into a precious metal currency, but there is no central bank regulating the total national money supply. In the 1970s and 1980s scholars developed theoretical models of free banking systems that maintained convertibility of bank notes into commodities such as gold and silver. These modes functioned without a central bank and much of current banking regulation. These scholars saw the free banking system as preferable to the so-called stop-and-go policies of the Federal Reserve System. The interest in free banking faded as the Federal Reserve showed more progress combating inflation.

See also: Central Bank, National Bank Act of 1864, Second Bank of the United States, Wildcat Banks

References: Rockoff, Hugh. 1975. *The Free Banking Era: A Reexamination.*

Rolnick, Arthur J., and Warren E. Weber. 1983. New Evidence of the Free Banking Era. *American Economic Review* 73, no. 5 (December):1080–1090.

Dowd, Kevin. 1996. *Competition and Finance: A Reinterpretation of Financial and Monetary Economics.*

Free Silver Movement

The free silver movement was a populist movement in the United States during the last quarter of the nineteenth century. "Free silver" meant that silver could be brought to the mint and struck into coins without a seigniorage charge; that is, without taking any of the precious metal to pay mint expenses. Also, the amount of silver that could be brought to the mint was to be unlimited. Before 1873 anyone who brought 3.7125 grains of silver to the mint could re-

ceive a legal-tender silver dollar, and the campaign for free silver fought for a return of these conditions.

Between the mid-1830s and 1873 the market price of silver exceeded the mint price of $1.29 cents per ounce; therefore, very little silver found its way to the mint. Silver dollars had largely disappeared from circulation when Congress enacted the Coinage Act of 1873, an act that made no provision for the coinage of silver, and put the United States on an unofficial gold standard. Proponents of free silver later condemned the act as the "Crime of '73."

The deletion of the silver dollar drew little attention at the time, but the United States was already in the clutches of a deflationary downswing that would last three decades. From 1870 until 1896 prices plunged 50 percent, a deflationary wave that hit hard at farmers in the West and South, where debt incidence stood at high levels. These groups quite rightly saw that a return to free and unlimited coinage of silver would raise the domestic money stock, raise prices, and reduce their debt burden. Much of the populist flavor of the free silver movement came from the hopes it lifted among large numbers of low-income farmers.

Silver prices felt an added deflationary force because the world was rushing toward a gold standard that left little role for silver as a monetary metal. Major silver discoveries in the American West further depressed the market for silver. From 1850 until 1872 the market price of an ounce of silver stood above $1.32, clearly above the mint price, but the price had slipped to $1.24 by 1874, and from there it tumbled to $0.65 by 1895. Silver-mining interests in the United States saw free silver as a way of increasing the demand for silver, and putting a floor under silver prices. They would have been delighted to sell silver to the Treasury for $1.29.

The free silver proponents achieved limited success in Congress. On 28 February 1878 Congress enacted, over a presidential veto, the Bland-Allison Act, which required the Treasury to coin between $2 million and $5 million worth of silver per month. The bill had begun as a free silver bill but had been amended to restrict the amount of silver the Treasury purchased. In 1890 the Sherman Silver Act required the Treasury to purchase $4 million of silver per month, and issue silver certificates. The Sherman Silver Act was blamed for sparking a crisis of confidence in the American monetary system, and

Nero (the Fifty-Fourth Congress) plays the fiddle (free silver) while the nation burns in this 1896 cartoon. (Library of Congress)

Europeans began withdrawing gold from the United States. President Cleveland, a staunch advocate of the gold standard, prompted Congress to repeal the silver purchase provisions of the Sherman Silver Act.

The silver controversy loomed as a major issue in the presidential election of 1896, coinciding with the nadir of the 30-year deflationary wave. William Jennings Bryan won the Democratic nomination after his famous "Cross of Gold" speech, denouncing the gold standard, and defining himself as the free silver candidate. Bryan lost the election and in 1900 the United States went squarely on the gold standard.

About this time the book *The Wizard of Oz* came out as a monetary allegory of the issues raised by the free silver movement. Bryan ran for president again in 1900, but prices were inflating, and the silver issue was losing its punch. Bryan lost again, and he would run again in 1908 without success.

The free silver movement died out with the return of prosperity at the turn of the century. The silver-mining interests, however, continued to exert a disproportionate share of power into the twentieth century. Until the 1960s dimes, quarters, and half dollars contained 90 percent silver. Treasury silver stocks fell as the industrial demand for silver grew and by 1970 the half dollar was silverless.

See also: Bimetallism, Crime of '73, "Cross of Gold" Speech, Wizard of Oz

References: Friedman, Milton. 1992. *Money Mischief: Episodes in Monetary History.*
Nugent, Walter T. K. 1968. *Money and American Society, 1865–1880.*

French Franc

The French *franc* is the monetary unit of account in France, just as the U.S. dollar is the monetary unit of account in the United States. It was the first decimalized currency system in Europe, except for Russia.

French francs were first coined in 1803. Before the decimalized franc was introduced, the French currency system was based upon the Carolingian system, in which 1 *livre* equaled 20 *sols,* which in turn equaled 240 *deniers.* In 1793 the French revolutionary government decided to replace the Carolingian system with a decimal system. In 1795 the livre was replaced with a franc equaling 100 *centimes.* These changes meant little amidst revolutionary chaos, but Napoleon's government began striking francs based on the new system in 1803.

The French Monetary Law of 1803 put the franc on a bimetallic system with the silver to gold ratio, per unit of weight, equal to $15^1/_2$ to 1. Coin pieces of 5 francs and less were struck in silver, and gold coins came in denominations of 20 francs and 40 francs. One franc equaled 5 grams of silver. The smallest denomination coin authorized by the act was a quarter franc. During the wars of the French Revolution and Napoleon France imposed its new currency system on conquered states. In 1798 France reorganized the freshly conquered Switzerland as the Helvetian Republic with a unified currency system in which 1

Swiss franc equaled 10 *batzen,* which in turn equaled 100 *rappen.* With the downfall of Napoleon the Swiss threw off their imported currency system, but in 1850 they readopted the French system voluntarily. The Netherlands had also seen the French system imposed from without, but abandoned it in 1814. When Belgium won its independence from the Dutch in 1830 the Belgians reestablished the French system. Italy adopted the French system in 1861, but named its money of account the *lira* rather than the franc. One lira equaled 1 franc. Under different names, the French system became the basis of currencies in Greece, Spain, Rumania, Bulgaria, and Finland. Although the British pound sterling dominated international trade in the nineteenth century, the French franc was the most influential currency in Western Europe.

By the beginning of the nineteenth century, France had acquired a horror of inflation from two firsthand experiences. The hyperinflation of the French Revolution was still a fresh memory, further bolstering French resolve to maintain the stability and integrity of the franc. The French maintained the metallic content of the franc for 125 years. During the Napoleonic Wars the franc experienced milder fluctuations than the pound sterling, perhaps because Napoleon's war indemnities helped supply the gold and silver to maintain the franc's parity. France suspended convertibility of the franc in Revolution of 1848 and during the Franco-Prussian War of 1870–1871. Following the Revolution of 1848 convertibility was resumed in 1850 and during the whole episode the franc had only depreciated mildly. After the Franco-Prussian War France was burdened with heavy war reparations and the political situation was clouded by the episode of the Paris Commune, which put Paris under the control of working-class revolutionaries. Nevertheless the franc fluctuated only within a narrow range, and convertibility was resumed in 1878.

In 1865 France, Italy, Switzerland, and Belgium formed the Latin Monetary Union, which fought to preserve a unified, bimetallic monetary system in the face of the growing prestige of England's gold standard. Declining silver prices made the bimetallic standard untenable, and France abandoned silver in 1873. By 1878 France was officially on the gold standard.

Under the gold standard the franc lost a bit of its reputation for soundness. The French authorities were hesitant to allow an outflow of gold, and insisted upon their right to pay out badly worn 10-franc gold coins and 5-franc silver coins. All European countries effectively suspended the gold standard during World War I, but the franc emerged from the war weaker than the pound sterling and suffered speculative attacks. In 1926 the franc stabilized at about one-fifth prewar parity. From 1927 until 1931 the franc was undervalued and the pound sterling overvalued, putting an end to speculative attacks on the franc. With the onset of the Great Depression, England, Japan, and the United States devalued their currencies, leaving the franc overvalued. The Gold Bloc countries, mainly consisting of members of the old Latin Monetary Union, clung to the gold standard and France, the leading member, remained on the gold standard until 1936. After World War II the franc went through a series of official devaluations under the Bretton Woods fixed-exchange regime, the last occurring in 1968.

During the post–World War II era, the West German mark rose to become the preeminent European currency, partly because West Germany, compared to England and France, kept inflation subdued. In the 1990s France tamed its inflation and the German mark was buffeted by the turmoil of merging the two Germanys. As a consequence the French franc regained some lost ground as one of the leading European currencies. In May 1998 members of the European Union announced plans to launch a European currency, called the *euro,* to replace the individual national currencies, including the French franc and the German mark.

See also: Decimal System, Deutsche Mark, Dollar, Monetary Law of 1803, Pound Sterling, Swiss Franc

References: Caron, Francois. 1979. *An Economic History of Modern France.*

Einzig, Paul. 1970. *The History of Foreign Exchange.* 2d ed.

Kindleberger, Charles. 1984. *A Financial History of Western Europe.*

Weatherford, Jack. 1997. *The History of Money.*

French Livre
See Bank of France, Bronze Standard of Ancient Rome, Carolingian Reform, French Franc, French Revolution Hyperinflation

French Revolution Hyperinflation
The famous English economist John Maynard Keynes, commenting upon an observation of Lenin, wrote:

> Lenin is said to have declared that the best way to destroy the Capitalist System was to debauch the currency. Lenin was certainly right. There is no subtler, no surer means of overturning the existing basis of society than to debauch the currency. The process engages all the hidden forces of economic law on the side of destruction. And does it in a manner which no one man in a million is able to diagnose. (Keynes, 1920)

No doubt Lenin and Keynes were familiar with the role of inflation during the French Revolution.

In October 1789 the French National Assembly found itself in a desperate situation. Tax revenue fell far short of expenses, and the government survived day by day with advances from the Bank of Discount, a bank that largely loaned funds to the government. The bank declared itself out of funds, and the assembly needed resources to complete the Revolution. The assembly met the financial crises with two important and interrelated measures. It confiscated church lands and it created an "extraordinary treasury" charged with raising 400 million *livres* by selling *assignats,* which were certificates of indebtedness bearing 5 percent interest. The government announced its intention to sell the church property and take assignats in payment. The church property in effect served as collateral for the assignats.

The assignats met with less than a hearty reception because it was not clear which lands would be sold to creditors. In August 1790 the assembly turned assignats into bank notes and added an extra 800 million livres to the issue. The decree specified that the total number of assignats in circulation should never exceed 1,200 million livres. The new assignats bore no interest and could be acquired by anyone, whereas the first issue was available only to creditors of the government. Instead of just liquidating the national debt, the government took to issuing assignats to pay for deficit spending.

By mid-1792 the inflation horse was definitely out of the barn; prices rose 33 to 50 percent while wages lagged far behind. In January 1793 a mob stormed stores in Paris and in February a scarcity of

A two-thousand-franc note issued during the French Revolution. (Smithsonian Institution, National Numismatic Collection)

soap sparked further riots. Mobs also obstructed grain shipments. In 1794 the government implemented a system of price controls known as the Law of the Maximum. People who refused to accept assignats in payment or accepted them (or paid them) at a loss, could be fined 3,000 livres and imprisoned six months for the first offense. The fine and imprisonment could be doubled for the second offense. Speculation in specie and assignats could bring six years' imprisonment, and forestalling was punishable by death. A forestaller was a person who withheld necessary commodities from circulation. Nevertheless, farmers and manufactures hoarded goods, and the specter of famine rose up for the spring. In December 1794 the government abandoned price controls, prices soared, and assignats fell to less than 3 percent of their face value.

The Convention, the governing body at that stage of the Revolution, acknowledged the fall of the assignats in June 1795. The nominal value of each successive issue was reduced according to a scale of proportions. In July of the same year the Convention ordered in-kind payments for half of the land tax and rents. Peasants stopped bringing produce to market to avoid accepting assignats. Speculation became rampant while inflation ruined creditors and

savers. As prices outpaced wages and workers suffered, speculative profits created a new class of ostentatious rich who stood in stark contrast to the destitution of the lower classes. Prices outpaced wages and workers suffered. Inflation reached its peak as the Directory took power. Each day saw prices rise hourly, and each night paper money came off the press for issuance the following day. Paper money issues doubled in four months, for a total of 39 billion livres in assignats.

In February 1796 the Directory discontinued the assignats. It tried an issue of land warrants, which were good for the purchase of national property at an estimated price without competitive bidding. The sale would be to the first taker. The public had lost faith in paper money, however, and in July 1796 the government decided to return to specie. Inflation continued to ravage the economy until the advent of Napoleon in 1799. Apparently, his wars brought in more than they cost and his government improved the efficiency of taxation, ending the government's need to promiscuously print paper money.

Since the experience of the French Revolution, hyperinflation has been associated with revolutionary change. It played a role in the rise of Hitler to power in Germany, the Communist Revolution in

Like precious metals and shells, fur served more than ornamental purposes. (Smithsonian Institution, National Numismatic Collection)

China, and the Bolshevik Revolution in Russia. The American Revolution also had a hyperinflationary episode.

See also: American Revolution Hyperinflation, German Hyperinflation, Inflation and Deflation, Russian Revolution Hyperinflation

References: Harris, S. 1930. *The Assignats.*
Keynes, John Maynard. 1920. *The Economic Consequences of Peace.*
Lefebvre, Georges. 1964. *The French Revolution.*
Paarlberg, Don. 1993. *An Analysis and History of Inflation.*
Theirs, M. A. 1844. *The History of the French Revolution.*

Fur Money

Not surprisingly, the most northern and coldest countries of the world have made use of furs as a medium of exchange and store of value, particularly among the societies that advanced beyond the barter stage.

The most highly developed system of fur currency existed in medieval Russia, where the word for money was *kuna,* stemming from the skin of the marten *(kunitza).* The marten is a close relative of the sable, and its soft, thick, valuable fur is called sable. The use of fur currency stretched as far back as the eighth century A.D. The grand dukes of Moscow furnished furs to pay traveling expenses of ambassadors sent to foreign countries. Russian law codes from the eleventh and twelfth centuries suggest a fixed ratio between fur currency and silver coins. These codes made fines payable either in 5 metal kuna or two skins.

At first skins had to be complete to be acceptable in trade, including snouts and paws. As the demand for money expanded with trade, snouts, claws, and ears functioned as money. Eventually one-inch circles of skin with a government stamp met the need for a medium of exchange. These one-inch stamped circles may have been convertible in whole skins at a government depot, but the evidence is scanty.

Squirrel skins and hare skins also circulated as money, at least in certain areas. The smallest of the early Russian coins, the *polushka,* got its name from hare-skin currency. *Ushka* was the Russian word for "hare skin," and *pol* meant half, suggesting it took two *polushka* coins to equal one hare skin.

The *kuna* monetary standard endured in Russia until late in the Middle Ages, lasting until 1409 in Pskov and until 1411 in Novgorod. Merchants of the Hanseatic League in Novgorod accepted Russian fur currency as an instrument of trade.

As Russia phased out its fur currency in favor of metallic currency, the northern colonies of the New World discovered the value of furs as a form of money. In 1673 the Council of Quebec decreed that bearskins be accepted in payments. On 17 September 1674 the same council defined moose skins as acceptable money, declaring that "no one is entitled to refuse them in payment of debt." The records of the Hudson Bay Company show that furs continued to serve as money until the mid-nineteenth century. The company would sell a rifle to an Indian for a stack of beaver skins that reached as high as the rifle was tall. Twenty beaver skins bought a horse at Fort Saskatchewan in 1854, and one beaver skin a scalping knife. The various trading posts of the Hudson Bay Company counted their sales in terms of the number of beaver skins they collected, converting the values of other skins to beaver equivalents at a fixed ratio. Other skins have also served as money. The district of the Yukon used the skin of a mature land otter as a unit of value before beaver skins took over.

Furs shares many of the characteristics of other commodities that societies have recognized as money. Like precious metals and shells, furs sometimes met ornamental needs. Beaver skins also had religious significance for some Indian tribes. Also, furs resembled livestock in supplying the practical needs of survival in northern societies often besieged by harsh winters. These characteristics, combined with durability and ease of transportation, made furs a workable currency in remote areas where metallic currency was in short supply.

See also: Commodity Monetary Standard, Leather Money

References: Del Mar, Alexander. 1899. *History of Money in America.*

Einzig, Paul. 1966. *Primitive Money.*

G

GDP Deflator
See Value of Money

German Hyperinflation
The German hyperinflation of the early 1920s stands as a constant reminder of the monetary insanity lurking beneath the surface of modern systems of money and banking. The German money supply grew during and after World War I. In June 1914 the German marks in circulation stood at 6,323 million, but by December 1918 the number of marks in circulation had grown to 33,106 million. Prices over the same time span more than doubled. Germany had financed the war largely by monetizing government debt rather than raising taxes or borrowing in capital markets.

After the armistice in 1918 German marks in circulation continued to expand and by December 1921 German currency in circulation stood at 122,963 million marks. Prices then were slightly over 13 times the 1914 level. Prices now began to catch up with money growth. By June 1922 German marks in circulation had risen to 180,716 million, but prices were now over 70 times the 1914 level. The Reichsbanks abandoned all pretense of monetary control as marks in circulation rose to 1,295,228 million by December 1922. By June 1923 the number had increased to 17,393,000 million.

After June 1922 price increases broke into runaway inflation. By December 1922 prices stood at 1,475 times their 1914 level, and prices stood 19,985 times their 1914 level by June 1923. Prices were ris-

A Berlin woman starts the morning fire with German marks, as it is cheaper than buying fuel. (Library of Congress)

ing so fast that workers were paid at half-day intervals and rushed to spend their wages before they lost their value. Customers at restaurants would negotiate prices in advance because prices could change before the meal was served. Grocery shoppers rolled to the store wheelbarrows laden with sacks of

A German note for 500 million deutschmark issued shortly after World War I. (Smithsonian Institution, National Numismatic Collection)

money, which was also balled up and used for fuel. Prices continued to rise into November 1923. A newspaper that sold for 1 mark in May 1922 rose in price to 1,000 marks in September 1923. By 17 November 1923 the same newspaper sold for 70 million marks.

In December 1923 the money supply and prices stabilized. The German government reformed its monetary affairs, issuing a new unit of currency called the *rentenmark,* equal to 1 trillion marks. The new currency was issued by the Rentenbank, which replaced the Reichsbank as the note-issuing bank. The only asset of the new bank was a mortgage on agricultural and industrial land, and the paper money issue of the new bank was strictly limited.

The inflation began with the stress of wartime finance. After World War I Germany needed to restock its warehouses with imported raw materials and pay war reparations. This led to an outflow of German marks and a depreciation of the German mark in foreign exchange markets. This depreciation caused inflation in the prices of imports, and the inflation spread to the rest of the economy. The Reichsbank kept the money supply rising faster than prices to ward off unemployment. The French occupation of the Ruhr aggravated the matter considerably. The German government encouraged passive resistance, banned reparation payments, and printed money to pay striking miners. The French blockaded the area and Germany lost the tax revenue.

The German experience with hyperinflation was the most spectacular the world had seen. Since World War II Germany can boast of one of the best records for controlling inflation of any advanced industrialized country. In the book *Economic Consequences of Peace* (1920) John M. Keynes saw the inflation trends and commented:

> By a continuing process of inflation, the governments can confiscate, secretly and unobserved, an important part of the wealth of their citizens.... While the process impoverishes many, it actually enriches some. The sight of this arbitrary rearrangement of riches strikes not only at security, but at confidence in the equity of the existing distribution of wealth.

Many observers blame the episode of German hyperinflation for creating the political conditions that led to the rise to power of Hitler. Partly because of the German experience, modern societies consider price stability an important ingredient of social stability.

See also: American Revolution Hyperinflation, French Revolution Hyperinflation, Inflation and Deflation, Russian Revolution Hyperinflation

References: Paarlberg, Don. 1993. *An Analysis and History of Inflation.*

Parsson, Jens D. 1974. *Dying of Money: Lessons from the Great German and American Inflations.*

Webb, Steven B. 1989. *Hyperinflation and Stabilization in Weimar Germany.*

Ghost Money

During the late medieval period, money units of account arose that did not correspond to real or tangible pieces of money or coin. Some historians have labeled as "ghost" money units of account without real counterparts. Some of the ghost money owed its origin to coins that were minted in the past, but were no longer minted or found in circulation. Two important units of account, however, the pound and the shilling, began as ghost money.

King Pepin the Short of France, father to Charlemagne, decreed that a pound weight of silver be struck into 240 *pennies*. He also introduced the shilling as a unit of account equal to 12 pennies, comparable in value to the popular Byzantine *solidus*. In the Carolingian system, one pound equaled 20 shillings or 240 pennies. The only coin that was actually minted for several centuries, however, was the penny, and the pound and shilling remained only money units of account or ghost money. Rather than recording 2,400 pennies in a ledger, or pricing a good at 2,400 pennies, merchants found it much easier to write 2 pounds. The silver weight of pennies dropped in time but a pound remained the equivalent of 240 pennies, losing all connection with a pound in weight of silver. The shilling was also a money unit of account for several centuries. England minted its first shilling during the 1500s.

In 1252 Milan began minting gold florins equivalent to 120 pennies. Perhaps because of the debasement of pennies, the value of the florin rose to 384 pennies and remained at that value for 60 years. A ghost florin emerged that was equal to 384 pennies, meaning that a florin came to signify 384 pennies. Later the value of the real florin rose to 768 pennies, leaving a real florin at twice the value of the ghost florin. Venice and Genoa developed ghost money in a similar fashion.

In Florence the florin also established itself, after a period of stability, at a rate of 384 pennies, another ghostly multiple unit of account. The Florentines, however, kept the real florin as a unit of account, and

made the penny a ghost penny equal to 1/384 florin, and the shilling, also a ghost, 1/29 florin.

The subject of ghost money touches on an issue always important to debtors and creditors—the stability of the purchasing power of a unit of money. Debtors invariably prefer contracts expressed in depreciating units of account, while creditors prefer contracts expressed in a stable coin. Put differently, debtors in Milan preferred to pay off debts in ghost florins rather than real florins. Creditors wanted to receive payment in real florins. Depreciating units of money and ghost monies created the same divergence of interest of debtors and creditors as found in modern societies suffering inflation.

See also: Carolingian Reform

References: Chown, John F. 1994. *A History of Money.*

Cipolla, Carlo M. 1956. *Money, Prices, and Civilization in the Mediterranean World.*

Evans, A. 1931. Some Coinage Systems of the Fourteenth Century. *Journal of Economics and Business History* 3.

Glass-Steagall Banking Act of 1933 (United States)

The Glass-Steagall Banking Act, more than any other piece of banking legislation, shaped the development of the current banking system in the United States. One of the numerous acts of economic reform passed in the first 100 days of Franklin Roosevelt's administration, it sought to revive confidence in the banking system and reduce bank competition for depositors' money.

In 1931 the position of banks in the United States caught the attention of the eminent economist John Maynard Keynes, who described it as the weakest element in the whole situation. Suspensions of deposit redemptions by banks had been averaging about 634 banks per year before the depression, already a high level. The banking crisis deepened with the onset of the economic crisis. Depositors pulled money out of banks, sometimes sending it abroad, sometimes hoarding it in homes. Gold reserves declined. From 1929 to 1933 over 5,000 banks suspended redemption of deposits. One-third of all U.S. banks failed during the depression. President Hoover saw the banks as a victim of a crisis in confidence. To prevent panic from spreading, President Roosevelt in March 1933 ordered all banks to close for a week.

On June 16 1933 the Glass-Steagall Banking Act

became the law of the land. To help restore confidence in banks, the act banned deposit banks from engaging in investment banking. Investment banks buy newly issued stocks and securities from corporations and resell them to the public for a profit, playing a key role in marshaling capital corporations. After the stock market crashed, banks that had invested depositors' money in stocks had no way to recover their investment and were forced into bankruptcy. The ban on investment banking remains in effect today, but has been weakened by innovations in the organization of the banking industry, and many people in Congress think it should be repealed. This divorce between deposit banking and investment banking does not exist in many countries, including Germany, France, Switzerland, and the United Kingdom.

The Act also gave the Federal Reserve System the power to regulate interest rates on savings and time deposits. This provision, known as Regulation Q, helped keep the cost of funds down for financial institutions. Another provision of the Glass-Steagall Banking Act prohibited interest-earning checking accounts. The payment of interest on checking accounts increased bank competition for deposits. This added competition might have driven some banks into bankruptcy. The deregulation of financial institutions in the 1980s phased out Regulation Q and removed the ban on checking accounts that pay interest.

The Federal Deposit Insurance Corporation (FDIC) owes its existence to the Glass-Steagall Banking Act. This corporation insures deposits from bank failure up to a maximum limit. All banks that are members of the Federal Reserve System must buy deposit insurance from the FDIC. Today virtually all commercial banks insure deposits with the FDIC. After the savings and loan crisis in the 1980s, the FDIC took over responsibility for furnishing deposit insurance to the thrift institutions. Deposit insurance helps maintain the public's confidence in the banking system.

Large numbers of bank and thrift failures during the 1980s showed that financial institutions remained vulnerable to disinflation and recession. The Glass-Steagall Banking Act went a long way toward instilling resiliency and public confidence in the banking system.

See also: Depository Institution Deregulation and Monetary Control Act of 1980, Federal Reserve System

References: Baye, Michael R., and Dennis W. Jansen. 1995. *Money, Banking, and Financial Markets: An Economics Approach.*
Schlesinger, Arthur M., Jr. 1960. *The Age of Roosevelt.*

Goat Standard of East Africa

John Maynard Keynes in Volume 1 of his *Treatise on Money,* published in 1930, says that:

A district commissioner in Uganda today, where goats are the customary native standard, tells me that it is a part of his official duties to decide, in cases of dispute, whether a given goat is or is not too old or too scraggy to constitute a standard goat for the purposes of discharging a debt.

Often goats shared with cattle the role of currency, a store of value, and standard of deferred payment in Uganda well into the twentieth century. Like many livestock standards, the rate at which goats and cattle could be traded for each other was fixed. The goats circulated more easily in subsistence economies and were often used to buy weapons and salt. Goats could be loaned out for interest; a chief might send a herd of goats to be kept by his subjects, and receive every third kid born to the herd as interest. The government also fixed fines payable in goats.

In Tanzania 25 goats were equivalent to 1 cow or ox, and 1 goat equaled 1 hoe. The exchange rate between goats and oxen varied between districts. The Masai rated 1 ass at 5 goats, an iron spear at 2 goats, and a big cattle bell or a small ax at 1 goat. They also paid bride money in goats.

In equatorial Africa goats often served as a store of value and a standard of deferred payment, but not a medium of exchange. Bride money was paid in goats and sheep; in order for a man to marry, he had to be able to borrow goats and sheep.

Societies living closer to the threshold of survival found food items useful as money because food was what everyone needed, and a large share of each individual's activity was devoted to securing food. Therefore food items were an obvious choice as a readily acceptable medium of exchange. The problem with much food, such as grain, was that it was perishable, hampering its usefulness as a store of value, one of the important functions of money. Livestock not only made excellent food, but also reproduced, solving the problem of perishability, and even earning a crude form of interest. Therefore livestock could serve both as a medium of exchange and a store of value. Because livestock could be counted on to maintain their value, creditors preferred to define debts in terms of livestock. Livestock shared with other commodities one important defect as a medium of exchange. The quality of livestock varied because of age and health and people invariably sought to repay debts with inferior animals, creating conflicts of the sort referred to in the quotation from John Maynard Keynes. Also livestock are often bulky and difficult to transport.

Livestock money is not necessarily a symptom of primitive economics and culture. Remote areas often suffer shortages of coins and other forms of money and turn to commodities as a medium of exchange. The American colonies resorted to commodities as money at a time when the world economy was flush with supplies of precious metals from the New World. The Massachusetts Bay Colony enacted a law for cattle being driven to Boston for payment of taxes, providing "if they be weary, or hungry, or fall sick, or lame, it shall be lawful to rest and refresh them for a competent time in any open place, that is not corn, meadow, or inclosed for some particular use" (Nettels, 1934).

See also: Cattle, Commodity Monetary Standard
References: Einzig, Paul. 1966. *Primitive Money.*
Nettels, Curtis P. 1934. *The Money Supply of the American Colonies Before 1720.*

Gold

Gold, the most enduring, highly valued, and universally accepted monetary metal, is a chemical element represented by the symbol "Au" on the periodic table. A lustrous yellow metal, soft and malleable, gold does not tarnish or corrode, and is found in nature in a relatively pure form. From earliest times up to the present, the search for gold in nature has remained a never-ending quest. Man's earliest chemical researches were inspired by a desire to find a means of converting other metals into gold.

Because it did occur in pure form, gold was one of the first metals that drew man's attention, but it was too soft to be a practical metal for making weapons and farming tools. As a metallic medium for artistic work, however, gold had no rivals and elaborate artistic productions in gold rank among the most prized relics of antiquity.

Gold's role as a monetary metal probably has its

roots in the perception, widespread in ancient cultures, that gold was a divine substance. That gold suffered no deterioration with time and that its color resembled the color of the sun may have encouraged the belief that gold was a sacred substance. Gold adornments were a necessary part of religious temples, further underlining the connection between gold and the gods.

The ancient Egyptians held gold to be sacred to Ra, the sun god, and vast quantities of gold went into the tombs of the divine pharaohs. A religion of ancient India taught that gold was the sacred semen of Agni, the fire god, and Agni's priests accepted gold as a gift for priestly services. The Incas of South America saw gold and silver as the sweat of the sun and the moon, and these precious metals adorned the walls of their religious temples. After the Spaniards took the Indians' gold and silver the natives substituted foil paper, and threw gold and silver-colored confetti into the air. The Maya of the Yucatan threw gold, silver, and jade sacrifices into their gods' cenotes. (The cenotes were deep pools of water formed when a limestone surface collapsed.)

The legend of El Dorado propelled Spain into one of the greatest searches in history, ending with the exploration and conquest of much of the Americas. El Dorado was the name of an Indian who ruled a town near Bogota, Colombia. According to legend, El Dorado celebrated festivals by plastering his body with gold dust, and plunging himself into Lake Guatavita at the end of the festival to wash off the gold, and make the gold a gift to the gods. His subjects also threw gold and other valuables into the lake. The legend of El Dorado grew, and the Spanish, Portuguese, and German explorers went in search of the golden Eldorado, a city in a land fabulously rich in gold. El Dorado himself was never found, but Eldorado came to mean a land of gold populated by several cities rich in gold. The English explorer Sir Walter Raleigh went in search of one of these cities.

Because gold was always in demand as a religious donation or sacrifice, it had an unlimited demand and was always valued. It was an excellent store of value because it did not tarnish or corrode, and it was divisible into units of any size, making it useful for exchanges of varying magnitudes, and making change. The high value of gold per unit of weight made gold more transportable than other commodities that might serve as money. For these reasons, gold became the basis for the most famous commodity standard in history, the gold standard, a monetary standard that dominated the world monetary system from the 1880s until 1914.

See also: Fort Knox, Gold Dust, Gold Rushes, Gold Standard
References: Green, Timothy. 1981. *The New World of Gold.*
Marx, Jennifer. 1978. *The Magic of Gold.*
Weatherford, Jack. 1997. *The History of Money.*

Gold Bullion Standard

Under a gold bullion standard, countries hold reserves of gold in the form of bars rather than coins, removing gold from monetary circulation in the form of coinage. Instead each country establishes an official price of a fixed weight of gold in terms of its own currency. The United States was on a gold bullion standard from the 1930s until 1971, and the official United States price of gold was $35 per ounce, committing the United States Treasury to selling gold at that price.

The gold bullion standard was a means of stretching existing supplies of gold, which were not sufficient to support the international monetary system at prevailing price levels. The famous British economist David Ricardo had first suggested the idea after the Napoleonic Wars.

Under a gold bullion standard, private citizens can only hold gold for industrial purposes, such as dentistry or jewelry manufacture. Monetary gold is owned by the government and is used solely to settle international transactions. Countries without substantial gold reserves can function on a gold exchange standard, while countries with significant gold reserves remain on a gold bullion standard.

The world began to move toward a gold bullion standard after World War I, when the world's trading partners sought to return to a version of a gold standard. With the complete breakdown of the gold exchange standard in the 1930s, the world moved toward a gold bullion standard. The gold bullion standard allowed countries to manage domestic currency supplies somewhat independently of international gold flows, giving governments more flexibility to meet the crisis of depression.

At the end of World War II the world's trading partners established the Bretton Woods system, putting most nations on a gold bullion standard. The United States emerged from World War II owning most of the noncommunist world's gold. Under the Bretton Woods system, the United States defined the value of the dollar in a fixed weight of gold. The United States agreed to buy and sell gold at a rate of $35 per ounce, and most other nations set the value of their own unit of money equal to a certain value in U.S. dollars.

The post–World War II gold exchange standard came to an end in 1971 when the United States stopped converting dollars into gold. By 1971 foreign central banks held more dollars than the United States could redeem in gold without substantially devaluing the dollar.

See also: Bretton Woods System, Gold Exchange Standard, Gold Reserve Act of 1934
References: De Vries, Margaret Garritsen. 1987. *Balance of Payments Adjustment, 1945–1986: The IMF Experience.*
Kindleberger, Charles P. 1984. *A Financial History of Western Europe.*

Gold Dust

During the Alaskan gold rush gold dust became a circulating currency in parts of Alaska. Silver coinage and other small coinage was nonexistent, so in its place little packets of gold dust, sealed in writing paper similar to medicine powders, passed as current money. The packets contained a fixed weight of gold dust, and the value of the enclosed gold was written on the outside of each packet. The packets came in popular denominations, such as one-dollar or two-dollar denominations, and some of the packets were known to circulate for two years.

The Alaskan gold dust currency demonstrates how societies will identify a medium of exchange when nothing else is available, but gold dust currency has a long history. In the tenth century the Japanese began circulating bags of gold dust. Later Japanese merchants began wrapping gold dust in small paper packets. The units were the *ryo,* the *bu,* and the *shu.* The bags of gold dust equaled about 10 *ryo.* After learning that a certain amount of gold dust seeped from the opened end of the bag, the Japanese began melting down the gold dust into gold bars. In the nineteenth century the people of Tibet used as currency gold dust by weight.

For part of the nineteenth century gold dust was virtually the only metallic money in Ghana. A farthing's worth of gold could be scooped up on the tip of a knife, and an ounce of gold dust equaled three to four British pounds. The government received taxes in gold dust and employed special weighing scales that gave an advantage to the government.

In the eighteenth and nineteenth centuries gold dust by weight circulated as money in the islands in and around the Indonesian Archipelago. As early as the sixteenth century gold dust acted as currency in the Philippines. The gold-producing districts of Siam made use of gold dust as currency into the twentieth century. In nineteenth-century Siam, a tube of gold dust, 10 centimeters long and the diameter of a thumb, could purchase a buffalo. Some Malayan tribes packed gold dust of uniform weight in pieces of cloth, and circulated these cloth packets as coins.

Africa also furnished examples of gold dust by weight circulating as currency. In Arguin of Spanish Sahara, on the west coast of Africa, an ancient Arabic unit of weight, the *mitkhal,* survived as a unit of weight of gold dust. The mitkhal was a monetary unit of account, but it does not appear that gold dust circulated as money on a significant scale. For a while gold dust by weight was the favored medium of exchange in the Ivory Coast.

See also: Gold, Gold Rushes, Gold Standard
References: Einzig, Paul. 1966. *Primitive Money.*
Stuck, Hudson. 1932. *Ten Thousand Miles with a Dog Sled.* 2d ed.

Gold Exchange Standard

Under a gold exchange standard a nation's unit of money is convertible at an official rate into a unit of money of a pure gold standard nation—that is, a nation that maintains the convertibility of its unit of money into gold at an official rate.

A gold exchange standard became a popular monetary standard after World War I when many nations could not marshal the gold reserves to support a gold standard. In 1922 Britain proposed at a Genoa conference the adoption of an international monetary system organized with major nations holding reserves only in gold and the remaining nations holding reserves in foreign currencies. Governments (or central banks) would hold reserves to redeem domestic currencies at official rates as a means of guaranteeing currency value. Although the adoption of an international monetary system failed to materialize from the Genoa conference, many countries individually went on a gold exchange standard. Nations of the British Commonwealth often defined their currencies in terms of the British pound. Other nations defined their currencies in terms of the currencies of nations they were dependent upon politically. The gold exchange standard of the post–War World I era ended when the world's major trading partners abandoned the gold standard early in the 1930s.

Critics of the gold exchange standard following World War I and World War II contend that it encouraged dominant nations to incur balance of payments deficits as a method of infusing the rest of the world with additional monetary reserves. Britain ran balance of payments deficits in the post–World War I era and the United States ran balance of payments deficits under the Bretton Woods system. A balance of payments deficit allows a nation to buy goods and investments from the rest of the world with payment in domestic currency never used to claim domestic goods. Historically, the gold exchange standard helped the world maintain the discipline of a gold standard when world supplies of gold were not keeping pace with the need for international monetary reserves.

See also: Gold Standard, Gold Standard Act of 1925, Gold Standard Amendment Act of 1931
References: Kindleberger, Charles P. 1984. *A Financial History of Western Europe.*
McCallum, Bennett T. 1989. *Monetary Economics: Theory and Policy.*

Gold Mark of Imperial Germany

The gold *mark* of Imperial Germany, the ancestor to the *Deutsche Mark,* burst upon the world in 1871 with the adoption of the gold standard in imperial Germany.

Before "iron and blood" (John Maynard Keynes in the *Economic Consequences of Peace* [1920]) forged the German Reich in 1871 from 30 loosely confederated independent states, Germany was split into seven separate currency areas. Six of the areas were on a silver standard and one was on a gold standard. Soon after the Zollverein, the German customs union, first began to emerge in 1818 pressures arose for a unified German coinage and monetary system. In 1837 southern members of the Zollverein established the *gulden* or *florin,* equivalent to $^1/_{24.5}$ Cologne mark of silver, as a common monetary unit. Northern members in 1838 responded with the adoption of the Prussian *thaler,* fixed in value at $^1/_{14}$ Cologne mark of silver, as a common unit of currency. The Dresden convention fixed the exchange ratio at 4 thalers to 7 gulden. In 1857 the members of the Zollverein and Austria formed a coinage union that replaced the Cologne mark of silver with a *Zollpfund* (customs union pound) of 500 grams. The Zollpfund was equivalent to 30 thalers, 52 $\frac{1}{2}$ South German florins, or 45 Austrian florins, with each currency unit convertible to the other at the fixed ratio. Austria dropped out in 1866, leaving two rival monetary units, the thaler and the gulden, competing for the monetary hegemony of the members of the Zollverein. German commercial interests continued to push for a unified monetary system based upon one currency rather than multiple currencies trading at fixed exchange rates.

Following the formation of the Reich in 1871 the German government enacted monetary reform that put Germany on the road to the gold standard, and establishment of the mark as the money unit of account. The mark had been a money of account on the Hamburg exchange, equivalent to one-third a Prussian thaler. On 4 December 1871 the German Reichstag enacted monetary legislation, the first three sections of which read:

> Sec. 1. There shall be coined an imperial gold coin,
> 139 $\frac{1}{2}$ pieces of which shall contain one pound of pure gold.
> Sec. 2. The tenth of this gold coin shall be called a "mark" and shall be divided into one hundred "pfennige."
> Sec 3. Besides the imperial gold coin of 10 marks (Sec. 10) there shall be coined imperial gold coins of 20 marks, of which
> 69 $\frac{3}{4}$ pieces shall contain one pound of pure gold. (Laughlin, 1968)

On 9 July 1873 the Reichstag took action that officially put Germany on a gold standard. The first section of the act read: "Sect. 1. In place of the various local standards now current in Germany, a national gold standard will be established. Its monetary unit is the 'mark,' as established in Sec. 2 of the law dated December 4, 1871" (Laughlin, 1968).

A war indemnity that Germany extracted from France after the Franco-Prussian War helped furnish the gold reserves that enabled Germany to adopt the gold standard. Germany also began selling silver to bolster its gold holdings. Either Germany correctly saw the coming of the gold standard, and was only acting in step with the times, or perhaps the commercial success of England had elevated the prestige of the gold standard in the eyes of Germany.

At the time of Germany's monetary reform, England and Portugal were the only countries on a gold standard, which is why Germany's action was of an extraordinary nature. The gold standard became virtually universal in Europe between 1875 and 1880. The United States went on a de facto gold standard in 1879, Austria-Hungary adopted the gold standard in 1892, and Russia and Japan in 1897. The era from 1875 until 1914 is regarded as the golden era of the gold standard.

The mark of imperial Germany lasted until the monetary reform that followed Germany's episode of post–World War I hyperinflation. In 1923 the *Rentenmark* replaced the mark at a rate of 1 rentenmark to 1,000 million marks. In 1924 Germany enacted another monetary reform that replaced the rentenmark with the *Reichmark,* and after World War II the reichmark was abolished in favor of the *Deutsche Mark.* In the post–World War II era the deutsche mark of the Federal Republic of Germany became the strongest currency in Europe. The new European currency, the *euro,* launched 1 January 1999, will eventually replace the German mark, the French franc, and other major European currencies, if present plans are realized.

See also: Gold, Gold Standard
References: Chown, John F. 1994. *A History of Money.*
Kindleberger, Charles P. 1984. *A Financial History of Western Europe.*
Laughlin, J. Laurence. 1968. *The History of Bimetallism in the United States.*

Gold Reserve Act of 1934 (United States)

The Gold Reserve Act of 1934 nationalized all monetary gold in the United States. Only the Treasury could own gold and buy and sell gold. The act also limited the power of the president to reduce the gold weight equivalent of a dollar, and the day after the passage of the Gold Reserve Act President Roosevelt fixed the gold equivalent of the dollar at $35 per ounce of gold, where it remained until 1971.

The act also established a stabilization fund of $2 billion, put at the disposal of the secretary of the Treasury, to support the purchase and sale of foreign currencies as needed to stabilize the value of the dollar.

The groundwork for the enactment of the Gold Reserve Act began with the banking crisis in March 1933 that led President Roosevelt to suspend banking operations for four days. Before banks were reopened the government required that all commercial banks turn over to the Federal Reserve System all gold and gold certificates and furnish lists of all persons who had withdrawn gold or gold certificates since February 1. The Federal Reserve issued Federal Reserve Notes in exchange for gold and gold certificates. The export of gold and speculation in foreign exchange was banned and one month later individual ownership of gold and gold certificates was likewise banned. The Treasury purchased privately held gold in the United States at a price of $20.67 per ounce, the price that had prevailed with few fluctuations for 100 years. The value of the dollar on foreign exchange markets depreciated 15 percent when the U.S. dollar was no longer redeemable in gold.

The World Economic and Monetary Conference, held in London during June and July 1933, sought to forge an agreement for the stabilization of international currencies and the eventual return to an international gold standard. Even members of the United States delegation could not agree among themselves, and President Roosevelt undermined the conference by announcing that the United States would manage its monetary policy to meet the needs of its domestic economy rather than fulfill conditions set for international monetary cooperation.

Abandonment of the gold standard in the United States aroused fears of inflation, inspiring references to the French Revolution and post–World War I Germany. Nevertheless, there were voices of support. Winston Churchill, responding to the United States' severance from the gold standard, called the action "noble and heroic sanity." On 3 July 1933 John Maynard Keynes responded to Roosevelt's announcement in an article (with the headline "President Roosevelt is magnificently right"), referring to the new law as a challenge to us to decide whether we propose to tread the old unfortunate ways, or to paths new to statesmen and to bankers but not new to thought. For they lead to the managed currency of the future" (Schlesinger, 1959).

Churchill later observed, perhaps overstating the case:

The Roosevelt adventure claims sympathy and admiration from all who are convinced that the fixing of a universal measure of value not based upon rarity or abundance of any commodity but conforming to the advancing powers of mankind, is the supreme achievement which at this time lies before the intellect of man. (Schlesinger, 1959)

The Treasury began, through the New Deal era Reconstruction Finance Corporation, to purchase gold domestically and later in international markets, driving up the price of gold in dollars, which effectively devalued the dollar in terms of gold. As the price of gold was rising Roosevelt fixed the price officially at $35 per ounce. The increase in the dollar price of gold substantially increased the value of the government's gold holdings, creating a windfall profit for the government that supplied funds for the Treasury's stabilization fund and later for the U.S. contribution to the World Bank and International Monetary Fund.

In the 1970s the United States government stopped selling gold to foreign central banks at $35 per ounce, ending the fixed exchange rate between dollars, gold, and foreign currencies. The price of gold was allowed to fluctuate freely, and the ban on the domestic ownership of gold was lifted.

See also: Bretton Woods System, Gold, Gold Standard, Gold Standard Amendment Act of 1931
References: Chandler, Lester V. 1971. *American Monetary Policy, 1928–1941.*
Myers, Margaret G. 1970. *A Financial History of the United States.*
Schlesinger, Arthur M., Jr. 1959. *The Coming of the New Deal.*
Schwartz, Anna J. 1997. From Obscurity to Notoriety: A Biography of the Exchange Stabilization Fund. *Journal of Money, Credit, and Banking* 29, no. 2 (May): 135–153.

Gold Rushes

Nineteenth-century gold discoveries sparked gold rushes—manias that rival, if not eclipse, the major speculative crazes that periodically rock financial markets. England adopted the gold standard following the Napoleonic Wars, and the United States was on a de facto gold standard after 1834. The discovery of gold in California in 1848 and in Australia in 1851 increased the world's monetary gold reserves from 144 million pounds sterling in 1851 to 376 million

MINES D'OR DE LA CALIFORNIE.

DESCRIPTION DU PAYS.

La Californie est un pays d'une grande étendue. C'est une presqu'île bornée au nord par la terre ferme dont elle fait partie, à l'est par la province du nouveau Mexique et le golfe de Californie ou mer Vermeille qui la sépare du continent, sur la partie méridionale, et au sud et à l'ouest par la mer Pacifique. Elle a 600 lieues de longueur ou 267 myriamètres, et dans divers endroits 40, 80, 120 et 160 kilomètres de largeur. C'est Cortès qui découvrit cette vaste péninsule. Les Indiens qui habitent ces contrées ont embrassé le christianisme, ils ont une grande douceur de caractère, et ils sont d'une grande probité. Il est rare même qu'il se commette un meurtre parmi eux. La population de la presqu'île est évaluée à 500,000 habitants. Ce pays est très-abondant en gibier, en poissons de toutes espèces. La fertilité du sol dépasse toute idée. Le froid n'y est jamais grand et les chaleurs y sont tempérées. Ce pays est très-abondant en mines d'or, on y fait la pêche de perles fines sur ses côtes. La Californie appartient aux Etats-Unis.

DÉCOUVERTE DES RICHES MINES D'OR DE SACRAMENTO EN CALIFORNIE.

Sur la fin de Février 1848, un ouvrier nommé James Marshall travaillait à construire une scierie sur l'embranchement d'une petite rivière, Américan-Forck, à 50 milles environ du fort de Sutter, où il travaillait aux fondations, lorsqu'il découvrit tout-à-coup des morceaux d'or qui brillaient au soleil; il les retira de l'eau, ils étaient d'un volume considérable. Donnant encore quelques coups de pioche, il en rencontra d'autres et en quelques jours il en réalisa pour de très-fortes sommes. Le bruit de cette découverte se répandit aussitôt, tous les habitants se mirent à la recherche de ce métal précieux, et on en trouva depuis cette époque pour plus de 500 millions de francs. L'or est mêlé à la terre dans des endroits, dans d'autres il roule avec le sable dans les ruisseaux et les rivières. Le colonel Masson cite en son rapport que deux hommes en ont recueilli en quelques journées pour 17,000 dollars (le dollar vaut 5 fr.) Un fermier ayant fait travailler durant quelques jours, a réalisé un bénéfice de 17,000 dollars. Un ouvrier ne travaille pas à moins de 20 dollars par jours. On peut voir, par cette relation véridique puisée aux meilleurs renseignements, que ces mines abondantes ouvriront une nouvelle voie au commerce et à l'industrie. Aussi des navires se frètent-ils de tous côtés pour porter en ces contrées lointaines des productions de toutes espèces et rapporter en retour ce métal précieux qui donnera l'activité à nos fabriques et qui développera de plus en plus l'industrie qui est la vraie mine d'or de la France.

Air: Bon voyage, M. Dumolet.

Courez vite !
Une mine d'or
A l'exploiter, bons Français, vous invite ;
Courez vite !
Une mine d'or
A pour vous tous dans sou sein un trésor.

I.
Vers ce beau ciel où Dieu vous accompagne,
Partez joyeux, ne prenez aucun soin.
Dans ce pays, vrai pays de cocagne,
L'or du Pérou tiendrait un petit coin.
Courez vite ! etc.

II.
Fermez les yeux et laissez-vous conduire ;
Là, l'on ne boit qu'ambroisie et que miel ;
Lorsque chez nous il faut les faire cuire,
Là, les oiseaux tombent rôtis du ciel.
Courez vite ! etc.

III.
Là, l'ouvrier, plus que millionnaire,
Sous sa chaussure a pour clous des rubis ;
Là, l'indigent, vrai mylord d'Angleterre,
A plus d'écus qu'un banquier de Paris.
Courez vite ! etc.

IV.
Là, les fauteuils sont rembourrés d'hermine,
De doux ressorts sauront vous y bercer ;
Là, sur le sol payé de mousseline,
Jamais piéton ne craint de se blesser.
Courez vite ! etc.

V.
Une liqueur digestive et légère,
Du gastronome aiguisant l'appétit,
Vingt fois par jour lui permet bonne chère
Car il se vide aussitôt qu'il s'emplit.
Courez vite ! etc.

VI.
Dans ce pays le blé croît sans semence,
L'hiver est chaud comme chez nous l'été ;
Huit fois par an la moisson recommence,
L'arbre fleurit le jour qu'il est planté.
Courez vite ! etc.

VII.
Là, ce n'est plus un bonheur d'être riche ;
Là, chaque endroit brille comme un miroir ;
L'or pleut partout, et loin d'en être chiche,
On n'y tient plus, à force d'en avoir.
Courez vite ! etc.

VIII.
Mais tous ces biens de la Californie,
Français, ne sont pas toujours le bonheur ;
On est heureux aussi dans sa patrie,
Quand l'ambition ne dévore pas le cœur.
Courez vite ! etc.

Fabrique d'Images de DEMBOUR et GANGEL, à Metz, et à Paris, rue Serpente, 7

The California gold rush was an international sensation, as this French broadside by Dembour & Gangel makes clear. (Art Resource) pounds sterling in 1861, a increase of 161 percent over a 10-year period. The gold discoveries enabled the United States to become an official gold standard country, and supplied the monetary reserves for the world to adopt the gold standard in the last quarter of the nineteenth century. Following the gold discoveries, a silver monetary standard became the mark of a low-income country.

On 4 January 1848 James W. Marshal found gold on land in California owned by a Swiss man named Sutter. The discovery occurred nine days before the United States signed a treaty with Mexico making California, New Mexico, Arizona, Nevada, and Utah part of United States territory. The secret soon leaked out—not in time to prevent the signing of the treaty—and gold fever infected the residents of San Francisco and Monterey, most of whom went straight to the gold mines, leaving their houses empty. Workers left employers and employers decided to join their workers mining for gold. Soldiers deserted and ship captains were afraid to make port for fear that sailors would leave for the gold mines. Some ships lay stranded in harbors, deserted by sailors who took up prospecting. The population of California had increased to 92,560 by June 1850, a sixfold increase. By November 1852 the population stood at 269,000 and by 1856 the population had topped half a million. Wages at unheard-of levels lured immigrants, who were content to leave the actual mining to others and take jobs as cooks or fill other skilled positions. Of course, the price of life's necessities also soared.

The repercussions of the Australian gold discoveries were a bit mild compared to the California experience. An emigrant who had already prospected in California began in 1851 searching for gold in the Northern Bathurst region of Australia, an area geologists believed to contain gold. Gold was discovered, but the mines were scattered, a factor that—coupled with a well-established sheep industry—blunted the demographic effects of the strike.

Something of the effect of these gold discoveries can be gleaned from the words of Karl Marx, who in 1859 mentioned in the preface to his *Contribution to the Critique of Political Economy* that the gold discoveries were a factor encouraging him to continue his studies of capitalism. He wrote:

The enormous material on the history of political economy which is accumulated in the British Museum; the favorable view which London offers for the observation of bourgeois society; finally, the new stage of development upon which the latter seemed to have entered with the discovery of gold in California and Australia, led me to the decision to resume my studies from the very beginning and work up critically new material. (Vilar, 1976)

The late 1890s saw another round of gold discoveries. America's monetary gold stock more than doubled between 1890 and 1900, thanks to discoveries in Alaska and northeast Canada, South Africa, and Australia. A new cyanide process for extracting gold from low-grade ores also added to gold production.

In 1896 gold was discovered in the Klondike area of Canada, along the Yukon River, on a scale comparable to the California gold discoveries. Twelve dollars worth of gold could be separated in a dish full of sand. Thirty thousand prospectors, crossing a mountain range in Arctic conditions, arrived after a heroic trial of endurance that could match the hardships of any expedition or human migration in history. Dawson City was born, where miners held out against disease and starvation, and salt fetched its weight in gold. Gold was found in other provinces, and Canada became the world's third-largest gold producer.

Under the gold standard a shortage of monetary gold stocks led to falling prices between 1875 and 1895, making gold that much more valuable. As prices fell the scramble for gold increased in intensity. Gold discoveries eased monetary tightness, allowing prices to rise, reducing the value of gold and the intensity of the search for gold.

See also: Gold, Gold Dust, Gold Standard
References: Benton, Pierre. 1954. *The Golden Trail.*
Green, Timothy. 1982. *The New World of Gold.*
Littlepage, Dean. 1995. *The Alaska Gold Rush.*
Vilar, Peter. 1976. *A History of Gold and Money, 1450–1920.*

Gold Standard

Under a gold standard, the value of a unit of currency, such as a dollar, is defined in terms of a fixed weight of gold and bank notes or other paper money are convertible into gold accordingly. Although the monetary systems of individual countries have been based on the gold standard at times, all the economically advanced countries of the world were on the gold standard for a relatively brief time—roughly from 1870 to 1914, sometimes called the period of the classic gold standard.

The coinage of gold dates back to 700 B.C. in the Mediterranean world, and it continued during the Roman Empire. Gold coinage disappeared from Europe during the Middle Ages, but during the thirteenth century Florence popularized gold coinage among Italian cities. The influence of the Italian cities seems to have brought the practice of gold coinage to England, where it caught on, particularly after the mid-fourteenth century. Charles II introduced a new English gold coin called a *guinea* in 1663. From England gold coinage then spread to the rest of Western Europe.

At the opening of the nineteenth century, no European country was on a gold standard or had developed a gold standard system. England and other countries coined both gold and silver and set the conversion ratio at which gold could be exchange for silver. England was still officially on a sterling silver standard, but in the eighteenth century the English government overvalued gold relative to silver, causing an outflow of silver and an inflow of gold and lifting gold to a position of preeminence in England's monetary system.

In normal times banks redeemed paper money out of reserves of specie (precious metal coinage), but during the wars with revolutionary France and Napoleon, the Bank of England suspended the redemption of its bank notes in specie. After Napoleon's defeat in 1815, Parliament turned its attention to the resumption of specie payments, and passed the Coinage Act of 1816. This act placed England definitely on the gold standard, while the rest of Europe remained on a silver or bimetallic standard. In 1819 Parliament passed the Act for the Resumption of Cash Payments, which provided for the resumption by 1823 of the convertibility of Bank of England bank notes into gold specie. By 1821 the gold standard was in full operation in England. Except for England, most countries operated bimetallic systems until the 1870s. Under a bimetallic system both gold and silver coins circulated as legal-tender mediums.

The English banking system evolved toward the use of Bank of England bank notes as reserves for commercial banks, and the Bank of England became the custodian of the country's gold reserves. The Bank of England learned to protect its gold reserves by adjustments in interest rates, using its bank rate and open market operations to raise interest rates and stem an outflow of gold. Higher interest rates attracted foreign capital that could be converted into gold, and lower interest rates had the opposite effect. Low interest rates were the natural results of a gold inflow.

By the end of the 1870s France, Germany, Holland, Russia, Austro-Hungary, and the Scandinavian countries were on the gold standard. The bimetallic system became awkward because official conversion ratios between gold and silver often differed from the ratio that existed in the precious metals market. Gold discoveries in California and Australia flooded markets for precious metals and gold began to replace silver as the circulating medium in France and other European countries. The wars and revolutions of the mid-nineteenth century again forced governments into issuing inconvertible paper money. Governments often restored convertibility by establishing the gold standard. If the gold standard had a golden age, it was between 1870 and 1914, when it acted as a brake on the issuance of paper money. If prices in Country A rose faster than prices in Country B, residents of A would start buying more goods from Country B. Gold would flow out of Country A into Country B, increasing the money supply in Country B and decreasing it in Country A. These money supply changes lowered prices in Country A and raised prices in Country B. These adjustments restored equilibrium, eliminating the need for further gold flows, and stabilizing prices at an equilibrium level.

World War I brought an end to the gold standard, partly because the export of gold was not feasible after 1914, and partly because governments wanted the freedom to print extra paper money to finance the war effort. The end of World War I set the stage for an international scramble for gold as countries tried to reestablish national gold standards. Britain and France kept their currencies overvalued in terms of gold, hurting the competitiveness of their export industries in foreign markets and causing recessions at home.

The economic debacle of the 1930s spelled the end of the gold standard for domestic economies. Governments wanted the freedom to follow cheap money policies in the face of severe depression. The

United States Gold Reserve Act of 1934 authorized the United States Treasury to buy and sell gold at a rate of $35 per ounce of gold in order stabilize the value of the dollar in foreign exchange markets. This legislation laid the foundation for the world to return to the gold standard for international transactions after World War II. The value of the dollar was fixed in gold, and the value of other currencies was fixed in dollars. The system only became fully operational after World War II, when most countries lifted bans on the exportation of gold. This gold exchange standard for international transactions remained in effect until 1971.

In 1971 the United States, after experiments with devaluation, suspended the conversion of dollars into gold as the only means of stemming a major outflow of gold. Abandonment of the gold standard preceded the strong worldwide surge of inflation in the late 1970s, and critics attributed the inflation to the loss of discipline provided by the gold standard. The inflation of the 1970s can be attributed to many factors, such as shortages of important commodities, powerful unions, monopolistic pricing, and undisciplined monetary growth.

Most economists see the gold standard as a relic of history. In the absence of the gold standard, governments and monetary authorities enjoy more flexibility to adjust domestic money stocks to meet the needs of domestic economies. The experience of the 1980s and 1990s suggests that countries can control inflation without the gold standard.

See also: Dollar Crisis of 1971, Gold Standard Act of 1900, Gold Standard Act of 1925, Gold Standard Amendment Act of 1931

References: Bordo, Michael D., and Forrest Capie. 1993. *Monetary Regimes in Transition.* Davies, Glyn. 1994. *A History of Money.*

Gold Standard Act of 1900 (United States)

The Gold Standard Act of 1900 put the United States for the first time explicitly on the gold standard, removing all traces of the bimetallic standard based upon gold and silver. The United States remained on a gold standard until 1933.

The world's major trading partners had been moving toward the gold standard since England adopted the gold standard in 1821. Portugal adopted gold as its standard in 1854, even making British sovereigns legal tender, and Canada went on the gold standard in 1867. After Germany adopted a gold standard in 1873 silver began to lose ground as a monetized commodity. The United States and France ended free minting of silver soon after Germany acceded to a gold standard. Austria-Hungary adopted a gold standard in 1892 and Russia and Japan did so in 1897.

In 1873 the United States ended free minting of silver in legislation that provoked no controversy at the time, but later social protest and silver interests kept the United States on a limited bimetallic standard. The uproar inspired a book, *The Wizard of Oz,* a monetary allegory of the advantages of monetized silver. The proponents of silver wanted to return to the free minting of silver, meaning that the Treasury stood ready to buy silver at $1.29 per ounce, above the then-prevailing world market price of silver. A return to a policy of free minting of silver would have increased domestic money supplies and eased the burden of a world trend of deflation that was making itself felt in the United States. At the Democratic Convention in 1896 William Jennings Bryan, referring to the enemies of silver and proponents of a gold standard, exclaimed: "You shall not press down on the brow of labor this crown of thorns, you shall not crucify mankind upon a cross of gold."

Bryan lost the presidential election to William McKinley, who favored a gold standard but was slow to take action, knowing that feelings ran high on the issue. The Spanish-American War galvanized public support for McKinley and shifted the issues that held the attention of the voting public. On 14 March 1900, five days before the next Democratic Convention, McKinley signed the Gold Standard Act. Bryan, renominated as the presidential nominee of the Democratic Party, launched a vigorous campaign, again favoring free minting of silver, but lost a second time. McKinley's reelection seemed to ratify the adoption of the gold standard in the United States.

Probably, increased world production of gold, and particularly increased United States gold reserves, accounts for the United States becoming the most powerful convert to the gold standard. Early in the 1890s the United States exported gold to the rest of the world, but late in the 1890s an excess of exports over imports changed the United States to an importer of gold. A substantial increase in tariffs on imported goods may have caused the trade surplus, coupled with a general revival of the world economy. Also, world supplies of gold rose significantly, partly due to new discoveries in Alaska, Africa, and Australia and partly due to a new cyanide process that made lower-grade ores a profitable source of gold. The annual world output of gold grew from 5,749,306 ounces in 1890 to 12,315,135 ounces in 1900, and the United States' monetary gold stock doubled over the same interval.

The act unequivocally defined the value of the dollar in terms of gold alone, without reference to another metal. The dollar was defined as equal to "twenty-five and eight-tenths grains of gold nine-tenths fine." Responsibility for maintaining parity fell to the secretary of the Treasury. No gold certificates were to be issued under $20, and silver remained as a subsidiary coinage and currency, with 90 percent of silver certificates remaining under $10.

The act also set up a system of reserves for national banks and substantially reduced the amount of capital needed to establish a national bank. These measures had the expected effect of increasing the quantity of bank notes in circulation, which rose from $349 million in 1901 to $735 million in 1913. These measures were also intended to make the supply of bank notes more elastic as the needs of trade varied. The elasticity of the currency, or lack thereof, remained a source of economic instability, leading to the establishment of the Federal Reserve System in 1913.

The United States remained on the gold standard until 1933 when the United States government, facing the debacle of the Great Depression, needed more flexibility in its handling of monetary matters. Like many governments around the world at that time, the United States government felt that a domestic money supply, completely uncoupled from domestic gold supplies, could be adjusted as needed by the Federal Reserve System to meet the needs of trade.

See also: Gold Standard, Gold Reserve Act of 1934

References: Davies, Glyn. 1994. *A History of Money*.
Hepburn, A. B. 1924. *A History of Currency in the United States*.
Myers, Margaret G. 1970. *A Financial History of the United States*.

Gold Standard Act of 1925 (England)

The Gold Standard Act of 1925 returned England to the gold standard after the disruption of World War I, signaling the beginning of a new gold standard era that lasted until 1931.

England's commercial supremacy and financial leadership had secured the gold standard as the international monetary standard between the 1870s and 1914, the years of the classic gold standard. If there was a headquarters for the international gold standard, it was England, and the return of England to gold after World War I was anxiously awaited.

England had not officially gone off the gold standard during World War I, but the risk of transporting gold under wartime conditions effectively put an end to the convertibility of pounds into gold. After April 1919 the export of gold was strictly prohibited except for freshly mined gold imported from other parts of the empire.

To study the financial aspects of postwar reconstruction the British government in 1918 had appointed a committee, soon called the Cunliffe Committee after its chairman, Lord Cunliffe, governor of the Bank of England. Nine of the 12 members of the committee were traditional bankers, perhaps accounting for the deflationary recommendations of the committee. From the outset the Cunliffe Committee assumed that England should return to the gold standard, and that the value of the pound should be fixed at its prewar value. The recommendations of the committee were phased in over a 10-year period, including the return to the gold standard in 1925.

Wartime inflation had continued at the war's end, lifting the 1920 price level threefold higher than the 1913 price level. In 1920, however, the postwar boom hit the skids, and by 1922 prices were less than twice the 1913 price level. The bout of deflation was temporary but prophetic, and the Cunliffe Committee would have done well to heed the warning.

With the help of loans from the Federal Reserve Bank of New York and a United States banking syndicate, England returned to the gold standard. The ban on the export of gold was lifted and the Gold Standard Act of 1925 made the pound convertible into gold at prewar parity. Unlike the classic gold standard of the prewar years, gold coins no longer circulated domestically, and the public could only convert Bank of England bank notes into gold bars. To meet the needs of international finance the Bank of England could have gold minted into gold coins, but the English public could not demand the convertibility of bank notes into gold coins.

Perhaps the fateful mistake of the act was the return of the pound to its prewar value. The pound needed to depreciate to enhance the competitiveness of English exports in foreign markets, and to diminish the competitiveness of imported goods in English markets. England's industry could not compete with German industry and industry from other parts of the world. England's economy settled into a sluggish recession, marked by militant labor-management clashes, struggling along until the more devastating collapse occurred in the 1930s.

The Bank of England had to keep domestic interest rates up to make the pound valuable in foreign markets, restricting the desire to convert pounds into gold, and keeping England in possession of its gold reserves. But domestic economic problems limited the ability of the Bank of England to raise domestic interest rates to protect its gold reserves. A conflict between the need to improve domestic economic conditions and the need to support the pound put the Bank of England in a difficult position. In 1931 the conversion of pounds accelerated, causing a drain on England's gold reserves. The English government suspended its gold standard with the Gold Standard Amendment Act of 1931. England, and the world's trading partners, never returned to domestic gold standards after the debacle of the 1930s. Later in the 1930s a gold standard for international transactions was established, lasting until 1971.

See also: Gold Exchange Standard, Gold Standard, Gold Standard Amendment Act of 1931, Gold Reserve Act of 1934

References: Feavearyear, Sir Albert. 1963. *The Pound Sterling.* 2d ed.

Kindleberger, Charles P. 1984. *A Financial History of Western Europe.*

Moggridge, D. E. 1969. *The Return to Gold, 1925.*

Gold Standard Amendment Act of 1931 (England)

The Gold Standard Amendment Act of 1931 is a rather euphemistic title for an act that marked the end of the international gold standard. The gold standard had provided the world with a stable monetary system from the 1870s until 1914, and was regarded as the ideal monetary system in the aftermath of World War I. In the pre–World War I era, Britain had been the major proponent and custodian of the gold standard, and the departure of Britain from the gold standard permanently removed the world from the gold standard.

Despite the interruption of World War I the world had by the mid-1920s returned to a gold standard that combined elements of a gold bullion and gold exchange. Countries held international reserves to redeem national currencies at official rates, and these reserves took the form of gold or leading foreign currencies, mainly British pounds and American dollars, which were "as good as gold." The United States held gold reserves well in excess of what was needed to satisfy foreign claims, but in Britain foreign claims exceeded domestic gold reserves, making Britain vulnerable to an international liquidity crisis.

After World War I Britain not only committed itself to returning to the gold standard, but also sought to fix the pound at its pre–World War I value, which was equivalent to $4.86 in the United States. In 1925 Britain returned to the gold standard with the pound at pre–World War I parity in terms of gold and foreign currencies, leaving the pound overvalued in the new international order. The overvaluation of the pound made British exports more expensive in foreign markets and foreign imported goods less expensive in British markets, increasing the supply of goods in Britain relative to demand. Deflationary effects of overvaluation in Britain caused strikes, unemployment, and recession, and forced on the British government added social spending, leading to larger budget deficits. The Bank of England kept interest rates high to attract foreign capital, and discourage withdrawal of foreign funds, together minimizing pressure to redeem pounds into gold. High interest rates also helped keep the British economy depressed.

With the onset of the Great Depression of the 1930s many smaller countries lost export markets and began to draw on reserves of foreign currencies to pay for imports. Bank failures in Austria and Germany weakened confidence in foreign currencies, encouraging redemption of foreign currencies into gold. France, perhaps sensitive to the feeling that the leading powers held reserves in gold and that secondary powers held reserves in foreign currency, took every opportunity to convert its holding of pounds and dollars into gold.

Britain first negotiated loans with the central banks of France and the United States, seeking to bolster its reserves and weather a mounting crisis of confidence in the pound. Later the British government arranged another loan from private sources, but only after restricting government deficit spending, and curbing expenditures on unemployment compensation and wages of government workers. The loans, however, were only stopgap measures, and the drain on Britain's gold reserves continued.

On Saturday, 19 September 1931, the British government decided to suspend gold payments, effective the following Monday, 21 September. The act was rushed through Parliament on 21 September and read, "Until His Majesty by Proclamation otherwise directs subsection 2 of section one of the Gold Standard Act of 1925 shall cease to have effect." The Gold Standard Act of 1925 had returned Britain to the gold standard.

Australia, New Zealand, Brazil, Chile, Paraguay, Uruguay, Venezuela, and Peru had already suspended gold payments. Within a few weeks most of the world's trading partners abandoned the gold standard or restricted foreign currency transactions. By the end of 1932 only the United States, France, Belgium, Switzerland, and the Netherlands remained on the gold standard and maintained freedom of transaction in foreign currencies. The United States abandoned the gold standard in 1933, followed by the remaining European countries in 1936.

See also: Gold Reserve Act of 1934, Gold Standard, Gold Standard Act of 1925

References: Chandler, Lester V. 1971. *American Monetary Policy: 1928–1941.*

Chown, John F. 1994. *A History of Money.*

Feavearyear, Sir Albert. 1963. *The Pound Sterling.*

Goldsmith Bankers

The goldsmiths of seventeenth-century London developed banking in its modern form. The goldsmiths united into one business activity functions such as: maintaining safe storage of gold, silver, and deposits of money; loaning out deposits of money (as well as their own money); transferring money holdings from town to town or person to person; trading in foreign exchange and bullion; and discounting bills of exchange. Before the goldsmith bankers these activities were scattered, often as sidelines or by-products of other trading activities. Around 1633 goldsmith banking arose as an indigenous form of banking in England. Before the gold-

smiths banking in London was the province of Italians, Germans, and particularly the Dutch.

The first step in the goldsmith evolution toward banking began when some goldsmiths became dealers in foreign and domestic coins. Goldsmiths who specialized as coin dealers became known as exchanging goldsmiths as opposed to working goldsmiths. The seizure of the mint in 1640 and the outbreak of civil war in 1642 sent people to goldsmiths in search of safety for jewelry, gold, silver, and coins. The civil war interrupted the normal goldsmith business of forging objects from gold and silver. Instead, goldsmiths developed facilities to store gold and silver deposits in safety. The goldsmiths maintained a running account of each depositor's holdings. They also conducted a profitable business loaning out depositors' gold, silver, and coins to government and private customers. To meet the demands from borrowers, goldsmiths turned to paying interest on deposits and offering time deposits.

The paperwork and record keeping of these activities laid the foundation for important innovations in banking. The bank note (paper money) evolved out of receipts for deposits at goldsmiths. The depositor got a receipt with the depositor's name and the amount of the deposit. These receipts soon became negotiable like endorsed bills of exchange. Modern banking began when these receipts were issued not just to those who had deposited money but also to those who borrowed money. Instead of bearing the name of a particular depositor or borrower, soon the receipts were issued to the "bearer." Thus the modern bank note came to life. The Promissory Notes Act of 1704 ratified the practice of accepting notes in exchange.

The goldsmiths were thus the first to develop checks. The British word "cheque" came from *exchequer,* the British term for "treasury." The cheques were named after the Exchequer orders to pay. The first cheques evolved out of bills of exchange and were called notes or bills. The courts confirmed the negotiability of endorsed bills and notes in 1697.

The paper records of credit transactions and transfers of funds evolved into a considerable supplement of the metallic money supply. By the time Adam Smith's *The Wealth of Nations* was published in 1776, bank notes in circulation exceeded metallic coins. The money supply of the capitalist economic system was no longer limited to the supply of precious metals.

See also: Bank, Check, Seizure of the Mint, Stop of the
   Exchequer
References: Challis, C. E. 1978. *The Tudor Coinage*.
Davies, Glyn. 1994. *A History of Money*.

Gold-Specie-Flow Mechanism

David Hume (1711–1776), one of the most famous
philosophers in Western civilization, was the first to
give a thorough and complete explanation of the
gold-specie-flow mechanism, which is the automatic
adjustment mechanism that balances the inflow and
outflow of gold under an international gold standard.

On a gold standard a country's money supply, including paper money, is directly proportional to domestic gold holdings, including bullion and gold
specie. When a country imports goods from abroad,
making payment causes gold to flow out of the importing country. When a country receives payment for
goods exported abroad, gold flows into the country. In
addition, investments in a foreign country cause gold
to flow out, destined for the country receiving the investment. When a country attracts foreign investment, gold flows in to pay for the investment.

David Hume addressed the problem of what happens when the outflow of gold, owing to imports and
investments in foreign countries, is unequal to the
inflow of gold from exports and foreign investment
attracted from abroad. He developed the gold-
specie-flow mechanism to explain the forces that
bring the outflow of gold into balance with the inflow of gold, stabilizing domestic money supplies.

If gold outflows exceed gold inflows, domestic
money supplies dwindle, putting downward pressure on domestic prices. As domestic prices fall, domestic goods become cheaper relative to imported
goods, decreasing gold outflows from imports. Also,
falling domestic prices lower the prices of domestic
goods in export markets, increasing gold inflows
from exports. Therefore, imports decrease and exports increase, closing the gap between the gold outflows and gold inflows.

If gold inflows exceed gold outflows, domestic
money supplies balloon, putting upward pressure on
domestic prices. Rising domestic prices render domestic goods less competitive in export markets, decreasing gold inflows from exports. Also, rising domestic goods prices lift the price of domestic goods
relative to imported goods, increasing gold outflows
from imports. Therefore, imports increase and exports decrease until the gap between gold inflows
and gold outflows has closed.

Hume's theory of the gold-specie-flow-mechanism
helped supply the theoretical foundation of the gold
standard as a stabilizing force in monetary affairs.

See also: Balance of Payments, Foreign Exchange Markets,
   Gold Standard, Mercantilism
References: Hume, David. 1955. *Writings on Economics*.
———. 1963. *Essays, Moral, Political, and Literary*.
Fausten, Dietrich K. 1979. The Humean Origin of the
   Contemporary Monetary Approach to the Balance of
   Payments. *Quarterly Journal of Economics* 93, no. 4
   (November): 655–673.

Great Bullion Famine

Fifteenth-century Europe encountered a severe
shortage of precious metals—particularly silver—
that scholars have named the Great Bullion Famine.
The worst years of the bullion famine lasted from
1457 until 1464. Evidence of price levels are scanty,
but E. J. Hamilton, author of a well-known study of
the sixteenth-century price revolution, found evidence that prices in Valencia and Aragon dropped as
much as 50 percent in gold equivalents, and 25 percent in silver equivalents from 1400 to 1500. Interest
rates that ranged between $4^7/_8$ and $8^3/_8$ percent during the first half of the fourteenth century in Italy,
rose to a range between 6 percent to over 10 percent
100 years later.

The reasons for the bullion famine lay in the depletion of silver mines located in what are now Germany, Austria, the Czech Republic, and Slovakia, and
a European trade deficit with countries of the Middle and Far East. Diminished European silver production began with the depopulation caused by the
Black Death epidemic of the fourteenth century, and
continued into the fifteenth century. A contributing
factor to the bullion famine was the strong tendency
to hoard precious metals in plate, cups, jewelry, and
treasures of coin. Falling prices rendered hoarding
precious metal a productive investment and hoarding was also a means of protection against coinage
debasement.

A European trade deficit with the Middle and Far
East existed because exotic goods from China and
India—spices, silks, cotton, and others—were
highly prized in Europe, but European products—
such as woolens from England—were not valued in
Eastern countries. Even falling European prices

could not erase the trade deficit. Precious metals, particularly silver, were strongly valued in the Eastern countries, and European precious metals sent to the East in payment for goods never returned in payment for exported European goods. Precious metals were a European export, and Eastern countries became a sinkhole for those metals. The Eastern countries exhibited the same strong propensity to save that now is associated with Japan, causing Japan to export goods to the United States without buying a comparable volume of United States goods.

Mints closed down all across Europe. A lack of bullion forced mints in the Rhineland to close one after another between 1440 and 1443. The English mint at Calais shut down permanently in 1442, and at one point the Tower of London housed the only mint in northwestern Europe that remained active. As early as 1392 the minting of silver in France had dropped to a trickle, and about the same time Sweden ended minting silver for 20 years. At the height of the bullion famine mints closed down in Flanders, Holland, Hainaut (southwestern Belgium), Dordrecht, and Valenciennes.

The bullion famine was one of the not-so-secret causes of the Age of Discovery. Portuguese explorations down the coast of Africa opened up new routes to sub-Saharan gold. Christopher Columbus in his diary of his first voyage mentions gold 65 times. After the mid-sixteenth century, the discovery of silver in Latin America put an end to the bullion famine, Europe entered an era of rising prices, and trade with the Eastern world reached a higher level of intensity.

See also: Ghost Money, Price Revolution in Late Renaissance Europe, Silver Plate

References: Davies, Glyn. 1994. *A History of Money*.
Day, J. 1978. The Great Bullion Famine of the Fifteenth Century. *Past and Present* 79.
Spufford, Peter. 1988. *Money and Its Use in Medieval Europe*.

Great Debasement

The Great Debasement (1542–1551) refers to the English Crown's policy of coinage debasement during the reigns of Henry VIII and Edward VI. Coinage debasement occurred when governments replaced to a significant degree the gold or silver content of coinage with a base metal such as copper. By reducing the value of gold or silver content relative to face value, governments extracted usable revenue from domestic money stocks. This stratagem was called debasement because each coin was worth less in terms of its precious metal content.

Normally, the face value of the coined money exceeded its production cost, including the cost of the precious metals. This difference, which the Crown earned as a profit, was called seigniorage. The Crown of England, like many governments, held an exclusive monopoly on the privilege to coin money from precious metals, and used the profits of seigniorage to help pay for government expenditures.

During the Great Debasement the English crown's profits from debasement rose to unreasonable levels. In March 1542 the value of the silver content of each English coin averaged 75 percent of each coin's face value. By March 1545 the value of the silver content had fallen to 50 percent, and by March 1546 to 33.33 percent. The value of each coin in silver content fell to only 25 percent of face value by the time the debasement had run its course in 1551.

During a period of coinage debasement, a mechanism called Gresham's law comes into play. Gresham's law is sometimes expressed as bad currency drives out good currency. Households and businesses will hoard the good (or undebased) coinage, and use the debased coinage to pay for goods and services. The result is that only the debased currency remains in circulation, and the good currency goes into hiding or is spent on goods from foreign countries where the debased currency is not legal tender and therefore not acceptable.

In 1551 the English government under Elizabeth I instituted a plan to retire the debased currency and replace it with currency the face value of which corresponded with its precious metal content. Because of Gresham's law, retiring the debased currency was a tricky affair because households and businesses tend to hoard good coinage and pay debts with debased coinage. To retire the debased currency the government enacted laws forbidding the outflow of good coinage to foreign markets, and ending the legal-tender status of the debased coinage beyond certain date.

During the gold standard era governments achieved the same purpose as debasement by increasing the paper money in circulation relative to the gold bullion held in reserves. Debasement, like printing excess paper money, was a secret form of taxation that monarchs could impose, often without receiving the approval of representative bodies such as Parliament. The secret tax made itself felt by increasing prices relative to measures of wages and other incomes.

An apologist for the debasement policies of the English Crown might point to the need to build up the English navy, and finance other public defense expenditures. Critics would answer that Henry VIII was fond of building palaces. Whatever the driving force of debasement, the public gradually lost faith in the ability of governments to manage money supplies without oversight from private financial sectors that are affected by monetary mismanagement. In the United States a quasi public-private agency, the Federal Reserve System, regulates the money supply, largely independent of the executive and legislative branches of government. Studies have shown that in the 1970s countries with independent monetary authorities experienced lower inflation rates than countries with monetary authorities dominated by government authority.

See also: Byzantine Debasement, Dissolution of Monasteries, Gresham's Law

References: Davies, Glyn. *The History of Money.* 1994. Gould, J. D. *The Great Debasement.* 1970.

Greek Monetary Maelstrom: 1914–1928

Between 1914 and 1928 Greece saw annual inflation rates vary from 85 percent to 11 percent, and monetary experiments that rank among the strangest in history.

The seeds of Greece's monetary disorder were sown in the middle to late nineteenth century, when the National Bank of Greece, founded in 1841, gradually acquired a virtual monopoly on the prerogative to issue bank notes and became the primary creditor of the government of Greece. The bank was founded as a private bank whose principal stockholder was the government and it dominated the monetary affairs of Greece, acting as a central bank until the establishment of a genuine central bank in 1928. The bank also made loans to the private sector.

Originally, the government conferred upon the National Bank the privilege to issue bank notes as long as the bank stood ready to convert its bank notes into gold. The government, however, suspended convertibility on four separate occasions: right after the 1848 revolutions, again from 1868 to 1870, from 1877 to 1884 when the government borrowed heavily, and last from 1885 to 1928.

Inflation reared its head during the prolonged era of suspended convertibility, but never reached the frenzied hyperinflation levels that characterized post–World War I Germany, Austria, Hungary, and Poland. Between 1914 and 1928 the cost of living index rose 868 percent, perhaps reflecting the threat of losing access to foreign capital that may have helped Greece keep a tight rein on its monetary affairs. Between 1895 and 1910 international financial pressure put Greece on a stricter monetary discipline, requiring the government to withdraw and burn 2 million drachmas in bank notes each year. This pressure came from imperialistic powers with vast financial resources, such as Britain, and served some of the same functions now performed by the International Monetary Fund. The Allies lifted these controls during World War I and even granted credits to Greece, allowing Greece to substantially increase the issuance of bank notes. The credits were never realized, further adding to the supply of unsecured bank notes in circulation.

The government budget of Greece was clearly in the surplus column at the opening of World War I, but by 1918 red ink had shown up in the deficit column. The costs of the war in Asia Minor sent the budget deficit soaring, and by 1922 the government was unable to raise additional revenue either from taxation or borrowing from traditional sources.

Under the duress of a deficit-ridden budget, the government of Greece carried out one of the most fantastic pubic finance schemes in history. On 25 March 1922 the government ordered all citizens to physically cut in half bank notes in their possession. One half of each bank note was to be retained by its owner and could continue to circulate at half of its face value. The owner was to surrender the other half to the government and receive in exchange a 20-year loan at $6\frac{1}{2}$ percent interest.

The National Bank of Greece exchanged with the government fresh notes for the canceled halves, making the whole process a means of raising a loan for the government. The government enacted a similar measure again on 23 January 1926, this time putting three-fourths of the value of the note in the hands of the owner, and the remaining one-fourth the government took in exchange for a 20-year loan at $6\frac{1}{2}$ percent interest. Despite, or because of, these

Greenbacks were the first paper money issued by the U.S. government. (Smithsonian Institution, National Numismatic Collection)

unorthodox financing measures inflation, after reaching a peak of 85 percent in 1923, steadily subsided until the end of the decade, even dipping into the negative range in 1930. The establishment of the Bank of Greece, a genuine central bank, began monetary rehabilitation, helping Greece to experience monetary stability during the decade of the Great Depression.

See also: Bisected Paper Money

Reference: Freris, A. F. 1986. *The Greek Economy in the Twentieth Century.*

Greenbacks (United States)

Greenbacks were the fiat money that the United States government issued during the Civil War. Fiat money, or inconvertible paper money, is money that cannot be converted or redeemed into a precious metal such as gold or silver. By the close of the Civil War greenbacks and related U.S. government notes accounted for about 75 percent of the money in circulation, largely displacing bank notes of state banks, the principal currency in circulation before the Civil War.

The United States government was not the first to issue inconvertible paper money during the Civil War, but was preceded by commercial banks. The secretary of the Treasury of the new Lincoln administration, Salmon Portland Chase, who came to that office without financial experience, possessed a naïve faith in "hard money." The government borrowed heavily from banks to finance the difference between $6 million in tax revenue and $25 million in

expenditures. When the government took out bank loans, it demanded payment in specie, and the specie was not redeposited in banks, but was removed from the banking system. Fears about the ultimate success of the war led the public to hoard specie. On 30 December 1860 banks in New York suspended specie payments on bank notes and deposits, and banks in other parts of the country soon followed. The government began issuing "demand notes" and the country was effectively put on an inconvertible paper standard.

On 30 December 1860 Congress entertained the first proposal for issuing legal-tender notes (fiat money) to defray government expenses. Bankers raised a howl about the government issuing fiat money and dispatched a delegation to advise the secretary of the Treasury and Congress on ways to finance the war. This delegation urged a program of heavy taxation and borrowing in long-term capital markets to finance government spending as an alternative to the issuance of fiat money.

Government officials weighed the alternatives: the issuance of legal-tender fiat money, or an issue of long-term government bonds. Given the poor credit reputation of the government, the paper money was bound to depreciate in value, but bonds would have to pay high interest rates to attract buyers. The government chose the issuance of fiat money, and the only remaining question for debate was whether Congress would clothe the fiat money with the legal status of legal-tender money.

On 25 February 1862 Congress adopted an act

providing for the issuance of notes that were lawful money and legal tender in payment of all debts public and private. The government issued $150 million of these notes, $50 million of which went to retire demand notes the government had already issued. The new notes were called greenbacks. The legal-tender provision contained two noteworthy exceptions. The government demanded payment of import duties in gold coin, and the government committed itself to paying in gold coin the interest earned from government bonds.

To dampen inflationary pressures the government devised means of diverting greenbacks from the spending stream. The greenbacks could be used to buy Treasury bonds paying 6 percent interest redeemable after 5 years, and maturing after 20 years. Also the Treasury accepted deposits of greenbacks, paying 5 percent interest, and redeemable with 10 days' notice. The option of converting greenbacks to Treasury bonds was removed in subsequent bills that authorized the issuance of additional greenbacks.

Prices more than doubled during the Civil War. In June 1864 Congress set a limit of $450 million on the issuance of greenbacks, a limit that was never exceeded. After the Civil War various interest groups dreaded the deflation that would likely follow the reduction of the supply of fiat money in circulation.

It was 1879 before the federal government began redeeming greenbacks with specie, and joined the world's major trading partners on a worldwide gold standard. The greenback experience was prophetic in light of the twentieth century's widespread adoption of inconvertible paper money.

See also: Legal Tender, Pacific Coast Gold Standard

References: Barrett, Don C. 1931. *The Greenbacks and Resumption of Specie Payments: 1862–1879.*

Nugent, Walter T. K. 1968. *Money and American Society, 1865–1880.*

Ritter, Gretchen. 1997. *Gold Bugs and Greenbacks: the Antimonopoly Tradition and the Politics of Finance in America.*

Gresham's Law

Gresham's law is often stated in a simplistic and aphoristic form as "bad money drives out good money." It means in practice that if two coins are in circulation, perhaps one silver and one gold, the public always wants to hoard the coin that has a face value equal to or less than the market value of the

Sir Thomas Gresham, from a portrait by Sir Antonio More. (North Wind Picture Archive)

coin's precious metal value. In turn, the public will use coins with a face value greater than their market value as precious metal to pay off debts and pay for goods and services. Coins with a face value less than the market value as precious metal can always be melted down and sold for a profit, causing these coins to disappear. The "bad money," sometimes called debased money, is the money with a face value greater than the market value of its precious metal content, and it becomes the medium of circulation. The "good money" is the money whose face value is comparable to the market value of its precious metal content, and holders of good money are reluctant to give it up. In a country with debased money circulating alongside good money, the latter tends to flow into the hands of foreigners, domestic hoards, or goldsmiths' melting pots, leaving only bad money in circulation, thus the phrase "bad money drives out good money."

Gresham's law owes its name to Sir Thomas Gresham, the foremost financial wizard of the Elizabethan era, who acted as a councilor to Elizabeth I and as the royal agent in European financial markets. England was on the silver standard and during the mid-sixteenth century, the silver value of England's silver coinage had dropped from 75 percent of face value to 25 percent. Only 3 ounces of silver was in a coin that had a face value equivalent to 12 ounces of silver. Elizabeth I inherited the confusion and monetary disorder of the debasement policies of her predecessors, who had practiced debasement to build up England's military defenses. Sir Thomas Gresham formulated Gresham's law to explain the difficulty of introducing good money in a monetary environment dominated by bad money, explaining how bad money would drive out the good money. Gresham explained that the government ran the risk of coining full-valued money that would only end up in the hands of foreigners and the goldsmiths while the bad money remained in circulation. Gresham devised a policy based on a quick recall, revaluation, and recoinage of debased money combined with severe legal penalties for melting down or exporting the new coinage.

Although Gresham received the credit for formulating a law still discussed in modern economic textbooks, he was not the first to put the law into words. Aristophanes, the great comedic playwright of ancient Greece, writing in 405 B.C., remarked concerning Athens, "In our Republic bad citizens are preferred to good, just as bad money circulates while good money disappears" (Angell, 1929). A French theologian, Nicholas Oresme (c.1320–1382) wrote a book, *A Treatise on the Origin, Nature, Law, and Alterations of Money,* in which he explained the operation of Gresham's law as one of the consequences of debasement.

In the modern world inflation of paper money has replaced debasement of coinage as a means of extracting more revenue for financially strapped governments. Gresham's law can sometimes be seen in operation in countries where domestic currencies are depreciating from inflation, and United States dollars are hoarded as a preferred currency.

See also: Great Debasement

References: Angell, Norman. 1929. *The Story of Money.* Chown, John F. 1994. *A History of Money.* McCallum, Bennett T. 1989. *Monetary Economics.*

Guernsey Market House Paper Money

Guernsey Island, second largest of the Channel Islands, home to the famous Guernsey dairy cows,

boasts of one of the more interesting paper money experiments in monetary history. The parliament of Guernsey Island, called the States, hit upon the scheme of issuing paper money to pay for the construction of public facilities, and in turn reclaiming the paper money in payment for rent on the use of the finished facilities.

In April 1815 the Guernsey States appointed a committee to investigate a proposal for enlarging the Guernsey meat market. The committee recommended the issuance of 1-pound State notes, beginning with a 3,000 pound issue. These one-pound notes were earmarked to pay the costs of material and wages for construction of the enlarged Guernsey meat market. According to the plan, those who used the building would have to pay rent in these one-pound notes. As these notes fell into the hands of the government of Guernsey as payment for rent, they would be destroyed, and therefore canceled. According to the committee report:

> Thus at the end of ten years, all the Notes would be cancelled and the States would be in possession of an income of 150 pounds per annum, which would be a return to the 3,000 pounds spent by them. Looked at from all sides, the scheme shows nothing but the greatest advantage for the public and for the States. (Angell, 1929)

In 1820 and 1821 the Guernsey States issued over 4,000 pounds in 1-pound notes to pay off its public debt. In 1826 the States authorized another paper issue of 1-pound notes to pay for Elizabeth College and parochial schools. This authorization set a limit of 20,000 pounds on notes in circulation.

In 1827 the States authorized another issue of 11,000 pound notes to pay for improvements to Rue de la Fontaine, a street adjoining the market. Again the rents related to the project would reclaim the notes, leading to their cancellation. Other note issues were approved.

In 1828 the States appointed the Finance Committee "to replace the used and worn-out Notes by new Notes, payable at the same time as the destroyed notes would have been." In 1829 a member of the Finance Committee observed that the volume of notes in circulation had risen to 48,183.

The Guernsey States experiment with paper money is one of the most interesting in history. It was a successful and productive use of a paper money issue that commanded value independent of a gold standard. It never climaxed in an inflationary finale that seemed to be the outcome of a merciless logic inherent in all the early issues of paper money. One important characteristic that distinguished the Guernsey paper money experiment from other early experiments was this: Unlike earlier paper money, often inspired by wartime expenditures, the Guernsey paper money issue went to pay for the production of durable, income-earning wealth. Therefore the nongold wealth of the community kept pace with the growth in paper money even though the amount of gold in the community may have declined.

Reference: Angell, Norman. 1929. *The Story of Money.*

Guns

Whenever European societies came into contact with primitive societies guns, particularly rifles, became a favorite article of trade. Guns were a virtual necessity in certain parts of the world, and they were durable, making them serviceable as a medium of exchange and store of value. Guns are sufficiently durable to be passed down from one generation to another, and even in the United States old guns are a favorite of antique collectors.

During the nineteenth century rifles in southwestern Africa served as a medium of exchange, and rich chiefs owned stores of rifles as a conspicuous form of wealth. In South Africa colonists found that rifles rivaled spirits as a preferred medium of trade with the natives. In parts of Mozambique rifles, ammunition, and gunpowder were media of exchange.

In regions of the Congo guns not only were used as a medium of exchange, but a monetary unit of one gun evolved and goods were priced in guns. Even though goods were priced in guns, guns were not involved in every transaction. Instead, goods were often traded for other goods whose value could be equated to the required number of guns. A *gun* came to represent a certain quantity of cotton cloth, some salt, brass wire, hoop iron, crockery, powder, spirit, and perhaps a big brass pan.

A fictitious rifle monetary unit also arose in Angola. Prices were quoted in rifles but payment was made in a basket of other goods of equivalent value. A basket of goods containing 50 to 60 items was necessary to pay for elephant tusks equaling one rifle in value.

Rubber plantations in Brazil paid Indian agricultural workers in cheap rifles that were only good for 40 to 50 shots. The short life expectancy of these rifles assured that the Indians would return to the plantation to work. An Indian fortunate enough to acquire a good gun would probably never be seen again. Indians in the United States also valued rifles, and eagerly exchanged other goods for rifles.

To a society that lives by hunting a gun is one of the most useful tools to be had. Also, intertribal warfare made the acquisitions of guns a necessity because tribes without guns were doomed to extinction.

See also: Commodity Money Standard
References: Einzig, Paul. 1966. *Primitive Money.*
Johnston, Sir Harry Hamilton. 1908. *George Grenfell and the Congo.*

H

High-Powered Money

High-powered money is sometimes called the monetary base. It includes all cash, even vault cash at commercial banks, and commercial bank deposits at Federal Reserve Banks, which are redeemable in cash. These assets are called reserves because commercial banks hold them to honor checking account withdrawals during times when withdrawals exceed new deposits. New loans are also made out of reserves in the sense that a bank with no reserves would have no funds to loan out. The term *high-powered* is a reference to the fact that a $1 increase in the volume of high-powered money will cause the most narrowly defined measure of the money stock to increase by about $2.50.

High-powered money is important because it represents net wealth to the private sector. In a contrast, checking account money, called demand deposits, represents an asset to the owner of the checking account, but represents a liability from the perspective of the bank, which owes that money to a customer on demand. The liability cancels out the asset, leaving a net effect of zero on the net wealth of the private sector. Commercial bank deposits at a central bank represent a liability to the central bank. However, a central bank is a government or quasi-government agency that is not considered part of the private sector.

The narrowest definition of the money stock, called M1, includes checkable deposits and circulating currency, but not vault cash at commercial banks. Because M1 includes checking deposits and excludes vault cash, it is possible for the supply of high-powered money to change without a change in a money stock measure such as M1. Normally, a 1 percent increase in the supply of high-powered money will lead to a 1 percent increase in M1, the most narrowly defined measure of the money supply in the United States.

The concept of high-powered money is important because central banks directly control high-powered money, and exert only indirect control over measures of the money supply, which are influenced by the willingness of commercial banks to make loans out of reserves.

See also: Bank, Central Bank, Legal Reserve Ratio, Monetary Aggregates, Monetary Multiplier

References: Baye, Michael R., and Dennis W. Janise. 1995. *Money, Banking, and Financial Markets: An Economic Approach.*
McCallum, Bennett T. 1989. *Monetary Economics: Theory and Practice.*

House of St. George

The House of St. George was a Genoese public bank, one of the first organized. It is regarded as a direct ancestor of the modern central banks, acting both as a state treasury and a private bank. During the sixteenth and seventeenth centuries the banking industry would briefly lift Genoa to the leadership of the capitalist world, with Genoese merchant bankers conducting business throughout Europe, making loans and transferring funds.

In a war with Venice during the fourteenth century, the city of Genoa had raised money from citizens in return for promissory notes. At the end of the war, Genoa pledged the customs dues from its port to redeem the notes. In 1407 the creditors organized themselves into a bank, the Casa di San Georgio, or House of St. George, appointed eight directors to watch after their investments, collected taxes, and made loans to the state. The bank's Renaissance palace can still be seen in the Piazza Caricmento.

The House of St. George was what Adam Smith called a bank of deposit. Coins from all parts of the world were deposited with the bank. The ownership of the deposits, called bank money, changed hands by bookkeeping entries at the bank in the presence of a notary, similar to the Bank of Amsterdam or Bank of Hamburg. Shares of stock in the bank also acted as a medium of exchange and changed hands through bookkeeping entries. The Genoese government paid interest on the public debt in three-year installments, and accounts of accrued interest that were payable also exchanged ownership in the capacity of money.

The House of St. George is credited with being the first bank to issue bank notes, not in specific denominations such as 100 or 1,000, but on an individual basis for large deposits. Each note was written out in hand, and the ownership could be passed on by endorsement. These handwritten notes could represent either a deposit of gold or silver, or shares of stock in the bank.

Genoa's control of European finances was brief. Repeated bankruptcies of the Spanish crown may have scared the Genoese bankers, or perhaps the Dutch and English demanded more involvement in the shipment and distribution of the precious metals from the New World. By 1647 Dutch ships carried Spanish silver directly to the Low Countries.

See also: Bank of Deposit, Bank of Venice, Bill of Exchange
References: Colwell, Stephen. 1965. *The Ways and Means of Payment.*
Homer, Sidney. 1977. *A History of Interest Rates.* 2d ed.

Human Heads

Sporadic evidence suggest that humans heads served as a store of value and medium of exchange in the southwest Pacific, particularly in areas where human flesh was eaten.

An eleventh-century Arab text, *'Aja'ib al-Hind*, mentions that the inhabitants of islands near Suma-

tra made use of human heads as a medium of exchange. A fifteenth-century Venetian traveler, Nicolo de' Conti, found human heads serving as currency on Sumatra. He observed that "In one part of the island called Battrech [Batak] the inhabitants eat human flesh. They keep human heads as valuable property, store up the skull and use it as money. When they desire to purchase any article, give one or more heads in exchange for it according to its value" (Williams, 1997). The practice of using human heads apparently survived for several centuries on Batak. In the nineteenth century white traders on Batak were accused of capturing people, severing their heads, and using their skulls as money to pay for sandalwood.

Borneo is also a place where human heads allegedly served as currency. The evidence is a bit soft, but on occasion the headhunters on Borneo were known to hold out their trophies when the white traders' goods reached a certain level of temptation.

Human head currency belongs on the fringe of monetary history. Like gold, silver, and copper, human heads were adaptable to ornamental purposes. Ornaments are usually adapted to be carried without tying up hands and pockets, and can serve a dual purpose if the ornaments are acceptable as a medium of exchange. The evolution of articles that serve a dual role as money and ornaments expresses the need to economize on the expenditure of time, energy, and resources.

See also: Manilla
References: Einzig, Paul. 1966. *Primitive Money.*
Williams, Jonathan, ed. 1997. *Money: A History.*

Hungarian Post–World War I Hyperinflation

In the aftermath of World War I, Hungary, one of the successor states to the Austro-Hungarian Empire, saw inflation advance into a hyperinflationary stage, multiplying prices by a factor of 263 between January 1922 and April 1924.

In addition to owing war reparations, Hungary inherited an economy facing shortages and uprooted from traditional trading relationships. The erection of new national barriers restricted trade between regions of the former Austro-Hungarian Empire. To complicate the economic turmoil, A Bolshevik revolution threw Hungary into monetary confusion; the revolutionaries seized the plates for one- and two-crown Austro-Hungarian bank notes and ran the printing presses liberally in support of their cause. A right-wing regime supplanted the Bolsheviks, but through 1924 the government continued to finance between 20 and 50 percent of government expenditures with issues of paper money.

The Hungarian section of the Austro-Hungarian bank was spun off as the State Note Institute, a note-issuing bank under the authority of the minister of finance. The State Note Institute exchanged its notes, the Hungarian *krone,* for the notes of the Austro-Hungarian bank, and even the notes issued by the Bolshevik government.

Total notes and deposit liabilities of the State Note Institute grew by a factor of 85 from January 1922 until April 1924, the time frame over which prices increased by a factor of 263. The percentage growth in prices exceeded the percentage growth in the money supply, reflecting the effects of the flight from the krone. As prices escalated, Hungarian residents sought to spend krones before they lost value, raising the velocity of circulation, adding further fuel to the inflationary spiral. To restrict Hungarians from using krones to buy assets denominated in more stable foreign currencies, the Hungarian government established the Hungarian Devisenzentral as part of the State Note Institute. This agency was responsible for making it difficult or illegal for Hungarians to own foreign currency.

The end of the inflationary episode in Hungary came when the League of Nations arranged an international loan for Hungary conditioned upon government policies committed to balanced budgets and a central bank independent of government authorities. The reparation committee also gave up its claim on Hungary's resources. The broad outlines of the reconstruction of Hungary's finances mirror closely the Austrian experience. The new central bank, the Hungarian National Bank, was able to continue increasing the supply of paper krones, but these krones were now backed by gold, other foreign assets, and commercial paper.

Inflation stabilized in December 1924 and the krone ended its slide on the New York foreign exchange market.

The Hungarian inflation experience underlines the importance of expectations in monetary affairs. The assurance of a return to responsible government policies was sufficient to bring a quick halt to inflationary momentum.

See also: American Revolution Hyperinflation, Austrian Hyperinflation, French Revolution Hyperinflation, German Hyperinflation, Inflation and Deflation, Polish Hyperinflation

References: Sargent, Thomas J. 1993. *Rational Expectations and Inflation.* 2d ed.

Wicker, E. 1986. Terminating Hyperinflation in the Dismembered Hapsburg Monarchy. *American Economic Review* 76, no. 3: 350–364.

Hungarian Post–World War II Hyperinflation

From July 1945 until August 1946 hyperinflation raged in Hungary on a scale more spectacular than Germany's hyperinflation experience following World War I. When the German hyperinflation was stabilized in 1923 the government issued a new mark equivalent to 1 trillion of the depreciated marks. On 1 August 1946 Hungary replaced its depreciated *pengo* with the *florint* at a rate of 1 florint to 400 octillion pengos. Although Germany's hyperinflation crisis lasted a bit short of two years, Hungary's post–World War II hyperinflation crisis ran its course in slightly less than a year.

Hyperinflation was not new to Hungary, which had shared in the hyperinflation frenzy that had afflicted Germany, Poland, and Austria at the end of World War I. Like its post–World War I experience, Hungary's post–World War II hyperinflation episode fit a familiar pattern in the history of hyperinflation. Episodes of hyperinflation usually occur during or immediately after a war, when the government is financing huge budget deficits, and supplies of goods have been disrupted. During Hungary's second hyperinflation experience, government revenue covered only 15 percent of government expenditures. The following schedule shows the increase of bank notes by the National Bank of Hungary that fueled the hyperinflation:

31 December 1945	765,400
1 January 1946	1,646,000
28 February 1946	5,238,000
31 March 1946	34,002,000
30 April 1946	434,304,000
31 May 1946	65,589,000,000
30 June 1946	6,277,000,000,000,000
31 July 1946	17,300,000,000,000,000,000

A Hungarian tax pengo note, 1946. (Smithsonian Institution, National Numismatic Collection)

Hungary's first effort to tame the inflation came in December 1945 when the government announced that notes of 1,000 or more pengos were banned unless special stamps were affixed to them. The stamps had to be purchased from the government at a cost of three times the face value of the notes. The owner of four 1,000-pengo notes had to give up three notes to buy a stamp to make the one note valid. The stamp requirement effectively reduced the number of notes in circulation by three-fourths. Inflation halted, and prices even fell for a few days, but by the end of December prices were rising so fast that employees hardly received their pay before they rushed to spend it.

On 1 January 1946 the government took an innovative approach to the inflation problem and created a new money of account, called the tax pengo, ostensibly to protect the government's tax revenue from an inflation loss between the time taxes were levied and the time of collection. The tax pengo equaled the regular pengo multiplied by a daily price index that measured the ratio of current prices to prices on 1 January 1946. Soon business transactions were paid in tax pengos, and on 10 January commercial banks began offering tax pengo deposits. With tax pengo deposits a customer deposited regular pengos in a bank. When the deposit was withdrawn the customer received the amount of regular pengos multiplied by the ratio of prices on the withdrawal date to prices on the date of deposit.

Multiplication by a price index ratio adjusted the pengo for loss in purchasing power. On 1 June 1946 the government issued tax pengo notes that circulated as paper money with values depending upon daily price ratio calculations. At this point the tax pengo had become a new indexed currency—indexed to the rate of inflation. The regular pengo rapidly depreciated in value relative to the tax pengo, but prices quoted in tax pengo remained stable until mid-April 1946.

In April prices began to escalate in tax pengo, and beginning on 20 June the depreciation accelerated rapidly. On 1 August 1946 the government issued the new florint, the convertibility into dollars of which was assured with reserves of gold, foreign currencies, and foreign securities. At that point Hungary's hyperinflation crisis ended. Hungary's official documents do not make it clear where these reserves originated.

The Soviet Union contributed to Hungary's hyperinflation crisis, probably in an effort to destroy Hungary's economy. In 1945 the Soviet army issued in Hungary the highest denomination bank note ever printed, a 100 quadrillion pengo note.

Hungary's second hyperinflation experience suggests that the only remedy for inflation is monetary discipline, restraint of monetary growth. Hungary's indexed currency failed because bank note circulation continued to race ahead.

See also: Austrian Hyperinflation, German Hyperinflation, Hungarian Post–World War I Hyperinflation, Inflation and Deflation, Polish Hyperinflation

References: Bomberger, W. A., and G. E. Makinen. 1983. The Hungarian Hyperinflation and Stabilization of 1945–1946. *Journal of Political Economy*, 91 no. 5: 801–824.

Nogaro, Bertrand. 1948. Hungary's Recent Monetary Crisis and Its Theoretical Meaning. *American Economic Review* (September): 526–542.

Paarlberg, Don. 1993. *An Analysis and History of Inflation*.

Siklos, P. L. 1989. The End of the Hungarian Hyperinflation of 1945–46. *Journal of Money, Credit, and Banking* 2: 132–147.

I

Icelandic Saga Money

During the medieval era the Icelanders were among the most literary people in Europe and left a written record in sagas that mirrored the manners, morals, and practices of their time. These sagas tell of blood feuds resolved with the payment of rings, usually silver rings, and of a monetary standard of cloth.

The cloth was called *wadmal,* spun from sheep wool and woven on handlooms. Virtually every Icelandic farm had the wherewithal to make its own wadmal. Values, including taxes, were expressed in units of wadmal, a piece of cloth 1 *ell* long and 2 wide. An ell was approximately the length of an arm.

Wadmal came in two standard qualities, a plain white cloth that carried the least value, and brown or brown-striped cloth that traded at a higher value. The term *wadmal* continued into the modern period as a measure of value for land. Early evidence shows that 120 ells of wadmal equaled $^1/_3$ mark of silver, but after 1280 cloth had appreciated to 96 ells of wadmal to $^1/_3$ mark of silver. The term *mark,* the monetary unit of account in modern Germany, originally referred to a length of cloth, but evolved into a measure of a certain weight of silver.

Large transactions brought into play metal rings, mainly silver and gold rings in later times. One account describes them as massy rings of gold with other rings hanging from them, suggesting that they were not intended to be worn on the finger. In Icelandic sagas rich persons generous with their wealth were ring givers, or breakers or scatterers of rings. In the Icelandic epic, *Burnt Nial,* the hero was known as "He that lavisheth rings in largesse," a reference to his generosity. Those who despised wealth were described as haters of rings. Before the arrival of silver and gold, segments of spiraled rings of metal were cut off, weighed, and passed as money.

References to chiefs or heroes distributing rings as acts of generosity can be found in the English medieval epic, *Beowulf,* and in Percy's *Reliques of Ancient English Poetry.* Ring money figures largely in the monetary history of Denmark and Sweden.

See also: Cloth, Commodity Money Standard
References: Einzig, Paul. 1966. *Primitive Money.* Quiggin, A. Hingston. 1949. *A Survey of Primitive Money.*

Inconvertible Paper Standard

An inconvertible paper standard is a monetary standard based on paper money, either bank notes or government currency that cannot be converted into any commodity or precious metal at an official rate. Inconvertible paper money is called fiat money and it bears a face value that may or may not be expressed in metallic terms.

The inconvertible paper standard evolved directly from precious metal standards. Originally paper money circulated as something resembling warehouse receipts representing titles to ownership of gold or silver safely secured with a goldsmith or bank. Exchanging titles of ownership was less risky and costly than physically transporting precious metals. From those warehouse receipts evolved bank notes, ancestors to the contemporary Federal

Reserve Notes and other bank notes of modern central banks.

War and other national emergencies often forced governments to put heavy claims on domestic gold and silver reserves, and in turn governments granted banks the privilege to suspend convertibility of bank notes into precious metal. England suspended convertibility during the Napoleonic Wars and the United States suspended convertibility during the War of 1812 and the Civil War. Suspended convertibility was invariably attended with some currency depreciation, but often the patriotic fervor of war helped maintain some monetary order. Government assurances of return to convertibility at war's end also helped protect currency values from a wave of inflation.

Two famous cases of paper money fiascoes occurred toward the end of the eighteenth century, the hyperinflations of the American and French Revolutions. France had already had one paper money disaster early in the eighteenth century with the episode of John Law's bank. The memory of these episodes acted as a constant reminder of the monetary insanity lurking beneath the surface of an inconvertible paper money standard, and encouraged governments to accept inconvertibility only as a temporary measure.

Between 1866 and 1881 Italy apparently made good use of inconvertible paper money to assist in the financing of economic development. The episode was called *Il Corso Forzoso*, or "forced currency," and it was accompanied by a modest depreciation of the lira of 10 to 16 percent. Nevertheless a new government felt the need to promise a return to convertibility, which was accomplished in 1881.

By the beginning of World War I the world was on a gold standard. Countries banned the export of gold, suspending convertibility for international trade, and the right of domestic convertibility was rarely exercised. At the end of the war returning to an international gold standard became an important goal of the world's major trading partners.

The world was on a gold standard in the early 1930s when worldwide depression shook the foundations of the international monetary system. It was during this era that inconvertible paper standards became virtually universal among the world's major trading partners. These countries went on inconvertible paper standards for domestic purposes but remained on a gold bullion standard for international purposes. In the United States private citizens could no longer convert dollars into gold, and private ownership of gold for anything but industrial purposes was illegal. The United States and other countries continued to redeem domestic currency into gold at the request of foreign central banks. After 1971 the world's major trading partners went on inconvertible paper standards for international as well as domestic purposes, severing the last ties with convertibility.

See also: Gold Reserve Act of 1934, Gold Standard, Gold Standard Amendment Act of 1931

References: Chown, John F. 1994. *A History of Money*. McCallum, Bennett T. 1989. *Monetary Economics*.

Independent Treasury (United States)

From the 1840s until 1863 the Independent Treasury, as it was called, divorced the government's fiscal operations from private sector banks. It accepted payment for public obligations—taxes—only in gold and silver specie and treasury notes, and operated its own depositories around the country. The Independent Treasury did not accept bank notes, and did not hold deposits in commercial banks. Its own depositories were separate from state banks.

The Independent Treasury was born of the freewheeling banking environment that flourished after the demise of the Second Bank of the United States. At first, the Treasury tried to supply a modicum of regulatory discipline by holding Treasury deposits in state banks and requiring special specie reserves for those deposits. The Treasury found, however, that its own deposits could be held hostage to overly aggressive lending policies of state banks, and on occasion the Treasury could not withdraw its funds. During this time gold and silver specie commanded a reverence in the eyes of a public that distrusted banks, bank notes, and even corporations themselves. Large segments of the public saw bank notes as a sham scheme of the "moneyed interests" to exploit the unwary, and the proponents of the Independent Treasury were "hard currency" people who wanted the government's business separated from banks and corporations.

The Sub-Treasury Act of 1840 became law during the presidency of Martin Van Buren, a staunch advocate of the hard currency policies that marked the presidency of his predecessor, Andrew Jackson. Daniel Webster stood flatly opposed to the bill, remarking on 12 March 1938 that "[t]he use of money is in the exchange. It is designed to circulate, not to be hoarded. To keep it that is to detain it is a conception belonging to barbarous times and barbarous governments" (Chown, 1994). Opponents of the bill saw it turning the Treasury into a hoarder of gold and silver, and throwing the private sector into a deflationary spiral. Banks held gold and silver specie to act as reserves for the redemption of bank notes. If the government began absorbing gold and silver specie, banks would be forced to contract the supply of circulating bank notes.

After heated political combat, Congress enacted the Sub-Treasury Act on 30 June 1840. It provided that in the first year one-fourth of public obligations, that is, taxes, should be paid in specie, and by 1843 100 percent of public obligations should be paid in specie. In 1843 Congress repealed the first Sub-Treasury Act.

In 1846 Congress enacted a second Sub-Treasury bill. This bill required that government offices accept only gold and silver specie and treasury notes (non-legal-tender paper money issued by the Treasury) in payment of public obligations. The Independent Treasury System lasted in some form until 1920. As early as 1863, however, the Treasury began to hold deposits in commercial banks.

In its pre–Civil War phase, the Independent Treasury proved that the fears of some of its critics were well founded. Problems arose because Treasury tax collections did not coincide with government expenditures. When tax collections rose above government payments, specie left private banks, and entered Treasury depositories, forcing banks to contract bank note circulation. When government payments overtook tax collections, specie flowed into the banking system, and banks issued more bank notes. The ebb and flow of specie from Treasury depositories imparted a cyclical motion to the supply of circulating bank notes, and acted to destabilize the economy. After the Treasury was allowed to maintain commercial bank deposits, the Treasury learned to conduct the government's fiscal operations without rocking the banking system.

The Independent Treasury System represents another episode in the paper money drama that would eventually define the terms on which the public would come to accept paper money. It represented a phase in which societies had come to accept precious metal coins, something that could not be taken for granted in ancient societies. Despite the acceptance of precious metal coins, feelings about paper money ran high, and suspicion about paper money gained ground quickly in hard times. Distrust of paper money left a social seam, often hidden, but always threatening to rip open and become a power force in political life.

See also: Free Banking, Specie Circular, Treasury Notes
References: Chown, John. 1994. *A History of Paper Money.* Hammond, Bray. 1957. *Banks and Politics in America from the Revolution to the Civil War.*

Indexation

Indexation is a method of controlling the income-redistributing effects of inflation.

Inflation is a decrease in the purchasing power of a unit of money. Households and businesses that supply commodities, credit, and raw materials under long-term contracts have revenues and incomes that are fixed regardless of what is happening to other prices. In an inflationary environment, revenues from long-term contracts diminish in real terms; that is, in real purchasing power.

Redistributive effects of inflation significantly harm important players in the economic system. With inflation, savers and lenders find their wealth losing value while in the hands of other households and businesses. The real losses to savers and lenders occur because their wealth is defined in terms of a unit of money that steadily, perhaps rapidly, buys less. Debtors stand to gain windfall profits from inflation that can reduce the value and burden of a debt, or, under hyperinflation, even eliminate a debt in practical terms.

Governments are suspected of generating inflation as a means of canceling vast public debts too large to service. In the aftermath of World War I the German government, shouldering a vast public debt from wartime expenditures coupled with war reparations, fueled an episode of hyperinflation that rendered its pubic debt null and void. The United States government emerged from World War II with a sizable public debt, perhaps removing government incentive to aggressively combat an inflation problem that continued until the early 1980s.

A system of indexation protects households and businesses whose wealth and income are at risk from inflation. Under indexation, escalator provisions automatically administer inflation adjustments to sources of income and assets fixed in money terms by contract. In the United States Social Security benefits automatically receive inflation adjustments geared to the Consumer Price Index, a limited application of the principle of indexation. Under a full-blown system of indexation, checking accounts, savings accounts, long-term and short-term bonds, mortgages, wages, and long-term contracts receive periodic adjustments to keep pace with inflation.

Some economists propose limited forms of indexation, applying only to government bonds and taxable income. This limited indexation automatically increases the maturity value of government bonds at a rate equivalent to the inflation rate, and withholds from government tax revenue paper profits due only to inflation. With limited indexation, government is spared the temptation to generate inflation as a means of canceling public debt, and levying a hidden tax.

As inflationary momentum increased during the 1970s prominent economists, such as Nobel Prize–winner Milton Friedman, proposed that the United States adopt a system of indexation. Brazil implemented a broad system of indexation, and Israel and Canada adopted indexation systems on smaller scales. Proponents of indexation felt it would lift the burden of forming accurate inflationary expectations and moderate economic fluctuations caused by discrepancies between actual and expected inflation. Strong anti-inflation policies often induce a bout of high unemployment because expected inflation remains high after the actual inflation rate has fallen. Indexation should moderate the high unemployment that often accompanies disinflation. Critics feel that the adoption of a system of indexation is equivalent to giving up the fight against inflation, and observe that inflation has often accelerated in countries practicing indexation. The United States never adopted indexation, and as other countries enacted market-oriented reforms, systems of indexation began to lose favor as another form of government interference.

See also: Brazilian Hyperinflation, Inflation and Deflation, Tabular Standard in Massachusetts Bay Colony

References: Fellner, William. 1974. The Controversial Issue of Comprehensive Indexation. In *Essays on Inflation and Indexation.*
Friedman, Milton. 1974. Using Escalators to Help Fight Inflation. *Fortune Magazine* (July).
Weaver, R. Kent. 1988. *Automatic Government: Politics of Indexation.*

Indian Rupee
See Cattle, Coconut Standard of Nicobars, Indian Silver Standard, Mughal Coinage

Indian Silver Standard
During the last quarter of the nineteenth century, when the world was abandoning bimetallism in favor of the gold standard, India adapted its silver standard to a modified gold system that held gold reserves to maintain the value of an entirely silver coinage.

The Indian currency system had always attracted the curiosity of the British. In 1772 the eminent economist Sir James Steuart advanced a recommendation to the East India Company "for correcting the DEFECTS of the present CURRENCY." John Maynard Keynes wrote his first book, *Indian Currency and Finance,* after serving on a committee studying India's monetary system.

A bit of the impression India's nineteenth-century monetary system left on contemporary British observers may be gleaned from a quotation of A. J. Balfour, later prime minister of England:

> What is the British system of currency? You go to Hong Kong and the Straits Settlements, and you find obligations are measured in silver; you go to England, and you find that obligations are measured in gold; you stop half way, in India, and you find that obligations are measured in something which is neither gold nor silver—the strangest product of monometallist ingenuity which the world has ever seen—a currency which is as arbitrary as any forced paper currency which the world has ever heard of, and which is as expensive as any metallic currency that the world has ever faced, and which, unhappily, combines in itself all the disadvantages of every currency which human beings have ever tried to form. (Chown, 1994)

"Symbols on Indian Coins." From 1835 to 1893, mints in India struck only silver coins. (Library of Congress)

Between 1835 and 1893, India practiced what in the United States was called free silver, a silver standard that allowed anyone to bring silver to the Indian mint for coinage. Only two coins were struck, the silver *rupee* and the silver half rupee, and only silver coins were legal tender. Gold was not legal tender and the mint did not strike gold coins.

As long as the European bimetallic system remained a viable monetary system, preserving a constant ratio of silver to gold of about 15.5 to 1, the Indian system functioned with a stable exchange rate between the silver rupee and Britain's gold pound sterling. India's silver rupee equaled 22.39 pence under Britain's gold standard. After Western trading partners began shifting over to the gold standard in the 1870s, the value of silver fell, adversely affecting the terms of trade of countries on the silver standard, mainly China, India, and Japan. Prices of both domestic and foreign goods rose in India, putting in a squeeze the household

budgets of civil servants and other groups on fixed incomes.

In an effort to raise the value of the silver rupee, the government suspended the private coinage of silver in 1893, hoping to manage the supply of silver currency and maintain its value in gold. The value of the silver rupee modestly climbed relative to gold to a rate of 1 shilling and 4 pence per rupee, or 15 rupees per British sovereign. The government stood ready to redeem silver rupees and paper rupees in gold at an official rate of 1 shilling and 4 pence in gold per rupee. The silver coinage now wore the aspect of a token coinage whose value was supported in the same manner as the value of paper rupees was supported. India became a gold standard country but its only circulating coinage was silver.

The limitation on Indian coinage of silver, coupled with high Indian interest rates needed to support the rupee internationally, depressed economic conditions in India and led to further calls for currency reform. In 1898 another government commission studied the problem and recommended that India bolster its gold reserves and issue gold coinage. These new reforms failed to bring monetary relief to India and in 1912 the British government formed the Royal Commission on Indian Currency and Finance, including among its members John Maynard Keynes, who would later become the most famous economist of the twentieth century. Keynes wrote a book on Indian currency in which he recommended that India remove gold coins from circulation and concentrate gold holdings in a state bank that would use the gold as reserves to support bank notes.

See also: Bimetallism, Gold Standard, Silver

References: Carter, Martha L. 1994. *A Treasury of Indian Coins.*
Chown, John. 1994. *A History of Money.*
Keynes, John Maynard. 1913. *Indian Currency and Finance.*
Laughlin, J. Laurence. 1968. *The History of Bimetallism in the United States.*

Inflation and Deflation

Inflation presents itself as an overall rise in the general price level, meaning that the average level of all prices is rising, rather than the prices of a select few goods and services. A closer examination suggests that inflation is a decrease in the value (purchasing power) of a unit of money, perhaps because of an increase in the supply of money relative to demand. Deflation is the reverse—a fall in the average level of prices. History appears to be inflationary, although episodes of deflation are numerous.

Inflation is measured by the growth rate in price levels calculated as weighted averages of prices of a spectrum of goods and services. In the United States the Gross Domestic Product Deflator (GDPD) measures the price level for all goods and services, including factory equipment and other goods bought by businesses, luxury goods, and goods bought by the government. Another index, the Consumer Price Index (CPI), measures the price level for goods and services that are associated with the basic cost of living, including food, gasoline, utilities, housing, clothes, etc.

Wartime government expenditures can nearly always be counted on to create inflationary pressures, as happened in the United States during World War II. At that time the U.S. government enacted wage and price controls to contain inflation. The price controls were lifted at the end of World War II, but inflation remained a problem throughout the cold war era. Inflation tends to become a problem whenever governments do not want to levy the taxes sufficient to support government expenditures.

Economists often see controlling inflation as a problem in maintaining the value of money, which rises in value, as the money supply is restricted. In the 1980s a prolonged reduction in the growth of the money supply ended the inflationary inertia in the United States economy.

A slow steady rate of inflation that is easily anticipated causes less disruption than high inflation rates showing substantial volatility. Inflation in the range of 300 percent annually or higher is called hyperinflation. This brand of galloping or runaway inflation is often associated with the complete breakdown of society.

The last quarter of the nineteenth century saw deflation in the United States and several European countries. Deflation puts a burden on debtors, who find it harder to earn money to repay debts that remain fixed in value as wages and profits fall. In the late nineteenth century debtor hardship attributable to deflation fueled a populist revolt in the United States that nearly propelled William Jennings Bryan to the presidency. Bryan decried the gold standard as "crucifying" mankind on a cross of gold. The supply of gold was not keeping pace with rapid increases in production due to technology, causing the supply of goods to increase faster than the supply of money. Prices fell and Bryan proposed to increase the coinage of silver, adding to the money supply and easing deflationary pressures.

See also: American Revolution Hyperinflation, French Revolution Hyperinflation, German Hyperinflation

References: MacCallum, Bennett T. 1989. *Monetary Economics: Theory and Policy.*

Sargent, Thomas. 1993. *Rational Expectations and Inflation.* 2d ed.

Weintraub, Sidney. 1978. *Capitalism's Inflation and Unemployment Crisis.*

Interest Rate

The interest rate can be regarded as the cost of money, expressed as a percentage. If the annual interest rate is 10 percent, an individual borrowing $100 for a year pays $10 interest. Decimalized currency systems substantially facilitated the calculation of interest. This is one reason countries rapidly adopted decimalized currency systems during the nineteenth century.

Theoretically, interest rates adjust to a level at which the interest earned on $100 invested in financial assets (for example, corporate bonds) equals the income earned from the ownership of $100 worth of capital goods (for example, tools, machinery, buildings). During the recovery phase of the business cycle interest rates tend to rise as capital goods become more productive, and in the recession phase interest rates tend to fall as capital goods lose productivity.

During early European history, religious authorities regarded charging interest as a sinful means of earning income. Governments either banned interest, or put a legal ceiling on interest rates. In the United States, state usury laws limiting interest rates were common as late as the 1970s. Most of them have now been repealed.

Historically, the highest peaks in interest rates have occurred during wartime. Interest rates reached historic levels during the Napoleonic Wars and during World War I. Wars are often the occasion for heavy government borrowing and high inflation, both of which are enemies to low interest rates. The legacy of the depression and wage and price controls helped keep a lid on interest rates during World War II, but the era of the cold war, from 1946 to 1983, saw

Paul Volcker speaks to protesters outside the Federal Reserve Building in Washington, D.C., 14 April 1980. (AP/Wide World Photos)

the longest upswing in interest rates occurring since the beginning of the eighteenth century.

Governments may act purposely to reduce interest rates as an antidote to depression. In 1998 the Federal Reserve System in the United States acted to lower interest rates to prevent a global financial crisis from spreading to the United States.

See also: Usury Laws

References: Barro, Robert J. 1987. Government Spending, Interest Rates, Prices, and Budget Deficits in the United Kingdom, 1701–1918. *Journal of Monetary Economics* 20 (September): 221–248.

Homer, Sidney. 1977. *A History of Interest Rates.*

International Monetary Conference of 1878

The International Monetary Conference opened in Paris on 10 August 1878. The conference was called at the request of the United States, which wanted to push for an international bimetallic monetary system. It utterly failed to live up to expectations. On 23 July 1878 the *New York Times* had printed an editorial with the heading, "Promoting the Federation of the World," suggesting that the conference would lead to the establishment of an international gold metric coinage unit and the new coinage unit would inculcate "true notions of the nature and purposes of money." The idea of an international coinage unit lingered in the background of the conference, partly as a pretext for some countries to attend the conference, but it never surfaced as a goal to be reached.

The seeds for the conference were sown with the passage of the Bland-Allison Act in the United States. This act began in Congress as a free silver act, but passed Congress, over a presidential veto, as an act requiring the Treasury to coin silver up to a fixed amount and asking the government to call an international conference to negotiate a world bimetallic standard. A world bimetallic standard would fix worldwide an official ratio of gold to silver. The United States hoped that if all governments set the same official ratio of gold to silver, the official world ratio would dominate the free market ratio, arresting the plunge of silver values in the free market.

The United States, possessing vast silver deposits, wanted to retain silver as a monetary metal, but the wealthier nations were rapidly shifting to a gold standard. England practiced "imperial bimetallism," maintaining herself on a gold standard, and India on a silver standard. Germany was selling off silver reserves after the adoption of the gold standard in 1871 and refused to attend the conference. The Latin Monetary Union countries, the largest being France, had ceased the coinage of silver because of its plunging value and were not favorably disposed toward resuscitating silver.

The representatives of the United States, isolated from the outset of the conference, found no crack in the diplomatic armor of the forces arrayed against a revival of bimetallism. A Dutch delegate suggested that the United States might look for monetary allies among the less-developed world (Latin America, Asia, etc.), hinting that the United States might belong with the less-developed countries itself and prompting a United States delegate to ask for a clarification. The European conference delegates offered to let the United States save face by turning the Conference into a series of sessions on coinage and bullion practices around the world, but the United States remained unswerving in its commitment to an international bimetallic standard.

On 28 August 1878 the conference delegates recessed for 45 minutes to let the European delegates reach an agreement on an answer to the American proposal. The European delegates flatly turned down the American proposal, saying that each nation, governed by its special situation, should set its own monetary standard.

The Conference of 1878 dropped the curtain on bimetallism, and by 1880 the world was squarely on a gold standard. The United States, the staunchest supporter of silver among the monetary powers, stood against the adoption of a bimetallic standard unless it was part of an international agreement.

The idea of an international monetary unit surfaced in the late nineteenth century and it is an idea that may yet be realized. Adoption of an international monetary unit would encourage international trade by reducing the risk of changing exchange rates between currencies and facilitating cost comparisons between goods produced in different countries. Europe has already launched a European currency, the *euro*, to replace national currencies in Europe, and the growth of international trade may push the world toward the adoption of an international monetary unit. Presently, the United States dollar fulfills some of the roles of an international monetary unit.

See also: Bimetallism, Latin Monetary Union

References: Bordo, Michael D. 1994. *Monetary Regimes in Transition*, ed. Forrest Capie.

Nugent, Walter T. K. 1968. *Money and American Society, 1865–1880*.

Willis, Henry Parker. 1901. *A History of the Latin Monetary Union.*

International Monetary Fund

The International Monetary Fund (IMF), is a supranational lending institution whose primary mission lies in furnishing short-term credit for countries suffering balance of payments deficits. Balance of payment deficits occur when a country's outflow of money from transactions with foreign countries exceeds its inflow. Like its sister institution, the World Bank, the IMF was born of the Bretton Woods Conference. That 1944 meeting of international monetary officials put foreign exchange markets under a system of fixed exchange rates—a system that lasted until 1971. The IMF began operations in 1946 and in 1964 it founded its headquarters in Washington, D.C. Although the mission of the World Bank lay in financing development and reconstruction projects, the IMF bore responsibility for loaning foreign currency reserves to countries on a short-term basis.

An excess of imports and investment in foreign countries relative to exports and domestic investment financed by foreign investors causes an excess outflow of a country's currency. This leads to currency depreciation in foreign exchange markets unless some type of market intervention occurs. A country can prevent currency depreciation by borrowing foreign currencies from the IMF and using these foreign currencies to purchase its own currency in foreign exchange markets, increasing the demand for its own currency and arresting its depreciation.

The funds of the IMF come from subscriptions of member countries, which contribute on the basis of such variables as national income and foreign trade. In 1946 member countries numbered 35, but by 1998 the number had grown to 182 countries. Soviet bloc countries did not join the IMF until after their transition to market countries. The United States has the largest quota of contributions and in 1998 contributed about 18 percent of all IMF funds. Each country contributes sums of its own currency, which serve as the IMF's lending capital. Out of these funds the IMF might make foreign currency loans to countries that use the proceeds to buy up excess amounts of their own currency in foreign exchange markets. The borrowing country puts up its own currency as collateral for such a loan.

Perhaps the greatest economic innovation of the IMF during the period of fixed exchange rates was the development of Special Drawing Rights (SDRs), sometimes referred to as "paper gold." By international agreement the SDRs are exchangeable for other currencies just as gold reserves.

Under the fixed exchange rate system the IMF loaned funds to countries that needed to intervene in foreign exchange markets to maintain the values of their currencies at the fixed rates. Under the floating exchange rate system the industrially developed countries had little need of the resources of the IMF. The IMF turned its attention to the less-developed countries, making longer-term loans to finance balance of payments of deficits, and granting soft loans to the poorest of the world's countries. These balance of payments deficits allowed these countries to import capital.

The oil price revolution of the 1970s not only pushed the fixed exchange rate system to the breaking point, but also put a heavy burden on the less-developed countries of the world, which responded by incurring large amounts of debt to foreign lenders. During the 1980s high interest rates increased the cost of servicing this debt, and reduced exports to the recession-ridden United States, decreasing the inflow of dollars needed to service this debt. Many of the less-developed countries also turned to inflationary policies at home, further endangering the investments of foreigners. Under these conditions the IMF assumed the thankless task of requiring these countries to follow responsible monetary and fiscal policies as a condition for receiving additional IMF credit. The IMF usually requires policies of high interest rates, depreciated currencies, and smaller budget deficits, translating as less social spending. Private lenders often refuse credit to countries that fail to follow IMF adjustment programs.

The decade of the 1990s kept the IMF unusually busy. The decade opened with Soviet bloc countries making the transition to market economies and needing domestic currencies convertible into hard currencies at stable exchange rates. The IMF provided expertise on the organization of central banks and supplied loans of hard currencies such as U.S. dollars to help these countries stabilize their currencies at stable exchange rates. In 1995 Mexico fell victim to a severe financial crisis, prompting the IMF to extend a record loan of over $17 billion dollars to that country. Toward the end of the decade global financial crisis was placing heavy demands on the resources of the IMF. By the end of 1998 Russia had received over $20 billion in loans, and $35 billion was committed to Korea, Indonesia, and Thailand to assist with the Asian financial crisis.

See also: Bretton Woods System, Dollar Crisis of 1971, World Bank

References: Myers, Robert J., ed. 1987. *The Political Morality of the International Monetary Fund.*

Polak, Jacques J. 1994. *The World Bank and the International Monetary Fund: A Changing Relationship.*

Iron Currency

Although iron currency has been regarded as primitive for 2,000 years, it survived into the modern period. Iron spits circulated as money in Greece before the advent of silver currency, and Sparta remained on an iron currency standard throughout the golden age of Greece. Sparta's iron currency was deliberately intended to make the accumulation of monetary wealth awkward.

Julius Caesar's writing, *Gallic Wars,* mentions an iron currency in Britain. Unfortunately, the texts of the various manuscripts of Caesar's work are not

Iron currency. (Smithsonian Institution, National Numismatic Collection)

consistent, and scholars have split on the meaning of the text, some claiming the iron currency was iron rings and others that it was iron bars. Archeological evidence seems to have decided the issue in favor of iron bars. No iron rings have been found from that time period but other iron objects, including iron bars, have been discovered. These iron bars were apparently unfinished sword blades.

The monetary unit for this currency seems to have been about 11 ounces of iron. Some pieces weighed as little as one-quarter of the standard unit, and others as much as four units. It is possible that the value of the bars was determined by length rather than weight.

During the nineteenth century iron bars were circulating as money in the Congo. Europeans complained about the high transportation cost of these bars. Apparently, it took one man to carry just 8 shillings' worth of money. The iron bars came in lengths of one foot and were extremely heavy. One of the Congo tribes, the Bakongo, were particularly noted for coveting these iron bars.

Iron hoes have circulated as money in regions of India, Africa, and Indochina. Iron hoes were the smallest monetary unit in the Bahnars at one time. During the nineteenth century, iron, mainly in the shape of hoes, circulated in the remote areas of Sudan. The Chiga of western Uganda made hoes their unit of account without making use of them as a medium of exchange or store of value. In Portuguese East Africa a hoe standard replaced a cattle standard, and some hoes circulated only as currency and were never used as agricultural implements. In the French Congo, iron bars, shovels, hoes, blades, and iron double bells played the role of currency. In mid-nineteenth-century Nigeria, 40 iron hoes could buy a slave.

Iron is not as immune to the elements as the precious metals and does not have the same aesthetic appeal. It does not seem to have had religious significance, such as did silver and gold. Nevertheless, it is a very practical metal, making it attractive as money in societies that have not mastered metallurgy to the same extent as the industrially developed societies.

See also: Commodity Monetary Standard, Spartan Iron Currency

References: Einzig, Paul. 1966. *Primitive Money*.

Islamic Coinage
See Arab Dinar, Ottoman Empire Currency

Italian Lira
See Carolingian Reform, Corso Forzoso, Quattrini Affair

Ivory
The tusks of elephants are composed of ivory, a substance much in demand throughout history for its durability and beauty. The demand for ivory has nearly become the downfall of elephants, which have been decimated in large numbers for the sake of their tusks.

The role that ivory has played as money is rather limited in spite of the fact that its aesthetic qualities and durability give it some of the same attraction as precious metals. In mountain villages on the island of Ili Mandriri in the Indonesian archipelago islanders used ivory as a store of value and mark of social status. An individual's social standing was a function of the number and size of ivory tusks that he or she owned. It appears that not too far in the murky past ivory also served as a medium of exchange. In the post–World War II era the islanders stilled used ivory as the main form of bride money.

Before the arrival of Arabian traders, tribes in Uganda cut ivory discs that served as a favored form of money. Although anyone was free to cut ivory discs, no one could kill elephants or possess ivory without the king's permission, and cutting ivory discs required special skills possessed only by a few people. In effect, the king had a monopoly on the supply of ivory discs.

During the time of German colonization of equatorial Africa fines were set in ivory, eventually leaving the colonial administration with a large stockpile. There is also evidence of an ivory monetary unit in Gabon. In Loma a 100-pound chunk of ivory represented a monetary unit for large transactions, but it was a fictitious unit and in reality represented an assortment of European goods. In the Nama tribe of southwest Africa, ivory represented a stable export, and acted as a medium of exchange.

Ivory has functioned as money primarily in Africa. Famous African explorer John H. Speke, who discovered Lake Victoria as the source of the Nile, mentioned the use of ivory as money in his book *The Discovery of the Source of the Nile.* Henry M. Stanley in his book *In Darkest Africa* tells of treasuries of ivory and his own use of ivory to pay for services rendered by tribes. He also wrote of raiding parties that captured slaves mainly to exchange the slaves for ivory. Ivory might have acted as money on a grander scale if it had commanded more religious significance for the Africans, or if the foreign ivory demand had not been so high relative to the domestic demand.

See also: Commodity Monetary Standard

References: Einzig, Paul. 1966. *Primitive Money.*
Speke, J. H. 1906. *The Discovery of the Source of the Nile.*
Stanley, Henry M. 1890. *In Darkest Africa.*

J

Juilliard v. Greenman (United States)

In the case of *Juilliard v. Greenman*, 110 U.S. 421 (1884), the United States Supreme Court ruled that Congress had the right to issue notes to be legal tender for the payment of public and private debt. Legal-tender notes are Treasury notes or bank notes that, in the eyes of the law, must be accepted in the payment of debts.

Under the Legal Tender Act of 25 February 1862 Congress authorized the issuance of United States notes as legal tender for all debts public and private, excepting custom duties and interest on the public debt, which were payable in coin. The United States Constitution had not explicitly conferred upon Congress the right to issue legal-tender notes, or other legal-tender paper money, and many doubted if legal-tender legislation was constitutional. The Constitution was framed while the memory of the hyperinflation episode of the Continental currency was still fresh.

Hepburn v. Griswold, 75 U.S. 603 (1870), was the first Supreme Court case to test the constitutionality of legal-tender notes. The Court found that the issuance of legal-tender notes amounted to an impairment of contracts without due process of law, which was forbidden by the Constitution and therefore unconstitutional. Contracts were abridged because a creditor had to accept depreciated notes rather than coin. Interestingly, Chief Justice Chase, who wrote the majority opinion, was secretary of the Treasury when the notes were issued at his strong urging. Some observers felt that Chase changed his mind to improve his chances for a presidential bid.

The *Hepburn* decision did not stand long. In *Parker v. Davis*, 79 U.S. 457 (1871), the Court—enlarged with two new appointees—ruled in favor of Congress's power to issue legal-tender notes, but the decision drew heavily on the exigencies of war and left in doubt the constitutionality of the issuance of legal-tender notes in peacetime.

In 1878 Congress repealed an earlier act providing for the retirement of outstanding legal-tender notes (greenbacks) and provided for the reissuance of these notes. Because these notes were reissued in peacetime, the constitutional authority of Congress to maintain their legal-tender status remained in doubt.

When *Juilliard v. Greenman* came before the Supreme Court in 1884 the Court held that Congress had the authority to issue legal-tender notes even in peacetime. The majority opinion argued that Congress had the authority to issue legal-tender notes under its constitutional power "to raise money for the public use on a pledge of the public credit," including the power "to issue, in return for the money borrowed, the obligation of the United States in any appropriate form of stock, bonds, bills, or notes adapted to circulation from hand to hand in the ordinary transactions of business" (110 U.S. at 432). The majority opinion also argued that the power to confer legal status on money derived from the rights of sovereignty as understood when the Constitution was framed.

The decision of *Juilliard v. Greenman* settled the question of the authority of Congress to provide a national currency for the United States.

See also: *Case of Mixt Monies,* Legal Tender

References: Breckinridge, S. P. 1969. *Legal Tender.*

Dunne, Gerald T. 1960. *Monetary Decisions of the Supreme Court.*

Hepburn, A. Barton. 1967. *A History of the Currency of the United States.*

Meyers, Margaret G. 1970. *A Financial History of the United States.*

K

Knights of the Templars

The Knights of the Templars, a religious order of knights devoted to liberating the Holy Land from infidels, developed an international banking network in the twelfth and thirteenth centuries. At the opening of the fourteenth century, the vast wealth of the Templars fell prey to the king of France, who greedily launched a campaign of persecution, complete with burnings at the stake.

The Military Order of the Knights of the Temple of Solomon, founded in Jerusalem in 1181, lived next to the ruins of Solomon's Temple and took on the task of keeping the Holy Land safe for pilgrims. Eventually owning castles all the way from England to Jerusalem, the Knights kept highways and sea lanes to the Holy Land open. After the fall of Jerusalem, the Templars retreated to Cyprus.

The Templars themselves followed an ascetic regimen, eating only two meals a day to the sound of scriptural readings and observing vows of chastity. On the battlefield a strict warrior code steeled the Templars to face death without flinching and left no room for surrender or defeat. Even as the Templars rose to become an international banking power, individual knights were forbidden to own money. A Christian burial was withheld from knights found with unauthorized money at death, condemning them to eternal damnation.

A series of papal bulls granted the Templars the privilege to retain the spoils of war. Also, like other religious orders, they received bequests, gifts, and donations. King Henry II of England made a handsome donation, hoping to find forgiveness for the murder of Thomas à Becket. Their castles provided safe and secure storage for money and other valuables, and their role as protector of highways and sea lanes enabled the Templars to transport income from their European estates to their headquarters in Jerusalem.

From providing depositories of safekeeping and transportation of valuables, the Templars expanded into banking, loaning money in Europe for delivery in Jerusalem, and financing kings and other knights. They held valuables of other knights and executed their wills. Philip II of France organized a force for the Crusade of 1190 and left his revenues to be managed by the Templars. The Templars' castles offered a complete range of banking services, and popes and kings sought the financial services of the Templars.

The Templars' headquarters in Paris boasted one of the largest treasure stores in Europe. Philip IV of France ran into financial difficulty and resorted to currency debasement more than once. He also removed the Templars from management of his finances. But only the vast treasure of the Templars could supply Philip with the gold and silver needed to reform France's debased currency. Philip opened a vicious war of words with the Templars, accusing them of devil worship, sexual perversion, sex with corpses of noblewomen, and impregnating virgins in order to harvest their infants to make sacred oil. The alleged practice of sodomy among the Templars purportedly led to the fall of Jerusalem, an obvious reference to the destruction of Sodom and Gomorrah.

After confessions extracted by torture, Templar knights were burned at the stake. Philip pressured Pope Clement V to abolish the order on 22 March 1312. In abolishing the order the pope gave the treasury of the Templars to other religious orders, particularly the Hospitalers. The French government managed to extract a large share of the treasure that went to the Hospitalers as compensation for prosecuting the Templars. With the memory of the fate of the Templars still fresh, the Hospitalers yielded to Philip's pressure.

The destruction of the Templars left a void in international banking that was soon filled on a smaller scale by the bankers of the Italian Renaissance.

See also: Dissolution of Monasteries, Papal Coinage

References: Barber, Malcolm. 1978. *The Trial of the Templars.*
Burman, Edward. 1996. *Supremely Abominable Crimes: the Trial of the Knights Templar.*
Weatherford, John. 1997. *The History of Money.*

L

Labor Notes

Labor notes, a unique monetary experiment in early nineteenth-century England, bore a face value equivalent to a certain number of hours of work. The notes were the brainchild of Robert Owen (1771–1858), a successful textile manufacturer in England who rose to fame as a utopian socialist reformer at the beginning of the Industrial Age. He is famous in the United States for involvement with New Harmony, Indiana. In 1825 Owen purchased 30,000 acres of land in Indiana and launched New Harmony as a cooperative society, a project that would cost him 80 percent of his fortune before he abandoned it.

In 1832 Owen was publishing a penny journal, *The Crisis,* in which he publicized his plan to form an association for the exchange of all commodities upon the principle of the numbers of hours of labor embodied in each commodity. All commodities that required the same amount of labor to produce were to be traded evenly, and other commodities were to be exchanged at ratios ruled by the number of hours of labor required to produce each one. If it took two hours of labor to produce product A and one hour of labor to produce product B, then it took two units of product B to purchase one unit of product A. Owen adapted his plan from the labor theory of value, a widely accepted concept among nineteenth-century economists, which held that all value comes from labor.

To carry out his plan, Owen opened the Equitable Labor Exchange on 3 September 1832 at a building called the Bazaar on Gray's Inn Road, London. Producers and manufacturers brought goods to the exchange, and received in return labor notes equal to the amount of labor required to produce the goods. The labor notes could be used to buy other goods at the exchange, which were priced based upon the hours of labor that went into producing each good. Exchanges opened in different regions, and one of the largest was in Birmingham, where two series of labor notes were issued in denominations of 1, 2, 5, 10, 50, and 80 labor-hours.

The exchanges were short-lived. It was a utopian idea that could not compete with a market system that incorporates all the available information that affects the prices of goods and services. Owens closed down the London exchange in March 1834 and paid off a 2,000-pound deficit the exchange had run up.

References: Angell, Norman. 1929. *The Story of Money.* Beresiner, Yasha. 1977. *Paper Money.* Birchall, Johnson. 1994. *Co-op: the People's Business.*

Land Bank System (American Colonies)

During the first half of the eighteenth century, land banks infused paper currency into the economies of the American colonies, helping to relieve the shortage of money that hampered trade and industry. Aside from two short-lived exceptions, these were public banks, functioning under the auspices of colonial governments.

Land banks loaned paper money to citizens who put up collateral in the form of some sort of real estate, such as farmland or houses in town. Borrowers ran the risk of forfeiting their property in the event of default, although the land banks, as public institutions, enjoyed reputations for extending the terms for debtors in difficulty. The real estate nevertheless stood as security maintaining the value of the paper money, and foreclosure was a legitimate weapon. When foreclosure failed to produce sufficient revenue to redeem the paper currency, then governments were usually obliged to make good the paper money. The borrowers paid interest on the loans, which in most colonies went to pay governmental expenses. Often a local public board of property-owning citizens acted as a loan board, approving and disapproving loans as it saw fit. In other cases provincial officials at a higher level made these decisions. These boards or officials received an allotment of paper currency for issuance in a given locality.

During the seventeenth century several proposals were floated for organizing private land banks in the American colonies, particularly in Massachusetts, but invariably the colonial assemblies refused to grant charters for these private ventures. In 1712 South Carolina led the way in the land bank movement when it established the first public land bank in the American colonies. Other colonies quickly followed the example set by South Carolina. Massachusetts founded a land bank in 1714, Rhode Island in 1715, New Hampshire in 1717, New Jersey and Pennsylvania in 1723, North Carolina in 1729, Maryland in 1731, Connecticut in 1732, and New York in 1737.

The English government viewed all colonial paper money as a threat to English creditors who faced severe loses if colonists sought to wipe out debts with a round of inflation. In 1720 royal governors in America received orders from London to suspend the operation of any land bank, pending approval from the Privy Council. Both American and English officials, however, were slow to take action. The land bank in Massachusetts remained in operation until 1730 and the land banks in the other colonies until 1740.

The saga of the land banks is another chapter in the struggle of the American colonies to fill the vacuum in the colonial money supply left by the outflow of hard specie in payment for European imports. England aggravated the money shortage by squashing efforts to mint coins in the colonies and severely restricting the authority of colonial governments to issue paper money. After the American Revolution, the Articles of Confederation granted state governments authority to establish mints and issue paper currency. The United States Constitution gave Congress sole authority to coin money and regulate the money supply.

See also: Franklin, Benjamin, Massachusetts Bay Colony Paper Issue

References: Chown, John F. 1994. *A History of Money*. Ernst, Joseph Albert. 1973. *Money and Politics in America*. Thayer, Theodore. 1953. The Land-Bank System in the American Colonies. *Journal of Economic History* 13, no. 2: 145–159.

Larin

The *larin* was a Persian coin that acted as international currency in the Indian Ocean trading area in the sixteenth through eighteenth centuries. For reasons unknown, the city of Lar in Iran gave its name to the larin, but the coin seems never to have been minted in that city. The larin was a silver coin.

As coins go the larin was a bit unusual, even for a period as early as the sixteenth century. Rather than a coin struck from a circular blank of metal, the larin was made of a strip of silver wire, bent in two, and stamped with circular or rectangular dies. The Safavid Shah Tahmasp, ruler of Hormuz, now southern Iran, struck the first larins during the mid-sixteenth century. India and Ceylon also minted larins, as did Arabia under the Ottomans, but the larins struck by the Safavids traded at a premium, owing to the purity of their silver metal.

In the sixteenth and seventeenth centuries larins were overvalued in terms of silver content, and silver flowed into Persia from European trade with the Levant. The law required Persian merchants receiving foreign coins to bring all these coins to the mint to be restruck as larins. The merchants had to pay the mint charge but the overvaluation of the larin offset these costs.

During the seventeenth century the Spanish *real*, forebear to the U.S. dollar, began to displace the larin in Indian Ocean and Far Eastern trade. Persian merchants smuggled in Spanish reales and Persian caravans and sea-going vessels laden with reals left Persia for trade with India. Early in the eighteenth century the Iranian and Indian currency was unified and the new currency was called the *rupee*, but by then Spanish reals dominated world trade.

See also: De a Ocho Reales, Ottoman Empire Currency
References: Braudel, Fernand. 1981. *Civilization and Capitalism: 15th–18th Century.* Vol. I.
Williams, Jonathan, ed. 1997. *Money: A History.*

Latin Monetary Union

One of the early efforts to establish a uniform and universal coinage, equally acceptable in all countries, led to the formation of the Latin Monetary Union. The union itself came to life through the work of a conference held in Paris, France, in 1865. In addition to France, three other countries, Italy, Switzerland, and Belgium, participated in the conference, all three of which were on the French bimetallic system. This conference was the first international meeting on monetary affairs.

Under a bimetallic system silver and gold coins circulated as money and the government set the value of silver relative to gold at a fixed ratio. Before the conference the value of silver was rising, causing holders of silver to buy gold and leading to the disappearance of silver. Switzerland debased the value of its silver coins to address the problem, and France responded by banning the acceptance of Swiss coins in public offices. The immediate technical problem facing the conference participants was the overvaluation of silver. Under the bimetallic system of the Latin Monetary Union, 15.5 ounces of silver stood equal to 1 ounce of gold in all member countries.

The conference participants saw the treaty creating the Latin Monetary Union put into effect on 1 August 1866. The States of the Church (the lands in central and north-central Italy that were ruled by the pope) joined the union later in 1866, followed by Bulgaria and Greece in 1867. Member countries minted gold pieces in denominations only of 100, 50, 20, 10 and 5 *francs.* They also minted silver pieces in denominations of 5, 2, and 1 francs and 50 and 20 silver *centimes.* Each country minted coins that were made legal tender and circulated throughout the union.

In 1867 France called another conference to discuss the establishment of a uniform world monetary system. Hopes of expanding French influence and prestige may have supplied the motive that pushed Louis Napoleon to call the conference. The need to keep the bimetallic monetary standard alive and working in the face of competition from England's gold standard may also have been a contributing factor.

The United States accepted the concept of a world monetary union and made a case for France to begin minting a 25-franc gold piece. Spokesmen for the United States, whose arguments for the 25-franc piece fell on deaf ears in France, observed that:

> [S]uch a coin will circulate side by side everywhere and in perfect equality with the half eagle of the United States and the sovereign of Great Britain. These three gold coins, types of the great commercial nations, fraternally united and differing only in emblems, will go hand in hand around the globe freely circulating through both hemispheres without recoinage, brokerage, or other impediments. This opportune concession of France to the spirit of unity will complete the work of civilization she has had so much at heart and will inaugurate that new monetary era, the lofty object of the international conference, and the noblest aim of the concourse of nations, as yet without parallel in the history of the world. (Chown, 1994)

The conference ended without reaching an agreement, only passing a resolution to meet again. England had refused to support the plan for a world monetary union, but did establish a Royal Commission on International Coinage to study the findings of the conference. The commission acknowledged the advantages of an international currency, citing that:

> Small manufacturers and traders are deterred from engaging in foreign transactions by the complicated difficulties of foreign coins by the difficulty in calculating the exchanges, and of remitting small sums from one country to another. Anything tending to simplify these matters would dispose them to extend their sphere of operations. (Chown, 1994)

Nevertheless, the commission cited numerous practical considerations that stood in the way of forming an international currency.

The commercial success of Great Britain persuaded the major trading partners of the world that the gold standard was the wave of the future. The fate of the bimetallic system of the Latin Monetary Union was sealed when France lost the Franco-Prussian War and had to pay war reparations to Germany. The war reparations enhanced Germany's gold reserves, giving Germany the wherewithal to follow England's example and adopt the gold standard. The value of silver dropped sharply, and the members of the Latin Monetary Union had to restrict the coinage of silver. The union wobbled on until the 1920s when the strains of war and diverging gold and silver prices put an end to the system.

The idea of a European monetary union, complete with a European central bank, became a reality on 1 January 1999 when the European Central Bank launched the *euro*. The euro does not presently circulate as bank notes or coins, but only as money of account. It will eventually circulate as bank notes and coins, and will replace major European currencies, such as the German mark and the French franc. This monetary union with its uniform currency will end the risk of fluctuations in foreign exchange rates and the inconvenience of converting domestic money into foreign exchange, thus easing the path for the growth of international trade.

See also: Bimetallism, Euro Currency, International
   Monetary Conference of 1878
References: Chown, John F. 1994. *A History of Money*.
Davies, Glyn. 1994. *A History of Money*.
Willis, Henry Parker. 1901. *A History of the Latin Monetary
   Union*.

Law, John

In the *Wealth of Nations* (1776) Adam Smith observed that "[t]he idea of the possibility of multiplying paper money to almost any extent was the real foundation of what is called the Mississippi scheme, the most extravagant project of banking and stock-jobbing that perhaps the world ever saw." John Law was the author of the Mississippi scheme. He was a Scottish financier who felt that Scottish industry languished from a lack of money. He conceived the notion that a bank could issue paper money equal in value to all the land in a country. The Scottish Parliament was not interested, but the new regent of France, Philippe d'Orleans, saw Law's theories as a way out of the bankrupt finances of France. Philippe authorized Law to establish the Banque Generale (1716). Among other things, this was the first bank to issue legal-tender paper money. It accepted de-

posits, paid interest, and made loans. The value of its paper money was defined in terms of a fixed weight of silver. In April 1717 taxes were made payable in the bank's paper money.

In 1717 Law secured a royal charter to launch the Mississippi Company. This was a trading company organized to exploit the Mississippi basin. Law sold 200,000 shares of this new company to the public. The price stood at 500 *livres* per share, but three-fourths of the payment could be made with government notes at face value. These government notes were then worth one-third of their face value. The shares found a ready market in holders of depreciating government notes eager for a piece of a profit-making enterprise. Law became bolder with success and instructed his bank to buy the royal tobacco monopoly and all French companies devoted to foreign trade. These companies he combined with the Mississippi Company for the complete monopolization of French foreign trade.

In 1718 Law's bank was reorganized as the Banque Royal, and the government made the bank's paper money legal tender. By 1720 the combination of trading companies known as the Mississippi Company was amalgamated with the bank. The Banque Royal bought up the national debt by exchanging it for shares in the Mississippi Company. Turning the national debt into shares of the Mississippi Company set the example that was soon copied by the South Sea Company in England. The prices of the shares in the Mississippi rose to fantastic heights on a wave of speculative frenzy. Law's bank continually increased the supply of paper money, much of which was used to bid up the shares in the Mississippi Company. When prices of commodities rose 100 percent and wages 75 percent between 1716 and 1720, the public lost faith in the value of paper money.

In the meantime things were not going well for the Mississippi Company. There were no precious metals to be found and no attraction could induce families to emigrate to the Mississippi basin. Profits fell far short of expectations.

In 1719 the price of the stock peaked and the downward spiral began. Those in the know sold their stock at the peak and redeemed their bank paper money with gold. As the sell-off gained momentum Law's bank issued paper money to buy the shares of stock. Holders of paper money besieged the bank, demanding silver or gold and several people were killed in the confusion. Law himself was forced to leave France and he passed his declining years as a professional gambler in Venice.

The Mississippi Bubble left a deep distrust of paper money and big banks in the mind of the French people. Nearly a century elapsed before France was willing to try paper money again. Learning the pitfalls of paper money has been a slow process in modern capitalist countries. Angola, Argentina, and Bolivia rank among the countries that have experienced hyperinflation in the post–World War II era.

See also: Caisse d'Escompte, French Revolution
   Hyperinflation
References: Minton, Robert. 1975. *John Law: The Father of Paper Money.*
Murphy, Antoin E. 1997. *John Law: Economic Theorist and Policy Maker.*
Schumpeter, Joseph. 1939. *Business Cycles.* Vol. I.
Spiegel, Henry W. 1971. *The Growth of Economic Thought.*

Law of the Maximum
See French Revolution Hyperinflation,
Wage and Price Controls

Leather Money
Leather money should perhaps be regarded as the most immediate precursor of paper money. It was usually issued as an emergency measure under the stress of war.

The extinct city of ancient Carthage issued a leather-wrapped money before the wars with Rome. The leather wrapping was sealed and the substance inside the wrapping remained a mystery.

Better documentation exists for the use of leather money in France and Italy as an emergency measure. In Normandy Philippe I (1060–1108) used as money pieces of leather with a small silver nail in the middle. Leather currencies also appeared under Louis IX (1266–1270), John the Good (1350–1364), and Charles the Wise (1364–1380). It is not clear whether these leather currencies bore an official stamp. Foreign ransoms had impoverished France of its metallic currencies, necessitating the development of an inferior substitute.

In 1122 Doge Domenico Michaele, ruler of Venice, financed a crusade by paying his troops and fleets in money made of leather with an official stamp. In 1237 the emperor Frederick II of Sicily, one

of the first European monarchs to reestablish gold coinage after the long hiatus of the Middle Ages, paid his troops in stamped leather money during the sieges of Milan and Faventia. In 1248 at the siege of Parma he again paid troops in leather money. Frederick's money was converted into silver at a later date.

Leather money bearing an official stamp bore a close kinship to modern paper money. English history furnishes a few references to leather money. In a speech to Parliament in 1523 Thomas Cromwell commented in referring to the expenses of sending an expedition to France:

> Thus we should soon be made incapable of hurting anyone, and be compelled, as we once did to coin leather. This, for my part, I could be content with; but if the King will go over in person and should happen to fall into the hands of the enemy—which God forbid—how should we be able to redeem him? If they will naught for their wine but gold they would think great scorn to take leather for our Prince. (Einzig, 1966)

Reports exist of leather money on the Isle of Man during the sixteenth and maybe seventeenth centuries. A description of the Isle of Man published in 1726 states that leather currency had a history on the Island of Man, and that men of substance were allowed to make their own money up to a limit.

See also: Chinese Leather Money, Fur Money,
   Leather-Wrapped Money of Carthage, Siege Money
References: Einzig, Paul. 1966. *Primitive Money.*
Quiggin, A., and A. Hingston. 1949. *A Survey of Primitive Money.*

Leather-Wrapped Money
of Ancient Carthage
The city of Carthage, an ancient Phoenician city in North Africa near the present site of Tunis, was the major rival to Rome during the third and second centuries B.C. It was destroyed by Rome in 146 B.C. in the third and last of the famous Punic Wars. Aeschines, an immediate disciple of Socrates in the fifth century B.C., wrote in his *Dialogues of Socrates:*

> The Carthaginians made use of the following kind (of money): in a small piece of leather, a substance is wrapped of the size of a piece of

four-drachmae; but what this substance is, no one knows except the maker. After this, it is sealed (by the state) and issued for circulation. (Angell, 1929)

Apparently, removing the leather wrapping rendered the pieces worthless. Other classical authors make reference to the leather-wrapped money of Carthage, but make no mention of the nature of the mysterious substance inside the wrapping. More recent scholars have speculated that the "leather" was more likely a parchment, and that the enwrapped substance was either tin or a compound of tin and copper. Perhaps the government of Carthage maintained the value of this fiat money by restricting its supply.

The murky history of the leather-wrapped money of Carthage reveals little about the dates of its circulation, or its success as a stable currency. In the third century B.C. Carthage was the richest Mediterranean city, but no history of Carthage written by Carthaginians has come down to us. This wrapped money may have been the short-lived product of the exigencies of war. Presumably, the Carthaginians no longer needed a fiat money after the opening of the gold and silver mines in Spain early in the fifth century. Carthaginian conquest of Sicily, from which Carthage learned coinage, and control of western Mediterranean sea trade brought on a century-long duel to the death between Rome and Carthage.

The metal currency of the Carthaginians was undistinguished, particularly in light of the high standards set by Greek coinage. The Carthaginians do deserve credit for introducing the equivalent of a paper money in the ancient world of the Mediterranean. In the history of Western civilization the ancients understood the debasement of metal coinage exceedingly well, but only Carthage is credited with developing anything resembling a paper money. China may have predated Carthage in paper money development, but well-documented evidence of paper money in China occurs after the Carthaginian innovation of leather-wrapped money.

See also: Ancient Chinese Paper Money, Chinese Leather Money, Leather Money

References: Angell, Norman. 1929. *The Story of Money*. Smith, R. Bosworth. 1913. *Carthage and the Carthaginians*.

Legal Reserve Ratio

A legally required reserve ratio is one of the important central bank instruments for changing the stock of money in circulation. The reserve ratio is the fraction of customer deposits banks hold in the form of assets that satisfy a legal definition of reserves. In the United States only vault cash or deposits at a Federal Reserve Bank may legally serve as reserves. A reduction in the legally required reserve ratio, allowing banks to loan out more depositor funds, leads to an expansion of the money stock. Raising this ratio reduces the money stock.

Commercial banks accept deposits of funds from customers. On a given day the fresh deposits approximately offset withdrawals from earlier deposits, leaving the bank with an average level of deposits available for loans to customers. Banks keep a fraction of these deposits as reserves to keep the bank solvent during those intervals when fresh deposits fall short of withdrawals. Without government regulation of reserve requirements, banks often fall prey to the temptation to trim reserves too thinly and come up short of funds if depositors suddenly place heavy demands for cash withdrawals. Because reserves are funds that are not invested, and therefore not earning income, banks have an incentive to hold reserves to a minimal level.

In the United States the Banking Act of 1935 authorized the Board of Governors of the Federal Reserve System to vary the legally required reserve ratio within prescribed limits. Before the Act of 1935 legal reserve ratios were set by statute. From 1935 until 1980 the Board of Governors could change the reserve requirements of commercial banks that were members of the Federal Reserve System, which included all commercial banks with national charters. State banks remained subject to state statutory reserve requirements until 1980. The Depository Institution Deregulation and Monetary Control Act of 1980 gave the Board of Governors authority to set reserve requirements for all depository institutions. The legal reserve ratio is usually set well below 20 percent. In 1992 the Board of Governors reduced the ratio from 12 to 10 percent.

If the level of deposits in a bank rises by $1,000, and the legal reserve ratio is 10 percent, the bank has to retain only $100 as reserves and can loan out the other $900. If the reserve ratio is cut for all banks, each bank can immediately loan out more funds.

Furthermore, as deposits at each bank grow from the lending at other banks, each bank can loan out a share of new deposits. The cumulative effect of these actions on the ratio of customer deposits to vault cash and deposits at the Federal Reserve Banks can be dramatic. If the legal reserve ratio decreased from 20 percent to 10 percent, the ratio of customer deposits to vault cash and deposits at the Federal Reserve Banks could double. Because bank deposits account for the lion's share of money supply measures, a reduction in the legal reserve ratio can sharply increase the money stock. An increase in the legal reserve ratio can have an equally blunt impact on the money stock in the opposite direction.

Significant controversy arose out of one of the early policy actions using legal reserves requirements. In 1936 commercial banks were flush with reserves, representing a potential for substantial increase in lending and monetary growth. The United States economy was still inching out of the depression, but the banking system brimming over with reserves aroused inflationary fears. The Board of Governors virtually doubled reserve requirements to mop up excess reserves. In 1937 the recovery stalled out, nosing the economy over into another recession, and many observers put the blame at the feet of the improper use of legal reserve requirements by the Board of Governors.

Today legal reserve ratios are one of the less important means of regulating monetary growth. Small changes in legal reserve ratios have powerful effects and create management difficulties for banks. Open market operations have become the most important means of regulating the money stock in the United States. Open market operations have to do with central bank purchases and sale of government bonds. When a central bank purchases bonds with new funds, the money stock increases.

See also: Bank, Central Bank, Federal Reserve System, Monetary Multiplier, Open Market Operations
References: Baye, Michael R., and Dennis W. Jansen. 1995. *Money, Banking, and Financial Markets.*
Klein, John J. 1982. *Money and the Economy.* 6th ed.

Legal Tender

Money is legal tender when creditors are legally obliged to accept it in payment of debts. The words "This note is legal tender for all debts, private and public," appears on all Federal Reserve Notes, mean-

ing that these notes are acceptable in payment of taxes or other obligations owed to the government and also that creditors must accept the notes in payment of all private debts.

In the expression *legal tender* the word *tender* means "offer," as when an individual tenders his resignation. The term *tender* with reference to money arose out of actions of creditors against debtors in English courts. A debtor could "tender" to the creditor the amount he or she thought was owed to the creditor. If the creditor thought the sum tendered unacceptable, the debtor could deposit the sum with the court, which would decide if the tender met the debtor's obligation.

The legal-tender quality of a unit of money can be restricted. The American colonies issued paper money that was acceptable for the payment of public debts, but not private debts. The colonial governments committed themselves to accepting the money in payment of taxes, but did not require private creditors to accept it in payment of debts. Currently in the United States the dime is legal tender for all debts up to $10.

English sovereigns arrogated to themselves the privilege of coining money and stipulated penalties for refusing to accept the king's coinage at face value. Orders from the crown went so far as to require the acceptance of pennies that had been halved and demanded that anyone refusing to accept half pennies should be seized for contempt of the king's majesty, imprisoned, and exposed to public ridicule in a pillory.

Although the English government threw the full weight of its sovereign power behind its coinage, disputes between creditors and debtors continued to raise questions, leaving with the courts the final authority for establishing the legal-tender quality of money. An important court case in 1601, *The Case of Mixt Monies,* set the legal-tender quality of money on firm footing when it demonstrated that creditors had to accept in payment for debts the money that was legal tender when the debt was paid, as opposed to the money that was legal tender when the debt was incurred.

The Constitution of the United States specifies that: "No state shall coin money; make anything but gold and silver coin a legal tender in payment of debts." Prior to 1862 no paper money in the United States commanded the legal-tender status. Never-

Only in 1883 did the U.S. Supreme Court rule in favor of the federal government's right to issue legal tender paper money, an event commemorated by the "Legal Tender Polka." (Library of Congress)

theless the government often accepted bank notes and treasury notes in payment of taxes and public land sales, giving the paper money some legal-tender qualities. In 1862, amidst the fiscal crisis of the Civil War, the United States government issued paper money that was legal tender for all private debts, and many, but not all, public debts. The power of the government to issue legal-tender paper money was challenged in the courts, but the wartime crisis clouded the issue at first. When paper money continued to circulate after 1878 the legal-tender issue came before the Supreme Court, and in 1883 the Court ruled in favor of the power of the federal government to issue legal-tender paper money. In 1890 the federal government issued the first paper money that was legal tender in payment of all private debts and all payments owed to the government.

Economists have not always written approvingly of governments using their power to adjudicate disputes to render money legal tender. The famous economist John Stuart Mill wrote in his *Principles of Political Economy* (Book III, chapter vii):

Profligate governments having until a very modern period never scrupled for the sake of robbing their creditors to confer upon all other debtors a license to rob theirs by the shallow and impudent artifice of lowering the standard; that least covert of all modes of knavery, which consists in calling a shilling a pound that a debt of a hundred pounds may be canceled by the payment of one hundred shillings.

When governments become major debtors they have an incentive to change the standard to pay off the debts, and in the twentieth century governments have printed up legal-tender paper money to cancel large public debts, the post–World War I government of Germany being the most notorious case. Despite the latent possibility for abuse, governments worldwide issue legal-tender paper money, which poses no problems as long as the supply is restricted to noninflationary levels.

See also: *Julliard v. Greenman* (United States)
References: Breckinridge, S. P. 1903. *Legal Tender.*
Dunne, Gerald T. 1960. *Monetary Decisions of the Supreme Court.*
Myers, Margaret. 1970. *A Financial History of the United States.*

Lex Aternia-Tarpeia of 454 B.C. (Rome)

With the Lex Aternia-Tarpeia of 454 B.C., sometimes called the Tarpeian law, the Romans took a historic step toward replacing livestock money with metallic currency. In 454 B.C. Rome sent three commissioners to Athens to study Athenian laws. Before Solon's reform of Athenian law in 600 B.C. the laws of Draco had provided for payment of fines in cattle and sheep. One of Solon's contributions to Athenian law was a provision that allowed fines expressed in cattle and sheep to be paid in metallic money. Among the outcomes of the Roman commissioners' visit was the Tarpeian law. Prior to the Tarpeian law the Romans fixed fines in livestock. Culprits guilty of minor offenses paid a fine of 2 sheep, while grave offenses drew fines ranging up to 30 oxen.

According to the Tarpeian law, payments defined in oxen could be paid in copper *asses*. The Roman *aes* or *as* began as a pound of copper, although it suffered the fate of many metallic currencies as the copper content was steadily reduced by law. It may have been measured in lengths of rods and was not coined until the fourth century B.C. The Tarpeian law valued an ox at 100 copper asses, and a sheep at 10 asses. In 452 B.C. the Romans drew up a constitution, the Twelve Tables of Law, which again called for penalties to be paid in copper and gold units without mentioning cattle.

Probably a major factor pushing the Romans toward greater reliance on metallic currency was the need to pay soldiers and government expenses in a more acceptable currency. Coins had circulated in Greece since the eighth century B.C. and Athens had begun coining money at the end of the seventh century.

Nearly 20 years after the Tarpeian law, in 430 B.C., the Roman Senate enacted the Lex Julia-Papiria, which mandated that metallic currencies replace payments in cattle. According to Cicero, this law came about because "the Censors had, through the vigorous imposition of fines of cattle, converted many private herds to the public use," and therefore "a light tax in lieu of a fine of cattle was substituted."

Compared to other Mediterranean societies, the Romans were slow to adopt metallic currency and coinage. Nevertheless, copper slowly superseded cattle as the principal standard of value, and the Romans sought to preserve the link between the cattle standard and the copper standard by stamping the first Roman copper coins with figures of cattle. The copper standard of the ancient Romans has left some vestige in modern language. In English the words "estimate" and "esteem" are derived from the Latin word *astimare,* which originated from expressing values in copper asses.

See also: Bronze Standard of Ancient Rome, Lex Flaminia of 217 B.C., Solon

References: Burns, A. R. 1927. *Money and Monetary Policy in Early Times.*

Einzig, Paul. 1966. *Primitive Money.*

Lex Flaminia of 217 B.C. (Rome)

The famous English economist, John Maynard Keynes, wrote in his *Treatise on Money,* Vol. I (1930):

> Nor am I aware of any chartalist change of standard, expressly designed to benefit the State at the expense of the public, earlier than the second Punic War—Rome being the first original to add

this instrument to the armoury of statecraft. From that time on chartalist changes of standard, generally in the form of debasement, sometimes for one purpose and sometimes for another, are the favorite theme of historians.

As early as the sixth century B.C. Athens had changed its monetary standard to relieve debtors, but not to benefit the government. Although a thorough study of ancient history would probably turn up earlier examples of currency debasement for the benefit of a government, historians have cited the Roman debasement during the Punic Wars as the fateful beginning of a series of currency debasements that had completely debauched the Roman currency by the second and third centuries A.D.

In 338 B.C. the Roman government issued copper coinage to replace cattle as the medium of exchange. The unit of measure was the *as,* equal to one pound of copper. The coins bore the image of an ox, a sheep, or a hog, and were called *pecunia,* from *pecos,* the Latin word for "cattle." In A.D. 269 the government minted two silver coins: the *denarius,* equal to 10 asses, and the *sestertius,* representing $2\frac{1}{2}$ asses.

There is sketchy evidence of currency manipulation during the First Punic War. According to Pliny, the Roman government eliminated its public debt during the time of the First Punic War (268–241 B.C.) by reducing the aes to two ounces of copper. A. R. Burns (1927) states that "the only certain and important currency reduction under the Republic was made during the second Punic war (218–201 B.C.)."

The Lex Flaminia of 217 B.C. provided for the reduction of the legal weight of the as from two ounces to one, and for the reduction of the legal weight of the denarius, decreasing it from one-seventy-second to one-eighty-fourth of a pound of silver. Also, the law raised the value of the denarius from 10 asses to 16 asses, and for military pay a denarius was to be paid for every 10 asses due.

Later, during the Second Punic War, the government issued silver-plated copper coins that passed for denarii. These coins left the mint looking just like sterling silver coins, but even the barbarians that traded with Rome preferred the older silver coins. By mid-second century the Roman Republic was issuing full-bodied metal coins. The Roman Empire hastened its own deterioration with currency debasements, climaxing in a brief episode of wage and price controls at the beginning of the fourth century.

The spread of state-managed paper money made currency debasements an obsolete method of financing government expenditures in excess of tax revenue.

See also: Augustan Monetary System, Edict of Prices of A.D. 301, Roman Empire Inflation

References: Burns, A. R. 1927. *Money and Monetary Policy in Early Times.*

Frank, Tenney. 1940. *An Economic Survey of Ancient Rome.* Vol. I.

Harl, Kenneth. 1996. *Coinage in the Roman Economy, 300 B.C. to A.D. 700.*

Liquor Money

Perhaps some measure of the importance of stimulants and depressants to civilization can be seen in the use of these goods as money. Stimulants such as coffee, tobacco, and cocoa beans have served as money, and alcohol—a depressant—has also fulfilled the functions of money in some societies.

During the nineteenth century, gin circulated as money in Nigeria. A bishop reported that it was impossible to buy food in parts of the Nigerian Delta, unless one could offer gin in payment. Bottles of gin changed hands for years, eluding human consumption. Members of a commission on native races, visiting the home of a chief in the central province, saw a stockpile of cases of gin, some cases exceeding 30 years of age. Gin functioned as a store of value, with chiefs holding large stocks of gin as a treasure. Gin owed part of its popularity as a form of wealth to the government's practice of steadily raising the taxes on imported spirits, rendering domestic stocks more valuable. Although there is no evidence that prices were fixed in gin, signifying gin as a standard of value, gin served as a medium of exchange and store of value. The government banned the importation of spirits during World War I, ending the use of gin money, and opening a period of a silver currency shortage.

In Australia rum served as the medium of exchange of choice during the late eighteenth and early nineteenth centuries, a time in Australian history known as the "period of the rum currency." Metallic currency was in short supply, a common problem among remote colonies, including the 13 American colonies along the eastern seaboard. Adding to the currency shortage in Australia was the thinking among English authorities that a convict colony did not need to be provided with money. Trade brought in a limited number of Spanish dollars that were used to pay for imports, and rum could be found in the cargo of every ship that came into port.

Rum met the need for a domestic medium of exchange in Australia. Farmers sold their produce for rum, workers expected to be paid in rum, convicts performed additional work for payment in rum, and law enforcement authorities offered rewards in rum for the apprehension of criminals. Rum functioned better as a medium of exchange than as a store of value. Its value fluctuated with the size of the last shipment, and its owners often fell prey to the temptation to drink it, rather than save it to buy other goods. Although Europeans accepted rum in payment for goods and wages, there no evidence that the aborigines accepted rum in payment, unlike the American Indians who were reported to have had a fondness for whiskey.

Beer has found a place among the ranks of currencies. Some tribes in Uganda are reported to have made payments in homemade beer, and tribal workers to have accepted beer in payment of wages. The consecration of a goat or the manufacture of a shield cost a pot of beer, and the barber charged a pot of beer and one chicken. There is no evidence that these tribes used beer as a store of value, but there is some evidence in Angola that during the 1980s imported beer served as a store of value.

The use of liquor as money gives added meaning to the New Testament admonishment that the "love of money is the root of all evil." One would expect liquor money to challenge the physical and moral strength of a society in ways that other currencies would not. Many societies have held up objects of reverence as money, such as whales' teeth on the Fiji Islands, or even gold and silver in ancient Western societies. In Angola the cynicism of war may deserve some credit for the use of imported beer as money. Also, colonial domination by other cultures may be a factor in the use of liquor money in Australia and Nigeria.

See also: Beer Standard of Marxist Angola, Commodity Monetary Standard

Reference: Einzig, Paul. 1966. *Primitive Money.*

Shann, E. O. G. 1948. *An Economic History of Australia.*

Liverpool Act of 1816 (England)

The Liverpool Act of 1816 officially put England on the gold standard and provided for a subsidiary silver coinage to complement the gold coinage and bank notes that dominated England's money supply. It gave silver a role to play in a monetary system in which the monetary standard was defined in terms of gold.

During the eighteenth century England was technically on a bimetallic standard, but the market price of silver stood above the mint price for most of that era, and consequently no silver was brought to the mint for coinage. England had in practice settled into a gold standard and silver coins were in short supply. After 1785 the market price of silver tumbled, and silver flowed to the mint in large amounts for coinage, threatening to upset an unofficial gold standard that met with the approval of the English government. Parliament hastily enacted legislation that prohibited the mint from purchasing silver for coinage, circumventing the possibility that silver would oust gold as the predominant monetary metal. By 1797 the financial stringencies of war with Revolutionary France had forced England onto an inconvertible paper standard that lasted until 1821, encompassing the period of the Napoleonic Wars. As pressure mounted for a return to the gold standard, a complementary movement gathered strength to reform the silver coinage.

As early as 1798 the government had appointed the Committee of the Privy Council on the State of the Coinage, but the committee failed to reach quick agreement and chose not to make recommendations until the war ended. In 1816 the committee made its report, recommending the coinage of both gold and silver, but also recommending that the monetary standard be defined in terms of gold only, thus officially ratifying a century-old gold standard. The committee's recommendations left the weight and denominations of gold coins unchanged.

The committee recommended a return to silver coins, but only as a subsidiary coinage. Silver coins were to be regarded as representative coins, legal tender for payments of no more than 40 shillings. The committee recommended that the mint purchase silver for 62 shillings per pound, but coin the silver at a rate of 66 shillings per pound. That is, the face value of the silver coins struck from a pound of silver was equal to 66 shillings. The committee hoped that the slight increase in face value per unit of silver weight would make the melting down and export of silver coins unprofitable. Also, the remaining silver content, which was still significant, would discourage counterfeiters.

The government adopted the committee's recommendations without delay in the Liverpool Act of 1816. This act made silver coins an important component of England's money supply until 1947, when England removed all precious metal content from its "silver" coinage. Beginning in 1947 England's "silver" coinage has been composed of cupro-nickel alloy, a copper and nickel alloy.

See also: Bank Restriction Act of 1797, Gold Standard
References: Chown, John F. 1994. *A History of Money*. Feavearyear, Sir Albert. 1963. *The Pound Sterling*. Jastram, Roy W. 1981. *Silver: The Restless Metal*.

Lombard Banks

Lombard banks were banks that accepted deposits of goods and issued credits on account. These credits could pass from one person's account to another's as a medium of exchange. The term *Lombard* probably came from the importance of Italian bankers in the early history of the London financial market, sometimes referred to as Lombard Street, just as Wall Street signifies the financial center of New York. In early English history, *Lombard* was another name for "Italian." According to Webster's dictionary *Lombard,* broadly speaking, can refer to a banker, moneylender, bank, or pawnshop.

In 1661 Francis Cradocke published a pamphlet, *Wealth Rediscovered,* in which he proposed the establishment of banks secured by things other than precious metals or financial assets. Among the commodities he advanced as possible securities were jewels, "rich pictures or hangings," silks, iron, sugar, wines, tobacco, and land. He recommended dividing the kingdom into a hundred districts, and each district would have a "standing and constant Bank or Registry" that registered all lands, houses, and rents, and granted credit upon the basis of land, goods, or pawns.

In 1676 Robert Murray published a proposal for a Lombard banking scheme, entitled *A Proposal for the Advancement of Trade,* in which he argued for the establishment of a "Bank and Lombard united." Under his plan people would deposit their "dead stock" in magazines, and receive credit on account that could be exchanged as money. He recommended awarding credit on account up to "two-thirds or three-fourths of their value according to the quality thereof." In explaining the credit on account, Murray explained that:

[N]o more is required than what is already practised in Banks here and abroad, where men deposite Money and obtain the Bank-Credit, which generally passeth in Receipts and Payments without the real issuing of Money, the Money remaining as a Pawn or Ground of Security in the Cash-Chest, or else imployed by the Banker to his own Benefit. (Richards, 1929)

The most famous economist of the era, William Petty, put in a good word for Lombard banks in his *Treatise of Taxes and Contributions* (1662). He wrote, "If public Loan Banks, Lombards, or Banks of Credit upon deposited Plate, Jewel, Cloth, Wooll, Silke, Leather, Linnen, Mettals, and other durable Commodities were erected, I cannot apprehend how there could be above one-tenth part of the Law-suits and Writings as now there are" (Richards, 1929). Lombard banks were sometime called Banks of Credit.

In 1682 the city of London established the Bank of the City of London, which acted primarily as a Lombard bank. Despite the noble mission of the bank, which was to pay down the city's debt to the Orphans' Fund, the experiment collapsed suddenly.

Lombard banks were a hybrid of pawnshops and deposit banks. Unlike pawnshops of today, Lombard banks issued credits that could circulate as money, adding to the money supply. Although pawnshops, called Lombards, had a long history, it is not clear that Lombard banks of the sort proposed in the seventeenth century ever developed far beyond the theory stage. Nevertheless, the Bank of England, created by an act of Parliament in 1694, was authorized to conduct a pawnbroker's business, reflecting the influence of Lombard banking schemes at the time.

See also: Bank, Bank of England, Land Bank System
References: Nevin, Edward, and E. W. Davis. 1970. *The London Clearing Banks.*
Richards, R. D. 1929. *The Early History of Banking in England.*

Lydian Coinage

Writing at mid-fifth century B.C. the Greek historian Herodotus in his *History* observes of the Lydians, "So far as we have any knowledge, they were the first nation to introduce the use of gold and silver coin, and the first who sold goods by retail." Subsequent research suggests that China may have edged out Lydia as the birthplace of round coins, but Lydia still receives priority for beginning the coinage of money that has evolved down to the present day. The date when Lydia hammered or struck the first true coins cannot be identified with certainty, but was probably around 800 B.C.

The kingdom of Lydia lay on the western coast of what is now Turkey, separated from ancient Greece by the Aegean Sea. Sardis, the capital of Lydia, was a clearinghouse for trade between Mesopotamia and Greek cities along the coast. According to Herodotus, "Lydia, unlike most other countries, scarcely offers any wonders for the historian to describe, except the gold dust, which is washed down from the range of Tmolus" (Herodotus, 1952). According to Greek myth the river Pactolus, near Sardis, owed its rich deposits of gold to Midas, who bathed in it to wash away his fateful golden touch that even turned his food to gold. Lydian rivers washed a natural amalgam of gold and silver down from the mountains, and left deposits of silt that the Lydians panned, capturing a light yellow precious metal that was called *electrum* because of its amber cast. Later the Lydians learned to separate the gold and silver content of

Early Lydian coinage bore images on only one side. (Smithsonian Institution, National Numismatic Collection)

electrum. They also substantially advanced the art of ascertaining the gold content of metal.

The main purpose of the first coins was to facilitate trade by providing state authentication of the purity and weight of precious metals, an important medium of exchange. The ancestor to the Lydian coins was a bean-shaped *dump* of electrum that served as Lydian coins at the opening of the seventh century. Soon these dumps acquired a punch mark on one side and, later, an inscribed mark on the other side, signifying that the government vouched for the purity and weight of the precious metal content. By midcentury these dumps began to take on the characteristics of round coins, stamped on both sides with clearly identifiable figures. One side of the coins bore the resemblance of a lion's head, the symbol of the ruling Mermnad dynasty of Lydia.

The development of coinage in Lydia did not end the production of gold bars of uniform size. Herodotus (1952) tells of a Lydian king, Croesus, who, a century after the appearance of the first coins, caused "a vast quantity of gold to be melted down, and ran it into ingots, making them six palms long, three palms broad, and one palm in thickness."

From Lydia the production of finished coins passed to Greece, where it developed very rapidly. Athens was minting coins by 575 B.C. and by the fifth century B.C. minted coins in Greece had come to rival other art forms in their beauty. From Greece the coinage of money passed to Rome and Western Europe and for the next 2,000 years money to most people in the Western world meant coins. By the twentieth century, Western Europe had spread the practice of coining money to the rest of the world, making coinage one of the epochal innovations in financial history.

See also: Cappadocia, Croesean Reform

References: Einzig, Paul. 1966. *Primitive Money.*
Head, Barclay Vincent. 1967. *The Coinage of Lydia and Persia.*
Herodotus. 1952. *History.*
Williams, Jonathan, ed. 1997. *Money: A History.*

M

Macmillan Committee
See Bank of England

Mahogany Logs
During the eighteenth century British Honduras made use of mahogany logs as the chief circulating medium of exchange and standard of deferred payment. Mahogany log currency was bulky, and part of the motivation for legally sanctioning mahogany log currency was a desire to create additional demand for a locally produced product.

The first legal sanction to mahogany log currency seems to have come in April 1765 with an act that read: "[W]hoever shall be found guilty of profane cursing or swearing shall forfeit and pay for every such offense the sum of 2s. 6d. in Jamaica currency or the same value in merchantable unchipped logwood."

Further legitimacy to logwood currency was added in May 1766 when all debts were made payable in logwood, except in contracts specifying another means of payment. One estimate suggests that logwood currency was officially overvalued relative to Jamaica currency on the order of 300 percent, causing a Gresham's law action in which bad money (overvalued logwood) drove out good money (Jamaica currency), and aggravating the shortage of metallic currency evident in all colonies and remote areas.

Creditors had just cause to complain of repayment of debts in overvalued logwood, and in 1784 the government resolved that all future business dealings would be conducted in Jamaica currency, and that debts could be repaid in logwood but at an official rate that mirrored current prices of logwood.

Mahogany log currency belongs in the same category as tobacco currency in Virginia and sugar currency in the West Indies. In remote areas that are short of metallic currency a staple export earning metallic currency in foreign trade was the next best thing to metallic currency itself.

See also: Commodity Money, Commodity Monetary Standard

References: Chalmers, Robert. 1972. *A History of Currency in the British Colonies.*
Quiggin, A. Hingston. 1949. *A Survey of Primitive Money.*

Manilla
One of the most enduring of the primitive metallic currencies was the *manilla* currency of West Africa. Manilla currency took the form of copper or brass anklets, bracelets, or front sections of necklaces. This currency served a dual purpose, acting both as articles of personal adornment and as currency that could be effortlessly carried. Nigeria and the areas along the Bay of Guinea made widespread use of manilla currency into the post–World War II era.

The use of manilla currency stretches back into the mists of history, with no sure origin. Some accounts credit the Phoenicians, famous Mediterranean traders and navigators before the ascendancy of the Greeks and Romans. Metallic bracelets

Manilla served as articles of personal adornment as well as a medium of exchange. (Smithsonian Institution, National Numismatic Collection)

were their favorite medium of exchange, and their ships traveled from Ireland to the coast of West Africa. The Phoenician bracelets may have been the origin of manilla currency, putting the beginning of manilla currency around the eighth or ninth century B.C. The manilla currency also resembles some ornaments worn by the ancient Celts, which may also have had a Phoenician origin.

Another theory of the origin of manilla currency points to the bolts, clamps, and other metal devices from shipwrecked Portuguese vessels. These salvaged pieces seemed to hold a special charm for the natives along the Guinea coast. The Portuguese explored the western coast of Africa during the fifteenth century and used manilla currency to trade with the natives. From 1504 to 1507 Portugal sent 287,813 manillas to just one trading station on the Guinea coast. A slave cost between 8 and 10 manillas, and 1 manilla could purchase a big elephant tooth.

The linguistic origin of the term *manilla* may be traceable to a mixture of Phoenician and Irish words. A more likely possibility is that the word *manilla* stems from the Spanish and Portuguese words for "little hand" (from the Latin *manus*).

As early as 1902 the British government took steps to phase out the use of manilla currency. Outsiders trading with Nigeria continued to find it necessary to trade in manilla currency until 1949, when manilla currency was officially withdrawn from cir-

culation. The official close to the era of manilla currency was later celebrated with the issuance of special postal stamps.

See also: Copper
References: Davies, Glyn. 1994. *A History of Money.* Einzig, Paul. 1966. *Primitive Money.*

Maravedis
See Vellon

Massachusetts Bay Colony Mint

The Massachusetts Bay Colony boasted of the first and only mint in the American colonies before the American Revolution. The colonial economies fought against a currency shortage that acted as a brake on economic activity. The largest component of the circulating coin in the colonies was the Spanish dollar or pieces of eight, but all currency tended to leave America faster than it came in because of the huge need for imported products from Europe. There were no local coins per se, and the mint of Massachusetts was erected on the initiative of the Massachusetts colonial government to meet the need for a colonial currency.

The mint was erected in 1652 and remained in operation for 30 years, eventually falling victim to the royal displeasure of the English Crown. Apparently, it was subject to the orders of the General Court of Massachusetts. The first order issued on 27 May 1652 said:

> That all persons whatsoeuer have libertie to bring into the mint house, at Boston, all bullion, plate, or Spanish coyne, there to be melted and brought to the alloy of sterling siluer by John Hull, master of the sd. Mint, & his sworne officers, & by him to be coyned into twelue pence, six pence, & three pence peeces. (Watson, 1970)

These silver coins were of small denominations for the time.

The mint house was a square building constructed of wood, measuring 15 feet on each side, and 10 feet high. The coins were legal tender in the area under the jurisdiction of the General Court.

The Massachusetts mint debased its coins about 22 percent relative to the silver content of English coins of the same denominations. The officials of

Massachusetts approved of this debasement in an effort the keep the coins from going to Europe in payment for American imports of foreign goods. The European merchants, however, simply raised the prices of their products in Massachusetts coin, and there remained the problem of hard specie leaving the American colonies.

The English government complained about debasement of the coins, contending that coinage should be uniform throughout the empire. To be sure, the English government occasionally changed the silver content of its own coins, but was unwilling that the silver content could vary among colonies. It also objected to the coinage of copper or other inferior metals that would solely support internal trade.

The operation of the mint contributed to the friction that led the English government to revoke the first charter of the Massachusetts Bay Colony in 1684, which was the last year that the mint operated. Other colonies asked for permission to establish mints, but the English government refused. The coins from the mint continued to circulate in the American colonies until after the Articles of Confederation authorized individual states to establish mints. The constraints that a coin shortage placed upon the colonial economy helped lift the discontent of the colonists to a revolutionary pitch.

See also: Massachusetts Bay Colony Paper Issue
References: Nettels, Curtis P. 1934. *The Money Supply of the American Colonies before 1720.*
Terranova, Anthony, 1994. *Massachusetts Silver Coinage.*
Watson, David. 1970. *History of American Coinage.*

Massachusetts Bay Colony Paper Issue

The colonial government of the Massachusetts Bay Colony has the dubious distinction of being the first to issue paper money in America. The first hesitant steps toward the issuance of paper money occurred in 1676 when the colonial government raised a loan from provincial merchants and issued treasury receipts as an acknowledgment of debt, expecting these receipts to circulate as currency. Public lands secured the loan.

In 1690 the Massachusetts Assembly enacted legislation that authorized the government to issue paper money. The immediate circumstance that forced the hand of the assembly was the need to pay

soldiers returning from a war expedition into Canada. Paper money is similar to many other inventions in that pressures of war often serve to speed up its development and acceptance, a theme that can be explored into the twentieth century.

Although war expenditures provided the immediate pretext for the paper money issue, broader concerns helped create a political environment receptive to the issuance of paper money. In 1686 the governor's council cited the "great decay of trade and obstructions to manufactures and commerce in this country, and multiplicity of debts and suits thereupon, principally occasioned by the present scarcity of coin" (Nettels, 1934). William Penn later commented that "the want of money to circulate trade has put Boston herself upon thinking of tickets to supply the want of coin" (Nettels, 1934). The law of 1690 also mentioned "the present poverty and calamities of the country, and through a scarcity of money, the want of an adequate measure of commerce" (Nettels, 1934).

Historically, paper money has either taken the form of bank notes, precursors to the modern Federal Reserve Note in the United States, or bills issued directly by government treasuries. The Massachusetts paper money was of the latter variety. The government issued the paper money and levied taxes that could be paid with the paper money. As long as the paper money issue was commensurate with the tax levy, the money maintained its value.

The first bills issued by the Massachusetts colonial government were not legal tender for all debts. The legislation of 1692 specified that the bills be accepted "in all payments equivalent to money," effectively making the bills legal tender. Bills issued between 1702 and 1712 were not legal tender, although after 1710 these bills could be used to stay out of debtors' prison until legal-tender currency could be obtained.

The Massachusetts paper money held its value reasonably well until 1713. Bills issued in 1709 were not redeemable in taxes until four years beyond the issue date, and the period of redemption for paper money issued between 1710 and 1712 was postponed for six or seven years. During the interim between issuance and redemption the bills earned 5 percent interest, but many more bills were issued than were needed to pay taxes. The bills depreciated in value and hard specie flowed out in foreign trade.

In 1716 the assembly established a public bank that issued bank notes secured by land.

In 1748 over 2 million pounds of paper money were in circulation when Massachusetts received a large reimbursement from England for war expenses, and used the proceeds to redeem paper money at about 20 percent of its face value. Gresham's law that bad money drives out good money had played out its ruthless logic in Massachusetts as paper money virtually displaced the specie. After 1720 the English government began to restrict the ability of colonial governments to issue paper money with legal-tender status. Experiences of the colonial governments with paper money led members of the Constitutional Convention to endow the Congress of the federal government with the sole privilege to coin money.

See also: Land Bank System, Tabular Standard in
    Massachusetts Bay Colony
References: Galbraith, John Kenneth. 1975. *Money, Whence
    It Came, Where It Went.*
Hepburn, A. Barton. 1924. *A History of Currency in the
    United States.*
Nettels, Curtis P. 1934. *The Money Supply of the American
    Colonies before 1720.*

Mat Currency of Samoa

Prior to World War II mats were the closest things to currency on the islands of Samoa. The women of Samoa wove mats of two to three yards square, investing months and sometimes years making a single mat. In British currency the mats ranged between 2 and 40 shillings in value. Samoans paid the wages in mats for artisans engaged in constructing houses and boats. Private ownership of land was vague, and rent took the form of gifts in mats. The bridegroom and his friends received a large number of mats at the celebration of the wedding. Chiefs married several women, in part to get their hands on more mats.

The value of the mats varied with the quality of material, and perhaps equally important, with historical and sentimental associations. Mats that had been used as the "top mat" at a wedding, or conclusion of a peace treaty, acquired a sentimental and historical significance that enhanced their value in the eyes of Samoans, despite wear and tear and the normal deterioration of age. The governor of Samoa during the period of German colonialism received a

request that mats be rendered unpawnable because of their sacredness and significance. Mats endowed with special historical and sentimental significance became heirlooms that were rarely traded, but ordinary mats were exchanged frequently.

These mats had no fixed negotiable value, falling short of a completely evolved medium of exchange in that important area. Some of their uses, however, bore a closer resemblance to modern money. At election time candidates for king and chief distributed mats to voters, and whoever could afford to distribute the most mats stood the best chance of winning the election. After the election, successful candidates received mats as gifts from the people. Samoans did fix fines and blood money in mats, and assuaged the feelings of angry husbands with gifts of mats.

Having no fixed negotiable value, mats could not function as a monetary unit of account, an important function of money. However, mats did function as a medium of exchange, and a store of value. Samoans saved mats for their children to inherit.

Mat money may owe its origin to the collectivist nature of Samoan society. Private ownership was not well defined. Land was vaguely claimed by individuals, but movable objects, including modern money, had to be given up at the request of a friend or family member, and taking movable objects without permission was also common. Mats, however, acquired sentimental attachments that lifted them above the vulnerability of other movable objects, and made them the only possible means of storing value.

See also: Commodity Monetary Standard
References: Einzig, Paul. 1966. *Primitive Money.*
Quiggin, A. Hingston. 1949. *A Survey of Primitive Money.*

Medici Bank

The Medici Bank, perhaps the most famous bank of Renaissance Italy, rose to the top rank of European financial institutions during the fifteenth century. It accepted time deposits, the sum of which was several times larger than the invested capital, and was a lending institution. This was unlike some of the exchange banks of the time that were primarily involved in fund transfers associated with international trade. The Medici Bank was the chief bank for the Curia, and it had branches in the major cities of Italy, as well as London, Lyons, Geneva, Bruges, and Avignon.

In Renaissance Italy openly charging interest (usury) was prohibited, but interest charges were hidden in bills of exchange through which foreign currency was purchased for delivery at a future date. Profit was at the mercy of the foreign exchange markets. What was called a dry exchange involved no transfer of goods or foreign exchange and effectively guaranteed interest to the lender. In 1429 dry exchanges were outlawed in Florence, but the law was suspended at least temporarily in 1435, right after the Medici became the de facto, if not legal rulers, of Florence. The Medici Bank was organized as a partnership with the Medici family being the largest investor in the parent company and the parent company being the largest investor in the branch partnerships. The parent company functioned like a modern holding company. The system of branch banks was organized such that one branch could be declared independent by rearranging accounts. Such arrangements protected the parent bank from the bankruptcy of individual branches due to localized economic difficulties.

Members of the Medici family entered the Florentine banking business in the latter 1300s. In 1393 Giovanni di Bicci de' Medici (1360–1429) took ownership of the Roman branch of a bank owned by one of his Florentine cousins. He removed the headquarters of his bank to Florence in 1397, the official founding date for the Medici Bank. At the time Rome was a source of funds, whereas Florence offered a better market for making loans. By 1402 the Medici Bank had opened a branch bank in Venice, another important outlet of investment opportunities. By then the bank boasted a total of seventeen employees at its headquarters in Florence, five of whom were clerks.

In the fourteenth and fifteenth centuries wool and cloth industries were the export mainspring of the Florentine economy. In 1402 the Medici Bank loaned 3,000 florins (nearly one-third of its original capital) to finance a Medici family partnership to produce woolen cloth. The year 1408 saw the establishment of a second and more successful shop for producing woolen cloth. In addition to banking, the Medici traded wool, cloth, alum, spices, olive oil, silk stuffs, brocades, jewelry, silver plate, citrus fruit, and other commodities, diversifying their risks by investing in a range of ventures.

In 1429 Giovanni di Medici died, passing the management of the bank into the hands of his eldest son, Cosimo. Under Cosimo's leadership the Medici Bank became the largest banking house of its time. In 1435 the bank opened a branch in Geneva, the first branch beyond the Alps. The Medici opened another woolen cloth manufacturing shop and acquired a silk shop in 1438. The Medici Bank opened a branch in Bruges in 1439, and branches in London and Avignon in 1446. The Milan branch was opened in 1452 or 1453. The Geneva branch was transferred to Lyons in 1464.

When Cosimo died in 1464 the bank had passed its peak. An invalid son, Piero de' Medici, assumed management of the bank. According to Machiavelli, he began calling in loans, causing a contraction in credit and numerous business failures. Piero died in 1469. Piero's son, Lorenzo the Magnificent, was a great statesman. He had a humanistic education without business training or experience. He turned the management of the bank over to managers, and the bank gradually lost ground. On Lorenzo's death in 1492, his son, Piero di Lorenzo, assumed control of the Medici political and business interests in Florence. Piero had neither business nor political acumen, and in 1494 the Medici were ousted from Florence. The bank, already tottering on bankruptcy, was confiscated, and was not successful under its new owners.

See also: Bank of Venice, Florentine Florin, House of St. George, Quattrini Affair

References: Bullard, Melissa M. 1980. *Filippo Strozzi and the Medici: Favor and Finance in Sixteenth-Century Florence and Rome.*
Goldthwaite, Richard A. 1995. *Banks, Palaces, and Entrepreneurs in Renaissance Florence.*
Roover, Raymond de. 1966. *The Rise and Decline of the Medici Bank: 1397–1494.*

Mercantilism

The first principle of mercantilism can be found in the idea that the greatness and power of a state are determined by the abundance of money (precious metals). This stock of money grows with what is now called a favorable balance of trade. The exports of home commodities should exceed in value the imports of foreign commodities, and this positive balance of trade is settled with the importation of money or precious metal.

Historically, this supply of gold and silver acquired through a positive trade balance made it easier for monarchs to raise funds either by loans or taxes. An edict in 1603 of Henry IV, king of France, stated that the arts and manufactures were to be encouraged as the only means of preventing the exportation of precious metals out of the kingdom and the resulting enrichment of other countries.

Adam Smith's *Inquiry into the Nature and Causes of the Wealth of Nations* discussed mercantilism at length. He described the "restraints on importation" along with the "encouragements of exports" by which a nation could turn the balance of trade in its favor. Restraints on imports, in the form of duties or prohibitions, were applied to the import of such foreign goods as could be produced domestically. They could also be directed to the imports from countries with which an unfavorable balance of trade existed. Goods that were imported for the purpose of reexport could enter duty free, and the encouragements to exports took the form of subsidies for the production of exportable goods, advantageous commercial treaties, and the establishment of colonies.

Smith strongly attacked the logic of the mercantilist system. He argued that a high per capita output played a much larger role than the stock of domestic precious metal in determining a nation's economic welfare. John Maynard Keynes in his book *The General Theory* (1936) referred to "what now seems to me to be the element of scientific truth in mercantilist doctrine. At a time when domestic authorities had no direct control over the domestic interest rate the effect of a favorable balance of trade on the influx of precious metals was their only indirect means of reducing the domestic rate of interest and so increasing the inducement to home investment."

In modern times Japanese economic policy has been described as mercantilist. The Japanese have maintained a favorable balance of trade and have enjoyed above-average economic growth.

See also: Balance of Payments, Foreign Exchange Markets, Gold-Specie-Flow Mechanism

References: Gomes, Leonard. 1987. *Foreign Trade and the National Economy: Mercantilist and Classical Perspectives.*
Keynes, John Maynard. 1936. *The General Theory.*
Nussbaum, Frederick. 1935. *A History of the Economic Institutions of Modern Europe.*

Mexican Peso
See De a Ocho Reales

Milled-Edge Coinage

A milled-edge coin has various forms of graining, ribbing, or serrulation around its circumference. In an Order of Council of May 1661 Charles II, king of England, set forth that all coin was to be struck as soon as possible by machinery, with grained or lettered edges, to stop clipping, cutting, and counterfeiting. As the order reveals, the motivation for the serrulated edges lay in the search for a means to discourage clippers, who removed bits of precious metal from the edges of coins, diminishing the metal content of coins without rendering them completely unacceptable in exchange. Hammered coins minted by hand produced coins of irregular shape that invited clipping.

Mechanized minting began in Italy, which may also have been the birthplace of the milled edge. Mechanized minting passed from Italy to France and Germany, and then to Spain and England. In 1553 Eloy Mestrell fled from Paris where he was engineer to the mint, and arrived in London, bringing knowledge of the methods of a horse-powered mill that turned out uniform blank coins, stamped with uniform images, and a milled-edge circumference. The machine for milling the edge made use of counterrotating hand screws. Mestrell's coins that survived are of impressive quality, but he faced strong opposition from established moneyers. After an inquiry yielded adverse findings, Mistrell was relieved of his duties at the mint, and six years later he was hanged for counterfeiting.

The Paris mint again lost talent to London in 1625 when Nicholas Briot, chief engraver in Paris, left France out of frustration over the opposition of the established moneyers. Between 1631 and 1640 Briot minted silver coins with milled edges, but hammered coins still dominated English coinage. In 1649 Pierre Blondeau, an engineer from the Paris mint, arrived in London. Blondeau had developed an inexpensive and practical method of producing the milled edge, prompting Louis III of France to ban the minting of hammered coins in 1639. In England Blondeau minted a token quantity of milled-edge coins. Apparently, both Briot and Blondeau returned to France after the Commonwealth government refused to progress beyond the experimental stage with the new methods of coinage.

After the Restoration returned Charles II to the throne, he recalled Blondeau from France, and awarded him a 21-year contract to develop and apply methods for making milled and engrained edges. The contract for turning out blanks and stamping fell to three Flemish brothers, John, Joseph, and Phillip Roettier. In 1663 the Tower mint produced a one-pound coin that signaled the beginning of mechanized minting in England.

Methods for minting coins with the serrulated or corrugated edge also passed from France to Spain. In the English colonies and early United States, the Spanish milled dollar was among the most popular and widely circulated coins, passing as legal tender for brief periods. The Spanish milled dollar established the dollar as the principal unit of currency in the United States.

The practice of milled-edge coinage continues to the present day. In the United States, coins in denominations larger than a nickel have milled edges.

See also: Cellini, Benvenuto, Da Vinci, Leonardo

References: Challis, C. E., ed. 1992 *A New History of the Royal Mint.*

Craig, J. 1953. *The Mint: A History of the London Mint from* A.D. *287 to 1948.*

Feavearyear, Sir Albert. 1963. *The Pound Sterling.*

Mississippi Bubble
See Law, John

Mondex System
See Debit Card

Monetarism
Monetarism is a school of macroeconomic theory emphasizing the causal role of the money stock in aggregate economic fluctuations, and holding that the key to aggregate economic stability lies with a steady, noncyclical growth path in the money supply. The aggregate economic system experiences upswings and downswings manifested in such statistics as the unemployment rate. These cyclical swings are a response to imbalances between the total demand for all goods and services relative to the total supply, as opposed to imbalances between supply and demand in individual markets, such as the market for automobiles.

According to monetarism, the aggregate economic system has strong intrinsic tendencies to gravitate toward a full-employment equilibrium,

and these tendencies will assert themselves in the absence of shocks to the money stock growth rate. If the money stock growth rate is stable, the aggregate economic system will mirror that stability. Economists who adhere to the tenets of monetarism are called monetarists.

In policy terms monetarism means that central bank monetary policy should set target rates of growth of money stock measures, and rather single-mindedly pursue those targets. Keynesian monetary policy, the orthodox policy in the 1950s and 1960s, emphasized interest rates as a target of monetary policy, raising interest rates to slow down the economy and reducing interest rates to speed things up. Monetarists contended that the Keynesian policies took the focus off the money stock and replaced it with subjective ideas about what interest rates should be. According to monetarism financial markets should determine interest rate levels.

Monetarism rose to prominence in the 1970s as inflation began to eclipse unemployment as the most dreaded economic problem. Monetarists contended that the relationship between inflation and money stock growth was virtually a one-to-one relationship, and that money stock growth was feeding the inflation. Monetarists clung to the money stock theory as the sole explanation of inflation, excluding the possible role of government budget deficits, powerful unions, monopolistic corporations, harvest failures, and shortages of key raw materials.

Although restricted money stock growth seemed a plausible antidote against inflation, the first effects of restricted money stock growth were seen in rising unemployment rates rather than falling inflation rates, making the tactic a touchy matter in democratic societies subject to the moods of voters. A president no less conservative than Richard Nixon preferred to give wage and price controls a try rather than put the economy on a prolonged diet of restricted money stock growth.

The decade of the 1980s saw what might be called a monetarist experiment. The governments of Margaret Thatcher in the United Kingdom and President Reagan in the United States imposed strict monetarist policies of restricted money stock growth in an effort to break the back of double-digit inflation. In the United States the prime interest rate soared to 20 percent, and unemployment reached double-digit levels. Thatcher's policies put the

United Kingdom through similar rigors. The tight money policies put these economies through recessions deeper than any economic contraction since the 1930s.

Monetarist policies succeeded in bringing down inflation rates, and unemployment rates began to fall back, suggesting that monetarist policies were succeeding. Nevertheless, in October 1987 stock markets crashed in New York and London, and central banks began increasing money stock growth to reinflate world financial markets. Contrary to monetarists' expectations the added money stock growth did not trigger another round of inflation. During the 1990s inflation has been less than expected based upon money stock growth, casting a bit of doubt on monetarism.

At the very least it can be said that monetarism brought a stoical quality to economic policy making that was needed to endure the pain of disinflating the economies of the world. Notwithstanding the departure in the 1990s from monetarist policies based upon strict, steady growth rates in money stocks, inflation rates have steadily subsided, perhaps reflecting the policy effects of new knowledge gained from the monetarists' theoretical explorations.

See also: Central Bank, Equation of Exchange, Monetary Theory

References: Friedman, Milton. 1969. *The Optimum Quantity of Money, and Other Essays.*

Mankiw, N. Gregory. 1997. *Macroeconomics.* 3d ed.

McCallum, Bennett T. 1989. *Monetary Economics: Theory and Policy.*

Monetary Aggregates

Monetary aggregates measure the money stock, which is defined as the sum of highly liquid assets that serve either as a medium of exchange, standard of value, or a store of value. Money supply measures in terms of monetary aggregates are necessary because many assets serve the same purpose as currency; for example, checking accounts, savings accounts, etc. Therefore, operational measures of the money stock must take these assets into consideration.

In the United States the monetary aggregate denoted M1 is the most narrowly defined measure of the money stock, and a broader measure, denoted M2, includes everything in M1 plus additional assets. M3 is even a broader measure, including everything in M1 and M2 and more.

M1 includes all the currency not held by the Treasury, Federal Reserve Banks, foreign financial institutions, and commercial banks, plus an array of checkable deposits and travelers' checks. Currency included in M1 is the currency circulating as a medium of exchange. Commercial bank vault cash is excluded because it is represented in depositors' accounts, and summing the vault cash with customer checking accounts would be counting those funds twice. The largest share of checkable deposits are called demand deposits, because the bank owes that money to the depositor on demand, without prior notice or other conditions. Bank customers often call these accounts checking accounts. Another checkable account is the negotiable order of withdrawal (NOW) account, an interest-bearing account at thrift institutions that resembles a savings account but has checking privileges. Automatic transfer service (ATS) accounts, which automatically transfer funds from an interest-bearing savings account to a checking account as needed, are also included as checkable deposits in M1, as are Credit Union Share Drafts (CUSDs).

Checkable deposits owned by other depository institutions, the U.S. government, foreign banks, and other official institutions are excluded from M1. M1 therefore represents highly liquid assets acceptable as a medium of exchange. Often cash is preferred over checks for small transactions, but for large transactions checks are preferred over cash.

M2 includes everything in M1 plus small repurchase agreements (less than $100,000), money market deposit accounts and money market mutual fund accounts when minimum deposits are less than $50,000, and savings and small time deposits (less than $100,000). A repurchase agreement is an arrangement under which a commercial bank sells a government bond to a large depositor and agrees to buy it back at a higher price in the future, overnight in some cases. It is an underhanded means of paying interest, and grew into prominence when regulations forbade interest rate ceilings on checking accounts. Money market deposit accounts and money market mutual fund accounts require high minimum deposits, pay high interest, and allow only checks written above a certain amount, such as $500. M2 does not include deposits held in tax-exempt retirement accounts, or those owned by the federal government, foreign governments, or commercial banks. M2 embraces assets less liquid than the assets included in M1, but assets that can readily be converted into cash.

M3 includes everything in M2, but adds large re-purchase agreements and time deposits, eurodollar accounts, large time deposits, and money market mutual fund accounts held by institutions. Eurodol-lar accounts are accounts owned by U.S. residents at foreign branches of U.S. banks worldwide, and all banking offices in Canada and the United Kingdom.

An even broader monetary aggregate is L. L in-cludes everything in M3 plus short-term treasury bonds, commercial paper, U.S. savings bonds, and bankers' acceptances. Commercial paper is an unse-cured promise to pay. It is sold at a discount from a face value and matures in a short time, no more than nine months. Bankers' acceptances, meaning a bank accepts (or guarantees) another firm's promise to pay, provide short-term financing for commercial trade.

M3 and L are less liquid assets than M1 and M2, but they represent readily accessible purchasing power, and are therefore included in the broader de-finitions of money.

See also: Certificate of Deposit, Eurodollars, Federal Reserve System, Money Market Mutual Fund Accounts, Negotiable Order of Withdrawal Accounts

References: Baye, Michael R., and Dennis W. Jansen. 1995. *Money, Banking, and Financial Markets: An Economics Approach.*
Federal Reserve System. 1998. *Federal Reserve Bulletin* (January).
McCallum, Bennett T. 1989. *Monetary Economics: Theory and Policy.*

Monetary Law of 1803 (France)

The French Monetary Law of 1803 ratified the *franc* as the French money of account and established France on a bimetallic system.

From the Carolingian monetary reform in the eighth century until the French Revolution, the *livre* was the money of account in France. Under the Car-olingian system each livre consisted of 20 *sols,* and each sol consisted of 12 *deniers.* These basic provi-sions of the Law of 1803 were first passed in Calonne's law of 1785, named after a comptroller general of French finances. The chaos of revolution disrupted the implementation of Calonne's law, but on 7 October 1793 France acted on the precedent set by the United States and Russia, and established a decimal monetary system. In 1795 the French revolu-tionary government changed the name of the money of account from livre, to franc. In 1799 the terms *franc, dixieme,* and *centime* replaced *livres, sols,* and *deniers* as the official units required in accounting.

The Law of 1803 fixed in law the provisions of Calonne's law, based upon a decimal monetary sys-tem with the franc as the French monetary unit. The franc had two legal equivalents, one in silver and the other in gold. The law declared that "Five grams of silver, nine-tenths fine, constitute the monetary unit, which retains the name of *franc.*" The law also pro-vided that the mint strike silver coins in denomina-tions of a quarter franc, half franc, three-quarter franc, 1 franc, 2 francs, and 5 francs.

After declaring the specifications and denomina-tions of the silver franc, the law stated that "There shall be coined gold pieces of twenty *francs* and of 40 *francs.*" The 20-franc Napoleon coin weighed 6.45 grams, making a gold franc equal to 0.3225 grams of gold. The defined metal contents of the silver franc and the gold franc established a bimetallic system in which a gram of gold was 15.5 times as valuable as a gram of silver.

Both gold and silver coins were legal tender, and unlike the old livres each coin bore a stamp of its value. Anyone, including a foreigner, was free to bring gold and silver to French mints for coinage. The law specified that:

> The expense of coinage alone can be required of those who shall bring material of gold and silver to the Mint. These charges are fixed at nine francs per kilogramme of gold, and at three francs per kilogramme of silver. When the material shall be below the monetary standard, it shall bear the charges of refining or of separation. (Laughlin, 1968)

Just as England became the headquarters for the gold standard during the nineteenth century, France became the staunch defender of bimetallism. A bimetallic ratio of between 15 and 16 to 1 continued until the 1870s when the value of silver began to fall significantly, forcing France and other bimetallic countries in Europe off the bimetallic standard in favor of the gold standard. The United States aban-doned bimetallism in favor of the gold standard dur-ing the same period.

See also: Bimetallism, Decimal System, French Franc, Latin
    Monetary Union
References: Chown, John. 1994. *A History of Money.*
Laughlin, J. Laurence. 1968 *The History of Bimetallism in the
    United States.*
Vilar, Pierre. 1976. *A History of Gold and Money, 1450–1920.*

Monetary Multiplier

The monetary multiplier shows the multiple by
which the money stock can expand given an initial
infusion of fresh funds into the banking system.

A central bank, such as the Federal Reserve System, can infuse additional funds into commercial
banks by purchasing government bonds owned by
commercial banks or commercial bank customers.
The central bank can also loan funds to commercial
banks, but purchasing bonds has a more permanent
impact.

A customer of a commercial bank sells a bond to
the Federal Reserve System, taking the proceeds of
the sale and depositing it in an account at the commercial bank. Under a fractional reserve system of
banking, the commercial bank has to hold only a
fraction of the new deposit, say 20 percent if the
legal reserve ratio is 20 percent, and the remainder
the commercial bank can lend to a borrowing customer. Whatever amount is loaned out is likely to be
deposited in either the bank making the loan, or
more likely, in another bank. The bank that receives
this second deposit originating from the bank loan
only has to keep a fraction of the new deposit, and
can lend the remainder. Therefore a second loan will
be made.

The customer that first sold a bond to the Federal
Reserve System still has the proceeds of that sale in
the form of a bank deposit, and two subsequent
bank deposits have been created, causing a magni-
fied expansion of the money supply, the bulk of
which is bank deposits. The expansionary process
will continue, as the proceeds of a second loan will,
in all probability, land in a bank deposit, giving another bank a new deposit from which it can make a
loan. Each bank that receives a new deposit must
hold a fraction of the new deposits as reserves, and
may lend the remainder.

Because each subsequent new deposit is smaller
than the previous new deposit, the cumulative expansion of new deposits slows to a halt. The monetary multiplier shows how far bank deposits could
theoretically expand under ideal conditions. If the
monetary multiplier is five, then an initial infusion
of $1,000 of fresh funds into commercial banks
could lead to a maximum expansion of bank deposits of $5,000.

The simplest monetary multiplier is calculated
by taking the reciprocal of the legal reserve ratio. A
legal reserve ratio of 20 percent produces a monetary multiplier of five. This simplest multiplier ig-
nores the possibility that banks may purposely
maintain a reserve ratio above the legal reserve ratio,
or that some funds loaned out by a bank may leak
into circulation, never to be deposited in another
bank. In practice the actual monetary multiplier will
be less than the theoretical monetary multiplier
based only on the legal reserve ratio.

More complicated multipliers incorporate a currency to deposit ratio to adjust for the leakage of
cash into circulation.

The funds that the Federal Reserve System in-
jects into commercial banks is sometimes called
high-powered money, because a series of commercial banks making loans will multiply that initial in-
jection of funds into a much larger money stock increase. The monetary multiplier also shows that the
money supply is not entirely in the hands of the Federal Reserve System, but expands and contracts with
the eagerness of commercial banks to make loans,
giving the commercial banks as much influence on
the money supply as the printing presses at the Bureau of Engraving.

See also: Bank, High-Powered Money, Legal Reserve Ratio
References: McCallum, Bennett T. 1989. *Monetary
    Economics.*
McConnell, Campbell R., and Stanley L. Brue. 1998.
    Economics. 14th ed.

Monetary Theory

Monetary theory, an important subarea of macroeconomics, proposes to explain the relationship between the money stock and the macroeconomic system. Macroeconomics is the part of economics
concerned with the economy as a whole, as opposed
to individual industries or sectors. Fluctuations in
the economy as a whole, that is, in aggregate output,
cause fluctuations in the unemployment rate, interest rates, and average prices.

Monetary theory analyses the role of money in
the macroeconomic system in terms of the demand

for money, supply of money, and the natural tendency of the economic system to adjust to a point that balances the supply and demand for money, a point that is called monetary equilibrium. One sector of the macroeconomic system is conceived as the monetary sector, and the monetary sector has a natural tendency to converge to monetary equilibrium.

A phenomenon such as inflation can be attributed to an excess of the supply of money relative to the demand. Excess money supply causes the value of money to drop, which manifests itself as higher prices, causing each unit of money to buy less. A stock market crash can be attributed to an excess demand for money relative to supply, causing stockholders to sell stocks to raise money. Theoretically, the macroeconomic system converges to equilibrium and one necessary condition for macroeconomic equilibrium is monetary equilibrium.

Monetary theory usually assumes as a rough approximation that the money supply is fixed by monetary authorities, and can be changed as necessary for the public's interest. The demand for money, however, is outside the control of public officials and is a function of other economic variables, particularly aggregate income, interest rates, the price level, and inflation. Aggregate income determines the amount of money households and businesses plan to spend in the near future. Households and businesses hold money because they plan to buy things in the near future.

Money holdings of households and businesses that will not be needed for purchases in the near future may be invested in long-term assets (stocks and bonds) that earn income. Money holdings earn little or no income. When money holdings are used to purchase stocks and bonds, the demand for money decreases, and the demand for stocks and bonds increases. Rising interest rates decrease money demand as money holdings are drawn into the purchase of bonds. Falling interest rates cause bonds to become less attractive, raising the demand for money.

Like rising interest rates, inflation means that money can be put to better use in other places, perhaps in the purchase of gold, silver, or real estate. Inflation reduces the demand for money, but deflation makes hoarding money an attractive investment, increasing the demand for money. Higher price levels, however, will eventually increase the demand for money, as money is needed to finance more costly transactions. Inflation reduces the demand for money at first, but when the inflation ceases, the demand for money will level out at a higher level than existed before the inflation started.

When monetary authorities change the money supply, the macroeconomic system adjusts to bring the demand for money in line with the supply of money. If the money supply is increased while the economy is in a recession, the extra money will probably flow into the stock and bond markets, stimulating business. As the economy expands, income grows, and the demand for money grows, catching up with the supply of money and restoring monetary equilibrium. If the money supply is increased while the economy is at full employment, the extra money will cause an increase in the demand for goods relative to supply. Prices will go up until the real (inflation adjusted) value of the money supply has fallen sufficiently to stop the inflation.

Monetary theory supplies the theoretical foundation for monetary policy, which has to do with the regulation of the money supply growth rate. Economists disagree as to whether the money supply growth rate should be speeded up and slowed down to meet the apparent needs of the economy, or whether the money supply growth rate should remain at a fixed amount, probably between 3 and 5 percent per year. Many contemporary economists argue that a fixed money supply growth rate is the best guard against inflation and economic instability.

See also: Equation of Exchange, Monetarism, Value of Money, Velocity of Money

References: Mankiw, N. Gregory. 1996. *Macroeconomics.* 3d ed.

McCallum, Bennett T. 1989 *Monetary Economics.*

Monetary Unions of Ancient Greece

In the ancient Greek world groups of smaller cities that had common trading interests and were too small to support individual mints formed monetary unions. These unions minted coins that were legal tender in all the member cities, which also split the profits from the coinage. These union coins might be struck in one federal mint, or several member cities might operate mints that shared in minting the union coinage. Often one side of these union coins bore a common symbol of the monetary union and the reverse side bore a symbol of the city where the coin was issued. Coins issued at different mints under the authority of a monetary union possessed a uniform weight and purity. These coins served as an international currency in their trading area, restricting the need for moneychangers, and avoiding the business hazards of fluctuations in foreign currency markets.

A monetary convention between Phocea and Mitylene, adopted around 400 B.C., represents one of the few agreements for a monetary union whose details survived for our inspection. The prerogative for striking coins alternated between each city on an annual basis. Each year one city closed its mint while the mint in the other city met the need for coins that year. These cities agreed to issue electrum coins identical in weight and purity, but without a uniform emblem, and the coins from either mint were legal tender in both cities.

At the end of the fifth century a group of towns and tribes on the western coast of Greece formed a monetary union, but knowledge of this union is limited to what can be gathered from the coins. Its coins were based on the silver *stater* of Corinth, a popular coin in the trading area around Italy and Sicily, and its coins bore identical images; a head of Athena on the obverse side, and Pegasus on the reverse side. This union thrived until the second century B.C. when the Roman invasion put an end to it.

The cities of Boeotia, north of Attica, joined into a monetary union that lasted from early times until the coming of Rome. The union began coining silver and later added a uniform bronze coinage. Although struck at different mints, the coins were uniform in weight and purity, and bore on the obverse side a badge that represented the union and on the reverse side a symbol of the city of origin.

One of the largest of the monetary unions federated as many as 43 cities at one time, including Corinth, Argos, and Lacedaemon. Its silver coins dominated trade within the Peloponnese from 280 B.C. to 146 B.C. when the area became a Roman province.

These unions were sometimes the by-products of military alliances. Mobilization of an army always created a demand for coinage, and armies were instrumental in spreading coinage. Also, cities that patronized the same religious temples, or sacred games and festivals, were more likely to issue a federated currency that supported shared activities.

The strengths of a monetary union remain very real in areas such as Europe, where small but sophisticated economies function in close geographical proximity. In 1998 the European Monetary Union planned the final step toward monetary unification with the introduction of a single European currency.

See also: Aeginetan Silver Standard, Attic Silver Standard, Corinthian Silver Standard, Euro Currency, Snake

References: Burns, A. R. 1927. *Money and Monetary Policy in Early Times.*
Carridice, Ian. 1995. *Greek Coins.*

Money Market Mutual Fund Accounts

Money market mutual fund accounts (MMMFA) arose during the 1970s as a financial innovation designed to circumvent Regulation Q, a federal rule that limited the interest rate payable on checking and savings accounts to less than 6 percent.

The high inflation rates of the 1970s put unreasonably low government ceilings on checking and savings account interest rates. Ninety-day treasury bills were exempt from interest rate ceilings, but these bills were only available in denominations of $10,000, outside the reach of the small saver. Other large denomination financial instruments, such as commercial paper and banker's acceptances, were also inaccessible to small savers.

Mutual funds raise capital by selling shares to investors, and invest the capital in an array of assets. They distribute the income from these investments to shareholders, minus management and other fees. Money market mutual funds sell shares to investors, but the value of shares is manipulated to remain at a fixed amount, such as $1 per share. The proceeds from the sale of shares are invested only in safe, short-term assets, such as U.S. treasury bills, giving small savers access to the high earnings of the high-denomination assets.

Small savers can often open a MMMFA with a small investment, maybe as little as $500 but usually between $2,000 and $4,000. As long as a minimum investment is maintained, the shareholder of a MMMFA enjoys limited check-writing privileges, generally in minimum amounts of $500 against their share holdings. A MMMFA is technically not a deposit subject to the regulations of a depository institution, but the accounts are managed to act as a deposit with check-writing privileges. Although an MMMFA cannot boast of the safety of deposits insured by the Federal Depository Insurance Corporation (FDIC), MMMFAs often invest a high proportion of their capital in U.S. treasury bills, giving them the same guarantee of the federal government as deposit insurance.

With check-writing privileges, MMMFAs began to serve same purposes as checking accounts, an important component of the money supply. Between 1976 and 1992 MMMFAs grew from $2.4 billion to $360 billion, due to the movement of deposits from checking and savings accounts. The Federal Reserve System includes MMMFA accounts in M2, a monetary aggregate economists often consider the best operational definition of the money supply.

On 14 December 1982 banks received authorization to offer money market deposit accounts (MMDAs), which offer depositors comparable interest rates on assets similar to MMMFAs and have the added advantage of protection from the FDIC. At first MMDAs grew rapidly at the expense of MMM-FAs, and the depository institutions regained ground lost to MMMFAs. By the 1990s MMMFAs had established themselves as an important monetary asset, but the volume of MMMFAs remained below the volume of the MMDAs.

See also: Certificate of Deposit, Monetary Aggregates, Negotiable Order of Withdrawal Accounts

References: Baye, Michael R., and Dennis W. Jansen. 1995. *Money, Banking, and Financial Markets: An Economics Approach.*
Klein, John J. 1986. *Money and the Economy.* 6th ed.

Money Superstitions

Various sorts of money, particularly in the Far East, have been thought to possess special powers, bringing good luck or ill, sometimes associated with meaningful inscriptions. *Zhouyuan tongbao* coins, tenth-century Chinese coins struck from bronze, purportedly possessed the power to cure illness and aid in childbirth. These coins may have owed some of their alleged special powers to the bronze statues taken from over 3,000 Buddhist temples to furnish the bronze for the mint. The inscription on these coins read, "everywhere—new beginning, circulating treasure."

The Chinese also made coin swords by tying coins to an iron rod. These swords were supposed to drive away illness and evil spirits. To make coin swords the Chinese favored coins issued by the Kangxi emperor (1662–1723). This emperor reigned a full 60 years, and his name came to be associated with good health. His grandson, Qianlong, also reigned as emperor for 60 years, and his coins, the *Qianlong tongbao* coins, were also in demand to fashion sword coins.

The Chinese were also prone to bury coins with the dead for use in the afterlife, a practice condemned by the government. The Chinese went so far as to issue "hell notes," paper money to be buried with the dead to pay for necessities in the next life. The Hong Kong Chinese still print up imitation paper money in the form of notes issued by the Bank of Hell, at least some of which are denominated in "dollars," and millions of these notes are burnt at the Chinese New Year. Even checks are written on the Bank of Hell to honor ancestors.

References: Angus, Ian. 1974. *Paper Money.*
Williams, Jonathan, ed. 1997. *Money, A History.*

Moneyer

Before the mechanization of coinage mints were staffed by moneyers, who physically struck the coins. In England at least, moneyers seemed to have owned their own tools. In 1484 Robert Hart, an English moneyer, bequeathed to his apprentice "my anvil, 4 hammers, a mallet, a pair of tongs, an hamnekyn, and 2 pairs of shears."

Moneyer as an organized trade or skill stretches back to the ancient world. In the Roman Empire moneyers were members of a hereditary profession, recruited mainly from families holding high positions in government. A member of the moneyer caste could not resign without furnishing someone to take his place. In Rome, as in later societies, trust and character were an important qualification for the profession of moneyer. The same skills that allowed a moneyer to strike coins meeting official specifications could be put to work to forge counterfeit coins, or to debase official coinage at a secret profit to the moneyer.

English moneyers organized themselves into a company or guild and elected a leader, the provost, who could call a meeting of the moneyers at any time and impose mild disciplinary penalties. New recruits to the company had to serve as apprentices

Before mints were mechanized, coins were struck using hammers, anvils, and tongs. (Library of Congress)

for seven years and take an oath to serve the company and the Crown loyally. The warden of the mint paid the provost, who in turned paid individual moneyers. Mints lay idle portions of the year and moneyers came to work only when the mint was in operation. The most important mint in medieval England was the Tower mint, and moneyers from the Tower mint were assigned to local mints in other parts of England. A few localities provided housing for moneyers while they were engaged at the mint. Some of the moneyers worked for goldsmiths when the mint lay idle, and judging from their debts, moneyers were not poor people.

Codes of law in medieval England regulated the conduct of moneyers. One provision stipulated that a moneyer found guilty of issuing debased or light coin should have the offending hand severed and fastened to the mint. Although the profits from forgery were high, the risks were also substantial. At Christmas in 1124 Henry III summoned all moneyers to Winchester, where, according to the Anglo-Saxon Chronicle, within a period of 12 nights all were mutilated. According to the Margam Annals, 94 were punished. By the close of Henry's reign 19 out of 30 mints had shut down, probably because of a shortage of moneyers.

In the seventeenth century mechanization began to replace the moneyers. Moneyers were now supervisors who oversaw the work of laborers operating machinery. The term *moneyer* does not seem to have been used in the United States. It was still applied to English mint workers into the nineteenth century,

but it fell into disuse in the twentieth century. Today there are no craftsmen working at mints who bear the title "moneyer."

See also: Cross Coinage, Milled-Edge Coinage
References: Challis, C. E. 1978. *The Tudor Coinage.*
———, ed. 1992. *A New History of the Royal Mint.*
Freeman, Anthony. 1985. *The Money and the Mint in the Reign of Edward the Confessor, 1042–1066.*

Montesquieu

Charles Louis de Secondat, Baron de La Brede et de Montesquieu, wrote one of the most famous books in history, *The Spirit of Laws* (1748), in which he touched on the role of money in shaping laws.

Montesquieu's book appears on every list of great books. The lessor-known full title of the book, almost rivaling Montesquieu's modest name, was *On the Spirit of Laws, or On the Relations Which Must Exist between the Laws and the Constitution of Each Government, the Manners, Climate, Religion, Commerce, etc.* The book proposed to demonstrate that the character and tendency of laws (the spirit of laws) owed their origin first to climate and geography, and then to the physiology, economy, government, religion, morals, and manners of the people. The framers of the American Constitution copiously quoted *The Spirit of Laws* in their writings. Catherine the Great of Russia thought *The Spirit of Laws* should be "the breviary of sovereigns," and expected those helping revise Russia's laws to read extracts that she furnished.

Montesquieu briefly addressed the subject of money and how the evolution of money influences the civil laws of a people. His inquiry led him to these conclusions:

When a people have not the use of money, they are seldom acquainted with any other injustice than that which arises from violence; and the weak by uniting, defend themselves from its effects. They have nothing there but political regulations. But where money is established, they are subject to that injustice which proceeds from craft—an injustice that may be exercised in a thousand ways. Hence they are forced to have good civil laws, which spring up with the new practices of iniquity.

In countries where they have no specie, the robber takes only bare moveables, which have not mutual resemblance. But where they make use of money, the robber takes the signs, and these always resemble each other. In the former nothing can be concealed, because the robber takes along with him the proofs of his conviction; but in the latter it is quite the contrary.

. . . The greatest security of the liberties of a people who do not cultivate the earth is their not knowing the use of money. What is gained by hunting, fishing, or keeping herds of cattle cannot be assembled in such great quantity, nor be sufficiently preserved, for one man to find himself in a condition to corrupt many others: but when, instead of this, a man has a sign of riches, he may obtain a large quantity of these signs, and distribute them as he pleases.

The people who have no money have but few wants; and these are supplied with ease, and in an equal manner. Equality is then unavoidable; and hence it proceeds that their chiefs are not despotic.

Unlike a modern monetary theorist, Montesquieu was concerned with the deeper social and anthropological significance of money, and suggests that the innovation of money contributes to social inequality, a theme that can be heard in the most ancient literature on the subject. He does not seem quite willing to give the innovation of money a ringing endorsement. In another section of his work, however, he says, "Should you ever happen to be cast by some adventure among an unknown people; Upon seeing a piece of money you may be assured that you have arrived in a civilized country. The culture of lands requires the use of money."

See also: Barter
Reference: Montesquieu, Charles De Secondat, Baron De. 1952. *The Spirit of Laws*. Trans. Thomas Nugent.

Mosaic Silver Standard

The Law of Moses makes numerous references to the silver *shekel* as means of payment. The twenty-seventh chapter of Leviticus describes monetary substitutes that could free a person dedicated to the service of the Lord. It reads:

The Lord said to Moses, Say to the people of Israel, When a man makes a special vow of persons to the Lord at your valuation, then your valuation of a male from twenty years old up to sixty years old shall be fifty shekels of silver, according to the shekel of the sanctuary. If the person is a female, your valuation shall be thirty shekels. If the person is from five years old up to twenty years old, your valuation shall be for a male twenty shekels, and for a female ten shekels. If the person is from a month old up to five years old, your valuation shall be for a male five shekels of silver, and for a female your valuation shall be three shekels. And if the person is sixty years old and upward, then your valuation for a male shall be fifteen shekels, and for a female ten shekels. . . . If a man dedicates to the Lord part of the land which is his by inheritance, then your valuation shall be according to the seed for it; a sowing of a homer of barley shall be valued at fifty shekels of silver.

Later in the Book of Leviticus guilt offerings were also defined in shekels of silver.

Although the Ancient Hebrews held gold in high esteem for religious purposes, they did not use it as a type of money. The book of Leviticus gives detailed accounts of the use of gold for religious ornamentation, describing altars overlaid with gold, and a plate of pure gold fastened on Aaron's turban, engraved with the words "Holy to the Lord."

Silver probably replaced livestock as a form of money among the early Hebrews. The ancient Hebraic word for "lamb," *kesitah,* appears in the Old Testament in contexts that indicate it was a monetary unit. The kesitah was probably a weight of silver equivalent to the price of a lamb, though it could have been a coin bearing the image of a sheep. The latter is an unlikely possibility because the Hebrews adopted coinage relatively late. The ancient Hebraic word for "livestock," *mikhne,* also meant "purchase," lending more credence to the theory that the early Hebrews had a sheep or lamb standard.

The Old Testament throws some light on the religious aspect of the origin of money. Before governments replaced tribes as the principal source of authority, religious authorities were the most able to sanction a commodity as a medium of exchange.

See also: Babylonian Grain and Silver Standard, Phoenician Weight Standard
References: Einzig, Paul. 1966. *Primitive Money.* *The New Oxford Annotated Bible.* 1973.

Mughal Coinage

The Mughal emperor Jahangir (1605–1627) wrote in his diary of his new coinage bearing signs of the zodiac:

> Previous to this the rule of the coinage was that on the face of the metal they stamped my name, and on the reverse side the name of the place and the year of the reign. At this time, it entered my mind that in the place of the month they should substitute the figure of the constellation which belonged to that month. (Williams, 1997)

One of Jahangir's coins bore a resemblance to himself with a cup of wine in his hands, a significant departure from Islamic coinage practice.

Evidence of Indian coinage prior to Alexander the Great's invasion (329–325 B.C.) is scanty, but Indian coinage may have appeared soon after the invention of coinage in Lydia. Whatever the date, early Indian coinage seems to follow Greek models, and Alexander can be credited with spreading the techniques of Greek coinage in India. Indian coinage spread eastward in the wake of Indian culture and religion, and by the thirteenth century could be seen as far away as Indonesia and the Philippines.

In the sixteenth century the Mughals descended upon India from the northwest, establishing an Islamic kingdom. Under Islam a new ruler could expect to have his name mentioned at the daily Mosque prayers, and have the privilege to issue coinage bearing his name.

The money of account of the Mughals was the silver *rupee,* which also dates back to sixteenth-century India. To be accepted as money, coins had to bear the name of the current Mughal emperor, a custom that persisted even after the Mughal emperor existed in name only and the Mughal empire had splintered into autonomous kingdoms. Roughly 300 types of rupee circulated when the British reformed India's currency and standardized the rupee early in the nineteenth century.

The silver rupee was the money of account in India under the Mughals. (Smithsonian Institution, National Numismatic Collection)

Under the Mughal system moneychangers, called *shroffs,* played a prominent and necessary role in monetary transactions. All large transactions required the presence of shroffs to count each coin and assign discounts according the wear of each coin and the time and location that each was struck.

Late in the eighteenth century the British introduced mechanical coinage into India. Mechanical coinage had been universal in Europe since 1700. In 1835 the British reformed India's currency and standardized the rupee, ending the multitude of rupees and the need for shroffs. The British continued the practice of issuing coins in the name of the Mughal emperor, a necessary condition to make coins acceptable. Under the prestigious influence of the British Empire, the rupee became the standard unit of currency in the Persian Gulf and southern Arabia, and spread as far south as British East Africa, and Natal in South Africa.

See also: Arab Dinar, Ottoman Empire Currency

References: Carter, M. L., ed. 1994. *A Treasury of Indian Coins.*
Williams, Jonathan, ed. 1997. *Money: A History.*

N

Nails

In the most famous of books on economics, *Wealth of Nations,* published in 1776, Adam Smith wrote that "there is at this day a village in Scotland where is not uncommon, I am told, for a workman to carry nails instead of money to the baker's shop or the alehouse."

Smith goes on to speculate why metals have been the money of choice for many countries. According to Smith:

> [M]en seem at last to have been determined by irresistible reasons to give the preference for this employment to metals above every other commodity. Metals can be kept with as little loss as any other commodity, scarce anything being less perishable than they are, but they can likewise, without any loss, be divided into any number of parts, as by fusion those parts can easily be reunited again, a quality which no other equally durable commodities possess, and which more than any other quality renders them fit to be the instruments of commerce and circulation. The man who wanted to buy salt, for example, and had nothing but cattle to give in exchange for it, must have been obliged to buy salt to value of a whole ox, or a whole sheep at a time. If, on the contrary, instead of oxen or sheep, he had metals to give in exchange for it, he could easily proportion the quantity of the metal to the precise quantity of the commodity which he had immediate occasion for.

Nails provide many of the advantages of metallic currency without requiring a mint. (Smithsonian Institution, National Numismatic Collection)

There is some evidence that nails served as money in one of the nineteenth-century French coal fields. Nails were perhaps a convenient form of a metallic currency, functioning without the service of a mint, and putting the metal in a form that was equally serviceable as a medium of exchange or as a practical commodity.

See also: Iron Currency
References: Einzig, Paul. 1966. *Primitive Money.*
Smith, Adam. 1952. *Wealth of Nations.*

National Bank Act of 1864 (United States)

The National Bank Act of 1864 gave the United States a uniform currency, universally accepted at par, sparing merchants the necessity to consult bank note detectors to appraise the value of various bank notes received from customers. Bank note detectors were regularly published booklets showing the discount on each bank note.

Before the National Bank Act of 1864 the United States had no permanent and uniform national currency but only a confusing medley of state bank notes trading at various discounts, usually depending upon the distance from the issuing bank. The National Bank Act established a system of note-issuing national banks, with national charters, to compete with the state banking system, which was regulated by separate banking regulations in individual states.

The National Bank Act bore a striking similarity to much of the states' free banking regulations, allowing any group of five or more persons meeting certain capitalization requirements to obtain a national charter. Capital requirements varied from $50,000 to $200,000, depending upon the size of the city the bank proposed to serve. Larger cities required larger capitalization. A third of the capital, or $30,000, whichever was smaller, had to be held as United States government bonds deposited with the comptroller of the currency, a new position created to supervise the national banking system. In exchange for the government bonds, the bank received national bank notes. Aside from other advantages, the new national banking system created a market for United States government debt.

The act provided for a hierarchy of reserve banks that led to a pyramiding of reserves in New York, creating an unstable link between the banking system and Wall Street financial markets. Country banks had to meet a 15 percent reserve requirement, three-fifths of which could be deposited in banks located in 18 large cities designated as redemption centers. The act subjected banks in the redemption centers to a 25 percent reserve requirement, half of which could be deposited with New York banks. The reserve requirement was the fraction of outstanding checking accounts or other deposits that a bank had to keep as reserves—vault cash or a reserve deposit at an acceptable institution.

Separate legislation effectively gave national banks a monopoly on the privilege to issue bank notes. In 1862 Congress put a 2 percent tax on the issuance of state bank notes. In 1866 Congress in-creased the tax to 10 percent, putting an end to the profits of state bank notes, and leaving only national bank notes in circulation. About one-fourth of the state banks in northern states survived the National Bank Act and the tax on state bank notes. In the later 1800s the substitution of the personal check for bank notes brought a resurgence of the more gently regulated state banks.

The National Bank Act significantly advanced the monetary system in the United States, but it made no provision for a lender of last resort to act as a safety net during financial crises. Concern over recurring financial crises led the United States to further centralize its monetary system with the establishment of the Federal Reserve System in 1913.

See also: Federal Reserve System, Greenbacks
References: Hepburn, A. B. 1924. *A History of the Currency of the United States.*
Myers, Margaret G. 1970. *A Financial History of the United States.*
Selgin, George A., and Lawrence H. White. 1994. Monetary Reform and the Redemption of National Bank Notes. *Business History Review* 68, no. 20 (Summer): 205–243.

Negotiable Order of Withdrawal Accounts

Negotiable order of withdrawal accounts, usually called NOW accounts, are interest-bearing checking accounts offered by banks, and particularly thrift institutions, in the United States. The so-called M1, the narrowest definition of the money supply in the United States, includes NOW accounts. NOW accounts came about from a process of regulatory evolution rather than consciously thought-out planning for the monetary system.

The Glass-Steagall Act of 1933 banned payment of interest on checking accounts, reflecting the depression-era thinking that interest-paying checking accounts had contributed to the high incidence of bank failures. Payment of attractive interest rates on checking accounts was one means banks used to attract depositors away from other banks, and banks that lost a large quantity of deposits faced bankruptcy.

Because savings and loan and other thrift institutions were not authorized to issue demand deposits, the zero-interest rate ceiling on demand deposits did not directly affect them. Thrift institutions were authorized to issue passbook accounts and regular savings accounts, which allowed customers to deposit funds or make withdrawals anytime during business hours. Technically, thrift institutions could require a seven-day notice before allowing the withdrawal of funds from these accounts, but in practice this requirement was usually waived.

The first NOW accounts were offered in 1972 by the Consumer Savings Bank in Worchester, Massachusetts, a mutual savings bank. Massachusetts had mutual savings banks, which were insured by a state insurance fund and therefore independent of the regulations imposed on the federally insured depository institutions. By 1970 Massachusetts savings banks were already authorized to waive a 30-day withdrawal notice for regular savings accounts, and depositors could walk into a savings bank and transfer funds to a third party by using counter checks devised for that purpose. The Worchester bank only proposed changing the location at which the third-party draft was written. The idea came before the Massachusetts Supreme Judicial Court, and the court took two years before deciding that the Consumer Savings Bank had a point. After 1972 NOW accounts spread rapidly among mutual savings banks in Massachusetts. Regulatory bodies allowed NOW accounts to penetrate the rest of New England, and then New York and New Jersey. Title III of the Depository Institution Deregulation and Monetary Control Act of 1980, called the Consumer Checking Account Equity Act, authorized the savings and loan industry to offer NOW accounts nationwide. The act also authorized credit unions to issue similar accounts called share drafts. Theoretically, share drafts pay dividends rather than interest, but the practical implications are the same.

Before the introduction of NOW accounts, savings deposits at thrifts fluctuated with opportunities to earn interest in other types of financial investments. A period of rising interest rates was invariably attended with a withdrawal of funds from savings deposits at thrift institutions. The availability of interest on NOW accounts eased some of the pressure on depositors to find investments for their money outside of the thrift institutions. NOW accounts increased the costs of funds to thrift institutions, but also have added stability to savings accounts. From the consumer's standpoint, accounts that pay interest are not as vulnerable to inflation, because the interest earned offsets the deterioration in purchasing power from inflation.

See also: Certificate of Deposit, Depository Institution Deregulation and Monetary Control Act, Monetary Aggregates, Money Market Mutual Fund Accounts
References: Rose, Peter S. 1986. *Money and Capital Markets.* Woerheide, Walter J. 1984. *The Savings and Loan Industry.*

New York Safety Fund System

The New York Safety Fund System represents one of the early efforts to protect the public from bank failures and an ancestor to the Federal Depositary Insurance Corporation in the United States. The Safety Fund System required that banks chartered by the state of New York contribute to a safety fund to pay for the redemption of bank notes issued by failed banks.

Under the pre–Civil War banking system individual banks issued their own bank notes, which in principle they stood ready to redeem in specie. Bank notes played the role that checking accounts play in the modern banking system. When banks failed the public could no longer convert the bank notes of failing banks into gold and silver coins. In the modern banking system, bank failures, in the absence of deposit insurance, leave the banking public unable to withdraw bank deposits in cash.

The legislature enacted the New York Safety Fund Act on 2 April 1829 and the system remained in effect until the era of free banking that began in 1838. Some of the public skepticism toward banks at the time can be read in the wording of the act, which referred to a bank as a "monied corporation." The act required that each bank annually contribute $1/2$ percent of its capital to a fund until the bank's contribution to the fund equaled 3 percent of its capital. The interest earned on the fund, after allowances for administering the fund, was paid back to the banks. When a bank failed, the safety fund paid the debts of the failing bank, but the fund did not reimburse the owners of the bank for loss of capital. The Act put the administration of the fund in the hands of three commissioners, one appointed by the governor, and two by the banking community. The Act provided that a bank could be liquidated if the bank was two months behind in its contribution to the safety fund, had sustained a loss of half of its capital stock, had suspended specie payments on its bank notes for 90 days, or had refused access to bank commissioners. The act also required that bank officers pledge an oath that a bank's stock was not purchased with a bank's own bank notes, a common abuse of banking laws at the time.

The safety fund system worked well until 1837, but the crisis of 1837 was more than the fund could handle. The safety fund appears to have remained in existence into the era of free banking, but not on sound footing. In 1842 the act was revised to remove the safety fund from responsibility for bank deposits and debts, but maintained the fund's responsibility for bank notes.

R. Hildreth, writing in 1837 on the banking system, commented on the safety fund, saying: "it does not level the root of the evil; and it has the obvious defect of taxing the honest for the sins of the fraudulent" (Chown, 1994).

See also: Central Bank, Free Banking, National Bank Act of 1864, Suffolk System

References: Chown, John. 1994. *A History of Money.*
Hepburn, A. Barton. 1924. *A History of the Currency in the United States.*
Myers, Margaret G. 1970. *A Financial History of the United States.*

O

Oedipus Tyrannus

Oedipus Tyrannus, a dramatic poem touching on the theme of paper money, was written by Percy Bysshe Shelley (1792–1822), the English poet famous for such poems as *Ode to the West Wind*.

Oedipus was the hero in a Sophoclean tragedy who blinded himself in a fit of painful self-revelation. The name *Oedipus* referred to his feet, made misshapen by a thong binding when he was a discarded baby. Shelley's poem is presented as a translation of a Greek tragedy, but bears a closer resemblance to one of Aristophanes' comedies. Shelley translated *Oedipus Tyrannus* as *Swellfoot the Tyrant*. Swellfoot reigned in Thebes over a kingdom of pigs who remained firmly under his heel. His queen, Iona Taurina, lay under a reproach of some crime, presumably promiscuity. The queen had been driven from land to land by a gadfly, and her impending return has brought to mind a prophecy that:

Boeotia, choose reform or civil war!
When through the streets, instead of hare with dogs,
A Consort Queen shall hunt a King with Hogs,
Riding on the Ionian Minotaur.

The play was an allegory of the English royal politics at the time. When George III died in 1820 the Prince of Wales was crowned in a ceremony that banned his wife, Princess Caroline, who had been investigated for adultery, from attendance. The peo-ple of England championed the cause of Princess Caroline, who in vain tried to attend the coronation and died a week later. Shelley regarded Princess Caroline as "a vulgar woman, with all those low taste, which prejudice considers as vices" (Reiter, 1967). His judgment of the king was no kinder, writing that the king, "no less than his ministers, are so odious that everything, however disgusting, which is opposed to them, is admirable" (Reiter, 1967).

In Act I Swellfoot stands before the statute of the goddess of famine, praying:

Thou to whom Kings and laurelled Emperors,
Radical-butchers, Paper-money millers,
Bishops and Deacons, and the entire army
Of those fat martyrs to the persecution
Of stifling turtle-soup, and brandy-devils,
Offer their secret vows!

When the pigs bemoan their fate and ask for clean straw and hogwash, an infuriated Swellfoot orders that the sows be spayed, and when the pigs run wild he orders them killed. The king's councilor, fearing for the safety of the kingdom, observes:

The troops grow mutinous—the revenue fails—
There's something rotten in us—

Mammon, the priest of the goddess of Famine, answers:

Do the troops mutiny? —decimate some
  regiments;
Does money fail? come to my mint—coin paper,
Till gold be at a discount, and ashamed
To show his bilious face, go purge himself,
In emulation of her vestal whiteness

Mammon's daughter, Banknotina (a reference to banknotes), inherited his estate, called Fool's Paradise, and consisting of funds in "fair-money, bonds, and bills." Later in the poem a reference is heard of "kings and priest and lords, who rule by vizers, sceptres, bank-notes, words."

The poem ends with the queen leading a rebellion of pigs against Oedipus, his councilors and allies, hinting at an outcome as lawless and merciless as the French Revolution. The prophecy of civil war in Boetia had come true.

Shelley wrote *Oedipus Tyrannus* toward the end of England's first experience with inconvertible paper money, which lasted from 1797 until 1821. His play sounded a theme that would often recur—the association between extravagant abuse of paper money and political and social conditions that lead to revolution.

See also: *Faust, Wizard of Oz*
References: Reiter, Seymour. 1967. *A Study of Shelley's Poetry.*
Shelley, Percy Bysshe. 1922. *Dramatic Poems of Percy Bysshe Shelley.*

Open Market Operations

Open market operations are the most important means of expanding and contracting money supplies in modern monetary systems regulated by central banks. Central banks, such as the Federal Reserve System in the United States, regulate money supplies as a means of maintaining economic stability and price stability.

To infuse additional money into the United States economy, the Federal Reserve System purchases United States government bonds, paying for the bonds with freshly created funds added to commercial bank deposits at Federal Reserve Banks. Commercial bank deposits at Federal Reserve Banks, coupled with vault cash, make up what is called high-powered money, because a system of commercial banks, making loans, can expand customer demand deposits by some multiple of the volume of high-powered money.

To withdraw money from circulation in the United States economy, the Federal Reserve system sells from its holdings of United States government bonds, and withdraws the proceeds of the sales from circulation and the banking system, leading to a contraction of money supplies.

The Bank of England may have been the first to regulate credit markets along the lines of modern open market operations. Late in the nineteenth century the Bank of England would borrow funds in the London money market as a means of raising interest rates.

The Federal Reserve System apparently discovered by accident the practice of open market operations as an instrument of monetary control. The Federal Reserve Act of 1913 did not specifically address open market operations but did empower individual Federal Reserve Banks to buy and sell securities with "such purchases to be made in accordance with rules and regulations prescribed by the Federal Reserve Board."

An economic slowdown in the 1920s reduced the demand for Federal Reserve Bank loans to commercial banks. Federal Reserve Banks began buying government securities in the open market as a means of acquiring income-earning assets, compensating for the loss in the discount loan business to commercial banks. At first individual Federal Reserve Banks (there are 12 Federal Reserve Banks) separately purchased government securities, occasionally pitting individual banks against each other in bidding for securities. The Federal Reserve Banks collectively decided to coordinate all purchases of government securities through the New York Federal Reserve Bank. In 1922 the then Federal Reserve Board, since renamed the Board of Governors of the Federal Reserve System, established a special committee, composed of board members and officials of the Federal Reserve Banks, to make decisions about open market operations. The comparable committee is now called the Federal Open Market Committee.

The Federal Reserve Banks soon learned the impact of open market operations on money supplies, interest rates, and credit conditions, but the Board remained split on the wisdom of open market operations until the 1930s. During the Great Depression of the 1930s open market operations began to play a larger role in monetary policy. By the end of World War II open market operations had become the most important tool in the central bank arsenal of monetary controls.

See also: Central Bank, Federal Reserve System

References: Anderson, Clay J. 1965. *A Half-Century of Federal Reserve Policymaking, 1914–1964.*

Baye, Michael R., and Dennis W. Jansen. 1995. *Money, Banking, and Financial Markets: An Economics Approach.*

Klein, John J. 1986. *Money and the Economy.* 6th ed.

Operation Bernhard

The scale of Operation Bernhard dwarfs all other counterfeiting operations in the history of paper money. Nazi Germany counterfeited British 5-pound bank notes and later 50-pound bank notes to fund its foreign intelligence operations. Operation Bernhard got its name from Bernhard Kruger who headed a workshop in which Germany's security service forged passports, motor licenses, university degrees, and other personal documents.

Counterfeiting as a weapon of war stretched well back into the nineteenth century, and at the beginning of World War II Britain had dropped forged German food and clothing coupons over Germany and had made awkward attempts to counterfeit German marks. Germany's technical mastery of counterfeiting, however, far surpassed all preceding operations.

The decision to counterfeit money went all the way to Adolf Hitler, who approved counterfeiting British pounds in his own handwriting but with the proviso, "[D]ollars, no. We're not at war with the United States." Germany stuck to counterfeiting Bank of England bank notes even after the United States entered the war, but toward the end of the war German apparently prepared plates to counterfeit French francs and United States dollars.

The practical problem of counterfeiting British bank notes was broken down into three separate parts: (1) production of paper identical to paper in British bank notes, (2) construction of plates identical with Bank of England plates, and (3) devising a numbering system.

After finding that rags made from Turkish flax produced paper almost identical to Bank of England bank notes, the Germans hit upon the expedient of sending the rags to factories to get dirty first, and then cleaned the used rags before using them to make bank note paper. Engravers spent seven months making plates that matched the original prints even when enlarged twentyfold. The numbering problem was the last to be solved. Apparently, the necessity of developing a numbering system that would blend in with the British numbering system posed the most troublesome obstacle. The finished plates were among the most closely guarded secrets in Germany.

Later in the project the German counterfeiters attacked the problem of making the notes age. As printed notes age, the oil in the printing ink begins to seep into surrounding areas, blurring the quality of the print. German counterfeit notes were not aging properly until the Germans learned to treat their printing ink with chemicals to make it seep into surrounding areas, producing an aging effect.

After the technical problems were solved, the Germans sent an agent to the Swiss, carrying a bundle of counterfeit notes and a letter from the Deutsche Reichsbank asking the Swiss to find out if the notes were forged. When the Swiss replied that the notes were genuine without a doubt, the agent feigned a lingering suspicion and asked the Swiss to check with the Bank of England. The Bank of England also returned a reply that the notes were genuine.

At first the German government planned to use an infusion of counterfeit notes to ruin the British economy, but efforts to inject large quantities of notes into circulation led to diplomatic embarrassments, and the German government dropped the plan. Then Germany's secret intelligence service decided to use counterfeit notes to finance its operations, and that is how the counterfeit notes were put into circulation.

The Bank of England bank notes were counterfeited at the Sachsenhausen concentration camp. Three hundred prisoners, some of them experts in forgery, took part in the project, and for a time these prisoners produced 400,000 notes per month. About 130 million British pounds were counterfeited in bank notes. As the demand for counterfeit money increased, the Germans began to counterfeit 50-pound notes.

Both the Germans and the Allies kept Operation Bernhard a secret. Because of the circulation of counterfeited bank notes, the Bank of England withdrew all notes of 10 pounds or above in 1943 and changed the paper of the 5-pound note in 1944. In May 1945 notes from 10 pounds to 1,000 pounds ceased to be legal tender.

Toward the end of the war the Germans dumped counterfeiting supplies and a vast quantity of notes into the Toplitzee, a lake in Austria. Large numbers of floating notes fueled rumors of the dumping and the Allies sent divers into the lake, but no bank notes were recovered. The first public knowledge of Operation Bernhard came in 1952 when *Readers Digest* carried an article about it, and gradually more knowledge of the operation came to light. Only in 1959 did divers finally recover the vast quantities of notes and printing supplies. Notes recovered from the lake were indistinguishable from genuine Bank of England notes.

Apparently, some of the notes continued to circulate until 1955 when the Bank of England went to colored notes, and its older notes ceased to be legal tender. Some evidence suggests that as late as 1961 these notes were sold behind the Iron Curtain to people looking for a store of wealth until the communist regimes fell.

See also: Counterfeit Money

References: Beresiner, Yasha. 1977. *Paper Money*.
Burke, Bryan. 1987. *Nazi Counterfeiting of British Currency during World War II: Operation Andrew and Operation Bernhard*.
Pirie, Anthony. 1962. *Operation Bernhard*.

Optimal Currency Area

In the post–World War II era economists raised the issue of the optimal currency area, which is that area that stands to gain from an independent currency. The issue grew in importance as Europe made plans to establish an all-European currency, the *euro*, to replace individual national currencies such as the German mark, French franc, and Swiss franc. Although Europe is merging into one large currency area, the breakup of the Soviet Union has held out the spectacle of a large currency area splintering into smaller currency areas, as new nations such as Ukraine replaced rubles with their own currency.

One theory of optimal currency areas emphasizes the importance of resource immobility. Consider two areas, one with a high unemployment rate and another with a low unemployment rate. If labor is a mobile resource, the unemployed workers will migrate to the area with the low unemployment rate. If labor is not mobile, due to distance, national laws, or language differences, then differences in currency exchange rates between the two geographical areas

can serve some of the same purpose, assuming the two areas have their own separate currencies. The area with high unemployment can lower the value of its currency, making its exports cheaper to the area with low unemployment. Also, the lowered currency value will increase the cost of imports to the high-unemployment area, encouraging domestic consumers to buy locally produced goods. Therefore, adjustments in the exchange rate will increase the demand for goods produced in the high-unemployment area, and lower the demand for goods produced in the low-unemployment area, indicating that areas with immobile resources should have their own currency. According to this criterion, Canada is probably too large to have a single currency because of the vast distance between the east coast and west coast, making mobility difficult. Among members of the European Union, reductions in barriers restricting the flow of capital and labor between countries preceded the introduction of the euro in 1999.

Another theory of optimal currency areas looks at the importance of internal trade relative to trade with outsiders. In the case of Europe, this theory looks at the size of trade between European countries, such as France and Germany, relative to the size of trade between Europe as a whole and outsiders, such as the United States. An area that trades a great deal with itself, and not so much with the rest of the world, should qualify as an optimal currency area, and have its own currency. Under this criterion, Canada again would not constitute an optimal currency area if regions in Canada traded largely with the United States, rather than with other regions in Canada. If regions in Canada trade mostly with other Canadian regions, then Canada benefits from having its own currency. This criterion leaves the case of Europe somewhat in limbo, because Europe trades significantly within itself, but also trades significantly with outsiders.

Another criterion for an optimal currency area is that the area must have institutions that can make political and technical decisions for the area as a whole. Nation states are the most obvious currency areas for this reason. Canada obviously qualifies as an optimal currency area under this criterion. Europe has moved toward political integration, including the election of a European Parliament, making Europe much more suitable as an optimal currency area.

See also: Euro Currency, European Currency Unit, Snake,
References: McKinnon, Ronald I. 1963. Optimal Currency
     Areas. *American Economic Review* 53: 717–725.
Melitz, Jacques. 1996. The Theory of Optimal Currency
     Areas. *Open Economies Review* 7, no. 2 (April): 99–116.
Mundell, Robert A. 1961. A Theory of Optimal Currency
     Areas. *American Economic Review* 51: 637–665.

Optional Clause
See Bank of Scotland, Scottish
Banking Act of 1765

Ottoman Empire Currency

At its height the Ottoman Empire ruled present-day
Turkey, the Middle East, North Africa, including
Egypt, and southeastern Europe. By World War I the
Ottoman Empire had largely disintegrated, and after
the war the core of the empire was organized as the
republic of Turkey. Although the Sunni-Ottoman dynasty dates back to the thirteenth century, the empire became a power to be reckoned with after the
capture of Constantinople in 1453. Perhaps the most
famous sultan of the Ottoman Empire was Suleiman
the Magnificent (1520–1566), whose conquest in the
sixteenth century gave the Ottoman Empire control
of East-West trade.

   The prime coins of the Ottoman Empire were the
akce, silver coins that provided the basis of monetary calculations for prices and wages. Suleiman's architect earned 55 akce per day. A niche for smaller
coins was filled by the *dirham,* with its quarter, and
the *manghir,* which were copper. The most important gold coin was the *ashrafit,* patterned after the
Venetian *ducat.* To compete with Austrian *talers,*
which rapidly gained acceptance in areas of the empire, Suleiman III (1687–1691) minted a silver coin
known as the *qurush.*

   To meet the coinage needs of the empire, the Ottomans purchased blank coins from Austria and the
Dutch. Unlike other Islamic coinage, which often
bore religious inscriptions, Ottoman coins bore inscriptions of the Sultan's titles. One coin bore an inscription that translates as "sultan of the two lands
and lord of the two seas."

   Mechanized methods of minting coins first appeared in Turkey in the mid-nineteenth century, two
hundred years later than the widespread adoption of
these methods in Europe. Iran saw its first mechanized mint established in Tehran in 1876. In the
twentieth century European mechanized mints
supplied coins for colonized areas of the Ottoman
Empire.

   Paper money also made its debut in the mid-
nineteenth century. The Ottomans led the way with
the issuance of notes in Turkey, setting an example
that was soon followed by other provinces of the empire. Iran waited until the late 1880s to issue bank
notes. Colonial powers often introduced paper
money, paving the way for newly independent countries to issue their own paper money. In the twentieth century the paper money issued in countries of
the old Ottoman Empire was often printed in European countries. A British firm, De La Rue, printed
paper money for Iraq until the invasion of Kuwait in
1990 cut Iraq off from Europe.

See also: Mughal Coinage
References: Ehrenkreutz, A. S. 1992. *Monetary Change and
     Economic History in the Medieval Muslim World.*
Williams, Jonathan, ed. 1997. *Money: A History.*

P

Pacific Coast Gold Standard

California and Oregon remained on a gold standard during the 1862 to 1879 period when the rest of the country transacted business on an inconvertible paper standard. During the Civil War the Confederate government abandoned all monetary discipline and flooded the South with Confederate paper money. In 1862 the North began issuing inconvertible greenbacks, and only in 1879 provided for the redemption of greenbacks in gold and silver specie. During the 1862 to 1879 period Gresham's law drove all gold and silver coins out of circulation in the East, but state laws and organized business interests kept gold in circulation on the Pacific coast. The Pacific coast could boast of no less than $25 million of gold and silver coins in circulation during the period when the rest of the country used paper money as a medium of exchange and standard of value.

Before the Civil War both California and Oregon relied exclusively on gold and silver coins, as opposed to bank notes, to circulate as money. When greenbacks were first issued, bank notes accounted for almost half of the circulating money in the East. The constitutions of both California and Oregon banned the issuance and circulation of paper money, and banks were forbidden to create "paper to circulate as money."

Aside from legal barriers to the circulation of paper money, merchants collectively agreed not to accept greenbacks on par with gold. The merchants of San Francisco agreed to neither receive nor make payment in greenbacks at any rate other than the greenback market value in terms of gold. They set prices in gold and accepted greenbacks at whatever discount the market dictated. When leading merchants in Portland agreed to accept greenbacks at the going rate in San Francisco, merchants throughout Oregon enforced the same policy. The merchants in Portland went so far as to circulate an announcement that customers who insisted upon paying debts in greenbacks would find their names on a blacklist of the Portland merchants' association. Commercial ostracism awaited any businessperson who paid a business debt in greenbacks, that is, who "greenbacked" a creditor. Banks in California and Oregon refused to accept deposits in greenbacks, and newspapers worked to keep down the circulation of greenbacks.

After the federal government began issuance of greenbacks, the legislatures of both California and Oregon enacted measures allowing people to contract debts in either coin or greenbacks, but requiring that payment be made as specified in the contract. The Oregon legislature enacted legislation requiring the payment of state and local taxes in only gold and silver coin, ruling out greenbacks. The California Supreme Court ruled that greenbacks were not acceptable in the payment of state and county taxes.

Organized opposition to greenbacks triggered a bitter debate on the Pacific coast. Critics charged that repudiation of greenbacks was tantamount to refusing to share in the financial burden of the Civil War. Crowding all the greenbacks on to the East Coast caused faster depreciation of the greenbacks, putting a greater burden of inflation on the East Coast. Although prices in greenbacks doubled over the course of the Civil War, Oregon prices in gold increased only 25 percent.

Two factors may help explain opposition to greenbacks on the Pacific coast. First, gold discoveries in California had already given that region a taste of inflation caused by increases in the money supply. A paper issue would only accelerate money growth, contributing to further inflation. Second, as a gold-producing region, the Pacific coast did not want to encourage the use of any other form of money. As abundant gold production drove out silver money, the Pacific coast moved essentially to a gold standard between 1862 and 1879, a unique exception to the paper standard that reigned in the rest of the country.

See also: Gold Rushes, Gold Standard, Greenbacks

References: Greenfield, Robert L., and Hugh Rockoff. 1996. Yellowbacks Out West and Greenbacks Back East: Social-Choice Dimensions of Monetary Reform. *Southern Economic Journal* 62, no. 4 (April): 902–915.

Lester, Richard A. 1939. *Monetary Experiments.*

Moses, Bernard. 1892. Legal Tender Notes in California. *Quarterly Journal of Economics* 7 (October): 1–25.

Papal Coinage

The Roman papal court rose to become a significant European financial center in the late Middle Ages and the papal mint, called the *Zecca*, was a major focus of curial activity. The famous Renaissance artist and architect, Donato Bramante, built a new mint for Pope Julius II. Another Renaissance architect of some renown, Antonio da Sangallo the Younger, later remodeled the mint, his facade remaining on the building to this day. The Renaissance popes needed money to pay soldiers, hire artists, and build monuments and buildings, and the papal mint often furnished the coins to make payment.

The popes minted gold and silver coins. The principle gold coin of the Renaissance era was the gold *ducat of the Chamber,* named after the Apostolic Chamber that handled the financial affairs of the papacy. The gold ducat was preceded by the gold *florin of the Chamber,* approximately equivalent in value to the ducat. In 1530 the papal mint issued a new coin,

the *scudo d'oro in oro,* a coin that in value fell short of the ducat by a small margin. A papal ducat equaled about one-third of a Tudor pound sterling. The papal mint struck silver coins called *carlina,* and later, *giulii,* that equaled approximately one-tenth the value of a ducat.

The papal treasury and Roman treasuries tended to accumulate precious objects, and during times of financial stress, treasures were melted down and minted. Under Innocent III, the opening of a sepulchre of a noble lady of imperial Rome brought to light a golden brocade on her robes, which was promptly sent to the mint and melted down.

The papal court of Rome drew income from benefices across Europe, and the Apostolic Chamber expected payment in its own coinage, partly to protect itself from payments in mixed and depreciated silver money. Princes usually made payments in gold and the lower classes in silver. The combined gold and silver sent to Rome raised the ire of northern Europe, leading to charges that the Roman Church was bleeding Europe white.

Papal coinage was noted for its beauty, a trait not surprising in light of the celebrated Renaissance artists who applied their gifts to coinage at the papal mint. The most eminent was Benvenuto Cellini, the Renaissance goldsmith and sculptor, and author of a famous autobiography. Perhaps less known is Francesco Francia, who struck coins so distinguished by their beauty that they became collectors' items, and sold at premiums soon after his death. Vasari, in his *Lives of the Most Eminent Painters, Sculptors, and Architects,* says of Francia that he was "so pleasant in conversation that he could divert the most melancholy individuals, and won the affection of princes and lords and all who know him."

Papal coinage is among the more modern manifestations of a familiar theme in monetary history. Temples and religious institutions usually have had the inside track on the accumulation of gold and silver. Because of the reverence for these institutions, the treasures of these institutions are usually safe from theft and extortion. (This reverence did not keep the papacy from losing much of its treasure during the Sack of Rome in 1527.) The moral leadership of these institutions can also add credibility to the precious metal purity of coinage. Historically, these institutions have often held a stronger claim of trust on the public than kings and princes.

Phoenicians, pictured here in Arrival of Solomon's Fleet, *were slow to accept coinage, preferring to trade in precious metals by weight and fineness. (North Wind Picture Archive)*

Today the Vatican issues its own paper money, in francs and lire, which is noted for beautiful pictorial and religious themes.

See also: Cellini, Benvenuto, Temple Coinage of Ancient Greece

References: Cellini, Benvenuto. 1931. *The Life of Benvenuto Cellini.*

———. 1967. *The Treatises of Benvenuto Cellini on Goldsmithing and Sculpture.*

Partner, Peter. 1976. *Renaissance Rome, 1500–1599.*

Ryan, John Carlin. 1989. *A Handbook of Papal Coins.*

Phoenician Weight Standard

The Phoenician weight standard bore a strong resemblance to the Babylonian system. Both systems expressed money values in *shekels* and *talents,* and both systems were bimetallic monetary regimes. In the Phoenician standard, a gold shekel was worth 15 silver shekels, weighing 112 grains each. A talent may have begun as the weight that one person could lift, but the Phoenicians and Babylonians fixed the value of the talent in terms of a set number of shekels.

One of the puzzles of monetary history is that the Phoenicians, who ranked among the most highly commercialized peoples of the ancient Mediterranean, hardly merit a footnote in the history of coinage, accepting it very slowly. The Phoenicians devoted themselves to commercial pursuits and found a place in history for inventing the alphabet. By contrast Lydia, a pastoral society that was a poor candidate for commercial innovations, became the birthplace of modern coinage.

It was not a shortage of gold or silver that hampered the development of coinage in Phoenicia, at least according to reports in the Old Testament. The first book of Kings says:

At the end of twenty years, in which Solomon had built the two houses, the house of the Lord and the king's house, and Hiram, king of Tyre [a Phoenician city] had supplied Solomon with cedar and cypress timber and gold, as much as he desired. . . . Hiram had sent to the king one hundred and twenty talents of gold. . . . King Solomon built a fleet of ships. . . . And Hiram sent with the fleet his servants, together with the servants of Solomon; and they went to Ophir, and brought from there gold, to the amount of four hundred and twenty talents; . . . The prophet Zechariah says: "Tyre has built herself a rampart, and heaped up silver like dust, and gold like the dirt of the streets."

John Maynard Keynes, the most famous economist of the twentieth century, observed in his *Treatise on Money* that coinage seemed to hold no charm for some of the societies of the ancient world, and held out the following suggestion:

The stamping of pieces of metal with a trade mark was just a piece of local vanity, patriotism, or advertisement with no far-reaching importance. It is a practice which has never caught on in some important commercial areas. . . . The Semitic races, whose instincts are keenest for the essential qualities of money, have never paid much attention to the deceptive signatures of mints, which content the financial amateurs of the North, and have cared only for the touch and weight of the metal. It was not necessary, therefore, that talents or shekels should be minted.

Evidence of Phoenician coinage appears during the middle of the fifth century B.C. Coinage had been in use for 200 years in the trading area of the Aegean Sea, and Athens had been coining money for 100 years.

The Phoenicians were famous as navigators and distant traders, perhaps often bringing them into contact with peoples who would be satisfied with nothing less than weighing precious metal and verifying its fineness on the spot. Such people would have been more suspicious of coinage whose fineness and weight was certified by the seal of a government in a distant land. Also, justly or unjustly, the Phoenicians were known to be sharp, aggressive, and sometimes unscrupulous traders, rendering it unlikely that traders in distant lands would accept Phoenician coins without questioning their quality in terms of weight and fineness. These factors may account for the slowness of the Phoenicians to adopt coinage.

See also: Babylonian Grain and Silver Standard, Mosaic Silver Standard

References: Betlyon, John Wilson. 1982. *The Coinage and Mints of Phoenicia: the Pre-Alexandrine Period.*
Burns, A. R. 1927. *Money and Monetary Policy in Early Times.*
Einzig, Paul. 1966. *Primitive Money.*
Keynes, John Maynard. *Treatise on Money.*

Pig Standard of New Hebrides

Until the eve of World War II pigs played the role of money in the New Hebrides. The pig standard of New Hebrides was more than another livestock standard that combined a ready source of food with a store of wealth. In the New Hebrides boar hogs with curved tusks conferred status in a unique economic, political, and social system. On some islands, neutered pigs qualified, if they also grew tusks. The length of the tusks was the crucial quality determining the value of pigs, rather than weight or condition of the animal. Islanders removed two teeth from the upper jaw, causing the tusks to grow longer, adding to the pig's value.

The special role of pigs as sacrificial victims at feasts raised them above the category of a common source of food, endowing them with a special cultural significance that substantially increased their value as a store of wealth. Islanders gauged a man's wealth by the number of boars in his possession, which enabled him to make handsome contributions to sacrifices and feasts. They were too valuable for the small change of everyday transactions, which were facilitated by other exotic forms of money, such as mats, shells, quartzite stone money, and feathers. Pigs were used to buy land, pay workers (including magicians, dancers, and mortuary officials), purchase brides, and pay blood money, ransoms, and fines for violating taboos. Debts were defined in terms of pigs, and a large share of the murders on the islands arose from disputes over pig debts.

The social life of the islanders was dominated by men's clubs or secret societies. To purchase a bride, gain admission to a secret society, or earn promotion within a secret society, young men borrowed pigs, probably from relatives. A young man already in a secret society borrowed pigs from fellow members. A person acquired power by being able to loan pigs to those who needed to borrow them. Interest on debts was paid not by returning to the lender more pigs than were originally borrowed, but by returning pigs with longer tusks. Because pigs became more valuable as their tusks grew, interest on debts was paid by returning to the lender pigs with longer tusks. The rate of interest was determined by the growth of the tusks.

In the 1930s pigs with quarter-circle tusks fetched 4 English pounds, half-circle tusks 6 pounds, three-quarter-circle tusks between 10 and 15 pounds, and full-circle tusks over 30 pounds. Pigs with tusks extending beyond one circle, perhaps a circle and a half, commanded premium prices.

The pig standard of New Hebrides shows that cultural and religious factors can outweigh utilitarian factors in raising up a commodity to serve as a medium of exchange in universal demand. Livestock standards are founded in the reality that people must find food on a daily basis, rendering them receptive to accepting edible livestock in exchange. Having a large reservoir of livestock, as a source of food, however, can become a status symbol, further enforcing the value of the livestock as money. In the New Hebrides the length of a pig's tusks bore no relationship to its food value, but the tusks became a status symbol that acquired a cultural life of its own, making tusk length the lynch pin of the monetary standard.

See also: Cattle, Goat Standard of East Africa
References: Cheesman, Evelyn. 1933. *Backwaters of the Savage South Seas.*
Einzig, Paul. 1966. *Primitive Money.*
Humphreys, C. R. 1983. *The Southern New Hebrides: An Ethnological Record.*

Plato (427–347 B.C.)

Plato ranks with Socrates and Aristotle as the most famous of the Greek philosophers during the golden age of Athens. Of the three, Plato was the most idealistic, and even today Plato is probably the most widely read philosopher among college philosophy students. Plato is less well known for being one of the first influential political philosophers to propose a system of token money.

Plato's vision of the ideal state had no room for democracy, private property, competitive markets, or the institution of marriage. In one of the enduring lines in philosophical literature, Plato shares his secret for reforming society:

Until philosophers are kings, or the kings and princes of this world have the spirit and power of philosophy, and political greatness and wisdom meet in one, and those commoner natures who pursue either to the exclusion of the other are compelled to stand aside, cities will never have rest from their evils.

One of Plato's ingredients for an idealized society has been realized on a large scale in contemporary society. In the *Laws* Plato describes the monetary system of his reformed society:

Further, the law enjoins that no private man shall be allowed to possess gold and silver, but, only coin for daily use, which is almost necessary in dealing with artisans, and payment of hirelings, whether slaves or immigrants, by all those persons who require the use of them. Wherefore our citizens, as we say, should have a coin passing current among themselves, but not accepted among the rest of mankind; with a view, however, to expeditions and journeys to other lands—for embassies, or for any other occasion which may arise of sending out a herald, the state must also possess a common Hellenic currency. If a private person is ever obliged to go abroad, let him have the consent of the magistrates and go; and if when he returns he has any foreign money remaining, let him give the surplus back to the treasury, and receive a corresponding sum in the local currency. And if he is discovered to appropriate it, let it be confiscated, and let him who knows and does not inform be subject to curse and dishonor equally with him who brought the money, and also to a fine not less in amount than the foreign money which has been brought back.

Plato's proposal for monetary reform based upon a token currency may show the influence of Sparta on his thinking. Sparta made use of huge, unwieldy iron discs as money, hoping to elude the vices associated with money—class warfare—corruption, personal debauchery, etc. In the early ages of economic evolution, money was viewed with distrust, a contributor to moral decay. The New Testament says "The love of money is the root of all evil."

Although Plato's token money played a positive role in his utopian society, realistically, most token money has appeared in time of war and revolution, when governments were strapped for funds and debased currency as a means of transferring wealth from private citizens to government. Only in the twentieth century have properly managed systems of token fiat money symbolized advanced achievement in economic development, typical of the most prosperous economies in times of peace and stability.

See also: Spartan Iron Currency
References: Plato. 1952. *The Dialogues of Plato.*
Weatherford, Jack. 1997. *The History of Money.*

Playing-Card Currency of French Canada

The French colonies shared with the English colonies the problem of insufficient money to transact the volume of business that was possible in a land with bountiful resources. French Canada turned to using playing cards as paper money to cope with a currency shortage.

Wheat, moose skins, beaver skins, and wildcat skins are among the commodities that belonged on the list of mediums of exchange in seventeenth- and eighteenth-century Canada. In 1713 the English soldiers stationed at Nova Scotia, which France had just ceded to England, petitioned the English authorities to end the practice of paying soldiers in rum, asking "that they be payd in money, or Bills, & not in Rum or other Liquors, that cause them to be Drunk every days, and Blaspheme the name of God" (Lester, 1935). In 1740 the accounts of a storekeeper in Niagara showed a "deficit by 127,842 *cats*" (Lester, 1935).

In 1685 the colonial authorities faced a cash-flow crisis that led to the issuance of ordinary playing cards as a form of paper money. During that year the French government ended its practice of appropriating and sending funds to French Canada in advance of a budget period. The funds for 1685 did not reach Quebec until September, leaving the civil and military authorities in Canada to fend for themselves for the first eight months of the year. By June 1685 the authorities saw the necessity of issuing some sort of paper money that they could redeem when fresh funds arrived from France. The absence of suitable paper and printing facilities to produce paper money forced the expedient of using playing cards. Each denomination of paper money was associated with playing cards of a certain color and cut into a certain shape. It was a system easily understood by the generally illiterate population. Also, the colonial agent of the treasurer wrote the denomination upon each card, and, with the governor general and the intendant, signed each card. As long as the French government sent adequate funds once a year to redeem the playing-card money, prices in the new currency remained steady.

The authorities acted to discourage counterfeiting. In 1690 a surgeon found guilty of counterfeiting was condemned "to be beaten and flogged on the naked shoulders by the King's executioner" (Lester, 1939). He got six lashes of the whip in each "customary square and place." After surviving this ordeal the surgeon saw himself sold into bondage for three years. Later, the crime of counterfeiting drew the death penalty, often by hanging.

When hostilities broke out between France and England, France stopped sending silver coin to Canada for redemption of playing-card money. Instead, the authorities redeemed playing-card money with bills of exchange drawn payable in silver coin in Paris. The merchants in Canada made use of these bills of exchange to pay for supplies imported from France.

Like many other early experiments with paper money, war proved to be the greatest enemy to the integrity of the playing-card system. The supply of playing-card money stood at 120,000 *livres* in 1702 when war erupted between England and France. By 1714, one year after the war ended, the supply stood at more than 2 million livres. During the war France began paying the bills of exchange in paper money rather than silver coin, and prices in Canada entered a spiral of inflation. In 1714 the French government offered to redeem all the playing-card money in silver coin at half its face value. The program of redemption took place over a five-year period and after 1720 the playing-card money was declared worthless.

From 1730 to 1763 the French government again issued card money in Canada, but the cards were blank cards rather than playing cards. The second issue of card money was again reasonably successful until war put a strain on resources.

The use of playing-card money seems a far-fetched expedient for a New World that had supplied the Old World with an abundance of precious metals for coining money. Unlike the Spanish colonies, however, the French and English colonies were not rich in deposits of precious metals. The episode of playing-card money shows the flexibility, adaptability, and inventiveness of an expanding economic system to raise up something to serve as a medium of exchange. It is also a reminder of the role of culture in identifying a suitable medium of exchange. The sensibilities of the New England Puritans would have been shocked at accepting playing cards as a form of money.

See also: Inconvertible Paper Standard, Siege Money
References: Beresiner, Yasha. 1977. *A Collector's Guide to Paper Money*.
Heaton, Herbert. 1928. Playing Card Currency of French Canada. *American Economic Review* (December).
Lester, Richard A. 1939. *Monetary Experiments*.

Polish Hyperinflation

In January 1921 the Polish wholesale price index stood at 25,139, indicating that prices were over 251 times their level in 1914, the base year in which the index equaled 100. By February 1924 the index had risen to 248,429,600, an increase of 988,223 percent in a bit over three years. That growth rate in prices is equivalent to a 50-cent newspaper rising in price to nearly $5,000. In the aftermath of World War I Poland was a country newly formed from territories formerly belonging to Germany, Austro-Hungary, and Russia.

The Polish episode of hyperinflation was born of large government deficits incurred by the fledgling Polish government freshly constituted following World War I. Germany's economic rape of Polish machinery and raw materials would have put even the most foresighted economic policy to the test. Furthermore, the armistice of 1918 left Poland locked in a costly war with the Soviet Union, a struggle that continued until the fall of 1920. Aside from heavy claims on scarce Polish resources, the Polish government fell heir to a grab bag of currencies—Russian rubles, crowns of the Austro-Hungarian bank, German marks, and Polish marks issued by the Polish State Loan Bank, an institution Germany established to regulate Poland's monetary affairs. Under these circumstances, hardly any government could turn away from the temptation to run the printing presses.

Between October 1918 and February 1924 circulating bank notes grew 60,090,040 percent, and the Polish mark steadily decreased on foreign exchange markets. The Polish government took command of the Polish State Loan Bank, which financed the government's budget deficits by issuing bank notes.

Unlike Austria and Hungary, Poland reformed its finances without help from an international loan, although an international loan was granted in 1927 to prop up the Polish mark in foreign exchange markets. In January 1924 the government invested the minister of finance with broad power to balance the government's budget. The minister of finance established the Bank of Poland, replacing the Poland State Loan Bank, as an independent central bank issuing notes secured with reserves in gold or foreign assets denominated in stable currencies that equaled 30 percent of the value of the notes. Whereas the government budget deficit in 1923 accounted for over 50 percent of government expenditures, in 1924 the government reported a balanced budget. The government also created a new currency, the gold *zloty*, worth 1.8 million paper marks.

The Polish wholesale price index stabilized early in 1924 and the Polish mark stabilized in foreign exchange markets about the same time. The rather quick adjustment of inflation to responsible monetary and fiscal policies affirms the power that expectations wield over monetary affairs. Late in 1925 a lax central bank policy led to another spurt of inflation and currency depreciation that lasted a year before the central bank pulled in the monetary reins.

See also: Austrian Hyperinflation, German Hyperinflation, Hungarian Post–World War I Hyperinflation, Inflation and Deflation
References: League of Nations. 1946. *The Course and Control of Inflation*.
Sargent, Thomas J. 1993. *Rational Expectations and Inflation*. 2d ed.

Pontiac's Bark Money

Pontiac was an Ottawa Indian chief and intertribal leader who organized the Indian resistance to British control in the aftermath of the French and Indian War in North America. The Indian resistance, known as Pontiac's War (1763–1764), gave rise to one of the first examples of siege money in America.

The French defeat in the French and Indian War had left the Great Lakes area in control of the British who were less hospitable to the Indians. The Indians also discovered that the British were the thin edge of the wedge of an aggressive settler movement. As friction developed between the British and the Indians, Pontiac organized virtually every Indian tribe from Lake Superior to the lower Mississippi, and launched a coordinated and simultaneous assault against 12 British forts in the area. Each tribe attacked the nearest British fort, and Pontiac laid siege to the fort at Detroit.

Pontiac's siege of Detroit lasted from May

through October, and, unlike the assaults on most of the other forts, ended in failure. Nevertheless, while the siege was in process Pontiac had recourse to an interesting experiment in money. In October Pontiac issued "notes" in payment for supplies his warriors needed to continue the siege. These notes were none other than pieces of birch bark. Each bark note bore two images, an image of the item that Pontiac wanted to purchase with it, and a figure representing the otter, which he adopted as his totem or hieroglyphic signature. Apparently, Pontiac fulfilled his commitment to redeem all the notes after the war and the notes were withdrawn from circulation, but the details of how this was done are sketchy.

Pontiac's confederation of Indian tribes achieved a momentary success, but in 1766 Pontiac, seeing the inevitable superiority of the British, negotiated a peace treaty. His expedient of bark money probably indicates how far European practices had influenced the Indians rather than the evolution of ancient Indian practices. The French trappers and hunters, who still had strong connections with the Indians, had agitated against the British, and the bark notes bear a striking resemblance to various sorts of token money or inconvertible paper money that governments often issue during wartime. By the time of Pontiac's War, the British colonies had issued vast quantities of paper money to finance the French and Indian War.

See also: Siege Money

References: Del Mar, Alexander. 1899. *The History of Money in America.*

Parkman, Francis. 1899. *The Conspiracy of Pontiac and the Indian War after the Conquest of Canada.*

Postage Stamps

Postage stamps have served as money in areas as diverse as America, Europe, and the Far East. During the American Civil War merchants, struggling with a shortage of small coins, began the practice of making small change with postage stamps. Daily purchases of stamps increased fivefold in New York City alone, and individual stamps circulated until they became too dirty and tattered for recognition. John Gault, a Boston sewing-machine salesman, proposed the encasement of stamps in circular metal discs with transparent mica on one side showing the face of the stamp. Soon the metal side of the discs was bearing inscriptions of advertisements; one series of

In the United States, postage stamps enclosed in circular metallic cases substituted for coins. (Smithsonian Institution, National Numismatic Collection)

encased stamps bore the slogan, "Ayer's Sarsaparilla to Purify the Blood." Denominations of encased stamp money ranged from 1 cent to 90 cents, and one rectangular encasement had three 3-cent stamps, making a 9-cent coin.

The government took up the idea of postage money and begin issuing postage currency in denominations of 5-, 10-, 15-, and 50-cent stamps, and some of the postage currency was even perforated around the edges to resemble stamps. The postage currency soon dropped any association with postage stamps and became simple fractional currency in denominations of 3 cents to 50 cents and bearing the inscription "Receivable for all U.S. stamps."

The British South Africa Company issued stamps affixed to cards bearing the statement, "Please pay in cash to the person producing this card the face value of the stamp affixed thereto, if presented on or after the 1st August 1900. This card must be produced for redemption not later than 1st October 1900."

Either during or immediately after World War I postage stamps circulated as money in Germany, Austria, France, Russia, Italy, Norway, Denmark, Belgium, Greece, and Argentina. Germany and Austria imitated the American practice of encasing the stamps in a circular metal disc with a transparent face, and a reverse side bearing an advertisement. France issued similar discs, but put a numeral on one side indicating the value of the encased stamp. Russia issued stamps on stout cards that bore the inscription "On par with silver currency." The Russian stamps were intended to circulate as money, but could also be used as postage stamps.

During World War II Ceylon and the Indian state of Bundi issued small change in the form of cards printed with contemporary stamps. In 1942 Filipino guerrillas fighting the Japanese issued 5-peso notes to which stamps of the appropriate amount were affixed.

In both World War I and World War II the British government declared postage stamps legal tender, but the stamps were never encased for special protection, or affixed to a special card.

Postage stamp money has usually emerged as money for domestic circulation when wartime finance has mobilized hard currency for purchasing military goods abroad.

See also: Shinplasters
References: Angus, Ian. 1975. *Paper Money.*
Beresiner, Yasha. 1977. *A Collector's Guide to Paper Money.*
Coinage of the Americas Conference. 1995. *The Token: America's Other Money.*

Potin
See Celtic Coinage

Potosi Silver Mines

Potosi, a desolate plateau 12,000 feet above sea level, now in Bolivia, was the site of a virtual "silver mountain," discovered in the sixteenth century. As a flood of silver poured into Europe, in England and Spain the word *Potosi* became synonymous with "wealth," as in France the word *Peru* symbolized wealth, because that area of Latin America was then called Peru.

In the aftermath of Columbus's discovery of America, until 1530, Europe imported substantial quantities of readily accessible gold from the New World, but silver was not significantly in evidence. After 1530 silver production in the New World reached significant levels, but still was dwarfed by the gold imports following Pizarro's conquest of the Incas between 1531 and 1541.

Europeans discovered the silver mountain of Potosi in 1545, a time when silver was still a highly favored metal in the Middle and Far East; a unit weight of silver exchanged for twice as much gold in the Eastern world as in Europe. Also, existing silver deposits were playing out, putting silver in strong demand. The base of the silver mountain measured six miles in circumference. The windy, dusty plateau of Potosi nourished a few fields of potatoes amid an otherwise agricultural wasteland. From an uninhabited desolate plateau, Potosi grew to a sizable city, boasting a human population of 55,000 by 1555, and climbing to a peak of 160,000 by 1610. Everything to meet the needs of this population had to be brought in, and a journey to Lima, the capital of Peru, took two and a half months.

Even high wages could not compensate for the prohibitive cost of living and arduous living conditions that the new immigrants faced at Potosi. To supplement a voluntary labor force, the *mita* system of forced labor required Indian villages within a certain radius of Potosi to send a quota of conscripted or drafted young men to work in the mines. The work was harsh and labor in the silver mines came down through history as a symbol of Spanish oppression of the Indians. One eyewitness tells the following account of the plight of the Indian miners:

> The only relief they have from their labors is to be told they are dogs, and be beaten on the pretext of having brought up too little metal, or taken too long, or that what they have brought is earth, or that they have stolen some metal. And less than four months ago, a mine-owner tried to chastise an Indian in this fashion, and the leader, fearful of the club with which the man wished to beat him, fled to hide in the mine, and so frightened was he that he fell and broke into a hundred thousand pieces. (Vilar, 1969)

In 1563 rich mercury deposits were discovered at Huancavelica, located between Potosi and Lima, Peru. Convenient accessibility to mercury enabled the Spanish to employ the mercury amalgam process of silver extraction, substantially increasing the productivity of low-quality silver ore left after the richest veins were mined.

Much of the silver found its way to the East to cover Europe's balance of trade deficit, and some of the silver was shipped directly from the New World to China. China enjoyed an economic boom until silver shipments fell off in the 1640s, plunging China into a depression. In Europe the infusion of silver fueled the price revolution, the century-long wave of inflation that engulfed Europe from 1540 until 1640.

Spain came to view the flood of silver less as a blessing from heaven and more as the curse of the devil. In the seventeenth century, Spain entered into a phase of monetary disorder that could rival any of the modern periods of inflation. Spain squandered its newfound wealth on costly wars, royal extravagance, and the growth of churches, convents, and ecclesiastics. By the second half of the seventeenth century, Spain had reverted to the Bronze Age, its coinage minted from copper.

See also: Great Bullion Famine, Price Revolution in Late Renaissance Europe, Silver

References: Davies, Glyn. 1994. *A History of Money.*

Flynn, Dennis O. 1996. *World Silver and Monetary History in the 16th and 17th Centuries.*

Vilar, Pierre. 1969. *A History of Gold and Money, 1450–1920.*

Pound Sterling

The *pound sterling* is the currency unit for the United Kingdom and has a longer continuous history than any other currency. For 1,300 years the pound has been the currency unit of England, never replaced by a "new pound" or any other change of name signifying a break with the past. Even the French *franc,* dating back to 1803, is a youngster compared to the pound sterling. The German *Deutsche Mark* came into being immediately following World War II.

Around the time of William the Conqueror, the English government began striking coins from a silver alloy containing 925 parts of pure silver per 1,000. Debased coins appeared occasionally, but Norman and English kings always returned to the silver alloy containing over 92 percent pure silver, which came to be known as the "ancient right standard of England." Early in the twelfth century the English called their silver pennies *sterling.* The reputation of the English silver coinage for consistent fineness gave rise to the term *sterling silver.*

The English currency system traces its ancestry directly to the Carolingian currency reform. Charlemagne's father, Pepin, established a silver standard that made one *livre* (pound) equal to a pound weight of silver. Also, 240 silver *denarii* (pennies) equaled a pound, and 20 *shillings* equaled a pound. In the English version of the Carolingian system, one pound equaled 20 shillings, which equaled 240 pence. The Carolingian system did not remain intact long on the Continent, particularly regarding the silver content of the pound, but it came to England with the Norman Conquest, where it survived longer than anywhere else. Only in 1971 did the United Kingdom decimalize its currency, making 100 pence equal to a pound.

Over the first eight centuries of its existence, the pound lost two-thirds of its silver content, averaging a depreciation of 0.13 percent per annum. After 1696 the silver content of the pound remained steady until 1817 when England officially adopted the gold standard, and silver coinage became only subsidiary. During the nineteenth century the pride of the

Originally, pound *referred to a pound of silver, but by 1696 the pound had lost two-thirds of its silver content. (Smithsonian Institution, National Numismatic Collection)*

British currency was the gold *sovereign*, equal to 20 shillings or 1 pound. The sovereign and half sovereign continued in circulation until 1914.

During the nineteenth century the pound sterling began to wear the aspect of an international currency. Although the pound sterling played no special role on continental Europe, the currencies of other European countries financed trade only within colonial empires, leaving the field free for the pound sterling to become the dominant international currency.

After World War I England made a frantic, and briefly successful, effort to return to the gold standard at the prewar parity, which was 3 pounds, 17 shillings, and $10^1/_2$ pence per fine ounce. In truth, England needed to devalue the pound sterling, and failure to do so helped usher in the Great Depression in England. In the Gold Standard Amendment Act of 1931 England abandoned the gold standard, and other countries had to decide to keep their currencies tied to the pound sterling, remain on the gold standard, or follow an independent policy. The Commonwealth countries, excepting Canada, the English colonies, Portugal, and the Scandinavian countries, elected to keep their currencies linked to the pound sterling, and these areas became known as the sterling area.

The pound sterling emerged from World War II as second only to the United States dollar as an international currency. In the post–World War II era the prestige of the pound sterling suffered from currency devaluation, and the United States' vast gold stock, combined with production facilities undamaged by war, gave the U.S. dollar the preeminent position as the international currency.

England's long history of conservatism in monetary matters may explain why the United Kingdom has been slow to participate in the European movement toward monetary union. In May 1998 members of the European Union announced plans to launch a European currency to replace the national currencies of several European countries, including France and Germany. Britain refused to go along and currently plans to retain its own national currency, the pound sterling.

See also: Act for Remedying the Ill State of the Coin, Bank of England, English Penny, Gold Standard, Gold Standard Act of 1925, Gold Standard Amendment Act of 1931, Liverpool Act of 1816

References: Chown, John F. 1994. *A History of Money.*

Davies, Glyn. 1994. *A History of Money.*

Feavearyear, Sir Albert. 1963. *The Pound Sterling: A History of English Money.*

Horton, Dana S. 1983. *The Silver Pound and England's Monetary Policy Since the Restoration, Together with the History of the Guinea.*

POW Cigarette Standard

A unique form of commodity money surfaced in the Nazi prisoner-of-war (POW) camps during World War II. Cigarettes came to fulfill all the functions of money; a medium of exchange, unit of account, standard of deferred payment, and store of value.

The Red Cross furnished the prisoners with cigarettes along with food, clothing, and other goods. The goods were distributed without precise knowledge of individual needs and taste, giving prisoners an incentive to barter unwanted goods for goods that more closely met their needs. A situation in which trade can considerably raise individual welfare is fertile ground for the emergence of a money commodity, and in the POW camps cigarettes came to play the role of money.

Prisoners set prices in cigarettes. Shirts cost 80 cigarettes, and one prisoner would do another prisoner's laundry for two cigarettes. Even nonsmoking prisoners kept a store of cigarettes to buy other goods and services, and prisoners built up supplies of cigarettes as savings, making cigarettes a store of value—another function of money. Cigarettes met the need for a standard of deferred payment. Debts were also run up in cigarettes, particularly gambling debts, and prisoners bought goods and services on credit, promising to pay out of future allocations of cigarettes.

As a monetary commodity cigarettes possessed many advantages. Their value was maintained by a strong consumer demand; they were somewhat durable, not perishable; and to make change they could be subdivided from a box to individual packages and even to individual cigarettes.

The history of POW cigarette money furnishes examples of a wide range of monetary phenomenon. Gresham's law could be seen in the tendency for inferior cigarettes to remain in circulation while prisoners hoarded higher-quality cigarettes. Sometimes prisoners debased the currency by removing tobacco in the middle of the cigarette and replacing it with inferior material. A diminished (or expectation of a diminished) influx of cigarettes caused a fall in the velocity of circulation as prisoners hoarded cigarettes, which were becoming more valuable as prices in cigarettes fell. An added infusion of cigarettes, or rumors of an added infusion, brought a rise in velocity, dishoarding, and rising prices in cigarettes. Even banks were established that issued bank notes convertible into cigarettes, but unfortunately the bank notes were often easily forged. Communal stores emerged that were capitalized in cigarettes, and paid dividends in cigarettes.

The history of cigarette money continued after the war. In postwar Germany a cigarette standard emerged, particularly in transactions between Germans and British and American troops. In the late 1980s in the Soviet Union packs of Marlboro brand cigarettes served as a medium of exchange in a large underground economy that had lost faith in the *ruble*.

See also: Commodity Monetary Standard, Gresham's Law
References: Einzig, Paul. 1966. *Primitive Money*.
Radford, R. A. 1945. The Economic Organization of a POW Camp. *Economica* (November): 189–210.

Price Revolution in Late Renaissance Europe

Historians call the wave of inflation that swept Europe during the sixteenth and seventeenth centuries the Price Revolution. It is seen as revolutionary in character partly because it followed a long period of stable prices, and partly because the prevailing view at the time was that prices and wages should be matters of fairness and justice rather than functions of supply and demand. By the mid-seventeenth century the inflation had ceased in most countries, followed by a century of stable or even falling prices.

Economists have mostly ascribed the influx of gold and silver from the New World as the cause of the inflation. An increase in the supply of anything, including money, relative to its demand causes its value to go down. A reduction in the value of a unit of money translates as inflation to the public. Scholars in other areas seem less satisfied with this single explanation. The timing of the beginning, the peak, and the end of the inflation only roughly corresponds with the timing of dates for the influx of gold and silver. The economist Jean Bodin (1530–1596) listed five reasons for the inflation: (1) the abundance of gold and silver, (2) monopolies, (3) scarcity

of goods caused by exports and waste, (4) the luxury of kings and nobleman, and (5) the debasement of coin. He regarded the abundance of gold and silver as the principal reason.

The inflation struck Spain the hardest, quadrupling prices within a century. In England from 1580 to 1640 prices of necessities rose 100 percent while wages inched up only 20 percent. England's first series of humane poor laws came into being in the midst of the Price Revolution. The acceleration in prices reached a peak in most countries between 1540 and the 1570s. Wages and rents fell behind prices and profits soared. Entrepreneurs ploughed these profits into new industries and new ventures of trade, speculation, and building, laying the foundation for further economic expansion.

See also: Gold, Inflation and Deflation, Potosi Silver Mines, Silver
References: Flynn, Dennis O. 1996. *World Silver and Monetary History in the Sixteenth and Seventeenth Centuries*.
Hamilton, E. J. 1934. *American Treasure and the Price Revolution in Spain, 1501–1650*.

Private Paper Money in Colonial Pennsylvania

In 1766 eight Philadelphia mercantile houses issued short-term, interest-bearing promissory notes that circulated as a medium of exchange. The experiment was short-lived but represents the first instance of private money in what was to become the United States.

The colonial economies suffered from a shortage of currency. Parliament forbade the coinage of money in the colonies, and the enactment of the Currency Acts of 1751 and 1764 restricted the authority of colonial governments to issue paper money. In addition, colonial economies invariably faced an excess of imports over exports, and an outflow of metallic currency paid for the extra imports, further leaving the colonial economies impoverished of currency. Colonial governments lobbied for the repeal of the Currency Act of 1764, not because of a need to finance budget deficits, but because a currency shortage was strangling the colonial economies.

By 1766 the shortage of colonial currency led to an appreciation of colonial currency relative to British pounds sterling, putting at a disadvantage export merchants who earned British pounds sterling in exports and had to convert British money back into colonial money to purchase colonial goods for export. The currency appreciation enhanced the incentives for creating fresh supplies of colonial currency that could be used to purchase colonial goods for export to earn British pounds.

Eight Philadelphia mercantile companies saw an opportunity to issue private notes, easing the shortage of a circulating medium of exchange and purchasing domestic produce at good prices for profitable export. These firms issued 30,000 pounds in short-term, interest-bearing promissory notes to pay for "Wheat and other Country Produce." The notes were payable in nine months in British sterling pounds.

A public outcry rose up against the issuance of private paper money for profit. Nearly 200 provincial merchants put an advertisement in the *Pennsylvania Gazette* on 11 December 1766 declaring that they would not accept these notes in payment for goods. A month later the inhabitants of the city and county of Philadelphia petitioned the General Assembly, the Pennsylvania colonial legislature, pleading that the privilege to issue money belonged only to the legislature. Eventually the king's attorney general and solicitor general took up the issue and declared that the notes were probably not illegal, but the notes were withdrawn in the face of a strong negative public reaction.

After the War of Independence private banks began to issue bank notes, but during the colonial period the issuance of paper money remained strictly a government prerogative.

See also: Currency Act of 1764, Land Bank System
References: Ernst, Joseph Albert. 1973. *Money and Politics in America, 1755–1775.*
Yoder, Paton S. 1941. Paper Currency in Colonial Pennsylvania. Ph.D. dissertation, Indiana University.

Promissory Notes Act of 1704 (England)

The Promissory Notes Act of 1704 officially established promissory notes as negotiable instruments. A promissory note is negotiable when it can be transferred to a third party by an endorsement, usually in the form of a signature of the recipient of the note. Because the bank note is a direct descendant of the promissory note, the Act of 1704 furnished the legal prerequisites for the use of bank notes as a medium of exchange.

In seventeenth-century England people deposited gold in the safekeeping of goldsmiths, who in return issued something like a warehouse voucher made out to the owner of the gold. It was a receipt for a deposit of gold. Rather than exchange gold in trade it was much easier to exchange warehouse receipts, giving rise to the custom of making these receipts transferable by endorsement. Promissory notes originated from these receipts. The wording on promissory notes entitled a certain person, or the "bearer," of the note, to a fixed amount of gold on demand. The custom arose of transferring the ownership of promissory notes with signature endorsements. The ownership of these notes might change over and over as long as there was room for more endorsements. With promissory notes changing hands through repeated endorsements, invariably disputes came before the courts involving cases in which someone did not want to redeem an endorsed promissory note, or in which the recipients of endorsed promissory notes did not receive the same consideration as the initial recipients of the notes. For promissory notes to circulate as a medium of exchange, it was necessary that the holders of endorsed notes suffer no disadvantages when demanding that notes be paid in gold. That is, the promissory notes had to be negotiable. The courts waffled on the issue of the negotiability of promissory notes, forcing Parliament to take action.

Parliament named the law An Act for giving like Remedy upon Promissory Notes, as is now used upon Bills of Exchange, and for the better Payment of Inland Bills of Exchange. The act provided that promissory notes payable to order, or bearer, were legally binding obligations, assignable by endorsement to new holders, and new holders could sue in the courts for enforcement of their rights. Parliament cited the benefits to trade and commerce accruing from the provisions of the act.

The first step toward the evolution of bank notes came when goldsmiths dropped the names of individuals entitled to gold, and instead made the unnamed "bearer" of the note entitled to a fixed amount of gold. The rise of engraved notes completed the transition to bank notes. Indorsed checks also became negotiable instruments by virtue of the Act of 1704. With the legal status of notes clarified, bank notes grew in popularity. Adam Smith observed in *The Wealth of Nations,* published in 1776, that bank money had surpassed metallic money in quantity of circulation, marking a turning point in monetary history.

See also: Check, Goldsmith Bankers

References: Beutel, Frederick K. 1938. The Development of Negotiable Instruments in Early English Law. *Harvard Law Review* 51, no. 5: 813–845.

Nevin, Edward, and E. W. Davis. 1970. *The London Clearing Banks.*

Rogers, James S. 1995. *The Early History of the Law of Bills and Notes: A Study of the Origins of Anglo-American Commercial Law.*

Propaganda Money

As a circulating medium, money has drawn the attention of political organizations looking for a vehicle to spread propaganda. In times of war and social turmoil paper money is particularly susceptible to becoming a medium for bearing revolutionary messages.

In 1967 the Chinese Communist Party instigated riots against the Hong Kong government and put to use the circulating money of Hong Kong to propagate messages discrediting the government. The communists were exploiting a touchy economic situation associated with the devaluation of the pound sterling and subsequent devaluation of the Hong Kong dollar. Hong Kong was a colony of the British government at the time.

The Hong Kong and Shanghai Banking Corporation issued notes in Hong Kong, and the communists took in $10 and $100 notes and overprinted messages calculated to inflame the populace against the government. In the top left-hand corner the overprinted $10 notes bore the famous figure of John Bull with outstretched hands and a gaping mouth. Behind his head in Chinese characters was the message, "He is so greedy that he swallows money." At the bottom of the overprinted $10 notes were two Chinese characters meaning "Devaluation." On the reverse side of the $10 bank notes the communists overprinted a text heavily sprinkled with words such as "imperialism," "banditry," and "fascism," and describing the British exploitation of Hong Kong that led to the devaluation of the Hong Kong dollar.

The communists overprinted the $100 notes with a caricature of a pirate with a sack of protruding $100 notes thrown over his back. Printed on the sack were the words "Open Banditry." In the center of the bill the communists overprinted the message, "Worth only 94.30 dollars after devaluation." On the reverse side the communists overprinted a text ending with the rallying cry, "fellow brothers: in order to survive we must unite together and fight to the end against the British in Hong Kong."

During the Vietnam War peace protesters in the United States drew peace symbols and slogans on dollar bills. At the height of the peace protests the Federal Reserve Banks withdrew the bills bearing antiwar messages. During World War II the British authorities overprinted German military notes with propaganda messages derogatory of Adolf Hitler.

Metallic coinage may have begun as a means of advertising seaports, and the use of propaganda money demonstrates that money is a vehicle for communication. Propaganda money defaces a symbol of government—usually images hallowed by time that are typically placed on paper money—and at the same time propagates a message that discredits the government.

See also: Siege Money

Reference: Beresiner, Yasha. 1977. *Paper Money.*

Q

Quattrini Affair

The *quattrini* was one of the three silver coins that circulated in fourteenth-century Florence. The quattrini affair refers to a devaluation of the quattrini in 1371 that set in motion a course of events leading in 1378 to a popular uprising and a brief dictatorship of the proletariat.

The Florentine money of account was the *lira*, originally meaning a pound of silver, and in the Florentine currency system 240 *denarii* equaled 1 lira, 60 quattrini equaled 1 lira, and 8 *grossi* also equaled 1 lira. Florence also minted the *florin*, a gold coin that circulated mainly in international trade and among the wealthiest members of society. The exchange rate between silver coins and florins varied with the silver content of silver coins.

The money stock of a fourteenth-century Italian city-state consisted of a varying medley of domestic and foreign coins and the rate of coinage depended on the amount of private silver brought to the mint. Private persons took their silver to city-state mints that struck coins with the greatest excess of face value per weight of silver. A city-state such as Florence could debase the silver content of its currency, increasing the face value of its coinage relative to silver content, and attract more silver to its mint. The system encouraged cities to engage in competitive devaluation, and devaluation became a plague that spread from one city to another.

Florentine authorities balked at currency devaluation, and by the mid-fourteenth century the coinage of denarii, quattrini and grossi came to a halt because no silver was brought to the mint. Currency from Pisa invaded the Florentine economy, driving out Florentine currency in accordance with Gresham's law that bad money drives out good. In 1366 the Florentine authorities gave way and slashed the silver content of the *denaro*, the most overvalued of the Florentine coins, by 36 percent. The authorities also banned the circulation of petty foreign currency, apparently under the expectation that the ban would have no practical significance.

Next Florentine grossi and quattrini came under pressure as Pisan grossi and quattrini with the same face value but less silver content were exchanged for the Florentine coins. Florentine grossi stood only slightly above Pisan grossi in silver content, and in 1366 Florence debased the grossi by 2.5 percent, a sufficient debasement to bring Florentine grossi into parity with Pisan grossi.

The Florentine quattrini, overvalued relative to Pisan quattrini by a good 18 percent, now came under pressure. The Florentines had sought to avoid devaluing the quattrini because local prices were most often quoted in quattrini and the whole domestic price structure and monetary stability depended upon quattrini. The invasion of devalued Pisan currency again forced the hand of the Florentines, and in 1371 the silver content of Florentine quattrini fell by 18 percent and Florentine denarii by 5 percent.

Silver flowed into Florentine mints with the rise

in face value relative to silver content, and soon a boom in the coinage of quattrini and denarii was under way. As supplies of quattrini and denarii soared, the forces of currency depreciation made themselves felt with a merciless logic, in time sending a thunderclap through the Florentine economy.

The florin rose in value as the silver content of the silver coinage fell, prices rose faster than wages, and discontent rose to a boiling point among the minor artisans. In 1378 Michele di Lando, a barefoot workingman, led the wool carders in a proletarian revolution against the financial oligarchy that ruled Florence. The revolutionaries dismissed the government officials, established a dictatorship of the proletariat, and set out to reform society, repealing laws against unionization, enfranchising unions of lower-paid workers, imposing a 12-year debt moratorium on debts of wage earners, and reducing interest rates. Businesses fought back by closing down and recruiting outside forces to overthrow the government. The

proletarians split into factions between more conservative skilled labors and unskilled labors sympathetic with communistic ideas. An armed force from the countryside overthrew the government in 1381, but not before the government had melted down large quantities of quattrini in an effort to end the pressures for currency depreciation.

The quattrini affair gives some support to Lenin's comment that the best way to destroy the capitalist society is to debauch its currency. Inflation and monetary instability have attended all major revolutions, including the French Revolution, the Russian Revolution, and the Chinese Revolution.

See also: Florentine Florin
References: Cipolla, Carlo M. 1982. *The Monetary Policy of Fourteenth-Century Florence.*
Chown, John F. 1994. *A History of Money.*
Goldthwaite, Richard A. 1980. *The Building of Renaissance Florence: An Economic and Social History.*

R

Radcliffe Report

In 1957 the British government formed a committee "to inquire into the working of the monetary and credit system, and to make recommendations." In August 1959 this committee issued a report called the Radcliffe Report after the committee chairman, Lord Radcliffe, that played down the importance of keeping the growth of the money stock within strict limits. The report became a symbol of the kind of government views of monetary policy that let inflation accelerate and develop a momentum of its own in the 1970s. According to Glyn Davies (1994), "No official report has ever in British history (nor I believe elsewhere) shown such skepticism regarding monetary policy in the sense of trying to control the economy by controlling the quantity of money."

The report was sprinkled with such exaggerated statements as:

> the authorities . . . do not regard the supply of banknotes as being the only, nor nowadays the only important, supply of money, and the Government's function in issuing notes is simply the passive one of ensuring that sufficient notes are available for the practical convenience of the public.

The report cited two main factors that impaired the operational significance of regulated money stock growth. The first factor was the importance of monetary substitutes that were always ready to come forth and fill gaps in the money supply. Obvious examples of money substitutes, or near-monies, were savings accounts and government bonds. The report stressed that it was an individual's liquidity position, rather than money holdings, that shaped that individual's spending decisions. An individual with modest money holdings might nevertheless be in a very liquid position financially.

The second factor hampering the effectiveness of regulated money stock growth was the velocity of circulation. An increase in velocity has the same economic impact as a money stock increase, and changes in velocity can offset changes in money stock growth. The flavor of the report's findings is captured in the following passages:

> If, it is argued, the central bank has both the will and the means to control the supply of money . . . all will be well. Our view is different. It is the whole liquidity position that is relevant to spending decisions. . . . The decision to spend thus depends upon the liquidity in the broad sense, not upon immediate access to money. . . . *Spending is not limited to the amount of money in circulation.*
>
> In a highly developed financial system the theoretical difficulties of identifying "the supply of money" cannot be lightly swept aside. Even when they are disregarded, all the haziness of the connection between the supply of money and the level of total demand remains: the haziness that lies in the impossibility of limiting the velocity of circulation. (Davies, 1994, his emphasis)

The findings of the Radcliffe Report essentially threw out the control of the money stock in the arsenal of weapons against inflation, a weapon that was sorely needed in the 1970s. The views expressed in the report became economic orthodoxy in the 1960s, and treated as the accepted view in economics textbooks. As inflation mounted in the 1970s, the views of the Radcliffe Report came under increasing criticism, and by the 1980s the quantity theory of money had largely supplanted the views of the Radcliffe Report. The quantity theory of money emphasizes the connection between the quantity of money and inflation.

See also: Bank of England, Deutsche Bundesbank, Equation of Exchange, Monetarism, Velocity of Money
References: Davies, Glyn. 1994. *A History of Money.*
United Kingdom. 1959. *Report of the Committee on the Workings of the Monetary System*, Cmnd. 827.

Real Bills Doctrine

The real bills doctrine holds that if banks make loans only to finance short-term commercial transactions, the money supply will expand and contract to meet the needs of trade and fluctuations in the money supply will not be a source of economic instability leading to either inflation or deflation. The self-liquidating nature of these loans, and their use to finance the production of goods and services, allegedly checks the rise of inflationary forces. The doctrine found favor with Adam Smith and it has commanded some interest to the present day.

To appreciate the doctrine one must first understand that when banks advance loans, the money supply expands. When banks allow money to build up as vault cash or other forms of reserves, the money supply contracts.

The real bills doctrine first broke into public debate in England during the Napoleonic Wars. Under the stress of wartime finance, England had suspended the convertibility of bank notes into precious metal, putting England on an inconvertible paper standard comparable to inconvertible paper standards in the United States or England today. So-called bullionists argued that the money supply should remain proportional to precious metal reserves, such as gold reserves, to maintain its value and avoid inflation or deflation. Antibullionists defended the suspension of convertibility on the grounds of the real bills doctrine and attributed

problems of rising prices and currency depreciation to other causes. After the Napoleonic Wars England established a gold standard and a new monetary debate developed between the banking school and the currency school. Both schools supported the gold standard but the banking school felt that banks should have the flexibility to make loans according to the real bills doctrine, allowing the money supply to expand and contract to meet the needs of trade. The currency school made the case that the money supply should remain proportional to gold reserves, and should only change as gold flowed in and out of the country.

In the early stages of development the Federal Reserve System followed the real bills doctrine in practice. During the post–World War II era the real bills doctrine and similar doctrines have lost credibility in favor of proposals to increase the money supply at a fixed rate, such as 3 to 5 percent per year, to encourage the economy to mirror the same stability.

See also: Bank Restriction Act of 1797, Banking School, Currency School, Monetarism, Radcliffe Report
References: Klein, John J. 1986. *Money and the Economy.* 6th ed.
Perlman, Morris. 1989. Adam Smith and the Paternity of the Real Bills Doctrine. *History of Political Economy* 21, no. 1 (Spring): 77–90.
Spiegel, Henry W. 1971. *The Growth of Economic Thought.*

Regulation Q
See Eurodollars, Glass-Steagall Banking Act of 1933

Reichmark
See Gold Mark of Imperial Germany, Rentenmark

Rentenmark

The *Rentenmark* was the currency that the German government issued in the aftermath of the hyperinflation that occurred in Germany immediately following World War I. Hyperinflation had completely discredited the mark, leaving the price of something as simple as a newspaper at 70 million marks. Toward the end of 1923 the rentenmark replaced the mark as a new, stable currency.

A costly war and heavy war reparations had left Germany virtually bankrupt, and without the gold and foreign exchange reserves needed to support a paper currency. Usually, governments seeking to restore monetary stability had arranged foreign loans that allowed them to issue a new currency convertible at an official rate into gold and foreign exchange. Germany, lacking access to foreign loans, faced the challenge of establishing a new currency that would command the confidence of the public without the backing of significant reserves of gold and foreign exchange.

Germany handled these monetary difficulties in much the same spirit that France handled similar difficulties in the past. Early in eighteenth-century France John Law's Banque Royal had issued paper money on the security of land in Louisiana, a financial venture that set the stage for France's first paper money debacle. Later the revolutionary French government issued paper money called *assignats,* backed by land confiscated from the church. At first the church land was reserved for sale to owners of *assignats,* but too many *assignats* were issued and the plan ended in a storm of hyperinflation.

The Deutsche Rentenbank, a new bank of issue organized to issue rentenmarks, held collateral in the form of agricultural and industrial mortgages. Theoretically, the agricultural and industrial mortgages could have been liquidated and the proceeds used to redeem the rentenmarks, but in practice such a liquidation would have been difficult. One rentenmark was worth 1 billion of the old marks.

In addition to reforming the currency the German government reformed its fiscal affairs, balancing the budget in terms of rentenmarks and ending government dependence on the central bank to purchase government bonds. The German government, by getting its own house in order, diffused the pressure for inflationary finance. In turn the Rentenbank, by strictly limiting the issuance of rentenmarks, ended the spiral of inflation, showing the world that gold and foreign exchange reserves were not necessary for a stable, noninflationary currency. The experience of the rentenmark underlined the role of government fiscal mismanagement as the force that invariably fuels hyperinflation.

Late in 1924 Germany received a sizable loan under the Dawes Plan, enabling it to reorganize the Reichbank, which had suspended the issuance of bank notes after the formation of the Rentenbank. The Reichbank again took over responsibility for issuing bank notes and the rentenmark was renamed the *Reichmark.* The reichmark was convertible into gold but gold coins did not circulate as currency, a system that spread to the rest of the world during the 1930s. Following World War II the reichmark was discontinued and replaced by the *Deutsche Mark.*

Although land-secured paper money had twice led France into the chaos of hyperinflation, Germany had embarked upon a land-secured system of paper money determined to contain inflationary pressures. Germany's experience with the rentenmark demonstrated that a society may avoid inflation and stabilize the value of a currency by strictly limiting currency supplies. By strict monetary discipline, Germany's experiment succeeded where similar efforts had failed.

See also: Deutsche Mark, German Hyperinflation, Gold Mark of Imperial Germany

References: Davies, Glyn. 1994. *A History of Money.*
Kindleberger, Charles P. 1984. *A Financial History of Western Europe.*
Stolper, Gustav. 1967. *The German Economy: 1870 to the Present.*

Report from the Select Committee on the High Price of Bullion

The so-called Bullion Report, published on 8 June 1810, ranks with the most famous documents in the history of monetary theory. The report was actually written by Henry Thornton, a prominent banker and economist. Thomas Malthus and David Ricardo, the most famous economists of the day, rallied to support the conclusions of the report, which cited fiat money (money inconvertible into a precious metal at an official rate) as the cause of the high price of bullion. Actually, the first volley had come from the pen of Ricardo, who wrote newspaper articles and pamphlets on the subject, one entitled *The High Price of Bullion* (1810).

During the French Revolution and Napoleonic Wars the Bank of England suspended convertibility of bank notes into metallic coinage and precious metal, an action that would become common practice during future wars but was then unprecedented. Inflation measures calculated from price indices were unavailable at the time, but the price of gold bullion in British pounds soared and the British pound depreciated relative to other European currencies in foreign exchange markets. Discussions on the high price of bullion and currency depreciation led to the appointment of a select committee to make an inquiry.

The current state of knowledge of monetary theory would have the finger of suspicion immediately turn to the issuance of fiat money, but at the threshold of the nineteenth century other causes were cited for the high price of bullion and the depreciation of the British pound. To the observation that the high price of gold was due to increased demand for gold to supply French armies, the report answered:

> Your Committee is of the opinion that in the sound natural state of the British currency the foundation of which is gold no increased demand for gold from other parts of the world however great or from whatever causes arising can have the effect of producing here for a considerable period of time a material rise in the market price of gold. . . . It was to be expected that those who ascribed the high price here to a great demand abroad, would have been prepared to state that there were corresponding high prices abroad. . . . [I]t does not appear that during the time when the price of Gold bullion was rising here as valued in our paper there was any corresponding rise in the price of Gold bullion in the market of the Continent as valued in their respective currencies. (Chown, 1994)

The select committee was equally unimpressed with theories that attributed the depreciation of the pound to harvest failures, Napoleon's blockade, subsidies of foreign allies, and support of armies in foreign lands. In the words of the report:

> From the foregoing reasoning relative to the state of the Exchanges if they are considered apart, Your Committee find it difficult to resist an inference that a portion at least of the great fall which the Exchanges lately suffered must have resulted not from the state of trade but from a change in the relative value of our domestic currency. But when this deduction is joined with that which your Committee have stated respecting the market price of Gold, that inference appears to be demonstrated. (Chown, 1994)

The report recommended a return to convertibil-ity as soon as possible, but the exigencies of war outweighed the logic of the report and a resumption of convertibility had to wait until 1821.

The bullionist controversy demonstrated the difficulty of pinpointing the causes of currency depreciation and inflation. Often the blame was laid at the feet of shortages, greedy labor unions, monopolies, and speculators, when a more careful examination placed the cause in undisciplined growth in money stocks. The report recommended a return to convertibility as a means of maintaining monetary discipline.

See also: Bank Restriction Act of 1797, Monetarism, Gold Standard, Real Bills Doctrine
References: Chown, John. 1994. *A History of Money*. Spiegel, Henry W. 1971. *The Growth of Economic Thought*.

Reserves
See Bank, Forestall System, High-Powered Money, Legal Reserve Ratio, Monetary Multiplier, National Reserve Act of 1864

Resumption Act of 1875 (United States)

The principal objective of the Resumption Act of 1875 was to provide for the resumption of specie payments on greenbacks, the fiat paper money born of the Civil War, which was still current in the 1870s.

The act had three important sections. The first section provided for the retirement of the fractional paper currency that been current since the Civil War. The fractional paper currency was in denominations of 10, 25, and 50 cents. The Act of 1875 provided for the issuance of subsidiary silver coin to replace the fractional currency. This provision was a bow to the silver interests because only gold coins circulated at the time.

The second section got rid of seigniorage, or mint charges, on the coinage of gold, a provision that pleased the mining interests.

The third section of the act removed limitations on the total number of bank notes that national banks could issue, a provision that met the demand for what then was called free banking. The Treasury was to retire greenbacks in an amount equal to 80 percent of the increase in national bank notes, until greenbacks in circulation fell to 300 million.

The third section took up the heart of the legislation, the redemption of greenbacks. After 1 January

1879 greenbacks were redeemable in coin when brought to the assistant treasurer at New York in sums no less than $50. The act also authorized the secretary of treasury to "issue, sell and dispose of, at not less than par, in coin" any of the bonds authorized under existing legislation.

A certain amount of pessimism surrounded the Resumption Act of 1875. Many opponents felt that resumption was not feasible, that people would show up in mass to exchange greenbacks for gold, that it would trigger an unbearable contraction of the money supply, and that Congress would not stand firmly in favor of resumption. In 1878 a bill to repeal the Resumption Act failed to pass Congress by a narrow margin, and Congress did raise from 300 million to 346 million the maximum number of greenbacks that could remain in circulation. Nevertheless, the expected eagerness to exchange greenbacks for gold had been overstated, and resumption took place without difficulty.

The term *coin* in the legislation was generally assumed to refer to gold coins. In 1878 the Bland-Allison Silver Purchase Act made silver legal tender, opening up the possibility that bonds sold to raise coin—gold coin—could be redeemed in silver. Advocates of silver felt that redemption of bonds was legitimate, but the proposal aroused strong opposition. President Hayes in his veto message on the Bland-Allison Act (the act was passed over a presidential veto) cited the large number of bonds the government had sold. He noted that the bonds were sold for gold, and that the bondholders expected the bonds to be redeemed in gold, and would not have bought the bonds otherwise. In the words of his veto message:

National promises should be kept with unflinching fidelity. There is no power to compel a nation to repay its debts. Its credit depends upon its honor. The nation owes what it has led or allowed its creditors to expect. (Watson, 1970)

Despite the provisions of the Bland-Allison Act making silver legal tender, the United States government maintained its commitment to redeem public bonds in gold.

The Resumption Act of 1875 is one of the important pieces of coinage legislation in United States history because it ended an era of fiat money.

See also: Bland-Allison Silver Repurchase Act, Free Silver Movement, Greenbacks
References: Carothers, Neil. 1930. *Fractional Money.*
Hepburn, A. Barton. 1967. *A History of Currency in the United States.*
Meyers, Margaret G. 1970. *A Financial History of the United States.*
Ritter, Gretchen. 1997. *Gold Bugs and Greenbacks: The Antimonopoly Tradition and the Politics of Finance in America.*
Watson, David K. 1970. *History of American Coinage.*

Return to Gold: 1300–1350

During the first half of the fourteenth century Europe saw gold currency displace silver currency as the primary circulating medium. The Carolingian reform of the eighth century had ended gold coinage in Europe, and for over 400 years Europe had contented itself with minting the silver *denarius,* a small denomination coin, predecessor to the modern penny. A critical development in returning Europe to gold coinage was the discovery of Hungarian gold deposits around Kremnica in Slovakia, which became producing mines around 1320.

In the mid-thirteenth century Florence and Genoa had introduced gold coinage and Venice followed later in the century with the gold *ducat* to rival the Florentine *florin*. Dependence upon African gold restricted the supply of the early Italian gold, limiting its circulation to the Mediterranean area.

After 1320 Hungarian gold grew in abundance, enabling Charles Robert of Anjou, king of Hungary, to began minting gold coins in 1328. These gold coins imitated the Florentine florin and were the first gold coins minted north of the Alps. An exchange of Bohemian silver for Hungarian gold enabled John the Blind of Luxemburg, king of Bohemia, to began coinage of gold florins coincidentally with the Hungarian coinage as part of a Hungarian-Bohemian monetary cooperation.

Hungarian gold profusely poured into Italy in exchange for Italian goods and services. In 1328 Venice effectively abandoned a silver standard in favor of a gold standard, and coinage of the gold ducat began to vastly outstrip the silver *grossi*.

In the 1330s France and England borrowed from Italian bankers large sums of gold florins to finance wars. The pope also subsidized France with vast sums of florins, and in 1337 France began minting large quantities of it own gold coin, the *ecu*.

Gold coinage began on a large scale in the Low Countries around the same time. In 1336 the mint of Flanders began striking large quantities of gold coins, and the mints of Brabant, Hainault, Cambrai, and Guelders first struck gold coins in 1336 and 1337.

Most of the German mints striking gold coins during the fourteenth century were located in the valleys of the Rhine and Main. One important exception, Lubeck, the principal city of the Hanseatic League, received royal permission to mint gold and silver coins in 1340. In 1342 Lubeck began striking gold Lubeck coins.

England had made an abortive effort to coin gold pennies in 1257, roughly coinciding with the appearance of gold coinage in Italy. England's second and more successful effort at gold coinage began in 1344. Edward III engaged Florentine mintmasters and issued a gold coin, the *leopard*, which proved unsuccessful because its official value in terms of silver exceeded its market value. After adjustments in metal content, Edward II minted another gold coin, the *noble*, valued at 6 shillings and 8 pence. Nobles, half nobles, and quarter nobles became important components of English coinage.

Scotland first launched a gold coin in 1357, but the first gold coinage failed, and a successful gold coinage had to wait until the end of the century.

As gold coinage spread silver coinage took on the role of subsidiary coinage suitable for small, local transactions, a role the silver continued to play until alloyed token currency replaced full-bodied metallic currency.

See also: Augustalis, Florentine Florin, Gold, Venetian Ducat
References: Chown, John. 1994. *A History of Money*. Spufford, Peter. 1988. *Money and Its Use in Medieval Europe*.

Rice Currency

The history of rice currency takes into scope geographical areas as diverse as the Far East and the American colonies, and touches upon familiar subjects in the history of money, including debasement, Gresham's law, paper money, and religious associations.

The most developed system of rice currency emerged in feudal Japan. At the opening of the seventeenth century Japan added up its wealth, measured in *koku* of rice, and found the country's wealth equivalent in value to 28,000,000 kokus. After the sixteenth century copper, gold, and silver circulated alongside rice but values were expressed in rice, debts were contracted in rice, and taxes were collected partly in rice and partly in metallic money. Workers received rice in payment for work, and the retainers and attendants of feudal lords received stipends in rice.

Large landowners issued rice notes, maintained large storehouses to redeem those notes, and often sought to redeem the notes at harvest season to make room for the new crop. When they discovered that some of the note bearers never claimed the rice, they began, in the manner of the goldsmith bankers, to issue more notes than they could actually redeem in rice. After a rash of abuses, the Tokugawa banned this practice in 1760.

Rice currency shared an inconvenience common to commodity money—it was bulky to transport for large commercial transactions. With the growth of trade Japan began to supplant rice currency with metallic money, but not without hearing from the political philosophers, who saw metallic money as the opening wedge for all kinds of evil. Perhaps these philosophers echoed the Confucian emphasis on social stability and saw metallic money as a revolutionizing influence. Other ancient societies, including Sparta of ancient Greece, saw metallic money as an immoral influence. Rice currency survived in some of the remote villages of Japan up to the eve of World War II.

In the nineteenth century local governments in Burma measured their revenue in baskets of rice. The Burmese ate the good rice and circulated as money the inferior broken rice unsuitable for food or seed, giving history another example of currency debasement and Gresham's law.

Rice was the most important primitive currency in the Philippines. In 1775 the Sultans of Magindan collected taxes from the Philippines in unthreshed rice. The prime monetary unit was a handful of unthreshed rice, called *palay*. A scale of denominations of palay rose from 1 handful to 1,000 handfuls. A day's wage of a mountain wood gatherer was five handfuls.

Some of the Philippine tribes endowed rice with religious significance. No women could enter a rice storehouse, and men had to perform certain religious rituals before entering.

In 1739 the colony of South Carolina enacted a law that made rice an acceptable means for paying taxes. The following year the colonial government collected 1.2 million pounds of rice. The government issued "rice orders" to public creditors, which were redeemable after taxes were collected in rice at a rate of 30 shillings per 100 pounds of rice. These rice orders circulated as money, and long-term contracts were struck in terms of rice.

As a commodity rice was relatively light, making it easier to transport than some commodities, and it could be stored up to eight or nine years. Rice could serve the monetary functions of a medium of exchange and store of value better than most monetary commodities, which accounts for its relatively rich history as a form of money.

See also: Commodity Monetary Standard, Virginia Tobacco Act of 1713
References: Brock, Leslie V. 1975. *The Currency of the American Colonies, 1700–1764.*
Einzig, Paul. 1966. *Primitive Money.*

Riksbank (Sweden)

The Riksbank or Bank of Sweden, the oldest central bank in the world, was the first European bank to issue bank notes. The English goldsmiths issued receipts that circulated as money but the Riksbank was the first bank to issue paper money.

The Riksbank came into being in 1656 as a private bank split into two departments. One department was an exchange or deposit bank organized along the lines of the Bank of Amsterdam. It accepted deposits of coins and precious metals, and these bank deposits changed ownership without precious metals or coins leaving the bank. They served as money, and were backed up by 100 percent reserves of precious metals. The second department was a lending bank.

The Riksbank issued its first bank notes in 1661. Other banks had already pioneered the use of bills of exchange and transferable bank deposits that supplemented the circulation of coins. Sweden turned to bank notes as a medium of exchange because payments in copper, which served as money in Sweden, were bulky and heavy even for domestic transactions. Sweden adopted copper as the basis for money in 1625, perhaps because Sweden boasted of the largest copper mine in Europe and the Swedish government owned a share of it. Copper mines paved the way for bank notes when, for convenience and

utility, they began paying miners in copper notes that could be redeemed for copper at the mines. These notes were preferable to copper coins and traded at a premium.

In 1668 ownership of the Riksbank passed into the hands of the government, making it the oldest central bank in operation today. By the early 1700s bank notes were no longer a rarity in Europe. The Bank of England was chartered in 1694 for the purpose of making loans and issuing bank notes, and by 1720 France was learning the disastrous consequences of issuing bank notes without discipline.

In 1789 the Riksbank began issuing government currency, and the Riksbank Act of 1897 conferred upon the Riksbank a monopoly on the issuance of currency in Sweden. As late as 1873 the number of central banks in the world remained in single-digit territory, but by 1990 more than 160 central banks dotted the financial landscape, the oldest being the Riksbank.

See also: Bank of England, Bank of France, Central Bank
References: Bank for International Settlements. 1963. *Eight European Central Banks.*
Kindleberger, Charles P. 1984. *A Financial History of Western Europe.*
Samuelsson, Kurt. 1968. *From Great Power to Welfare State: 300 Years of Swedish Social Development.*
Sveriges Riksbank. 1994. *Sveriges Riksbank: the Swedish Central Bank, a Short Introduction.*

Roman Aes
See Bronze Standard of Ancient Rome

Roman and Byzantine Law
Roman and Byzantine law dealt rigorously with coinage abuses such as counterfeiting and irrational discounts applied to coins, setting a brutal standard that would survive into the nineteenth century.

The earliest counterfeiting law preserved in the Codex Theodosianus came from the emperor Constantius II in A.D. 343. It reads:

Emperor Constantius Augustus to Leontius, Praetorian Prefect
A reward having been offered to informers, let every counterfeiter of solidi that can be found, or that is exposed by any man, be immediately and without any delay delivered over to the burning flames. (Hendy, 1985)

The *solidus* was a Roman and Byzantine gold coin first issued by the emperor Constantine. Other laws prescribed the same punishment for clipping solidi or passing counterfeit solidi in transactions.

Despite the rigorous brutality of the law, the death penalty seems rarely to have been carried out during the fourth century. The Easter amnesties of 367, 368, and 380 excluded certain crimes such as treason, sorcery, murder, adultery, or rape, but made no reference to counterfeiting, suggesting that counterfeiting was considered a less serious crime. After 381 counterfeiters are expressly excluded from amnesties, indicating that counterfeiting was definitely a capital crime. Roman law sometimes treated counterfeiting as an act of treason, which was always a capital crime. Counterfeiting copper coinage drew lessor penalties, such as confiscation of property.

The Romans and Byzantines faced a puzzling coinage problem that would seem irrational in a more financially sophisticated age. Some of the solidi were valued not according to gold content but according to the size or other characteristics of the images on the coins. Touching on this subject, the Codex of Theodosianus preserves a law issued by the Emperor Constantine in 317. It reads:

Emperor Constantine Augustus to Leontius, Praetorian Prefect

All solidi on which Our face and venerability is to be found are to be valued and sold at one price, however diverse the extent of the image. For that which is spread out with a larger representation of Our face is not worth more, and that which is contracted with a smaller portrait is not to be thought worth less, when the same weight is present, and if anyone should suppose otherwise he is to be capitally punished either by being handed over to the flames or by some other death-carrying instrument. [And indeed he that should nibble away the extent of the outside edge of a solidus, so as to diminish the total of its weight, or should replace a stamped solidus with a false imitation in a sale, is to suffer in the same fashion.] (Hendy, 1985)

Apparently, solidi bearing a smaller portrait of the emperor were passing at a discount compared to solidi bearing a larger portrait, and solidi bearing images of past emperors or relations of the current emperor circulated at a discount compared to solidi bearing a portrait of the reigning emperor.

The legendary brutality of the Romans may account for the harsh penalties levied against counterfeiters. In nineteenth-century England, however, counterfeiters of paper money faced hanging. Counterfeiting has always been a serious offense.

See also:: Counterfeit Money, Edict of Prices of A.D. 301
References: Grierson, P. 1956. The Roman Law of Counterfeiting. In *Essays in Roman Coinage Presented to Harold Mattingly.*
Hendy, Michael F. 1985. *Studies in the Byzantine Monetary Economy.*

Roman Empire Inflation

During the third and fourth centuries A.D. inflation in the Roman Empire rose to astronomical numbers, aiding and abetting those internal forces of economic, political, and social decay that made the empire easier prey for the barbarians.

Early in the first century A.D. Augustus had minted full-valued gold and silver coins. In the following two centuries the Roman emperors slowly whittled down the weight of the coins, and reduced the fineness of the silver coins. In the second century A.D. the silver content of the *denarius* sank to 75 percent during the reign of that philosophic prince, Marcus Aurelius. By mid-third century creeping inflation had gradually lifted prices about threefold.

Early in the third century the Caracalla replaced the silver denarius with a new silver coin, 50 percent silver in content, called the *Antoninianus.* At midcentury this coin still contained 40 percent silver, but thereafter debasement gathered momentum at a heady pace and reached a climax under Gallienus, emperor between A.D. 260 and 268. The silver content sank to 4 percent, and prices—already triple the first-century level—finishing the third century at 50 to 70 times higher than the first-century price level.

The political stage mirrored the monetary disorder, or vice versa. In a space of 40 years, starting with the assassination of Gordian in A.D. 244, 57 emperors donned the imperial purple, until the accession of Diocletian in A.D. 284 ended the revolving door for the imperial title.

The root cause of the inflation could be found in the fiscal affairs of the Roman government. The government paid its expenses in coins and had no major credit market in which to raise funds when expenditures exceeded tax revenue. Perhaps because of the inertia of tradition or political opposition, tax rates could be changed only with great difficulty. The more notorious emperors found it easier to raise funds by condemning wealthy senators and citizens on trumped-up charges and confiscating their estates, than to raise taxes. The remaining alternative was debasement of the currency.

When Aurelian assumed the reins of power in A.D. 270, facing galloping inflation, he adopted a currency reform that was almost as good as printing paper money. He simply raised by about two and one-half times the nominal or face value of the silver-plated copper coins that had replaced the silver coins of the empire. Under his reign the treasury began supplying sealed bags that contained 1,000 of these silver-plated coins. During this inflationary ordeal the government kept the gold coins much purer, but it paid its expenses in silver-plated coins, which were legal tender.

Diocletian was the first emperor to aggressively combat the rampant inflation. He came to power in A.D. 284, amidst an economy flooded with inferior coinage, and in A.D. 295 he put in place a major reform of the currency, issuing full-weight pure gold and silver coins. His *aureus* equaled one-sixtieth of a pound of gold, and his pure silver coin equaled one-ninety-sixth of a pound of a silver. His coins were comparable in weight and fineness to the coins in Nero's time, when prices were 100 times lower. Inflation continued to surge through the Roman economy and, perhaps out of frustration, Diocletian resorted to wage and price controls in A.D. 301. Raising prices above legal levels became a capital offense, and inflation may have begun to slow a bit.

Constantine became emperor early in the fourth century. He eased up on the wage and price controls, and continued Diocletian's policy of increasing the value of the currency. He minted a coin called the gold *solidus,* equal to one-seventy-second of a pound of gold. This coin maintained its value for 700 years, becoming one of the most famous coins in history. After making Christianity the official faith in A.D. 313 Constantine looted the pagan temples of vast quantities of gold to supply his mints. The government mints, however, continued to turn out huge amounts of the debased copper coins, and the added supply of gold may have added fresh fuel to the fires of inflation. The debased denarii continued to fall in value. By the mid-fourth century in Egypt 1 gold solidus equaled 30 million denarii. By then the government protected itself by collecting taxes in gold or in kind. The mass of the population paid the penalty for the inflation while the wealthy hedged against inflation by investing in gold and land. The inflation began to decelerate toward the end of the fourth century, but by then the empire was tottering in the face of a barbarian onslaught. The Visigoths captured Rome in A.D. 410 and in A.D. 476 Odoacer the Barbarian replaced the last Roman emperor, Romulus Augustulus. Constantinople continued to mint the solidus.

See also:: Augustan Monetary Standard, Edict of Prices of A.D. 301, Inflation and Deflation

References: Duncan-Jones, Richard. 1998. *Money and Government in the Roman Empire.*
Frank, Tenney. 1940. *An Economic Survey of Ancient Rome.* Vols. I–VI.
Jones, A. H. M. 1974. *The Roman Economy.*
Paarlberg, Don. 1993. *An Analysis and History of Inflation.*

Rossel Island Monetary System

Rossel Island, about 200 miles southeast of New Guinea, can lay claim to one of the most novel and complicated primitive monetary systems, one in which time was a significant factor in measuring the value of goods. The actual pieces of money had been handed down virtually unchanged to successive generations since time immemorial and allegedly were of divine origin.

Rossel money split into two variations. *Dap* money came in single polished pieces of shells, and *ko* money in sets of 10 discs made from shells. Dap money covered a larger range of values, and stretched into the smallest values, whereas ko money exchanged hands in the larger transactions. These two variations bore some gender connotation; dap money was looked upon as men's money and ko money as women's money. Some goods were only priced in one type of money, and other goods in a combination of dap and ko money.

The system of denominations of shells of different values made the Rossel money unique among primitive currencies. The actual names were a bit clumsy but 22 different values are represented. For simplification it is easiest to regard the lowest denomination as number 1, the next lowest denomination as number 2 and so on, until the largest denomination of number 22 is reached. Dap came in all 22 denominations, but ko came only in denominations of numbers 8 through 22. One denomination was not a multiple of other denominations, and no one denomination was equivalent to a fixed number of other denominations, contrary to the United States monetary system in which 100 pennies equal a dollar. A good costing a number 10 could not be purchased with anything but a number 10, and not in a multiple of smaller denominations.

The differences in value between denominations were based on the amount of time one denomination would have to be loaned out before repayment could be required in another denomination. If a number 10 was loaned out for a length of time, the loan had to be repaid in a number 11. A loan of a number 10 for longer lengths of time called for repayment in a number 12, or a higher denomination, depending upon the length of the loan.

Transactions involved a highly elaborate system of credit. Suppose individual A sought to purchase a product priced at number 10 in dap, and this individual owned denominations below number 10 and above No. 10, but not in number 10. This individual would borrow a number 10, and would repay the loan in the future with a denomination higher than a number 10, as a means of paying interest. This individual would not mind this arrangement, having the opportunity to loan out his own dap denominations and earning interest also. If a number 22 was loaned out, an initial interest payment was made in a smaller denomination, and in the future the loan was repaid with another number 22. A special class of brokers arranged these necessary transactions.

The currency units, or shells, of the higher-valued denominations (number 18 and above) were known on an individual basis by active financial traders. Only seven currency units of denomination number 22 were in existence, all owned by chiefs. The higher values were considered sacred. When a number 18 exchanged hands the parties involved crouched down. Numbers 19 to 22 were kept enclosed, always protected from the light of day.

References: Armstrong, W. E. 1924. Rossel Island Money: A Unique Monetary System. *The Economic Journal* 34: 424–429.

Einzig, Paul. 1966. *Primitive Money*.

Royal Bank of Scotland

The Royal Bank of Scotland, like the Bank of England, began when a group of holders of public debt received a royal charter to incorporate as a banking institution. Parliament granted the royal charter creating Scotland's second public bank on 31 May 1727. The Scottish Parliament had chartered Scotland's first public bank, the Bank of Scotland, on 17 July 1695, before the unification of Scotland and England. In the Rebellion of 1715 the Bank of Scotland had appeared to stand on the Stuart side, a point frequently recalled by those who wanted to create a rival bank, the Royal Bank of Scotland. Parliament later chartered a third Scottish public bank, and also encouraged the growth of private banks. Scotland promoted competition among banks to a much greater extent than England, pioneering the development of free banking, which flourished in the United States in the first half of the nineteenth century.

The Royal Bank of Scotland earned a place in the history of money and banking when it developed the antecedents of overdraft privileges. In his famous book, *An Inquiry into the Nature and Causes of the Wealth of Nations,* perhaps the most famous book on economics, Adam Smith attributed this important banking innovation to the public banks of Scotland. Although he does not credit a single bank for the innovation, his description captures the spirit of the innovation in the language of the day:

> They invented, therefore, another method of issuing their promissory notes; by granting what they called cash accounts, that is by giving credit to the extent of a certain sum (two or three thousand pounds, for example) to any individual who could procure two persons of undoubted credit and good landed estate to become surety for him, that whatever money should be advanced to him, within the sum for which the credit had been given, should be paid on demand, together with the legal interest. Credits of this kind are, I believe, commonly granted by banks and bankers in all different parts of the world. But the easy terms upon which the Scottish banking companies accept of repayment, are so far as I know, peculiar to them, and have, perhaps, been the principal cause, both of the great trade of those companies and of the benefit which the country has received from it.

Other authors, such as Glyn Davies, confer the credit for this innovation to the Royal Bank of Scotland, and cite this innovation as the beginning of the flexible overdraft. The Royal Bank of Scotland (now called the Royal Bank of Scotland, Limited) remains one of the leading commercial banks of Scotland.

See also: Bank of Scotland, Scottish Banking Act of 1765
References: Checkland, S. G. 1975. *Scottish Banking: A History, 1695–1973.*

Davies, Glyn. 1994. *The History of Money.*

Smith, Adam. 1952. *An Inquiry into the Nature and Causes of the Wealth of Nations.*

Rum Currency
See Liquor Money

Russian Paper Money
See Yeltsin's Monetary Reform in Russia

Russian Revolution Hyperinflation

In the aftermath of the Bolshevik seizure of power (1917), Russia experienced a bout of hyperinflation comparable to the hyperinflation of the French Revolution, sending prices to levels more than 600 million times higher than their 1913 levels. The only limitation on the quantity of paper rubles printed was the supply of ink and paper.

The Imperial Russian Government resorted to inflationary finance to sustain itself through World War I. On the eve of World War I Russia boasted of the largest gold reserves in Europe, which backed 98 percent of the Russian bank notes in circulation. The Treasury held large gold reserves to back paper rubles. Tax revenue from taxes levied on the manufacture and sale of alcohol, one-fourth of the Treasury's revenue, fell because of a newly enacted law against alcohol consumption. Tariff revenue also dropped significantly with the onset of war. Instead of direct taxes and internal war bond financing, the government turned almost exclusively to paper money and foreign loans to finance the war.

On 27 July 1914 the government suspended specie payments on paper rubles. The gold reserve requirement for the issuance of bank notes also came to an end. The government doubled the supply of paper money at the beginning of the war when it issued an additional 1.5 billion rubles. The issuance of paper money continued until the supply had increased fourfold by January 1917. The issuance of

paper money increased 100 percent in France and 200 percent in Germany over the same time frame.

This wartime finance led to monstrous price increases, and set a precedent that the Bolsheviks would continue to accelerate the Revolution. Inflation forces remained dormant through the first half of 1915 because the war blocked exports, which increased domestic supplies. Toward the end of 1915 inflation began to accelerate rapidly, and by the end of 1916 prices were four times higher than their 1913 levels. From 1913 to October 1916 the price of wheat flour rose 269 percent, buckwheat by 320 percent, salt by 500 percent, meat by 230 percent, and shoes and clothes by 400 to 500 percent. The cost of living grew two or three times faster than wages, and food and fuel shortages were common in urban areas. Workers formed cooperatives to purchase food and other necessities at lower prices. The government helped maintain order by threatening to induct into the army anyone who caused trouble.

Worker discontent became the political base that drove the revolution. Long lines of people waited to buy bread, and by the time workers were off work the shops no longer had bread on the shelves. The anger of the workers mounted as food and fuel became scarce, and strikes erupted in Petrograd, the largest industrial center.

In 1917 the revolution began in earnest. Nicholas I abdicated in March 1917 followed by the Bolsheviks' seizure of power in October 1917. Throughout 1917 prices rose more rapidly, topping 7.55 times their 1913 level by October 1917. The supply of rubles in circulation rose to 19.6 billion, compared to 2.4 billion in the first half of 1914. After the October coup, the tax system fell apart and the new government counted on the printing presses to finance government spending. In 1918 notes were printed in denominations up to 10,000 rubles. By October 1918, prices had grown to 102 times their 1913 level, and to 923 times in October 1919.

In May 1919 the government completely unleashed the supply of paper money. The only restriction upon printing of fresh paper money was the supply of ink and paper. The government used gold holdings to buy printing supplies abroad. Nearly 50 percent of the Treasury's budget went for the cost of printing paper money. In 1919 the supply of paper money in circulation grew to 225 billion. In 1920 it reached 1.2 trillion and doubled again in the first half of 1921. In 1921 notes were issued with face values up to 100,000 rubles. By 1923 prices were 648,230,000 times their 1913 level.

In 1922 a new ruble was introduced that was equal to 10,000 of the old rubles. This currency reform did not halt inflation and in 1923 a newer ruble was introduced that equaled 1,000,000 of the 1922 rubles. Also, the government introduced a parallel currency called the *chervonetz* that was linked to gold. This currency remained in circulation until 1928.

Revolutions are often attended with episodes of hyperinflation. The French Revolution, the American Revolution, the Bolshevik Revolution, and the Communist Revolution of China were attended with episodes of hyperinflation.

See also: American Revolution Hyperinflation, French Revolution Hyperinflation, German Hyperinflation, Inflation and Deflation

References: Hasegawa, Tsuyoshi. 1981. *The February Revolution: Petrograd, 1917.*
Paarlberg, Don. 1993. *An Analysis and History of Inflation.*
Pipes, Richard. 1991. *The Russian Revolution.*

Russian Ruble

See Decimal System, Russian Revolution Hyperinflation, Tzarist Russia's Paper Money

S

Salt Currency

The word *salary* stems from the Latin word *salarium,* meaning "salt money." The Romans paid soldiers, officers, and civil administrators an allowance of salt, and *salarium* came to be a term for military pay after salt was no longer used to pay soldiers.

Marco Polo in *The Travels of Marco Polo,* writing at the end of the thirteenth century, tells of Chinese salt money in the province of Kain-Du. In the words of Polo:

> In this country there are salt springs, from which they manufacture salt by boiling it in small pans. When the water is boiled for an hour, it becomes a kind of paste, which is formed into cakes of the value of two pence each. These, which are flat on the lower, and convex on the upper side, are placed upon hot tiles, near a fire, in order to dry and harden. On this latter species of money the stamp of the grand khan is impressed, and it cannot be prepared by any other than his own officers. Eighty of the cakes are made to pass for a saggio of gold. But when these cakes are carried by traders amongst the inhabitants of the mountains, and other parts little frequented, they obtain a saggio of gold for sixty, fifty, or even forty of the salt cakes, in proportion as they find the natives less civilized. (Polo, 1987)

Ethiopia offers the most recent example of a society circulating salt as money, a practice that lasted into the twentieth century in remote areas. As early as the sixteenth century visiting European explorers noted the use of salt as money. Bars of salt money were called *amole,* after the Amole tribe that first introduced salt money to the Ethiopians. The bars of rock salt bore a marked resemblance to a whetstone, 10 to 12 inches in length, $1\frac{1}{2}$ inches thick, and black in color, perhaps from handling. They weighed about a pound. Referring to a millionaire, Ethiopians say "he eateth salt." During the nineteenth century Richard Burton visited Harar and observed that a slave cost a donkey-load of salt bars.

Twentieth-century reports on the value of salt bars varied, some putting the exchange rate of salt bars at less than 7 bars per dollar, and others reporting as many as 48 bars per dollar. In some areas the bars could be broken up for small change, and Ethiopians enjoyed a reputation for accurately gauging the amount to break off.

The Ethiopians are known for having a strong attraction to the taste of salt, but the black bars were not used for consumption. White salt of a finer quality met the needs for seasoning and the black bars were reserved for monetary uses.

The use of salt as money gives added meaning to the phrase "worth his salt." In virtually every quarter of the globe examples can be found of salt circulating as money at some point in history. It is one of those commodities universally in demand. Following the inflationary chaos of the Bolshevik Revolution, salt was the main standard of value, medium of exchange, and store of value in Moscow.

See also: Commodity Monetary Standard
References: Einzig, Paul. 1966. *Primitive Money.*
Marco Polo. 1987. *The Travels of Marco Polo.*
Williams, Jonathan, ed. 1997. *Money: A History.*

Sandalwood

Sandalwood served as a unit of account and means of payment in nineteenth-century Hawaii. Sandalwood is a hard, light-colored, close-grained wood that in Southeast Asia is ceremonially burned in funeral rights of Hindus, Buddhists, Parsis, and Muslims. Early in the nineteenth century sandalwood became the major Hawaiian export, and a Hawaiian ruler, King Kamehameha, owed his rise to power to income derived from the export of sandalwood to the Orient.

During the heyday of the sandalwood trade, merchants and exporters kept accounts in terms of *piculs* of sandalwood, making sandalwood the unit of account, rather than metallic currency such as the Spanish dollar, the international currency at the time. A picul was originally the amount of wood a man could carry, but evolved into an oriental measure of weight between 132 and 140 pounds.

Hawaiian chiefs purchased foreign goods on credit, making payment in promissory notes payable in sandalwood.

These promissory notes were not issued as payment for token amounts. A Hawaiian ruler purchased eight sailing ships at a price of $300,000 and made payment in promissory notes payable in sandalwood. The first quarter of the nineteenth century saw massive Hawaiian debt pile up that was payable in sandalwood. In 1826 the United States government sent a sloop of war to forcibly arrange for the payments of these debts. Every man found himself assessed with a head tax payable either in half a picul, or in four Spanish dollars. The debts were paid in full, but soon afterward the supply of Hawaiian sandalwood dried up.

Sandalwood money belongs in the category of tobacco money in Virginia, or sugar money in the West Indies. Metallic money was often in short supply in the remote areas of the world, and commodities tended to surface that could fill the role of money.

See also: Commodity Monetary Standard, Mahogany Logs, Virginia Tobacco Act of 1712

References:
Bradley, Harold Whitman. 1968. *The American Frontier in Hawaii.*
Einzig, Paul. 1966. *Primitive Money.*

Savings and Loan Bailout (United States)

In August 1989 Congress enacted the Financial Institution Reform, Recovery, and Enforcement Act. This legislation furnished funds to redeem insured deposits at failed Savings and Loan institutions (S&Ls) and created the Resolution Trust Corporation, an agency responsibly for liquidating the assets of failed savings and loans. The bailout was expected to cost the federal government $160 billion over a 10-year period and maybe as much as $500 billion over 40 years.

Between 1988 and 1991 over 1,000 S&L institutions failed, putting out of business approximately one-third of all the S&Ls in the United States. The Federal Savings and Loan Insurance Corporation (FSLIC), the agency responsible for insuring deposits at S&Ls, ran out of money to redeem insured deposits at these institutions. In effect, the S&L collapse bankrupted the FSLIC.

During the 1970s, a period of rising inflation in the United States, S&Ls faced strict legal limits on the interest rates that depositors could earn on S&L deposits. S&Ls paid low interest rates on deposits and made relatively low interest loans on home mortgages.

During the 1980s the United States economy made the transition from an inflation economy to a disinflation economy, and the S&L industry also changed from a highly regulated industry to a deregulated industry. The deregulation of the S&Ls lifted the interest rate ceilings of S&L deposits, and allowed S&Ls to enter the business of consumer and commercial loans. Interest rates escalated rapidly in the early 1980s under the pressure of a tight, anti-inflation, monetary policy, squeezing S&Ls that held low interest mortgages while paying high interest rates on current deposits.

Savings and loans tried to save themselves by turning to riskier consumer and commercial loans that paid higher interest rates. When depression struck in the oil and real estate industry in the last half of the 1980s, S&Ls began to fail rapidly.

The S&L collapse in the United States uncovered

an unsuspected weakness in deposit insurance: fully insured depositors had no incentive to favor S&Ls with conservative investment policies over S&Ls with risky investment portfolios. That is, depositors had no incentive to keep track of investment practices of individual S&Ls, allowing them a free rein to finance risky business ventures.

Another provision of the Financial Institution Reform, Recovery, and Enforcement Act placed responsibility for insuring S&L deposits with the Federal Deposit Insurance Corporation (FDIC), the agency that has always insured commercial bank deposits. The FDIC is devising a plan to vary the insurance premiums that financial institutions pay according to the riskiness of loan portfolios. Under such a plan financial institutions that carry high-risk loan portfolios pay higher deposit insurance premiums.

See also: Depository Institution Deregulation and Monetary Control Act of 1980, Glass-Steagall Act of 1933
References: Barth, James R. 1991. *The Great Savings and Loan Debacle.*
Long, Robert Emmet, ed. 1993. *Banking Scandals: The S&Ls and BCCI.*

Sceattas
See English Penny

Scottish Banking Act of 1765

The Scottish Banking Act of 1765 established the legal foundations that enabled Scotland to pioneer the development of free banking, a system of banking that flourished in the United States before the Civil War. Under a system of free banking no one bank, usually called a central bank, claims a monopoly on the issuance of bank notes, as the Federal Reserve System enjoys in the United States. Instead, each private bank issues its own bank notes, and maintains the convertibility of its notes into gold or silver, or other commodity, depending upon the monetary standard. Under free-banking systems the privilege to start a new bank is removed as far as possible from political processes.

The Act of 1765 was entitled "An Act to prevent the inconveniences arising from the present method of issuing notes and bills by banks, banking companies, and bankers, in that part of Great Britain called Scotland." The act authorized all "banks, banking compa-

nies and bankers" to issue bank notes, and for a century the issuance of bank notes became the defining characteristic of Scottish banks. In England the Bank of England had a monopoly on the privilege to issue bank notes in London. In Scotland the Bank of Scotland and the Royal Bank of Scotland campaigned to give themselves a monopoly on the issuance of bank notes, but the public sided with the small banks wanting to maintain the privilege to issue bank notes.

The act forbade the issuance of bank notes with a face value less than 20 shillings (or 1 pound sterling). The smallest note issued by the Bank of England was 5 pounds sterling, but small note issues had circulated widely in Scotland, some as small as 5 shillings, or even 1 shilling. In Scotland a shortage of small change created a vacuum that low denomination bank notes filled.

The Act of 1765 also forbade the so-called optional clause. In 1730 the Bank of Scotland, to protect itself from bank runs, began printing on its notes the optional clause, stating that the bank could either redeem the bank notes on demand, or defer redemption for up to six months. The clause also stated the interest rate that bank notes would earn if redemption was deferred. The notes only bore interest for the time redemption was suspended. To encourage banks to follow safer banking policies, optional clauses were banned.

Scotland's free banking system did not exactly find smooth sailing. Several banks failed in 1772, including the Ayr Bank that Adam Smith described in the *Wealth of Nations*. Notwithstanding a few bank failures, Smith sang the praises of Scotland's banking system, and noted the expansion of Scottish commerce that had coincided with the development of banking. During the Napoleonic Wars, Parliament came to the rescue of the Bank of England and Bank of Ireland by ordering the suspension of their bank note convertibility. The banks of Scotland, however, maintained the convertibility of their bank notes and never had to throw themselves upon the government for protection.

See also: Bank of Scotland, Free Banking, Royal Bank of Scotland
References: Checkland, C. G. 1975. *Scottish Banking, A History: 1695–1973.*
Colwell, Stephen. 1859. *The Ways and Means of Payment.*
Kroszner, Randy. 1995. *Free Banking: The Scottish Experience as a Model for Emerging Economies.*

Sealed Coin Purses

During the Roman and Byzantine Empires sealed purses of coins circulated as money in larger transactions. Early coinage was primitive, and gold coins changing hands needed to be first weighed and counted—a time-consuming process for large monetary transactions. Sealed purses contained a quantity of metallic coinage, mainly gold and silver, already counted and weighed, thus expediting the process of handling large transactions.

Evidence of sealed purses of coins first appears in legal documents during the third century A.D. The precipitous debasement in the second half of the third century may have accelerated the practice of substituting sealed purses for loose coins. On the one hand, debasement encouraged hoarding of full-bodied coins, and sealed purses were a convenient form for holding large quantities of coins. On the other hand, debasement substantially increased the number of debased coins involved in individual transactions, adding a further incentive to bunch coins in purses. Debased coins as well as full-bodied coins were put in sealed purses. The number of coins in these purses ranged from 20 up to 2,000. At first, officials of the state reserved the right to count, weigh, and seal up purses of coins. Later, private bankers enjoyed the privilege of sealing up purses of coins with an official inscription stating the number and weight of the enclosed coins.

Sealed purses of money also protected coins from the natural loss of wear and tear. Moneychangers often applied a discount to a quantity of coins as an allowance for loss of weight from such wear, and sealing money in purses, with an official inscription vouching for the weight of the coins, was a means of avoiding payment of such a discount.

The process of sealing purses of coins lent itself to a certain amount of corruption, because the main objective was to enable the exchange of sealed purses of money without having to recount the contents of the sealed purses at each transaction. Individuals engaged in sealing purses would skim off a bit of the precious metal for themselves before sealing the purse. Edict XI of Justinian, dated 559, addressed various abuses attributable to those engaged in sealing purses of money. The edict required that gold coins sealed in Egypt be reckoned on the same measures current in Constantinople. The edict mentioned that some individuals were sealing purses marked with higher sums than were actually contained in the purse. The edict required that the amount inscribed on the purse be no more than the true weight of the gold sealed up, and that anyone marking a sum greater than the enclosed gold faced the death penalty. Government officials who were a knowing party to the corrupt sealing of purses also faced the death penalty.

Evidence of sealed purses exists for as late as the eleventh century. The use of sealed purses of coins became a boon to future archeologists in search of numerous specimens of coins from the same time period.

See also: Leather-Wrapped Money of Ancient Carthage

References: Hendy, Michael F. 1985. *Studies in the Byzantine Monetary Economy.*

Johnson, A. C., and L. C. West. 1949. *Currency in Roman and Byzantine Egypt.*

Second Bank of the United States

The Second Bank of the United States met the need for a central bank in the United States between 1816 and 1836. During the War of 1812 state banks suspended the conversion of bank notes into specie. At that time each bank issued its own paper money and held specie (gold and silver coins) to redeem its paper money. Today banks issue checking accounts and hold paper money to redeem the checking accounts. When the banks suspended specie payments in 1814, six months before the war ended, the federal government had no way to pressure them to return to convertibility. The Second Bank of the United States bore a strong resemblance to the First Bank of the United States, which had lost its charter in 1811 because of constitutional questions and foreign ownership. At the time many questioned if Congress had the authority to grant a charter of incorporation, much less sanction a monopoly. The First Bank of the United States provided monetary discipline by demanding that all bank notes deposited with it be redeemed in specie by the bank that issued them. As the government began to miss the monetary discipline enforced by the First Bank of the United States, critics—mainly followers of Jefferson and Madison—began to soften their constitutional objections and came to support the creation of the Second Bank of the United States. Now the Jeffersonian Republicans were supporting such a bank instead of the New England Federalists.

Congress approved the charter for the Second Bank of the United States early in 1816 and President Madison signed the bill on April 10 of that year.

The Second Bank was capitalized at $35 million. The government owned one-fifth of the stock and appointed 5 of the 25 directors. Shares of stock were sold at a price to attract broadly based ownership. Foreign-owned stock had no voting rights and large shareholders were limited to 30 votes. Subscribers could pay as little as one-fourth in specie and the remainder in government securities.

The Second Bank got off to a wobbly start. In 1818 a House committee investigated the bank. It then had $2.4 million in specie to support $22 million in demand liabilities. The bank was on the verge of suspending specie payments itself. The investigating committee discovered that the Second Bank had extended loans to its own stockholders who used stock in the bank as collateral. This practice enabled speculators to buy stock in the Second Bank by using the bank's own money. The officers of the bank had speculated in its stock, and the Second Bank had also been slow in demanding specie payments on notes issued by state banks.

The Second Bank's poor management had consequences for the economic contraction in 1818. The bank's effort to bring its own house in order hastened the economic downturn. The Baltimore branch failed. It had made bad loans and its officers had speculated in its stock. The president of the Second Bank resigned and Langdon Cheves assumed the leadership of the bank (1819). His conservative administration put the bank on firm financial footing. Nicholas Biddle succeeded Cheves in 1823. Biddle's understanding of the role of a central bank put him ahead of his time. He placed the public responsibilities of the bank above the private interests of its stockholders. In 1834 a French traveler termed the Second Bank the *banque centrale*.

The Second Bank forced the state banks to maintain specie payments for their bank notes. To reduce money in circulation the Second Bank accumulated specie. The bank increased the money in circulation by making more loans. The bank's practices made enemies of state banks in the West and South, which resented its regulation of state bank notes. These banks tended to expand the supply of bank notes in circulation beyond what their reserves of specie could be counted on to redeem.

The state banks had a powerful ally in President Andrew Jackson. Biddle and his advisers saw the hostility to the bank gathering momentum. Rather than wait for the Second Bank's charter to expire in 1836, they asked Congress for a renewal of the charter in 1832. The bill for rechartering the bank passed the House and the Senate. President Jackson vetoed the bill.

Critics charged that the bank put too much power in the hands of officials who were neither elected directly by the people nor responsible to elected officials. In addition, paper money had not yet established itself in the confidence of the voters. President Jackson himself was a "hard money" person. The public saw paper money as the culprit in depressions. In his veto message President Jackson stated:

> Equality of talents, of education, or of wealth cannot be produced by human institutions ... but when the laws undertake to add to these natural and just advantages artificial distinctions . . . to make the rich richer, and the potent more powerful, the humble members of society—the farmers, mechanics, and laborers—who have neither the time nor the means of securing like favors to themselves, have a right to complain of the injustice of their Government. (Schlesinger, 1945)

Jackson's rhetoric may bear the stamp of the demagoguery of the frontier politician rather than the best thinking of the time. Perhaps the best-educated and most cosmopolitan of all the presidents, Thomas Jefferson, described his opinion of banks in this way:

> I have ever been the enemy of banks; not of those discounting cash; but of those foisting their own paper into circulation, and thus banishing our cash. My zeal against those institutions was so warm and open at the establishment of the [First] bank of the U.S. that I was derided as a Maniac by the tribe of bank-mongers, who were seeking to filch from the public their swindling and barren gains. (Cappon, 1959)

With the establishment of the Federal Reserve System in 1913 the United States finally came to terms with the idea of a central bank. By then the role of central banks in maintaining economic stability was better understood, and banks were better accepted than they were in Jefferson's day.

See also: Bank of England, Bank of France, Central Bank, Federal Reserve System, First Bank of the United States
References: Brown, Marion A. 1998. *The Second Bank of the United States and Ohio, 1803–1860: A Collision of Interests.*
Cappon, Lester, ed. 1959. *The Adams-Jefferson Letters.*
Meyers, Margaret G. 1970. *A Financial History of the United States.*
Schlesinger, Arthur M., Jr. 1945. *The Age of Jackson.*
Timberlake, Richard H. 1978. *The Origins of Central Banking in the United States.*

Seigniorage

Seigniorage is the profit or revenue raised through coining or printing money. The word *seigniorage* stems from the French *seigneur*, a word for "feudal lord," referring to feudal manors that often exercised the privilege to mint coins in the Middle Ages. In modern societies the rights of seigniorage belong to government.

Historically, kings, dukes, counts, bishops, or city-states exercised the privilege to coin money. The coinage usually bore the name, symbol, or portrait of the responsible ruler who guaranteed the weight and purity of the precious metal content. Originally, seigniorage was the mint's share of the coins that were struck from precious metals brought to the mint by private citizens. Some authorities define seigniorage more narrowly as the profit that mints earn from coinage of precious metals supplied by citizens.

Mints operated on the principle that private citizens brought precious metals to them, and they then tested the metal for weight and purity. A private citizen that brought precious metal meeting mint standards either received coins that had already been struck, or received the coins struck from the precious metal that he or she brought to the mint. Minted coins were worth more than equivalent amounts of precious metal because they were much more convenient for transacting business, sparing the need to weigh and evaluate the precious metal. Today a gold coin such as South Africa's Krugerrand enjoys a market value exceeding the market value of its gold content. By adding value to the coined metals, a mint could get by with taking a cut for itself.

Early in European monetary history governments began minting bullion brought to mints without deducting seigniorage, minting free of charge. England began the practice of free coinage in 1666. Under England's system a citizen could bring gold bullion to the mint, wait until the mint turned bullion into coins, or take the bullion to the Bank of England and receive gold coins immediately at a discount of less than one-half of 1 percent.

The development of government paper money opened new opportunities for seigniorage because the face value of paper money far exceeds the value of the paper as raw material. When the government prints additional paper money, it makes the paper money already in circulation worth less. Prices rise, in effect imposing a tax on existing money balances in the hands of the public.

The dependence upon seigniorage revenue varies substantially among modern governments. The United States government raises about 3 percent of government revenue from seigniorage, but Italy and Greece raise over 10 percent of government revenue from seigniorage. Seigniorage often accounts for 50 percent or more of government revenue in countries caught in a spiral of hyperinflation. The chief cause of hyperinflation is excessive government dependence upon revenue from seigniorage, rather than from taxes or borrowing.

See also: Cross Coinage, Great Debasement
References: Chown, John F. 1994. *A History of Money.*
Fischer, Stanley. 1982. Seigniorage and the Case for a National Money. *Journal of Political Economy* 90 (April): 295–313.

Seizure of the Mint (England)

The Seizure of the Mint refers to an episode in 1640 in which Charles I, reigning king of England from 1625 to 1672, intercepted the flow of coins from the mint to the government's major creditors, the goldsmiths and merchants. Minting coins had become such a booming business under Charles I that the Tower Mint could not keep up, causing Charles I to open branch mints throughout the kingdom.

Charles I was always in need of money despite a treaty with Spain that assured him of abundant supplies of bullion. On one occasion Charles I forced the East India Company to sell him its entire stock of pepper on credit, payable after two years. Charles I bought the pepper at a price of 2 shillings 1 pence per pound, and then turned around and sold it for

1 shilling 8 pence per pound, raising instant cash in a roundabout credit transaction that angered the merchants of London. On two occasions the Privy Council blocked proposals that Charles I advanced to increase the mint profits by debasing the coins, a favorite stratagem of monarchs for squeezing more resources from subjects. Debasing the coin meant reducing the precious metal content in coins with a given face value.

The machinery of public finance was a bit primitive during the reign of Charles I. The government's creditors, mainly goldsmiths and merchants, claimed freshly minted coins when they became available. In 1640 Charles I stopped the flow of coins from the mint, planning to use the coins for his own expenditures, and instead promised to pay the Crown's creditors 8 percent interest on his outstanding debt. A howl rose up from goldsmiths and merchants who wanted their money immediately, causing Charles I to relent and send two-thirds of the coins to the Crown's debtors. Charles I kept one-third of the coins and promised to pay his creditors 8 percent for six months.

Charles I eventually paid the creditors in full, but only after the merchants and goldsmiths had lost faith in the government's management of monetary affairs. Already there was talk of setting up a national or public bank, and the incident of the mint seizure convinced influential people that the government could not be trusted with direct power over such a bank. The Bank of England came into being in 1694, and developed as a private institution that nevertheless enjoyed close ties with the government.

See also: Bank of England, Stop of the Exchequer
References: Challis, C. E., ed. 1992. *A New History of the Royal Mint.*
Craig, J. 1953. *The Mint: A History of the London Mint from* A.D. *287 to 1948.*

Shekels
See Babylonian Grain and Silver Standard, Cappadocia, Mosaic Silver Standard, Phoenician Weight Standard

Sherman Silver Act of 1890 (United States)

The Sherman Silver Act of 1890 nearly doubled the government's monthly purchase of silver, and provided for the issuance of legal tender Treasury notes in payment of silver.

The Coinage Act of 1873 made no provision for the coinage of silver dollars, an omission that became an angry point of contention as deflation and depression spread in the late nineteenth century, and silver interest saw silver prices steadily decline. A "free silver" movement sprang up calling for unlimited coinage of silver. The Bland-Allison Act of 1878 provided for restricted purchase of silver and coinage of silver dollars, but silver prices continued to fall, and agitation for "free silver" mounted strength. The Sherman Silver Act of 1890 extended the monetization of silver about as far as possible without embracing "free silver," and returning to a bimetallic gold-silver standard.

Silver certificates spared the U.S. government the expense of minting silver coins. (Smithsonian Institution, National Numismatic Collection)

The act called for the Treasury to purchase 4,500,000 ounces of silver per month at market prices as long as the market prices did not exceed $1.29 per ounce, the historic mint price since 1837. The Treasury was to pay for the bullion in treasury notes in denominations not less than $1 or more than $1,000. These Treasury notes were legal tender for all debts, private and public. The act made these notes redeemable in either gold coin or silver coin, depending upon the discretion of the Treasury. The act only required the Treasury to coin quantities of silver bullion as needed to redeem Treasury notes.

The act authorized the issuance of Treasury notes to save on coinage expenses. Since the market value of silver fell short of its official price, silver was preferred over gold in the payment of government obligations. Silver dollars tended to return to the Treasury as fast as they were issued, notwithstanding the Treasury's practice to ship the silver coins to distant places at no cost. Complaints were heard about the storage costs and inconvenience of the silver dollars. Before the Act of 1890 the government was issuing Treasury notes that were not legal tender.

The Sherman Silver Act passed the Congress after a "free silver" bill had already passed the Senate. Apparently one motivation for enacting this legislation was to avoid what gold standard defenders saw as a worst alternative, a free silver bill.

Since the United States and the countries of Europe were on either a defacto or an official gold standard in the 1890s, gold coin was preferred over silver coin. Banks tended to ask the Treasury to redeem treasury notes in gold coin, and the Treasury obliged. The Treasury's gold reserves dwindled while silver reserves grew. Foreigners who had purchased American securities with gold became fearful that these securities would be redeemed in silver, at a rate well below the market value of silver. Foreigners began to sell American securities, taking payment in gold and causing a gold outflow to Europe. In 1893, after the government had to sell bonds to raise gold reserves, Congress repealed the Sherman Silver Act. The Treasury stopped purchasing silver except for subsidiary coinage, and the flight of capital from the United States ceased. The Gold Standard Act of 1900 officially put the United States on the gold standard.

See also: Bimetallism, Bland-Allison Silver Repurchase Act, Crime of '73, Free Silver Movement, Gold Standard Act of 1900
References: Friedman, Milton. 1992. *Monetary Mischief.*
Hepburn, A. Barton. 1967. *A History of Currency in the United States,*.
Jastram, Roy W. 1981. *Silver: The Restless Metal.*
Myers, Margaret G. 1970. *A Financial History of the United States.*

Shillings
See Carolingian Reform, Ghost Money

Shinplasters

Shinplasters are small-denomination bank notes or forms of paper money. The face value of shinplasters is usually less than $1. The name probably arose from similarities to plasters used on sore shins.

The term goes back at least to the early nineteenth century, when some bank notes in the United States were issued for as little as 12.5 cents. In 1834 Senator Thomas Hart Benton, a famous "hard currency" advocate who referred to himself by the nickname Old Bullion, was heard to say, "What! Do you want a coroner's jury to sit and say, 'Old Bullion died of shinplasters'?" (Schlesinger, 1945).

Adam Smith in the *Wealth of Nations* does not mention shinplasters per se but devotes a good deal of attention to discouraging the issuance of small denomination notes. According to Smith:

Where the issuing of bank notes for such very small sums is allowed and commonly practiced, many mean people are both enabled and encouraged to become bankers. A person whose promissory note for five pounds, or even for twenty shillings, would be rejected by everybody, will get it received without scruple when it is issued for so small a sum as a sixpence. . . . It were better, perhaps, that no bank notes were issued in any part of the kingdom for a smaller sum than five pounds. Paper money would then confine itself . . . to circulation between the different dealers [wholesalers]. . . . Where paper money is confined to circulation between dealers and dealers, as at London, there is always plenty of gold and silver. Where it extends itself to a considerable part of the circulation between dealers and con-

"Shinplasters" was the name given to U.S. paper money in denominations of less than $1. (Smithsonian Institution, National Numismatic Collection)

A mock shinplaster depicts Andrew Jackson (riding a pig) and Thomas Hart Benton (on an ass) heading for a precipice while chasing the "Gold Humbug" butterfly, representing their efforts to restrict the amount of paper money in circulation. Martin Van Buren (riding a fox) cleverly avoids the disaster. (Library of Congress)

sumers, as in Scotland, and still more in North America, it banishes gold and silver almost entirely from the country. (Smith, 1952)

In 1829 England banished bank notes of less than 5 pounds. In the United States a Treasury circular of April 1835 disallowed the acceptance of notes under $5 for payment of federal obligations. In February 1836 the Treasury extended the ban to notes under $10, and prohibited banks holding U.S. government deposits from issuing such notes. In April 1836 Congress enacted legislation banning notes under $20.

In April 1862 the Congress authorized the issuance of a paper currency in fractional units of a dollar. At first the currency took the form of postal stamp designs engraved on notes but later took other forms. This fractional currency could be exchanged for legal-tender notes in amounts up to $5. In 1875 Congress provided for the replacement of fractional currency with subsidiary coinage.

In 1870 a shortage of silver coins led the Dominion Government of Canada to issue paper currencies in denominations of a fraction of a dollar, familiarly known as shinplasters because of their small size. The Canadian government discontinued the shinplasters in 1935 after issuing over 300 different varieties of shinplasters over the 65-year period.

The fact that history is inflationary may have put an end to shinplasters. The United States has attempted to replace the one-dollar bill with a coin, suggesting that the dollar bill is beginning to fall into the range of small change, in the same value range as the shinplasters.

See also: Inconvertible Paper Money, Postage Stamps
References: Angus, Ian. 1975. *Paper Money.*
Chown, John F. 1994. *A History of Money.*
Schlesinger, Arthur M. J. 1945. *The Age of Jackson.*
Smith, Adam. 1952. *An Inquiry into the Nature and Causes of the Wealth of Nations.*

Siege Money

During a siege coins and precious metal invariably go into hiding, in secret hoards, and cities under siege have often turned to a form of fiat money, usually paper money.

In 1574 the Spanish laid siege to the city of Leyden in the Lowlands. The city needed all the metal it could muster to manufacture arms, and even collected the metallic coinage to contribute to the effort. The burgomaster of Leyden issued small pieces of paper to take the place of coinage. These scraps of paper money predate by nearly a century the permanent introduction of paper money in Europe.

Several cities issued siege notes during the wars of the French Revolution and Napoleon. In 1793 the royalists in Lyons, France, revolted and took control of the city. The republican forces laid siege. The royalists printed crude notes on cardboard with the expression "The Siege of Lyon" and distributed them as money. In the same year Austria laid siege to the German town of Mainz, then under French control. The French authorities printed up a paper currency with the expression, "Siege de Mayence Mai 1793 2e de la Rep. France." In 1796 the city of Mantua in Italy

issued a siege currency when the city came under siege by Napoleon. Colburg, Prussia, issued siege currency in 1807 under the pressure of a Napoleonic siege. Also, several Italian cities issued siege currencies during the uprisings of 1848.

In 1884 the British government dispatched General Charles George Gordon to the Sudan to evacuate Egyptian forces from Khartoum, which was about to be overrun by Sudanese rebels. Gordon reached Khartoum in February 1884 and a month later the rebels laid siege to the city. The siege lasted until 26 January 1885 when the rebels took the city and killed the defenders, including Gordon. Gordon's death after a colorful career and heroic struggle made him a martyr, and the siege of Khartoum became one memorable episode in the history of the British Empire, the stuff of Hollywood movies.

One of the less well-known aspects of the siege of Khartoum was the issuance of a siege paper money. On his arrival, Gordon found the treasury of Khartoum empty, and within a few weeks Gordon issued emergency notes. Each note bore Gordon's signature. The first 50,000 notes he signed by hand, and the rest bore his printed signature. Gordon's signature accompanied a statement on each note saying that he (Gordon) was "personally responsible for the liquidation, and anyone can bring action against me, in my individual capacity, to recover the money." The total value of the notes was approximately 168,500 Egyptian pounds. About 2,000 specimens of these notes have survived, mostly in the hands of collectors.

The exigencies of sieges have forced governments to experiment with fiat money, helping to make way for the ascendancy of fiat paper money in the twentieth century.

See also: Inconvertible Paper Money, Pontiac's Bark Money
References: Beresiner, Yasha. 1977. *Paper Money.*
Weatherford, Jack. 1997. *The History of Money.*

Silver

Silver and gold were the most aristocratic of the monetary metals. Silver owes its chemical symbol, Ag, to its Latin name, *argentum,* meaning "white and shining." Ancient artisans found silver malleable, resistant to oxidation, and beautiful. It is one of the most reflective of all metals, under favorable conditions reflecting about 95 percent of the light striking its surface.

The use of silver for ornaments, jewelry, and a store of wealth stretches into the mists of ancient history. In the Book of Genesis, Abraham, after returning from Egypt, is described as very "rich in cattle, in silver, and gold." The laws of Moses put a silver value on men, cattle, houses, fields, and provisions. Silver seems to have been in greater use than gold as a monetary metal among the ancient Hebrews, but gold possessed greater religious significance. Hiram, king of Tyre, furnished gold for decoration of the Temple of Jerusalem.

The practice of coinage began in Lydia in the seventh century B.C. and crossed the Aegean Sea to ancient Greece, a country endowed with rich silver deposits. The Laurion silver mines furnished Athens with abundant supplies of silver, and the commercial leadership of Athens lifted the Attic silver standard to a position of dominance in Mediterranean trade. The Roman Empire debased its silver coinage, but maintained the purity and weight of its gold coinage. During the Middle Ages, the Byzantine world maintained its gold standard, but gold virtually disappeared from Europe. Silver remained an important monetary metal in India and the Far East. Given the disappearance of gold, the Carolingian reform of A.D. 755 put Europe on a silver standard that lasted until the end of the Middle Ages. Nevertheless, silver coinage was rare and often severely debased.

Gold coinage returned to Europe in the thirteenth century, but silver remained an important monetary metal. England moved firmly toward the gold standard only in the eighteenth century. On the Continent silver rivaled gold as a monetary metal until late in the nineteenth century.

The discovery of the New World infused vast supplies of silver throughout the world-trading system. It is not commonly appreciated that 98 percent of all the precious metal taken out of the New World was silver. Silver was a favored metal in India and the Far East, and some silver was shipped directly from Latin America to China. The Spanish silver dollar became a worldwide medium of exchange, remaining legal tender in the United States until the 1850s.

In the nineteenth century Europe and the United States began moving away from silver as a monetary standard, although silver continued in use as subsidiary coinage. The subsidiary coinage always kept the silver content sufficiently low to discourage melt-

ing down coins for profit. In China and India the silver standard survived into the twentieth century.

Although gold became the preeminent precious monetary metal during the nineteenth and twentieth centuries, silver may have an even longer and more varied history as money. Silver was light enough to be carried in ships, although overland transportation favored gold, which was lighter per unit of value. Silver, however, was next to gold in value per unit of weight. Gold was too precious for many ordinary transactions, but silver, between gold and copper in value, was light enough to be carried around in values useful for ordinary transactions. In addition, silver deposits, unlike gold, were scattered all over the earth, making silver very accessible.

See also: Chinese Silver Standard, Free Silver Movement, Indian Silver Standard, Mosaic Silver Standard, *Wizard of Oz*

References: Braudel, Fernand. 1981. *Civilization and Capitalism.* Vol. 1.

Flynn, Dennis O. 1996. *World Silver and Monetary History in the 16th and 17th Centuries.*

Jastram, Roy W. 1981. *Silver: The Restless Metal.*

Williams, Jonathan, ed. 1997. *Money: A History.*

Silver Certificates

See Free Silver Movement, Silver Purchase Act of 1934

Silver Plate

The silver plate that adorned the dinner tables of European nobility was treated as monetary reserves and frequently played that role. To help pay for the Seven Years War (1756–1763) Frederick the Great of Prussia requisitioned the silver plate from the royal palaces. He sent it to the melting pots at the mint, and minted it into 600,000 *thalers* at a rate of 21 thalers per Cologne *mark* of fine silver, rather than the usual 14 thalers. King Louis XIV of France also sent the royal plate to the mint to pay his troops.

In 1536 Henry VIII sent 20,878 pounds sterling of plate to the mint to furnish money urgently needed to pay troops. Later, in the last of the French wars, Henry VIII disgorged another 10,020 pounds sterling of plate for coinage, again furnishing money to wage war. Henry also confiscated vast amounts of ecclesiastical plate and sent it to the mint.

Those further down the social scale used plate to pay benevolences, subsidies, and tithes levied against them, and the mint could convert a quantity of plate into a coinage equivalent. Nobles needing funds to finance political intrigue sent plate to the mint. Plate was the closest thing to a near-money owned by English households in the sixteenth and seventeenth centuries, and at times the mint offered a premium to attract more silver plate to be coined. The government also legally mandated a higher standard of fineness for plate than for coinage, trying to prevent coinage from being melted down and fashioned into plate. That silver plate was associated with monetary affairs is revealed in a proclamation of the English king, Charles II, in 1661. It declared: "The nation had flourished for many hundred of years, famous for her constant silver standard and renowned for her plenteous stock of monies and magnificence of plate" (Einzig, 1966).

One common denominator in many types of money, whether it is human heads in Sumatra, or *manillas* in Africa, is that the money has ornamental value. Even coinage is sometimes converted into ornaments. The Argentine gauchos made leather belts a foot wide and studded with large silver coins from Peru. Although articles that serve the dual purpose of money and ornament are most common in primitive societies, silver plate in the stately homes of England was a vestige of ornamental money.

See also: Dissolution of Monasteries, Pound Sterling, Silver
References: Challis, C. E. 1978. *The Tudor Coinage.* Cripps, Wilfred Joseph. 1967. *Old English Plate.* Einzig, Paul. 1966. *Primitive Money.*

Silver Purchase Act of 1934 (United States)

Under the Silver Purchase Act of 1934 the federal government purchased large quantities of silver and issued silver certificates, significantly adding to the United States' monetary base. The act marked a renewed emphasis on silver as monetary metal, reversing a trend to demonetize silver, which had been evident since the late nineteenth century.

The deflation of the 1930s created fertile conditions for another silver movement, an echo of the nineteenth-century free silver movement. The monetization of silver appeared as a means of increasing the money stock and reinflating prices while remaining committed to precious metal money rather than fiat paper money. After the depression-driven

tumble in prices of all commodities, precious metal monetary standards of any stripe held little charm for governments. The silver-producing interests, however, still had sufficient political clout to advance silver as a partial answer to the woes of economic depression.

The Agricultural Adjustment Act of 1932 (AAA) had an amendment attached, the Thomas amendment, authorizing the president to return the country to a bimetallic standard that would define the dollar in both a gold equivalent and a silver equivalent, and provide for the unlimited coinage of gold and silver. The United States had been on a bimetallic standard from 1792 until 1873, and then populist political leaders had taken up the banner of the free silver movement, advancing the idea of reenfranchising silver as a monetary metal. By the turn of the century gold seemed to have won a clear victory over silver as a competing monetary standard, but the Great Depression of the 1930s intervened to dethrone the much-vaulted gold standard.

After the adoption of the Thomas amendment, the United States abandoned the gold standard, and President Roosevelt showed no indication that he planned to exercise his authority under the Thomas amendment. Silverites in Congress, those favoring a return to a bimetallic standard based on gold and silver, pressed ahead with new legislative proposals and Roosevelt finally compromised, sending a message to Congress that led to enactment of the Silver Purchase Act of 1934.

The act authorized the government to purchase silver until either the monetary value of the United States' silver stock equaled one-third of the value of its monetary gold, or the market price of silver climbed to the monetary value of $1.29 per ounce. Under the act the government purchased silver at market prices and made payment in silver coins and silver certificates, a form of paper money similar to Federal Reserve Notes. Soon after the passage of the act, the government nationalized domestic silver stocks at $0.50 per ounce. By 1938 the government had acquired 40,000 tons of silver, an amount that raised the issue of storage. The grounds of the West Point military academy became the home of a depository that held the silver until industry found a need for it in the 1960s.

The Silver Repurchase Agreement raised the world price of silver, and silver production increased in the United States. Rising silver prices put a hardship on the handful of countries still on a silver standard because it made the exports of these countries more expensive to the rest of the world, forcing these countries to undergo domestic deflation to remain competitive worldwide. China abandoned the silver standard in November 1935 and Mexico began exchanging its silver coins for paper. In 1936 and 1937 the United States government let the price of silver fall, but the trend toward demonetization of silver in silver standard countries had already established momentum. Because of its depression-inducing effects on silver-standard countries, the Act of 1934 actually reduced the monetary demand for silver abroad, canceling long-term benefits to the American silver industry. In the United States the monetization of silver had no inflationary effects because the government retired Federal Reserve Notes to compensate for the infusion of silver certificates.

In the 1960s the industrial demand for silver accelerated, lifting silver prices above the official price of $1.29 per ounce. The government began selling off its silver stocks. In 1963 Congress repealed the Silver Purchase Act of 1934 and authorized the issuance of Federal Reserve Notes in denominations of $1 and $2, enabling the government to retire silver certificates. The Coinage Act of 1965 allowed the government to substantially cut the silver content of its silver coinage, and thus further curtail its silver purchases. The final chapter on the demonetization of silver in the United States closed on 24 June 1968 when the right to redeem silver certificates expired.

See also: Bimetallism, Chinese Hyperinflation, Free Silver Movement, Sherman Silver Act of 1890, Silver

References: Friedman, Milton. 1992. *Monetary Mischief.*
Jastram, Roy W. 1981. *Silver: The Restless Metal.*
Rickenbacker, William F. 1966. *Wooden Nickels: Or the Decline and Fall of Silver Coins.*

Slave Currency

Slaves often served as a form of wealth in primitive societies, making slaves a suitable medium of exchange, particularly for large transactions.

In the modern era Africa provides the most evidence of the use of slaves as money. In the nineteenth century a slave was the unit of account in the Sudan. A standard unit was defined as a slave that met certain measurements. The value of a slave was equivalent to 30 cotton pieces, 6 oxen, or 10 dollars. In the Bagirmi country of equatorial Africa a slave of medium qualities, defined as a standard slave, served as a standard of value for large transactions. The prices of better slaves were some multiple of the standard slave. Wealth took the form of "heads," and a successful slave raid depreciated the value of the standard, causing the prices of commodities expressed in slaves to rise. In Ghana slave payments were made for large transactions, and slaves served as a standard of value. In Guinea slaves were the favored unit of account in large transactions, and kings charged European ships port dues ranging from 7 to 12 slaves, depending upon the number of masts on each ship. In Nigeria slaves ran a close second to cowries as the prime unit of currency. A report in the late nineteenth century said of the slave: "He has been the cheque book of the country and has been necessary for all large payments. Unfortunately he has a trick of dying while passing from hand to hand" (Einzig, 1966).

The standard of value was defined in terms of a slave of a certain age, and in the course of a transaction each slave was valued in terms of this standard slave. In Nigeria, slaves were the choice medium of exchange for large transactions, and rich men amassed wealth in slaves. In the Congo slaves passed in payment for goods, and met the need for a standard of value. The people of this area practiced cannibalism, and the value of a slave could not drop below the value of the pounds of meat that could be gotten from the slave if the owner ate his money. In seventeenth-century Angola a 20-year-old slave was a standard unit of value.

Some authors pin the blame for African slavery on the absence of a convenient currency. Slaves were mobile and often carried other forms of primitive money that was bulky and difficult to transport. Merchants brought slaves carrying other currencies on trading expeditions, and exchanged the slaves along with the other currencies for merchandise when the opportunity arose.

In early Cambodia slaves ranked with cattle, buffaloes, horses, pigs, and elephants as an acceptable means of paying fines. In early England values were occasionally estimated in slaves, and in Ireland a unit of account of one slave girl lasted well into the Christian era, long after the practice of trading human beings for goods had ended. People in western areas of

New Guinea priced calico and other traded goods in terms of slaves.

The use of slave money probably began when warriors took more captives in war than they could personally use, and therefore they traded these captives for goods. From this small beginning the practice of trading human beings evolved into the use of slaves as a type of money.

See also: Slave Currency of Ancient Ireland
References: Einzig, Paul. 1966. *Primitive Money*. Weatherford, Jack. 1997. *The History of Money*.

Slave Currency of Ancient Ireland

Although ownership of slaves represented wealth in slave-holding societies and slaves were popular subjects for barter, ancient Ireland made slave girls, called *kumals* or *ancillae,* a unit of account for measuring the values of goods and services. A legendary king in ancient Irish literature owned a chessboard, and each chess piece was said to equal 6 kumals in value. Queen Maeve, a figure in an epic poem dating from before the Christian era, boasted of a chariot worth thrice seven bondsmaids. During the fifth century in Ireland, St. Patrick wrote in his *Confessions:* "You know how much I have paid out to those who were judges in all the regions, which I have often visited; for I think that I have given away to them not less than the price of fifteen humans" (Einzig, 1966). The wording suggests that St. Patrick did not pay in slaves, but was using slaves as a standard of value for reckoning what he did pay. St. Patrick would not have used slaves as a means of payment. Under his guidance the Hiberian Synod decreed that retribution for the murder of a bishop or high prince demanded either crucifixion or payment of seven ancillae. The decree also required that if blood money was paid in specie, one-third must be in silver, a clear indication that ancillae were only a unit of account, and not a tangible means of payment.

Probably the second century A.D. saw the kumal transformed into an abstract unit of account. The laws under King Fegus, king of Uldah, required a blood money payment of "seven kumals of silver" and "seven kumals of land" for the murder of anyone under the king's protection. These laws clearly show that land and silver were mediums of exchange, and kumals were only a unit of account. These laws were set forth in two legal texts, the *Senchus Mor* and the

Book of Aicill, both of which contained a table legally sanctioning the kumal standard. According to this table:

8 wheat-grains = 1 pinginn of silver
3 pinginns = 1 screpall
3 screpalls = 1 sheep
4 sheep = 1 heifer
6 heifers = 1 cow
3 cows = 1 kumal

The example of slave-girl money in Ireland brings to the forefront four separate functions of money. Money serves as a medium of exchange, a store of wealth, a unit of account or measure of value, and a standard of deferred payment. The slave-girl money evolved into a unit of account only, while the other roles of money were filled by various commodities, land, and precious metals.

The origin of the social acceptance of the use of kumals as a medium of exchange may have stemmed from the prestige conferred by slave ownership. Also, slaves may have been regarded as the rightful spoils of war, and warriors capturing more slaves than they could employ were free to trade them for land, livestock, and goods and services that they needed. Perhaps the spread of Christianity in Ireland and the concept of Christian love helped liberate Ireland from the base practice of actually exchanging human beings in trade, making kumals less acceptable as a medium of exchange, but still sanctioned by tradition as a unit of account.

See also: Slave Currency
References: Einzig, Paul. 1966. *Primitive Money*. Nolan, Patrick. 1926. *A Monetary History of Ireland*. Powell, T. G. E. 1985. *The Celts*. New ed.

Snake

The so-called snake was a coordinated policy among European Community (EC) countries to constrict exchange rate variations between member countries to a narrower band than allowed by the International Monetary Fund (IMF). It was the first stage toward the monetary unification of Europe, a goal that appears now within reach with the introduction of a European currency unit, the *euro.* The snake system began in March 1972 and remained in operation until January 1979 when the European Monetary System (EMS) replaced the Economic and Monetary

Union (EMU). The EMS and its predecessor, the EMU, were agreements of cooperation in monetary affairs between members of the EC. The EMS took a further step toward monetary unification with the introduction of the European Currency Unit (ECU).

Early in the 1970s the IMF allowed the currencies of member countries to vary within a range of $2^1/_4$ percent above or below parity with the dollar, or $4^1/_2$ percent overall. The members of the EMU committed themselves to keeping the variation between European currencies to within $2^1/_4$ percent of each other and fluctuations in the aggregate of European currencies was kept with the $4^1/_2$ percent band of parity with the dollar. The European currencies became known as the "snake in the tunnel' because these currencies moved up and down together relative to other currencies. When the Belgium-Luxembourg monetary union kept its own currency fluctuations within a tighter range, then the "snake in the tunnel" began to reveal a "worm in the snake." When the fixed exchange-rate regime broke down in 1973, and the dollar floated freely, the European "snake in the tunnel," became the "snake in the lake."

The snake terminology survived in the EMS, in which a measure of exchange-rate divergence from other European currencies was treated as a warning sign or signal that intervention may be necessary. This warning sign was called the rattlesnake.

The snake was intended to keep EC currencies fluctuating in step with each other, a preliminary measure to the complete monetary unification of Europe. The transition to a European currency unit, the euro, to be managed by a European central bank, will remove the need for this sort of coordination, as the euro replaces the German mark, French franc, and other European currencies.

See also: Euro Currency, European Currency Unit, Optimal Currency Area

References: Kenen, Peter B. 1995. *Economic and Monetary Union in Europe.*
Padoa-Schioppa, Tommaso. 1994. *The Road to Monetary Union in Europe.*

Social Dividend Money of Maryland

More than half of the first paper money issued by the colony of Maryland flowed into the economy as a social dividend, equivalent to a gift to each inhabitant over 15 years of age. Historically, the major sources of paper money have been banks that issued it on the strength of promissory notes, and governments that issued it to finance government expenditures. Often governments have issued paper money during wartime when demands upon government spending are particularly heavy. Maryland's first experiment with paper money was unique for that era because its colonial government issued paper money solely for the purpose of stimulating the private economy, without feeling pressure to finance a portion of the public sector's budget.

Like other American colonies Maryland struggled against a shortage of currency that kept the colonial economy on a tight leash, limiting trade to what could be transacted with a limited money supply. England made no special provision to supply the colonies with coins and currency, and the colonies had to get by with what could be earned from trade with the rest of the world. To infuse additional coin into the local economy, the Maryland legislature in 1729 granted a 15 percent reduction in import and export duties if they were paid with imported gold or silver.

Maryland shared with Virginia an almost exclusive dependence upon tobacco, either to pay for foreign trade or as the principal medium of exchange in the local economy. In the eighteenth century, however, tobacco production outpaced demand and the price of tobacco on the world market steadily declined, accounting for the depression in Maryland's economy. Maryland's first proposal for issuing paper money was part of a scheme for limiting tobacco production in an effort to raise the price of tobacco. In 1731 the Maryland legislature enacted a law that provided for the issuance of 30,000 English pounds of paper money to pay for tobacco that would be taken out of production. For each 6,000 tobacco plants standing during the month of July, the owner was to burn and destroy 150 pounds of tobacco. In return for each 150 pounds of tobacco destroyed the owner received from the colonial government 15 shillings in paper currency. For some reason this plan was never implemented and the paper money never issued.

The Currency Law of 1733 provided for the social dividend money issue. It authorized the issuance of 90,000 English pounds, 48,000 of which were to be distributed as a "bounty of thirty shillings per taxable." That included all citizens over 15 years of age excepting ministers of the Church of

England, imported male servants, and slaves. The government issued the remaining 42,000 pounds as loans paying 4 percent interest and secured by real estate appraised at twice the value of the loans. The government levied a tax of 1 shilling and 3 pence per hogshead of tobacco exported from Maryland. The proceeds of this tax paid for investment in Bank of England stock, creating a fund for redeeming the paper money, beginning at the end of 15 years. Within 30 years the government planned to retire all the paper money.

The paper money issue helped finance an economic expansion in Maryland. The paper money depreciated in value moderately until 1748 when the government retired the first 30,000 English pounds. After 1748 the value of the paper money stabilized. The colonial government redeemed in shillings the entire issue of the paper money at face value, making Maryland's paper money experience the most successful in the American colonies.

See also: Land Bank System, Massachusetts Bay Colony Paper Issue

References: Brock, Leslie V. 1975. *The Currency of the American Colonies, 1700–1764.*

Lester, Richard A. 1939. *Monetary Experiments.*

Solidus
See Constantine I

Solon (CA. 630–560 B.C.)

Solon was a sixth-century Athenian lawgiver and poet who, according to a literary tradition, changed the Athenian monetary standard in an effort to extend relief to debtors. Subsequent research has cast doubt on the populist nature of Solon's monetary reforms, but the thrust of his reforms nevertheless eased the burden on debtors. He redeemed land that had been forfeited for indebtedness and freed citizens enslaved because of debt. His laws forbade loans that subjected the borrower to enslavement in case of default. In the life of Solon in Plutarch's *Lives of Noble Grecians and Romans* (1952) can be found the following passage, referring to Solon's monetary reforms:

Though some as Androtion, affirm that the debts were not canceled but the interest only lessened, which sufficiently pleased the people; so that they

named this benefit the Seisacthea, together with the enlarging their measure, raising the value of money; for he made a pound, which before passed for seventy-three drachmas, go for a hundred; so that, though the number of pieces in the payment was equal, the value was less; which proved a considerable benefit to those that were to discharge great debts, and no loss to the creditors.

Solon lived before the Greeks began writing history and ancient authors writing after the event disagreed on the nature of Solon's reforms. Aristotle's treatment of the same subject suggested that Solon's reforms raised rather than lowered the value of the drachma.

The literary and archeological evidence suggests that Solon began the coinage of silver money in Athens. Before Solon there is no evidence of Athenian coinage. It also suggests that before Solon two monetary standards dominated trade in the Greek world, the Euboic standard, and the Aeginetan standard, derived from the older Phoenician silver standard. Solon, himself of the merchant class, preferred the Euboic standard as the standard in use by most of Athen's trading partners. It seems that Solon urged the Athenians to adopt a standard that made Athenian coins most acceptable to trading partners. During the sixth century the Euboic standard spread rapidly and superseded the Aeginetan standard in most areas.

One of the far-reaching provisions of Solon's reforms provided that fines be remitted in currency rather than cattle or sheep as existing Athenian law provided, marking a turning point in the transition from livestock money to coinage. In 454 B.C. Rome sent three commissioners to Athens to study Athenian law. The 12 tables of Roman law drawn up in 456 B.C. did not mention penalties paid in cattle as in former times, but provided for payment in copper coins.

The history of Solon's monetary reforms, regardless of their true nature, opens a theme that is often replayed in monetary history—the secret war between debtors and creditors that invariably surfaces when monetary policies are up for discussion and revision. Policies that change the value of money, either directly by government decree or indirectly by inflation, always tilt the balance between debtors and creditors. When money loses its value, debtors win and creditors lose because the money they receive in repayment has lost some of its value. The opposite occurs when money gains in value.

See also: Aeginetan Silver Standard, Attic Silver Standard, Phoenician Weight Standard

References: Freeman, Kathleen. 1976. *The Work and Life of Solon.*
Milne, J. G. 1931. *Greek Coinage.*
Plutarch. 1952. *Lives of Noble Grecians and Romans.* Trans. Dryden.

Spanish Inconvertible Paper Standard

Spain stood aloof from the classical gold standard that brought monetary order to the world from the 1870s until 1914. In 1883 Spain abandoned convertibility of bank notes into precious metal and never returned to a metallic standard, even in the aftermath of World War I when most of the world's trading partners adopted a gold exchange standard.

In 1868 Spain adopted a bimetallic standard along the lines of the Latin Monetary Union. Like the union Spain fixed the official ratio of silver to gold at 15.5 to 1. In 1874 the government conferred upon the Bank of Spain a monopoly on the issuance of bank notes. The value of silver fell as the world turned to the gold standard, raising the free market ratio of silver to gold to 18 to 1 by 1876. Gresham's law set to work in Spain. Because gold could buy more silver abroad than in Spain, gold flowed out and silver displaced gold as domestic currency. Gold currency decreased from 1,131 million *pesetas* (the monetary unit of Spain) in 1874 to 736 million in 1883. Gold reserves in the Bank of Spain increased substantially until 1881, and then dropped precipitously in 1883.

The suspension of convertibility in 1883 may have been triggered by an international financial crisis, including a stock market crash in France and a deteriorating balance of trade for Spain. When Spain's gold reserves dropped to 60 percent of their 1881 level the government suspended convertibility.

Despite abandonment of the gold standard Spain's prices remained relatively stable; mildly deflationary during the world depression of the 1880s and early 1890s, and rising gently in the two decades before World War I. From 1883 until 1913 the Spanish wholesale price index (1913 = 100) rose from 89.5 to 100, an annual average increase substantially below 1 percent. The exchange rate of pesetas to British pounds rose significantly during the Spanish-American War, when the government ran large budget deficits, but returned to presuspension levels by the eve of World War I. Over the same time span the money supply grew at an average annual rate of 2 percent.

Spain eluded the severe monetary disorder many countries witnessed during experiments with inconvertible paper money. During the heyday of the classical gold standard Spain maintained monetary stability with inconvertible paper, providing lessons that are relevant today. Despite inconvertible paper money Spain's government engaged in only modest deficit spending, excepting the brief episode of the Spanish-American War. Spain invariably ran a trade surplus, exporting more goods and services than importing, and the Bank of Spain accumulated gold reserves, leading speculators to expect a return to convertibility. Spain's experience proved that monetary stability could be maintained without the much-vaunted gold standard.

Nevertheless, Spain paid a toll for not adopting the gold standard. The Bank of Spain kept interest rates in Spain above international levels, a necessary expedient to attract capital from countries considered safer because of the gold standard. Even with high interest rates Spain saw a reduction in foreign capital inflows. The higher interest rates also acted to retard domestic investment in Spain, further reducing indigenous economic growth.

Spain's experience from 1883 to 1914 was unique because it occurred when the gold standard was heralded as the guardian of monetary stability. During the twentieth century Spain has shared many of the difficulties of other countries on inconvertible paper standards. In the 1970s Spain's economy sank into the doldrums of stagflation, largely because the Bank of Spain issued bank notes to finance government deficits. In the 1980s Spain reformed its public finance and monetary policy, and now Spain enjoys one of the best records for monetary stability in Europe.

See also: Gold Standard, Inconvertible Paper Money, Latin Monetary Union

References: Bordo, Michael D., and Forrest Capie, ed. 1993. *Monetary Regimes in Transition.*
Martin-Acena, P. 1990. The Spanish Money Supply, 1874–1935. *Journal of European Economic History*, 19, no. 1.

Spanish Inflation of the Seventeenth Century

The seventeenth century almost from beginning to end saw Spain debase its silver coinage with copper and mint vast quantities of copper coins, causing inflation and shortages, punctuated with fits of deflationary policies and solemn promises of currency reform. Ironically, Spain struggled for nearly a century with debasement and inflation after exploiting vast gold and silver discoveries during the sixteenth century. The percent of Spain's domestic coinage made of copper rose to 92 percent, hardly believable in light of the influx of gold and silver from the New World in the sixteenth century.

At the beginning of the seventeenth century, Spain's government budget was bloated after years of financing wars and the royal pomp necessary for a great world power. Spain's revenues from gold and silver mines in the New World began trailing off, and the Spanish crown turned to minting copper coins to pay for heavy government expenditures. Spain's dependence on foreign treasure had perhaps already sapped vitality from domestic industries, rendering inflationary policies tempting in an economy that could not generate sufficient tax revenue to finance its government.

During the first quarter of the seventeenth century, the government's unbridled coinage of copper coins spawned a wave of inflation that drew public protest. The face value far exceeded the intrinsic value of copper coins and the crown was reaping the difference as a profit for minting the coins. By 1627 widespread inflation aggravated public anger over wheat and livestock shortages, pressuring the government to switch to a deflationary monetary policy. The nominal values of the copper coins were cut in half without compensating the holders of the devalued copper coins. The government began a practice of making solemn promises not to tamper with the currency—promises only meant to be broken.

In 1634 the government resumed a policy of inflationary finance. To save the expense of supplying copper to the mints, the government restamped the existing copper coins, raising the face value. Coins were called in several times and restamped, often doubling or tripling nominal values. Between 1627 and 1641 copper coins were inflated three times and deflated four times. In 1641 inflation reached a peak and silver was selling at a premium of 190 percent.

In 1642 the government undertook a brutal deflationary devaluation, reducing the face value of copper coins by 70 to 80 percent.

In 1651 the government, again short of money for military outlays, called in copper coins of one denomination and restamped them, quadrupling their face values. In 1652 the government returned to a deflationary monetary policy and devalued copper coins. This time the government compensated holders of devalued copper coins with interest-bearing bonds.

Counterfeiting contributed significantly to the depreciation of copper currency. After 1660 counterfeiting was punishable with the death penalty, and burning at the stake awaited those participating in the importation of counterfeit coins.

Monetary disorder reached a climatic crisis in 1680 with silver selling at a premium of 275 percent. The government issued a decree devaluing copper currency by half, equivalent to one-fourth its 1664 value. Prices plummeted 45 percent in a few months, forcing a harsh readjustment. The government began reducing the supply of copper coins, and had ceased minting copper by 1693. Monetary stability returned to Spain and lasted throughout the first half of the eighteenth century.

Nearly a century of monetary disorder ravaged the Spanish economy. The woolen industry in Toledo and the cargo ships sailing between Spain and the Indies shrank by three-fourths and some industrialized areas lost half their populations. Monetary chaos stifled private initiative, contributing to Spain's economic deterioration.

See also:: Copper, Great Debasement, Inflation and Deflation

References: Hamilton, Earl J. 1947. *War and Prices in Spain: 1651–1800.*
Paarlberg, Don. 1993. *An Analysis and History of Inflation.*
Vives, Jaime Vicens. 1969. *An Economic History of Spain.*

Spartan Iron Currency

In about 600 B.C. Lycurgus, the famous Spartan lawgiver, put into Sparta's constitution a provision that banned the circulation and possession of gold, silver, or other precious metals as a means of transacting business and replaced these forms of money with an iron currency, variously reported as being in the form of disc or bars. This provision was part of a plan of social reform intended to spare Sparta the evil consequences of wealth concentrated in the hands of a few citizens. According to Plutarch, Lycurgus, after effecting a land reform that spread out the ownership of that wealth, set to work reforming the currency. In Plutarch's *Lives of Noble Grecians and Romans* (1952) we read that Lycurgus:

> Not content with this [land reform], he resolved to make a division of their moveables too, that there might be no odious distinction or inequality left amongst them; but finding that it would be very dangerous to go about it openly, he took another course, and defeated their avarice by the following stratagem: he commanded that all gold and silver coin should be called in, and only a sort of money made of iron should be current, a great weight and quantity of which was very little worth; so that to lay up twenty or thirty pounds there was required a pretty large closet, and, to remove it, nothing less than a yoke of oxen. With the diffusion of this money, at once a number of vices were banished from Lacedaemon; for who would rob another of such a coin? Who would unjustly detain or take by force, or accept as a bribe, a thing that it was not easy to hide, nor a credit to have, or of any use to cut in pieces? For when it was just red hot, they quenched it in vinegar, and by that means spoilt it, and made it almost incapable of being worked.

Part of the motivation for the reformation of Sparta's currency may have been the discouragement of trade with foreigners, because there is no record of exchange rates between Sparta's iron currency and the coinage of other cities of the same era. It is unlikely, but possible, that Sparta was attempting to compensate for a shortage of domestic supplies of gold and silver, possessing no gold or silver mines of its own. Societies sometimes develop substitute monies when the growth of commercial activity is restricted by a shortage of money. The whole tenor of these reforms, however, seems to have been intended to limit the growth of commercial activity rather than promote it.

Lycurgus's reforms sound a familiar refrain in the ancient literature on money, variations of the biblical warning that "the love of money is the root of all evil." The use of money first spread in the seaport cities, such as Athens, where traders and sailors of all religions and creeds met at the crossroads of international trade. Exposure to foreign creeds, morals, and traditions often weakened the hold of domestic religions on the citizens of the seaport towns. Traders from all over the world, away from home, pockets full of money, made a ready market for all sorts of vices that thrived in these cities. The inland cities such as Sparta, dependent on agriculture rather than foreign trade, sought to protect themselves from the moral chaos that they saw as a direct result of the introduction of money and the massive inequality of wealth in the seaport cities.

History, however, was on the side of the societies that made use of money, and Sparta nearly disappeared as Athens grew to a world-class city.

See also: Barter, Iron Currency, Plato

References: Burns A. R. 1927. *Money and Monetary Policy in Early Times.*
Einzig, Paul. 1966. *Primitive Money.*
Plutarch. 1952. *Lives of Noble Grecians and Romans.*

Specie Circular (United States)

On 11 July 1936 President Andrew Jackson issued an executive order, called the Specie Circular, requiring payment in specie (gold and silver coins) for all government lands sold to the public. The government no longer accepted bank notes in sales of government land. The Specie Circular actually came from the pen of Senator Thomas Hart Benton, who unsuccessfully advanced a Senate resolution with the same intent. Jackson and Benton were both "hard currency" advocates, and Benton had supported Jackon's veto of the rechartering of the Second Bank of the United States. As the bank war raged in the Senate, Benton thundered:, "Gold and silver is the best currency for a republic, . . . it suits the men of property and the working people best; and if I was going to establish a working man's party, it would be on the basis of hard money; a hard money party against a paper party" (Schlesinger, 1945).

With the demise of the Second Bank, banking regulation was strictly in the hands of state governments. The proliferation of banks and the multiplication of bank notes fed a wave of inflation and a speculative frenzy in land. Banks in the East made loans on the condition that bank note proceeds were use to pay for land in the West, maximizing the chance that the bank notes would not find their way back to the lending bank for redemption. By accepting the bank notes in payment for land the government—in effect guaranteeing that bank notes could be redeemed in land—was underwriting the banking system. Benton roared in the Senate: "I did not join in putting down the Bank of the United States, to put up a wilderness of local banks . . . I did not strike Caesar to make Anthony master of Rome" (Schlesinger, 1945).

The speculative frenzy hit the skids in 1837 and Jackson's Specie Circular may belong with the immediate agents that brought down an overextended banking system. By increasing the demand for specie in payment for land, the government forced banks, which now found it more difficult to maintain specie reserves, to contract bank note circulation.

See also: Independent Treasury, Second Bank of the United States
References: Atack, Jeremy, and Peter Passell. 1994. *A New Economic View of American History.*
Schlesinger, Arthur M., Jr. 1945. *The Age of Jackson.*

Standard Drawing Rights

Special drawing rights (SDRs) are a form of fiat international monetary reserves that substitute for gold as monetary reserves in the international economy. The SDR also serves as an international monetary unit of account in the accounts of the International Monetary Fund (IMF).

SDRs were born of a shortage of international gold reserves that arose in the 1960s. Participants at the annual meeting of the IMF in 1967 at Rio de Janeiro drafted an agreement to issue SDRs. Member countries ratified the agreement in 1969, and the first allocations of SDRs came forth in 1970. Each country received allocations of SDRs proportional to its quota of funds contributed to the IMF. The IMF receives its lending resources from the contributions of member countries, which are assigned individual quotas based on such factors as national income and volume of international trade.

Physically, SDRs are bookkeeping entries in accounts with the IMF. Known in some circles as paper gold, SDRs can be created with the stroke of a pen. At first the value of SDRs were fixed in terms of gold. In mid-1974 the gold valuation of SDRs was dropped in favor of a system that defined SDRs in terms of a "basket" of major international currencies. In 1981 the basket was simplified to five currencies, the United States dollar, German mark, French franc,

Japanese yen, and British pound. The value of an SDR is based on a weighted average of the values of major international currencies. Every five years the IMF adjusts the weights, which determines the significance of each currency that enters into the value of an SDR. The IMF last adjusted the weights in 1995.

Individual countries may draw upon SDR accounts to settle international payments that could normally be settled with gold reserves or foreign exchange reserves. SDRs do not play a role in private international transactions, but, by international agreement, are accepted in intergovernmental transactions on a par with gold and foreign exchange. For example, the United States could buy French francs from France's central bank by paying for them by drawing upon its SDR account at the IMF. The United States might use the French francs to buy goods and services from France or buy U.S. dollars in foreign exchange markets, propping up the value of the dollar.

The value of SDRs fluctuates on a daily basis, reflecting the daily fluctuations in the values of currencies in foreign exchange markets. The daily values of SDRs are reported in the foreign exchange tables in publications such as the *Wall Street Journal*. In time SDRs should replace gold and the United States dollar as the principal international monetary reserve. Already the IMF uses SDRs rather than a specific national currency as a unit of account in financial reports. Some countries define domestic currencies in terms of SDRs.

See also: Bretton Woods System, International Monetary Fund
References: Daniels, John D., and Lee H. Radebaugh. 1998. *International Business.* 8th ed.
Daniels, John D., and David Vanhoose. 1999. *International Monetary and Financial Monetary Economics.*
Snider, Delbert. 1975. *Introduction to International Economics.* 6th ed.

State Notes
See Exchequer Orders to Pay, Greenbacks, Treasury Notes

Stop of the Exchequer (England)
In January 1672 Charles II issued a proclamation that suspended payment on tallies and Exchequer orders to pay, an action that became known as the

Stop of the Exchequer. The British treasury is called the Exchequer, because during the Middle Ages transactions with the British treasury took place in a room with tables covered by checkered cloth. The modern term *check* is a derivative of *exchequer*.

During the reign of Charles II the Exchequer discounted tallies and Exchequer orders to pay to goldsmith bankers, paying interest rates above 6 percent. Tallies were wooden sticks that represented a debt of the government and Exchequer orders to pay were paper orders that were replacing the wood tallies, which were a holdover from the Middle Ages. The goldsmith bankers paid 6 percent interest on near-money accounts (deposits not readily available on demand, such as modern certificates of deposit) in order to raise funds for discounting tallies and paper orders from the government. Tallies and paper orders were similar to some present-day government bonds that are bought at a *discount* (an amount less than face value), and can be redeemed at face value at some maturity date in the future. The government pledged to redeem the tallies and paper orders in a rotating order.

When the goldsmith bankers had no more money to loan out, and were no longer able to discount tallies and paper orders, Charles stopped redemption of the tallies and paper orders already held by the goldsmiths. This Stop of the Exchequer initially caused a run on the goldsmith bankers and many were eventually ruined by this action. Later the government honored about half of its debt to the goldsmith bankers.

The Stop of the Exchequer reminded people of the seizure of the mint in 1640 and created more doubt about government involvement in banking. It also cast a shadow on paper money, and postponed the development of an institution such as the Bank of England for another 20 years. The credibility of government money suffered a severe setback from this experience, and in England issuing paper money became the province of banks.

See also: Bank of England, Seizure of the Mint, Tallies
References: Davies, Glyn. 1994. *A History of Money.* Horsefield, J. K. 1982. Stop of the Exchequer Revisited. *Economic History Review*, 35, no. 4.

Suffolk System

The Suffolk System was the first effort to regulate private banking in the United States. Although banking regulation later became a government activity, the Suffolk System was born of a private initiative that saw a need to regulate country banks.

The Suffolk Bank of Boston first established the Suffolk System in 1819 and in 1824 six other Boston banks joined the system. The Suffolk System required country banks around Boston to deposit reserve balances totaling $5,000 in one or more of the seven Boston banks participating in the system. These reserve balances acted as a guarantee that country banks could always redeem their bank notes in specie.

In the pre–Civil War United States individual banks issued their own bank notes, rather than the current practice of issuing checkbooks or debit cards to accompany checking accounts. In today's United States economy, only the Federal Reserve System can issue bank notes. Under the banking system in which individual banks issued their own bank notes, financially sound banks could always redeem their bank notes in gold and silver coinage; therefore their bank notes circulated at face value, and were accepted in trade as equivalent to gold and silver coinage or other bank notes. Bankers, however, often fell prey to the temptation to issue more bank notes than was reasonable, considering the bank's gold and silver coin reserves. This left the public holding bank notes that they could not be confident would be redeemed in gold and silver coin. These bank notes circulated below par and anyone accepting one of these bank notes in trade risked taking a loss. Banks that often had to take bank notes as deposits were particularly vulnerable to sustaining a loss from bank notes issued by overextended banks.

The Suffolk System was designed to protect the public and Boston banks from country banks that issued more bank notes than they could be counted on to redeem in gold and silver coin. The Suffolk banks always accepted at par the bank notes of country banks that maintained reserves in the Suffolk System.

In the course of trade bank notes issued by country banks flowed into the hands of the Suffolk banks. The Suffolk banks then immediately presented these bank notes to the issuing banks for redemption, as a way of keeping the issuing banks honest. The Suffolk banks, however, treated the banks that kept reserves within the Suffolk System with a certain amount of consideration, allowing these banks to redeem their bank notes at a steady pace over time. Country banks refusing to keep reserves in the Suffolk System often found themselves suddenly presented with a large volume of their bank notes for immediate redemption, putting an intolerable strain on reserves of gold and silver coin. Without a legal sanction, the Suffolk System was able to coerce the country banks to participate in the Suffolk System.

By 1825 virtually all New England bank notes could be converted at face value in the bank notes of any other bank, or in gold and silver coin, due in no small part to the discipline enforced by the Suffolk System. From 1825 to 1860 New England boasted of the advantages of a uniform currency, a rare accomplishment at that stage of the history of paper money in America. The practice of centralizing reserves in a few banks made itself felt in the development of modern central banks such as the Federal Reserve System.

See also: Central Bank, Federal Reserve System, New York Safety Fund

References: Calomiris, Charles W., and Charles M. Kahn. 1996. The Efficiency of Self-Regulated Payments Systems: Learning from the Suffolk System. *Journal of Money, Credit, and Banking*, 28, no. 4 (November): 766–797.

Davis, Lance E., J. R. T. Hughes and D. M. McDougall. 1969. *American Economic History*.

Myers, Margaret G. 1970. *A Financial History of the United States*.

Sugar Standard of the West Indies

From the mid-seventeenth century sugar became the reigning monetary standard on the Leeward Islands, and to a lessor extent on Barbados and Jamaica. Jamaica, because of its importance as a naval base as well as a favorite of the buccaneers, was always furnished with a plentiful supply of coins, but nevertheless made use of sugar money. Barbados and the Leeward Islands perennially wrestled with coinage shortages, forcing the expedient of commodity money. Before sugar rose to the forefront, tobacco met the need for a medium of exchange and unit of account in the West Indies.

A Barbados law of 1645 concerning family prayers provided that "whomsoever shall swear or curse, if a master or freeman he shall forfeit for every offense 4 pounds of sugar; if a servant, 2 pounds of sugar" (Einzig, 1966). Fees and wages were also

measured and sometime paid in Muscovado or brown sugar at rates established by an act of the legislature. A rate of 10 shillings per 100 pounds of sugar prevailed for a while as the monetary standard of Barbados.

Sugar displaced tobacco a bit later on the Leeward Islands. Laws enacted in 1644 and 1688 declared that a fine of a 1,000 pounds of good tobacco in a roll awaited anyone found guilty of commerce with the heathen or Sabbath breaking by "unlawful gaming, immoderate and uncivil drinking—or any other prophane and illicious Labours of the Weekdays, as digging, hoeing, baking, crabbing, shooting and such like indecent actions" (Einzig, 1966).

The Leeward Islands turned to sugar as the monetary commodity after midcentury. In 1668 Montserrat paid an "able preaching Orthodox Minister" a salary of "fourteen thousand pounds of sugar or the value thereof in Tobacco, Cotton Wool, or indigo." The going rate for sanctifying a marriage was 100 pounds of sugar or "the value thereof in Tobacco, Cotton Wool or Indigo." For about 30 years the sugar standard on the islands maintained a stable parity for sugar, equating "five score pound of good dry merchantable Muscavado Sugar" to 12 shillings and 6 pence.

By the beginning of the eighteenth century metallic currency had made inroads into the Leeward Islands' monetary system. An act of 1700 provided that coinage could be substituted for commodities in payment of debts at a rate of:

12 shillings and 6 pence for 100 pounds of muscavado sugar
2 shillings for one pound of indigo
9 pence for one pound of cotton wool
1 $\frac{1}{2}$ pence for one pound of tobacco or ginger
(Einzig, 1966)

Sugar played a modest monetary role in the eighteenth century. On 24 August 1753 the assembly of Nevis considered, but failed to enact, legislation making sugar and other commodities legal tender for debts in an attempt to ease a shortage of metallic currency. In 1751 Jamaica, which did not have a coin shortage, enacted legislation making sugar legal tender "where both parties agree for payment in sugar and other produce of this kind." In 1756 up to two-thirds of a tax obligation in Antigua could be paid in sugar. In 1784 St. Christopher enacted revenue legislation stating that, "And whereas it may be burdensome and oppressive to the inhabitants of this Island to pay the amount in specie, be it enacted that the payment of the taxes aforesaid may be in cash, sugar, or rum at the option of the person or persons liable to pay the same" (Einzig, 1966).

By the end of the eighteenth century coins had edged out commodity money in the West Indies.

See also: Commodity Money, Commodity Monetary
    Standard
References: Einzig, Paul. 1966. *Primitive Money*.
Nettels, Curtis P. 1934. *The Money Supply of the American
    Colonies before 1720*.
Quiggin, A. Hingston. 1949. *A Survey of Primitive Money*.

Suspension of Payments in War of 1812 (United States)

The British attack on Washington in 1814 unnerved the public's confidence in a banking system that had overextended itself in the issuance of bank notes. Banks in the Washington area suspended payments on their obligations to redeem bank notes, touching off a round of payment suspensions that spread to every region except New England.

In the early banking system individual banks issued their own bank notes, which they were obliged to redeem in gold and silver coin (specie). Bank customers received bank notes instead of a checking account and checkbook, and each bank held reserves of coin to redeem bank notes, just as a modern bank holds vault cash and other reserves to redeem checking accounts. A suspension of payments meant that banks no longer redeemed their bank notes with specie, putting the United States on an inconvertible paper standard. An inconvertible paper standard is a monetary system based on paper money that cannot be converted into precious metal at an official rate.

The War of 1812 contributed only part of the pressure on the banking system that preceded the crisis. From 1799 until 1811 the First Bank of the United States oversaw the banking system and made sure that individual banks could redeem their bank notes in coin. In 1811 the First Bank lost its charter from the United States government, substantially removing what regulation there was of state-chartered banks. From 1811 to 1815 the number of banks increased from 88 to 208, and the value of

bank notes in circulation rose from $23 million to $110 million. The capitalization of the banking system only doubled during the same time, and most states allowed banks to issue bank notes without regard to capital or reserves. The circulation of bank notes had outgrown the supply of gold and silver, leaving the banking system floating on a thin film of public confidence. After the suspension of payments these bank notes circulated at discounted values, usually between 10 and 20 percent, but some notes from Kentucky banks were discounted 75 percent.

The United States government encountered difficulty financing the war because its bonds not only sold at a discount, but it received payment in depreciated bank notes. In addition to interest-bearing bonds, the Treasury issued $5 noninterest-bearing notes that were not legal tender but were acceptable as payment of taxes.

Congress soon regretted its decision not to renew the First Bank's charter, and in 1816 granted a charter for the Second Bank of the United States. The bank opened for business on 17 January 1817 and by February had negotiated agreements with state banks in major cities to resume redemption of bank notes in of gold and silver coins.

The suspension of payments put the United States on an inconvertible paper standard for over two years, a rather short time considering that England from 1797 until 1821 was on an inconvertible paper standard. Just as England avoided the excesses of the paper money of French Revolution, the United States during the War of 1812 avoided the excesses of paper money that arose during the American Revolution. Today, virtually all countries are on an inconvertible paper standard.

See also: Inconvertible Paper Standard, Second Bank of the
    United States
References: Chown, John F. 1994. *A History of Money*.
Hepburn, A. Barton. 1924. *A History of the Currency of the
    United States*.
Meyers, Margaret, G. 1970. *A Financial History of the United
    States*.
Timberlake, Richard H. 1978. *The Origins of Central Banking
    in the United States*.

Sweden's Copper Standard

Like most European countries, Sweden emerged from the medieval period on a silver standard. In 1625, however, Sweden monetized copper and switched to a

In 1720 a Danish diplomat wrote home that "a daler is the size of a quarto page." (Smithsonian Institution, National Numismatic Collection)

bimetallic standard based on copper and silver. As often happened under bimetallic systems, one metal currency drove out the other metal currency, and in Sweden's case copper currency displaced the silver currency in domestic circulation, putting Sweden on a copper standard. Sweden's copper standard remained technically in effect until 1776, but its operational importance ended in 1745 when Sweden introduced an inconvertible paper standard.

Sweden turned to a copper standard not because of any perceived commercial advantage, but because copper mining was an important industry in Sweden, and the Swedish government sought to increase the demand for copper. Gustavus Adolphus, king of Sweden from 1611 to 1632, felt that drawing copper into use as circulating money would reduce the supply of copper in world markets and lead to an increase in copper prices. Spain, then the foremost power in Europe, had furnished a recent precedent for the monetization of copper when it debased its own silver coinage with a copper alloy. *Vellon* was the name given to Spain's debased silver coinage, which in the first half of the seventeenth century became virtually all copper in content. Spain's de facto copper standard supplied the first stimulus to the copper industry, causing the Swedish government to look to the copper industry, which it controlled, as its main source of revenue.

Because the purpose of the copper standard was to create a domestic demand for copper, it would have served no purpose to reduce the copper weight

of the copper coinage relative to face value. Therefore, the copper coins were full-valued coins, with the face value of the coins close in value to the bullion value of the copper. Because copper per unit of weight was equal to about one-one-hundredth the value of silver, copper coins on average had to be about 100 times the size of silver coins, and the sheer size of the copper coins seems to have been the major drawback of Sweden's copper standard. In 1644 the Swedish government issued probably the heaviest coins in history, 10-*daler* copper plates weighing over 43 pounds each. In 1720 a Danish diplomat wrote home somewhat humorously about Sweden's copper coinage:

A daler is the size of a quarto page ... many carry their money around on their backs, others on their heads, and larger sums are pulled on a horsecart. Four riksdaler would be a terrible punishment for me if I had to carry them a hundred steps; may none here become a thief. I shall take one of these dalers back to you unless it is too heavy for me; I am now hiding it under my bed. (Heckscher, 1954)

The transportation of any sizable sum of copper coins required the use of wagons, and problems associated with the transportation of the tax revenue came to the attention of the highest councils in Sweden's government.

The copper standard failed to increase world prices of copper, apparently because Sweden increased domestic copper production to meet the increased demand for copper as coinage. Nevertheless, Sweden's copper standard did lead to Europe's first peacetime flirtation with paper money. Copper mines discovered that it was easier to pay miners in copper bills, representing ownership of copper, rather that the bulky copper itself. In 1661 Sweden saw its first bank notes based upon the copper coinage. These bank notes, the first in Europe, were an immediate success, being much more convenient than the bulky copper coinage. In 1656 Johan Palmstruch had received royal permission to form a bank and five years later his bank started issuing bank notes. Paper money experiments, however, seem to be especially vulnerable to the pitfalls of success. Palmstruch's bank overissued bank notes, the public staged a run on the bank, and the bank failed. The failed bank, however, was purchased and reorganized as the Riksbank, now the oldest central bank in Europe.

Despite the fear inspired by the collapse of Sweden's first note-issuing bank, in 1745 Sweden suspended its copper standard and issued irredeemable bank notes. Monetary disorder marked Sweden's paper-money experiment until 1776 when Sweden returned to a pure silver standard.

See also: Commodity Monetary Standard, Copper, Riksbank, Sweden's First Paper Standard

References: Heckscher, Eli F. 1954. *An Economic History of Sweden.*
Samuelsson, Kurt. 1969. *From Great Power to Welfare State.*
Weatherford, Jack. 1997. *The History of Money.*

Sweden's First Paper Standard

Between 1745 and 1776 Europe had its first experience with an inconvertible paper standard. Sweden had been the first European country to introduce bank notes early in the seventeenth century, but by the mid-eighteenth century England and France had both made use of bank notes, and France had furnished Europe with its first example of a paper money debacle. Neither England nor France had officially adopted a paper standard when the Swedish government put Sweden on an inconvertible paper standard.

In the eighteenth century Sweden had a parliamentary government, in which two parties vied for power. One party, the "Hats," identified with the exporting industries, the military, the nobility, and the monarchy, and generally favored policies of foreign expansion and increased influence abroad. By 1720 Sweden had lost its Baltic empire, much to the chagrin of the Hats, who wanted to maintain Sweden as a player in European politics. The other party, the "Caps," represented agricultural interests, and what might be called the commoners. The Caps' preference for policies of pacifism earned them the nickname Nightcaps, shortened to Caps, because they supposedly wanted to sleep while the great powers of Europe passed Sweden by.

Before the adoption of a paper standard, Sweden, home to vast copper reserves, had functioned on a copper standard. Copper, worth less than gold and silver per unit of weight, was bulky and awkward to transport in large monetary values, and Sweden turned to bank notes as a convenience. In the mid-seventeenth century Sweden saw its first suspension

of bank note convertibility and bank panic. Bank notes fell into disfavor at first, but the Swedish public found bank notes much more convenient than copper coinage, and bank notes returned to circulation by popular demand rather than government policy.

The Hats held the upper hand in Parliament from 1739 until 1765 and pursued a policy of inflationary war finance, a policy opposed by the Caps. Between 1741 and 1743 the financial strain of war with Russia prompted the Swedish government to look for salvation in the printing press. Because copper was bulky, the sheer cost of transporting copper enabled the government to vastly increase bank notes without triggering an export of copper coins. With copper reserves held intact, the convertibility of bank notes into copper was not immediately threatened.

The issuance of bank notes continued, partly for subsidies to manufacturers, and by 1745 the Swedish authorities imposed an inconvertible paper standard. Unlike the suspensions of payments in the seventeenth century, the public did not panic, but inflation rose to the forefront of economic problems. The Swedish currency depreciated on foreign exchange markets, making foreign goods much more expensive in Sweden and Swedish exports cheaper in foreign markets.

The inflationary policy irritated the Caps, who wasted no time kicking the monetary rudder in the opposite direction when they returned to power in 1765. The Caps imposed a deflationary policy. As Swedish currency appreciated in foreign exchange markets, foreign imports became cheaper in Sweden, but Sweden's export industries had to slash prices to remain competitive in foreign markets. Prices in export industries fell faster than wages and raw material prices, plunging the export industries into a depression.

Political opposition to the Caps' monetary policy mounted as economic distress defused throughout Sweden and the Caps fell from power in 1769. The Caps' experience with disinflation policies inspired a political drama that history would see replayed again whenever democratic governments imposed deflationary policies. Unemployment, bankruptcies, and virtually every other form of economic discomfort invariably accompanies disinflation and deflationary policies, and often democratic governments find it difficult to pursue these policies for extended time periods.

The Hats regained power and reverted to inflationary policies before the Caps returned briefly to power in 1771 through 1772. The political sphere began to mirror the turbulence in the economic sphere, and in March 1772 a bloodless coup d'etat engineered by the Hats displaced Sweden's parliamentary government with a constitutional monarchy. Sweden's parliament survived, shorn of much of its power, and the parties of the Hats and Caps disappeared. In 1776 Sweden established a silver standard, completely breaking with the copper standard and putting an end to inconvertible bank notes.

Sweden's eighteenth-century episode of monetary disorder demonstrates how a society, exhausted with war, may find inflationary policies attractive, and how these policies are associated historically with political instability.

See also: Inconvertible Paper Standard, Sweden's Copper
   Standard
References: Chown, John F. 1994. *A History of Money.*
Heckscher, Eli F. 1954. *An Economic History of Sweden.*
Samuelsson, Kurt. 1968. *From Great Power to Welfare State.*

Sweden's Paper Standard of World War I

During World War I Sweden sought to weaken the link between gold and domestic currency in an effort to tame inflationary forces. Sweden's policy was unprecedented, considering that the gold standard usually receives strongest support from those quarters where inflation is most feared. The nineteenth century had seen several countries abandon a silver standard to avoid currency depreciation, reacting to the depreciation of silver relative to gold, which was a stronger metal monetarily and clearly the preferred bulwark against inflation.

Sweden had adopted the gold standard in 1873. A gold standard country must stand ready to buy and sell gold at an official price in its own currency. A country's commitment to sell gold at an official price in its own currency puts a strict limit on the volume of paper money issued, acting as a guard against the issuance of inflationary levels of paper money. When a country suspends gold payments, as often happens during times of fiscal stress, such as wars, the country expects to see its currency depreciate, and domestic prices go up.

The other side of the gold standard is the commitment to buy gold at an official price, a commitment that Sweden suspended in February 1916. During World War I Sweden supplied war materials and supplies to the belligerents and often received gold in payment. Foreign currencies sold at a discount relative to the Swedish *krone,* and gold would have sunk in value relative to the krone if the Swedish central bank had not been committed to buy gold at the official price. The influx of gold and foreign currencies would not have created difficulties if Sweden's opportunities for importing foreign goods had increased proportionately with its accelerating opportunities for export. Wartime conditions, however, favored exports over imports.

Sweden found itself faced with a swelling domestic money supply, fueled by gold inflows, and a shrinking supply of goods for domestic consumption as exports rose relative to imports. The Swedish central bank saw itself having to buy large quantities of gold that paid no interest. Also gold was sinking in price worldwide, which acted to drag down the values of gold-standard currencies, such as the Swedish krone. These difficulties converged to push Sweden into unhinging itself from the gold standard.

Freed from an obligation to buy gold at an official price and to mint all gold brought to the mint, Sweden continued to import gold, but at reduced prices, and to augment the domestic money supply. Between the first quarter of 1916 and the last quarter of 1917 the circulation of paper money increased 62 percent and prices climbed 65 percent.

Although nullifying the gold standard did not spare Sweden from a bout of inflation, it restrained the levels that inflation reached. In the Stockholm foreign exchange market, the Swedish krone rose in value relative to the U.S. dollar, the Swiss franc, and the British pound. The krone rose about 10 to 25 percent above the value it commanded when it was on a strict gold standard, and Swedish coins were worth 10 to 25 percent more than the value of their gold content.

The Swedish experience of World War I was a reminder that precious metals do not offer fail-safe protection against inflation, as Europe discovered after the influx of gold and silver from the New World.

See also: Gold Standard, Sweden's First Paper Standard
References: Cassel, Gustav. 1922. *Money and Foreign
   Exchange after 1914.*
Lester, Richard A. 1939. *Monetary Experiments.*

Swiss Banks

Swiss banks enjoy a worldwide reputation for protecting the identity of depositors. This important characteristic helped Switzerland grow to one of the world's major banking centers in the twentieth century. Another factor contributing to the growth of Swiss banking is Switzerland's position of neutrality. On 20 May 1815 the Vienna Congress established the permanent neutrality of Switzerland among the European powers—a position the superpowers of the world honored through two great wars in the twentieth century.

Switzerland was not a pioneer in early European banking. Geneva was the first of the Swiss cities to become a banking center. By 1709 Geneva boasted of a dozen bankers who left a name in Swiss financial history, and Louis XIV floated loans in Geneva to finance his wars. Geneva bankers kept close ties with France and remained involved in financing French public debt until the end of the nineteenth century.

Basel developed a significant banking industry only in the nineteenth century. In 1862 the Basel Register listed 20 banks, 9 of which were exclusively devoted to banking.

Financial activity of various sorts appeared in Zurich during the sixteenth century. In 1679 an injunction from the city council prohibited a reduction of interest rates from 5 percent to 4 percent. Merchant bankers, who accepted deposits for investment in securities, appeared in the middle of the eighteenth century. Zurich waited until 1786 to see the formation of a bank in the broad sense. In 1805 the official register of Zurich reported two banks devoted exclusively to banking.

By the eve of World War I Switzerland ranked as one of the international financial centers. Six large banks, Swiss Credit Bank, Swiss Bank Corporation, Union Bank of Switzerland, Trade Bank of Basel, Federal Bank, and Swiss People's Bank, controlled a system of branches throughout Switzerland. These banks floated international loans for European governments and railroad and other industrial concerns in the United States. After World War I, inflation in the currencies of the former belligerents made Switzerland more attractive as a safe haven.

In the post–World War II era three of the big banking houses remained in business, the Swiss Credit Bank, the Swiss Bank Corporation, and the Union Bank of Switzerland. There was also a large network of smaller banks, rural loan associations, and branches of foreign banks. In 1968 Switzerland had a population of 6 million people and 4,337 banking offices, which added up to one banking office for every 1,400 individuals.

In the 1930s Switzerland enacted laws that strengthened the anonymity protection of depositors in Swiss banks. During that time some countries prohibited citizens from holding assets abroad on pain of criminal penalties, and even sent agents into Switzerland to track down assets owed by their own citizens. On the other hand, some people wanted to keep deposits in Switzerland in case they had to make a hasty departure from their homeland for political or racial reasons. Swiss banks began opening the so-called numbered accounts, which substantially reduced the number of bank employees who knew the name of a depositor. Also, the Swiss government claimed no right to pry into bank accounts either to collect information on its own citizens or the citizens of foreign countries. Governments around the world have lodged complaints against Swiss banks for holding deposits of foreigners evading taxes. Switzerland recently has yielded to pressure to open up information on deposits when criminal activity and tax evasion are involved.

In 1997 it came to light that Switzerland, thought to have been a neutral country in World War II, acted as a banking center for Nazi Germany, and that Swiss commercial banks had accepted three times as much gold in deposits from Nazi Germany's central bank as was originally thought. Jewish groups launched a class-action lawsuit in an effort to force Swiss banks to compensate Holocaust victims, emphasizing that Swiss banks held on to dormant accounts of Holocaust victims and laundered millions of dollars in gold stolen from Jews. On 12 August 1998 representatives of Holocaust survivors and Swiss banks announced a $1.25 billion reparation settlement to compensate Holocaust survivors and their heirs.

See also: Swiss Franc

References: Bauer, Hans. 1998. *Swiss Banking: An Analytical History.*

Cowitt, Philip P. 1989. *World Currency Yearbook.*

Fehrenbach, T. R. 1966. *The Swiss Banks.*

Ikle, Max. 1972. *Switzerland: an International Banking and Finance Center.*

New York Times. 1998. Settling Switzerland's Debts. 16 August, at 1.

Swiss Franc

Over the years Switzerland developed a legendary reputation for financial probity, helping to lift the Swiss *franc* above the crowd of national currencies and become a symbol of strength and monetary soundness. Internationally, it is a favored currency for hoarding money, partly because Swiss banking secrecy laws protect the anonymity of depositors in Swiss banks. International pressure has steadily eroded away some of the protection of anonymity afforded to depositors in Swiss banks, particularly for depositors engaged in criminal conduct.

In 1848 Switzerland adopted the French monetary system, preferring a coherent application of the decimal system. Switzerland had first tasted the French system during the Napoleonic era when France conquered Switzerland and turned it into the Helvetian Republic.

In 1860 Switzerland debased its subsidiary silver coins to prevent the exportation of its silver coinage. In 1865 Switzerland was one of the countries attending a conference in Paris that led to the formation of the Latin Monetary Union. Switzerland argued for the adoption of the gold standard and conversion of silver coinage into subsidiary coinage. The union agreement, however, provided for a bimetallic standard based on gold and silver. Switzerland, along with France, Italy, and Belgium, agreed to mint gold pieces only of 100, 50, 20, 10, and 5 francs. The union members agreed to mint a fully weighted 5-franc silver piece, but lower denomination silver coins became subsidiary coinage with reduced weight. Under the union agreement, coins from each country circulated freely in other union countries. After Germany adopted the gold standard in 1871 the Latin Monetary Union broke down, and the member countries adopted the gold standard.

During World War I the Swiss suspended the gold standard and the Swiss franc appreciated relative to the currencies of the belligerents, and even relative to the U.S. dollar. Following World War I Switzerland returned to the gold standard at its prewar parity and maintained parity through the 1920s and well into the 1930s.

During the Great Depression period Switzerland, along with France, Belgium, Holland, Italy, and Poland, organized a "gold bloc" that sought to withstand the pressures for devaluation. Switzerland devalued the Swiss franc long after the United States and Britain had devalued their currencies, and only after France had devalued the French franc in September 1936. The French franc and the Swiss franc were devalued by 30 percent.

During World War II the Swiss franc remained firm, but not as firm as during World War I. In July 1945 the Swiss franc traded at a 3 percent premium over the U.S. dollar. During the post–World War II era the Swiss franc remained strong relative to the dollar and Swiss authorities had to take steps to discourage demand for Swiss francs. Under the Bretton Woods System of fixed exchange rates, slightly over four Swiss francs were needed to purchase a U.S. dollar. After a system of floating exchange rates replaced the fixed exchange rate system in the 1970s the value of the Swiss franc rose relative to the dollar. In the late 1990s about 1.5 Swiss francs were needed to purchase a U.S. dollar.

Switzerland is home to the world's largest gold market, and Swiss residents have always enjoyed unfettered freedom to hold gold, unlike citizens in the United States where the government outlawed the domestic ownership of gold in the decades immediately preceding and following World War II. Bank notes in Switzerland are backed by a minimum of 40 percent gold reserves, suggesting that gold is still important in Switzerland, even though none of the world's major trading partners—including Switzerland—is now on a gold standard.

See also: Swiss Banks

References: Chown, John F. 1994. *A History of Money*. Cowitt, Philip P. 1989. *World Currency Yearbook*. Einzig, Paul. 1970. *The History of Foreign Exchange*. 2d ed.

Symmetallism

Symmetallism is a type of monetary system in which a standard monetary unit is equivalent to a fixed number of ounces of gold, coupled with a fixed number of ounces of silver. The standard monetary unit becomes equivalent to a bundle of two precious metals, combined in a fixed, unchanging proportion. As an illustration, the dollar might be set equivalent to 0.0242 ounces of gold, plus 0.3878 ounces of silver. The term *symmetallism* seems to have been coined by Alfred Marshall, a prominent economist around the turn of the century who proposed a symmetallic system as an answer to world monetary woes. Symmetallic systems were not without precedent, however, because the ancient kingdom of Lydia is credited with striking the first coins from a metal called electrum, which was a mixture of gold and silver found in a natural state.

During the last half of the nineteenth century, the world's major trading partners engaged in a monetary tug of war between a bimetallic system, based upon gold and silver, and a monometallic system relying strictly upon gold. England favored a gold standard, which eventually displaced a bimetallic standard that France and the United States had championed without success. The bimetallic system, like the symmetallic system, made use of two metals, but it set a fixed value for each metal in terms of the other metal. Under a bimetallic system a government might officially set the value of 15 ounces of silver as equal to 1 ounce of gold, and would stand ready to exchange gold for silver at this ratio. Because officially fixed values often varied from freely fluctuating market values, the bimetallic system worked less successfully in practice than in theory. In contrast to the bimetallic system, the symmetallic system does not fix a ratio of value between two metals, but fixes the value of a composite unit composed of a fixed quantity of each of two metals. A monometallic system circumvents the complications of two metals and fixes the value of a monetary unit in terms of a fixed weight of a single metal. Under the post–World War II monometallic gold standard, the United States officially fixed the price of an ounce of gold at $35.

The last quarter of the nineteenth century saw a spreading wave of mild deflation in the face of the strict discipline of a worldwide gold standard, in which the world gold supply did not keep pace with the monetary needs of an expanding world economy. Alfred Marshall held out the symmetallic system as a means of avoiding the awkwardness of the bimetallic standard, while adding to the world's stock of monetary metals, and venting deflationary pressures. He also argued that the value of a composite quantity of gold and silver would fluctuate less than the values of gold and silver separately. He advanced his proposal to the Gold and Silver Commission in the United Kingdom in 1888.

Marshall's proposal apparently made little impression on policy makers at the time, but academic economists found it a fruitful idea that could be expanded. They saw no reason why the number of commodities in the composite standard had to be limited to two, or why the commodities had to be precious metals. They extrapolated Marshall's concept into schemes that included all the commodities in the wholesale price index as part of the composite monetary commodity. These kinds of extensions of Marshall's idea surfaced in the 1980s as anti-inflation policies stood at the top of research agendas in economics.

See also: Bimetallism, Gold Standard
References: Friedman, Milton. 1992. *Monetary Mischief.*
Marshall, Alfred. 1987. Remedies for Fluctuations of General Prices. *Contemporary Review,* 51 (March): 355–375.
McCallum, Bennet, T. 1989. *Monetary Economics.*

T

Tabular Standard in Massachusetts Bay Colony

During two separate periods of rapid inflation, the Massachusetts Bay Colony put in practice a tabular standard in which debts payable in shillings were adjusted for changes in the purchasing power of the paper currency. Under the tabular standard, a 100 percent rise in the price level meant debtors owed twice as many shillings as they had borrowed. Without the protection of a tabular standard, the money that came back to creditors in repayment for loans had less purchasing power than the money they first loaned out.

The first experiment with a tabular standard occurred in 1742, when the legislature authorized a new issue of paper currency. At the same time the legislature enacted a so-called equity law, requiring the repayment of all debts of five years duration and contracted after March 1742 at a rate of $6^2/_3$ paper shillings to an ounce of silver. The most innovative portion of the law, however, empowered justices of the Massachusetts courts, in adjudicating disputes involving debts paid in paper currency, to "make Amends for the depreciating of said Bills from their present stated Value," which was $6^2/_3$ shillings to an ounce of silver. That is, the justices could force debtors to pay more than $6^2/_3$ shillings to an ounce of silver to compensate creditors for the erosion in purchasing power of their money while it was loaned out. (Creditors often do not fully anticipate inflation and do not charge enough interest to compensate for

inflation.) Every six months the purchasing power of the new bills was adjusted according to "the Rates that said Bills then commonly pass at in Proportion to Silver and Bills of Exchange payable in London."

Debtors complained that the equity law only considered the exchange ratio between paper shillings and silver, which might only reflect speculative activity, and ignored the cost of living in paper shillings, which was more pertinent to their lives. In 1747 the legislature amended the equity law to provide that "when any valuation shall be made of the bills . . . in pursuance of said act [1742] . . . regard shall be had not only to silver and bills of exchange, but to the prices of provisions and other necessaries of life" (Lester, 1939). This law did not remove all disagreement about the rate of depreciation of the bills, but it diffused the issue until 1749 when Massachusetts received from England a large reimbursement for war expenditures and began redeeming its paper money.

The colonial legislature faced similar problems during the American Revolution when Massachusetts soldiers complained that their pay, set at the time of enlistment, had lost all but a tiny fraction of its purchasing power. To encourage reenlistment, the legislature computed the original pay in terms of what it would buy in Indian corn, beef, sheep wool, and sole leather, and compensated the soldiers accordingly for the balance owed them in four bond issues, bearing 6 percent interest. The bond issues matured in 1781, 1782, 1783, and 1784, successively.

Soldiers refusing to enlist received similar bonds maturing in 1785, 1786, 1787, and 1788. The legislature indexed the principal and interest on these bonds to the prices of four staple commodities. A statement on the face of these bonds read:

> both principal and interest to be paid in the then current money of said state [Massachusetts], in a greater or less sum, according as five bushels of corn, sixty-eight pounds and four-sevenths parts of a pound of beef, ten pounds of sole leather shall then cost, more or less, than one hundred and thirty pounds current money, at the then current prices of the said articles. (Lester, 1939)

The advent of fiat paper currency opened the possibility of episodes of rapid inflation that was unheard-of in monetary systems based upon precious metal standards, such as gold and silver. Rapid bouts of inflation wiped out the claims of creditors against debtors, setting the creditors against the debtors, and making the hidden seam separating debtors and creditors a major point of social division and political discontent. Massachusetts Bay Colony demonstrated Yankee ingenuity in developing a scheme for balancing the interest of creditors and debtors at a time when inflationary finance was inevitable.

See also: Massachusetts Bay Colony Paper Issue
References: Fisher, W. C. 1913. The Tabular Standard in
    Massachusetts History. *Quarterly Journal of Economics*,
    27 (May): 417–454.
Lester, Richard A. 1939. *Monetary Experiments*.

Talent
See Babylonian Grain and Silver Standard,
Phoenician Weight Standard

Taler
The *taler* was originally a German coin equal to three German marks, but the word *taler* became a common name for currency that, in various guises, appeared in other languages and countries. The English word *dollar* evolved from *taler*, as did the Italian *tallero*, the Dutch *daalder*, and the Swedish and Danish *dalers*.

The first talers came from Jachymov, now a small village in the Ore Mountains in the western part of the Czech Republic. At the opening of the sixteenth

A taler. During the sixteenth century, German states and municipalities minted as many as 1,500 different types of talers. (Smithsonian Institution, National Numismatic Collection)

century Jachymov fell within the Holy Roman Empire and was administered under German authority. In 1516 the local ruler, Count Hieronymus Schlick, found a silver deposit close to his home. As early as 1519 Count Schlick, without official sanction, began minting silver coins in his castle, and on 1 January 1520 he received official approval to operate a mint. Minting silver into coins was probably more profitable than merely selling silver. Between 1534 and 1536 King Ferdinand I ordered the construction of an imperial mint in Jachymov. The building housing the imperial mint served as a museum as late as 1976.

The coins were first called *Joachimstalergulden* or *Joachimstalergroschen* after the German name for the valley, Joachimsthal, where they were minted. The names were shortened to *talergroschen*, and later to *thalers*, or *talers*.

With the stimulus of silver mining, Jachymov blossomed into a bustling community of 18,000 inhabitants. In 1568 a plague left its mark on this mining community, but the most severe devastation was wrought by religious intolerance. Jachymov became strongly Protestant, but the Bohemian monarchy was Catholic. Religious persecution killed the community, which could only boast of 529 inhabitants in 1613, and in 1651 the government moved the official mint to Prague.

In the first year of operation Count Schlick's mint

struck about 250,000 talers. During the years of peak production, between 1529 and 1545, the mines produced enough silver to mint 5 million talers. By the end of the century, Count Schlick's mint had sent about 12 million talers into circulation.

The coinage of talers spread throughout the German-speaking world. During the sixteenth century alone as many as 1,500 different types of talers found their way into circulation from various German states and municipalities. By 1900 as many as 10,000 different types of talers had been minted for metal currency and commemoration medals.

Maria Theresa, a famous Austrian empress of the eighteenth century, gave her name to the best known, longest circulating of all talers. In 1773 the Gunzburg mint first struck a taler bearing the image of Maria Theresa. After her death in 1780 subsequent talers were always dated 1780. After the dissolution of the Holy Roman Empire early in the nineteenth century the Austro-Hungarian Empire continued to mint the Maria Theresa talers with the 1780 date. Following the break up of the Austro-Hungarian Empire after World War I the Austrian Republic minted talers until Hitler invaded in 1937. Mussolini found Maria Theresa talers the favored coin in Ethiopia, causing Italy to mint its own talers between 1935 and 1937 in order to facilitate trade with Ethiopia. After World War II the Republic of Austria resumed the coinage of talers, still bearing the date of 1780. Austria continued to mint talers until 1975.

See also: Dollar

References: Nussbaum, Arthur. 1957. *A History of the Dollar.*
Weatherford, Jack. 1997. *The History of Money.*

Tallies (England)

In England tallies were wooden sticks that functioned as instruments of credit and exchange in public finance. The Exchequer (treasury) began using tallies in the Middle Ages, and by the humor of history the use of tallies survived into the early nineteenth century.

A tally was a wooden stick with notches denoting various sums of money. A notch the length of a man's hand denoted 1,000 pounds, while a notch the width of a man's thumb denoted 100 pounds. A simple V-shaped notch represented 20 pounds. The handle of the tally remained notchless. In a credit transaction, the notched segment of the wooden tally was split lengthwise down the middle and the handle remained with one half of the tally. The creditor kept the larger half with the handle, and the debtor kept the smaller half, called the foil. The two halves would match or "tally." The tallies were assignable, meaning creditors could transfer ownership of tally debts to third parties. In this connection tallies circulated as money.

Tallies entered into the British public finance system in two ways. First, a citizen owing taxes to the government might hand the Exchequer a tally, signifying a debt of taxes. The government would use the tally to pay for goods and services. The recipient of the tally presented it to the taxpayer who had the other half (the foil) and demanded payment. A second use of tallies in public finance occurred when the government issued tallies in payment for goods and services. In this instance the government was the debtor, and tallies originating from the government could be used in payment of taxes. Originally the government pledged future tax revenue from specific sources earmarked for redemption of these tallies. Later the government issued tallies to be redeemed from the general revenue. Tallies used as an instrument of government debt paid interest.

It was this second use of tallies that contributed to the growth of a primitive money market in London. Purveyors of goods to the government received

Tallies were wooden sticks that served as instruments of credit and exchange. (Smithsonian Institution, National Numismatic Collection)

tallies, and discounted them—that is they sold them at less than face value—to goldsmith bankers rather than using them in exchange, a practice that reached its zenith in the seventeenth century. The goldsmith bankers, in turn, expected the government to redeem at face value at some date in the future the tallies that they had purchased. Later, the Bank of England also discounted tallies, creating an even more ready market in tallies and adding to their acceptability in exchange.

By the seventeenth century tallies were already an anachronism, but they were not officially discontinued until 1834. In addition to assisting the emergence of the London money market, tallies reduced the need for money minted from precious metals and eased pressure on the English government to debase the coinage to finance excess government expenditures.

See also: Exchequer Orders to Pay
References: Davies, Glyn. 1994. *A History of Money*. Dickson, P. G. M. 1967. *Financial Revolution in England*. Feavearyear, Sir Albert. 1963. *The Pound Sterling: A History of English Money*.

Tea

The eminent Zen scholar, Daisetz T. Suzuki, in his book *Zen and Japanese Culture,* observes that "If tea symbolizes Buddhism, can we not say that wine stands for Christianity?" Commodities having religious significance have a propensity to take on the characteristics of money. Gold was often considered the metal of the gods and a favored gift to religious temples. Therefore it should be no surprise that tea surfaced as money in geographical areas where Buddhist culture exerted a potent influence.

In nineteenth- and early twentieth-century Tibet, which was a virtual citadel of Buddhism, sheep served as a measure of value, but Tibetans used tea as a medium of exchange. Tea bricks and sheep also acted the role of money in Sinkiang.

In the nineteenth and twentieth centuries tea bricks displaced sheep as currency in inner Asia, and particularly Mongolia. During the nineteenth century the Chinese paid Mongolian troops in tea bricks. Consumers went to the market with a sackful or cartload of tea bricks. A sheep cost between 12 and 15 bricks, and a camel between 120 and 150 bricks. Between 2 and 5 bricks could purchase a Chinese pipe. Credit transactions were negotiated in

tea bricks, and reports were heard of houses purchased with tea bricks. In Burma a tea brick was the monetary equivalent of a *rupee* and circulated as such.

The weight and size of tea bricks were not always consistent, but two main sizes predominated, one weighing two and one-half pounds and a larger one weighing close to five pounds. The bricks consisted of leaf stalks of the tea plant mixed with other herbs and glued with the blood of a steer or young bull. The inferior quality tea went into the production of tea bricks intended for monetary purposes, as if additional evidence was needed to validate Gresham's law. This unappetizing concoction was shaped into bricks and dried in an oven. Value per unit of weight was not a selling point for tea brick money. The transportation of $100 worth of tea required the sturdy back of a camel.

Asiatic Russia also furnished examples of tea brick money, particularly in areas near the Mongolian border. Goods were purchased and wages were paid in tea bricks. Sugar, iron goods, tools, and arms also circulated among various tribes, and in the 1930s jam became a favorite and circulated as a medium of exchange in these areas.

Evidence of tea money outside Asia is scanty. In medieval Russia tea became a form of payment for government officials. Paraguay under Jesuit rule was a barter economy, but there is evidence of tea currency, including for the payment of taxes.

Stimulants and depressants, concomitants of most if not all civilizations, show up frequently as money. Tobacco, cocoa beans, and various varieties of alcohol come to mind as obvious examples. Tea shares some of the characteristics of these commodities and carries a religious significance, rendering it a likely candidate to fill a monetary role.

See also: Commodity Monetary Standard
References: Einzig, Paul. 1966. *Primitive Money*. Quiggin, A. Hingston. 1949. *A Survey of Primitive Money*.

Temple Coinage in Ancient Greece

Before coinage became a monopoly prerogative of governments, religious temples minted coins in Greece, playing an important role in spreading the practice of coinage to the Greeks. The coinage of money on sacred temple grounds, under the direction of priests, brought to bear the full weight of religion and custom to protect the funds of the mint and assure the quality of the coins.

The famous religious shrines of ancient Greece and Rome acted as treasuries, including the temple of Athena at Athens, the temple of Apollo at Delphi, and that of Juno Moneta at Rome. Even the later Roman Republic, famous for clever statecraft, used shrines as repositories of public funds. The gold statues in the Parthenon and the bullion in the temple treasury were part of Athens' monetary reserve. Thucydides, in his famous *Peloponnesian War,* puts these words into the mouth of Pericles regarding the resources of Athens:

Apart from other sources of income, an average revenue of six hundred talents of silver was drawn from the tribute of the allies, and there were still six thousand talents of coined silver in the Acropolis. . . . This did not include the un-coined gold and silver in public and private offerings, the sacred vessels for the processions and games, the Median spoils, and similar resources to the amount of five hundred talents. To this he added the treasury of the other temples. These were by no means inconsiderable, and might fairly be used. Nay, if they were ever absolutely driven to it, they might take even the gold ornaments of Athene herself, for the statute contained forty talents of pure gold and it was all removable. (Thucydides, 1952)

The temple priests handled large amounts of precious metals, flowing in from gift offerings, and revenue from investments in land, mines, and other ventures. In addition to providing religious services, temple shrines became centers of trade, affording safe conduct to travelers to the temple and occasionally constructing sacred roads that led to the temple. Temples were dedicated to a particular deity that protected pilgrims. Temple coins may have begun as souvenirs for pilgrimages held at the time of sacred festivals. In time, temple districts during religious festivals began to wear the aspect of trade fairs, attracting merchants who saw the concentration of people as an opportunity to market their wares. Temples supplied the need for local coins to transact the burst of commercial activity. Pilgrims also needed coins to pay priests.

The influence of temple coinage accounts for the religious influence that is evident in Greek coinage. Coins minted in temples, under the auspices of temple priests, usually bore a sacred symbol associated with the patron deity that protected the temple, or perhaps an effigy of the deity. Coins struck in the temple of Zeus bore a thunderbolt, or an eagle, and coins struck in the temple of Apollo a tripod or lyre. The temple of Artemis stamped its coins with a stag or a wild boar, and that of Aphrodite with a dove or tortoise.

Religious themes remained a trait of Greek coins after civil authorities had assumed responsibility for coinage, perhaps reflecting the high esteem that temple coins enjoyed. Athenian coins bore the stamp of an owl, the sacred bird of Athene.

Some scholars have attached deep significance to the religious symbols stamped on temple coins, suggesting that the stamped symbols indicated the coins belonged to a specific deity, and were sacred to him or her. The symbols also assured the temple priests that the precious metal they received was of the same quality and quantity as the metal they paid out. The sacred symbols may also have helped establish the coins in the confidence of people, adding to the credit that the coins commanded.

Early in the sixth century B.C. minting coinage became the sole privilege of government authorities throughout the Aegean world.

See also: Temple Moneychangers, Temple of Juno Moneta
References: Burns, A. R. 1927. *Money and Monetary Policy in Early Times.*
Thucydides. 1952. *The Peloponnesian War.* Trans. Richard Crawley.
Williams, Jonathan, ed. 1997. *Money: A History.*

Temple Moneychangers

The moneychangers in the ancient world made a market in foreign exchange where merchants and traders bought currency of other countries to carry on trade. The New Testament tells a story of how Jesus entered the temple in Jerusalem, disdainfully overturned the tables of the moneychangers, and showed his indignation with the admonishment, "It is written, 'My house shall be called a house of prayer'; but you make it a den of robbers" (Luke, 19:46). This confrontation between Jesus and the temple moneychangers is another reminder that money in ancient times, particularly precious metal coins, was not embraced with open arms as a means of encouraging trade and securing prosperity. It was more often associated with the dark forces in society. Today, money is regarded as a necessary instrument of exchange in our complex economies, but the idea of moneychangers in the temple still leaves our moral sensibilities in a state of repugnance.

The multiplication of coins minted in various Greek cities, and in Lydia and Persia, created a demand for experienced specialists who were knowledgeable of the diverse weights, quality, and standards of foreign coins. They sat at tables in streets and marketplaces and fulfilled the role of bankers to their customers. In addition to trading foreign currency, they aided merchants in arranging foreign deals, and acted as the custodians of savings entrusted to them.

Temples became home to moneychangers for practical reasons. The temples had to build treasuries to keep safe the donations and offerings they received. The sacredness of the temple also gave an added sense of protection against would-be thieves. Businesses and wealthy individuals took to depositing their money and valuables in temples as a place of safety. Temples had an incentive to find ways to invest their own funds, and sometimes invested the funds of their patrons. Thus, some of the temples began to wear the aspect of banks, including paying interest on funds held in their custody. Temples issued their own money in the eastern parts of the Seleucid empire, which ruled most of Asia Minor, Syria, Persia, and Bactria from 312 to 64 B.C. In addition to coined money, gold, and silver, the temples also owned estates, cattle, and slaves.

The temples at Delos were known for their wealth. Cities deposited funds with temples, which in turn made loans to cities and private persons. The temples of Delos went so far as to hold deposits of clients while depositing their own funds in private banks. During the time of the Lydians and Persians the temple of Ephesus was the place of choice for kings, cities, and private individuals to keep money on deposit. A law of Ephesus of 85 B.C. makes a reference to loans of sacred funds and insolvent debtors of the temple. The temple at Jerusalem was wealthy when Seleucus IV, deep in financial difficulties, wanted to confiscate its treasury, exciting indignation because of its sacredness and the number of widows and orphans with deposits held by the temple.

Moneychangers resided in temples because the rights of private property had not been secured by law, and ancient societies were often embroiled in civil war, or ruled by arbitrary and capricious rulers. The sacredness of the temple helped secure the safety of precious metals in the midst of lawlessness.

Temple moneychangers may reflect a religious element in the origin of money that is often ignored. Commodities that developed as a medium of exchange often had religious significance. Livestock that served as money was also needed for sacrificial purposes and as payment to priests for religious services. Some societies regarded gold and silver as the metals of the gods, or special creations of the gods, making them especially appropriate as payment to priests or donations to temples. Charms that had magical powers were also struck from precious metals. The sperm whale teeth used as money on the Fiji Islands was called *tambua,* from which the word *taboo* is derived, meaning "sacred or forbidden for religious reasons." Because an unlimited demand existed for commodities acceptable as sacrifices to the gods, these goods maintained their value, making them useful as money.

See also: Temple Coinage of Ancient Greece, Temple of Juno Moneta

References: Rostovtzeff, M. 1941. *The Social and Economic History of the Hellenistic World.*
Williams, Jonathan. 1997. *Money: A History.*

Temple of Juno Moneta

The temple of Juno Moneta acted as the mint and treasury for the Roman government. From the name of the temple can be traced the English words *money,* and *mint.* The Spanish word for "coin," *moneda,* also stems from *moneta.* The month of June gets its name from *Juno.*

The most important of the Seven Hills of Rome was Capitoline Hill, a modest elevation even when compared to the other six hills, but at the crest of the hill stood the Capitol, the main temple of the empire. The center of the temple belonged to Jupiter Optimus Maximus, the king of the gods, but side chambers honored two other important deities, Minerva, the goddess of wisdom, and Juno, consort to Jupiter, and mother to Mars, the god of war.

Each of the Roman triad of gods came with different surnames reflecting different aspects of their heavenly responsibilities. Juno Regina reigned as the queen of heaven resembling Hera, wife of Zeus in

Greek mythology, and looked after the interests of women. Juno Pronuba oversaw marriage negotiations, and Juno Lucina guarded over expecting women. Labor and childbirth came within the province of Juno Sospia.

In the fourth century B.C., if we can believe Roman historians, the timely honking of sacred geese around Juno's temple on Capitoline Hill tipped off the Roman people that the Gauls were scaling the walls of the Roman citadel, also on Capitoline Hill, and that an attack was imminent. Out of this episode was born another Juno: Juno Moneta, from Latin *monere* (to warn).

Juno Moneta, patroness of the Roman state, took on various government responsibilities, including the issuance of money. When the Romans issued a new silver coin, the *denarius,* in 269 B.C. the temple of Juno Moneta minted the coins with an image of the goddess and her surname, Moneta.

The temple of Juno Moneta worked as a full-time mint, either melting down existing coinage and issuing freshly minted coins, or minting new supplies of gold and silver bullion. A constant stream of coins flowed from the mint, and the Latin word *currere,* meaning "to run" or "to flow," became associated with money, giving rise to the English word *currency*.

The temple of Juno Moneta furnishes another instance when ancient societies took advantage of the sacredness of temple grounds to protect treasures of precious metals. Temple coinage had a long history in Greece and Asia, but the mint in the temple of Juno Moneta owed its existence to the premeditated action of a powerful state government.

See also: Temple Coinage of Ancient Greece, Temple
    Moneychangers
References: Burns, A. R. 1965. *Money and Monetary Policy
    in Early Times.*
Weatherford, Jack. 1997. *The History of Money.*

Tobacco Notes
See Virginia Tobacco Act of 1713

Touchstone
Touchstones were stones used to test the purity of precious metals such as gold and silver. Touchstones were also called Lydian stones, after the country of Lydia, the birthplace of precious metal coinage and the first country credited with the use of touch-

stones. The spread of gold coinage particularly increased the profits that could be earned from adulterating and alloying gold coinage, and touchstones offered an inexpensive and useful test for purity of gold coinage. Both individuals and governments were known to reduce the purity of precious metals by alloying them with cheaper metals.

Touchstones were cut from black siliceous stone or opaque quartz, brown, red, or yellow in color, with a smooth surface, and convenient for holding in one hand. Ancient and medieval assayers tested the purity of gold or silver by rubbing the metal across a touchstone with sufficient pressure to leave a streak. Different metals left streaks of different colors. The color of the streak left on the touchstone by a metal of unknown purity could be compared with the color of a streak left by a piece of metal of known purity. Nitric acid was put on the streaks to dissolve impurities, and sharpen the contrast between the streaks of pure and impure metal. From this comparison an assayer rendered a judgment about the purity of a metal. Because differences in shades of color can be slight, the test involved a significant subjective component. Nevertheless, the test brought to light the more outrageous debasements, and was sufficiently accurate for most purposes.

Before the development of more advanced techniques the Goldsmiths' Company of the City of London kept test metals of known purity, called touch needles, for use in making touchstone tests. The company made available 24 gold needles for each of the traditional 24 gold carats. They kept similar pieces for silver.

Touchstone tests are not decisive in detecting silver alloyed with copper, but can be used to assay gold with some accuracy. By the fifteenth century the Tower mint in London was using a new method, cupellation, which makes use of the tendency of various metals to fuse at high temperatures. The new method using fire grew out of the experiments of the alchemists during the medieval era.

See also: Trial of the Pyx (England)
References: Davies, Glyn. 1994. *A History of Money.*
Marx, Jennifer. 1978. *The Magic of Gold.*

Trade Dollar
In 1873 Congress authorized the coinage of the trade dollar, a special silver dollar coin intended to facilitate trade between the United States and China, and

The U.S. trade dollar helped popularize the use of silver dollars in the Pacific Rim. (Smithsonian Institution, National Numismatic Collection)

to furnish a market demand for rising silver production in the Western states. At first the coin was legal tender only for up to $5, but Congress later withheld its legal-tender status. The Treasury stopped minting the trade dollar in 1877 and Congress officially discontinued the coin in 1887.

Trade between the United States and the Far East, particularly China and Japan, accelerated around 1869 through 1870, and a popular medium of exchange in the Pacific Basin was the Mexican silver dollar containing 416 grains of silver. The American silver dollar, containing $412\frac{1}{2}$ grains of silver (before discontinuance on 1873), was not competitive with the Mexican dollar. The state of California petitioned Congress to coin a silver dollar containing 420 grains of silver, hoping to draw to California the Chinese and Japanese trade then flowing to Mexico.

The Act of 1873, known in American folklore as the Crime of '73, discontinued the silver dollar as a standard of value in American coinage, but created the trade dollar strictly for commercial purposes with other nations. The act defined the value of the standard dollar strictly in terms of a fixed weight of gold, and silver coinage, excepting the trade dollar, remained only as a subsidiary coinage with a face value exceeding the market value of its bullion content. Apparently, Congress by accident gave the trade dollar a legal-tender status on par with the other subsidiary coinage, making it legal tender for debts up to $5. On 17 July 1876 Congress passed a joint res-

olution declaring that the trade dollar was not legal tender. The Treasury minted nearly $36 billion of these coins, and all but about $6 million of these coins were exported.

The trade dollar was ill starred from the outset. The traditional United States silver dollar remained in circulation, although new silver dollars were no longer minted. The old silver dollars, containing $7\frac{1}{2}$ grains less silver than the trade dollar, were legal tender, acceptable in payments of public debts, and the government was committed to maintaining their parity with the gold dollar. The trade dollar had more intrinsic value, but enjoyed none of these characteristics, giving rise to no small amount of confusion. Declining silver bullion prices put a tighter seal on the fate of the trade dollar, which commanded no official value and was worth only the market value of its silver content.

To put an end to an awkward situation, Congress on 19 February 1887 discontinued the coin and authorized the Treasury to accept trade dollars in exchange for standard dollars or subsidiary coinage for a period of six months. Congress further provided that the Treasury melt down the trade dollars received in exchange and recoin the silver content as subsidiary coinage. Over $7 million of trade dollars flowed into the Treasury for exchange. As a legacy of the trade dollar, many Pacific nations, including Australia and New Zealand adopted the name *dollar* for their domestic currency.

See also: Bimetallism, Crime of '73, Free Silver Movement
References:
Myers, Margaret G. 1970. *A Financial History of the United States.*
Nugent, T. K. Walter. 1968. *Money and American Society.*
Weatherford, Jack. 1997. *The History of Money.*

Trapesite Banking

Trapesite banking is the term for private banking that arose during the mid-fourth century in ancient Greece. The trapesite bankers themselves were called *trapezitai,* and the banking concerns were called *trapezai.* The Greek word *trapeza* means "table," a reference to the moneychangers' tables of the ancient world. The modern English word *bank* can be traced to the moneychangers' bench of the Middle Ages.

Our information about trapesite banking comes largely from speeches delivered in lawsuits arising out of the banking business. No less of a person than Demosthenes, the most famous orator of classical Greece has passed down speeches that shed light on the trapesite banking in his time. The most famous trapesite banker was Pasion of Athens, who came to Athens as an alien resident, and won his citizenship for the value of his services to the city of Athens. In one reference to Pasion's banking, Demosthenes says: "Of the deposits of the banks, eleven talents were interest-bearing" (Westermann, 1931).

Foreign exchange transactions accounted for a large share of the business of trapesite banks. Trapesite banks had correspondents in major cities of the ancient world and merchants could deposit money with a trapesite banker in one city and collect the money from a correspondent in another city. Merchants made use of this service to avoid the risks of traveling with large sums of money. These banks also acted as pawnbrokers. Demosthenes relates a story of a man who took drinking goblets—made of precious metal, no doubt—and a golden crown to a trapesite banker and received an advance. Demosthenes also mentions an instance in which Pasion received bronze vessels in exchange for an advance of 1,000 *drachmas.*

In one of his court speeches Demosthenes describes the deposit business of the trapesite bankers:

All the banks are accustomed when any private person has deposited money with them and wishes the bank to pay it to some man, to write first the name of the depositor, and the sum deposited, then in a marginal note: "It is to be paid to so and so." If they know the man by sight to whom they are to pay the money they write only "The money is to be paid to this man." If they do not know him by sight they also write an additional note stating what person will introduce the man who is to receive the money. (Westermann, 1931)

A system to write checks on deposits was unknown at the time. In the classical period of ancient Greece there is not even evidence of deposit transfers from one depositor's account to another depositor's account.

In the early phase of ancient Greece banking services were the province of the religious temples, the safest place to store precious metals and coinage when law and order was precarious. Trapesite banks represent the appearance of private initiative in banking, which soon began to leave the cocoon of the temples.

See also: Temple Moneychangers
References: Millett, Paul. 1991. *Lending and Borrowing in Ancient Athens.*
Rostovtzeff, M. 1941. *The Social and Economic History of the Hellenistic World.*
Westermann, William Linn. 1931. Warehousing and Trapesite Banking in Antiquity. *Journal of Economic and Business History.*

Treasury Notes

Treasury notes were interest-bearing treasury bonds that circulated as money in the pre–Civil War era in the United States. The notes were not legal tender but were accepted for payments owed the federal government, including tax obligations.

For the first two decades of its existence the new government of the United States steered clear of the issuance of government notes that circulated as money. The hyperinflation of the American Revolution remained a thought-provoking memory of the dangers of paper money, and Alexander Hamilton stood as a staunch opponent of Treasury issues of paper money.

By the War of 1812 Congress was in the hands of people without firsthand experience of the Revolutionary hyperinflation, and wartime demands for

The reverse of a $10 treasury note. (Smithsonian Institution, National Numismatic Collection)

resources pressed hard on government officials. On 30 June 1812 Congress authorized the issuance of $5 million of treasury notes, redeemable within one year, and paying $5^2/_5$ percent interest. The following years saw authorizations for additional issues, $5 million in 1813, $18 million in 1814, and $8 million in 1815. The notes circulated as money and were acceptable in payment of federal government taxes.

The Constitution had strictly forbidden the states from declaring any money other than gold and silver to be legal tender and did not expressly give the federal government authority to declare any money legal tender. Most people at the time felt that the issuance of legal-tender paper money was at best against the spirit of the Constitution, and at worst unconstitutional. On 12 November 1814 Congress entertained a resolution that read as follows: "That the treasury notes which may be issued as aforesaid shall be a legal tender in all debts due or which hereafter may become due between citizens of the United States or between a citizen of the United States and a citizen of any foreign state or country" (Breckinridge, 1969).

Congress brushed aside the idea of declaring treasury notes legal tender in a decisive 95 to 45 vote. After the war the government retired the notes. By 1817 only 2 percent of the total issue remained in circulation.

The money panic of 1837 sent the government into a budgetary tailspin, and Congress again authorized the issuance of treasury notes. The notes were to be redeemable in one year, and pay interest no greater than 6 percent. Some of these notes paid as little as 0.1 percent interest per year. In 1838 Con-

gress authorized the Treasury to reissue treasury notes that had been paid in for taxes or other government obligations, removing an important distinction between treasury notes and circulating paper money. Congress authorized similar issues in years leading up to and including the war with Mexico from 1846 to 1848. By 1850 the government had retired the treasury note issues, but in 1857 a budget crisis once again turned the government to treasury notes to meet a budget shortfall. These notes were earmarked for retirement until the budget crisis of the Civil War overtook budgetary policy. In 1862 the government began issuing legal-tender notes that were soon dubbed greenbacks.

The history of the treasury notes reveals how hesitant the federal government was to issue legal-tender paper money. Congress accepted without question that the issuance of treasury notes with the legal-tender function was beyond its power.

See also: Greenbacks, Legal Tender

References: Breckinridge, S. P. 1969. *Legal Tender.*

Hepburn, A. Barton. 1924. *A History of Currency of the United States.*

Kagin, Donald H. 1984. Monetary Aspects of the Treasury Notes of the War of 1812. *Journal of Economic History*, 44, no. 1 (March): 69–88.

Myers, Margaret, G. 1970. *A Financial History of the United States.*

Trial of the Pyx (England)

The Trial of the Pyx was a public trial or test of the purity of gold and silver coins that began in the thirteenth century and continued into the present day.

In 1982 Queen Elizabeth II and Sir Geoffrey Howe, chancellor of the Exchequer, attended the Trial of the Pyx in celebration of a custom marking its seven-hundredth anniversary. The oldest extant writ ordering a trial came at the behest of Edward I in 1282. Although similar tests were conducted at regional mints, the most meticulous and thorough tests were held for coins struck at the Royal Mint in London.

To conduct a trial a specified sample of coins of each denomination was set aside and stored in leather bags identified by the month of coinage. In 1485 a sample consisted of 10 shillings from every 10 pounds of gold and 2 shillings from every 100 pounds of silver. These leather bags were put in a chest, or pyx, hence the name "Trial of the Pyx." The pyx was locked with three keys, one held by the warden of the mint, a second by the comptroller, and a third by the master-worker. The crown could call for a trial every three months, but the trials were much less frequent.

To conduct a trial, the officers of the mint appeared before the Council in Star Chamber, together with the lord treasurer's clerk and officials of the Exchequer who brought the contracted specifications for the weights and fineness of coins. The pyx (or pyxs) was unlocked before the Council.

The Trial of the Pyx has always made use of the most advanced methods for assaying gold and silver, beginning in the earliest times with the use of the touchstone. A public jury of 12 lawful citizens and 12 members of the Goldsmith's Company of London actually conducted the public testing. If the jury held the coins to meet the prescribed standards, based upon the fineness of the bullion sent to the mint by the Crown, the master-worker received a letter of acquittance. If the coins fell short of the required weight and fineness, the master paid a penalty to the Crown proportionate to the profits the master skimmed off by reducing the purity of the coinage. Of course, the king was never brought before a public jury to test the purity of the precious metal he sent to the mint. Presumably the mint master assured himself of the purity of the metal supplied by the king.

The custom of the Trial of the Pyx bore witness to the ever-present danger of debasement of the coinage, either at the hands of the Crown, or at the hands of dishonest mint officials. The longevity of the custom stood as a reminder of the importance certain groups in society, particularly merchants and bankers, placed on the trustworthiness of the coinage. The Trial of the Pyx helped the English Crown control the temptation to debase the currency, contributing to England's reputation for sound currency and laying the foundation for England's commercial success.

See also: Touchstone
References: Challis, C. E. 1978. *The Tudor Coinage.* Davies, Glyn. 1994. *A History of Money.*

Tzarist Russia's Paper Money

Of the European countries only Sweden beat Russia to the punch on the issuance of government-sanctioned paper money inconvertible into precious metal. Perhaps it is no accident that Russia first saw paper money under Catherine the Great (1762–1795), whose wars broke the power of Turkey and made Russia a player among the powers of Europe. The first issue of paper money, called *roubles-assignats* appeared in 1768 to help finance the first Turkish war. Russia termed its paper money *assignats* before the French issued their own more-famous *assignats* during the French Revolution, which fueled one of the great hyperinflation episodes in history.

The government created two note-issuing Assignation Banks to issue the notes. The supply of *assignats* swelled as Catherine fought a second Turkish war and wars with Sweden, Poland, and Persia. For the first two decades the bourse exchange rate between assignat rubles and silver rubles traded close to par. Toward the end of the century the assignat rubles were trading at a 30 percent discount, and fluctuated around that level until the Napoleonic struggles increased the government's dependence upon paper money. By 1811 a silver ruble equaled 3.94 assignat rubles. The victory over Napoleon brought some improvement in confidence but the trading range remained between 3 and 4 assignat rubles per silver ruble for the following three decades.

Between 1839 and 1843 Russia, under Nicholas I, reformed its currency and issued new silver notes convertible into silver at a fixed rate. The assignat rubles were traded for the new silver notes at a rate of 3.5 to 1.

During the Crimean War (1854) the supply of paper rubles doubled and Russia suspended convertibility of its silver notes. The value of the ruble remained uncertain and fluctuated until the period 1868 through 1875, when the government succeeded in propping up the ruble. Again, a war disrupted best-laid monetary plans during the Turkish war of 1877 and 1878.

Until the adoption of the gold standard (1897–1899) the ruble traded at a modest 30 percent discount, but fluctuated sharply in foreign exchange markets, scaring away potential foreign investment.

Russian adopted the gold standard to attract foreign investors and bring in badly needed foreign capital.

See also: Inconvertible Paper Standard, Sweden's First Paper Standard

References: Crisp, Olga. 1976. *Studies in the Russian Economy Before 1914.*
Pintner, Walter McKenzie. 1967. *Russian Economic Policy Under Nicholas I.*

U

United States Eagle

See Coinage Act of 1792, Coinage Act of 1834, Coinage Act of 1853

Usury Laws

Usury laws either prohibit payment of interest on loans or set a maximum interest rate that lenders can charge. Historically, the medieval Catholic Church disapproved of charging interest on loans. As late as 1950 Pope Pius XII felt it necessary to reassure people that bankers earn their livelihood honestly. In the late medieval period the Church began to relent, allowing certain forms of credit involving the payment of up to 5 percent interest.

In the early history of France, the French crown often forced subjects to loan money to the crown at zero percent interest. Businesses worked around the Church's prohibition on interest. In 1311 Philip the Fair (IV), drawing a distinction between usury and trade loans made at fairs, set a maximum of $2^1/_2$ percent interest for commercial loans between fairs. (The annualized rate of this maximum equaled about 15 percent.) In 1601 Henry IV for reasons that were unclear issued an edict putting a $6^1/_4$ percent legal ceiling on interest rates. The edict was widely disregarded, but his government probably saw it as a way of promoting commerce. Under the regime of Cardinal Richelieu the crown issued a royal edict (1634) further reducing the legal rate of interest to $5^5/_9$ percent, citing the evil effects of high interest

rates that allow people to live on interest income instead of engaging in commerce.

During the time of Colbert, Louis XIV issued a royal edict (1665) lowering the maximum rate of interest to 5 percent. The discussion leading up to this edict was revealing. Feeling pangs of conscience for sanctioning the payment of interest, given the attitude of the Church, Louis XIV before issuing the edict held an informal meeting with five of the "most learned doctors" of The Sorbonne to discuss the matter. The dean of the faculty spoke first and said that such a weighty matter should be discussed at a meeting of the whole faculty. The faculty took up the subject in the light of Scripture, writings of Church fathers, the decisions of various councils, and decrees of popes. One of the doctors reported their findings saying that "no doctor of the Sorbonne could approve the proposition that one could take interest on money or set the rate thereof" (Cole, 1964.)

In 1766 a law attempted to lower the interest rates in France from 5 percent to 4 percent, but it was not obeyed, leaving interest rates in the 5 percent range until the French Revolution, when interest rate ceilings were abolished.

Even in England, the most commercialized of the European states, charging interest was a shady activity. Writing in the early 1600s the famous English philosopher and statesman, Francis Bacon, cited arguments of his day against usury, which he defined as "interest, not necessarily excessive." It was said "[t]hat the usurer is the greatest Sabbath-breaker, because his plough goeth every Sunday that the usurer breaketh the first law that was made for mankind after the fall which was in the sweat of thy face shalt thou eat bread—not in the sweat of another's face" (Bacon, 1969).

Under the reign of Elizabeth I, the English government enacted a usury law condemning but allowing a maximum of 10 percent interest to be paid. The wording of this law reflected the gradual change in the meaning of the word *usury*. Now the term *usury* referred to excessive interest. The legal interest rate ceiling in England remained at 10 percent from 1571 to 1624. From 1624 to 1651 the interest rate ceiling stood at 8 percent, and the period from 1651 to 1714 saw interest rates fall to 6 percent. An amendment to the usury law in 1715 reduced the ceiling to 5 percent, where it remained until the end of the eighteenth century. Parliament abolished the usury law in 1854. Interest rate ceilings did not apply to loans to the government.

In the United States individual states kept usury laws on the books into the 1970s. High inflation rates in the 1970s lifted interest rates well above state usury ceilings, and states repealed usury ceilings to prevent a disappearance of credit financing. The view has survived into the modern era that low interest rates contribute to economic prosperity. The proper method of securing low interest rates, however, is to provide for an ample supply of credit rather than putting a legal lid on interest rates. The ample supply of credit must come from savings rather than printing up new money, which can cause inflation.

See also: Interest Rate, Medici Bank

References: Bacon, Sir Francis. 1969. *Civil Essays*.

Clapham, Sir John. 1951. *An Economic History of Modern Britain*.

Cole, Charles Woolsey. 1964. *Colbert and a Century of French Mercantilism*.

Glaeser, Edward L. 1994. *Neither a Borrower, Nor a Lender Be: An Economic Analysis of Interest Restrictions and Usury Laws*.

Homer, Sidney. 1977. *A History of Interest Rates*.

V

Vales (Spain)

Vales were Spanish paper money notes issued in the late eighteenth century and the Napoleonic era, the first paper money issued in Spain. During the last half of the eighteenth century, the gold and silver mines of Spanish America supplied the lion's share of the world's precious metals, and mints in Spain and the Indies struck most of the coins. Vast gold and silver resources were of little avail when war interrupted the flow of trade with the New World, compelling Spain to turn to the issuance of paper money.

War between England and Spain, the major colonial powers in the New World, broke out in 1779. Charles III, king of Spain, refused, perhaps out of fear, to raise taxes to fight the war. Also a history of defaults and bankruptcies damaged the ability of the Spanish government to float bond issues. A royal decree of 20 September 1780 authorized the issuance of 16,500 vales, each with a face value of 600 *vellon pesos* and bearing 4 percent interest. A syndicate of Dutch, French, and Spanish merchants had offered to extend funds to the Spanish government in return for interest-bearing notes that passed as legal-tender money.

Once a year the vales were returned to the treasury for payment of interest, inspection for counterfeited issues, and renewal for another year. A holder of a vale endorsed it before passing it on in exchange, and the holder of a counterfeited vale was entitled to reimbursement from the last endorser.

The vales were legal tender for payment of taxes and other obligations to the crown, promissory notes and other private debts, and bills of exchange. Creditors had to accept vales even when specie had been stipulated in the contract's terms. Anyone refusing to accept vales as the equivalent of specie faced exile from Spain and exclusion from business dealings with Spain abroad. Vales had legal-tender status only for transactions equal to or exceeding 600 pesos, and recipients of salaries, wages, and pensions could refuse to accept them.

Other issues of vales followed on similar terms. The first issue drew a 10 percent commission to the syndicate supplying the funds, and subsequent issues drew a 6 percent commission.

The strains of the four-year war with England led to a modest overindulgence in paper money, and at times vales circulated at 15 to 20 percent discounts relative to specie. At the war's end, bullion and specie again flowed into Spain from the New World, and vales circulated at par again. The retirement of a portion of the vale issues further boosted their value. In 1781 the Bank of Spain was chartered partly as a means for the orderly retirement of paper-money issues, an unusual mission for the type of bank usually known for issuing paper money.

In 1793 war erupted with revolutionary France, and the Spanish government again balked at raising taxes. At the opening of the war vales were circulating at par and suffered little depreciation despite the

300 percent increase in the supply of vales over the course of the 28-month war.

When Spain went to war with England again in 1796 the strains of wartime finance reached the breaking point. After resisting the issuance of additional vales for the first three years of war, the Spanish increased the supply of circulating vales by 50 percent in 1799. The inflation cooker now boiled over, and vales began to depreciate relative to specie. When a government office began to redeem small amounts of vales in hardship cases, a riot ensued after people formed a long line, and some bought places in line. By 1801 vales had depreciated by 75 percent.

Monetary chaos continued in Spain as the Napoleonic struggle spread to Spain, first with occupation by Napoleon and then by the Duke of Wellington. By the war's end the value of the vales had fallen to 4 percent of their par value. After the war the government stopped printing vales and the inflation ceased.

See also: Bank Restriction Act of 1797, Inconvertible Paper Standard

References: Hamilton, Earl J. 1969. *War and Prices in Spain: 1651–1800.*

Kindleberger, Charles P. 1984. *A Financial History of Western Europe.*

Value of Money

The value of money has to do with the purchasing power of a unit of money. One approach to the measurement of money value is to look at its precious metal equivalent. Under a gold standard, a dollar should be worth approximately a dollar's worth of gold. Under a gold coin standard, the value of a dollar could drop below a dollar if the government reduces the gold content of its coinage relative to its face value. Under such circumstances it might be appropriate to say that a dollar is worth only 75 cents or 50 cents, based upon the value of its precious metal content.

Despite the widely hailed virtues of precious metal backing for money, the amount of precious metal a unit of money can buy is not the essential factor to individual consumers, who have to think of the cost of things they must buy to maintain themselves and their families. Furthermore, under an inconvertible paper standard such as that of the United States, where even the metallic coinage is token money, the value of money is divorced from any precious metal connection. The true measure of money value must be measured in terms of its purchasing power.

The value of money can only be measured relative to its value at a point in time. Assume that $1 is equal to $1 in 1987. If prices double from inflation in the following decade, and in 1997 it takes $2 to buy what $1 would have bought in 1987, then it would be appropriate to say that today's dollar is worth only 50 cents.

In practice government statisticians and economists calculate price indices, such as the wholesale price index, the consumer price index, or the GDP deflator, which show the ratio of a weighted average of prices in a given year over a weighted average of prices in some arbitrarily selected base year. If the base year is 1987, then the price index is set to 100 for that year. If prices go up 10 percent over the following year, then the price index for 1988 will be 110, indicating that it takes $1.10 to purchase what $1 would buy the year before.

In 1998 the United States GDP deflator (base year = 1987) stood at 137.33. The value of a dollar can be calculated by dividing 137.33 into 100 (100/137.33), which equals 0.73, indicating that a dollar was worth only 73 cents in 1998. Keeping the base year at 1987, the GDP deflator for 1970 equals 34.5. The value of the 1970 dollar equals 100/34.5, or $2.90, meaning a dollar in 1970 was worth $2.90 cents relative to a 1987 dollar. In this context it would be appropriate to say that a dollar in 1970 was worth $2.90.

For a currency to be useful as a store of value and standard of deferred payment, it must maintain its purchasing power. A general rise in prices, commonly known as inflation, can be interpreted as a decrease in the value of a unit of money.

See also: Inflation and Deflation, Monetary Theory

References: Klein, John J. 1986. *Money and the Economy.* 6th ed.

McCallum, Bennet T. 1989. *Monetary Economics.*

Variable Commodity Standard

Under a variable commodity standard a currency is officially redeemable in a certain amount of a commodity, such as gold, but the authorities may vary the redemption rate, depending upon other economic conditions. If the commodity is gold, the monetary authorities would vary the amount of gold the central bank stood ready to buy and sell for a unit of currency (e.g., a dollar) to maintain the value of the currency.

One of the legacies of the inflation-ridden 1970s and early 1980s was a renewed search for an inflation-proof currency. Issues surrounding the formation of the European Monetary Union and the planned development of a single European currency, focused additional attention on schemes of monetary reform. In the late 1980s numerous proposals for monetary reform surfaced that incorporated the concept of a variable commodity standard. The common theme in these proposals was the idea of a currency whose value is tied to a weighted basket of goods. The emphasis was on a currency not convertible into a fixed weight of gold, or other commodity, but convertible, at least indirectly, into a weighted basket of goods.

Irving Fisher made one of the first proposals for a variable commodity standard in 1926. He called it the compensated dollar and it required periodic adjustments to the rate at which dollars were redeemable into gold. The magnitude of the adjustments was based upon the deviations of the current dollar value of a basket of goods from the value of the same basket of goods at a point in time. The purpose of Fisher's proposal was to stabilize the value of the dollar in terms of a basket of goods, rather than a single commodity.

More recent proposals abandoned the idea of periodic adjustments in favor of a currency indirectly convertible into a weighted basket of goods at all times. Under these plans, the monetary authorities would constantly evaluate the value of a weighted basket of goods in terms of a weight of gold or other commodity, and would stand ready to redeem a unit of currency in the amount of gold needed to purchase the weighted basket of goods.

The weighted basket of goods in these schemes would be identical with the weighted basket of goods in a price index, such as the Wholesale Price Index (WPI). The weighted basket of goods might be viewed as a unit of a composite good composed of all the goods in the WPI, and combined in the same proportions as in the WPI. The variable commodity standard then is seen for what it is: A commodity standard that replaces gold or a single commodity with a composite of goods. If the value of a unit of currency (e.g., dollar) remained constant relative to its ability to purchase a unit of a such a composite good, then by definition the inflation rate would be zero.

The mechanics of these schemes have not been worked out satisfactorily, at least for operation over an extended period of time. Recent discussions of variable commodity standards, however, may indicate that the inconvertible paper standard may not represent the pinnacle stage of evolution in monetary standards and that in the eyes of some theoretical researchers there is room for improvement.

See also: Commodity Monetary Standard, Gold Standard, Symmetalism

References: Coats, Warren L. 1989. In Search of a Monetary Anchor: A New Monetary Standard. *International Monetary Fund Working Paper*. No. 82.
Fisher, Irving. 1926. *Stabilizing the Dollar*.
Schnadt, Norman, and John Whittaker. 1993. Inflation-proof Currency? The Feasibility of Variable Commodity Standards. *Journal of Money, Credit, and Banking*, 25, no. 2: 214–221.

Vellon

Originally, vellon was a mixture of copper and silver that became widely used for subsidiary coinage in Spain in the sixteenth, seventeenth, and eighteenth centuries. Over its history vellon took several forms. *Calderilla,* an early type of vellon, contained a variable but modest amount of silver, and was coined mainly in the sixteenth century. Another type of vellon, rich vellon, was coined mainly in the seventeenth century and contained a token 6.95 percent of silver. A pure copper vellon containing no silver or metal alloys also appeared in the seventeenth century.

Vellon was coined into units of *maravedis,* ranging from $1/2$ maravedi to 12 maravedis. The maravedi was a large Moorish coin that emerged as the smallest unit of account in the Castile monetary system.

Vellon coinage circulated before the era of paper money in Spain. Just as paper money bears a face value far in excess of the value of the paper, vellon coins bore face values far in excess of the value of their metal content. Seventeenth-century Spain saw one of the last great episodes of inflation before the development of paper money vastly multiplied the inflationary potential of modern monetary systems. As Spain debased vellon coinage to pure copper, vellon coins drove out silver and gold coins according to the merciless logic ordained by Gresham's law. The government called in vellon coins and restamped them at higher values and in time vellon was carried in bags to transact business.

In 1654 the government complained that owners of calderilla had not surrendered them as requested and ordered that within a month all calderilla should be used to pay government obligations or returned to the mint for restamping. Nobles who failed to comply within the specified time faced six years' imprisonment, and commoners faced a comparable sentence to the galleys.

Like modern paper money, counterfeiters saw vellon coinage as an opportunity to profit from differences in intrinsic values, based upon metal content, and extrinsic values, reflected in face values. On 29 October 1660 the government enacted a statue setting forth that: (1) counterfeiting, and efforts to import vellon counterfeited abroad, were capital offenses, (2) importing, receiving, or assisting the importation of counterfeit coins would lead to confiscation of importing vessels, forfeiture of goods, and burning at the stake, and (3) a mere failure to denounce smuggling and counterfeiting merited a sentence to the galleys and confiscation of goods.

Early in the eighteenth century Spain's government limited the legal-tender status of vellon to transactions under 300 *reales,* and placed the practice of selling gold and silver at a premium in a category with "theft, highway robbery, and counterfeiting," with penalties commensurate with the crime. Meanwhile economic growth had caught up with monetary policy, stabilizing the value of vellon coinage, and monetary order was for a time restored in Spain.

See also: Copper, Spanish Inflation of the Seventeenth Century

References: Grice-Hutchinson, Margorie. 1993. *Economic Thought in Spain: Selected Essays of Margorie Grice-Hutchinson.*

Hamilton, Earl J. 1969. *War and Prices in Spain: 1651–1800.*

Vives, Jaime Vicens. 1969. *An Economic History of Spain.*

Velocity of Money

The velocity of money is the average number of times per year that a unit of currency (e.g., U.S. dollar, Japanese yen, German mark, etc.) is spent on goods and services. From a theoretical perspective a percentage change in the velocity of money can have the same impact on prices or other economic variables as an equivalent percentage change in the money supply.

Sir William Petty (1623–1687) may have been the first writer on economics to describe the velocity of money. He advanced the plausible view that the velocity of money was determined by the frequency of people's pay periods. The famous philosopher John Locke (1632–1704) wrote on monetary economics and referred to the ratio of a country's money stock to its trade, a concept bearing a marked resemblance to velocity. By the mid-twentieth century, the concept of velocity was a cornerstone of monetary economics, which is the study of the relationship between the money supply and prices, interest rates, and output.

A measure of velocity can be calculated by dividing a measure of a nation's output (i.e., Gross Domestic Product or GDP) by a measure of the money supply. Between 1945 and 1981 one measure of velocity varied between two and seven. Whether velocity is stable or fluctuates in a narrow range, conditional upon stability in other parts of the economy, remains one of the important theoretical questions in monetary economics.

Under conditions of hyperinflation money loses its value quickly and people try to spend it faster. During the classic case of the German hyperinflation after World War I workers were paid at half-day intervals, and took off work to spend their wages before they lost their value. These are the conditions that set velocity soaring, further feeding the inflationary momentum that begins with excess money supplies.

A depression economy, particularly when coupled with falling prices, may lead households and businesses to hoard money because they are afraid that stocks and bonds are unsafe investments and perhaps because they hope to capture the benefits of falling prices. These conditions produce declining velocity, having the same effect as declining money supplies, sending the economy into a steeper descent.

Many modern economists argue that if the government stabilizes the money supply growth rate at a modest rate, perhaps 3 to 5 percent annually, velocity will also stabilize, and the growth path of the economy will mirror the stability in the monetary growth rate.

The Venetian ducat replaced the florin in the fifteenth century as the dominant international currency. (Smithsonian Institution, National Numismatic Collection)

See also: Equation of Exchange, German Hyperinflation
References: McCallum, Bennett T. 1989. *Monetary Economics.*
Sargent, Thomas. 1993. *Rational Expectations and Inflation.* 2d ed.

Venetian Ducat

During the late Middle Ages the Venetian *ducat* became the preferred international currency, sometimes referred to as the dollar of its time, a reference to the dominant role the United States dollar played in post–World War II international trade. By the fifteenth century the prestige of the gold ducat of Venice made it the standard for currency reform in Muslim and Christian nations of the Mediterranean. The Mamluk *ashraftil,* the Ottoman *altun,* and the Portuguese and Castilian ducat were based upon the Venetian ducat.

Venice first minted the gold ducat in 1284 at a weight and fineness of 3.5 grams of virtually pure gold (0.997 fine), a standard of purity and fineness that would be maintained until the end of the Venetian Republic in 1797. Gold coinage had disappeared in Western Europe after the eighth century, and the Italian city-states were the first European governments to renew coinage of gold. Florence and Genoa first struck gold coins in 1252, and Venice minted its ducat at the same weight and fineness as the Florentine *florin,* a coin that commanded the prestige of an international currency before it lost credibility when

the Florentine government minted issues of lighter weight. The florin also suffered from inferior imitations issued by other governments. The Venetian ducat clearly superseded the florin in the fifteenth century as the international currency par excellence.

Venice has been regarded as the birthplace of capitalism, a forerunner of capitalist cities such as Amsterdam and modern Hong Kong, economies whose only resources are good harbors and social and legal environments that favor commercial and financial activity. In Venice political power and social prestige had passed from the land-owning aristocracy, which still controlled most governments, to a class of hereditary mercantile families who jealously sought to preserve the position of Venice as an international trading center. Although feudal monarchies all too easily turned to currency devaluations, debasements, and seigniorage to finance government expenses, the mercantile oligarchy that ruled Venice weighed the long-term consequences and steadfastly maintained the integrity of its currency, symbolizing Venice's commitment to fair dealings. The Venetians lodged complaints against other governments for issuing inferior imitations of Venetian ducats, and allowed only Venetian citizens to work at the mint, discouraging foreign access to stamp patterns employed to strike the Venetian coins.

Venice was on a silver standard when ducats were first struck. At first the value of gold rose as gold was in greater demand at mints for coinage. In 1326, however, the value of gold dropped significantly, putting a hardship on debtors using gold ducats to pay debts defined in silver. The debtors, including banks needing to pay depositors and the government needing to pay bondholders, persuaded the officials to switch to a gold standard, fixing the gold price of silver at a rate that prevailed before the value of gold plummeted.

During the mid-fifteenth century, the value of gold rose relative to silver, and Venice returned to a silver standard. The name of the gold ducat was changed to *zecchino* and the term *ducat* came to refer to a unit of account, such as dollars are a unit of account in the United States. The Venetian mint began producing silver ducats.

In 1797 Venice lost its independence as a sovereign state at the hands of Napoleon, ending the long history of the Venetian ducat (zecchino) as one of the most trusted coins in monetary history.

See also: Augustalis, Florintine Florin, Return to Gold
References: Cipolla, Carlo M. 1956. *Money, Prices, and Civilization in the Mediterranean World.*
Lane, Frederic C. 1973. *Venice: A Maritime Republic.*

Lane, Frederic C., and Reinhold C. Mueller. 1997. *Money and Banking in Medieval and Renaissance Venice.* Vols. I–II.

Virginia Colonial Paper Currency

In the last half of the eighteenth century the colonial government of Virginia was the last of the colonial governments to have recourse to paper currency. Paper money was not completely new to Virginia because tobacco notes, essentially warehouse receipts for stored tobacco, had circulated as money since early in the eighteenth century. Later, however, the Virginia colonial government issued fiat paper currency that was declared legal tender.

The circumstances that pushed Virginia to the paper currency brink were hardly rare in the history of paper money. Robert Carter Nicholas, a member of the House of Burgesses at the time but not a friend of paper money, explained the rationale as follows:

Money, the acknowledged Sinews of War was necessary, immediately necessary; Troops could not be levied and supported without it; of Gold and Silver, there Was indeed some, what Quantity

Virginia's was the last colonial government to accept the idea of legal-tender paper money issued by the government. (Smithsonian Institution, National Numismatic Collection)

I do not know, in the Hands of Individuals, but The Publick could not command it. Did there not result from hence a Necessity Of our having Recourse to a Paper Currency, as the only Resource from which we Could draw Relief? (Brock, 1975)

The crisis that led to the issuance of paper currency was the encroachment of the French in what is now western Pennsylvania. After Major General George Washington returned from an expedition against the French and reported to the colonial governor about the military situation, the Virginia House of Burgesses in February 1754 authorized the treasurer to borrow 10,000 pounds at 6 percent interest. The treasurer reported back that there was no money to be had or borrowed. Metallic coinage, flowing out to Europe to pay for imports faster than it flowed in, was hard to come by in colonial Virginia.

At first the House of Burgesses balked at the issuance of paper money, but in May 1755 the Burgesses authorized the issuance of 20,000 pounds of legal-tender treasury notes for the use of General Edward Braddock. When Braddock's expedition met with disaster shortly thereafter, the Burgesses authorized another 40,000 pounds. Further issues were made in 1756. The legal-tender status of these notes drew protests, at first ineffective, from British merchants not wanting to accept depreciated paper money in payment of debts.

In 1757 the Burgesses seized upon the idea of slashing government expenditures by exchanging interest-bearing treasury notes for noninterest-bearing notes. It voted to issue 100,000 pounds in noninterest-bearing notes to retire the interest-bearing notes still in circulation. To attract additional support for the idea of noninterest-bearing notes, the Burgesses authorized the issuance of an additional 80,000 pounds in noninterest-bearing notes to aid in the war effort. Although not paying interest, these notes were legal tender and were to be retired in the payment of taxes.

After 1762 the exchange rate between Virginia's paper currency and the British pound began to rise significantly, meaning that more of Virginia's paper currency was needed to buy British currency, usually about 40 percent more. Thus, 140 pounds of Virginia paper currency was needed to buy 100 British pounds. This currency depreciation forced British creditors to accept cheap paper, which was legal tender, in payment of debts owed by Virginia's colonists. As Virginia's paper currency was convertible into ever fewer British pounds, British merchants became more impatient with their losses. Parliament finally passed the Currency Act of 1764, which banned paper money as legal tender in private and public debts. The act applied only to the colonies south of New England because the Currency Act of 1751 had applied similar principles to New England. Virginia continued to issue paper money until the Constitution of the United States put the authority to issue money with the federal government.

See also: Currency Act of 1751, Currency Act of 1764, Virginia Tobacco Act of 1713

References: Brock, Leslie V. 1975 *The Currency of the American Colonies: 1700–1764.*

Ernst, Joseph Albert. 1973. *Money and Politics in America, 1755–1775.*

Virginia Tobacco Act of 1713

The Virginia Tobacco Act of 1713 created the most advanced form of a commodity monetary standard found in the American colonies. Under the provisions of the act planters brought their tobacco to public warehouses, where it was weighed, graded, and stored. The planters received paper notes that were titles of ownership to the tobacco, and these notes circulated as money. Any recipient of these tobacco notes had the option of claiming the tobacco and taking possession of it.

The American colonies, struggling with a shortage of precious metal specie for transacting business, turned to several expedients, including allowing certain commodities to be acceptable in the payment of debts. Several of the northern and middle colonies had a whole list of commodities that could be used in the payment of debts at prices mandated by the government. The colony of Virginia, however, relied almost exclusively on tobacco as a medium of exchange to compensate for the shortage of specie. The government accepted tobacco in the payment of taxes and government officials and the Anglican clergy received payment in tobacco.

Tobacco as a medium of exchange, however, shared many of the defects of other commodities used for that purpose. For one thing, the quality of tobacco varied substantially and debtors always wanted to pay off debts with the lowest grade possible. Owners of tobacco also found ways to pass off lower grades of tobacco for higher grades. In 1705 the Virginia House of Burgesses enacted a law against passing off hogsheads of tobacco that had trashy tobacco packed underneath a top layer of quality tobacco. Another disadvantage of tobacco lay in its bulk and weight, which made it difficult to transport for the purposes of exchanging ownership.

The Tobacco Act of 1713 called for the construction of a number of public warehouses for the storage of tobacco. Each warehouse employed agents who weighed and graded the tobacco that a planter brought in for storage. The agents then issued to the planter notes or warehouse receipts vouching for the grade and quantity of the tobacco. These tobacco notes allowed the ownership of the tobacco to change hands without removing the tobacco. This form of tobacco money resolved many of the difficulties with the tobacco standard and decreased the inconvenience to those who received tobacco in payment of debts, effectively increasing the value of tobacco money.

The act drew strong protest from critics who were against any sort of cheap money or paper-money plan. Because of vehement opposition, the House of Burgesses was later forced to pass a law assessing penalties for burning the newly built tobacco warehouses. In 1730 the House of Burgesses enacted additional legislation that further strengthened the government's system for inspecting and grading tobacco and providing for the rejection of tobacco that failed to meet certain quality standards. This act made Virginian tobacco more attractive in export markets.

The system of tobacco notes worked sufficiently well to delay the introduction of real paper money in Virginia until 1755, making Virginia one of the last colonies to adopt paper money. Virginia's experience with the tobacco standard demonstrates that gold is not the only commodity that may serve as a monetary standard. Any commodity that is universally in demand and acceptable in trade can serve as a standard to support paper money.

See also: Commodity Monetary Standard, Commodity Money, Rice Currency, Virginia Colonial Paper Currency

References: Brock, Leslie V. 1975. *The Currency of the American Colonies, 1700–1764.*

Galbraith, John Kenneth. 1975. *Money: Whence it Came, Where It Went.*

Nettels, Curtis P. 1934. *The Money Supply of the American Colonies before 1720.*

W

Wage and Price Controls

Wage and price controls freeze wages and prices at a certain point in time, and perhaps establish procedures for gradually adjusting wages and prices. Episodes of hyperinflation and wars have most often laid the groundwork for the enactment of programs of wage and price controls. Inflation is rising prices, but also can be defined as a decrease in the purchasing power of a unit of money.

In 1793 the government of the French Revolution initiated a system of price controls that became known as the Law of the Maximum. A decree of 29 September 1793 empowered district administrations with the authority to set commodity prices at rates one-third higher than the levels of 1790. The decree granted municipal authorities the responsibility for setting wages at 50 percent higher than the 1790 level. In 1794 the Committee on Provisions issued an enormous schedule of the national Maximum, or price list. Each district added transportation costs, 5 percent profit for the wholesaler and 10 percent for the retailer, and then published a catalog of prices. Hoarding commodities to avoid selling at controlled prices was punishable by death. Despite the government's involvement in the forcible requisitioning of supplies, the controlled economy of the Revolution broke down. In December 1794 the government suppressed the Law of the Maximum.

The American colonies experimented with wage and price controls to cope with shortages in commodities and labor. In 1623 the governor of Virginia issued a proclamation fixing prices and profit rates. The proclamation issued a list of prices embracing goods ranging from Canadian fish to wine vinegar. A war with Indians apparently created a shortage of goods that led to the controls. The colonial government lifted the controls in 1641. In 1630 the Massachusetts Bay Colony enacted a schedule of wages for skilled workers, coupled with a limit on the markup for finished goods. In 1633 a law banning all "excessive wages and prices" displaced the scale of wages and limitation on markups.

The colonists turned again to wage and price controls to protect themselves from the wave of hyperinflation that struck the colonial economy during the War of Independence. The Continental Congress did not have the power to impose wage and price controls and remained split on the efforts of state governments to control prices and wages. The New England colonies enacted legislation to control prices, but the southern colonies demurred. Goods flowed to regions where prices remained free to rise with market conditions, and state efforts to control prices failed.

During the United States Civil War inflation surged in the northern states, and reached hyperinflation proportions in the Confederacy. Neither the North nor the South enacted a system of wage and price controls during that conflict, perhaps reflecting the ascendancy of laissez-faire economics during the nineteenth century.

During World War I virtually all the belligerent

powers resorted to systems of wage and price controls. By then inventions such as the typewriter had increased the administrative efficiency of governments. In the United States wholesale prices had risen 60 percent above their 1914 level when Congress declared war on Germany. The United States government made use of as many as eight government agencies to control prices. The War Industries Board controlled the prices of many basic raw materials. The Food Administration set the prices for many staple foods, such as wheat and livestock. Inflation slowed substantially, contributing to a general feeling that the controls were a success. The controls were lifted at the end of the war amid some talk that the controls should be extended to the peacetime economy.

In 1936 Germany imposed a comprehensive system of wage and price controls that remained in effect for 12 years. This system of controls was part of Germany's centrally planned economy that was directed toward military mobilization. When the Allied occupation governments kept the controls in place at the end of World War II, black markets sprang up to meet the needs for certain supplies. Germany's rapid economic growth began after the controls were lifted in 1948.

During World War II many countries established some form of wage and price controls to contain inflation. The United States went to a comprehensive system of wage and price regulation in 1942. The Office of Price Administration had to approve of price increases and a National War Labor Board approved of wage increases. The main effect of the controls in the United States lay in the postponement of inflation until after the war. The United States briefly turned again to wage and price controls during the Vietnam War.

The use of wage and price controls to suppress inflation runs the risk that black markets will emerge, and that producers will secretly reduce the quality of products to save money. The reduction in the quality of products, which forces consumers to buy them more frequently, defeats the purpose of the controls.

See also: American Revolution Hyperinflation, French Revolution Hyperinflation, Inflation and Deflation

References: Blinder, Alan S. 1979. *Economic Policy and the Great Stagflation.*

Rockoff, Hugh. 1984. *Drastic Measures: A History of Wage and Price Controls in the United States.*

Wampumpeag

Wampumpeag was a famous currency used by the American Indians, particularly but not exclusively along the eastern seaboard, and became widely accepted by the English colonists. The name of the currency, a bit of a mouthful, was usually shortened to *wampum.* The *peag* meant "beads" in the language of the Indians, and the *wampum* referred to the white color of the beads. The most common color was white but some of the beads were black. Wampum rose to the status of legal-tender currency in 1643 when Massachusetts set the value of the white beads at eight and the black at four to the penny for sums no more than 40 shillings. In 1649 Rhode Island set the value of black beads at four to the penny, but reduced the value in 1658 to eight to the penny regardless of the color of the beads. White beads, however, were taken in payment for taxes at six to the penny. As the white man with improved tools learned to manufacture wampum at a faster rate, the supply increased, and in 1662 Rhode Island ended the acceptance of wampum for payment of taxes.

The shells of clams and other similar bivalves furnished the raw materials for the manufacture of wampum. The estuarine rivers of the northeast of America and Canada made fertile breeding grounds for these clams and bivalves. A typical piece of wampum was a cylindrical bead about one-half inch in length, and about one-eighth to one-quarter inch in diameter. The beads were strung through a hole drilled lengthwise through each bead. The ornamental value of wampum remained an important part of its attraction as a medium of exchange. Wampum strings that traded as money were usually either 18 inches or six feet in length. They were usually counted in cubits and fathoms, but could be divided into smaller values. The black wampum usually traded at twice the value of the white wampum. Both the English and the Dutch made use of this currency. In 1644 Peter Stuyvesant, directory general of New Netherland, negotiated a loan of between 5,000 and 6,000 guilders in wampum, which was used to pay workers who were building a fort in New York.

Several factors caused wampum to gradually lose its value. The Stone Age technology of some of the tribes known for producing wampum had kept the supply somewhat in bounds. The colonists brought with them steel drills that substantially increased wampum production, and the colonists themselves

Like precious metals, wampum was valued for its use as personal adornment. (Smithsonian Institution, National Numismatic Collection)

began to manufacture wampum. Also, part of the value of wampum hinged upon its usefulness in the purchase of beaver skins. As these skins declined in value, wampum lost some of its value as well. In a matter of a few years the Indians saw the value of wampum fall by 50 percent, which they interpreted as efforts of the white man to cheat the Indian.

Nevertheless, in New England the demand for wampum remained strong into the eighteenth century. In 1760 J. W. Campbell built a wampum factory in New Jersey and boasted that one person could manufacture 20 feet of wampum per day. This factory remained in operation for 100 years. The manufacture of wampum still contributes to the tourist industry.

The history of wampum as money among the American colonists shows that advanced societies will find a medium of exchange when more official supplies of money are in short supply.

See also: Commodity Money, Manilla

References: Hepburn, A. Barton. 1924. *A History of Currency in the United States.*

Martien, Jerry. 1996. *Shell Game: A True Account of Beads and Money in North America.*

Taxay, Don. 1970. *Money of the American Indians, and Other Primitive Currencies of the Americas.*

Wendish Monetary Union

From the mid-fourteenth century to the mid-fifteenth century the Wendish Monetary Union maintained and guarded a common monetary standard for cities of the Hanseatic League. The Wendish Monetary Union ranks among the first of the European examples of monetary union, a distant ancestor to the contemporary European Monetary Union.

The Hanseatic League was an association of north German towns, mainly maritime towns and inland towns engaged in foreign trade, that dominated Baltic trade during the fifteenth century. The league negotiated trade concessions and monopoly privileges from foreign countries such as England, Norway, and Russia, often at the expense of local merchants. The league operated self-government trading compounds, called *kontors,* at trading centers such as London, and these kontors were shared by the merchants who were citizens of Hanseatic towns.

The Wendish Monetary Union was formed in 1379 and officially included only four cities of the Hanseatic League, Lubeck, Hamburg, Wismar, and Luneburg. Other towns adopted the standard unofficially, making the union influential over a broad area, including all of Scandinavia. The union regulated the currency of northern Germany until 1569 and its monetary system was based upon a silver standard.

The union struck a silver coin equivalent to the Lubeck mark, containing 18 grams of fine silver, and bearing the coats of arms of the four member towns. The union purchased the precious metal and supervised its coinage, including the activities of goldsmiths and the mint's employees. Compliance with the regulations of the union was voluntary, and regular reminders issued by the union suggest that it had a difficult time maintaining cooperation.

The spread of gold coinage in the fourteenth century was met with a less-than-hearty reception among the towns of the Hanseatic League. During the mid-fifteenth century in Wendish towns the penalty for buying goods with gold was confiscation of the goods. Apparently, the union feared the destabilizing effects of fluctuating exchange rates between gold and silver, perhaps reinforced by the union's own unsuccessful efforts to maintain a fixed ratio between gold and silver. In 1340 Louis IV, emperor of the Holy Roman Empire, granted Lubeck the privilege to mint gold coins, leading to the introduction of the Lubeck gold *florin,* which was comparable to the Florentine *florin* in weight and fineness.

Unlike many feudal governments the merchants of the Hanseatic League never sought to profit from currency debasement. Often governments dominated by merchant princes or commercial classes displayed a strong commitment to currency integrity, perhaps to help attract commercial activity. Venice, living on an empire of trade and finance, maintained the value of the *ducat* for over 500 years, and in the nineteenth century England became the staunch defender of the gold standard against bimetallism, which would have allowed debtors to substitute silver for gold in the repayment of debts.

See also: European Currency Unit, Latin Monetary Union, Monetary Unions of Ancient Greece

References: Dollinger, Phillipe. 1970. *The German Hanza.* Williams, Jonathan, ed. 1997. *Money: A History.*

Whale Tooth Money in Fiji

The case of whale tooth money on the island of Fiji shows how a commodity can become a symbol of wealth in a collectivist society in which most trade in goods takes the form of gift exchanges, omitting the need for a common standard of value. To the people of Fiji the polished ivory teeth of the sperm whale commanded a ceremonial value and sacredness that put them beyond the realm of a fixed value compared with other goods. The idea of pricing a wide range of goods in terms of whale teeth would not have occurred to the Fijians.

Captain James Cook first set forth the customs surrounding whale teeth in his *Journal* describing his voyages through the Fijian and Tongan Islands in 1774. The Fijians called the whale teeth *tambua,* a word that connoted a sacred sense of propriety, a positive sense of what was fitting, as well as a negative sense of what was not fitting. The negative side is captured in the modern meaning of the word *taboo.*

Whale teeth served as the principal store of wealth among the Fijians and were considered precious articles to receive in gift or barter exchanges. No one left unhappy who received a whale tooth in an exchange, making it a de facto medium of exchange for large purchases. In the nineteenth century a single whale tooth commanded sufficient value to barter for a large canoe. It could also purchase a bride, or serve as blood money in compensation for a murdered person. To a bride a whale tooth bore the same symbolic significance as an engagement ring today. According to some reports the power of a whale tooth clenched any accompanying request, whether it was for a specific gift, an alliance, or a human life.

Whale teeth were constantly oiled and polished, and even in the later nineteenth century were preferred to gold. After Fiji became a British Crown Colony in 1874 a native Fiji official of the government asked to be paid in whale teeth, rather than sterling silver or gold sovereigns, citing the added sense of prestige and authority commanded by the sacred attributes of whale teeth in the eyes of the Fijians. The ceremonial significance of the whale teeth survived into recent times. The officials of Fiji made a formal presentation of a whale tooth to the queen of England and the duke of Edinburgh when they visited Fiji in 1982.

The native Fijians were not acquisitive in the modern sense. They traded their surplus produce for particular things they wanted, and if they did not have a particular thing in mind, they let their surplus produce rot. Gold and silver coins held no charm for them when they were first introduced. Fijian whale teeth reveal possible religious and ceremonial roots to the evolution of money that precede the need for a convenient medium of exchange to finance trade.

References: Davies, Glyn. 1994. *A History of Money.* Einzig, Paul. 1966. *Primitive Money.*

Wildcat Banks (United States)

During the pre–Civil War era, wildcat banks, although technically legal, abused the bank note-issuing authority of state banks by issuing bank notes or paper money under circumstances that discouraged or rendered impossible conversion into gold and silver specie. The wildcat banks emerged in a banking system that allowed each bank to issue its own bank notes, which legitimate banks stood ready to redeem into gold and silver specie. As security for outstanding bank notes, state banking laws required banks to own federal or state government bonds, and keep them on file at a state auditor's office. The First Bank of the United States and the Second Bank of the United States had helped maintain an honest currency by forcing western banks and country banks to redeem their bank notes in specie.

In 1833 the demise of the Second Bank of the United States left the banking system without an important safeguard against the temptation of bankers to issue bank notes in excess of their reserves. Bank notes from distant localities circulated at varying discounts, depending upon the likelihood of redemption into specie. Newspapers published lists of good notes and bad notes, and periodicals appeared that were exclusively devoted to the values of bank notes.

Wildcat banks were usually formed without buildings, offices, or furniture, and required minimal amounts of capital. A group of investors would purchase bonds, often state bonds selling at a discount, and file the bonds with a state auditor, who authorized the investors to start a bank. The investors possessed the engraved plates and dies that were used to print the bank notes, and often printed bank notes equaling two or three times the amount of the bonds filed with the state. In practice, the legal requirement that the state auditor countersign each bill did not act as a brake on the issuance of bank notes.

Investors were known to start up wildcat banks with only enough money to buy engraving plates and dies and pay the cost of printing up the bank notes. Investors arranged through brokers to pay for the bonds after they were delivered to the state auditor's office. The investors then brought the freshly printed bank notes to the auditor's office, had them countersigned, and used them to pay for the bonds.

Although bank notes were theoretically convertible into gold and silver specie, wildcat banks were put in places difficult to find. In some cases an In-dian guide was necessary to find what was no more than a shanty located on an Indian reservation. The accessibility of a wildcat bank determined the discount at which its bank notes traded. Brokers dispatched agents to find remote banks and demand the redemption of bank notes into specie. Some of the wildcat banks stationed lookouts that threatened and intimidated strangers who might be seeking redemption of bank notes.

In the early days of American capitalism the supply of capital necessarily fell short of what was needed to exploit the virtually endless supply of natural resources. The wildcat banks contributed to mobilizing much-needed capital, but they cost the banking industry a bit of credibility with the public. Understanding the history that the banking industry has had to live down helps explain why it remains highly regulated.

See also: Free Banking, Second Bank of the United States

References: Dillistin, William H. 1949. *Bank Note Reporters and Counterfeit Detectors, 1826–1866.*

Dowd, Kevin. 1996. *Competition and Finance: A Reinterpretation of Financial and Monetary Economics.*

Knox, John Jay. 1903. *A History of Banking in the United States.*

Rockoff, Hugh. 1975. *The Free Banking Era: A Reexamination.*

Rolnick, Arthur J., and Warren E. Weber. 1983. New Evidence of the Free Banking Era. *American Economic Review*, 73, no. 5 (December): 1080–1091.

Wizard of Oz

The book *The Wonderful Wizard of Oz*, by L. Frank Baum, is one of the most famous of American children's stories and the inspiration of a movie classic that is shown annually on television in the United States. What is often lost in the movie is that the book, published in 1900, incorporated allegorically an important monetary debate in the United States in the 1890s.

The book was written against the background of the free silver movement in the United States. From 1880 until 1896 the United States saw the average level of prices fall by 23 percent, a strong downdraft of deflation that worked a severe hardship on debtors, mostly farmers of the South and West. The bankers and financiers concentrated in the Northeast benefited from the deflation. One proposal for mitigating the hardship of deflation was to supplement the money supply, then tied to the gold standard, with silver, creating a bimetallic standard of gold and silver to replace the gold standard. Under a bimetallic standard both silver and gold could be minted and circulated as money. The infusion of silver would put an end to deflation by increasing the amount of money in circulation.

The political agitation for a bimetallic standard was called the free silver movement. Its most memorable spokesman, William Jennings Bryan, four times a presidential candidate, said in one of the epochal orations in American history: "You shall not press down upon the brow of labor this crown of thorns, you shall not crucify mankind upon a cross of gold." The "cross of gold" referred to the gold standard.

In the *Wonderful Wizard of Oz,* the heroine Dorothy represents traditional American values—honesty, kindheartedness, and pluck. The cyclone, representing the free silver agitation, carries Dorothy to the land of "Oz," as in ounce (oz) of gold, where the gold standard reigns unchallenged. When Dorothy's house lands on the Wicked Witch of the East, the Witch dries up, leaving only her silver shoes, which become Dorothy's. The silver shoes (which were changed to ruby in the movie version) possess a magical power, representing the magical advantages of adding silver to the money supply.

Dorothy cannot find out how to return to Kansas, but learns that she should follow the yellow brick road that leads to the Emerald City. The yellow brick road represents the gold standard and the Emerald City represents Washington, D.C. On her journey to the Emerald City Dorothy is joined by the Scarecrow, representing western farmers, the Tin Woodman, representing the industrial worker, and the Cowardly Lion, representing William Jennings Bryan. The joints of the Tin Woodman had become rusty because the depression of the 1890s had put the industrial workers out of work.

The Cowardly Lion goes to sleep in the poppy field that represents all the issues, such as anti-imperialism and antitrust, that threatened to distract Bryan away from the central issue of the free silver movement in the 1900 presidential election.

Dorothy's group reaches the Emerald City, where everyone looks through green-colored glasses, as in money-colored glasses. Everyone in the city, including Dorothy's group, must wear the glasses and they are locked on with a gold buckle, another reference

to the gold standard. In other words, the financial establishment of the city required that everything be looked at from the perspective of money.

Dorothy and her friends reach the Emerald Palace, representing the White House, and Dorothy is led to her room through seven passages and up three flights of stairs, a reference to the Crime of '73, an act of legislation passed in 1873 that eliminated the coinage of silver. The next day the group meets the Wizard, who was probably Marcus Alonzo Hanna, the chairman of the Republican Party and the brains behind President McKinley's presidency. The Wizard sends the group to find and destroy the Wicked Witch of the West, which may have been President McKinley himself. Dorothy's group finds the Wicked Witch of the West, who, knowing the magical power of the silver slippers, snatches one of Dorothy's slippers in a trick. The separation of the silver slippers, destroying their magical power, refers to the efforts of the Republican Party to diffuse the silver issue by calling for an international conference on the subject. Dorothy angrily pours a bucket of water on the Wicked Witch of the West, destroying her, and getting back her slipper.

Dorothy with her friends returns to the Emerald City, expecting the Wizard to tell her how to return to Kansas. The Wizard turns out to be a fraud and Dorothy seeks out the Good Witch of the South. The South is ruled by a good witch because the South was sympathetic with the free silver movement. The Good Witch of the South tells Dorothy that she can return to Kansas if she clicks her silver slippers together three times, representing the magical power of silver to solve the problems of the western farmers, made possible by the support of the South.

Despite the agitation for free silver, the United States remained on the gold standard. Discoveries of gold in Alaska, Australia, and South Africa substantially increased the world supply of gold, ending the era of tight money. From 1896 until 1910 prices rose 35 percent in the United States, diffusing the social protest that found its expression in the *Wonderful Wizard of Oz.*

See also: Bimetallic Standard, Crime of '73, "Cross of Gold" Speech, Free Silver Movement, Gold Standard Act of 1900

References: Littlefield, Henry M. 1964. The Wizard of Oz: Parable on Populism. *American Quarterly*, 16 (Spring): 47–58.

Rockoff, Hugh. 1990. The *Wizard of Oz* as a Monetary
Allegory. *Journal of Political Economy*, 98, no. 4:
739–760.

World Bank

The World Bank, officially the International Bank for Reconstruction and Development, is the largest provider of development assistance to middle-income and low-income countries, directly financing projects and coordinating development assistance from other agencies. It also serves as a clearinghouse of ideas for promoting economic development, and publishes statistical data and research on the state of the world economy.

Aside from negotiating a fixed exchange rate system for international trade, the Bretton Woods Conference of 1944 organized the World Bank under the auspices of the United Nations. The delegates of the Bretton Woods Conference had in mind financing the reconstruction of war-torn Europe and Japan, and the development needs of the poorer areas of the world. On 25 June 1946 the World Bank opened his headquarters in Washington, D.C.

Member countries, now numbering more than 180, purchase stock in the World Bank, which also raises capital by selling bonds in private capital markets. Member governments guarantee the bonds, reducing the interest rate that investors demand and lowering the cost of capital to the bank. The United States is the largest shareholder and the president of the World Bank has always been from the United States.

The first quarter century of the bank's existence saw an emphasis on financing basic economic infrastructure needed to support industry. Between fiscal years 1961 and 1965 electric power and transportation projects accounted for 76.8 percent of the bank's lending. The bank continued to extend substantial loans to developed countries until 1967. After Robert McNamara assumed the presidency in 1968, the bank began to channel more resources into projects that directly relieve poverty, increasing bank lending on agriculture and rural development projects from 18.1 percent in fiscal year 1968, to 31 percent in fiscal year 1981.

In 1960 the International Development Association (IDA) came into being as a division of the bank that makes soft loans and interest-free loans to the poorest countries. These countries do not qualify for loans from the World Bank, whose lending philosophy is more conservative. Also affiliated with the World Bank is the International Financial Corporation (IFC), created in 1956 to raise private capital for financing private sector projects. The loans of the IFC are structured on a commercial basis with maturities ranging from 7 to 12 years.

The World Bank is perhaps the foremost world leader on economic development issues. In 1978 the World Bank began publishing the influential *World Development Report*, combining articles on current development issues and a statistical report of economic indicators for the nations of the world.

Until the 1980s the World Bank mainly financed public enterprises, but since then the bank has affirmed its commitment to financing private sector projects, and used its leadership to strengthen the private sector in Third World countries. The bank promotes reforms conducive to stable macroeconomic environments, and encourages privatization of public enterprises, environmental responsibility, and investments in basic health and education.

See also: Bretton Woods System, International Monetary
Fund
References: Ayres, Robert L. 1983. *Banking on the Poor: The
World Bank and World Poverty.*
Polak, Jacques J. 1994. *The World Bank and the International
Monetary Fund: A Changing Relationship.*

Y

Yap Money

The inhabitants of the island of Yap, one of the Caroline Islands in the central Pacific, adopted large, thick stone wheels for money, a primitive medium of exchange that survived into the post–World War II era. The inhabitants called this from of money *fei*. A study of the operation of this system of currency reveals interesting insights into the nature of money that are relevant for modern monetary systems.

The stone wheels ranged in diameter from a foot to 12 feet and the larger stones were virtually immovable. The hole in the center of the stone wheels varied with the diameter of the stone, and the smaller stones could slide over a pole and be carried. The stones were quarried from Palau, about 260 miles away, and sometimes from as far away as Guam. Stones could serve as *fei* only if they were made of a fine, white, close-grained limestone.

One of the interesting characteristics of this currency was that the owner did not have to take possession of it. In transactions involving these large stones, a buyer would give ownership of the *fei* to a seller in return for goods. The seller, however, would not actually take possession of the *fei*, but would leave it on the premises of the buyer of the goods. A mere acknowledgment that the seller owned the *fei* was all that was needed to signify its new ownership.

The logic of the Yap monetary system went so far as to acknowledge the wealth of a family on the strength of the ownership of a very large stone that had been lost at sea for several generations. According

Yap money was far too bulky to be carried on one's person. (Smithsonian Institution, National Numismatic Collection)

to tradition, an ancestor of this family had secured this *fei* and was towing it home on a raft when a storm rose, and the stone ended up at the bottom of the sea. Because all aboard the ship towing the raft testified to the size and quality of the stone, and that it was lost at no fault of the owners, the inhabitants of Yap agreed that the stone belonged to the family that lost it and that its market value remained unimpaired. Therefore the family enjoyed the purchasing power of this stone just as if it lay on their own property.

Another interesting anecdote related to the Yap monetary system occurred after the German government purchased the Caroline Islands from Spain in 1898. The German government wanted the natives of Yap to improve the roads and make them suitable for more modern vehicles. When the natives rather obviously neglected to improve the roads, the German government was faced with finding a way to fine the natives. Since removing *fei* was difficult, and the stones had no value outside of the island of Yap, the German government hit on the idea of sending an agent around to paint a black cross on the most valuable stones to signify a claim of the German government. The natives of Yap immediately set to work to improve the roads. After the German government was satisfied that the roads were improved, it sent an agent around to remove the crosses, and a great rejoicing rose up among the natives.

The value of the primitive money on the island of Yap depended upon the faith of its inhabitants. The idea of accepting money on faith must seem ridiculous to modern-day advocates of a gold standard as the necessary backbone of any paper-money system. The acceptance of paper money in our modern economies, shorn of the assurance of the gold standard, requires that people have faith that government will not mismanage the money supply, causing it to lose its value from inflation.

See also: Spartan Iron Currency
References: Angell, Norman. 1929. *The Story of Money.* Friedman, Milton. 1992. *Monetary Mischief.* Gillilland, Cora Lee C. 1975. The Stone Money of Yap: A Numismatic Survey. *Smithsonian Studies in History and Technology.* No. 23.

Yeltsin's Monetary Reform in Russia

Russia opened the 1990s in monetary chaos, manifested by soaring inflation, and a currency, the *ruble,* that had long been shielded from the free-market forces of foreign exchange markets. In foreign exchange markets, currencies are bought and sold with other currencies, as when Japanese yen are purchased with United States dollars.

Under economic reforms, prices, unfettered from state controls, took off, creating a ruble shortage that left some workers unpaid for months. Wages and pensions rose, and the Russian government cranked up the printing presses on a round-the-clock basis. For the month of July 1992 alone, the government printed up more rubles than the Soviet Union government had printed up in its last 30 years. To expedite the process, the government increased the largest denomination of the printed ruble from the 200-ruble note to the 1,000-ruble note. Coins also became available in higher denominations. Inflation reached its peak in 1992 when monthly inflation rates ran 15 percent, and prices increased 200 percent over the year.

In 1993 the government begin to step on the monetary brakes, but in ways that threw the country into deeper confusion. In July the government invalidated all rubles issued before 1993, and gave people only a few days to convert the old rubles into new rubles. It also put a limit on the number of old rubles that foreigners could convert into new rubles. Citizens could convert up to 35,000 old rubles into new rubles, and if they held additional rubles, these had to be put into savings accounts for six months. By the end of 1997 annual inflation had fallen to the 12 percent range, and the government announced a plan to lop off three zeros from the ruble. Effective 1 January 1998, in what was essentially an accounting reform, 1,000 rubles became 1 ruble, and all prices, balance sheets, debts, etc., were adjusted accordingly.

One legacy of the Soviet regime was tight control over the conversion of rubles into foreign currencies. Tourists were able to convert foreign currencies into rubles at a rate close to a black market rate, but set by the Russian Central Bank. Foreign-owned enterprises earning profits in rubles faced a special difficulty. If a foreign-owned company wanted to send profits home to the parent company, those profits had first to be converted from rubles to the home-country currency at a disadvantageous exchange rate set by the Russian government. To attract foreign investment, and integrate the Russian economy into the world economy, Russia had to make the ruble convertible into foreign currencies at free-market rates.

A loan from the International Monetary Fund helped the Russian government marshal the foreign exchange reserves needed to establish a convertible ruble. On 1 July 1992 the Russian government established a single exchange rate between the dollar and the ruble at an initial rate of 126.5 rubles per dollar. The responsibility for adjusting the rate fell to the Russian Central Bank, which planned to set a rate based upon twice-weekly currency auctions. After

July 1993 the Russian Central Bank pegged the ruble to the dollar in a crawling peg system that avoided wild fluctuations but allowed the ruble to depreciate over time relative to the dollar. In 1996 Russia further broadened the ruble market by allowing foreigners to buy and sell Russian government bonds in secondary markets. Russian government bonds, paying over 100 percent interest at times, constitute a major demand for rubles. Rubles must be purchased first before bonds can be purchased. The astronomical interest rates on Russian bonds were sometimes necessary to maintain a demand for Russian rubles. Despite high Russian interest rates, the ruble steadily declined relative to the dollar, falling to a rate of 6,200 rubles per dollar at the end of 1997. After three zeros were lopped off, the rate became 6.2 rubles per dollar.

In 1998 the Russian government again turned to the printing press to solve Russia's problems, putting pressure on the ruble in foreign exchange markets. The value of the ruble fell sharply in august, and to help cope with the crisis the government imposed a moratorium on payments on foreign debt, significantly adding to the severity of a global financial crisis. By the end of the year the ruble was trading at around 20 rubles per dollar.

See also: Foreign Exchange Markets

References: Hanke, Steve H. 1998. Is the Ruble Next. *Forbes* (9 March): 64–65.

Wall Street Journal. 1991. "Soviet Printing of Rubles Soared in 11-Month Period." 24 December, eastern edition, at A8.

———. 1992. "Russia, Facing Inflation, Plans Bigger Banknotes." 31 January, eastern edition, at A10.

———. 1992. "Russia Plans to Make Ruble Fully Convertible by August 1." 6 May, eastern edition, at A3

———. 1993. "Chaos in Russia Mounts." 26 July, eastern edition, at A8.

———. 1997. "Russia's Overhaul of Ruble Prompts Unease in Nation." 31 December, eastern edition, at A7.

Yen

The *yen* is the money of account for Japan, comparable to the dollar for the United States. By the 1990s the Japanese yen had become a major international currency, sharing the stage with the U.S. dollar, the German mark, and the ECU as determinants of international monetary values.

The Shinka Jorei (New Currency Regulations) of 1871 established the yen as the monetary unit in Japan. The Japanese derived the word *yen* from the Chinese word *yuan,* which meant "round thing," a reference to the U.S. and Mexican dollars that dominated East Asian trade at the time. The act set the yen equal to 0.05 ounces of gold, making the official Japanese price of an ounce of gold equal to 20 yen. At the time the official United States price of an ounce of gold was $20.67. The yen was intended to be equivalent to the Mexican dollar, the standard unit in Asian trade at the time. The yen began life as a decimalized currency; one-one-hundredth of a yen was called a *sen,* and one-tenth of a *sen* was called a *rin.*

Officially, Japan was on a bimetallic monetary system, but in practice the yen was on a silver standard. In 1877 a civil rebellion forced the government to issue inconvertible paper money to finance military expenditures. Inflation erupted and in 1882 the government established the Bank of Japan, partly to replace inconvertible paper money with bank notes convertible into silver. Following the Sino-Japanese war of 1894–1895, Japanese received in gold a large war reparation payment from China, providing a gold reserve sufficient for Japan to establish a gold standard. In 1887 a new currency law gave the Bank of Japan a monopoly on the privilege to issue bank notes, and put the yen on the gold standard.

At the beginning of World War I most developed countries, including Japan, abandoned the gold standard and prohibited the export of gold. Following World War I Japan, beset by economic turmoil, stumbled in its efforts to return to the gold standard. In 1930, on the eve of the Great Depression, Japan returned to the gold standard, only to have to abandon it again in 1931. The depression dealt a serious blow to the gold standard worldwide, and Japan turned to tight government regulation of its currency, which continued through World War II.

A wave of inflation engulfed Japan following World War II and the occupation authorities instituted a currency reform that withdrew old yen notes and issued new yen notes. In 1949 the exchange rate between the yen and the dollar was set at 360 yen per dollar. Under the Bretton Woods system, exchange rates were fixed at official rates, and the ratio of yen to dollars remained at 360 until 1971. Large trade surpluses enabled Japan to bolster its gold and foreign exchange reserves, paving the way for lifting all restrictions on foreign exchange transactions.

When a system of floating international exchange

rates displaced the fixed-rate Bretton Woods system in 1973, the yen began an upward career of currency appreciation. In 1970 it had taken 360 yen to purchase a dollar. By 1973 it took only 272 yen, and by the end of the decade it took only 219 yen to purchase a dollar. As the yen grew stronger, it took more dollars to purchase a yen, but despite that Japanese goods constituted a major competitive threat to U.S. industries. In 1984 the world's major trading partners agreed to intervene collectively in foreign exchange markets to appreciate the yen even further. Whereas it took 239 yen to purchase a dollar in 1985, by 1988 that number had fallen to 128 yen, a substantial increase in the value of the yen.

In the 1980s Japan took further steps to deregulate its financial system and to allow foreign firms to participate in Japan's financial markets. Japanese banks had become among the largest and most powerful in the world, and the yen emerged as a major international currency. By 1998 economic depression in Japan put downward pressure on the yen, and the yen traded at around 140 yen per dollar.

See also: Deutsche Mark, European Currency Unit, Dollar

References: Davies, Glyn. 1994. *A History of Money*.
Ohkawa, Kazushi, Miyorhei Shinohara and Larry Meissner, eds. 1979. *Patterns of Japanese Economic Development: A Quantitative Appraisal*.

Yuan
See Chinese Silver Standard

Bibliography

Acheson, A. L. K. *Bretton Woods Revisited*. Toronto: University of Toronto Press, 1972.

Allen, D. F. *Coins of the Ancient Celts*. Edinburgh, Scotland: University Press, 1980.

Anderson, Clay J. *A Half-Century of Federal Reserve Policymaking, 1914–1964*. Philadelphia: Federal Reserve Bank of Philadelphia, 1965.

Angell, Norman. *The Story of Money*. Garden City, NY: Frank A. Stokes Company, 1929.

Angus, Ian. *Paper Money*. New York: St. Martin's Press, 1974.

Appleyard, Dennis R., and Alfred J. Field, Jr. *International Economics*. Homewood, IL: Richard D. Irwin, Inc., 1992.

Aristotle. *Politics*. Translated by Benjamin Juwett. Chicago: William Benton Publisher, 1952.

Atack, Jeremy, and Peter Passell. *A New Economic View of American History*. New York: W. W. Norton, 1994.

Ayres, Robert L. *Banking on the Poor: The World Bank and World Poverty*. Cambridge, MA: MIT Press, 1983.

Bacon, Sir Francis. *Advancement of Learning*. Chicago: William Benton Publisher, 1952.

———. *Civil Essays*. 1625. Reprint, New York: P. F. Collier, 1969.

Barber, Malcolm. *The Trial of the Templars*. Cambridge, UK: Cambridge University Press, 1978.

Barrett, Don C. *The Greenbacks and Resumption of Specie Payments: 1862–1879*. Cambridge, MA: Harvard University Press, 1931.

Barro, Robert J. "Government Spending, Interest Rates, Prices, and Budget Deficits in the United Kingdom, 1701–1918." *Journal of Monetary Economics* 20 (September 1987): 221–248.

Barth, James R. *The Great Savings and Loan Debacle*. Washington, DC: AEI Press, 1991.

Bauer, Hans. *Swiss Banking: An Analytical History*. New York: St. Martin's Press, 1998.

Baye, Michael R., and Dennis W. Jansen. *Money, Banking, and Financial Markets: An Economics Approach*. Boston: Houghton Mifflin, 1995.

Behrman, Jere R. *Foreign Trade Regimes and Economic Development: Chile*. New York: National Bureau of Economic Research, 1976.

Benton, Pierre. *The Golden Trail*. Toronto: Macmillan, 1954.

Berdan, Frances F. *The Aztecs of Central Mexico: An Imperial Society*. New York: Holt, Rinehart and Winston, 1982.

Beresiner, Yasha. *A Collector's Guide to Paper Money*. New York: Stein and Day, 1977.

Berry, Jeffrey, M. *Feeding Hungary People*. New Brunswick, NJ: Rutgers University Press, 1984.

Betlyon, John Wilson. *The Coinage and Mints of Phoenicia: the Pre-Alexandrine Period*. Chico, CA: Scholars Press, 1982.

Beutel, Frederick K. "The Development of Negotiable Instruments in Early English Law." *Harvard Law Review* 51 (5): 813–845 (March 1938).

Bezanson, Anne. *Prices and inflation during the American Revolution, Pennsylvania, 1770-1790*. Philadelphia: University of Pennsylvania Press, 1951.

Bible, The New Oxford Annotated. New York: Oxford University Press, 1973.

Binswanger, Hans Christopher. *Money and Magic: Critique of the Modern Economy in the Light of Goethe's Faust*. Translated by J. E. Harrison. Chicago, IL: University of Chicago Press, 1994.

Birchall, Johnson. *Co-op: the People's Business*. New York: St. Martin's Press, 1994.

Birley, Robert, ed. *Speeches and Documents in American History*. Vol. III. London, UK: Humphrey Milford, 1943.

Blinder, Alan S. *Economic Policy and the Great Stagflation*. New York: Academic Press, 1979.

Board of Governors of the Federal Reserve System. *The*

Federal Reserve System: Purposes and Functions. Washington, D.C., 1984.

Bomberger, W. A., and G. E. Makinen. "The Hungarian Hyperinflation and Stabilization of 1945–1946." *Journal of Political Economy* 91 (5): 801–824 (1983).

Bordo, Michael, D. "The Classical Gold Standard: Some Lessons for Today." *Monthly Review.* (Published by the Federal Reserve Bank of St. Louis): 2–17 (May 1981).

———. *Monetary Regimes in Transiton.* Edited by Forrest Capie. Cambridge, UK: Cambridge University Press, 1994.

Bradley, Harold Whitman. *The American Frontier in Hawaii.* Gloucester, MA: Peter Smith, 1968.

Braudel, Fernand. *The Mediterranean.* Vols. 1 and 2. Translated by Sian Reynolds. New York: Harper and Row, 1972.

———. *Civilization and Capitalism.* Vols. 1–3. Translated by Sian Reynolds. New York: Harper and Row, 1981.

Bray, Nicholas. "Future Shop: No Cash Accepted." *Wall Street Journal,* 13 July 1995.

Breckinridge, S. P. *Legal Tender: A Study in English and American Monetary History.* 1903. Reprint, New York: Greenwood Press, 1969.

Brock, Leslie V. *The Currency of the American Colonies: 1700–1764.* New York: Arno Press, 1975.

Brown, Marion A. *The Second Bank of the United States and Ohio, 1803–1860; A Collision of Interests.* Lewiston, NY: Edwin Mellen Press, 1998.

Broz, J. Lawrence. *The International Origins of the Federal Reserve System.* Ithaca, NY: Cornell University Press, 1997.

Bullard, Melissa M. *Filippo Strozzi and the Medici: Favor and Finance in Sixteenth-Century Florence and Rome.* Cambridge, UK: Cambridge University Press, 1980.

Burke, Bryan. *Nazi Counterfeiting of British Currency during World War II: Operation Andrew and Operation Bernhard.* San Bernardino, CA: Book Shop, 1987.

Burman, Edward. *Supremely Abominable Crimes: the Trial of the Knights Templar.* London: Alison & Busby, 1996.

Burns, A. R. *Money and Monetary Policy in Early Times.* 1927. Reprint, New York: Augustus M. Kelly, Bookseller, 1965.

Calomiris, Charles W., and Charles M. Kahn. "The Efficiency of Self-Regulated Payments Systems: Learning from the Suffolk System." *Journal of Money, Credit, and Banking* 28 (4): 766–797 (November 1996).

Cameron, Rondo, with Olga Crisp, Hugh Patrick, and Richard Tilly. *Banking in the Early Stages of Industrialization.* London: Oxford University Press, 1967.

———, ed. *Banking and Economic Development: Some Lessons of History.* London: Oxford University Press, 1972.

Cappon, Lester, ed. *The Adams-Jefferson Letters.* Chapel Hill, NC: University of North Carolina Press, 1959.

Caron, Francois. *An Economic History of Modern France.* New York; Columbia University Press, 1979.

Carothers, Neil. *Fractional Money.* 1930. Reprint, New York: Augustus M. Kelley, 1967.

Carradice, Ian, ed. *Coinage in the Administration of the Athenian and Persian Empires.* Oxford, UK: B. A. R., 1987.

Carradice, Ian. *Greek Coins.* Austin, TX: University of Texas Press, 1995.

Carter, Martha L. *A Treasury of Indian Coins.* Bombay: Marg Publications, 1994.

Carter, T. F. *The Invention of Printing in China and its Spread Westward.* Rev. ed. New York: Columbia University Press, 1931.

Cassel, Gustav. *Money and Foreign Exchange after 1914.* New York: Macmillan, 1922.

Cellini, Benvenuto. *The Life of Benvenuto Cellini.* 1728. Translated by John Addington Symonds. New York: Liveright Publishing, 1931.

———. *The Treatises of Benvenuto Cellini on Goldsmithing and Sculpure.* Translated by C. R. Ashbee. New York: Dover Publications, 1967.

Challis, C. E. 1978. *The Tudor Coinage.* Manchester, UK: Manchester University Press, 1978.

Challis, C. E., ed. *A New History of the Royal Mint.* Cambridge, UK: Cambridge University Press, 1992.

Chalmers, Robert. *A History of Currency in the British Colonies.* 1893. Reprint, Colchester, UK: J. Drury, 1972.

Chandler, Lester V. *American Monetary Policy: 1928–1941.* New York: Harper and Row, 1971.

Chang, Kia-Ngau. *The Inflationary Spiral: The Experience in China, 1939–1950.* Cambridge, MA: M. I. T. Press, 1958.

Checkland, S. G. *Scottish Banking History: 1695–1973.* Glasgow, UK: Collins, 1975.

Cheesman, Evelyn. *Backwaters of the Savage South Seas.* London, UK: Jarrolds Limited, 1933.

Chou, Shun-Hsin. *The Chinese Inflation, 1939–1949.* New York: Columbia University Press, 1963.

Chown, John. *A History of Money.* London, UK: Routledge Press, 1994.

Cipolla, Carlo M. *Money, Prices, and Civilization in the Mediterranean World.* Princeton, NJ: Princeton University Press, 1956.

———. *Before the Industrial Revolution: European Society and Economy, 1000–1700.* 2d ed. New York: W. W. Norton, 1980.

———. *The Monetary Policy of Fourteenth-Century Florence.* Berkeley, CA: University of California Press, 1982.

Clapham, Sir J. *The Bank of England.* Cambridge, UK: Cambridge University Press, 1970.

Clough, Shepard B. *The Economic History of Modern Italy.* New York: Columbia University Press, 1964.

Coats, Warren L. "In Search of a Monetary Anchor: A New Monetary Standard." *International Monetary Fund Working Paper.* No. 82, 1989.

Coinage of the Americas Conference. *The Token: America's Other Money.* New York: American Numismatic Society, 1995.

Cole, Charles Woolsey. *Colbert and a Century of French Mercantilism*. Hamden, CT: Archon Books, 1964.

Colwell, Stephen. *The Ways and Means of Payment*. 1859. Reprint, New York: Augustus M. Kelley, 1965.

Cowitt, Philip P. *World Currency Yearbook*. New York: International Currency Analysis, 1989.

Craig, J. *The Mint: A History of the London Mint from A.D. 287 to 1948*. Cambridge, UK: Cambridge University Press, 1953.

Cripps, Wilfred Joseph. *Old English Plate*. 1878. Reprint, London, UK: Spring Books, 1967.

Crisp, Olga. *Studies in the Russian Economy Before 1914*. New York: Barnes and Noble, 1976.

Cummings, Richard. *The Alchemists*. New York: David McKay Company, 1966.

Dacy, Joe. "How to Spot Bogus Bills." *Nations Business* 81 (7): 30 (July 1993).

Daniels, John D., and Lee H. Radebaugh. *International Business*. 8th ed. Reading, MA: Addison-Wesley, 1998.

Daniels, John D., and David Vanhoose. *International Monetary and Financial Monetary Economics*. Cincinnati: Southwestern Publishing Co., 1999.

Davies, Glyn. *A History of Money*. Cardiff, Wales: University of Wales Press, 1994.

Davis, Lance E., Jonathon Hughes, and Duncan M. McDougall. *American Economic History*. Homewood, IL: Richard D. Irwin, 1969.

Day, J. "The Great Bullion Famine of the Fifteenth Century." *Past and Present* 79 (1978).

De la Balze, Felipe A. M. *Remaking the Argentine Economy*. New York: Council on Foreign Relations Press, 1995.

De Roover, Raymond. *The Rise and Decline of the Medici Bank: 1397–1494*. New York: W. W. Norton, 1966.

De Vries, Margaret Garritsen. *Balance of Payments Adjustment, 1945 to 1986: The IMF Experience*. Washington, DC: The International Monetary Fund, 1987.

Del Mar, Alexander. *The History of Money in America*. 1899. Reprint, New York: Burt Franklin, 1968.

Dillistin, William H. *Bank Note Reporters and Counterfeit Detectors, 1826–1866*. New York: American Numismatic Society, 1949.

Dollinger, Phillipe. *The German Hanza*. Stanford, CA: Stanford University Press, 1970.

Dowd, Kevin. *Competition and Finance: A Reinterpretation of Financial and Monetary Economics*. New York: St. Martin's Press, 1996.

Du Bois, Cora Alice. *The People of Alor: A Social-Psychological Study of an East Indian Island*. Cambridge, MA: Harvard University Press, 1986.

Duncan-Jones, Richard. *Money and Government in the Roman Empire*. New York: Cambridge University Press, 1998.

Dunne, Gerald T. *Monetary Decisions of the Supreme Court*. New Brunswick, NJ: Rutgers University Press, 1960.

Dupriez, Leon H. *Monetary Reconstruction in Belgium*. New York: Ding's Crown Press, 1946.

Durant, Will. *The Reformation*. New York: Simon and Schuster, 1957.

"Economic Climate Looks Good for Launch of New Currency." *Wall Street Journal*. Monday, May 4, 1998: A17–18.

Ehrenkreutz, A. S. *Monetary Change and Economic History in the Medieval Muslim World*. Aldershot, UK: Ashgate Publishing Co., 1992.

Eight European Central Banks. (Published under auspices of the Bank of International Settlements) New York: Frederick A. Praeger, 1963.

Einzig, Paul. *Primitive Money*. 2d ed. Oxford, UK: Pergamon Press, 1966.

———. *The History of Foreign Coinage*. 2d ed. New York: St. Martin's Press, 1970.

Ernst, Joseph Albert. *Money and Politics in America, 1755–1775*. Chapel Hill, NC: University of North Carolina Press, 1973.

Evans, A. "Some Coinage Systems of the Fourteenth Century." *Journal of Economics and Business History*, vol. 3, 1931.

Fausten, Dietrich K. "The Humean Origin of the Contemporary Monetary Approach to the Balance of Payments." *Quarterly Journal of Economics* 93 (4): 655–673 (November 1979).

Feavearyear, Sir Albert. *The Pound Sterling*. Oxford, UK: Clarendon Press, 1963.

Federal Reserve System. *Federal Reserve Bulletin*. January, 1998.

Fehrenbach, T. R. *The Swiss Banks*. New York: McGraw Hill, 1966.

Fellner, William. "The Controversial Issue of Comprehensive Indexation." In *Essays on Inflation and Indexation*. Washington, DC: American Enterprise Institute for Public Policy Research, 1974.

Fetter, F. W., and T. E. Gregory. *Monetary and Financial Policy in Nineteenth-Century Britain*. Dublin: Irish University Press, 1973.

Figueira, Thomas J. *The Power of Money: Coinage and Politics in the Athenian Empire*. Philadelphia: University of Pennsylvania Press, 1998.

Fisher, Irving. *The Purchasing Power of Money*. New York: Macmillan, 1911.

———. *Stabilizing the Dollar*. New York: Macmillan, 1926.

Fisher, W. C. "The Tabular Standard in Massachusetts History." *Quarterly Journal of Economics* 27 (May 1913): 417–454.

Fitzgerald, C. P. *China, A Short Cultural History*. London: Cresset Press, 1935.

Flynn, Dennis O. *World Silver and Monetary History in the Sixteenth and Seventeenth Centuries*. Brookfield, VT: Ashgate Publishing Co., 1996.

Frank, Tenney. *An Economic Survey of Ancient Rome*. Vols. 1–6. 1940. Reprint, Paterson, NJ: Pageant Books, 1959.

Freeman, Anthony. *The Money and the Mint in the Reign of Edward the Confessor, 1042–1066*. Oxford, UK: B. A. R., 1985.

Freeman, Kathleen. *The Work and Life of Solon*. New York: Arno Press, 1976.

Freris, A. F. *The Greek Economy in the Twentieth Century*. New York: St. Martin's Press, 1986.

Friedman, Milton. *The Optimum Quantity of Money, and Other Essays*. Chicago, IL: Aldine Publishing Company, 1969.

———. *Money and Economic Development*. New York: Praeger Publishers, 1972.

———. "Using Escalators to Help Fight Inflation." *Fortune Magazine*, July 1974.

———. *Money Mischief: Episodes in Monetary History*. New York: Harcourt Brace Jovanovich, 1992.

Gadsby, J. William. *Future of the Penny: Options for Congressional Consideration*. Washington, DC: The Office, 1996.

Galbraith, John Kenneth. *Money, Whence It Came, Where It Went*. New York: Bantam Books, 1975

Gillilland, Cora Lee C. "The Stone Money of Yap: A Numismatic Survey." *Smithsonian Studies in History and Technology* 23. Washington, DC: Smithsonian Institution Press, 1975.

Glaeser, Edward L. *Neither a Borrower, nor a Lender Be: An Economic Analysis of Interest Restrictions and Usury Laws*. Palo Alto, CA: Hoover Institution on War, Revolution, and Peace, Domestic Studies Program, 1994.

Goethe, Johann Wolfgang von. *Faust*. Translated by George Madison Priest. Chicago: William Benton Publisher, 1952.

Goldthwaite, Richard A. *The Building of Renaissance Florence: An Economic and Social History*. Baltimore, MD: Johns Hopkins University Press, 1980.

———. *Banks, Palaces, and Entrepreneurs in Renaissance Florence*. Aldershot, UK: Variorum, 1995.

Gomes, Leonard. *Foreign Trade and the National Economy: Mercantilist and Classical Perspectives*. New York: St. Martin's Press, 1987.

Gorton, Gary. *Clearinghouses and the Origin of Central Banking in the U.S.* Philadelphia: Federal Reserve Bank of Philadelphia, 1984.

Green, Timothy. *The New World of Gold*. New York: Walker and Company, 1981.

Greenfield, Robert L., and Hugh Rockoff. "Yellowbacks Out West and Greenbacks Back East: Social-Choice Dimensions of Monetary Reform." *Southern Economic Journal* 62 (4): 902–915 (April 1996).

Greider, William. *Secrets of the Temple: How the Federal Reserve System Runs the Country*. New York: Simon and Schuster, 1987.

Grice-Hutchinson, Margorie. *Economic Thought in Spain: Selected Essays of Margorie Grice-Hutchinson*. Edited by L. Moss and C. K. Ryan. Translated by C. K. Ryan and Margorie Grice-Hutchinson. Aldershot, UK: Elgar, 1993.

Grierson, P. "The Roman Law of Counterfeiting." In *Essays in Roman Coinage Presented to Harold Mattingly*. Edited by R. A. G. Carson and C. H. V. Sutherland. Oxford, UK: Oxford University Press, 1956.

Haak, Bob. *The Golden Age, Dutch Painters of the Seventeenth Century*. Translated and edited by Elizabeth Willems-Treeman. New York: Harry N. Abrams, 1984.

Hamilton, Earl J. *War and Prices in Spain, 1651–1800*. New York: Russell and Russell, 1947.

———. *American Treasure and the Price Revolution in Spain, 1501–1650*. New York: Octagon Books, 1965.

Hammond, Bray. *Banks and Politics in America from the Revolution to the Civil War*. Princeton, NJ: Princeton University Press, 1957.

Hammond, G. L. *Alexander the Great: King, Commander, and Statesman*. Parkridge, NJ: Noyes Press, 1980.

Harl, Kenneth. *Coinage in the Roman Economy, 300 B.C. to A.D. 700*. Baltimore, MD: Johns Hopkins University Press, 1996.

Harris, S. *The Assignats*. Cambridge, MA: Harvard University Press, 1930.

Hasegawa, Tsuyoshi. *The February Revolution: Petrograd, 1917*. Seattle, WA: University of Washington Press, 1981.

Head, Barclay Vincent. *The Coinage of Lydia and Persia*. San Diego, CA: Pegasus Publishing Co., 1967.

Heaton, Herbert. "Playing Card Currency of French Canada." *American Economic Review* 18 (4): 649–662 (December 1928).

Heckscher, Eli F. *An Economic History of Sweden*. Cambridge, MA: Harvard University Press, 1954.

Hendy, Michael F. *Studies in the Byzantine Monetary Economy*. Cambridge, UK: Cambridge University Press, 1985.

Hepburn, A. Barton. *A History of Currency in the United States*. 1924. Reprint, New York: Augustus M. Kelley, 1967.

Herodotus. *History*. Chicago: William Benton Publisher, 1952.

Higgins, Andrew. "Twilight Economy: Lacking Money to Pay, Russian Firms Survive on a Deft System of Barter," *Wall Street Journal*, 27 August 1998, at A1:1.

Hogendorn, Jan S. *Economic Development*. New York: Harper and Row, 1987.

Homer, Sidney, *A History of Interest Rates*. 2d ed. New Brunswick, NJ: Rutgers University Press, 1977.

Horsefield, J. K. "Stop of the Exchequer Revisited." *Economic History Review* 35 (4): 511–528 (1982).

Horton, Dana S. *The Silver Pound and England's Monetary Policy Since the Restoration, Together with the History of the Guinea*. New York: Garland Publishing, 1983.

Hume, David. *Writings on Economics*. Edited by Eugene Rotwein. Madison, WI: University of Wisconsin Press, 1955.

———. *Essays, Moral, Political, and Literary*. New York: Oxford University Press, 1963.

Humphreys, C. R. *The Southern New Hebrides: An Ethnological Record*. Cambridge, UK: Cambridge University Press, 1983.

Ikle, Max. *Switzerland: An International Banking and Finance Center*. Translated by Eric Schiff. Stroudsburg, PA: Dowden, Hutchinson, and Ross, 1972.

"In Marxist Angola, Capitalism Thrives, using Beer Standard," *Wall Street Journal*, 19 September 1988, at 1.

Israel, Jonathan I. *Dutch Primacy in World Trade: 1585–1740*. Oxford, UK: Clarendon Press, 1989.

Jackson, Kevin, ed. *The Oxford Book of Money*. Oxford, UK: Oxford University Press, 1995.

Jastram, Roy W. *Silver, The Restless Metal*. New York: John Wiley, 1981.

Johnson, A. C., and L. C. West. *Currency in Roman and Byzantine Egypt*. Princeton, NJ: Princeton University Press, 1949.

Johnston, Sir Harry Hamilton. *George Grenfell and the Congo*. 1908. Reprint, London, UK: Kraus Reprint, 1969.

Jones, A. H. M. *The Later Roman Empire: 284–602*. Vols. 1–2, Norman, OK: University of Oklahoma Press, 1964.

———. *The Roman Economy*. Totowa, NJ: Rowman and Littlefield, 1974.

Kagin, Donald H. "Monetary Aspects of the Treasury Notes of the War of 1812." *Journal of Economic History* 44 (1): 69–88 (March 1984).

Karouf, Jim. "Start the Presses: Euro Set to Debut." *Futures* 27 (9): 30 (1 September 1988).

Kenen, Peter B. *Economic and Monetary Union in Europe*. Cambridge, UK: Cambridge University Press, 1995.

Kennedy, Ellen. *The Bundesbank: Germany's Central Bank in the International Monetary System*. New York: Council on Foreign Relations Press, 1991.

Keynes, John Maynard. *Indian Currency and Finance*. London: Macmillan, 1913.

———. *The Economic Consequences of Peace*. New York: Harcourt, Brace and Howe, 1920.

Kindleberger, Charles P. *A Financial History of Western Europe*. London: George Allen and Unwin, 1984.

Klein, John J. *Money and the Economy*. 6th ed. San Diego, CA: Harcourt Brace Jovanovich, 1986.

Knox, John Jay. *A History of Banking in the United States*. New York: Bradford Rhodes and Company, 1903. Reprint, New York: Augustus M. Kelley, 1969.

Krieger, Herbert William. *Island Peoples of the Western Pacific: Micronesia and Melanesia*. Washington, DC: Smithsonian Institution, 1943.

Kroszner, Randy. *Free Banking: The Scottish Experience as a Model for Emerging Economies*. Washington, DC: World Bank, 1995.

Lane, Frederic C. *Venice: A Maritime Republic*. Baltimore, MD: Johns Hopkins University Press, 1973.

Lane, Frederic C., and Reinhold C. Mueller. *Money and Banking in Medieval and Renaissance Venice*. Vols. 1–2. Baltimore, MD: Johns Hopkins University Press, 1997.

Laughlin, J. Laurence. *A History of Bimetallism in the United States*. 1896. Reprint, New York: Greenwood Press, 1968.

League of Nations. *The Course and Control of Inflation*. Geneva: League of Nations, 1946.

Lefebvre, Georges. *The French Revolution*. Vols. 1–2. Translated by John H. Stewart and James Friguglietti. New York: Columbia University Press, 1964.

Lerner, Eugene M. "Inflation in the Confederacy, 1861–1865." In *Studies in the Quantity Theory of Money*. Edited by Milton Friedman. Chicago: University of Chicago Press, 1956.

Lester, Richard A. *Monetary Experiments*. 1939. Reprint, New York: Augustus M. Kelley, 1970.

Littlefield, Henry M. "The Wizard of Oz: Parable on Populism." *American Quarterly* 16 (Spring 1964): 47–58.

Littlepage, Dean. *The Alaska Gold Rush*. Santa Barbara, CA: Albion Publishing Group, 1995.

Long, Robert Emmet, ed. *Banking Scandals: The S & Ls and BCCI*. New York: H. W. Wilson, 1993.

Lopez, Robert S. *The Shape of Medieval Monetary History*. London: Variorum Reprints, 1986.

Mankiw, N. Gregory. *Macroeconomics*. 3d ed. New York: Worth Publishers, 1996.

Marshall, Alfred. "Remedies for Fluctuations of General Prices." *Contemporary Review* 51: 355–375 (March 1887).

Martien, Jerry. *Shell Game: A True Account of Beads and Money in North America*. San Francisco: Mercury House, 1996.

Martin-Acena, P. "The Spanish Money Supply, 1874–1935." *Journal of European Economic History* 19 (1), 1990.

Marx, Jennifer. *The Magic of Gold*. Garden City, NY: Doubleday, 1978.

Mattingly, Harold. *Roman Coins*. London: Methuen and Co., 1968.

McCallum, Bennett T. *Monetary Economics*. New York: Macmillan, 1989.

McConnell, Campbell R., and Stanley L. Brue. *Economics: Principles, Problems, and Policies*. 14th ed. New York: McGraw Hill, 1998.

McKinnon, Ronald I. "Optimal Currency Areas." *American Economic Review* 53 (1963): 717–725.

Meek, Charles Kingsley. *Law and Authority in a Nigerian Tribe: A Study in Indirect Rule*. London: Oxford University Press, 1950.

Meiselman, David. *Varieties of Monetary Experience*. Chicago: University of Chicago Press, 1970.

Millett, Paul. *Lending and Borrowing in Ancient Athens*. Cambridge, UK: Cambridge University Press, 1991.

Milne, J. G. *Greek Coinage*. Oxford, UK: Clarendon Press, 1931.

Minton, Robert. *John Law: The Father of Paper Money*. New York: Association Press, 1975.

Miskimin, Harry A. *Money, Prices, and Foreign Exchange in Fourteenth-Century France*. New Haven, CT: Yale University Press, 1963.

Mittra, Sid. *Central Bank Versus Treasury: An International Study*. Washington, DC: University Press of America, 1978.

Moggridge, D. E. *The Return to Gold, 1925*. Cambridge, UK: Cambridge University Press, 1969.

Montesquieu, Charles De Secondat, Baron De, *The Spirit of Laws*. 1748. Translated by Thomas Nugent. Chicago: William Benton, Publisher, 1952.

Moses, Bernard, "Legal Tender Notes in California." *Quarterly Journal of Economics* 7: 1–25 (October 1892).

Mundell, Robert A. "A Theory of Optimal Currency Areas." *American Economic Review* 51 (1961): 637–665.

Murphy, Antoin E. *John Law: Economic Theorist and Policy Maker*. Oxford, UK: Clarendon Press, 1997.

Myers, Margaret G. *A Financial History of the United States*. New York: Columbia University Press, 1970.

Myers, Robert J., ed. *The Political Morality of the International Monetary Fund*. New Brunswick, NJ: Transactions Books, 1987.

Nettels, Curtis P. *The Money Supply of the American Colonies before 1720*. 1934. Reprint, New York: Augustus M. Kelly, 1964.

———. *The Emergency of a National Economy*. Madison, WI: University of Wisconsin Press, 1962.

Nevin, Edward, and E. W. Davis. *The London Clearing Banks*. London: Elek Books, 1970.

Nogaro, Bertrand. "Hungary's Recent Monetary Crisis and Its Theoretical Meaning." *American Economic Review* 38 (4): 526–542 (September 1948).

Nolan, Patrick. *A Monetary History of Ireland*. London: P. S. King and Son, 1926.

Nugent, Walter T. K. *Money and American Society: 1865–1880*. New York: Free Press, 1968.

Nussbaum, Arthur. *A History of the Dollar*. New York: Columbia University Press, 1957.

Nussbaum, Frederick L. *A History of the Economic Institutions of Modern Europe*. 1935. Reprint, New York: Augustus M. Kelley, 1968.

Ohkawa, Kazushi, Miyorhei Shinohara, and Larry Meissner, eds. *Patterns of Japanese Economic Development: A Quantitative Appraisal*. New Haven, CT: Yale University Press, 1979.

Paarlberg, Don. *An Analysis and History of Inflation*. Westport, CT: Greenwood Press, 1993.

Paddock, Richard C. "Russians Bank of Bartering." *Los Angeles Times*, 28 December 1998, at A1:1.

Padoa-Schioppa, Tommaso. *The Road to Monetary Union in Europe*. Oxford, UK: Clarendon Press, 1994.

Parkman, Francis. *The Conspiracy of Pontiac and the Indian War after the Conquest of Canada*. 1899. Reprint, Boston: Little, Brown and Company, 1933.

Parrson, Jens D. *Dying of Money: Lessons from the Great German and American Inflations*. Boston: Wellspring Press, 1974.

Partner, Peter. *Renaissance Rome, 1500–1599*. Los Angeles: University of California Press, 1976.

Pereira, Luiz Carlos Bresser. *Economic Crisis and State Reform in Brazil*. London: Lynne Rienner Publishers, 1996.

Perlman, Morris. "Adam Smith and the Paternity of the Real Bills Doctrine." *History of Political Economy* 21 (1): 77–90 (Spring 1989).

Pintner, Walter McKenzie. *Russian Economic Policy Under Nicholas I*. Ithaca, NY: Cornell University Press, 1967.

Pipes, Richard. *The Russian Revolution*. New York: Alfred A. Knopf, 1991.

Pirie, Anthony. *Operation Bernhard*. New York: William Morrow and Co., 1962.

Plato. *The Dialogues of Plato*. Translated by Benjamin Jowett. Chicago: William Benton, Publisher, 1952.

Plutarch. *Lives of Noble Grecians and Romans*. The Dryden translation. Chicago: William Benton, 1952.

Polak, Jacques J. *The World Bank and the International Monetary Fund: A Changing Relationship*. Washington, DC: Brookings Institution, 1994.

Polo, Marco. *Travels of Marco Polo*. Edited by W. Marsden. New York: Dorset Press, 1987.

Postgate, John Nicholas. *Early Mesopotamia: Society and Economy at the Dawn of History*. Rev. ed. London: Routledge, 1994.

Powell, Ellis. *The Evolution of the Money Market: 1385–1915*. 1915. Reprint, New York: August M. Kelley, 1966.

Powell, T. G. E. *The Celts*. Rev. ed. New York: Thames and Hudson, 1985.

"Precarious Peso—Amid Wild Inflation, Bolivians Concentrate on Swapping Currency." *Wall Street Journal*, 13 August 1985, at 1.

Quiggin, A. Hingston. 1949. *A Survey of Primitive Money*. New York: AMS, 1949.

Radford, R. A. "The Economic Organization of a POW Camp." *Economica* 12 (48): 189–210 (November 1945).

Reiter, Seymour. *A Study of Shelley's Poetry*. Albuquerque, NM: University of New Mexico Press, 1967.

Richards, R. D. *The Early History of Banking in England*. 1929. Reprint, New York: Augustus M. Kelley, 1965.

Richter, Jean Paul, ed. *The Notebooks of Leonardo Da Vinci*. 1833. Reprint, New York: Dover Publications, 1970.

Rickenbacker, William F. *Wooden Nickels, Or the Decline and Fall of Silver Coins*. New Rochelle, NY: Arlington House, 1966.

Ritter, Gretchen. *Gold Bugs and Greenbacks: The Antimonopoly Tradition and the Politics of Finance in America*. Cambridge, UK: Cambridge University Press, 1997.

Roberts, Richard, ed. *The Bank of England: Money, Power, and Influence, 1694–1994*. Oxford, UK: Clarendon Press, 1995.

Rockhoff, Hugh. "The Free Banking Era: A Reexamination." *Journal of Money, Credit and Banking* 6 (1974): 146–157.

———. *The Free Banking Era: A Reexamination*. New York: Arno Press, 1975.

———. *Drastic Measures: A History of Wage and Price Controls in the United States*. Cambridge, UK: Cambridge University Press, 1984.

———. "The *Wizard of Oz* as a Monetary Allegory." *Journal of Political Economy* 98 (4): 739–760 (1990).

Rogers, James S. *The Early History of the Law of Bills and Notes: A Study of the Origins of Anglo-American Commercial Law*. New York: Cambridge University Press, 1995.

Rolnick, Arthur J., and Warren E. Weber. "New Evidence of the Free Banking Era." *American Economic Review* 73 (5): 1080–1090 (December 1983).

Rose, Peter S. *Money and Capital Markets*. 2d ed. Plano, TX: Business Publications, 1986.

Rostovtzeff, M. *The Social and Economic History of the Hellenistic World*. Vols. 1–3. Oxford, UK: Oxford University Press, 1941.

Ryan, John Carlin. *A Handbook of Papal Coins*. Washington, DC: J. C. Ryan, 1989.

Samuelsson, Kurt. *From Great Power to Welfare State: 300 Years of Swedish Social Development*. London: George Allen and Unwin, 1968.

Sargent, Thomas J. *Rational Expectations and Inflation*. 2d ed. New York: HarperCollins, 1993.

Sayers, R. S. *The Bank of England: 1891–1944*. Cambridge, UK: Cambridge University Press, 1976.

Schama, Simon. *The Embarrassment of Riches: An Interpretation of Dutch Culture in the Golden Age*. New York: Alfred Knopf. 1987.

Schlesinger, Arthur M., Jr. *The Age of Jackson*. New York: Book Find Club, 1945.

———. *The Age of Roosevelt*. Vols. 1–3. Boston: Houghton Mifflin Company, 1957–1960.

Schnadt, Norman, and John Whittaker. "Inflation-proof Currency? The Feasibility of Variable Commodity Standards." *Journal of Money, Credit, and Banking* 25 (2): 214–221 (1993).

Schumpeter, Joseph. *Business Cycles: A Theoretical, Historical, and Statistical Analysis of the Capitalist Process*. Vols. 1, 2. Philadelphia: Porcupine Press, 1939.

Schwartz, Anna J. "From Obscurity to Notoriety: A Biography of the Exchange Stabilization Fund." *Journal of Money, Credit, and Banking* 29 (2): 135–153 (May 1997).

Schwarz, Ted. *A History of United States Coinage*. San Diego, CA: A.S. Barnes, 1980.

Selgin, George A., and Lawrence H. White. "Monetary Reform and the Redemption of National Bank Notes." *Business History Review* 68 (20): 205–243 (Summer 1994).

"Settling Switzerland's Debts." *New York Times*, August 16, 1998: 1.

Shann, E. O. G. *An Economic History of Australia*. 1948. Reprint, Melbourne, Australia: Georgian House, 1963.

Shelley, Percy Bysshe. *Dramatic Poems of Percy Bysshe Shelley*. London: Florence Press, 1922.

Siklos, P. L. "The End of the Hungarian Hyperinflation of 1945–46." *Journal of Money, Credit, and Banking* 2: 132–147 (1989).

Slabaugh, Arlie. *Confederate States Paper Money*. 9th ed. Iola, WI: Krause Publications, 1998.

Smith, Adam. *An Inquiry into the Nature and Causes of the Wealth of Nations*. 1776. Chicago: William Benton Publisher, 1952.

Smith, R. Bosworth. *Carthage and the Carthaginians*. New York: Longman's, Green, and Co., 1913.

Smith, Vera C. *The Rationale of Central Banking*. 1936. Reprint, Indianapolis, IN: Liberty Press, 1990.

Snider, Delbert. *Introduction to International Economics*. 6th ed. Homewood, IL: Richard D. Irwin, 1975.

Solomon, Steven. *The Confidence Game: How Unelected Central Bankers are Governing the Changed Global Economy*. New York: Simon and Schuster, 1995.

Speke, J. H. *The Discovery of the Source of the Nile*. 1864. Reprint, London: Everyman's, 1906.

Spiegel, Henry W. *The Growth of Economic Thought*. Englewood Cliffs, NJ: Prentice-Hall, 1971.

Spufford, Peter. *Money and its Use in Medieval Europe*. Cambridge, UK: Cambridge University Press, 1988.

Stabile, Donald R. *The Origins of American Public Finance: Debates over Money, Debt, and Taxes in the Constitutional Era, 1776–1836*. Westport, CT: Greenwood Press, 1998.

Stanley, Henry M. *In Darkest Africa*. New York: Charles Scribner's Sons, 1890.

Stewart, A. *Faces of Power, Alexander's Image and Hellenistic Politics*. Berkeley, CA: University of California Press, 1993

Stolpher, Gustav. *The German Economy: 1870–Present*. New York: Harcourt, Brace, 1967.

Stuck, Hudson. *Ten Thousand Miles with a Dog Sled*. 2d ed. New York: Charles Scribner's Sons, 1932.

Sveriges Riksbank. *Sveriges Riksbank: the Swedish Central Bank, a Short Introduction*. Stockholm, Sweden: Sveriges Riksbank Information Secretariat, 1994.

Tavernier, Jean-Baptiste. *The Six Voyages of John-Baptiste Tavernier, Baron of Aubonne, through Tureky, into Persia and the East Indies*. 1677. Translated by J. Phillips. Reprint, London: Robert Littlefield and Moses Pitt, 1985.

Taxay, Don. *Money of the American Indians, and Other Primitive Currencies of the Americas*. New York: Nummus Press, 1970.

Terranova, Anthony. *Massachusetts Silver Coinage*. New York: American Numismatic Society, 1994.

Terrell, Henry S., and Rodney H. Mills. "International Banking Facilities and the Eurodollar Market." Staff Study No. 124. Washington, DC: Board of Governors of the Federal Reserve System, August 1983.

Thayer, Theodore. "The Land-Bank System in the American Colonies." *Journal of Economic History* 13 (2): 145–159 (1953).

Thiers, M. A. *The History of the French Revolution*. Vols. 1–5. 1881. Translated by Frederick Shoberl. Reprint, Freeport, NY: Books for Libraries Press, 1971.

Thucydides. *The Peloponnesian War*. Translated by Richard Crawley. Chicago: William Benton Publisher, 1952.

Timberlake, Richard Henry, *The Origins of Central Banking in the United States*. Cambridge, MA: Harvard University Press, 1978.

Toynbee, Arnold. *A Study of History*. Vol. 7. London: Oxford University Press, 1954.

Troxell, Hyla A. *Studies in the Macedonian Coinage of Alexander the Great*. New York: American Numismatic Society, 1997.

United Kingdom. *Report of the Committee on the Workings of the Monetary System.* Cmnd. 827. London: Her Majesty's Stationary Office, 1959.

Usher, Abbott Payson. *A History of Mechanical Inventions.* Rev. ed. 1929. Reprint, New York: Dover Publications, 1988.

Valdes, Juan Gabriel. *Pinochets' Economists.* Cambridge: Cambridge University Press, 1995.

Van Arsdell, Robert D. *Celtic Coinage of Britain.* London: Spink, 1989.

Van Houte, J. A. *An Economic History of the Low Countries: 800–1800.* New York: St. Martin's Press, 1977.

Vilar, Pierre. *A History of Gold and Money, 1450–1920.* Translated by Judith White. London: NLB, 1976.

Vives, Jaime Vicens. *An Economic History of Spain.* Princeton, NJ: Princeton University Press, 1969.

Wachter, Susan M. *Latin American Inflation.* Lexington, MA: Lexington Books, 1976.

Watson, David K. *History of American Coinage.* 1899. Reprint, New York: Burt Franklin, 1970.

Weatherford, Jack. *The History of Money.* New York: Crown Publishers, 1997.

Weaver, R. Kent. *Automatic Government: Politics of Indexation.* Washington, DC: Brookings Institution, 1988.

Webb, Steven B. *Hyperinflation and Stabilization in Weimar Germany.* New York: Oxford University Press, 1989.

Weinstein, Steve. "True Benefits." *Progressive Grocer* 77 (5): 80–86 (May 1998).

Weintraub, Sidney. *Capitalism's Inflation and Unemployment Crisis.* Reading, MA: Addison-Wesley Publishing Company, 1978.

Westermann, William Linn. "Warehousing and Trapesite Banking in Antiquity." *Journal of Economic and Business History.* 1931. Reprint, New York: Kraus Reprint Corporation, 1964.

White, Lawrence J. "The Partial Deregulation of Banks and other Depository Institutions." In *Regulatory Reform: What Actually Happened?* Edited by Leonard W. Weiss and Michael W. Klass. Boston: Little, Brown, and Company, 1986.

Wicker, E. "Terminating Hyperinflation in the Dismembered Hapsburg Monaarchy." *American Economic Review* 76 (3): 350–364 (1986).

Williams, Jonathan, ed. *Money: A History.* New York: St. Martin's Press, 1997.

Willis, Henry Parker. *A History of the Latin Monetary Union.* 1901. Reprint, New York: AMS Press, 1901.

Woerheide, Walter J. *The Savings and Loan Industry.* Westport, CT: Quorum Books, 1984.

Yeager, Leland B. "Stable Money and Free-Market Currencies." *Cato Journal* 3: 305–326 (Spring 1983).

Yoder, Paton S. "Paper Currency in Colonial Pennsylvania." Ph.D. dissertation, Indiana University, 1941.

Index

Italic numbers indicate illustrations.